Forensic Victimology

Forensic Victimology

Examining Violent Crime Victims in Investigative and Legal Contexts

Second Edition

Brent E. Turvey

Amsterdam ▪ Boston ▪ Heidelberg ▪ London ▪ New York ▪ Oxford ▪ Paris
San Diego ▪ San Francisco ▪ Singapore ▪ Sydney ▪ Tokyo

Academic Press is an imprint of Elsevier

Academic Press is an imprint of Elsevier
The Boulevard, Langford Lane, Kidlington, Oxford, OX5 1GB
225 Wyman Street, Waltham, MA 02451, USA

First edition 2009
Second edition 2014

British Library Cataloguing in Publication Data
A catalogue record for this book is available from the British Library

Library of Congress Cataloging-in-Publication Data
A catalog record for this book is available from the Library of Congress

ISBN: 978-0-12-408084-3

For information on all Academic Press publications
visit our website at **store.elsevier.com**

Printed and bound in the United States
14 15 16 17   10 9 8 7 6 5 4 3 2 1

Working together
to grow libraries in
developing countries

www.elsevier.com • www.bookaid.org

Contents

Preface
An Argument for Forensic Victimology

Brent E. Turvey

Victimology is a social science regarded as the scientific study of victims. It is a broad subject with many subcategories of research. Some of these are theoretical and some are applied.

The objective of this textbook is to provide readers with the basic principles and practice standards of *forensic victimology:* the scientific study of victims for the purpose of addressing investigative and forensic issues. It is intended to educate the student in an applied fashion and to act as a guide for victimologist practitioners who assist investigators and provide expert testimony in court. It gives readers the means and rationale for examining victims with a scientific mindset, as opposed to the mindset of a police officer, victim's advocate, or treatment professional.

Dr. Petherick and I collaborated on this text for the following reasons: there is really none other like it available; professionals are less and less encouraged to approach victims with the skepticism that science requires; and victimization is not always simple.

On Friday, March 11, 2005, at 9:00 a.m. in Atlanta, Georgia, a suspected rapist named Brian Nichols overpowered a courthouse deputy. As is customary, his handcuffs had been removed so that he could change from jail to civilian clothes for the jury. Nichols took the deputy's keys and gun and made his way to the courtroom where his trial was to be held. He entered at the back, through the private chambers of Judge Rowland Barnes. Nichols then shot Judge Barnes in the head, killing him. During his escape, Nichols also shot and killed Julie Brandau, the court reporter, and deputy sergeant Hoyt Teasley. (See Figure P-1.) Sometime later, Nichols shot and killed U.S. Customs Agent David Wilhelm, taking his badge, gun, and vehicle. By that time, a nationally publicized statewide manhunt was already under way.

According to Ashley Smith's initial statements to police, the following took place on Saturday, March 12, 2005, at around 2:00 a.m. Nichols encountered 26-year-old Smith in the parking lot of an apartment complex where she had just arrived home (Smith, 2005). He followed her after she parked and forced his way through her apartment door, with Smith at gunpoint. Nichols tied

xi

FIGURE P-1
Rescue personnel speed one of the victims of Brian Nichols' March, 2005 shooting spree into an ambulance waiting outside the Fulton County Courthouse in Atlanta, Georgia.

her hands and feet with masking tape and an extension cord. At one point, he forced her to sit in the bathroom with a towel over her head while he took a shower. He told her who he was, and she was afraid for her life.

But something unexpected happened: at 9:50 a.m., after seven hours of holding Smith hostage in her own home, Nichols allowed her to leave. She called 911. Shortly thereafter, Nichols was taken into custody by authorities. As explained in Mattingly (2005):

> Smith said Nichols eventually unbound her hands and feet and that he began to relax as they spoke for hours about religion and family—including Smith's 5-year-old daughter and her late husband, who was stabbed four years earlier and died in her arms.
>
> "I basically just talked to him and tried to gain his trust," she said.

Smith said she showed Nichols family photographs and read him passages from Rick Warren's bestselling book, *The Purpose Driven Life: What on Earth Am I Here For?*

After 6:00 a.m., Smith said she followed Nichols so he could hide [Agent] Wilhelm's truck and then took him back to the apartment in her car. She said that Nichols did not bring any weapons on the trip, and that she had her cellular phone but did not call police.

Smith said Nichols was "overwhelmed" when she made him a pancake breakfast and that the two of them watched television coverage of the manhunt.

Smith said Nichols allowed her to leave for a 10:00 a.m. visit with her daughter, who lives with Smith's aunt. Nichols gave her money, saying he was going to stay at her apartment for a "few days."

She dialed 911 about 9:50 a.m. and within minutes a SWAT team converged on the building. After several tense minutes, police saw Nichols waving a white T-shirt.

In subsequent interviews, Ashley Smith gave any and all credit for her survival directly to God, saying that among other things she also read to Nichols from the Bible. The religious community enjoined the sensational mainstream coverage of the case. With Smith's assistance, they promoted her successful use of faith to end Nichols' killing spree, save her own life, and demonstrate that even the most horrific among us cannot resist the word of God.

In the months that followed, Ashley Smith was hailed as a hero by the news media and local law enforcement for executing what some have referred to as a textbook hostage negotiation for her own release. She was also given more than $70,000 in reward money for her role in Nichols' capture. She even coauthored a 2005 memoir, *Unlikely Angel: The Untold Story of the Atlanta Hostage Hero*.[1] (See Figure P-2.)

However, in that memoir, Smith publicly revealed for the first time that there were crucial details she had withheld from her account. She was actually a methamphetamine addict who had spent time in a psychiatric facility and had given up custody of her child by the time that Nichols took her hostage. Moreover, her captivity by Nichols did not just include reading from religious works to gain his trust and calm him down; it also involved sharing some of her personal meth stash with him. These were details that had been omitted from her interviews with the religious and mainstream media. More importantly, she also failed to mention her meth addiction, possession, and sharing with Nichols to police until giving a supplemental interview to investigators months after the incident. In her memoir, she claims not to have used meth

---

[1]Ashley Smith's book was published by Zondervan, which also publishes the *NIV Study Bible*.

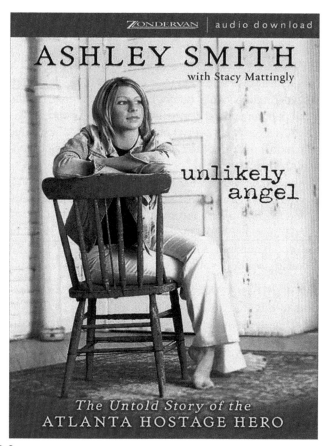

FIGURE P-2
Ashley Smith's coauthored memoir was published in 2005, the same year as her ordeal with Brian Nichols. In it, Smith admits for the first time details about her methamphetamine addiction and how she shared her drug stash with her captor.

with Nichols and asserts that being held hostage by him was the reason she ultimately decided to stop using altogether.

Despite her deception, the authorities let Smith keep the reward money and did not press charges against her for methamphetamine possession or false reporting. She also turned her story of survival into a credential as an author and motivational speaker. But the story does not end there. Nichols, whose capital murder trial has been postponed four times because of funding issues, has yet to face justice.[2]

---

[2]As of this writing, the defense has reportedly spent around $1.5 million and is out of money; the new judge has stopped jury selection until financial issues have been resolved; and the DA is suing the judge to remove himself from the case for being biased toward the defense.

In 2008, Smith was called by the prosecution to testify against Brian Nichols at his trial. She testified that she was a waitress and single mother battling drug addiction when Nichols took her hostage–and that she had received over $700,000 dollars in rewards and had joined the lecture circuit as a motivational speaker in relation to surviving the ordeal. While she admitted offering his drugs that she had in her possession, she denied using them with him. Brian Nichols was subsequently convicted of more than 50 charges in relation to his litany of crimes, and sentenced to life in prison without parole.

Again, victimization is not always simple.

REALISTIC VICTIMOLOGY

The Brian Nichols/Ashley Smith case illustrates how complex victimization can be. Victims are not theoretical, ideological, or archetypal constructs; they are people. They are susceptible to the same frailties and imperfections as the rest of us. Trying to examine victim behavior through any other lens is going to fog the truth and preclude actual understanding. Subsequently, as explained in Fattah (2000), there is a need to move toward what may be referred to as *realistic victimology* (p. 39):

> The current dominant view in victimology of a bad offender and a good victim, of an innocent victim and a guilty criminal, will slowly give way to the more realistic and defensible view of two human beings caught in a web of intricate social relationships and human emotions.

Victimization is not always simple. It does not always happen in a straightforward manner to the innocent, the honest, or even the law-abiding. Nor does it occur in a vacuum under controlled laboratory conditions. Because it involves real people with real lives and real problems, victimization occurs under convoluted circumstances and within or as a result of relationships that are equally complex.

The victimologist is challenged with establishing, examining, and interpreting the features of these complexities. In doing so, she must contend with corrupted and incomplete victim information, the overt falsity of victims and witnesses, and the unique social-political pressures that arise for and against every victim population imaginable. And that's when things are going well.

Dietrich Dorner, a cognitive psychologist, professor of psychology at the University of Bamberg, and author of *The Logic of Failure: Recognizing and Avoiding Error in Complex Environments* (Dorner, 1996), argues that there are three common features that make problems difficult to solve:

Complexity: When many interdependent features that cannot be understood exist in isolation.

Dynamics: When the environment changes over time, creating pressure.
Opacity: The lack of visibility of certain parameters needed to accurately characterize the situation or problem.

As we will learn throughout this text, it is reasonably safe to argue that victimology suffers from all these features to varying degrees. So how can victimologists make informed and useful examinations and interpretations under these conditions? What Dorner found in his research is that those who were able to solve complex problems gathered information before acting, thought systematically, reviewed their progress, and corrected themselves often. Those who made the most errors tended to cling to preconceived theories, did not correct themselves, and blamed others when things went wrong. The errors made in complex situations, Dorner surmised, were not a feature of human capability; rather they were a feature of poorly conceived reasoning and an overall human tendency for laziness.

Certainly Dorner's findings cannot be irrelevant to the questions posed in victimology. So how do victimologists apply them in their work? Before we can address that issue, we must first agree what victimology is and what it is not.

VICTIMOLOGY DEFINED

Victimology is intended to be the scientific study of victims (Drapkin and Viano, 1974). Currently, victimologists tend to find themselves operating within one of three main subgroups: general victimology, penal/interactionist victimology, and critical victimology.

General victimology is the study of all those individuals or groups who have suffered harm or loss, whether they are victims of a specific crime, general oppression, or a natural disaster. According to Mendelsohn (1976), this vast landscape includes victims of criminal offenders, the social-political environment, the natural environment, technology, and even those who victimize themselves. General victimologists are concerned with identifying or developing preventative measures, as well as tools for victim assistance. They not only want to study the characteristics and causes of victimization but also want to determine remedies.

Interactionist victimology, or penal victimology, is the study of the dynamics between victims and their offenders. It is limited, however, to those who have been the victims of a specific crime. Interactionist victimologists study the victims' participation in crime causation through their interaction with the offenders, the interaction between the victims and society, and the victims' subsequent role in the criminal justice system. Like the general victimologist, the interactionist intends to examine causes to develop remedies that favor the victims.

Critical victimology has developed in reaction to the way that victimology is defined and studied by the first two subgroups. It seeks to question how criminality and victimity are established, tolerated, and even sanctioned. The basic premise is that any mainstream view of victims perpetuates existing yet inadequate definitions of crime and victimization. This may be observed in the overemphasis in research and policy on certain types of crime and crime victims, because they are clearly defined and easier to grasp. This, in turn, results in a failure to study—let alone recognize—a host of both victim populations and their related social issues. It may also be observed in the way that a given justice system penalizes those who would elsewhere be viewed as victims, such as prostitutes who are selectively punished in some Western cultures and victims of rape may be punished in some Islamic cultures.

These victimology subgroups are alike in that they are ultimately oriented toward helping victims, in studying ways of "speeding up a victim's emotional recovery, overcoming adversity, reimbursing financial damages, promoting reconciliation between the injured party and the wrongdoer, and restoring harmony to a strife-torn community" (Karmen, 2004, p. 24). In other words, the professional compass in these subgroups points toward victim betterment. While this is an admirable goal and one well worth serving, it does not always promote an environment where scientific study is welcome.

THE PROBLEM

Contemporary victimologists can be found in many professions, including those associated with academia, the justice system, victim treatment, victim's advocacy, and politics. They routinely have a mandate to help victims above all other considerations, or for political reasons they may need to be perceived as having such a mandate. However, satisfying this ideological imperative often requires uncritical and unconditional regard for those who present themselves, or are presented contextually, as victims. When this political or functional need clashes with the reality of victim imperfection, the results to any given professional can be chilling. The pendulum of bias can swing widely for and against. Consider the effect that this has had on some prosecutors, as described in Pokorak (2007, pp. 710–712):

> Although the effect is not often discussed, through the combination
> of the prosecutor's unique "quasi-judicial" position that is freed from
> the normal constraints of a fiduciary relationship to an individual
> client, and the reality of a prosecutor's high volume of cases, the result
> is that prosecutors have little contact with victims. This dirty open
> secret starts with the initial years as a young prosecutor. During this
> period, the thoughtful exercise of prosecutorial discretion may not be
> developed, but rather it may be constrained by office structures and

policies that overload new prosecutors with large case loads of minor matters. In order to prevent serious consequences from mistakes made by inexperienced prosecutors, many prosecution offices regularize plea offers for these less serious, "routine" cases and significantly constrain discretionary decision-making by the new, overloaded members of the office. At this same time, a period of desensitization can occur among the newer members of the prosecution team. This takes the form of two separate, yet interrelated effects of high volume workloads. The first is the objectification of the defendant. Even though the prosecutor has a duty to the defendant as well as to all other members of the public, the reality of human interactions is that it is more difficult to argue that a person should be incarcerated if one knows that individual and sympathizes with his or her plight. Therefore, some prosecutors may be heard to refer to defendants in highly derogatory ways, such as "scumbag," "dirt bag," "animal," and worse.

At the same time this tendency to dehumanize the defendant is being adopted by young prosecutors emulating more experienced attorneys in their office; they begin to realize that the defendants and the victims in cases share many characteristics and sometimes switch roles. Because most crimes are intra-racial and intracommunity, Monday's defendant may also be Wednesday's witness and Friday's victim. Therefore, it is not a difficult leap from demonizing a defendant to treating victims with something less than complete respect.

Additionally, some victims can be very challenging to manage. Work, childcare, or economic constraints may prevent them from being readily available to meet to discuss and prepare the case or even to appear in court when needed. Ongoing relationships between the victim and the defendant also may severely complicate or compromise prosecutions. Certain victims may not present as good witnesses due to their lack of education, language proficiency, or simply because they are not good storytellers. At the same time, victims can be demanding—often calling to get status updates or seeking assistance in other, perhaps unrelated, areas of legal need.

In contrast to the access and communication barriers that might exist between prosecutors and victims, prosecutors, early on, learn to develop close relationships with police witnesses. For example, prosecutors in sexual assault cases have ready access to one or more police officers who help them put together and present their case. Often, these police witnesses interact with the prosecutors on a near-daily basis. Many police officers, in addition to being trained investigators and evidence handlers, are also specifically trained to serve as witnesses. Compared to these helpful professional witnesses, victims can seem to an overworked prosecutor like much more of a problem than an asset to the case development and prosecution strategy.

The result of these two acculturated responses—the dehumanization of defendants and the general impatience with many victims—is that prosecutors tend to rely on the police and investigators to manage victims during the bulk of pre-trial preparation. Simply put, prosecutors all too often would rather hear what a victim has to say from a police officer rather than from the victim herself.

At this point, the problem becomes clear to anyone actually trained as a scientist. Victimology is meant to be a scientific study. But bias that develops for or against victims because of routine contact with them can act as a wall to the mandates of scientific inquiry, namely the requirements of doubt and skepticism.[3]

This is a problem because some witnesses lie, some victims lie, and some people lie about being victims. Blind faith in a victim shields them from scientific inquiry; overt mistrust of victims shields others.

It should not take a scientist to put forth the premise that establishing the facts and defining the limits of evidence are preferable to falsity. In the social-political arena of victims and victimology, however, it does. As Goldberg explains (2003, pp. 17–18):

> There was a time when you could assume that an intelligent person looking for the truth was guided by the most basic of scientific intuitions: nature will give you a life if only you're going her way....
>
> In social science today we can no longer make this assumption. Even if we continue to assume we are dealing with intelligent people, we find no way to maintain the belief that such people act on an impulse to find the truth. Instead, we find large and increasing numbers of ideologues who act as if nature is not something to be discovered no matter what she should turn out to be, but a handmaiden whose purpose is to satisfy one's psychological and ideological needs. Lacking the rudimentary scientific impulse of self-refutation...the ideologue assesses truth not by concordance with reality, but by concordance with psychological and ideological need.

As detailed in Turvey (2006), for more than a century the investigative and forensic science literature has acknowledged the importance of establishing the relationships between the primary components of a crime in order to solve it. These supporting pillars relate directly to evidence that establishes the

---

[3]For a useful discussion, see "Science as Falsification" by Karl R. Popper's *Conjectures and Refutations* (1963, pp. 33–39).

relationships between *the victim, the suspect,* and *the crime scene.* This expansive body of work has given more than a small share of its pages to explaining the necessity of carefully investigating and documenting evidence as it relates to each, and determining the connections that can be reliably demonstrated. Establishing these pillars and the details of their relationships is, in fact, a threshold goal of all criminal investigation, so that criminal investigators and subsequent forensic examiners may adequately provide the foundation for any related court action.

When these pillars are not investigated, examined, and firmly established, the theories of a case are essentially unsupported. They are at best a weak guess, and at worst, the erroneous result of biasing influences such as politics, emotion, ignorant beliefs, and personal interest. As will be discussed presently, the solution proposed here is the application of *forensic victimology* as a necessary safeguard.

REINFORCING VICTIMITY

Doubt and skepticism are warranted in all realms of victimology, not just because they are mandated by good science, though that should be enough, but because of the manner in which any given system (e.g., school, employer, government, civil or criminal courts), culture (e.g., profession, family, religion, or region), or the general public responds to victims. Victims frequently need and are indeed entitled to counterbalance in the form of compensation for the loss and harm they suffer. However, these counterbalances invite abuse and can be a strong incentive for fraud.

Systemic Reinforcement

We must begin by acknowledging that many systems offer what may be viewed by some as incentives, even rewards, for suffering harm or loss, in the form of various compensations. These range from generally expecting less of victims and removing the barriers that are present in everyday challenges, to protecting them from responsibilities and liabilities, to direct financial reimbursement for a loss. As explained in Holstein and Miller, establishing oneself as a victim is one of the ways that someone can account for personal failures in an acceptable fashion (1990, p. 11):

> In the course of daily life, we all fall short of our, and others',
> expectations. The ways in which we depict, account for, and manage
> these failures is central to maintaining our public and self identities
> as competent practitioners of everyday life.... In addition to denying
> responsibility for particular actions, designating one's self, or another,
> as a victim provides an economical way of telling others that the

performance at hand should not be taken to exemplify the nature, quality, or potential of either the actor engaged in it, or the activity itself. Such practices help us maintain a sense of purpose and competence in the face of situational demands which might ostensibly give little evidence that goals are being accomplished or standards being upheld.

Children are trained to think this way the moment they step inside their first classroom. From grade school to grad school, students who become ill, suffer the death of a close relative, or befall some other personal tragedy are able to miss classes without penalty, skip or retake exams, hand in assignments after their due date, and may even receive some sympathy in their final grade. These lessons are then transferred from the classroom to the workplace. Employees who become ill, suffer the death of a close relative, or befall some other personal tragedy are often able to miss workdays with pay, push back deadlines, and be relieved or even excused from difficult responsibilities without shame or penalty. As further explained in Holstein and Miller (1990, p. 7):

> Victimization is a method for absolving persons of responsibility. When trouble emerges, an "innocent" party—the object of the injury or trouble—can be specified by assigning victim status to one or more persons, thus exempting them from blame.

In short, whether a student or a professional, one is constantly reinforced with the notion that being a victim freezes the normal course of daily events and thereby shifts responsibility and accountability, if only temporarily.

There are also explicit financial compensations for victimity. Victims can seek or threaten to seek legal remedy in civil court and thereby receive financial or other material remuneration directly from those they believe are responsible for their harm or loss. Additionally, various governments and private organizations have developed victim's assistance programs to provide money for everything from living expenses and lost wages to medical treatment and counseling.

This is a good time to point out that victim compensations are in place for at least two reasons: they are necessary, and they are humane. Compensations are necessary because in most cases when a person falls prey to illness and tragedy, it is beyond his or her control. Furthermore, we often assume that no one would intentionally cause himself or herself harm or loss—or at least we prefer to give people the benefit of the doubt. The subsequent prevailing wisdom is that we should not be penalized for our victimity, even when we fail to guard against it or do things to openly invite it. After all, bad things can happen to anyone. Systemic counterbalances can serve justice, restore a sense of fairness, and give a second chance when one is needed. Compensations are also humane, because victims may be in extreme pain or anguish. They may need time to heal or become whole before they can be expected to resume their life and the responsibilities that come with it.

Just as these systemic compensations are necessary and humane, their existence encourages some individuals to abuse them. Consider the following example.

CASE EXAMPLE:

Hurricane Katrina

At 7:10 a.m. EDT on August 29, 2005, Hurricane Katrina made landfall in Louisiana as a Category 3. Maximum winds were clocked at nearly 125 mph. It was the most destructive hurricane in U.S. history, obliterating, rending, and flooding buildings, homes, and lives all along the Gulf Coast. The victims of Katrina are estimated in the millions, including nearly two thousand dead, thousands more wounded, and hundreds of thousands displaced, along with those who also lost property totaling in the billions of dollars.

Attempts to get federal aid to the victims of Katrina ranged from inadequate to late to never. They also resulted in one of the largest collective opportunities for victim fraud in recent U.S. history. As explained in a 2006 report by Gregory D. Kutz, Managing Director of Forensic Audits and Special Investigations, and John J. Ryan, Assistant Director Forensic Audits and Special Investigations, both of the United States General Accounting Office (GAO) (Kutz and Ryan, 2006, p. 1):

> We estimate that through February 2006, FEMA made about 16 percent or $1 billion in improper and potentially fraudulent payments to registrants who used invalid information to apply for disaster assistance. Based on our statistical sample, we are 95 percent confident that the range of improper and potentially fraudulent payments is from $600 million to $1.4 billion. In our assessment of whether a payment was improper and potentially fraudulent, we did not test for other evidence of impropriety or potential fraud, such as insurance fraud and bogus damage claims. This means our review potentially understates the magnitude of improper payments made. Examples of fraud and abuse include payments to registrants who used post office boxes, United

FIGURE P-3

One of several FEMA debit card designs. Approximately 11,400 were distributed in Houston, Dallas, and San Antonio to those who claimed to be displaced victims of hurricane Katrina.

CASE EXAMPLE: *CONTINUED*

Parcel Service stores, and cemeteries as their damaged property addresses.

Absent proper verification, it is not surprising that FEMA continued to pay fictitious disaster registrations set up by GAO as part of our ongoing forensic audit. In one case, FEMA paid nearly $6,000 to one registrant who submitted a vacant lot as a damaged address. Below is a copy of a rental assistance check sent to GAO after FEMA received feedback from its inspector that the GAO undercover registrant did not live at the damaged address, and after a Small Business Administration inspector reported that the damaged property could not be found.

We also found that FEMA provided expedited and housing assistance to individuals who were not displaced. For example, millions of dollars in expedited and housing assistance payments went to registrations containing the names and social security numbers of individuals incarcerated in federal and state prisons during the hurricanes. In addition, FEMA improperly paid individuals twice for their lodging—paying their hotels and rental assistance at the same time. For example, at the same time that FEMA paid $8,000 for an individual to stay in California hotels, this individual also received three rental assistance payments for both hurricane disasters. Finally, we found that FEMA could not establish that 750 debit cards worth $1.5 million went to hurricane Katrina victims. We also found debit cards that were used for a Caribbean vacation, professional football tickets, and adult entertainment. [See Figure P-3.]

This example is not proof that everyone is dishonest, or even that most people are dishonest. Rather, it demonstrates that a significant percentage of the population is capable of varying levels of dishonesty and opportunism when the circumstances are in place and the appropriate controls are not. This remains true even during times of national crisis, when actual victims will be deprived of the benefits being defrauded. History has taught us that wherever there are sympathetic victims and corresponding efforts to assist them, there will be fraud.

Cultural Reinforcement

As we've already learned, cultural and public responses can be unconditionally warm and accepting for some victims. For others, they can be cold, judgmental, and rebuking. This may have to do with the nature of the crime, the nature of the victim, the nature of the offender, or unrelated elements present in the immediate climate. In their personal estimation of whether responses will be favorable, there are those who will be drawn to embellish, omit, or fabricate some or all of the details of their victimization. There are also those who are compelled to invent their victimization entirely.

Consider the following examples.

CASE EXAMPLE:

Tanja J. Morin

On July 17, 2006, 26-year-old Tanja J. Morin of Lancaster, Ohio, called 911 to report that her 2-year-old son, Tyler, was missing. She tearfully explained to the dispatcher: "The only way he could have went is through the back, and the only way you can get the fence open is if somebody kicks it from the outside.... Somebody had to come through the yard." The call was made at 10:51 a.m.

Continued

CASE EXAMPLE: *CONTINUED*

Tanja's husband, Michael, immediately came home from work to help in the search for Tyler. He found the couple's youngest child at 11:22 a.m., in a garbage dumpster less than a block away from their home.[4]

Had he been left in the dumpster much longer, the heat would have killed him; it was one of the hottest days of the year.

During the initial police investigation, the mother's kidnapping story succumbed to realistic victimology and fell apart. A nearby surveillance camera had captured the activity at and around the dumpster before, during, and after Tyler was reported missing. On the surveillance stills, Tanja can be seen walking hand-in-hand with her youngest son in the alley near the dumpster at 10:35 a.m. A minute later, she can be seen leaving toward her home alone.

Tanja confessed to detectives that she hadn't meant to hurt Tyler, only to create an emergency that would get her husband to come home from work. According to police, she told them, "He wanted to spend money today that we didn't have, and I was trying to think of a way he could come home so he didn't have to spend the money that he had."

Tanja was arrested that day and charged with attempted murder, child endangerment, and kidnapping. At first, she pleaded not guilty. The judge subsequently ordered her to submit to a psychiatric evaluation. In November 2007, she pled guilty to kidnapping, child endangering, and felonious assault charges.

In this case, the mother lived in a severely dysfunctional family in which she was apparently convinced that the benefits of creating a false crisis outweighed the potential consequences to her or anyone else. Taken at her word, she was actually a victim of her husband's financial irresponsibility and was acting with good intentions. Certainly, her actions were enough to warrant a psychiatric evaluation—something that would not necessarily occur to the court if a man were facing the same charges. In cases of domestic violence and even homicide, women are often treated by the justice system as victims in need of help, and men are viewed as aggressors deserving of punishment. Such distorted views, based on cultural archetypes, can result in diminished responsibility, or at least sympathy, for the mother.

The objective, scientific victimologist would refrain from taking this mother or any other alleged victim at her word, as this case and many others demonstrate that the institution of motherhood is not inviolate. Even a mother claiming to have the best intentions can put her child in a garbage dumpster and lie about it if she thinks there is something to be gained.

[4]The couple also had a six-year-old girl and a four-year-old boy.

CASE EXAMPLE:

D.C. Metro Police Officers Nathan Minor and Peter Snipes

Just after midnight on August 7, 2006, Eugene Radcliff was being treated at Howard University Hospital in Washington, D.C., subsequent to his arrest for possession of cocaine and unlawful entry. Officers Nathan Minor and Peter Snipes had been assigned to guard him. Radcliff escaped, and the two officers called for backup. As Segraves (2007) details:

> A call for help came into police dispatch from Snipes, a 10-year veteran of the force. Snipes said the prisoner had attacked his partner and escaped.

> The officers were giving chase through the Northwest D.C. neighborhood near the hospital and requested backup. A manhunt ensued as police canvassed the area.

But documents obtained by WTOP reveal a different story....

> In his original statement, Minor, who has been on the force since 2000, wrote: "The defendant kicked me in the midsection knocking me completely to the floor. I then saw the defendant running down the hallway of the hospital. I gave chase...I saw the defendant running northbound on Georgia Avenue."

> But according to an affidavit filed by an agent with the Metropolitan Police Internal Affairs Department, a witness said the prisoner "was not restrained...walked directly out of the hospital with no police officers near, and saw

CASE EXAMPLE: *CONTINUED*

no altercation between the prisoner and police officers."

In other words, witnesses reported that the prisoner simply left the hospital while the officers weren't looking—no fight or chase occurred. After an investigation was conducted into these conflicting accounts, Officers Minor and Snipes changed their story. In October 2007, they both pled guilty to making false statements, as explained in Alexander (2007, p. B3):

> Two D.C. police officers pleaded guilty yesterday to making false statements in an official report to cover up an incident in which they allowed a prisoner to escape.
> Officers Nathan Minor, 33, and Peter Snipes, 32, face up to 180 days in prison and $1,000 in fines, prosecutors said. The officers, both assigned to the 1st Police District, resigned

from the force as part of their plea agreements and remain free pending sentencing in D.C. Superior Court.

In this case, the officers attempted to establish themselves as victims to account for failure. They were responding to their perceptions of both law enforcement culture and eventual professional accountability. They did not want to appear weak or inept in the eyes of their fellow officers for letting a prisoner walk away, nor did they want to be held accountable for their incompetence by superiors. Rather than admit a mistake and ask for help, they contrived a story with the necessary elements to seem plausible, mitigate responsibility, and deflect scrutiny. They portrayed themselves as victims of a violent criminal made more dangerous by the involvement of drugs. However, they could not control the statements of impartial witnesses to the event.

CASE EXAMPLE:

New Hampshire v. Brian Shepherd

Work involving victims draws all kinds of people into related professions. Some are balanced and well adjusted, and others are not. The imbalanced and maladjusted seek to please their surroundings, to satisfy the demands of their professional culture against the limits of the facts and evidence. At the far end of the ethical spectrum, there are those who actively conceal, obscure, and avert evidence relating to a victim's character, history, or condition. They do so for a variety of reasons. For some, it is a matter of bias in favor of the victim, the police, the prosecution, or against the offender.[5]

For others, it is a matter of egoism or narcissism, of needing to be perceived as the hero, the rescuer, or the protector.

In January 2005, Brian Shepherd was convicted of Aggravated Felonious Sexual Assault.[6]

Shepherd and the co-accused, Matt MacDuff, were at a party at the home of the victim, Emily Thompson, on December 2, 2003. Early on at the party, Thompson reportedly advised Shepherd that she would like to have sex with him on the condition that he wore a condom, restating her desire throughout the evening.

Thompson participated in a number of drinking games and smoked marijuana at various times throughout the night. Because of her desire to make friends and fit in, Thompson drank more than she usually would have, and subsequently went into a back bedroom to lie down because of her level of intoxication. She later testified that she had lost interest in sex at this point.

At some point later in the evening, Thompson woke up and two men were engaging in simultaneous sexual penetration with her, though she couldn't identify who these men were. She testified that because of her level of intoxication she could not resist the assault. She noted that she heard MacDuff's voice but could not make out what he was saying. She then heard an unidentified voice say, "I think she is going to pass out again."

Thompson also testified that the next day she was unsure of what had happened in the bedroom; that she had a sense that something wasn't right but was not able to recall specific details. Over the next few days, she heard from friends and other partygoers that she had intercourse with multiple

Continued

CASE EXAMPLE: *CONTINUED*

male partners in the back of MacDuff's trailer. Because of these discussions, Thompson reported the assault to the police who interviewed both Shepherd and MacDuff. After initially denying any sexual activity, Shepherd later admitted to the intercourse but maintained that Thompson was both awake and consenting.

At trial, Shepherd called the co-accused (MacDuff), Detective Mulholland, and toxicologist JoAnn Samson as witnesses. Shepherd presented his theory that Thompson was awake, and that despite passing out several times, she had consented to having sex. The state argued the opposite; that Thompson was heavily under the influence, physically helpless, and therefore not able to resist.

On January 12, 2005, the jury convicted Shepherd. MacDuff was subsequently tried for the same crime, but the court dismissed the case. Shepherd later claimed that new evidence discovered during the MacDuff trial entitled him to a new trial.

After initially bringing the complaint to the attention of police, the victim was subjected to a sexual assault examination, performed by Dr. Wendy Gladstone. By way of introduction to Dr. Gladstone, consider the following background information:[7]

> Dr. Gladstone earned her medical degree from Columbia University before going on to Columbia Presbyterian Medical Center to complete her internship and residency. After residency, she trained for her sub-specialty interest, adolescent medicine, at Children's Hospital Medical Center in Boston. Dr. Gladstone is board certified by the American Board of Pediatrics and is a Fellow of the American Academy of Pediatrics. Dr. Gladstone came to Exeter in 1978 to join the Exeter Clinic. In 1982 she was co-founder of Exeter Pediatric Associates. She is currently an associate at Children's Hospital Medical Center and a member of the teaching staff at Harvard University Medical School. A member of the Society of Adolescent Medicine, the American Public Health Association, the American Professional Society on Abuse of Children, and the [New Hampshire] Attorney General's Task Force on Child Abuse and Neglect. Dr. Gladstone is the Medical Director of Seacoast HealthNet and was the President

> of the [New Hampshire] Pediatric Society from July 1996 [to] 1999.

As explained in *State v Brian Shepherd* (2007, pp. 3–4):

> MacDuff was tried by a different prosecutor and before a different judge to ensure that MacDuff's testimony, provided under a grant of immunity during the defendant's trial, would not be used against MacDuff in his own trial. On the day of jury selection, the prosecutor learned that Dr. Wendy Gladstone, who had performed a rape kit examination of the victim, had redacted certain portions of her progress notes from the version that she supplied to the State during discovery. Consequently, the State informed the court and MacDuff. As a result, the court conducted an in-camera review of the medical file and released the completed version of Dr. Gladstone's report to the attorney.
>
> The unprecedented report contained information regarding the victim's history of depression, including a list of counselors and therapists. In addition, the report contained a statement the victim provided during the exam in which she asked Dr. Gladstone not to inform the victim's mother of the sexual assault until after the victim had retrieved her clothing "in order to avoid a confrontation." The victim further explained that she expected her mother to be angry because they did not have a good relationship. The information contained in the complete report led to the discovery of other mental health records from Seacoast Mental Health and Coastal Counseling. These records revealed that the victim had been diagnosed with a mental health condition which caused her to exercise poor judgment, use impulsive behavior, and engage in dangerous and risky activities that could lead to injury.

Just to recap the situation, Dr. Gladstone performed a sexual assault exam on Thompson. Two men, Shepherd and MacDuff, were subsequently arrested and prosecuted for raping her. Dr. Gladstone, after performing the forensic examination, provided two different reports of her findings. The first report went to the prosecution and included all the necessary

CASE EXAMPLE: *CONTINUED*

victimological information including the complainant's mental health history and statements to her mother. The second report, a mirror of the first in most ways, did not contain the victimological information regarding the mental health history or the telltale page numbers.

In short, Dr. Gladstone crossed the line between forensic examiner and advocate. She delivered necessary contextual information to the prosecution that was deliberately withheld from the defense in their version of the report. Moreover, one cannot claim that this was a novice mistake, given Dr. Gladstone's background and credentials. As provided by the court (pp. 8–9):

> In this case, the court finds that Dr. Gladstone was acting as an agent of the State when she examined the victim and collected evidence for an eventual prosecution. Specifically, she is a member of the Attorney General's Task Force regarding Sexual Assault Protocols and she assisted in drafting protocols regarding interview techniques. In addition, she was trained in the proper procedure for evidence collection. Moreover, Dr. Gladstone testified that she examined the victim in this case with the intent to collect forensic evidence during her examination for eventual use at trial. She explained that she collected the evidence in a manner designed to protect the integrity of the chain of custody. Thus, her failure to disclose the complete report of her examination to the police or the County Attorney constituted a breach of the State's duty to the defendant.
>
> The court also finds that Dr. Gladstone knowingly failed to turn over her complete report. She testified at the hearing that she purposely redacted a portion of the first page of the report and the entire second page. In addition, the report she provided to the police was photocopied without page numbers and in a manner that made the document appear complete. As a result, no one involved in the case could have

made a request for further discovery because the document the doctor provided contained no indication that any information had been redacted.

> As a result of the court's finding that Dr. Gladstone knowingly withheld discoverable material (material she also admitted was important and relevant to the assault), the court must next consider whether the state can meet its burden to establish beyond a reasonable doubt that the omitted evidence would not have affected the verdict. As stated in its previous analysis, the omitted evidence led to the discovery of mental health records that provided information regarding the victim's state of mind. The defendant could have used the specific diagnoses contained in those records to rebut the victim's claim of non-consensual sexual intercourse. Given that the outcome of the case turned largely on a determination of whether the victim accurately described her level of consciousness and whether the defendant's claim of consensual sex was true, the state cannot meet its burden of establishing beyond a reasonable doubt that the omitted evidence would not have affected the verdict.

This case stands out as an example of intentional concealment of victimology by someone who is supposed to be an impartial forensic examiner. It is an abuse of the court's trust, and ultimately resulted in Brian Shepherd's conviction being overturned.

---

[5]This issue is explored further in Chapter 4, "Constructing a Victim Profile."
[6]Unless otherwise stated, this section is largely adapted from, and all quoted material is taken directly from, The State of New Hampshire v Brian Shepherd, *Rockingham Superior Court, Docket no. 04-S-1220, March 8, 2007; Court Decision by Justice Tina L. Nadeau.*
[7]Biographical material cited from Beansprout Networks at http://www.beansprout.net/, last downloaded July 20, 2007.

These examples serve to demonstrate that no victim culture or institution associated with the criminal justice system is wholly immune from the reinforcement that victimity can provide. None are beyond doubt, examination, critique, or redress. Not the institution of motherhood, or the "sacred bond" between a mother and her child; not the culture of law enforcement; and not the "objective" forensic examiner. Within each, there are those who are willing to distort or fabricate victimity because they perceive a cultural reward for doing so.

THE SOLUTION

Let's return to our original question: given that victimological evidence can be incomplete, ambiguous, and complex under the best of conditions, and given the possibility of falsity, how can the forensic victimologist make informed examinations and interpretations? How can we apply Dorner's lessons to the problems we face? Answering these questions is the purpose of this text.

As we've already stated, *forensic victimology* is the scientific study of victims for the purposes of addressing investigative and forensic issues. The social scientist researching victim–offender relationships; the investigator going though a victim's garbage or cellphone records; the criminal profiler reading a victim's diary or making a "friends and family" list; the forensic nurse taking a victim history or looking for evidence of injury; the reconstructionist examining a victim's toxicology or making a timeline of activities leading up to his or her demise; the psychiatrist or psychologist performing a mental health assessment; the medical examiner establishing a victim's place of employment or last meal—each collects, examines, and interprets evidence related to forensic victimology. Their work serves criminal investigation and anticipates courtroom testimony. Their findings and interpretations bear directly on determining whether there is a victim, precisely who the victim is, and the potential consequences for those who caused that person harm.

Forensic victimology is intended to serve the justice system by educating it. It is aimed at helping to provide more informed investigations, more scientific examinations, and more informed legal outcomes. All this serves the betterment of society as a whole, if one accepts that truth is better than fiction.

PURPOSE

Forensic victimologists include investigators, criminal profilers, crime reconstructionists, medical examiners, forensic nurses, and testifying academics—anyone who uses his or her knowledge of victimology to serve investigative or forensic ends. Because of the need for accuracy and reliability in these complementary spheres, forensic victimologists are best conceived as objective, dispassionate, and above all scientific examiners. They are critical and skeptical, and they put the establishment of fact before politics or any other consideration. To that end, they take nothing for granted, look for corroboration of any alleged victims' statements, seek out collateral sources of information, and investigate alternate or contributing motives for victim behavior. Most importantly, forensic victimologists are barred from assuming that alleged victims must have been victimized. For their purposes, victimity must be established unequivocally and may not be asserted simply for ideological purposes. They investigate as scientists, they report as educators, and they understand the gravity of their eventual courtroom testimony.

The purpose of this textbook is to distinguish the investigative and forensic aspects of victim study as a necessary adjunct to the practice of *victimology*. It identifies forensic victimologists in the investigative and forensic communities and provides them with methods and standards of practice needed to be of service. Forensic victimology is necessary because it provides a scientific balance against the idealization or demonization of victims, a filter for deception and false reporting, and a means for providing an objective threshold of relevance for victim information and opinions already at work in the criminal justice system.

References

Alexander K. 2 D.C. officers admit lying about escape. Washington Post October 2007;19:B3.

Dorner D. The Logic of Failure: Recognizing and Avoiding Error in Complex Environments. Cambridge, MA: Perseus Books; 1996.

Drapkin I, Viano E. Victimology: A New Focus. Lexington, MA: Lexington Books; 1974.

Fattah E. Victimology: past, present, and future. Criminologie 2000;33(1):17–46.

Goldberg S. Fads and Fallacies in the Social Science. New York: Humanity Books; 2003.

Holstein J, Miller G. Rethinking victimization: an interactional approach to victimology. Symbolic Interaction 1990;13(1):103–22.

Karmen A. Crime Victims: An Introduction to Victimology. fifth ed. Belmont, CA: Thompson/ Wadsworth; 2004.

Kutz G, Ryan J. Hurricanes Katrina and Rita Disaster Relief: Improper and Potentially Fraudulent Individual Assistance Payments Estimated to Be Between $600 Million and $1.4 Billion. Washington, DC: United States Government Accountability Office; 2006, GAO-06–844T June 14.

Mattingly D. Atlanta's 26 hours of fear. CNN.com; March 15, 2005. Available at: http://www.cnn.com/2005/LAW/03/14/atlanta.summary/index.html.

Mendelsohn B. Victimology and contemporary society's trends. Victimology 1976;1(1):8–28.

Pokorak J. Rape victims and prosecutors: the inevitable ethical conflict of de facto client/attorney relationships. South Texas Law Review, Spring 2007;(48):695–732.

Popper K. Conjectures and Refutations. London: Routledge and Keagan Paul; 1963.

Segraves M. Cops busted for false report, losing suspect. WTOP Radio 2007; September 13, Available at: http://www.wtopnews.com/index.php?nid=428&sid=1246487.

Smith A. Unlikely Angel: The Untold Story of the Atlanta Hostage Hero. Grand Rapids, MI: Zondervan; 2005.

Turvey BE. Beneath the numbers: rape and homicide clearance rates in the United States. Journal of Behavioral Profiling 2006;6(1).

About the Authors

Brent E. Turvey, PhD

Brent E. Turvey received a BS from Portland State University in Psychology, with an emphasis on forensic psychology, and an additional BS in History. He went on to receive his master's of science in Forensic Science after studying from the University of New Haven. He also earned his PhD in Criminology from Bond University.

Since 1996, Brent has consulted with many organizations, attorneys, and law enforcement agencies in the United States, Australia, Scotland, China, Canada, Barbados, Singapore, Korea, and Mexico on a range of rapes, homicides, and serial/multiple rape death cases as a forensic scientist and criminal profiler. In August of 2002, he was invited by the Chinese People's Police Security University (CPPSU) in Beijing to lecture before groups of detectives at the Beijing, Wuhan, Hanzou, and Shanghai police bureaus. In 2005, he was invited back to China to lecture at the CPPSU and to the police in Beijing and Xian—after the translation of the second edition of his text *(Criminal Profiling: An Introduction to Behavioral Evidence Analysis)* into Chinese for the university. In 2007, he was invited to lecture at the First Behavioral Sciences Conference at the Home Team (Police) Academy in Singapore, where he also provided training to their behavioral science unit. In 2010, he examined a series of sexual homicides for the Solicitor General of the Crown Office and Procurator Fiscal Service in Edinburgh, Scotland. And in 2013, he became the sponsor for the Criminal Profiling and Behavioral Analysis Unit of the Forensic Laboratory in cd. Juarez in Chihuahua, Mexico.

Brent has been court qualified as an expert in the areas of criminal profiling, victimology, crime scene investigation, sex crimes investigation, false reports, crime scene analysis, forensic science, and crime reconstruction in many courts and jurisdictions (state and federal) around the United States, in both civil and criminal matters—most often in capital murder cases.

Brent has published in numerous peer-reviewed journals and is the author of *Criminal Profiling: An Introduction to Behavioral Evidence Analysis*, first, second, third, and fourth editions (1999, 2002, 2008, 2011) and *Forensic Fraud* (2013).

He is also a co-author of *Ethical Justice* (2013); *Rape Investigation Handbook*, first and second editions (2004, 2011); *Crime Reconstruction*, first and second editions (2007, 2011), *Forensic Victimology* (2009), and *Forensic Criminology* (2010)—all with Academic/Elsevier Science.

Brent is currently a *Distinguished Member* of the Mexican Academy of Forensic Investigators; a *Board Member* of The International Association of Forensic Criminologists/Academy of Behavioral Profiling; a full partner, forensic scientist, criminal profiler, and instructor with Forensic Solutions, LLC; and an Adjunct Professor of Sociology Justice Studies at Oklahoma City University. He can be contacted via email at bturvey@forensic-science.com.

Jodi Freeman, MCrim

Jodi Freeman holds an honors bachelor degree in health sciences from the University of Western Ontario, Canada, with a double major in health sciences and criminology. She recently graduated from Bond University, Australia, with a master's degree in criminology. During her master's program, Jodi completed an independent study under Brent Turvey in the area of behavioral evidence analysis. In 2010, Jodi completed a crime scene analysis internship with Forensic Solutions, LLC. Working in this role, she continues to assist with research, casework, publications, and workshop facilitation. Jodi can be contacted at jodi.freeman@rogers.com.

Charla M. Jamerson, BSN, RN, MNS, SANE-A, CMI, III

Charla Jamerson received her bachelor's of nursing science from Excelsior College of Nursing in 2002 and her RN diploma from the Baptist School of Nursing Northwest in 1995. In 2003, she completed the graduate certificate program in forensic nursing and forensic internship at the University of Colorado, Colorado Springs. She subsequently completed a master's in nursing science and is a certified family nurse practitioner.

Charla is a registered nurse in the state of Arkansas; has been certified as a sexual assault nurse examiner (SANE) by the International Association of Forensic Nurses; and is certified as a medical investigator by the American College of Forensic Examiners. From 2000 to 2003, she was the director of forensic nursing and forensic nurse examiner at the Children's Safety Center in Springdale, Arkansas. From 2003 to 2006, she was the owner, director of Forensic Nursing Services, and head clinician of Jamerson Forensic Nursing & Investigative Services, Inc., in Fayetteville, Arkansas.

Charla graduated with her master's degree from the nurse practitioner program at Stony Brook University, New York, in 2013. She is currently a family nurse practitioner at Karas Urgent Care. She can be reached at cjame24152@aol.com.

Stan Crowder, PhD

Stan Crowder is a retired U.S. Army Military Police Colonel, and holds a PhD, an MBA, and a BS. During his military career, Stan served in numerous positions, including MP Commander, Chief of Investigations for the Inspector General of Georgia, Counter-drug Commander, Battalion Commander, and Chief of Personnel. He served seven years as a civilian police officer. He teaches at Kennesaw State University, Kennesaw, Georgia, where he has been teaching since 1999 and was selected as the 2007 recipient of the Betty Siegel teaching award.

Stan has published articles on various criminology and criminal justice teaching methods in peer-reviewed journals, and is also a co-author of *Ethical Justice* (2013) with Dr. Turvey.

Stan is currently the president of The International Association of Forensic Criminologists/Academy of Behavioral Profiling. He can be contacted at scrowder@kennesaw.edu.

Michael McGrath, MD

Michael McGrath, MD, is a Board Certified Forensic Psychiatrist, licensed in the State of New York. He is a Clinical Associate Professor in the Department of Psychiatry, University of Rochester School of Medicine and Dentistry, Rochester, New York, and Medical Director and Chair, Department of Behavioral Health, Unity Health System, Rochester, New York.

He has been researching and publishing in the areas of criminal profiling, false allegations, and victim psychology for the past two decades.

Dr. McGrath divides his time among administrative, clinical, research and teaching activities. His areas of expertise include forensic psychiatry and criminal profiling. He has lectured on three continents and is a founding member and a past president of The International Association of Forensic Criminologists/Academy of Behavioral Profiling. He can be contacted at mmcgrath@ profiling.org.

Shawn Mikulay, PhD

Dr. Shawn Mikulay is a Professor of Psychology at Elgin Community College in Elgin, Illinois, where he teaches coursework in general, forensic, developmental, and experimental psychology, human sexuality, and criminal profiling. Dr. Mikulay has been with Elgin Community College since 1995.

Dr. Mikulay received his doctorate of philosophy in Psychology from Northern Illinois University (1998). He received his master of arts in Psychology (1995) and master of science in Industrial Management (1996). During graduate school, he taught as an adjunct instructor at Concordia University, Kishwaukee College, Waubonsee Community College, and Elgin Community College. His research has been published in *Genetic, Social, & General Psychology Monographs, Educational & Psychological Measurement*, and the *Journal of Organizational Behavior*.

Dr. Mikulay's areas of research and expertise include workplace deviance, forensic victimology, behavioral analysis, offender modus operandi, and offender signature behavior. He is currently the vice president of The International Association of Forensic Criminologists/Academy of Behavioral Profiling. He can be contacted via email at smikulay@forensic-science.com.

Detective John O. Savino, NYPD (ret., 2007)

John Savino joined the New York City Police Department on January 26, 1982, and was promoted to detective in 1989. In a career that spanned 25 years, Detective Savino became one of the best sex crime investigators New York City had to offer. His career spanned all aspects of law enforcement, beginning with a short assignment as a uniformed police officer and his quick advancement to the Organized Crime Control Bureau in 1986. Detective Savino began developing his investigative skills while assigned to the Manhattan North Narcotics Division. His assignment to the narcotics division helped develop his ability and skills to interact with people from all walks of life. His experiences as an "undercover" officer helped develop his ability to gain the confidence and trust of the individuals he purchased narcotics from, and would later use those skills when interviewing victims and suspects during the thousands of investigations he was involved in.

For the last 18 years of his career with the NYPD, he was assigned to the Manhattan Special Victims Squad, where he investigated reports of sexual assault and child abuse occurring in the Borough of Manhattan. While assigned to the special victims squad, he rose to the prestigious rank of 1st grade detective. Detective Savino investigated thousands of reports of rape and sexual assault and investigated some of the most notorious and heinous sex crimes Manhattan has ever seen.

Detective Savino was chosen to rewrite the policy used for investigating sexual assaults by the New York City Police Department and was tasked with creating a training manual for newly assigned detectives to the Manhattan Special Victims Squad. During his assignment with the Manhattan Special Victims Squad, Detective Savino began lecturing at training classes held for rape advocates and emergency room personnel after he saw a need to bridge the gap between medical personnel and the police. He also created training material and provided training for uniformed officers and first responders on the proper response to a sexual assault, how to interact with a sexual assault victim, and how to preserve a crime scene properly.

In 2000, Detective Savino was the first detective in New York State to participate in the "John Doe" DNA indictment of a DNA profile for a suspect responsible for at least 16 sexual assaults since 1997, dubbed the "East Side rapist" by the New York City press. Detective Savino had been the lead investigator for many successful serial rape and pattern sexual assault investigations, and had conducted lectures for the New York State Police on proper procedures when investigating a serial rape case or pattern sex offender.

In September 2001, after the World Trade Center tragedy, Detective Savino, along with an elite group of detectives, was assigned temporarily to the New York City morgue for several months and assigned the difficult task of attempting to identify victims of the World Trade Center disaster. His skills, dedication, and attention to detail carried over to this assignment and led to the identification of numerous victims of the tragedy.

Since retiring in 2007, Detective Savino has continued his career in law enforcement and is now conducting complex financial and fraud investigations for a large state agency in Florida.

Angela N. Torres, PhD, ABPP (Forensic)

Angela Torres majored in psychology at the University of California, Berkeley. She then went on to complete her doctorate in clinical psychology with a forensic focus at Sam Houston State University in Huntsville, Texas. After course work, she was a pre-doctoral intern at the Federal Medical Center in Rochester, Minnesota. She then went on to become a post-doctoral fellow in Forensic Psychology at Central State Hospital in Petersburg, Virginia. She is board certified in Forensic Psychology by the American Board of Professional Psychology.

Dr. Torres is currently Chief Forensic Coordinator at the Central State Hospital for the Virginia Department of Behavioral Health and Development Services. Her specialties and research areas include sex offender risk assessment, gender/sexuality/cultural issues, malingering, and general forensic assessment.

CHAPTER 1

Victimology: A Brief History with an Introduction to Forensic Victimology

Brent E. Turvey[1]

KEY TERMS

Criminal investigation The process of gathering facts to be used as evidence and proof in a court of law.

The Dark Age In victimology, the area after the emergence of written laws and structured governments, where all offenses were viewed as perpetrated against the king or state, not against the victims or their family.

Forensic victimology The idiographic and nomothetic study of violent crime victims for the purposes of addressing investigation and forensic issues.

General victimology The study of victimity in the broadest sense, including those that have been harmed by accidents, natural disasters, war, and so on.

The Golden Age In victimology, the era thought to have occurred before written law, where victims played a direct role in determining the punishment for actions of another committed against them or their property.

Interactionist/penal victimology An approach to victimology from a criminological or legal perspective, where the scope of the study is defined by criminal law.

Reemergence of the victim The era in the middle of the twentieth century, when a small number of people began to recognize that those who were most affected by criminal acts were rarely involved in the criminal justice process. This led to the realization that victims were also being overlooked as a source of information about crime and criminals.

Sanctity of victimhood The belief that victims are inherently good, honest, and pure, making those who defend them righteous and morally justified.

Scientific method A way to investigate how or why something works or how something happened through the development of hypotheses and subsequent attempts at falsification through testing and other accepted means.

Victim A term used in the modern criminal justice system to describe any person who has experienced loss, injury, or hardship due to the illegal actions of another individual, group, or organization.

Victima A Latin word used to refer to those who were sacrificed to please a god.

Victimology The scientific study of victims and victimization, including the relationship between victims and offender, investigators, courts, corrections, media, and social movements.

Victim precipitation When a crime is caused or partially facilitated by the victim.

Victim prone Individuals who share a capacity for being victimized.

CONTENTS

---

[1]This chapter an update to material originally published in Turvey and Ferguson (2009).

1

Historically, the Latin term *victima* was used to describe animals or humans whose lives were destined to be sacrificed as an offering to a divinity. This was generally in relation to a religious ceremony, with females the preferred sacrifice for certain goddesses. The word *victima* was not used to suggest pain, suffering, or loss. Rather, it suggested a sacrificial role, preferably the result of consent; fear and panic from the intended sacrifice were regarded as bad omens (see generally Green, 2001). It wasn't until the nineteenth century that the word *victim* was used negatively, in connection with harm or loss in general (Spalek, 2006).

In the modern criminal justice system, the word *victim* has come to describe any person who has experienced injury, loss, or hardship due to the illegal action of another individual, group, or organization (see generally Karmen, 2012). The term *victimology* first appeared in 1949, in a book about murderers written by forensic psychiatrist Fredric Wertham (see Figure 1-1). It was specifically used to describe the study of individuals harmed by criminals (Karmen, 2012). In modern usage, the term *victimology* refers generally to the scientific study of victims and victimization, including the relationships between victims and offenders, investigators, courts, corrections, media, and social movements (Karmen, 2012).

Jan Van Dijk, a professor of victimology at Tilburg University, has proposed that there are currently two major types of victimology (1999): general victimology and penal victimology, with major differences stemming from the definitions used to identify victims. *General victimology* studies victimity in the broadest sense, including those that have been harmed by accidents, natural disasters, war, and so on (Van Dijk, 1999). The focus of this type of victimology is the treatment, prevention, and alleviation of the consequences of being victimized, regardless of the cause.

Interactionist (or penal) victimologists, on the other hand, generally approach the subject from a criminological or legal perspective, where the scope of study is defined by criminal law. According to Van Dijk (1999; p. 2) "the research agenda of this victimological stream combines issues concerning the causation of crimes with those relating to the victim's role in the criminal proceedings," where victims are only those who become such as a result of a crime. Generally speaking, this type of victimology advocates for victims, for their rights or in relation to certain types of prosecutions.

Victimology exists beyond just the narrow study of victims related to criminal offenders, however. It includes those that have suffered from violations of civil statutes as well—as the civil justice system is where victims can seek to be made legally whole (Crowder and Turvey, 2013). It is also the best place for victims to seek justice when law enforcement and prosecutors fail them.[2]

---

[2]This concept is discussed throughout the text and in greater detail.

FIGURE 1-1

Dr. Fredric Wertham (1895–1981) reading the first issue of *Shock Illustrated*. A psychiatrist for the New York Department of Hospitals connected with the Court of General Sessions, he is best remembered for his expert testimony in the trial of serial murderer Albert Fish and opposition to comic books. In 1954, he wrote a book titled *Seduction of the Innocents*, which argued that comic books were the lowest form of literature and a primary cause of juvenile delinquency—citing their depiction of sex, drugs, and violence. That same year, this book led to an official Congressional Inquiry that ultimately resulted in the "voluntary" creation of the Comics Code Authority (CCA) by the Comics Magazine Association of America. The CCA screened all comic books prior to publication, acting essentially as an industry censor.

According to Ezzat Fattah, PhD, an Egyptian prosecutor turned criminologist, as well as a leading author on the subject of victimology (Fattah, 2000; p. 24):

> [T]he study of victims and victimization has the potential of reshaping the entire discipline of criminology. It might very well be the long awaited paradigm shift that criminology desperately needs given the dismal failure of its traditional paradigms: search for causes of crime, deterrence, rehabilitation, treatment, just desserts, etc.

Of this there can be no doubt, yet the literature on victimology remains underdeveloped. There remains, unfortunately, a level of ignorance regarding the nature and even existence of victimology across the professional spectrums that intersect with the subject. Most notably, this occurs within the criminal justice system itself, which tends to be populated by those without a scientific, behavioral, or research background. A primer is therefore necessary.

The purpose of this chapter is to provide a brief history of victimology as it has evolved in relation to systems of justice until modern times, as a precursor to the development of forensic victimology as a subdiscipline. It then closes with discussions on the rationale for the investigative and forensic utility of victimology. If readers have not yet studied the *Prefaces* to both editions of this text in the front matter, now would be a good time to go back and do so.

HISTORY

It is important to understand how the field of victimology originated and then acknowledge how it has developed. To that end, this section involves a general overview of the victim's role in various systems of justice throughout history. It concludes with a more specific rendering of the contributions of relevant victimologists, their subsequent research, and its impact on the discipline.[3]

The idea of studying victims in relation to legal conflict is not new. In fact, it has been around for centuries in various forms. It just hasn't always been referred to as victimology.

Jerin and Moriarty (1998) contend that there are three distinct historical eras defining the victims' role within systems of justice: the *golden age*, the *dark age*, and the *reemergence of the victim*.

The Golden Age

In the so-called *golden age*, which Jerin and Moriarty suggest existed prior to written laws and established governments, tribal law prevailed. In much of tribal law, victims are said to have played a direct role in determining punishments for the unlawful actions that others committed against them or their property. It is reported to be a time when personal retribution was the only resolution for criminal matters. As such, victims sought revenge or demanded compensation for their losses directly from those who wronged them (Karmen, 2012; Shichor and Tibbetts, 2002).

Doerner and Lab (2011) go so far as to describe this tribal approach as a *victim justice system*, as opposed to a *criminal justice system*, explaining that (p. 2)

---

[3]As will become clear, the victimological literature has often been the product of advocates interested in victim rights, legal reforms, and various liabilities. This as opposed to those interested in objective study for the advancement of scientific knowledge. Therefore, some of the terminology used has been less than scientific and even partial. It is presented here purely in an effort to maintain the historical record.

> With rare exceptions, written laws did not exist...it was up to
> victims or their survivors to decide what action to take against
> the offender. Victims who wished to respond to offenses could
> not turn to judges for assistance or to jails for punishment. These
> institutions did not exist yet. Instead, victims had to take matters
> into their own hands.

This was not a time of objectivity or critical regard toward victims and their claims. Victims could define the extent of any loss or harm and then seek their own retribution. They would not necessarily be required to submit to an investigation or assessment by a disinterested third party or higher authority. Ostensibly, they seek their own justice without attendance to a formal burden of proof, with the victim's word set against that of the accused. In such a system, fault and consequence can become a strict matter of character, politics, and influence without representation or appeal.

Victim-driven approaches to justice became somewhat problematic as populations grew, and as families and groups expanded. The reason is partly that, in many instances, crimes were not suffered or inflicted against just one person. Depending on the nature of an offense, it might be harmful to an entire family, tribe, or culture. If the actual offender were not available to be punished, his or her kinsman might bear the responsibility for the harm that had been caused. Worse still, in some instances, successive generations would inherit any insult and injustice committed against the last—wrongfully victimized or wrongfully prosecuted alike. So the commission of a single crime had the potential to draw in many people. Resulting vendettas could lead to longstanding blood feuds between families or tribes for harms that may or may not have actually happened.

Eventually, many came to the realization that although it promoted strong family, clan, and even cultural loyalty, this form of justice did little to resolve conflict. The notion that a crime against one is a crime against many did not serve to alleviate the hardship endured by the individual victims. Neither did holding one kinsman responsible for the crimes of another. Rather, this scheme of justice expanded the harm of the original crime to people who weren't directly involved. It also resulted in cycles of revictimization as groups sought their share of vengeance back and forth (Shichor and Tibbetts, 2002). Rather than serving the victim, victim-driven justice actually made matters much worse.

For example, a long-practiced victim-oriented remedy to the problem of crime, debt, and related blood feuds is marriage: the mixing of blood from both sides to vest interests, pay back a loss, or end the need for retaliation. However, even in cultures in which tribal law maintains a foothold and such problems are common—as is the case in modern-day Afghanistan—this widely accepted "solution" is known to fail and actually create new victims. As explained in Tang (2007):

> Despite advances in women's rights and at least one tribe's move to outlaw the practice, girls are traded like currency in Afghanistan and forced marriages are common. Antiquated tribal laws authorize the practice known as "bad" in the Afghan language Dari—and girls are used to settle disputes ranging from debts to murder.
>
> Such exchanges bypass the hefty bride price of a traditional betrothal, which can cost upward of US$1,000. Roughly two out of five Afghan marriages are forced, says the country's Ministry of Women's Affairs.
>
> Though violence against women remains widespread, Afghanistan has taken significant strides in women's rights since the hard-line Taliban years, when women were virtual prisoners—banned from work, school, or leaving home unaccompanied by a male relative. Millions of girls now attend school and women fill jobs in government and media.
>
> There are also signs of change for the better inside the largest tribe in eastern Afghanistan—the deeply conservative Shinwaris. Shinwari [tribal] elders from several districts signed a resolution this year outlawing several practices that harm girls and women. These included a ban on using girls to settle so-called blood feuds—when a man commits murder, he must hand over his daughter or sister as a bride for a man in the victim's family. The marriage ostensibly "mixes blood to end the bloodshed." Otherwise, revenge killings often continue between the families for generations...
>
> About 600 elders from the Shinwar district put their purple thumbprint "signatures" on the handwritten resolution.
>
> More than 20 Shinwari leaders gathered in the eastern city of Jalalabad, nodding earnestly and muttering their consent as the changes were discussed last week.
>
> They insisted that women given away for such marriages—including those to settle blood feuds—were treated well in their new families. But the elders declined requests to meet any of the women or their families. "Nobody treats them badly," Malik Niaz said confidently, stroking his long white beard. "Everyone respects women."
>
> But Afghan women say this could not be further from the truth. "By establishing a family relationship, we want to bring peace. But in reality, that is not the case," said Hangama Anwari, an independent human rights commissioner and founder of the Women and Children Legal Research Foundation. The group investigated about 500 cases of girls given in marriage to settle blood feuds and found only four or

five that ended happily. Much more often, the girl suffered for a crime committed by a male relative, she said. "We punish a person who has done nothing wrong, but the person who has killed someone is free. He can move freely, and he can kill a second person, third person because he will never be punished," Anwari said.

A girl is often beaten and sometimes killed because when the family look at her, they see the killer. "Because they lost someone, they take it out on her," Naderi said.

There are no reliable statistics on blood-feud marriages, a hidden practice. When it happens, the families and elders often will not reveal details of the crime or the punishment.

Several years ago in nearby Momand Dara district, a taxi driver hit a boy with his car, killing him. The boy's family demanded a girl as compensation, so the driver purchased an 11-year-old named Fawzia from an acquaintance for US$5,000 and gave her to the dead boy's relatives, according to the Afghan Women's Network office in Jalalabad. Three years ago, Fawzia was shot to death, according to a two-page report kept in a black binder of cases of violence against women.

The story of Malia and the nine sheep illustrates the suffering of girls forced into such marriages. Malia listened as her father [Ahmad] described how he was held hostage by his lender, Khaliq Mohammad, because he could not come up with the money to pay for the sheep, which Ahmad had sold to free a relative seized because of another of Ahmad's debts. [See Figure 1-2.]

Ahmad was released only when he agreed to give Malia's hand in marriage to the lender's 18-year-old son. Asked how she felt about it, Malia shook her head and remained silent. Her face then crumpled in anguish and she wiped away tears. Asked if she was happy, she responded halfheartedly, "Well, my mother and father agreed..."

Her voice trailed off, and she cried again. Does she want to meet her husband-to-be? She clicked her tongue—a firm, yet delicate "tsk"—with a barely perceptible shake of her head. The answer was no.

The theory is not entirely unsound—join groups or families and their interests to stop the cycle of retaliation and end the need for generational vendettas. However, in reality, such marriages can create a whole new set of victims when arranged or coerced in opposition to the desires of those involved. In such cases, the "good news" is different for everyone.

In any event, the notion that this time period or its related practices represent some kind of *golden age* of discretionary justice for any but a favored few seems misplaced, if not entirely mythical. Certainly, some victims were free to accuse those who harmed them and seek the vengeance they desired. This would naturally result in increased false reporting. Moreover, there might not be anyone

FIGURE 1-2

As described in Tang (2007): "Nazir Ahmad said he was forced to pay a debt of less than $200 by betrothing his [16 year old] daughter Malia, third from left. From left to right Malia's father, sister, Malia, and her mother, during an interview with Associated Press in their home in Jalalabad, Afghanistan, Sunday, July 1, 2007."

to protect them from the consequences if they did make a report, true or not, let alone protect them from the accused. Consider the following realities of this type of justice:

- The less power or perceived character one had, the less able to report and sustain sympathy for actual victimization.
- The more power or perceived character one had, the more able to abuse the power of accusation (make false allegations for personal gain).
- Given the absence of any standard of evidence, and the known fallibility of eyewitness accounts, the likelihood of being wrong in one's accusations was necessarily high.
- Making an accusation could result in generations of retaliation, including dishonor for children and grandchildren.
- Committing a crime could result in generations of retaliation, including dishonor for children and grandchildren.
- In patriarchal systems, women and children were often forced to pay the price of crimes committed by their adult male kinsman, becoming victims without any voice or recourse.

The list of inequities does not end here, but the point is that this was not a golden age for victims or offenders by any stretch of the imagination. Although it might look good to some through the distance of time, the sword of justice swings erratically and irrevocably under such circumstances. It also favors only the favored.

The Dark Ages of Victimology

It has been argued that the so-called *dark ages* of victimology were a result of the emergence of structured local governments and the development of legal statutes. Such laws and governments were a byproduct of more stable economic systems. They were made possible by urbanization, the industrial revolution, and the rise in power of the Roman Catholic Church (Karmen, 2012; Shichor and Tibbetts, 2002). As families moved away from their farms and into cities, neighborhoods became depersonalized. The old tribal systems, based on culture and kinship, were no longer viable (Doerner and Lab, 2011).

In these criminal-oriented justice systems, offenses were increasingly viewed as perpetrated against the laws of the king or state, not just against a victim or the victim's family. Eventually, focus shifted toward offender punishments and rights, as opposed to victim rights and restoration. Subsequently, as formal systems of criminal justice rose and spread, victim involvement eroded to little more than that of witness for the police and prosecution (Doerner and Lab, 2011; Karmen, 2012). As explained in Doerner and Lab (2011; p. 3):

> The development of formal law enforcement, courts, and correctional systems in the past few centuries has reflected an interest in protecting the state. For the most part, the criminal justice system simply forgot about victims and their best interests.

One result of this ongoing evolution is that modern criminal justice systems do not necessarily seek to help the victim in a given case. As subsequent chapters discuss, those in power invariably create laws to protect cultures, societies, and institutions. In modern Western cultures, for example, society at large is the intended beneficiary of criminal law: the criminal justice systems seek to separate criminals from society, to deter others from acting criminally via ever-harsher punishments, and ultimately to prevent future victimizations. Whether this is actually being accomplished is a matter of debate, and individual victims are often required to seek remedy for the harms they suffer in civil court, owing to failed or inadequate law enforcement efforts.

Reemergence of the Victim

A so-called *reemergence of the victim* occurred in the 1950s and 1960s, when a small number of people began to recognize that those who were most affected by criminal acts were rarely involved in the process. Unsettled with the fact that victims' rights and needs had gone by the wayside, they fought to bring this disparity to the public's attention (Karmen, 2012). It soon became the consensus among various groups, including journalists, social scientists, and those involved directly with the criminal justice system, that "victims were forgotten figures in the criminal justice process whose needs and wants had been systematically overlooked but merited attention" (Karmen 2012; p. 38; see also Mawby, 1982).

During the same time, a collection of sociologists, criminologists, and legal scholars came to the same realization—that victims were being overlooked as a source of information about crime and criminals. Their interest in studying victims is what ultimately led to the birth of traditional victimology as a discrete scientific endeavor. While victims' rights were gaining attention, victimology, in its early years, did not seek to address the needs of victims and alleviate their suffering. Rather, it came from a desire to better understand the victim's role in the criminal act, relationship to the offender, and culpability (Doerner and Lab, 2011). It is from this research that the field of criminology formally spawned the subspecialty of victimology, and by the early 1970s courses on the subject were being taught at universities across the United States. As announced and described in *Time Magazine* (1971):

> At its last conference, the International Criminological Society included a special session on the behavioral patterns of victims. For the first time in the U.S., three courses in victimology are being offered, one at the University of California, the others at Northeastern University and at Boston University Law School. A major book on the subject is nearing publication, and an international conference devoted solely to victimology has been scheduled for Jerusalem in 1973.
>
> Most behavioral scientists agree with University of Montreal Criminologist Ezzat Abdel Fattah, who contends that "there are people who attract the criminal as the lamb attracts the wolf." Some of these victims are masochistic or depressed; Criminologist Hans von Hentig described them as longing "lustfully" for injury.
>
> Others, says Northeastern University Victimologist Stephen Schafer, have certain personality traits—for example, the Kennedys' ambition for power—that invite attack by "offending the offender." Israeli Criminologist Menachem Amir, who set up the victimology course at Berkeley, cites cultural factors: to participate in certain lifestyles, such as prostitution and drug addiction, is to court trouble. There are some occupations, too, that are likely to attract violence: cab driver, bank teller, and policeman, among others. The motivation for seeking these jobs sometimes includes an unconscious need to be a victim, or a wish to defy fate.

The type of crime often fits the behavior that provoked it. Theft, for instance, is often stimulated by the victim's negligence, swindles by his greed, and blackmail by his guilt. Murder can be invited by belligerence: in 1969 a national study of bus drivers showed that three who were killed during robberies had vowed not to let "any punk kid" rob them, and had carried and tried to use guns in violation of company rules. In other cases, suicidal wishes have provoked murder—a phenomenon that the mother of Congressional Medal of Honor Winner Dwight Johnson may have recognized when she surmised that her son, shot while committing a holdup, had "tired of life and needed someone else to pull the trigger."

Much of the initial research in victimology remains foundational to questions that are still being asked today. A brief discussion of the early victimologists and their thinking is therefore warranted.

KEY FIGURES

As mentioned, the origins of scientific victimology can be attributed to a few key figures in criminology, including *Hans von Hentig, Benjamin Mendelsohn, Stephen Schafer,* and *Marvin Wolfgang* (Karmen, 2012). Their early work represents the first attempts to study the victim–offender relationship in a systematic fashion, however misguided by generalizations, personal bias, and professional agendas. Each is discussed in turn, as their approaches to victim study are arguably the most relevant to modern concerns.

Hans von Hentig (1887–1974)

A criminologist in Germany during the first half of the last century, Hans von Hentig sought to develop crime prevention strategies. Having researched the factors that predisposed one to criminality, he began to wonder what might cause a victim to become a victim. He ultimately determined that certain victim characteristics did play a role in shaping the crimes suffered (Doerner and Lab, 2011; Meadows, 2007).

Specifically, Von Hentig believed that some victims contributed to their own victimization by virtue of many converging factors, not all of which were in their control. Von Hentig described his beliefs to the mainstream media in *Time Magazine* (1948):

> The characteristics and forces that tend to make a man a criminal...are diverse and complicated. A contributing factor may be ugliness, deafness, a physical handicap...
>
> Victims, Dr. Von Hentig believes, are born or shaped by society much as criminals are. ... Some types of criminals are attracted to slum

areas; so are their victims. Feeblemindedness, common among some types of criminals, is also common among their victims.

...certain characteristics of law-abiding citizens arouse a counter reaction in the criminal. The inexperienced businessman, for example, invites embezzlement; the nagging wife is flirting with murder; the alcoholic is a natural for robbery. Thus the victim becomes the "tempter."

To his credit, Von Hentig was perhaps the first to systematically study the role victims could play in the crimes committed against them (Van Dijk, 1999). He later published *The Criminal and His Victim: Studies in the Sociobiology of Crime* (1948), which contained a chapter devoted solely to discussing these theories. Von Hentig argued for acknowledging the responsibility some victims had in becoming victimized. He even developed a system of categorizing victims along a continuum that depended on their contribution to the criminal act, though his terminology would now be considered offensive to some.

Von Hentig originally classified victims into one of 13 categories, which could easily be described as a list of characteristics that increase victim vulnerability or exposure to danger (adapted from pages 404–438):

1. *The Young:* Von Hentig was referring to children and infants. From a contemporary point of view, children are physically weaker, have less mental prowess, have fewer legal rights, and are dependent on their caretakers (e.g., parents, guardians, teachers, and day-care providers); they also have the potential to be exposed to a wider range of harm than adults. Moreover, they are less able to defend themselves and sometimes less likely to be believed should they report abuse. This includes children who suffer emotional, physical, and sexual abuse at home because of abusive parents (often under the influence of drugs and alcohol); children who are bullied at school because of some aspect of their appearance or personality; and children who are forced into acts of prostitution or sold into slavery by impoverished parents. Each suffers different levels and frequencies of exposure to different kinds of harm.

2. *Females:* Von Hentig was referring to all women. From a contemporary point of view, many women are physically weaker than men. Many have been culturally conditioned, to varying degrees, to accept male authority. And many women are financially dependent on the men in their lives (e.g., fathers, male family members, husbands, and boyfriends). To make matters worse, many Western women are conditioned to believe that their value is associated with their bodies, or specifically, their sexuality or reproductive capability. In extreme cases, perceptions of failure in these areas can lead to low self-esteem, depression, substance abuse, promiscuity, and prostitution, resulting in varying exposure to harm.

3. *The Old*: Von Hentig was referring to the elderly. In a contemporary sense, they have many of the same vulnerabilities as children: they are often physically weaker, mentally less facile, and may be under someone else's care. This can expose them to a range of harms, from the theft of personal property to physical abuse. However, they are also particularly vulnerable to confidence scams, as they can have greater access to money and property, along with poor memory and a sense of pride that may combine to prevent them from reporting loss.

4. *The Mentally Defective and Deranged*: Von Hentig was referring to the feeble-minded, the mentally ill, drug addicts, and alcoholics. Those who suffer from any of these conditions are likely to have an altered perception of reality. As a consequence, depending on the level of their affliction, personality, and environment, these potential victims may harm themselves and others to varying degrees. They may also suffer many of the same general kinds of exposures as children and the elderly.

5. *Immigrants*: Von Hentig was referring to foreigners unfamiliar with a given culture. In reality, any people traveling to a culture different from their own are subject to varying gaps in communication and comprehension. This can, depending on where they go and whom they encounter, expose them to all manner of confidence schemes, theft, and abuse, to say nothing of prejudices. It is compounded by the presence of language barriers, religious conflicts, and cultural differences that can result in behavior that is unintentionally offensive. This is true whether the situation involves an American traveling to Asia; a Mexican visiting relatives in California; or a someone from Calcutta immigrating to London.

6. *Minorities*: Von Hentig was referring to the "racially disadvantaged," as he put it. What this truly means is prejudice. Groups against which there is some amount of bias or prejudice by another may be exposed to varying levels of abuse and violence depending on the tensions present on a given day.

7. *Dull Normals*: Von Hentig was referring to "simple-minded persons," as he put it. Essentially, these are people who border mental handicap. From a contemporary viewpoint, we might consider them as having the same types of exposure to harm as those who are mentally defective and deranged.

8. *The Depressed*: Von Hentig was referring to those with various psychological maladies that cause them to withdraw inward. From a contemporary viewpoint, those who are depressed may expose themselves to all manner of danger, intentional and otherwise. They also tend to have less of a social support system, in that they may not be as likely or able to reach out for help from others. Additionally, they may take medication that alters perception, affects judgment, and impairs reasoning.

9. *The Acquisitive:* Von Hentig was referring to those who are greedy and looking for quick gain. In other words, those focused on acquiring wealth and possessions. Such individuals may suspend their judgment, or intentionally put themselves in dangerous situations, to get the things of value that they desire.

10. *The Wanton:* Von Hentig was referring to promiscuous individuals. People who engage in indiscriminate sexual activity with many different partners expose themselves to different levels of disease and varying personalities. Some of these personalities may be healthy and supportive; some may be narcissistic, possessive, jealous, and destructive.

11. *The Lonesome or Heartbroken:* Von Hentig was referring to widows, widowers, and those in mourning. From a contemporary standpoint, loneliness is at epidemic proportions, with more than half of marriages ending in divorce, the rise of the culture of narcissism since the late 1970s (see Lasch, 1979), and diminishing intimacy skills across all cultures. This category does not apply only to those in mourning; those who are lonely or heartbroken are prone to substance abuse, and can be easy prey for con men, the abusive, and the manipulative.

12. *The Tormentor:* Von Hentig was referring to the abusive parent. In contemporary terms, there are abusive caretakers, intimates, and family members of all kinds. Such abusers expose themselves to the harm they inflict, the resulting guilt and angst, and the potential for their victims to fight back. For example, an abusive mother who gets drunk and punches a child exposes herself to the dangers of injuring her hand, of misjudging her strike and even her balance, of feeling bad about it, and of the child punching back.

13. *The Blocked, Exempted, or Fighting*: Von Hentig was referring to victims of blackmail, extortion, and confidence scams. In such cases, the attention of law enforcement, and any subsequent publicity, is something that these victims wish to avoid. They find a means of dealing with the crimes being committed against them (e.g., giving in to demands) without avoiding harm or loss—and without involving the authorities.

From a research point of view, these are interesting and even somewhat useful classifications with important theoretical implications, although the terminology is sometimes inappropriate. However, the case-working victimologist must study each victim to determine the extent to which such a classification has a bearing on the harm suffered within a particular crime. Some children are smart and fast; many women are strong and self-assured; some of the elderly are quick and resourceful; immigrants and travelers can learn languages and customs; and the "blocked" may decide to go to the police. In short, many of the generalizations suggested in this typology may not hold when applied to a specific crime or victim.

Benjamin Mendelsohn

Benjamin Mendelsohn was a French-Israeli lawyer who began studying victims in 1947 (Karmen, 2012). While working for the defense on a rape case, he became interested in the correlations between rapists and their victims. He found that there was often a strong interpersonal relationship between the two, and that it could lead some victims to unknowingly invite or even cause their own victimization (Meadows, 2007). He referred to this as *victim precipitation*.[4]

Mendelsohn ultimately believed that many victims shared an unconscious capacity for being victimized, and referred to this as being *victim prone*. Similar to Von Hentig, Mendelsohn developed a typology that categorizes the extent to which a victim is culpable in his or her own demise. However, while Von Hentig's typology explains victim contribution based on personal characteristics, Mendelsohn's typology uses situational factors. Mendelsohn's six victim types, as adapted from Meadows (2007; p. 22) are as follows:

1. *Completely innocent victim:* This person exhibits no provocative or contributory behavior prior to the offender's attack.
2. *Victim due to ignorance:* This person unwittingly does something that places him or her in a position to be victimized.
3. *Voluntary victim:* Victims make a conscious and deliberate choice to suffer harm or loss. This includes suicides, or those injured while participating in high-risk activities crimes such as drug abuse or prostitution (see Figure 1-3).
4. *Victim more guilty than the offender:* The victim provokes a criminal act (e.g., throws the first punch to start a fight but ends up the loser).
5. *Most guilty victim:* This person is the initial aggressor, but due to circumstances beyond his or her control ends up the victim (e.g., attempts to rob a convenience store but is shot by the storeowner).
6. *Simulating or imaginary victim:* This person is a pretender, or false reporter. No crime has happened yet the person reports suffering harm or loss.

The danger with Mendelsohn's typology is that it doesn't always apply that well to actual cases. It does have some important conceptual value, in showing a continuum of possible victim culpability or precipitation. However, if applied broadly, simplistically, and without careful investigation into the facts, it could be misused. Before these descriptors can be applied to a specific case, attention must be paid to the details. This means accepting that not every prostitute or drug user is a voluntary victim; not every bar fight involves a more guilty or most guilty victim; and not everyone who fails to exhibit provocative behavior prior

---

[4]Doerner and Lab explain (2011; p. 7): "Victim precipitation deals with the degree to which the victim is responsible for his or her own victimization."

FIGURE 1-3

A Chinese prostitute is found by authorities in a Guangzhou hotel room with two men. Were she to become the victim of a crime or contract a venereal disease, as have many prostitutes, those using Mendelsohn's typology might be tempted to dismiss her as a *voluntary victim*. This description may or may not be accurate. For instance, many prostitutes around the world are sold or tricked into sex work by relatives and brothel owners at a very young age, and then become captive by circumstances that they cannot control.[5] In some cases they are broken in to the trade with beatings, rape, and other forms of torture. Eventually, they can become trapped by fear, shame, poverty, addiction, and disease.

---

[5]The United States is no stranger to the problem of *human trafficking*, which is among the most profitable forms of organized crime in the world. According to Srikantiah (2007; p.162–163): "Trafficking is modern-day slavery. Men, women, and children from developing countries are trafficked to industrialized countries for forced prostitution, forced labor, and other forms of exploitation. Increased globalization, including cheaper transportation and communication methods, has resulted in increased migration, including increased trafficking in persons. According to U.S. government estimates, up to 800,000 people are trafficked across international borders annually, and up to 17,500 people are trafficked into the United States each year. These victims include men, women, boys, and girls. The majority of trafficked persons are women and girls, who are more vulnerable to trafficking because of a greater susceptibility to poverty, illiteracy, and lower social status. Individuals are typically trafficked from poor countries, often in the global South, to wealthier countries. Trafficking is an extremely profitable international criminal enterprise, ranking third in profits after the arms and drug markets. The International Labour Organization estimates that human trafficking generates $31.6 billion in organized crime profits annually."

to an attack is completely innocent. While Mendelsohn's typology is interesting in theory, its application to specific cases can be problematic, if not entirely inappropriate, when contextual information is not investigated and considered.

Stephen Schafer, PhD

Dr. Stephen Schafer was a professor of sociology at Northeastern University in Boston, Massachusetts. In 1968, he published what is regarded by some as the first textbook on the subject of victimology, *The Victim and His Criminal: A Study in Functional Responsibility*. According to Van Dijk, this work was significant to the advance of victimology, as it was an "independent study of the relationships and interactions between offender and victim, before, during, and after the crime" (1999; p. 2). Schafer's study involved interviews with criminals and aimed to build upon the typologies presented in previous works by focusing on victim culpability.

According to Doerner and Lab (2011), Schafer proposed seven types of victim responsibility (or victim precipitation), which are essentially a variation on the work of Von Hentig (1948):

1. *Unrelated victims:* No victim responsibility
2. *Provocative victims:* Victim shares responsibility
3. *Precipitative victims:* Some degree of responsibility
4. *Biologically weak victims:* No responsibility
5. *Socially weak victims:* No responsibility
6. *Self-victimizing:* Total victim responsibility
7. *Political victims:* No responsibility

In reviewing this typology, we find it to be less of an inclusive measure and more of an incomplete list of circumstances that mitigate victim responsibility because they increase general vulnerability. While it is true that lines are drawn between the *provocative*, the *precipitative*, and the *self-victimizing*, from the examples cited in the literature, it is unclear how these categories would be applied to a specific case, as the defining elements are highly subjective. Also, Schafer has inappropriately defined (and therefore presumptively assumed) the specific responsibility of each victim type. There appears to be no room for mitigating circumstances once a victim is put in a particular slot, which is what a pedantic or bureaucratic victimologist could do with this labeling system.

Socially weak victims, such as immigrants, are regarded as having no responsibility, but what if they are shot while robbing a convenience store? *Biologically weak victims,* such as the elderly, are also regarded as having no responsibility, but what if they are abusing alcohol and become rancorous precipitative drunks, only to start a physical altercation at home that they lose? As discussed throughout this text, the relationships between victims and criminals are far too complex for such rigid presumptions.

However problematic, Dr. Schafer's contribution to the field of victimology must not be dismissed. As Young and Stein explain: "The importation of victimology to the United States was due largely to the work of the scholar Stephen Schafer, whose book *The Victim and His Criminal: A Study in Functional Responsibility* became mandatory reading for anyone interested in the study of crime victims and their behaviors" (Young and Stein, 2004; p. 2). With his research, our efforts have the benefit of being that much more informed.

Marvin E. Wolfgang, PhD

Dr. Marvin Wolfgang was a professor of criminology, legal studies, and law at the Wharton School, and founding director of the Sellin Center for Studies in Criminology and Criminal Law, at the University of Pennsylvania (see Figure 1-4). According to Doerner and Lab (2011), Wolfgang was the first to present empirical research findings as support for his theories of victimology. In his work *Patterns of Criminal Homicide* (1958), Wolfgang presented the results of his study of police homicide records, which concluded that over a quarter of the homicides in the city of Philadelphia between 1948 and 1952 involved some element of victim contribution and participation (Doerner and Lab, 2011). He even went so far as to label one type of homicide *victim-precipitated*, where

FIGURE 1-4
Dr. Marvin Wolfgang, a pioneer of quantitative and theoretical criminology, died in 1998 at the age of 73.

the initial physical violence or threat of physical violence came from the victim, not the offender (Shichor and Tibbetts, 2002). This concept of victim precipitation has since been used to study many violent crimes, but it loses some of its validity when property and sex crimes are considered, since provocation by the victim becomes much more subjective in such cases (Shichor and Tibbetts, 2002).

VICTIM STUDY: PAST TO PRESENT

As we have described, the formal discipline of victimology was born out of a desire to study victims for the purpose of answering social and legal questions regarding cause and culpability. Liu explains (2006; p. 175): "victimologists consider how victims help create the conditions in which they are victimized, how victims contribute to and even provoke their own victimization, and the demographic relationship between victims and offenders."

On the one hand, victimology began as a preventative issue relating to social health: what can we do to avoid becoming a victim today, and what can we do to reduce the number of victims tomorrow? On the other hand, it was a matter of legal consequence: to what extent did the victim contribute to his or her own demise with respect to circumstances, ignorance, negligence, or intentional provocation? Victimology was the beginning of an attempt, however imperfect, to peel back the layers of the onion and expose the dynamics of the victim–offender relationship. But the political climate has changed how we study victims today.

Modern texts on the subject of victimology, many of them cited in this chapter, have moved away from asking questions that might reveal victim falsity and weaken related advocacy or criminal prosecutions. Rather, they tend to focus on victim statistics, the impact of crime, the need to enhance victim rights, victim compensation, and ways to develop new victim remedies. Furthermore, they offer broad yet thin reference to victim groups by crime type, in accordance with the Uniform Crime Reports (UCR, to be discussed in Chapter 2). Some texts do not achieve even that level of coverage, being little more than compilations of various writings by authors with diverse views and agendas without organization or theme.

In short, current victimology texts presume victimhood for all of the numbers that apply and provide little that would help inform an objective or critical investigation into the facts and dynamics of a particular victim–offender relationship. In this current perspective, crime is regarded as a social disease with victimology acting as its socio-statistical thermometer—taking the temperature of victim groups and providing a speculative lens for various causes. We understand that this is a genuinely important role and one that must not be completely abandoned by the field. Somebody has to look at the numbers and give voice to the available empirical trends.

However, it must be acknowledged that despite the collection of victim data, the use of victim statistics, and the politics of victim sympathy, such approaches to victimology can regularly be found lacking in actual science. In fact, they may even be viewed as biased, or as pandering to victims, advocates, bureaucracies, and their respective agendas. Certainly, these voices need the floor, but not the whole floor and not the whole agenda.

Any victim bias is a problem when studying victims of crime: pro-victim and anti-victim alike. However, a pro-victim bias in victimology is currently being rewarded because it is socially and politically inoffensive, and because it maintains the much-needed sanctity of victimhood. Without a presumptive showing regarding the *sanctity of victimhood*,[6] some investigators become lax and apathetic, some prosecutors are loath to go to trial, and some juries are hesitant to convict. As a consequence, anything that gets in the way, whether it be research asking politically inappropriate questions, investigations that might reveal negative victim information, or forensic examinations that might disprove victim claims, is too often regarded as off-limits for mainstream victimologists.

Victimologists, to achieve any scientific threshold, must be free to remain skeptical, inquisitive, and above all, objective. They cannot be attached to a particular sociocultural view or agenda; they cannot be working to achieve satisfaction or remedies for the victim; and they cannot assume the existence of victimhood. Victimologists must be free to question and interpret victim evidence as it is found. As a counterbalance to the victimologists who are in the business of taking temperatures of crime victim populations, often amidst a host of biasing influences including pressure to maintain the sanctity of victimhood, there must be those free to doubt and seek proofs in individual cases. This is the considered role of *forensic victimology*.

FORENSIC VICTIMOLOGY: AN INTRODUCTION

Although many diverse aspects of victim study are encapsulated within general victimology, interactionist victimology, and critical victimology, there is one concept that has been largely overlooked in the related literature to date.

---

[6]*The sanctity of victimhood* refers to the belief that all victims are universally good, honest, and pure, making those who defend them righteous and morally justified in any action they take. Conversely, it suggests that those who doubt victim accounts are immoral and unjust. Ultimately, it also requires victims to meet an unrealistic standard of near perfect victimity. It is anathema to the scientific method.

Forensic victimology,[7] the idiographic and nomothetic study of violent crime victims for the purposes of addressing investigative and forensic issues, has been an implicit feature of the field since its inception. However, forensic victimology is often inappropriately folded in with treatment, punishment, and even advocacy-oriented goals. Expropriated from scientific study and commonly disguised as professional compassion to serve nonscientific agendas, explicit discussions of what may be viewed as forensic victimology by behavioral scientists have been limited.

Forensic victimology is a subdivision of *interactionist victimology,* in which victims are defined by having suffered harm or loss due to a breach of law. It involves the thorough, critical, and objective outlining of victim lifestyles and circumstances, the events leading up to their injury, and the precise nature of any harm or loss suffered. The purpose of this text is to provide readers with an applied understanding of the principles and practice of forensic victimology, to define it as an explicit area of scientific victim study, and to outline its value to investigative and forensic purposes.

Purpose

The primary goals of those involved with other fields of victimology commonly relate to the restoration of victims in some fashion. They work at empowering victims; returning victims to the state they were in prior to suffering harm or loss; or making them feel comfortable again, and satisfied that justice has been served (Williams, 2004). Again, these are important functions.

Forensic victimology, however, does not seek to assist with victim advocacy or promote victim sympathy. Nor is the forensic victimologist invested in restoring victims and making them whole. However, there is a heightened awareness that the victim evidence gathered, as well as subsequent interpretations, may be used by others for these purposes at a later time.

It is essential to appreciate that forensic victimology is an applied discipline as opposed to a theoretical one. The forensic victimologist seeks to examine, consider, and interpret particular victim evidence in a scientific fashion to be able to answer investigative and forensic (i.e., legal) questions. In that capacity, forensic victimologists serve investigations and court proceedings by endeavoring to do the following (adapted from Turvey, 2011; pp. 168–169):

1. *Assist in understanding elements of the crime.* By studying the victim, the examiner is better able to understand the relationship between a victim

---

[7]The term *forensic victimology* was originally defined in Petherick and Turvey (2008). However, the general purpose and practice are as old as criminal investigation itself.

and his or her lifestyle and environment, and subsequently of a given offender to that victim. Victimology provides the context for the victim–crime scene interaction, the offender–crime scene interaction, and the victim–offender interaction.

2. *Assist in developing a timeline.* Retracing a victim's last known actions and creating a timeline are critical to understanding the victim as a person, understanding the victim's relationship to the environment, understanding the victim's relationship to other events, and understanding how the victim came to be acquired by an offender.

3. *Define the suspect pool.* In an unsolved case, where the identity of the offender is unknown, a thorough victimology specifies the suspect pool. The victim's lifestyle in general and his or her activities in particular must be scrutinized to determine who had access to that victim, what they had access to, how and when they gained and maintained access, and where the access occurred. If we can understand how and why an offender has selected known victims, then we may also be able to establish a relational link of some kind between the victim and that offender. These links may be geographic, work related, schedule oriented, school related, hobby related, or they may be otherwise connected. The connections provide a suspect pool that includes those with knowledge of, or access to, the related area.

4. *Provide investigative suggestions.* A thorough victimology compiled in the investigative stage will offer suggestions and provide direction for an investigation. Such suggestions may include interviewing those in the specified suspect pool, interviewing witnesses about discrepancies in their statements or contradictions with timeline information, and examining or re-examining any physical evidence that may have been overlooked during the initial investigation.

5. *Assist with crime reconstruction.* By understanding the victim's behavioral patterns, the examiner is better equipped to complete a thorough crime reconstruction. Knowing why a victim was in the location where he or she was acquired, or what the victim was doing in that location, provides the examiner with context. Contextual information is vital for accurately inferring the most reasonable behaviors to have taken place in relation to a crime or at a crime scene.

6. *Assist with contextualizing allegations of victimization.* Developing a clear and factually complete victim history will provide context to the allegations of victimization. Victimological information may also help to support or refute the allegations of victimization.

7. *Assist with the development of offender modus operandi.* Knowledge of the victim's pattern of behavior in relation to the location where the victim was acquired may assist with the development of the offender's

modus operandi (MO), specifically in victim selection.[8] For example, an offender who is trolling for victims may choose to acquire an opportunistic victim at a location with increased victim availability and vulnerability, such as a busy pub with intoxicated patrons. This information tells us about the offender's MO or the choices made during the commission of the crime.

8. *Assist with the development of offender motive.* Without a thorough examination of victim history, the examiner may overlook important victimological information that may reflect an offender's motivation. For example, an examiner can only appropriately establish a list of items missing from a crime scene if it is known what the victim had in his or her possession at the time of victimization. Without this information, a profit-oriented motivation may be improperly disregarded for lack of knowing what is actually missing.

9. *Assist with case linkage.* When an examiner is determining whether a series of crimes can be behaviorally linked, victim selection is an important behavioral factor that cannot be ignored during a linkage analysis. A study of the victims across a series of cases may reveal a unique connection between the victims, or the exposure levels of the victims may allow the examiner to support or refute a linkage.

10. *Assist with public safety response.* If we can understand how and why offenders have selected their previous victims, then we have a better chance of predicting the type of victim they may select in the future. This will allow the appropriate public safety messages to be delivered to the public with the aim of reducing the exposure levels of those affected individuals. For example, an offender who enters multiple residences through unlocked windows may prompt a public safety message to be delivered to affected communities warning them to lock their windows and doors.

11. *Educate the court.* In cases in which the victimology has a bearing on specific legal issues, the forensic victimologist is best situated to examine case-specific evidence and provide informed opinions for consideration by a judge or jury, whenever deemed necessary by the court. It is understood that investigative and forensic venues are quite different in scope, structure, and function. The questions they need answered are particular to their unique geographical variations. They also represent very different standards of evidence. What may be investigatively useful speculation or theory at one point may lack the sufficiency for subsequent

---

[8]As explained in Turvey (2011; p. 153): "All criminals have a *modus operandi* (or MO, method of operation) that consists of their habits, techniques, and peculiarities of behavior."

court-worthy opinions. Given the capacity for investigative work to find its way into court, this distinction must be ever-present and crystal clear.

Philosophy

The philosophy of forensic victimology is that victim facts are preferable to victim fictions; that victim evidence must be gathered and examined in a consistent, thorough, and objective fashion as with any other form of evidence; and that interpretations of victim evidence must comport with the tenets of the scientific method, whether examining the results of a rape kit or assessing victim risk.

The guiding principle for studying victims in investigative and forensic contexts is this: a comprehensive understanding of the victims and their circumstances will allow for an accurate interpretation of the nature of their harm or loss, and it will also teach us about their offender. The less we know about the victim, the less we know about the crime and the criminal. Consequently, the way we collect and develop victim evidence is just as important as our eventual interpretations: they must not be weak, narrow, or based on unproved assumptions. With this as our standard, it is not possible to avoid the fact that the best way to objectively build knowledge and render valid interpretations is through the *scientific method.* As explained in Turvey (2008; p.45):

> The scientific method is a way to investigate how or why something works, or how something happened, through the development of hypotheses and subsequent attempts at falsification through testing and other accepted means. It is a structured process designed to build scientific knowledge by way of answering specific questions about observations through careful analysis and critical thinking. Observations are used to form testable hypotheses, and, with sufficient testing, hypotheses can become scientific theories. Eventually, over much time, with precise testing marked by a failure to falsify, scientific theories can become scientific principles. The scientific method is the particular approach to knowledge building and problem solving employed by scientists of every kind. ...
>
> It is important to explain that scientists use the scientific method to build knowledge and solve problems; its use defines them. If one is doing something else, then one is not actually a scientist. Faigman et al. (1997, p. 48) warn: "Not all knowledge asserted by people who are commonly thought of as scientists is the product of the scientific method."

It follows that to meet the requirements of a scientific study, forensic victimology must be conducted with a scientific mindset by those properly educated and trained to employ the scientific method. Any other approach is out of step with this philosophy, serving some other purpose or rationale.

Rationale

Forensic victimology is intended to serve the justice system by educating it. It is aimed at helping provide for informed investigations, requiring scientific examinations of victim evidence presented in court, and more informed legal outcomes. As with any other forensic discipline, it does not take sides, and it does not seek to intrude on the ultimate issues of guilt, innocence, or victimity. Further explanation is necessary.

As described in Dienstein (2005; p. 160), *criminal investigation* is the process of gathering facts to be used as evidence and proof in a court of law. Without an investigation, the facts will be absent and proofs will be impossible to attain. Schultz (2005; p. 122) explains that prior to being tested in the courtroom, a competent investigation will gather or prepare evidence of the following: "knowledge or proof that a crime has been committed; the existence of a victim(s)…an approved report of the investigation answering the questions of who, what, where, when, why and how; and evidence that has been identified and preserved for the prosecutor." Only then may investigators proceed with their case to the district attorney for prosecutorial consideration.

In the investigative realm, forensic victimology provides for the consistent recognition, collection, preservation, and documentation of victim evidence, all of which will be detailed in subsequent chapters. Questions are asked, context is established, and history is documented. Each piece of victim evidence is scrutinized by investigators and then acted upon again and again until it is an exhausted possibility. This informs the nature, scope, and depth of the investigation. It can also lead to the discovery of additional relevant or dispositive evidence. Ultimately, forensic victimology assists with answering the question of whether and how criminal charges and civil liabilities may be appropriate, which is going to be decided by the court.

More and more, criminal and civil trials alike require the assistance of forensic experts to introduce and explain various kinds of evidence to the jury. To do so, a potential witness must first be qualified as an expert by the court. According to Lilly (1987; p.483):

> [A]n expert witness possesses knowledge and skill that distinguishes him from ordinary witnesses. Presumably, he is in a position superior to the other trial participants, including the jury, to draw inferences and reach conclusions within his field of expertise.

Significantly different from investigative opinions, which are dynamic and often rendered in haste with incomplete information amid ongoing efforts to gather facts, forensic opinions are those expert findings regarding the state of the record held to such a level of confidence and certainty that they may be presented in court as best evidence.

In the forensic realm (which necessarily involves and therefore must continuously anticipate the courtroom), forensic victimology is a form of evidence that informs the nature, scope, and depth of any legal proceedings to be decided by the trier of fact (a judge or jury). When presented by a forensic expert, it involves the scientific interpretation of various kinds of victim evidence gathered during the investigation and any subsequent analysis. Ultimately, it assists with demonstrating the actual limits of victim evidence—which criminal or civil theories it supports and which it refutes.

CASE EXAMPLE:

Investigative and Forensic Utility of Forensic Victimology

In May of 2009, 23-year-old Rocky Moody of Richmond County, Georgia, was shot to death (see Figure 1-5). He had been employed by the Augusta National Golf Club as a landscaper, and had served in the Georgia National Guard. He was shot in the chest one time with a rifle. The killing occurred at his home, where he lived with his father, 55-year-old Robert Moody.

The shooting occurred subsequent to an argument between Rocky Moody and his father. An investigation by police revealed that the argument had become heated; that Rocky Moody had punched his father several times; and that he had bitten his father on the arm, causing a visible injury. Shortly thereafter, Robert Moody was hospitalized and underwent several surgeries to treat necrotizing fasciitis, which is believed to have been caused by multiple bites from his son that night.

Relevant to establishing the context of the shooting, law enforcement investigated Rocky Moody's criminal history, which was extensive. As reported in Johnson (2012):

> Rocky Moody had a criminal history in Richmond County going back to 1997, when he would have been 9, according to his sheriff's office file.
>
> Although the law does not allow the release of reports on a juvenile, authorities can say there were 14 juvenile reports involving Moody between 1997 and 2006.
>
> In 2005, *The Augusta Chronicle* interviewed Moody after his graduation from the Georgia National Guard's Youth Challenge Academy.
>
> Moody, 17 at the time, admitted to making mistakes but said, "I was always judged by my past."
>
> ...A year later, Moody was in the Richmond County jail on charges of theft by taking,

according to his file. Police said Moody took a Toyota Camry from Surrey Tavern. The car had been left unlocked with the keys in the ignition. It was found abandoned the next day at Eisenhower Park.

> Since turning 18, Moody was arrested at least five times. Charges included drug offenses, theft by taking, theft by taking motor vehicle, driving under the influence and family violence battery.

Robert Moody was arrested and charged with murder and weapons possession in relation to his son's death. However, he missed his initial court dates due to the aforementioned hospitalization and surgery.

Establishing the criminal history of the victim in this case provides important contextual details that could be used to support a theory of self-defense. These same details could also be used as potential mitigating circumstances in sentencing, in the event that the father is convicted of any crimes. In fact, the logic of making an arrest and bringing murder charges in this case is questionable when considered in light of the injuries sustained by the father, the victim's history of drug use, and the victim's violent criminal background.[9] Taking this case to trial, and achieving a conviction, requires the existence of other evidence that overwhelms these victimological considerations—or the successful exclusion of victim history as evidence altogether.

---

[9]*Victim toxicology (e.g., presence of drugs and alcohol in the victim's system), which should have been tested in relation to the autopsy, would be used by investigators to shed light on the victim's state of mind that evening. The importance of victim toxicology as an investigative and forensic tool is discussed throughout this text.*

CASE EXAMPLE *CONTINUED:*

FIGURE 1-5
Rocky Moody was shot to death by his father subsequent to an argument in their home. This 2005 photograph depicts then-17-year-old Moody shaking hands with Gen. William T. Nesbitt during the graduation ceremony for the Georgia National Guard's Youth Challenge Academy at Augusta's civic center. It provides a sharp contrast to the many photos taken in association with Moody's arrests for violent and drug-related offenses over the years.

SUMMARY

In the sphere of criminal justice, the word *victim* describes any person who has experienced injury, loss, or hardship due to the illegal action of another individual or organization. *Victimology* refers to the scientific study of victimization, including the relationships between victims and offenders, investigators, courts, corrections, media, and social movements. There is a clear gap in the victimology literature, however: little research or attention is paid to the idiographic and nomothetic study of violent crime victims for the purposes of addressing investigative and forensic issues as originally described in Turvey (2008). This type of analysis may be referred to as *forensic victimology*, which differs markedly from traditional forms of general or interactionist victimology.

Forensic victimology is the objective study of victims, with a focus on impartially and completely describing all aspects of their life and lifestyle to gain a better understanding of how they came to become victimized, how the crime took place, and their relationship with the offender. The purpose of forensic victimology is aimed at accurately, critically, and objectively describing the victim to better understand victims, crime, criminals, and forensic issues. Moreover, forensic victimology does not seek to restore victims to the state they were in prior to being victimized, nor does it wish to assign blame to victims. Forensic victimology is designed to look beneath victim stereotypes, in a scientific manner, to improve the understanding of the dynamics of the criminal act as well as the victims themselves.

The philosophy behind studying victims in investigative and forensic contexts is that a complete understanding of victims and their circumstances will allow for a comprehensive and correct interpretation of the nature of their harm and loss. It will also provide insight into the plans and motives of those who committed the offenses against them. Like all types of evidence, victim information is of much more use if it is developed and interpreted in a consistent and scientific fashion.

The aim of forensic victimology is therefore to assist in providing informed investigations, to require scientific examinations of victim evidence that is intended for court, and to result in more informed legal outcomes. Forensic victimology does not take sides, and it does not seek to intrude on the ultimate issues of guilt, innocence, or victimity. It is applied discipline, intended to be employed as an objective scientific practice.

QUESTIONS

1. Name three of Hans von Hentig's 13 categories of victims.
2. True or False: Since the end of the "golden age" of victims, there have been no further blood feuds among families and cultures.
3. Choose one: Mendelsohn's typology for categorizing victims is problematic because it relies on
   a. personal characteristics
   b. situational characteristics
   c. demographic characteristics
4. It is difficult to study _____ and _____ crimes through the lens of victim provocation because they involve more subjectivity.
5. Define forensic victimology.
6. Describe how *forensic victimology* differs from other types of victimology.
7. Name three ways that forensic victimologists serve investigations and court proceedings.
8. Describe the scientific method.

REFERENCES

Crowder, S., Turvey, B., 2013. Ethical Justice: Applied Issues for Criminal Justice Students and Professionals. Elsevier Science, San Diego.

Dienstein, W., 2005. Criminal investigation. In: Bailey, W. (Ed.), The Encyclopedia of Police Science, second ed. Garland Publishing, New York, pp. 160–162.

Doerner, W., Lab, S., 2011. Victimology, sixth ed. Anderson Publishing, Cincinnati, OH.

Faigman, D.L., Kaye, D.H., Saks, M.J., Sanders, J., 1997. Modern Scientific Evidence: The Law and Science of Expert Testimony, Vol. 2. West Publishing, St. Paul, MN.

Fattah, E., 2000. Victimology: past, present, and future. Criminologie 331, 17–46.

Green, M., 2001. Dying for the Gods. Tempus Publishing, Stroud, UK.

Jerin, A., Moriarty, L., 1998. Victims of Crime. Nelson Hall Publishers, Chicago.

Johnson, B., 2012. Murder victim Rocky Moody had criminal history. Augusta Chronicle, June 4; http://chronicle.augusta.com/news/crime-courts/2012-06-04/murder-victim-rocky-moody-had-criminal-history

Karmen, A., 2012. Crime Victims: An Introduction to Victimology, eighth ed. Wadsworth, Toronto.

Lasch, C., 1979. The Culture of Narcissism. W.W. Norton, New York.

Lilly, G., 1987. An Introduction to the Law of Evidence, second ed. West Publishing, St. Paul, MN.

Liu, J., 2006. Victimhood. Missouri Law Review 71, Winter; pp. 115–175.

Mawby, R.I., 1982. Crime and the elderly: a review of British and American research. Current Psychological Research 2 (3), 301–310.

Meadows, R., 2007. Understanding Violence and Victimizations, fourth ed. Prentice Hall, Upper Saddle River, NJ.

Shichor, D., Tibbetts, S., 2002. Victims and Victimizations: Essential Readings. Waveland Press, Long Grove, IL.

Spalek, B., 2006. Crime Victims: Theory, Policy, and Practice. Palgrave Macmillan, New York.

Srikantiah, J., 2007. Perfect victims and real survivors: the iconic victim in domestic human trafficking law. Boston University Law Review 87, February; pp. 157–211.

Tang, A., 2007. Afghan girls traded for debts, blood feuds. USA Today, July 9; http://usatoday30.usatoday.com/news/world/2007-07-09-afghan-girls_N.htm

Time Magazine, 1948. Go ahead, hit me. September 20 http://www.time.com/time/magazine/article/0, 9171, 799202,00.html

Time Magazine, 1971. Is the victim guilty? July 5 http://www.time.com/time/printout/0, 8816, 905314,00.html

Turvey, B., 2011. Criminal Profiling: An Introduction to Behavioral Evidence Analysis, fourth ed. Elsevier Science, San Diego.

Turvey, B., Ferguson, C., 2009. Victimology: a brief history with an introduction to forensic victimology. In: Turvey, B., Petherick, W. (Eds.), Forensic Victimology, Elsevier Science, San Diego.

Turvey, B., Petherick, W., 2008. Victimology. In: Turvey, B. (Ed.), Criminal Profiling: An Introduction to Behavioral Evidence Analysis, third ed. Elsevier Science, San Diego.

Van Dijk, J.M., 1999. Introducing victimology. Paper on the Ninth Symposium of the World Society of Victimologyhttp://rechten.uvt.nl/victimology/other/vandijk.pdf

Von Hentig, H., 1948. The Criminal and His Victim: Studies in the Sociobiology of Crime. Yale University Press, New Haven.

Williams, K., 2004. Textbook on Criminology, fifth ed. Oxford University Press, New York.

Young, M., Stein, J., 2004. The history of the crime victims' movement in the United States. National Organization for Victim Assistance, U.S. Department of Justice Grant Number 2002-VF-GX-0009, Decemberhttp://www.ojp.usdoj.gov/ovc/ncvrw/2005/pg4c.html

CHAPTER 2

Victimity: Entering the Criminal Justice System

Brent E. Turvey

KEY TERMS

Availability heuristic A procedure used to judge the commonality, frequency, or likelihood of events; answering a question of probability by asking whether examples come readily to mind.

Bad Samaritans Those who fail to help victims. This may be the result of apathy, distrust, or fear of involvement with respect to the victim or situation as it presents itself.

Bystander apathy The failure of anyone in a crowd of witnesses to help a victim in unambiguous distress.

Clearance rate The percentage of cases cleared by arrest or exceptional means.

Compassion fatigue A caregiver's decreased ability to be empathetic or bear the pain and anguish of clients.

Criminality The state, quality, or fact of being a victim.

Double victimization The harm and loss suffered by a victim, first from an attacker and second from a criminal justice system that either fails its promise to assist or protect or entirely neglects the victim.

Downgrading (or misclassifying) evidence Changing the status of evidence, which occurs when a serious offense is entered into the system and reported as something less serious.

Duty of care Professional obligations to adhere to a reasonable standard of care while performing any acts that could harm others.

Good Samaritans Those who respond to a victim's peril and injuries, notify the authorities, and become eventual witnesses when Emergency Medical Services (EMS) or law enforcement arrives.

Idiographic knowledge The study of the concrete, or the examination of individuals and their actual qualities; concentrates on specific cases and the unique traits of functioning of individuals.

Law enforcement The branch of the criminal justice system that is legally commissioned to respond to crime.

Mandated reporters Those bound by law to report evidence of crime, abuse, or neglect.

Nomothetic knowledge The study of the abstract, or the examination of groups and universal laws.

Secondary victimization The lack of control and subsequent trauma that victims may experience when they are harmed by or dissatisfied with the criminal justice system. Essentially the same as double victimization.

Unfounding Changing the status of a case, which occurs when an investigator decides that a complaint is false or baseless.

Forensic Victimology. http://dx.doi.org/10.1016/B978-0-12-408084-3.00002-8

Victim advocate A liaison between a victim and/or the victim's family and the criminal justice system.

Victim discouragement The act of deliberate dissuasion of victim complaints.

Victimity The state, quality, or fact of being a victim.

Mendelsohn (1963) describes *victimity* as being the opposite of criminality. *Criminality* refers to the state, quality, or fact of being criminal. Therefore, victimity refers to the state, quality, or fact of being a victim. The purpose of this chapter is to describe what this concept means in an applied sense. This means coverage of what victimity involves as those suffering harm or loss enter the criminal justice system. It also means appreciating the documentary record of evidence that is created along the way.

Understanding how the criminal justice system documents victim evidence is necessary for at least two reasons. First, it contextualizes the available information—when it is collected, how it is collected, and why it is collected. This context helps examiners to determine the nature and weight of what may or may not be found during subsequent forensic examinations. The more that is known about what is involved in the creation of victim-related documentation, the better any related judgments and inferences will be. Second, unless one has been the victim of a crime or works directly with victims in the justice system, the only frames of reference that come to mind are residual images from film and television. This is a very real problem for theoretical victimologists, or for those working in a research setting.

Film and television provide an unreliable yet popular frame of reference that creates a misinformed *availability heuristic*. As Sunstein (2005) explains, people are not always that critical, that deliberate, or that bright. In fact, many are intellectually lazy, reaching only for the explanations and reasons within their immediate cognitive vicinity. In other words, they use under-informed thought processes and are often incapable of knowing any better (pp. 990–991):

> It is well known that individuals do not always process information well. They use heuristics that lead them to predictable errors; they are also subject to identifiable biases, which produce errors. A growing literature explores the role of these heuristics and biases and their relationship to law and policy. For example, most people follow the representativeness heuristic, in accordance with which judgments of probability are influenced by assessments of resemblance (the extent to which A "looks like" B). The representative heuristic helps explain what Paul Rozin and Carol Nemeroff call "sympathetic magical thinking," including the beliefs that some objects have contagious properties and that causes resemble their effects. The representativeness heuristic often works well, but it can also lead to severe blunders.

People also err because they use the availability heuristic to answer difficult questions about probability. When people use this heuristic, they answer a question of probability by asking whether examples come readily to mind.

The *availability heuristic* is in play when judgments are made based on what one can remember rather than on complete or more reliable information. As discussed, it is used for judging the commonality, frequency, or likelihood of events. There is simply no greater influence on the availability heuristic than film and television. The popular media provides false or distorted examples to populate our memory, which are inappropriately accepted as accurate and reliable in the absence of actual knowledge or experience.

In our study of victims, we need to move past market-driven archetypes and cultural stereotypes; we need to understand who victims are and what they are actually up against as they enter the justice system. We need to know the hurdles they must clear, how they are perceived and treated, and how information about them is being gathered and disseminated. This chapter attempts to address some of these issues.

First, we discuss what it takes to become a victim in the criminal justice system in the most general terms. Then we touch briefly on the role of law enforcement, of mandated reporters, and of victim's advocates. Next, there is a review of the more realistic contact that victims can have with witnesses, emergency services, and the police. The concepts of *bystander apathy, double victimization,* and *duty of care* are discussed. The chapter closes with an evaluation of the frailty of crime victim data, which is gathered based on documentation subsequent to all the above.

VICTIMS IN THE JUSTICE SYSTEM

Before victims can enter the criminal justice system, the crime or crimes committed against them must be reported to law enforcement (see Figure 2-1). This can happen in one of several ways:

- The victims report the crime directly to authorities themselves (immediately or eventually).
- Another victim involved in the same crime can report it directly to authorities, and other victims are identified during the investigation.
- The investigation of a criminal suspect can reveal the existence of victims who have not reported the crimes committed against them.
- A third party can report the crime to authorities, after being told by a victim (e.g., parent, intimate, doctor, teacher, stranger, or witness).

Victims report crime for a variety of reasons. They may seek an end to the harm that is being caused to themselves or to others; to help catch and punish

FIGURE 2-1

In January 2012, New York City consolidated its emergency call system so that emergency call takers and dispatchers from the NYPD, FDNY, and Emergency Medical Dispatch services would be located on the same floor and use the same technology to improving inter-agency communications and emergency response efforts. In 2010, the system received around 10.4 million calls, nearly 40% of which were accidental dials. The new system can handle about 50,000 calls per hour, which is 40 times more than is needed on an average day (Press Release, 2012).

an offender; to prevent future crimes; to facilitate the recovery of property; and sometimes they report unwillingly because doing so is unavoidable (e.g., when the harm they suffer requires medical attention or is seen by too many witnesses).

As this information suggests, not every person who suffers harm or loss reports it to law enforcement, even if he or she is able. In fact, the U.S. Bureau of Justice Statistics (Berzofsky, Krebs, and Smiley-McDonald, 2012) estimates that "52% of all violent victimizations, or an annual average of 3,382,200 violent victimizations, were not reported to the police"; that "a third (34%) went unreported because the victim dealt with the crime in another way, such as reporting it to another official, like a guard, manager, or school official"; and that "almost 1 in 5 unreported violent victimizations (18%) were not reported because the victim believed the crime was not important enough" (p. 1).[1]

---

[1] These frequencies should be regarded as a reference point only. The specific frequencies are unknown and widely presumed to be much higher.

Crime victims may decide not to report because[2]

- They consider it a personal matter and do not want the attention.
- They have reported it to another authority and no longer perceive a duty to report it themselves.
- They do not think it is important enough to report it to the police.
- They think reporting the crime will take too much time.
- They believe the police will not care, will not be competent, or may be biased against them.
- They feel there is a lack of evidence and that they will not be believed.
- They feel that they might be blamed for what happened.
- In cases involving theft, they might have recovered their valuables and consider the matter closed.

Consider the perspective of victims of sexual assault, described in Kanter (2005; pp. 277–278):

> At a very fundamental level, the experience of rape defies the ability of the victim to seek help and the ability of those around her, including the legal system, to respond to her needs. Rape, whether seen as a means of gender, race, class, age or other forms of oppression, is also a devastating attack on the physical, psychological and sexual integrity of the individual victim. Furthermore, the most common forms of rape—rape by those known to the victim—involve a betrayal of trust that adds to that devastation. It is not uncommon for victims to be immobilized by the trauma of rape and its psychic aftermath.
>
> Yet few individuals not victimized themselves can comprehend the destructive impact of non-stranger rape, particularly on adolescent girls and college age women. This impact is compounded by the fact that this form of rape is the least acknowledged by society and least punished by the legal system. Except in some cases of stranger rape, victims often fail to acknowledge their own victimization. When they do, they often blame themselves for the assault. In the case of young women, their inexperience in sexual situations combined with a normal adolescent desire to experience sex adds both to their vulnerability to attack and their subsequent feelings of personal responsibility. Feelings of shame, guilt and personal responsibility increase if one adds to this mix the common presence of alcohol and drugs. In these situations, the response of those adults who might offer understanding, support and protection (i.e., parents, teachers, law enforcement) is often quite the opposite, and they too blame the victim just as she blames herself.

---

[2]See generally Berzofsky, Krebs, and Smiley-McDonald (2012); and Truman and Planty (2012).

Ultimately, victims will make a cost–benefit analysis about reporting crime when the decision is theirs alone. Some will report, some will keep quiet, and others will be forced to come forward against their will. However, the decision of whether to report crime is not always entirely up to the victim.

MANDATED REPORTERS

Mandated reporters are professionals who have regular contact with the vulnerable and the criminal. This includes those professions that intersect with sex offenders, addicts, prisoners, parolees, children, the elderly, and victims of domestic violence. Mandated reporters are required by law to report any evidence of crime, abuse, or neglect that crosses their path. A short list of mandated reporters, which varies by state, can include the following:

- Corrections employees
- Probation and parole officers
- School employees (e.g., administrators, teachers, and guidance counselors)
- Daycare workers
- Clergy
- Social workers
- Children's advocates
- Law enforcement employees
- Attorneys and other legal professionals
- Healthcare professionals (e.g., doctors, nurses, pharmacists, and physicians' assistants)
- Mental health professionals (e.g., psychologists, psychiatrists, therapists, and counselors)
- Welfare

Mandated reporters are required to inform the authorities when crimes are disclosed to them by victims. They are also required to report any crimes that they witness, and may even receive training to spot signs of criminality, abuse, and neglect.

Typically, mandated reporters are required to report any information and findings to the appropriate government agency, which will then initiate its own investigation. For example, in cases of child abuse and neglect, they may be required to report any evidence or suspicions directly to an agency akin to Child Protective Services (CPS). The process is explained in Lukens (2007; pp. 201–202):

> After a report of suspected child abuse or neglect is made, either anonymously or by a mandated reporter, a social worker from CPS makes an initial determination whether the information provided in

the report is sufficient to warrant further investigation. Most reports are screened out at this initial stage. If the CPS worker decides to investigate, the next step is a visit by a CPS investigator to the home where the parent, child, and any other adults who live in the household are interviewed. Based on the results of this investigation, the next phase involves a determination whether there has actually been abuse or neglect. If abuse or neglect is "substantiated," either the family begins CPS supervision while the child remains in the home, or if there is risk of danger to the child, then the child is removed from the family and placed in foster care. Removal can be voluntary or involuntary; unless there is imminent danger to the child, in which case CPS will move for immediate removal on an emergency basis. If abuse or neglect is "unsubstantiated," however, the case will likely be closed in the CPS system.

There are legal penalties for failing in the duty to report, both criminal and civil. In a civil context, this can mean being held responsible, financially, for any harm that results from a failure to report. In a criminal context, this can mean being charged with a crime, assessed fines, and jail time (in more severe cases).

CASE EXAMPLE:

Irene Hinojosa,

George de la Torre Jr. Elementary School, Los Angeles Unified School District

Consider the case of Irene Hinojosa, the former Principal of George de la Torre Jr. Elementary School in the Los Angeles Unified School District (see Figure 2-2). According to published allegations, she was made aware of inappropriate teacher behavior toward students and failed in her duties as a mandated reporter. As detailed in Blume, Flores, and Winton (2013):

A now-retired principal twice failed to report accusations of sexual misconduct by a teacher who this week was charged with molesting 12 students at a Wilmington elementary school, officials said.

In 2002 and 2008, the principal was told that the teacher, Robert Pimentel, 57, inappropriately touched a student. But the principal failed to tell law enforcement authorities, as required by law, said L.A. schools' Supt. John Deasy.

The Los Angeles Police Department began investigating Pimentel only last March, when they learned of more recent allegations at George de la Torre Jr. Elementary School.

LAPD Capt. Fabian Lizarraga said Thursday that detectives will launch an investigation into whether the principal, Irene Hinojosa, should face charges for failing to report alleged abuse. She could not be reached for comment Thursday.

It remains unclear why Hinojosa did not tell authorities about the accusations. The 2008 allegation also occurred at De la Torre, where she was principal. The 2002 allegation was made when Pimentel was a teacher and Hinojosa the principal at Dominguez Elementary in Carson, Deasy said.

At De la Torre, volunteer Magdalena Gonzalez said Thursday that Hinojosa had been made aware of several questionable incidents involving Pimentel.

Continued

CASE EXAMPLE: *CONTINUED*

FIGURE 2-2

In 2013, retired Principal Irene Hinojosa was accused of failing to report complaints of student abuse to authorities, committed by one of her teachers a George de la Torre Jr. Elementary School. That teacher, Robert Pimentel, was arrested and suspended from teaching in March of 2012. Former Principal Hinojosa now faces the possibility of criminal charges related to her alleged inaction, and is currently under investigation by prosecutors.

Three years ago, she said, a girl told her parent that Pimentel had playfully spanked students. Gonzalez also said she and other volunteers saw Pimentel pull on a student's bra strap during a fifth-grade graduation ceremony.

Gonzalez alleged that Hinojosa was dismissive of their complaints and that she allowed Pimentel to have students in his classroom during recess and lunch despite their misgivings. "We told her he was touching the girls," Gonzalez said in Spanish.

School employees are required by law to report allegations of sexual misconduct to police. They also are supposed to report such issues to their supervisors, according to school district policies.

According to Guzman-Lopez (2013), the school district ultimately verified the allegations against Hinojosa and disciplined her administratively. Failure to report under these circumstances could constitute a misdemeanor that is punishable by a maximum of six months in jail, a $1,000 fine, or both. However, conviction requires prosecutors to prove the mandated reporter suspected that a child had been abused or neglected, but took no action to notify the authorities. This has been, historically, a difficult threshold to clear with respect to educators (Romo, 2013). It comes down to whether the accused reporter believed the accusations being made, which they can claim lacked credibility for any number of reasons. Whether or not criminal allegations are proved, the Los Angeles Unified School District faces potential civil liability from both the alleged actions of the teacher and the ex-principal.

CASE EXAMPLE: *CONTINUED*

Ironically, while laws exist to designate mandated reporters and penalties for failing to report, many professionals go about their work unaware of either. Yet, even when they are informed of a reporting duty as prescribed by law, they may be untrained or unwilling to get involved. These failures are not always a matter of apathy and ignorance.

Additionally, as explained in Lukens (2007), some mandated reporters do not report incidents of suspected child abuse or neglect because of concerns that CPS will be associated with the process (p. 181):

> [T]he chief explanations for under-reporting suspected incidents are the perception by professionals that (1) the child welfare system is overtaxed; (2) intervention by the child welfare system will not resolve the matter satisfactorily; and (3) engagement with the system may be detrimental to the child. Moreover, it is possible that some children simply may not come to the attention of mandated reporters (e.g., very young children not enrolled in school and medical neglect situations where the child is not seen routinely by care specialists), and some may not exhibit any signs of trouble or may be reticent about revealing it (e.g., many of the instances of

sexual abuse or emotional neglect). In sum, despite the broad reach of the mandatory reporting system, too many children remain in harm's way because they have not been identified by the child welfare system.

The reality is that CPS workers tend to be jaded, undertrained, and overtaxed. Moreover, there is a lot of subjectivity and caseworker autonomy in the CPS process, at least in practice. Subsequently, professional views regarding CPS range from too complacent or apathetic in cases of obvious abuse and neglect; and too swift to take children from parents in cases in which there are other options.

Similar problems exist among other mandated reporter professions. The reason is that related professionals can come to suffer from what is referred to as *compassion fatigue*. This is defined as (Adams et al., 2006, p. 104) "the formal caregiver's reduced capacity or interest in being empathic or bearing the suffering of clients and is the natural consequent behaviors and emotions resulting from knowing about a traumatizing event experienced or suffered by a person." Those suffering from *compassion fatigue* essentially stop caring about their professional and ethical obligations with respect to custodial obligations, victims, administrative rules, and the law.

THE ROLE OF LAW ENFORCEMENT

Law enforcement is the branch of the criminal justice system that is legally commissioned to respond to crime (Sullivan, 1977; Kappeler, 2006). It is composed of various municipal, state, and federal agencies that are required, by law, to develop strategies and deploy personnel within an established jurisdiction that[3]

- Facilitate the prevention of crime
- Respond to criminal complaints
- Investigate unsolved crime
- Arrest suspected criminals
- Recover stolen property

---

[3]This section was originally published in Turvey and Crowder (2013).

Specific obligations and functions vary, in accordance with individual agency policy as well as local statutes. However, law enforcement agents are generally responsible for keeping the peace, protecting the citizenry, and representing justice (Kleinig, 1996; Kappeler, 2006; Wolfe and Piquero, 2011). These virtues, and related principles, are often a feature of the sworn oaths or pledges that officers must take when receiving their police credentials. They generally relate to maintaining professional integrity, protecting citizens and property, faithfully enforcing the laws of their state, and upholding the U.S. Constitution (International Association of Chiefs of Police, 2011). Specific values, missions, or creeds can be found on the backside of an officer's credentials, on the side of an officer's patrol car, or on their department's website.

As readers will learn, the role of law enforcement is not always in harmony with the needs or desires of victims. When there is a conflict between the two, the victim will invariably lose all initial skirmishes. Furthermore, we will learn that police agencies do not necessarily hold, practice, or even perceive a duty of care to the victims of crime, despite conventional public belief to the opposite. This duty, in extreme cases, may even need to be compelled with civil litigation.

THE ROLE OF VICTIM ADVOCATES

A *victim advocate*, when assigned to a given case, is intended as a liaison between a victim and/or the victim's family and the criminal justice system. Advocates facilitate the arrangement of resources, interviews, and the gathering of victim information. They act as go-betweens to help coordinate services from state agencies and private organizations that may be of benefit. Advocates also tend to serve the unhappy role of explaining the peculiarities of the criminal justice system to victims as they enter and are repeatedly failed by it.

Victim advocates can be found in many agencies that intersect with the criminal justice system, including the police department, the prosecutor's office, hospitals, rape crisis clinics, and various state and nonprofit organizations that contract services with the aforementioned. Depending on the resources of their particular jurisdiction, police or prosecutors may recommend victims to any one of their own in-house advocates or to outside state and nonprofit agencies, as they perceive the need. However, law enforcement goals may not be entirely benevolent in this effort; they may just want victims out of the way to avoid the conflicts that can arise, as described in Goodrum (2007; p. 746):

> For the bereaved victim, the case represents a new and extremely traumatic event, one in which all information and evidence seems critical. For detectives, the case represents one of many. Erez and Rogers (1999) argue that experience desensitizes legal professionals to the horror and tragedy observed in victims. This desensitization

when compared to bereaved victims' hypersensitivity may create differences of opinion on the significance of some information, and these differences of opinion may create additional conflict.

As the point of contact, a victim advocate becomes a source, if not *the* source, of details about the case. This is a slippery slope, as the police may or may not be forthcoming with complete or accurate case-related information. A conflict arises when victims and family members need this information to regain their sense of the world, and nobody that knows anything will return phone calls. This issue is discussed in Goodrum (2007) as it relates to cases involving bereaved family members and victims of homicide (pp. 747–748):

> During the early stages of the murder case, many bereaved victims believed that someone in law enforcement knew (and could tell them) exactly how their loved one died. They wanted to know all of the details surrounding their loved one's last few moments of life and the manner of death. In her advice to mental caregivers of bereaved victims, Rando (1993) explained bereaved victims' compulsive need to understand the specifics of the death and their effort to find meaning in the loss as "related to the need to restore control...and a sense of justice and order to the world."
>
> Social psychologists relate this type of reaction to the Just World Hypothesis (Lerner, 1980), which argues that people will use their belief that the world is a fair and just place to make sense of difficult or harmful situations.
>
> The search for information represents an attempt to find an explanation for the death that upholds notions of justice. A crime victims' advocate with eleven years of experience counseling victims (primarily bereaved victims) and promoting victims' rights explained:
>
> Victims want the truth, no matter how painful it is; they need the truth, instead of going around the truth. They can deal with the truth a lot better than keeping them wondering [about how their loved one was murdered].
>
> Detectives and counselors tried to answer bereaved victims' questions as best they could and within the limits of their policies. A victim services counselor with more than five years of experience explained:
>
> When the families are wanting information, they meet with the primary detective on the case, and I am also present. Because, of course, he knows all the details, and he knows what he can disclose at the time and what he can't.
>
> This counselor further explained that she asked detectives not to share any information about the case with her that could not also be shared with the family "because I don't want to be lying to them [about what we know and don't know]."

Victim advocates are subsequently enlisted to give victims and their families a perceived sense of empowerment, hope, or control in a situation that may in reality offer very little of either. They also provide victims with a human point of contact that has no sensitive case information or authority. Advocates serve primarily to comfort and coordinate logistical details of aid, upcoming interviews, and eventual legal proceedings. Their inability to provide more eventually leaves a bitter taste in the mouth of most crime survivors, driving them to withdraw from the justice system in exasperation.

FIRST CONTACT

As already mentioned, initial contact between victims and the justice system is typically made via the police or a witness. The police are part of the criminal justice system, and witnesses may or may not choose to participate in it. Both are gatekeepers after a fashion, and can present significant hurdles that must be cleared in order for the victim to successfully initiate a criminal investigation, let alone receive aid and comfort. The following sections do not discuss what happens when things go smoothly, rather they reveal what can happen in the real world of people and responders when victims are ignored, dismissed, or disbelieved.

Victims and Other People

A rape victim may knock on a stranger's door and ask her to call the police; an assault victim may be found half conscious in an alley by a passerby; or a teacher may be the first to discover a shooting victim at a school. In such cases, initial contact between the victim and the criminal justice system is not through the police but rather fellow citizens who are in the right place at the right time to be of service. These *Good Samaritans* respond to victim peril and injuries, notify the authorities, and become eventual witness when Emergency Medical Services (EMS) or law enforcement arrives. That is, unless they are unwilling to get involved.

In the case of *Bad Samaritans*, their failure to help victims may be the result of apathy, distrust, or fear of involvement with respect to the victim or situation as it presents itself.[4] This fear may involve the danger associated with attempting a rescue (e.g., fear of diving into freezing water to rescue a drowning child; fear of pulling a crash victim from a burning vehicle), or it may be related to the consequences for any actions once they get involved (e.g., fear of reprisal from a vengeful offender; fear of litigation from a thankless victim). To be clear, not all of those unwilling to get involved should be viewed as uncaring or selfish.

---

[4]The author has worked more than one case involving a naked or partially clothed victim approaching a stranger's home after being sexually assaulted, only to be met by an understandably shocked and distrustful occupant. However, compassion typically wins out in these scenarios.

CASE EXAMPLE:

Bystander Apathy, Redux

With situations that involve a group of people, the reluctance of potential Samaritans to get involved with victims of crime is more common. The larger the group, the more common. The failure of those in a crowd of witnesses to help a victim in unambiguous distress is sometimes referred to as *bystander apathy*. As Scott explains (2003; pp. 39–40):

> On March 13, 1964, Catherine (Kitty) Genovese reached her apartment in Queens, NY, at 3:30 a.m. Suddenly, a man approached with a knife, stabbed her repeatedly, then raped her. When she screamed, "Oh my God, he stabbed me! Please help me!" lights came on and windows opened in nearby buildings. Seeing the lights, the attacker fled; but when no one came to Genovese's aid, he returned to stab her repeatedly and rape her again. The attack lasted more than 30 minutes and was witnessed by 38 neighbors. One couple pulled chairs up to their window and turned off the lights so they could get a better view. No one called police until the attacker departed for good. When the neighbors were questioned about their lack of intervention, they could not explain it.
>
> The reporter who first publicized this story, and later made it the subject of a book, assumed the bystander apathy was caused by big-city life (Rosenthal [1964]). He presumed people's indifference to their neighbors' troubles was a conditioned reflex in crowded cities such as New York. After this incident, many experiments were conducted by social psychologists in an attempt to determine causes of this so-called "bystander apathy" [Latane and Darley, 1970(a); (b)]. This research actually discredited the reporter's conclusion, finding that several factors other than big-city life contribute to bystander apathy....
>
> A key contributor to the bystander effect is a presumption that someone else should assume the responsibility. For example, many observers of the Genovese attack likely assumed that another witness would call police or attempt to scare away the assailant. Perhaps some observers waited for a more capable witness to come to the rescue.

The notion of diffused responsibility as a contributing factor in such cases is further supported in Miller and Clinkinbeard (2006; pp. 12–14):

> Psychological research involving bystander intervention has indicated that individuals are not always willing to help, even when they have the ability to do so.
>
> In a classic social psychological study, college students witnessed another participant (actually an undercover researcher) in the study suffer from an epileptic seizure. Some students were led to believe that they were the only person aware of the situation, while other students were led to believe that others were also aware of the situation. The investigators found that those who were alone were more likely to help and to help in a timelier manner than participants who believed that others were aware of the situation. Diffusion of responsibility, the phenomenon in which [the] presence of other individuals lessens the amount of individual responsibility experienced, is used to explain this bystander apathy.

A contemporary example of bystander apathy is the case of LaShanda Calloway in Wichita, Kansas, as described in Hegeman (2007):

> As stabbing victim LaShanda Calloway lay dying on the floor of a convenience store, five shoppers, including one who stopped to take a picture of her with a cell phone, stepped over the woman, police said.
>
> The June 23 situation, captured on the store's surveillance video, got scant news coverage until a columnist for *The Wichita Eagle* disclosed the existence of the video and its contents Tuesday.
>
> "It was tragic to watch," police spokesman Gordon Bassham said Tuesday. "The fact that

Continued

CASE EXAMPLE: *CONTINUED*

people were more interested in taking a picture with a cell phone and shopping for snacks rather than helping this innocent young woman is, frankly, revolting."

The woman was stabbed during an altercation that was not part of a robbery, Bassham said. It took about two minutes for someone to call 911, he said. Calloway, 27, died later at a hospital.

The Calloway case is markedly different from the Genovese case in that there were no screams for help and no sexual component. In addition, while some bystanders in the market simply ignored the victim, others took photos and video of Calloway that were subsequently posted to *YouTube* (www.youtube.com). The particular bystanders were able to emotionally detach from the moment with some ease, objectify the victim, and view her demise as a source of entertainment for themselves and others.

Victims and Law Enforcement

As Goodrum (2007) explains, there is an inherent "power struggle" between the victims of crime and law enforcement officers charged with its investigation. Victims come from a personal and emotional context, in which they are looking to satisfy needs related to their harm and loss. Law enforcement comes from an objective and professional context, in which in the worst instances, behavior can border on dismissive and even apathetic (Goodrum 2007; p. 753):

> Underlying this struggle is the issue of power, and the issue of power emerges repeatedly in research on all types of victims and at all stages of the criminal justice system. In this study, bereaved victims felt powerless because law enforcement workers—as agents of the criminal justice system—controlled the entire investigation process. They determined the bereaved victim's access to the deceased's body; they also determined the direction and extent of the information flow in the case. Law enforcement workers' control and bereaved victims' relative lack of control in the case frustrated and upset many bereaved victims and hindered their recovery from the crime. Thus, despite the implementation of victims' rights legislation in states across the United States, rights whose purpose is ostensibly to empower victims, the relationship between victims and law enforcement workers remains largely unequal.

Even with the best of intentions, the role of the police is often in direct conflict with the needs of the victim, as Goodrum further explains (2007; pp. 729–730):

> Police officers, prosecutors, and judges repeatedly indicate that maintaining an objective and unemotional approach to criminal cases proves important to their work (Erez and Rogers, 1999), to upholding

the rule of law (Erez and Laster, 1999), and to the maintenance of a professional (i.e., stoic) demeanor (Goodrum and Stafford, 2003). This approach often means that criminal justice workers see themselves as crime-solvers, not victim helpers, and this definition restricts the amount of time they interact with victims and the types of interaction they choose to take (see Stenross and Kleinman, 1989). Prosecutors handling rape cases tend to focus on presenting evidence that will persuade judges and jurors that a rape really happened, not on emotionally preparing victims for their witness testimony (Konradi, 1997). Detectives and prosecutors view their role, the victim's role, and criminal cases from a perspective that conflicts with and may even harm victims (see Kondradi, 1997; Martin and Powell, 1995).

Victims invariably need different levels of assistance, counseling, advice, logistical information, and comfort. Police and their prosecutorial counterparts may be unable or unwilling to provide any of these. Moreover, many assurances given to the victim by the police in the early stages of an investigation are soon forgotten, having been dispensed for the purpose of comfort only. Whether it is assurances about investigative action or the eventual sentencing of offenders, Doerner and Lab parse no words when stating (Doerner and Lab, 2011, p. 63): "What it boils down to is that the system is not making good on its promises."

In fact, to keep the justice system moving, prosecutors are apt to eventually plead cases down to avoid going to court altogether, especially if they have large caseloads and competent investigations have not been performed at the outset.

Aside from initial promises regarding investigative action and offender sentencing, when police and prosecutors do provide information to the victim, it may be incorrect or out of date. This can be the result of miscommunication, bureaucratic snafus, and even personnel turnover. For example, a victim may be assigned a case officer who continually changes without the victim's knowledge as staff are transferred, sent on training, or take extended vacations. Each time the victim calls to inquire about the status of his case, he may need to speak with a new person and explain his circumstances all over again.

Additionally, it is not uncommon for a victim to receive a subpoena from the prosecutor's office with no explanation or pretrial interview; set aside time in her schedule and show up for court; and then sit waiting for several hours before she learns that she wasn't needed at all. Nor is it uncommon for prosecutors to harass victims who are unwilling to be helpful with the power of subpoena, to compel testimony that is favorable to their theories of the case. The effect of these and similar circumstances on a victim's sense of trust, worth, and value in the investigative process can be quite devastating.

Double Victimization

The cumulative ineptness, ignorance, apathy, and even belligerence of those in the criminal justice system can result in what has been referred to as *double victimization,*[5] as Doerner and Lab explain (2005; p. 55):

> First, they suffer at the hands of their criminals. Then, by participating in the criminal justice system, they risk even more damage. By making a choice to avoid the system, victims are able to minimize their losses.

Goodrum (2007; p. 747) goes into further detail, referring to the subsequent lack of control perceived by victims in this context as *secondary victimization*[6]:

> Feeling a lack of control over the criminal justice process can increase victims' feelings of powerlessness and lead to a sense of further victimization (Kilpatrick and Otto, 1987). Psychologists refer to this type of further victimization as a secondary victimization or trauma, which may negatively affect well-being (Rando, 1993). Social psychologists find that having a sense of personal control over situations positively affects well-being (Mirowsky and Ross, 1989), and Amick-McMullan et al. (1989) found a positive association between satisfaction with the criminal justice system's management of the murder case and bereaved victims' psychological well-being. The idea that victims' involvement in the criminal justice system would help restore control and facilitate healing seems like a good one but not if the involvement does not occur in the ways that victims want or expect. Indeed, none of the eleven victims' rights in this state [state name omitted from study] afford victims the explicit right to give information to the police about their criminal case or to have that information be taken seriously.

It is important to point out that the cumulative harms and losses felt by victims from injuries suffered while in the criminal justice system can be personal, physical, mental, emotional, and financial. And the weight of this loss is not made easier with the passage of time, especially when left unresolved.

Duty of Care

Duty of care refers to obligations imposed on professionals requiring that they adhere to a reasonable standard of care while performing any acts that could foreseeably harm others. It is a legal concept that relates to the liability of

---

[5]*Double victimization* refers to the harm and loss that a victim suffers first from the attacker, and second from a criminal justice system that either fails in its promise of assistance or protection, or ignores the victim entirely.

[6]*Secondary victimization* refers to the lack of control and subsequent trauma that victims may experience as they are increasingly harmed by or dissatisfied with the criminal justice system.

agencies and individuals charged with various professional functions, such as doctors and hospitals, mental health professionals and clinics, police officers and departments, security guards and firms, teachers and schools, and others.

Litigation against police agencies across the United States has revealed diverse liability for local law enforcement, and often reduced standards that must be met—if they may be held accountable at all (not every police agency as a whole may be held civilly liable for its negligence or misconduct, even when it is not in dispute; however, individual officers and governments may). As Miccio explains (2000; pp. 142–143):

> The modern view of municipal liability for police conduct is narrowly constructed. This doctrine of public duty shapes legal relationships among the police, society, and individual citizens. Under the public duty doctrine, police are not under an affirmative obligation to respond to individual citizen needs. Consequently, because a duty is owed to the public generally, there is no particularized duty of care allocated to individuals.

This issue of liability is a recurrent theme that runs throughout this chapter and the rest of this text. However, some specific examples are warranted at this point.

CASE EXAMPLE:

New Port Richey

Consider the case of a 41-year-old woman in New Port Richey, Florida, twice raped by the same stranger in her own home between 1998 and 1999, as reported in Davis (2002b):

> The first attack occurred in the victim's New Port Richey home on Dec. 5, 1998. The woman, her left eye swollen shut and her mouth bloody with 15 broken teeth, told police she had been brutally beaten, bound, gagged and raped at knifepoint by a stranger.

New Port Richey police detectives, however, did not believe her account and accused her of not telling the truth. "I believe that you were battered," Detective Jackie Pehote told the victim, who had a black eye and 15 broken teeth, "but I do not believe it happened the way you say" (Davis, 2002a). Subsequently, a semen sample taken from the victim sat in a refrigerator at the department instead of being sent to the forensic laboratory for testing. New Port Richey police also failed to test evidence collected from the

woman's house. Two weeks later, the police department declared the investigation inactive (Davis, 2003b).

Twenty-nine days after the first attack, the same offender raped the victim again, but not before tripping a burglar alarm installed after the first attack, which the police responded to. The rapist hid inside the victim's home until the police left; they did not enter the premises. Once the police were gone, he attacked the victim (Davis, 2003a).

While interviewing the victim after this second rape, Detective Pehote asked her: "How could you be so stupid to move back into your house?" Pehote remained in doubt of the victim's rape allegations because of inconsistencies in her statements; she was convinced that a lover had battered the victim after consensual sex (Davis, 2003a).

Three days after the second attack, a milk crate filled with items stolen during the rape was delivered back to the victim's house with a note asking her for a date.

Four months after the second rape, the victim recognized her attacker in a convenience store. His name was John A.

Continued

CASE EXAMPLE: *CONTINUED*

Casteel (see Figure 2-3), and he lived three blocks from her home. Casteel had recently been released from prison after serving 14 years for a 1983 rape. In August of 2001, after a four-day trial, a jury convicted John A. Casteel of raping the woman in under an hour. DNA tests linked him to both crimes. He was sentenced to life in prison without parole.

In November of 2002, the victim filed suit against the city of New Port Richey and the two detectives who had handled her complaints, alleging that the second rape could have been prevented if police had properly investigated the first. The victim accused them of negligence and intentional infliction of emotional distress.

The attorney for the victim argued, among other things, that police failed in their duty to protect the victim (Davis, 2003a): "given the totality of the circumstances, police had a responsibility to protect the woman after the first rape, especially when they responded to the burglar alarm just before the second attack."

The attorney for the city of New Port Richey argued that no such duty exists (Davis, 2003a):

> Peter Walsh, the city's attorney for the civil case, argued Thursday that under the law, "there is no duty that New Port Richey owes to a citizen

to protect them from a criminal." The detectives, he said, "owed no special duty to catch this crook and perform a perfect investigation."

Both of the detectives who worked the case were cleared after an internal affairs investigation conducted by Captain Martin Rickus found no wrongdoing (Davis, 2002a):

> "Some people may not feel that this approach should be used when dealing with a rape victim," Rickus wrote. "But it is also important that investigators make logical connections between what they are told by victims and what they observe."

The report criticized another detective, William Barrus, for waiting seven months before submitting for testing a semen sample taken from the woman after the first rape.

The report recommends that officers be given clear guidelines outlining the steps to be followed in submitting evidence. It also recommended a sergeant be added to the detective bureau to supervise investigations.

FIGURE 2-3
John Casteel is sentenced to life in prison without parole.

CASE EXAMPLE: *CONTINUED*

However, Detective Barrus was cited for failing to submit the semen sample from the cases in a timely fashion. He waited seven months. John Casteel's DNA had been in a state database since 1996. Furthermore, the internal affairs report also uncovered false testimony that Detective Pehote had given in an unrelated death investigation. She claimed under oath that she had not threatened to arrest the wife of the primary suspect in that case during an interrogation. A videotape of the interrogation proved otherwise. Captain Rickus said that she simply became confused under cross-examination and forgot about the threat.

When this false testimony from Detective Pehote came to light, the suspect, who had originally been charged with first-degree murder, was allowed to plead guilty to manslaughter (Davis, 2002a).

Detective Pehote was also found to have given false testimony in the Casteel case (Davis, 2001): "In the Casteel case, she testified in a deposition that the Police Department at one time had no tape recorders....

In fact, the department has never been without tape recorders, [Capt. Darryl] Garman [New Port Richey Police Department spokesman] told the Times."

In June of 2003, Pasco-Pinellas Circuit Judge Stanley Mills begrudgingly ruled that no matter how poor any investigation might have been (Davis, 2003b):

> the police cannot be held liable for negligence. Florida courts have made it clear, the judge said, that public safety agencies and their employees cannot be sued over discretionary judgments made during the course of an investigation, regardless of the consequences.

Further attempts at appeal by the victim were ultimately unsuccessful.

In summary, it is generally publicized and perceived that law enforcement has a duty to protect life and property. However, its role can actually contribute to double victimization and secondary victimization with no legal requirement of a duty of care to victims of crime or the general public. Victims of crime do not always understand this, nor is it likely to be explained by those guiding them through the criminal justice system.

VICTIM CRIME DATA

In the study of victims and victimity, as with any subject, there are two major approaches to research and the development of knowledge. The first is *nomothetic knowledge,* or the study of the abstract, which involves the examination of groups and universal laws. The second is *idiographic knowledge,* or the study of the concrete, which involves the examination of individuals and their actual qualities. Idiographic study concentrates on specific cases and the unique traits or functioning of individuals.[7]

According to Hurlburt and Knapp (2006; p. 287): "Psychologists use the term 'idiographic' to refer to the characteristics of unique individuals and 'nomothetic'

---

[7]In scientific research settings, it goes without saying that not all knowledge derived nomothetically results in universal laws or even useful generalizations. Occasionally, the best we may hope for is to develop a theory or theories about the group under study. Such theories may not apply outside the study group. Knowing the difference—and saying it out loud—is an indication of scientific honesty. However, crime stats are generally used outside a research setting, and by those with little or no training in science, statistics, or the limits of research.

to refer to universal characteristics." Moreover, they explain that these terms have been a part of the American psychological landscape since as early as 1898. Consequently, these concepts have a history of application from which we can learn.

Nomothetic research refers to studies that are conducted on groups; *idiographic research* refers to studies that are conducted on individuals. In terms of victimology, it is fair to say that there are nomothetic methods and idiographic methods. A primary goal of idiographic victimology is to study and determine the unique characteristics of the particular victims that have suffered harm or loss as the result of a specific crime. The primary goal of nomothetic victimology studies is to accumulate general, typical, common, or averaged characteristics of victim groups. These characteristics are abstract in the sense that they do not necessarily exist in each individual case; they represent the theoretically possible and at best probable. The problems come when nomothetic methods and results are used inappropriately to make overly confident inferences or conclusive interpretations about individual victims—in other words, applying broad nomothetic knowledge to answer narrow idiographic questions.

Forensic victimology is oriented toward idiographic victim study; however, nomothetic victim data may be used to develop theories or provide a point of fundamental reference with the appropriate caveats. In the absence of actual knowledge about victims, many researchers and some caseworkers invest heavily in the perceived authority of victim statistics. The following sections further contextualize the real-world limitations of such nomothetically compiled victim data.

The UCR Program

Each year, the FBI's Uniform Crime Reporting (UCR) program compiles and publishes this aggregated crime data. The FBI publishes three other annual reports: *Crime in the United States, Law Enforcement Officers Killed and Assaulted,* and *Hate Crime Statistics.* According the FBI, these crime statistics are generated by assembling data that is received from "over 18,000 city, university/college, county, state, tribal, and federal law enforcement agencies voluntarily participating in the program" (FBI, 2013).

However, there are significant problems with UCR data, as conceded in Maltz (1999; p. iv):

> The quality of the data provided to the FBI, however, is uneven. Reporting to the FBI remains for many jurisdictions a voluntary activity; although many States now mandate that agencies report crime and arrest data to them (which they then forward to the FBI), even in those States local agencies do not always comply. Moreover, despite the efforts of the FBI to maintain their quality, there are many gaps in the data that make their use questionable. While this has had limited impact in the past, the fact that the UCR data have, for the first time, been used to allocate Federal funds brings issues about data quality to center stage.

UCR data, and its integrity, is relevant to our interests. The reason is that much of the victim and offender data cited in the criminology and criminal justice literature comes from these and other related crime statistics. There are essentially three big problems with UCR data: *victim underreporting, agency failure to report,* and *crime data falsification.* Each is discussed in turn.

Victim Underreporting

As mentioned previously in this chapter, most crime is not reported. This has a significant impact on crime statistics; specifically, we are left without a very accurate sense of how often which crimes occur and against which victim populations. What does exist are at best low estimates providing limited insight. This is not to say that we can't know anything from this data, only that was is known is greatly minimized and therefore uncertain with respect to frequencies.

Failure to Report: No Numbers

Although submitting crime data to the UCR is voluntary, law enforcement agencies that wish to qualify for federal funding are required to participate. Still, not every law enforcement agency compiles crime data each year, and not every agency that does compile statistics actually submits them to the FBI (Regoli, Hewitt, and Maras, 2012). This is true even when there are state laws mandating compliance.[8] This is especially true if certain crime rates are too high (e.g., rape or homicide), certain clearance rates are too low, and the agency does not want this information made public because it could make the agency appear otherwise ineffectual.

For example, among the many types of data collected are those related to police agency clearance rates.[9] An agency's *clearance rate* is the percentage of cases cleared by arrest or exceptional means. According to the Uniform Crime Report (UCR, 2012; pp. 1–2):

> **Cleared by arrest**
>
> In the UCR Program, a law enforcement agency reports that an offense is cleared by arrest, or solved for crime reporting purposes, when three specific conditions have been met. The three conditions are that at least one person has been:
>
> - Arrested.
> - Charged with the commission of the offense.
> - Turned over to the court for prosecution (whether following arrest, court summons, or police notice).

---

[8]More than 36 states have laws on the books mandating participating in the UCR program (Maltz, 1999).
[9]This section is adapted from material originally presented in Turvey and Savino (2011).

In its clearance calculations, the UCR Program counts the number of offenses that are cleared, not the number of persons arrested. The arrest of one person may clear several crimes, and the arrest of many persons may clear only one offense. In addition, some clearances that an agency records in a particular calendar year, such as 2011, may pertain to offenses that occurred in previous years.

Cleared by exceptional means

In certain situations, elements beyond law enforcement's control prevent the agency from arresting and formally charging the offender. When this occurs, the agency can clear the offense exceptionally. Law enforcement agencies must meet the following four conditions in order to clear an offense by exceptional means. The agency must have:

- Identified the offender.
- Gathered enough evidence to support an arrest, make a charge, and turn over the offender to the court for prosecution.
- Identified the offender's exact location so that the suspect could be taken into custody immediately.
- Encountered a circumstance outside the control of law enforcement that prohibits the agency from arresting, charging, and prosecuting the offender.

Examples of exceptional clearances include, but are not limited to, the death of the offender (e.g., suicide or justifiably killed by police or citizen); the victim's refusal to cooperate with the prosecution after the offender has been identified; or the denial of extradition because the offender committed a crime in another jurisdiction and is being prosecuted for that offense. In the UCR Program, the recovery of property alone does not clear an offense.

In another example, according to the UCR (2010), there were 76,276 forcible rapes reported by law enforcement agencies across the United States in 2009. Of these, 41.2% were cleared by arrest or exceptional means. This means that the remaining rapes were not cleared.

A law enforcement agency's clearance rate is essentially its report card. It is the one way that a community can begin to understand whether their police are doing a good job—more than just responding to 911 calls. Higher clearance rates are believed to be reflective of efficient and effective police investigations. Lower clearance rates are believed to reflect the opposite.

Regardless of crime type, the total number of law enforcement agencies reporting crime data statistics varies from state to state, and from year to year. Additionally, the FBI accepts crime data from any reporting agencies seeking to remain compliant with state laws and federal grants up to a year late. But it generates UCR reports prior to these deadlines. This means that published UCR crime data does not always reflect the total data from all reporting agencies—even under the best circumstances.

Falsification: Bad Numbers

In addition to those providing no crime data, there are also law enforcement agencies reporting inaccurately and creatively, which hides increased crime rates, lowered solve rates, and any other problems with the numbers. Sometimes this is the consequence of error. Sometimes this is the result of fraud.

With respect to erroneous and incomplete crime data submission, Maltz (1999) offers the following discussion of causes (pp. 16–17):

> [P]olice agencies may not provide complete (or any) reports to the FBI. The agencies may be delinquent or incomplete in their reporting of crime for a number of reasons:
>
> - Some agencies experienced natural disasters that prevented them from getting their data in on time (or in some instances, at all).
> - As has been the case with other public agencies, budgetary restrictions on the police have meant that some agencies have had to cut back on services. Although crime reporting is considered an essential function because it provides information about community safety to the public, some agencies that are especially strapped may forgo these routine clerical activities so as to ensure that sufficient resources exist for patrolling the streets.
> - Retirements, promotions, and other personnel changes may mean that the person experienced in the preparation of UCR crime and arrest data is replaced by someone
>   - who has little experience in its preparation (and consequently makes numerous errors)
>   - who is not given sufficient training
>   - who gives the task a low priority
>   - or who doesn't prepare the data in a timely manner.
> - With respect to training, some jurisdictions may rely completely on handbooks on UCR reporting produced by the Program Support Section, and there may be ambiguities in the reports that require more complete descriptions than are included in the handbooks.
> - Phasing in a new reporting system or computerization of the old system may cause delays or gaps in the crime reporting process....
> - Small agencies with little crime to report may feel it unnecessary to fill out reports that are filled almost entirely with zeros....
> - A State may have offense definitions that are incompatible with UCR definitions, leading to data being submitted but not accepted.

Thus, there are a number of reasons that crime reports may be incomplete, late, or in error.

The problems identified in Maltz (1999) remain relevant concerns to modern criminologists, criminal justice professionals, and policymakers, as found in research into crime data collection conducted by Friedmann, Rosenfeld, and Borissova (2010; p. 7):

> The criminal justice system lags behind other social service providers and the private sector in the development, timely dissemination, and use of reliable statistical indicators to monitor, predict, and prevent crime. Deficiencies in the nation's crime data infrastructure deny policy-makers the ability to make decisions based on sound and timely information. In contrast, health, education, business, and economics possess readily available data for forecasting and planning. Too often in criminal justice data are not compiled in standardized formats suitable for policy development or program evaluation without time-consuming, repetitive, and costly compilation and analysis efforts. In smaller agencies large amounts of data are still collected by hand and few agencies are able to routinely share comparable data across jurisdictions. Moreover, law enforcement data are generally devoid of other relevant attributes (such as census information) and are reported in tabular or aggregate formats that are not suitable for policy-relevant research. These problems indicate a demonstrable need for improvements in criminal justice data collection, analysis, and dissemination methods to facilitate better strategic choices and policy decisions.

With respect to intentionally falsifying or manipulating crime data, there are a number of ways that this can occur.[10] Common methods includes *downgrading*, *misclassifying*, and *unfounding* complaints. In other cases, police may even actively *discourage* a victim from making a complaint.

Downgrading and *misclassification* occur when a serious offense is entered into the system and reported as something less serious. For instance, consider the crime of first degree rape. It might be improperly downgraded to a lesser sex crime (e.g., forcible touching) associated with less serious charges. Or, it could be misclassified as an assault without a sexual component. As reported in Toor (2012), the New York City Police Department has had problems with downgrading for years:

> Citywide figures on felony crimes would be at least 13 percent higher if police officers and their commanders were not downgrading or refusing to take crime reports on a widespread basis, according to two criminologists who closely monitor the NYPD.

---

[10]This section is adapted from Turvey and Savino (2011).

"This is a super-conservative figure," John Eterno, a retired NYPD Captain who is chair and associate dean of graduate studies in criminal justice at Molloy College, said in an interview. "We're talking about a very extensive level of manipulation that would affect the index-crime numbers," which cover murder, rape, robbery, felony assault, burglary, grand larceny and auto theft.

These are the crimes the department focuses on in Compstat, the crime-analysis program that Mr. Eterno and his partner, Eli B. Silverman, a Professor Emeritus at John Jay College of Criminal Justice who has studied police departments around the world, have criticized for departing from its initial mission to deploy resources effectively.

The pair wrote in their recent book, "The Crime Numbers Game: Management by Manipulation," that Compstat had been twisted into a forum where top commanders bully mid-level subordinates into coming up—honestly or not—with ever-decreasing crime statistics and ever-increasing indicators of police activity such as stop-and-frisk encounters.

Mr. Eterno and Mr. Silverman extrapolated the minimum figure of 13 percent under-reporting from a survey of about 2,000 retired police officers from all ranks. That study confirmed the results of a survey of retired Captains they did in 2008 showing that pressure to fake crime numbers had intensified sharply under Mayor Bloomberg and Police Commissioner Raymond W. Kelly.

"It demonstrates the reliability and the validity of our analysis," Mr. Silverman told THE CHIEF-LEADER. "It confirms every kind of anecdotal stuff we've been hearing over the past three years. It's solid evidence that pressure is increasing."

Unfounding occurs when an investigator decides that a complaint is false or baseless. This is a legitimate label for some criminal complaints, but should not be arrived at without the benefit of a comprehensive investigation. Consider the following report, which discusses these and similar practices in Philadelphia and Baltimore (Fenton, 2010):

More than half of nearly 100 rape reports that Baltimore Police decided were false or baseless have been reclassified as rapes or other sex crimes, according to an audit presented Wednesday to a City Council panel.

The findings came from a review prompted by a *Baltimore Sun* analysis that exposed flaws in the way police handled sex offense investigations. Baltimore has long led the nation in the proportion of rape reports classified as "unfounded"—meaning the incident did not happen.

Mayor Stephanie Rawlings-Blake said the audit, along with other comprehensive changes in recent months, "has forever changed and improved the way sexual assault cases are investigated in Baltimore, ensuring that all victims of sexual assault have their complaints investigated fully and are treated with dignity and respect."

Rawlings-Blake asked the panel in late June to evaluate recent reports of rape and sexual crimes. The Sexual Assault Response Team, which includes police, prosecutors and victim advocates, reviewed 98 rape investigations classified as unfounded between January 2009 and August 2010. It found that 52 should be considered rapes or other sex crimes.

It may be necessary for the diligent investigator to remind any supervisors applying inappropriate pressure of the name of the officer that is going on the report and the courtroom consequences that can result from making a false or incomplete statement in it.

Those cases and others will get a fresh look from new detectives, but officials stressed that the reclassifications have yet to produce arrests.

The audit constituted one piece of the city's rape-reporting overhaul. Police instituted new policies, making sure all sexual-assault reports were referred to a specialized unit and could not be dismissed on the scene. Commissioner Frederick H. Bealefeld III also selected a new commander for the sex offense unit, sent detectives to training and obtained grant money to beef up investigations. A U.S. Senate subcommittee convened a hearing on the topic....

Statistics indicate that the new policies are having an impact. Reported rapes in Baltimore had been on the decline for years, dropping at a much faster rate than the national average and fueling skepticism among critics and victim advocates. Through the first half of 2010, rape reports had declined by 15 percent, compared with the same period a year earlier.

But as of Nov. 1, with the changes in effect, rape reports were up 48 percent compared with the same time last year, police figures show. Those figures do not yet include the cases the review team said should be reclassified.

Advocates say that a long-standing police culture that resulted in aggressive questioning of those making rape reports—sometimes leading them to recant their accounts in frustration—is changing.

"For me, the biggest thing is the shift in attitude toward an appreciation that the process needs to be more victim-centered," said Gail Reid, director of victim services for Turn Around, a Towson-based group that works with victims of sexual assaults. "That process requires collaboration, and I don't think it's an easy thing to do. We have a lot of work ahead of us."

Baltimore officials looked to cities that had grappled with similar problems, visiting Philadelphia, where a women's group continues to review sex crimes after major flaws were uncovered in the late 1990s. The review of unfounded cases paired sex-offense detectives with victim advocates from Turn Around. They tracked down victims and offered to reinvestigate cases, while members of the response team pored over case files and discussed whether the case had been properly classified.

"When there was disagreement among members, the recommendation was made to reopen the case," said Col. Dean Palmere, the Police Department's chief of detectives.

Of the 98 rape claims reviewed, 26 cases were reclassified as rapes or attempted rapes, with 26 others reclassified as sex offenses or possible sex offenses. Forty-four of the cases had been properly classified as false, officials said, and two were downgraded from rapes to assaults.

Members of the team reviewed some 911 calls for sex crimes, as well as a random sampling of other sex offenses. Those cases turned up additional crimes that had been improperly classified. In all, 135 cases were reviewed, with 71 reclassified, including the 28 that will now be considered rapes. Sixty-four were found to have been properly labeled "unfounded."

Improper unfounding is the lazy investigator's means of avoiding having to conduct a proper, and comprehensive, investigation. Unfortunately, it is a short cut that is all too common.

Victim discouragement in this context is the act of deliberate dissuasion of victim complaints. In such cases, a supervisor or an investigator will attempt to convince victims that filing a report would not be in their best interests. Law enforcement may tell victims things such as "you will have to go to court and tell your story a bunch of times," "this is going to take a lot of time," "it's your word against his," or "we will have to look into your background and everything will come out, maybe embarrassing you and your family." Given sufficient discouragement, many victims can be talked out of filing a report. At the very least, they are being told that law enforcement is not enthusiastic about conducting an investigation, let alone getting involved. This is, of course, improper on every level.

Problems with downgrading, unfounding and victim discouragement have been so prevalent in some jurisdictions (e.g., Milwaukee, Wisconsin [Barton, 2010]. and New York City, New York), with respect to sex crimes, that preventative reforms have been necessary. For example, the New York City Police Department has determined that patrol officers will no longer be allowed to respond first to sex crimes (Parascandolar, 2010):

Patrol officers will no longer be the first to respond to reported sex crimes, leaving the initial interviews to detectives from the special victims unit. The NYPD, in response to complaints from advocacy groups and rape counselors, also will increase the number of available SVU investigators. Some complained that victims' allegations too often were ignored or classified as less serious crimes.

In response to the criticism, the Police Department conducted an internal review of how it handled such crimes. The review turned up problems in only 19 of the 1,922 cases. Still, Police Commissioner Raymond Kelly decided to make changes. One of the most persistent complaints from advocates was that patrol officers who interviewed victims at hospitals often weren't sensitive enough. "I think that's a valid concern," Kelly said Wednesday.

This move by the NYPD is an acknowledgment that the department perceives cultural problems with its patrol officers that can be addressed only with drastic measures and not just training.[11]

Consider also the following examples from over the past decade. Each represents the manipulation or misrepresentation of crime data, if not more.

CASE EXAMPLE:

Robert Bayardo, MD, Travis County Medical Examiner's Office, Texas

The Travis Country Medical Examiner's Office (TCMEO) in Austin, Texas, under the direction of Chief Medical Examiner Robert Bayardo, was no stranger to controversy (see Figure 2-4). This includes a potential impact on frequency of reported homicides. In 2004, an investigation was performed that "found no evidence of improprieties" at the TCMEO for numerous instances of death misclassification, among other allegations. This scandal involved the inappropriate labeling of some deaths caused by police officers as *accidental* instead of *homicide*. As reported in Smith (2004):

> Travis Co. Judge Sam Biscoe on Monday announced the end to a month-long county investigation into allegations that the office of Travis Co. Medical Examiner Roberto Bayardo has improperly handled its investigations into 11 minority Austinites killed by Austin police officers since 1998. "Based on our review of the issues…and after our review of the information received from the [ME's] office, we have found

> no evidence of improprieties that would justify an official investigation at this time," Biscoe said.

> Rev. Sterling Lands filed a complaint with Biscoe in July, asking that he investigate 11 "senseless and unprovoked killings" of minorities by APD officers. Lands said he was concerned that in each case Bayardo's office ruled that the deaths were "justified or unrelated to any unjustified actions by law enforcement," he wrote on July 30. Further, Lands said, he was concerned about the "countless numbers of blacks who are incarcerated" based in part on court testimony provided by examiners with the ME's office. Lands also raised questions about whether the doctors had perjured themselves and whether each of the examiners had been "properly accredited and credentialed" over the past two decades.

---

[11] Readers may wish to investigate the bizarre case of Adrian Schoolcraft. A New York Police Department whistleblower, Officer Schoolcraft was committed to a mental ward by his supervisors because he complained about manipulating sexual assault crime statistics and the policy of talking victims out of filing complaints. He and other NYPD whistleblowers recorded supervisors giving orders to enforce illegal quotas and manipulate crime data. Now he is suing the NYPD (for a complete archive, visit the Village Voice online at http://www.villagevoice.com).

CASE EXAMPLE: *CONTINUED*

FIGURE 2-4

Dr. Robert Bayardo, MD; former Chief Medical Examiner (retired in 2006), Travis County Medical Examiner's Office.

Biscoe said that upon receiving the complaint, he immediately contacted Bayardo and asked that his office gather the relevant documents for review. Bayardo did that, reviewed the materials, and then met with Biscoe, county Emergency Services Coordinator Danny Hobby, and county commissioners for further review of the cases and to answer questions. In short, Biscoe said, they didn't find anything wrong.

A primary issue of concern for Lands is that several of the 11 cases he cites were adjudged by Bayardo to be not homicides but accidental deaths—thus (arguably) reducing the likelihood of consequences for the police involved. In a memo to Biscoe, Hobby, and the commissioners, Bayardo wrote that his office was able to locate autopsy reports for eight of the 11 individuals Lands referred to, but that he didn't have enough identifying information

to locate the other three. Of the eight cases, four deaths were ruled homicide—in each case the victim died from gunshot wounds—and the other four were ruled accidental.

In those four cases, Bayardo said, the underlying cause of the victim's death was the "acute toxic effects" of drugs, which were exacerbated during the struggles with police. "Whenever a person is under the influence of a drug like cocaine, the heart is susceptible" to bursts of adrenaline, he said at a Monday press conference. If the victims hadn't been on drugs, he said, they likely would not have died during their altercations with police. But both Bayardo and Biscoe noted that there is an ongoing national "issue" over whether such deaths should be classified accidental—laying the responsibility for death at the feet of the deceased—or classified as homicide, shifting the blame elsewhere.

Continued

CASE EXAMPLE: *CONTINUED*

The classification of those deaths as homicides does make sense, said Bayardo, "because the direct cause of death is the injury, not the drugs." Indeed, Bayardo pointed to an issue summary prepared this year by the College of American Pathologists that addresses the issue. "[I]f one accepts that the struggle contributes to death, it is difficult to argue against a ruling of homicide," the summary reads. "Such a ruling does not necessarily imply intent, nor is it meant to imply 'murder' or wrongdoing on the part of police." Still, Biscoe said, the justice system provides at least six "checks and balances" for cause of death in addition to the ME's opinion—such as the grand jury process, the district attorney, judges, and juries. That was the only place where Biscoe suggested that Lands' various allegations may be well-founded.

Bayardo and his examiners only testify in murder cases—all told, approximately 38 cases each year—Biscoe said, so they couldn't be responsible for the incarceration of "countless" blacks. Moreover, there is nothing to suggest the MEs have perjured themselves—"this complaint is too general to provide an appropriate response," Biscoe wrote in a press release. "To our knowledge, this claim is untrue and without factual support." Regarding accreditation, for a "short period" of time earlier this year, Deputy Medical Examiner Elizabeth Peacock's state license was "not in good standing," after Peacock let her dues lapse; however, Biscoe said the autopsies she performed during that time period are still good, and there's no indication that she'll be reprimanded for continuing to work during the lapse.

Lands, who was pleased with the timeliness of Biscoe's response to his initial complaint, was nonetheless displeased with the judge's "findings." And, he told KVUE-TV, he is not impressed with Biscoe's decision to let the ME investigate itself. And he said it's "ridiculous to me that anyone would buy" the line that the ME's opinions are "checked" by the grand jury process or by the district attorney. To Lands, the way to ensure fairness and accuracy is to employ a third party to observe autopsy proceedings in cases involving confrontation with police.

The net effect of misclassifying homicides as accidental deaths, which Dr. Bayardo appears to admit was possible, is that overall homicide rates and officer-involved deaths will seem lower. Moreover, any officers involved in deaths that are not classified as homicides are essentially exempt from otherwise mandatory review for negligence or excessive use of force. This is separate from the overt errors that may infect crime data resulting from victim misidentification and inaccurate causes of death.

It also bears noting that in the first half of 2006, all three of the TCMEO's forensic pathologists (including Dr. Bayardo) resigned within a few months of each other (Smith, 2006). This mass exodus occurred subsequent to an external audit that was ordered at the tail-end of 2005 because of numerous high profile errors, including the following (Smith, 2005):

- In December 2003, the office released the wrong body for cremation. Instead of sending 38-year-old Paul Williams, they released 39-year-old Rayford Floyd, whose family had wanted a burial. Travis Co. Medical Examiner Roberto Bayardo told the *Statesman* Floyd's body had been incorrectly labeled. "We are very sorry this happened," he said. "I had thought we were foolproof."
- In June 2004, the office misidentified the charred remains of an 81-year-old woman as those of a 23-year-old man. In his autopsy report, former Deputy Medical Examiner Vladimir Parungao identified the remains as those of Clayton Wayne Daniels, noting that he'd found a "small segment of penis" and a small amount of urine in the bladder that he matched to Daniels. Unfortunately, the corpse was that of an already dead—and embalmed, buried, and then exhumed—woman, leaving Burnet Co. officials (for whom the ME's office had conducted the examination) wondering if the ME's office actually examined the body. "They've got some serious explaining to do," Burnet Co. attorney Eddie Arredondo told the *Houston Chronicle.*

CASE EXAMPLE: *CONTINUED*

- In June 2005, the office mistakenly reported that 18-year-old Daniel Rocha, who was shot and killed by police on June 9, was drug-free at the time he was killed. After APD questioned the results, the ME's office performed a second, more discriminating toxicology, which revealed there was a small amount of marijuana in Rocha's bloodstream when he was killed.
- In August 2005, the office reported that Randy "Biscuit" Turner died from cirrhosis caused by alcohol abuse. After learning that Turner didn't drink alcohol, the office reversed its finding to reflect that the

cirrhosis was caused by Hepatitis C. The alcohol found in Turner's system, the office subsequently reported, was the result of body decomposition.

These types of errors erode the quality of the crime data that may be reported to the FBI's UCR. However, they also have a toxic impact on the lives of victims and undermine public confidence in the competence and objectivity of the ME's office. It is therefore fair to say that these circumstances serve to diminish victim confidence in the justice system as a whole—especially when they do not result in consequences for those involved.

CASE EXAMPLE:

San Antonio Police Department, Texas

The San Antonio Police Department has had problems collecting and reporting crime data for years. As reported in Kriel (2008):

The San Antonio Police Department incorrectly tallied the city's homicide statistics, wrongly calculated how many slayings police solved and failed to update its homicide clearance rates, an audit released Thursday concludes. Some other crimes also were miscounted in the 18-month period evaluated by the report.

Police Chief William McManus ordered the audit after the *San Antonio Express-News* published a series of reports questioning the department's homicide clearance rates for 2006.

In those articles, officials provided three wildly different rates, casting doubt on the department's ability to accurately keep and report its statistics. A clearance rate represents a percentage of cases solved and can be a measure of a police agency's performance.

The department has had problems with how it submits its crime numbers to the FBI for years. In 2002, the FBI rejected the department's overall clearance numbers because the figures were so low. Thursday's report, released by the city auditor's office,

evaluated statistics from January 2006 through June 2007.

It blamed antiquated computer programs, a lack of written procedures, insufficient training and a host of clerical errors. It found the SAPD "has no true central records function in place to ensure accuracy, completeness and compliance" with guidelines set forth by the FBI.

"This was embarrassing for us," said Deputy Chief Geraldine Garcia, who oversees the department's handling of records. Previous ways of reporting data "obviously weren't very effective," she said.

The audit did show the reporting of homicide numbers and related clearances "generally" complied with the FBI's Uniform Crime Reporting criteria. But it also highlighted several errors. Justifiable homicides, such as officer-involved shootings and cases of self-defense, were routinely classified incorrectly, causing the department to tally a lower amount of reported homicides than actually occurred. In 2006, for example, eight justifiable homicides weren't included in the department's figures. Neither was one negligent homicide and

Continued

CASE EXAMPLE: *CONTINUED*

another homicide in which the cause of death was undetermined. That would have increased the reported homicides to 129....

The audit also found some officers were counting an offense as cleared when an arrest warrant was issued, rather than when an arrest was made. In addition, officials failed to routinely update their clearance rates. SAPD's Web site originally reported only 36.1 percent of slayings were solved in 2006. When reporters questioned this figure, officials hastily ordered a hand count, which determined 50.4 percent of the homicides had been cleared.

Around the same time, however, the Department of Public Safety released a 40 percent clearance rate for SAPD—a number DPS said was based on the Police Department's own figures. According to the audit, 50.8 percent of homicides were solved in 2006.

The department also over-reported the number of homicides cleared in 2006 and 2007, by two and three homicides, respectively. Though the discrepancies are small, they underline the larger issue of correctly reporting crime statistics. One homicide, for example, was counted in two subsequent years and another was considered solved when it wasn't.

Michael Gilbert, a University of Texas at San Antonio criminologist, said the audit reflects a data-entry problem rather than an attempt to willfully manipulate the figures. "These are things you want the Police

Department to know and you want them to fix," he said. However, he added that having perfect data is almost impossible.

The complete audit (Gonzales, 2008) is available online at http://www.sanantonio.gov/cityauditor/reports/FY2008/AU07-011.pdf. These types of errors, which are similar to those reported in the previous example of Travis County, essentially undermine the value of FBI UCR crime statistics to the criminal justice system as a whole. Although it is true that perfect data is impossible, the failure to train law enforcement in the proper methods of data collection and reporting remains a significant issue everywhere.

The overreliance on victim crime data from the FBI as meaningful or conclusive has reached near fetishistic levels in the criminology literature. While such data provides useful reference points for the purpose of generating theory, fixation on nomothetic crime data is rarely helpful in answering specific questions about the characteristics and qualities of specific victims. It is hoped that examples in this chapter leave readers with a genuinely informed sense of how fallible—or at least vulnerable—crime data can be to all manner of manipulation.

The realities associated with crime reporting, and the resultant crime statistics, also serve to demonstrate the very real difficulties that many victims must overcome. They must successfully file a complaint, get the police to believe them, and then hope that there is sufficient law enforcement motivation to initiate an investigation. These are only the first hurdles that must be cleared in order to seek justice—and success, as we have begun to learn, is not guaranteed.

SUMMARY

Victims face many challenges as they enter the criminal justice system. Not everyone who can help them will. Not everyone who is supposed to help them is able, willing, or even technically required to do so. And not everyone who claims to be helping is making things better. As a result of the cumulative effects of an overburdened justice system, apathy from professionals and bystanders alike, and double victimization, victims are often reluctant to report crime or even request the help of authorities. In addition, these limitations and the other contextual problems discussed should prevent victimologists from relying too heavily on any victim-related crime data that may be gathered and submitted by law enforcement.

QUESTIONS

1. What are some of the problems with the crime rate and victimological literature to date?
2. Explain the availability heuristic.
3. Why might victims choose not to report crime? Give four reasons.
4. What are some examples of mandated reporters?
5. True or False: The primary role of law enforcement is to enforce the law, not to protect the public.
6. Explain the role of the victim advocate.
7. What is bystander apathy?
8. Explain the difference between double victimization and secondary victimization.

REFERENCES

Adams, R.E., Boscarino, J.A., Figley, C.R., 2006. Compassion fatigue and psychological distress among social workers: a validation study. American Journal of Orthopsychiatry 76 (1), 103–108.

Amick-McMullan, A., Kilpatrick, D., Veronen, L., Smith, S., 1989. Family survivors of homicide victims: theoretical perspectives and an exploratory study. Journal of Traumatic Stress 2 (1), 21–35.

Barton, G., 2010. Police to improve sensitivity training. Milwaukee Journal-Sentinel, July 9; Available at: http://www.jsonline.com/news/milwaukee/98133094.html

Berzofsky, M., Krebs, C., Smiley-McDonald, H., 2012. Victimizations Not Reported to the Police, 2006–2010. U.S. DOJ, Bureau of Justice Statistics, August, NCJ 238536, Washington, DC.

Blume, H., Flores, A., Winton, R., 2013. LAUSD principal failed to report alleged molestation by teacher. Los Angeles Times, January 24; Available at: http://articles.latimes.com/2013/jan/24/local/la-me-0125-teacher-20130125

Davis, C., 2001. Detective's actions face inquiry. St. Petersburg Times, October 2; Available at: http://www.sptimes.com/News/100201/news_pf/Pasco/Detective_s_actions_f.shtml

Davis, C., 2002a. Handling of rape cases is upheld. St. Petersburg Times, February 7; Available at: http://www.sptimes.com/2002/02/07/TampaBay/Handling_of_rape_case.shtml

Davis, C., 2002b. Victim sues in handling of rape. St. Petersburg Times, November 19; Available at: http://www.sptimes.com/2002/11/19/Pasco/Victim_sues_in_handli.shtml

Davis, C., 2003a. Judge may toss suit in rape. St. Petersburg Times, May 30; Available at: http://www.sptimes.com/2003/05/30/Pasco/Judge_may_toss_suit_i.shtml

Davis, C., 2003b. Victim of rape dealt setback in court. St. Petersburg Times, June 26; Available at: http://www.sptimes.com/2003/06/26/news_pf/Pasco/Victim_of_rape_dealt_.shtml

Doerner, W., Lab, S., 2005. Victimology, fourth ed. Anderson Publishing, Cincinnati, OH.

Doerner, W., Lab, S., 2011. Victimology, sixth ed. Anderson Publishing, Cincinnati, OH.

Erez, E., Laster, K., 1999. Neutralizing victim reform: legal professionals' perspectives on victims and impact statements. Crime and Delinquency 45, 530–553.

Erez, E., Rogers, L., 1999. Victim impact statements and sentencing outcomes and processes. British Journal of Criminology 39 (2), 216–239.

FBI, 2013. Uniform Crime Reports. Federal Bureau of Investigation Website, Available at: http://www.fbi.gov/about-us/cjis/ucr

Friedmann, R., Rosenfeld, R., Borissova, N., 2010. Improving Crime Data Project. The Statistical Analysis Bureau at Georgia State University, Atlanta, GA, NIJ Grant #2002-RG-CX-K005, May; Available at https://www.ncjrs.gov/pdffiles1/nij/grants/237988.pdf

Gonzales, p, 2008. Audit of the San Antonio Police Department Uniform Crime Reporting Process. Project No. AU07-01, Office of the City Auditor, City of San Antonio, Issue Date: January 28; Available at: http://www.sanantonio.gov/cityauditor/reports/FY2008/AU07-011.pdf

Goodrum, S., 2007. Victims' rights, victims' expectations, and law enforcement workers' constraints in cases of murder. Law and Social Inquiry 32, Summer; pp. 725–757.

Goodrum, S., Stafford, M., 2003. The management of emotions in the criminal justice system. Sociological Focus 36 (3), 179–196.

Guzman-Lopez, A., 2013. Lawyers for alleged victims of LA Unified teacher say higher up knew of accusations. Southern California Public Radio, March 21st; Available at: http://www.scpr.org/blogs/education/2013/03/21/13019/lawyers-for-alleged-victims-of-la-unified-teacher/

Hegeman, R., 2007. Police: shoppers stepped over victim. Associated Press, July 4; Available at: http://abcnews.go.com/US/wireStory?id=3342724

Hurlburt, R.T., Knapp, T.J., 2006. Munsterberg in 1898, not Allport in 1937, introduced the terms 'idiographic' and 'nomothetic' to American psychology. Theory and Psychology 16 (2), 287–293.

International Association of Chiefs of Police, 2011. What is the law enforcement oath of honor? The International Association of Chiefs of Police website, Available at: http://www.theiacp.org/PoliceServices/ExecutiveServices/ProfessionalAssistance/EthicsWhatistheLawEnforcementOathofHonor/tabid/150/Default.aspx

Kanter, L., 2005. Invisible clients: exploring our failure to provide civil legal services to rape victims. Suffolk University Law Review 38, 253–289.

Kappeler, V., 2006. Critical Issues in Police Civil Liability, fourth ed. Waveland Press, Long Grove, IL.

Kilpatrick, D., Otto, R., 1987. Constitutionally guaranteed participation in criminal proceeding for victims: potential effects on psychological functioning. Wayne Law Review 34, 17–28.

Kleinig, J., 1996. The Ethics of Policing. Cambridge University Press, New York.

Konradi, A., 1997. Too little, too late: prosecutors' precourt preparation of rape survivors. Law and Social Inquiry 22, 1–54.

Kriel, L., 2008. Audit raps SAPD death stats. San Antonio Express-News, February 1.

Latane, B., Darley, J.M., 1970a. Group Inhibition of Bystander Intervention. Journal of Personality and Social Psychology 10 (1968), 215–221.

Latane, B., Darley, J.M., 1970b. The Unresponsible Bystander: Why Doesn't He Help? Appleton-Century-Crofts, New York.

Lerner, M., 1980. The Belief in a Just World: A Fundamental Delusion. Plenum Press, New York.

Lukens, R., 2007. the impact of mandatory reporting requirements on the child welfare system. Rutgers Journal of Law and Public Policy 5 (1), 177–233.

Maltz, M., 1999. Bridging Gaps in Police Crime Data. U.S. DOJ, Bureau of Justice Statistics, September, NCJ 176365, Washington, DC.

Martin, P., Powell, R.M., 1995. Accounting for the "second assault": legal organizations' framing of rape victims. Law and Social Inquiry 19, 853–890.

Mendelsohn, B., 1963. The origin of the doctrine of victimology. In: Drapkin, I., Viano, E. (Eds.), Victimology, D.C. Heath, Lexington, MA.

Miccio, G.K., 2000. Notes from the underground: battered women, the state, and conceptions of accountability. Harvard Women's Law Journal 23, 154–171, Spring.

Miller, M., Clinkinbeard, S., 2006. Improving the Amber Alert System: Psychology Research and Policy Recommendations. Law and Psychology Review 30, 1–21, Spring.

Mirowsky, J., Ross, C., 1989. Social Causes of Psychological Distress. Aldine de Gruyter, Hawthorne, NY.

Parascandola, R., 2010. SVU investigators to be first on sex-crime scenes, NYPD says. New York Daily News, December 23; Available at: http://www.nydailynews.com/news/crime/svu-investigators-sex-crime-scenes-nypd-article-1.474571

Press Release, 2012. Mayor Bloomberg announces completion of major milestones in 911 system overhaul sought by the city for decades. New York City Police Department, Public Safety Answering Center, January 5; Available at: http://www.nyc.gov/html/nypd/html/pr/pr_2012_01_05_psac_911.shtml

Rando, T., 1993. Treatment of Complicated Mourning. Research Press, Champaign, IL.

Regoli, R., Hewitt, J., Maras, M., 2012. Exploring Criminal Justice: The Essentials, second ed. Jones & Bartlett Learning, Boston, MA.

Romo, V., 2013. School principals who fail to report abuse are rarely prosecuted. Southern California Public Radio, February 8; Available at: http://www.scpr.org/programs/take-two/2013/02/08/30435/school-principal-failure-to-report-abuse-lausd/

Rosenthal, A.M., 1964. Thirty-Eight Witnesses. McGraw-Hill, New York.

Scott, G., 2003. People-based safety. Professional Safety 48 (12), 33–43.

Smith, J., 2004. Biscoe defends the M.E. The Austin Chronicle, September 3; Available at: http://www.austinchronicle.com/news/2004-09-03/227271/

Smith, J., 2005. Trouble at the ME's office. The Austin Chronicle, December 2; Available at: http://www.austinchronicle.com/news/2005-12-02/315716/

Stenross, B., Kleinman, S., 1989. The highs and lows of emotional labor: detectives' encounters with criminals and victims. Journal of Contemporary Ethnography 17, 435–452.

Sullivan, J., 1977. Introduction to Police Science, third ed. McGraw-Hill, New York.

Sunstein, C., 2005. Group judgments: statistical means, deliberation, and information markets. New York University Law Review 80, 962–1049, June.

Toor, M., 2012. Survey: retired cops say NYPD crime stats fudged. The Chief-Leader, July 24; Available at: http://thechiefleader.com/news/open_articles/survey-retired-cops-say-nypd-crime-stats-fudged/article_6bcbd6bc-cc58-11e1-9840-001a4bcf6878.html

Truman, J., Planty, M., 2012. Criminal Victimization, 2011. U.S. DOJ, Washington, DC Bureau of Justice Statistics, October, NCJ 239437.

Turvey, B., Crowder, S., 2013. Ethical Justice. Academic Press, San Diego.

Turvey, B., Savino, J., 2011. Rape Investigation Handbook, second ed. Elsevier Science, San Diego.

UCR, 2010. Crime in the United States, 2009. U.S. Department of Justice, Washington, DC Federal Bureau of Investigation, September.

UCR, 2012. Offenses Cleared. Crime in the United States, 2011, U.S. Department of Justice, Federal Bureau of Investigation, September, Washington, DC.

Wolfe, S., Piquero, A., 2011. Organizational justice and police misconduct. Criminal Justice and Behavior 38 (4), 332–353.

CHAPTER 3

911 Emergency Response

Stan Crowder and Brent E. Turvey[1]

KEY TERMS

Excited utterances (or spontaneous declarations) Spontaneous statements made, it is believed, before the person speaking has had time to contrive something to his or her own advantage. Excited utterances are exceptions to hearsay rules under the Sixth Amendment that can be admitted in court.

Enhanced 911 (E911) The improved emergency response system. It routes each call to the appropriate 911 jurisdiction or answering point while simultaneously providing the caller's location and phone number to dispatchers.

Nine-one-one (911) The number that people in the United Stated call to obtain assistance from government-funded agencies that provide police, fire, and emergency medical services. It is a number that is reserved for emergencies only; therefore, it is intended to triage citizen requests for immediate rescue from dire circumstances.

As we discussed in the preceding chapter, victims generally enter the criminal justice system when the crimes committed against them are reported to law enforcement. There are many ways that this can happen. A mechanism familiar to most is the 911 emergency response system.

The purpose of this chapter is to provide readers with an applied sense of what 911 emergency response is and does; the challenges faced by 911 dispatchers when dealing with callers in distress; and the problems that have and continue to plague 911 emergency response systems in general, from personnel issues to funding shortages.

It bears mentioning up front that public reports of 911 systems, operators, and supervisors often portray the negatives or failures. This reality cannot be ignored, as it is necessary for understanding the uphill battle that many victims

CONTENTS

---

[1]While having served in a variety of positions to aid victims, the authors have not worked as 911 operators. One author (Crowder) sometimes assisted in the old-style "radio room" when his wife was on duty at the county police headquarters as a "call taker" or "dispatcher," but those were the analog days of yesteryear. In addition, the authors have worked numerous investigations in which 911 recordings have played a significant role in case resolution. For these reasons, it was agreed that a review of 911 Emergency Response, and related victim interaction and impact issues, was necessary for inclusion in the present text.

Forensic Victimology. http://dx.doi.org/10.1016/B978-0-12-408084-3.00003-X

confront when seeking aid and justice from government-funded agencies. It is also necessary for identifying issues within 911 systems that require attention or remedy. Therefore, this chapter does not shrink from providing that perspective. However, it is also the goal of the authors to present the importance of responsive and competent 911 operators to victims, case resolution, and crime reduction.

911: HISTORY, ROLES AND RESPONSIBILITIES

Nine-one-one (911) is the number that people in the United States call to obtain assistance from government funded agencies that provide police, fire, and emergency medical services. It is a number that is reserved for emergencies only; therefore, it is intended to triage citizen requests for immediate rescue from dire circumstances. Common examples include calls from citizens who have just been victimized (e.g., a burglary, robbery, or sexual assault); calls from citizens reporting crimes that they have observed (sometimes while the crimes are still in progress); calls from citizens reporting a fire in their home or that of a neighbor; and calls from citizens reporting an injury suffered by themselves or a loved one. As with most government services, 911 is largely funded by local, state, and federal tax revenue.

History

The idea for a universal emergency number first took shape in 1957, when the National Association of Fire Chiefs suggested an easy-to-remember phone number to report fires. The notion was formalized in 1967, when the President's Commission on Law Enforcement and Administration recommended the establishment of a nationwide number for emergencies of all types. The Federal Communications Commission (FCC) sought the assistance of the American Telephone and Telegraph Company (AT&T) to implement the program; in 1968, AT&T selected 911 as the nationwide emergency contact number. The first 911 phone call was made on February 16, 1968, in Haleyville, Alabama, by Senator Rankin Fite. With Congressional support and mandates, the 1970s era kicked off the growth of 911. Now E911 service is available for about 95% of America with 240 million calls made annually to 911.

Enhanced 911

Enhanced 911, or *E911*, is the improved emergency response system. It routes each call to the appropriate 911 jurisdiction or answering point while simultaneously providing the caller's location and phone number to dispatchers. E911 is also capable of providing caller phone number and physical location information for calls made from cellular phones. However, E911 is not available in all areas of the United States. As will be discussed, some agencies have limited emergency response systems, whereas others have none.

Duties

The 911 operators, sometimes referred to as dispatchers, have specific obligations and responsibilities to their callers (see Figure 3-1). Although these duties vary from system to system, most of them are universal. They are as follows:

- *Take the call*: Dispatchers are responsible for taking the calls that they receive. If a call comes in to their station, and they are able, they must answer. They may not ignore the call or hang up abruptly without cause, no matter who makes the call or where it originates. By answering, they are also take responsibility for the disposition of the call.
- *Get caller information quickly*: Dispatchers must rapidly acquire certain basic information from the caller, to ensure a timely and appropriate response. This information includes caller name, location, the nature of the emergency, and whether there is anyone armed or injured on site. Typically, dispatchers will follow a required script to elicit this information, such as "911, please state the nature of your emergency" and "tell me exactly what happened." If the call is not related to an emergency, dispatchers will direct the caller to use nonemergency numbers.
- *Triage the call*: If it is determined that a call is related to an emergency, dispatchers must quickly decide which services to send and from where. This means that they must have the caller's information; understand

FIGURE 3-1
A dispatcher takes emergency calls at her station for 911 at the Department of Safety in Denver.

the essential nature of the emergency; and have an awareness of which available police, fire, and medical services are closest to the caller. Effective triage normally happens within the first 30 seconds of answering the call.

- *Provide a call summary:* Once the decision has been made on how and where to triage an emergency call, dispatchers must summarize the pertinent details in their system for distribution to responding agencies. As outlined in a memorandum by Carl Simpson, Director of Denver 911 (2012; p. 2):
  - Police dispatchers will be dispatching first responders based on the information in the snapshot; therefore, the operator's snapshot must appropriately reflect the basic nature of the call including, and when available, time frame, weapon, accident details, and injury information.
  - The snapshot is generally the caller's response to "tell me exactly what happened" and may or may not contain, on initial utterance, any weapon, time frame, or injury information. If safety and time frame information is not included in the initial statement, the operator will immediately ask the applicable questions and document those details in the comments of the incident.
- *Stay on the line:* Generally, dispatchers are admonished to stay on the line with child and victim callers until first responders have arrived on the scene. If the call is terminated voluntarily on the caller's end, that may require no further immediate action on the operator's part. However, if the call drops out, or if it is interrupted before the dispatcher has received complete information, then the operator may be obligated to make efforts to reconnect with the caller. Additionally, if help is not immediately on the way, the operator may be obligated to stay on the line, providing comfort, reassurance, and even emergency first aid instructions when the situation calls for it.
- *Update information:* Dispatchers must stay in touch with first responders to be able to update information in their system with respect to each call they've taken throughout their shift. This information then becomes available to other responding agencies as they need it to make informed operational decisions. These updates are added as comments to the file or case number associated with the initial call.
- *Avoid nonpertinent detail:* Dispatchers should avoid adding "unnecessary information to the incident convoluting their comments or quote callers use of profanity or slang in their comments" and further avoid adding in "opinion, discussions, or other detracting, non-pertinent statements" (Simpson, 2012; p. 3). Such additions to the narrative, apart from being unnecessary, can muddy or even poison the record of events with subjective and erroneous information. This assists responders in their professional assignments and may actually cause delays as first responders work to parse through lengthy personal commentary for important specific details.

- *Maintain a professional attitude:* Dispatchers have tremendous power to influence not just prevailing case assumptions, but also the professional attitudes of those from other responding agencies. Their professionalism can set the tone from the outset, demonstrating a propensity for thoroughness, information sharing, and follow-up. As a consequence, those with other responding agencies can learn that 911 Emergency Response expects certain tasks be accomplished in a certain fashion; that certain conduct and speech are not acceptable; and that they either grow accustomed to being professionally prepared or they grow accustomed to being on record with a lack of it. Unfortunately, unprofessional conduct leads by example from 911 as well, so at the very least, this must be avoided.

Throughout this entire process, dispatchers must be ever mindful of the reality that their job is to help callers and victims in distress. It is very likely that callers will be in an extreme emotional state and perhaps even in severe pain. This includes callers who are upset and crying, frightened, enraged, entering a state of shock, in a state of panic, or any of the preceding throughout the call. Managing such calls therefore requires both professionalism and empathy.

Violations of these and related protocols can result in dispatcher suspension and even termination, as will be discussed shortly.

THE 911 CALL AS AUTHORITY AND EVIDENCE

As everything we have discussed up to this point suggests, 911 is currently an integral, and inextricable, component of the criminal justice system. This is true for a number of reasons.

With 911 dispatchers serving as front-line emergency responders, they have great power with respect to shaping all other responding agency impressions, conclusions, and attitudes. For example, 911 may receive a call reporting a suicide or some other unattended death. If this label is treated as an authoritative conclusion and does not lead to a competent death investigation, a homicide may go undetected. Dispatchers have an obligation to be mindful that words like *homicide, suicide,* and *accident* have tremendous forensic implications, and they should therefore avoid using them whenever possible. In this way, they will not invite other agencies to be derelict in their own duties by simply agreeing with an early label to avoid work and related paperwork.

Also, everything that 911 dispatchers say and do is logged in to or recorded by the system, along with a recording of every conversation that they have with every caller. As such, 911 calls become important documentary evidence of statements, caller knowledge, the occurrence of background events recorded during the call, and timelines.[2] Consequently, 911 recordings are used every day by investigators, attorneys, and the courts as evidence to inform decision making, implicate suspects, and even to exonerate the innocent.

For example, the verbal exchanges between 911 dispatchers and callers have an impact on grand jury verdicts, criminal prosecutions, and sentencing in court due to the "excited utterance" exception to the admissibility of hearsay evidence. *Excited utterances*, or *spontaneous declarations*, are exceptions to hearsay rules under the Sixth Amendment and can be admitted in court (Greenberg, 2004). They are spontaneous statements made, it is believed, before the person speaking has had time to contrive something to his or her own advantage. Viewed as a part of the criminal incident, the call may be made while the crime is in progress or in the immediate aftermath of the incident. Again, because there has been no opportunity for the caller to consider, review, and falsify the account of events, the courts generally allow a 911 call to be entered into evidence under the excited utterance exception.

EMERGENCY SYSTEM CHALLENGES

Every 911 emergency response system experiences universal challenges. The top three tend to be personnel, budgets, and false alarms. We consider each of them in turn.

Issues with Dispatch Personnel

Briefly, it is necessary to discuss common management and supervisory issues with dispatch personnel. As with any emergency responder agency, 911 has an ethical obligation to hire, retain, and promote only those employees with the proper education, training, or experience. A failure in this area can be disastrous.

Furthermore, 911 has an ethical obligation to ensure that each employee is sufficiently trained for the work he or she is assigned. Some agencies have stringent training and certification requirements for their dispatchers. They don't want people answering calls who can't handle what is inevitably going to be thrown at them. Other agencies have little to no training requirements; they are also likely to be only a lawsuit away from losing their municipal liability insurance (unless they already have and are forced to self-insure).

---

[2]One of authors (Turvey) worked a shooting case that involved a drug deal gone wrong, resulting in a homicide. Audio of the shots, along with important gunshot timeline information, was captured by the cellphone of a passerby who called 911 after the initial shot was fired. This recording, made because of a call to the 911 system, served as powerful evidence with respect to the author's subsequent forensic reconstruction.

The reality is that being a 911 dispatcher is stressful and demanding. Without the proper education, training, and accompanying support from management, this difficult job becomes almost impossible to do effectively. Support from management means avoiding political appointments, getting all the staff trained, giving them adequate supervision, and getting rid of those who shouldn't be there. This includes those dispatchers engaged in conduct that evidences their incompetence, their apathy, or their own mental distress.

For example, 911 dispatchers are at risk for becoming overwhelmed by *compassion fatigue,* as are all first responders, discussed previously in Chapter 2. This can cause negative interactions between a jaded dispatcher and distressed callers at the very least. At the worst, it can result in negligent failure to respond adequately (or at all) to caller distress, resulting in the loss of life.

Additionally, there can be very real mental health consequences for dispatchers who are constantly bombarded with violence and trauma, as explained in Lilly and Pierce (2012; p. 135):

> Continued exposure to trauma increases risk for both depression and PTSD. This may be particularly true for individuals with work-related exposure to trauma such as 911 telecommunicators, a group with significant exposure to work-related trauma that has received limited empirical attention.... Symptoms of PTSD and depression were significantly related to peritraumatic distress, self-worth, and benevolence of the world. Analyses revealed that the relationship between peritraumatic distress and both current depression and PTSD was significantly stronger for individuals who reported more negative assumptions about the benevolence of the world and self-worth.

In other words, the constant exposure to traumatic events experienced by 911 dispatchers can lead to the symptoms of post-traumatic stress disorder (PTSD), especially if they already view the world and themselves in a negative fashion. A negative attitude compounds the stress of their *secondary victimization.*[3]

Managers, supervisors, and co-workers must be trained to identify the behaviors that are associated with these forms of mental distress—and to take them seriously. In this way, they can report it properly or take action before something gets missed or someone gets hurt. Given these concerns, failure to provide adequate training and supervision at every pertinent level can have disastrous results.

---

[3]See discussion in Chapter 2.

Budgetary Issues

It should be noted that due to budget shortages in the face of increasing demands for emergency response, some agencies have been forced to limit their 911 emergency services. Sometimes these shortages occur because of reduced federal funding; sometimes they occur because local citizenry refuse to pass the necessary levies; and sometimes it is a combination of both reasons.

A more general budgetary issue has to do with how 911 emergency response contracts are negotiated with cellphone service providers. In 1996, the FCC mandated that wireless carriers set up systems with tracking technologies to find callers. These carriers spent billions to meet the requirement, and the FCC threatened fines of up to $2.2 million for AT&T missing required implementation deadlines (Murphy and Ridgway, 2002). However, these carriers (e.g., Verizon, AT&T, and T-Mobile) prefer to negotiate regional package deals with state governments, rather than having to hammer out contracts with each individual city or county system. They have lobbyists who work hard to ensure this very thing. From their point of view, such an arrangement makes sense.

When the state gets a lump sum of funds for 911, meant to be divided among individual municipal agencies, there is no guarantee that this money will make it to the local level. In fact, there is a good chance that it won't. State governments can and will dig in to any available funds for other projects, regardless of how they were collected or why. For example, in Rhode Island, where a state budget operates the 911 system, a past governor and general assembly diverted two-thirds of the funds collected from traditional phone line and wireless line surcharges and then cut their budget (Barmann, 2008).

Whatever the case for local budget shortfalls, 911 emergency response has been dramatically affected in the following ways across the nation: reduced or no response to "lesser" crimes; reduced staffing; reduced or no training for dispatchers; reduced hours of availability for emergency response; and the elimination of emergency response services to rural areas altogether. Consider the following examples.

The Chicago Police Department has stopped responding to lesser crimes, as reported in Spielman (2013):

> Chicago is implementing a dramatic change in 911 dispatch to free the equivalent of 44 police officers a day to respond to the most serious crimes. As of Sunday, police officers are no longer responding in person to reports of a vehicle theft, garage burglary, or crime where the victim is "safe, secure and not in need of medical attention" and the offender is "not on the scene and not expected to return immediately."
>
> Instead, those 911 calls are being transferred to the Chicago Police Department's Alternate Response Section, staffed by officers on light

duty. Police reports will be taken over the phone. If necessary, evidence technicians will be assigned later.

Last year, the Alternate Response Unit processed 74,000 reports. Crime victims had the option of filing reports on the phone or they could insist on an in-person response and wait until a squad car was free. Now, they won't have that option. That's expected to more than double the number of case reports taken over the phone—to 151,000 a year—and free the equivalent of 44 officers a day for patrol and to respond to more serious crimes.

City Hall says dispatchers have been told to transfer calls if: the offender is gone, not expected to "return immediately" and an officer is not needed for a prompt investigation; an officer on the scene would "not result in an immediate arrest" and the victim is safe, secure and not in need of medical attention.

All "non-criminal" reports will be taken over the phone, including lost property and damage caused when a window is broken or a tree falls on property. Police will also no longer respond in person to a variety of criminal reports, including: vehicle or other theft; garage burglaries; bogus checks; lewd, obscene or threatening phone calls without "imminent danger"; simple assault and animal bites.

Deputy chief-of-patrol Steve Georgas said law enforcement agencies across the nation are searching for ways to use their resources more efficiently.

In Cincinnati, Ohio, it has come to light that many 911 operators have little or no medical training. Hiring them saves money, but it also requires these untrained personnel to hang up on callers without providing them with aid or comfort, as reported in Keefe and O'Keefe (2013):

The startling fact that some 911 operators in Cincinnati have no or only partial medical training comes amid a city budget crunch that has left a hiring freeze on the Emergency Communications Center (ECC), which runs the city's 911 operations.

Rhonda Andrews was having a heart attack when her sister called 911 for help. "I could have died that day," Andrews said. "My heart had stopped three times."

The 911 call for Andrews lasted barely more than a minute. "No one gave us any instructions…they just hung up," Andrews said.…

"I want to hear the person, a strong person, say 'take her, lay her down, do this, do that,'" Andrews said. "Instead I heard, 'OK, they're coming. Bye.'"

Two current Cincinnati dispatchers without the proper training whose identity the I-Team is keeping a secret said they are often assigned to answer 911 calls. "I start the fire department and get off the phone to answer other emergencies," Dispatcher One said of how she responds to medical calls.

"It's sad and scary at the same time," Dispatcher Two said. "It's scary because you don't know what's going to happen to those people. And it's sad because you put yourself in their shoes and how would you feel if that was you?"

"It keeps me up at night because I've gotten calls that I could not handle with the training given to me," Dispatcher One said.

To get to other waiting calls, dispatchers said they were told by their supervisors not to stay on the line if they are not trained....

Consider the more serious debacle in rural Josephine County, Oregon, which voted down a tax levy that would have saved it from the current crisis, described in Templeton (2013):

Last year, the Josephine County sheriff's department lost a multi-million dollar federal subsidy for timber dependent counties. The sheriff laid off 23 deputies and eliminated the entire major crimes division. [See Figure 3-2.] Of the six deputies left, two are limited to patrolling federal forest lands and the Rogue River because of the way they are funded. After the cuts, the Sheriff put out a press release warning victims of domestic violence to "consider relocating to an area with adequate law enforcement services."

Then, on August 18 of last year, a woman in Cave Junction placed this call.

911 Emergency tape:

Woman: "My ex-boyfriend is trying to break into my house. I'm not letting him in but he's like, tried to break down the door and he's tried to break into one of the windows."

The threat she was reporting was real. Her ex, a man named Michael Bellah, eventually pleaded guilty to kidnapping, assault, and sex abuse for what he did when he got inside the house. The woman has asked us not to use her name. When she called 911, she explained that Bellah had hurt her before.

Woman: "He put me in the hospital a few weeks ago and I have been trying to keep him away."

The call came in on a Saturday at 4:58 in the morning. Because of the staffing limitations, Josephine County deputies are only available 8 a.m. to 4 p.m., Monday through Friday. So the dispatcher transferred her call to the state police....

The Oregon State Police say their primary responsibility isn't responding to 911 calls like this one. It's traffic safety, patrolling the highways. But in the rural parts of Josephine County, the State Police are often the only law enforcement agents available on the weekends.

FIGURE 3-2
From Mortenson (2012): "Erin Maue, a statistician and public information officer with the Sheriff's Office, stands among several uniforms, which were turned in this week after several members of the Josephine County Sheriff's Office were laid off."

Since the county layoffs, their office in Grants Pass has received about 3 times as many calls as in the past. But it's a small office. Here's a recording of the state police dispatcher's response to the woman's call for help that day.

State police tape: "Uh, I don't have anybody to send out there. You know, obviously, if he comes inside the residence and assaults you, can you ask him to go away? Do you know if he's intoxicated or anything?"

Woman: "I've already asked him. I've already told him I was calling you. He's broken in before, busted down my door, assaulted me."

The State Police dispatcher stays on the phone with the woman for 10 minutes and 21 seconds. She asks if Bellah has a weapon. The woman says no. She tells the dispatcher there's already a warrant out for Bellah's arrest.

Dispatcher: "Is he still there?"

Woman: "Yes, he is."

The dispatcher tells the caller to try to hide in the house. And four times in total she says there isn't anyone who can help.

Dispatcher: "Once again it's unfortunate you guys don't have any law enforcement out there."

Woman: "Yeah, it doesn't matter, if he gets in the house I'm done."

According to police records, a few minutes later Michael Bellah used a piece of metal to pry open the woman's front door. He choked her, and sexually assaulted her. Later that day he was arrested by the State Police.

Because 911 emergency response systems are funded largely by local tax dollars, every system is a reflection of the tax revenues supporting it—similar to the way that schools are funded. In the same way, then, it is possible to have a high-tech and well-staffed 911 system with competent personnel in an affluent county. Meanwhile, a nearby county with the same population, but lower average per capita income, will have a system that is low-tech, understaffed, poorly trained, and otherwise running on fumes.

False Alarms

False alarms are a huge problem for any emergency response system. Accidental calls alone (e.g., misdials, pocket dials, and accidental child calls) can represent up to 40% or more of the total call volume in a given system, as mentioned in the preceding chapter. This can reduce response time and limit, or eliminate, responder availability for actual emergencies. And that doesn't even address what it actually costs in dollars. Such issues become even more pertinent in systems that are already underfunded and physically strained.

Intentional false reports are another problem altogether and receive a better discussion in Chapter 9, "False Allegations of Crime." However, suffice it to say that prank calls to 911 are not at all unheard of. In fact, the recent trend of *swatting* demonstrates that the practice is alive and well in some regions.[4]

THE CONSEQUENCES

As this chapter has demonstrated, when 911 emergency response systems experience shortcomings with respect to budgets, personnel, or management, victims are the ones who pay the most direct price. The reason is that there are

---

[4]*Swatting* refers to making a false report to 911 Emergency Response regarding a home invasion, armed gunman, or some other criminal threat that requires an equivalent response from law enforcement, specifically the dispatch of their Special Weapons And Tactics (SWAT) unit. In the Los Angeles area, for example, it is becoming increasingly common to *swat* celebrity homes by making false reports to 911 with cellphones. It has become problematic enough that police have warned they will charge anyone engaging in *swatting* with a felony.

not many second chances during an emergency, and the harm that is suffered is often terrible, if not entirely irrevocable. Specific consequences are as follows:

- Emergency response to victims can be delayed or nonexistent.
- More victims can suffer from more crime or extended episodes of victimization.
- Victims can die waiting for a response or due to the negligence of those involved in the response.
- The 911 dispatchers can suffer mental health consequences that go unrecognized and unattended, leading to more of the above.
- Criminals can become emboldened by reliable delays in emergency response.
- The public can lose confidence in the emergency response system and vote to defund it, making a bad situation worse.

It is therefore necessary to ensure that emergency response systems are properly funded, staffed, and managed to ensure that calls and cases are resolved swiftly, with the protection of victims in mind. Predictably competent responsiveness will, in turn, lead to crime reduction, which keeps the public trust and best assures that voters will not forget responders when voting on related tax levies.

CASE EXAMPLE:

911 Operator Angie Rivera

Every day, in every city around the United States, there are 911 dispatchers providing vital aid and assistance to victims of violent crime. Few better examples of such efforts exist than that of dispatcher Angie Rivera (see Figure 3-3), as reported Tugman (2013):

A California teen was home alone when burglars broke into her house. She quickly and quietly ran to a closet to hide and called 911 for help. The suspects were just feet away from her at one point. Doyin Oladipupo was home alone when three burglars broke in. She says, "I was so, so scared. I could see them."

The quick-thinking 15-year-old grabbed a phone and called 911. She hid behind clothes in her mother's closet, the robbers so close the 911 operator could hear them on the phone. As she hid, the thieves stole right in the closet, right next to her. The 911 operator was cool, calm and quiet.

It is life frighteningly mimicking art. In the film, "The Call," amazingly out just last week, Halle Berry plays a 911 operator in a similar situation. For this 15-year-old and her mother, it was a very happy ending.

The dispatcher, Angie Rivera, takes as many as 200 calls a day, never one like this. She says, "I won't lie, I did shed a couple of tears, just the adrenaline release, just knowing she was safe. You know, when we take these calls, we don't know how they're going to end."

Police arrived, found her and even arrested the three burglars still in the driveway in a stolen car.

Ms. Rivera credits the good outcome despite the high stress in no small part to the victim, who she reports did everything right in this terrible situation.

Continued

CASE EXAMPLE: *CONTINUED*

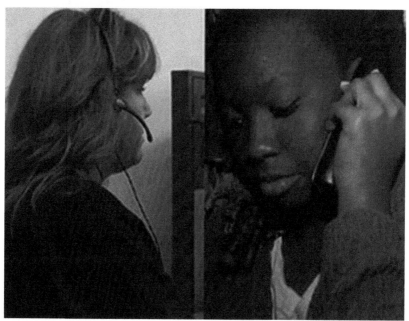

FIGURE 3-3
Dispatcher Angie Rivera pictured alongside the girl she helped through a home invasion, Doyin Oladipupo.

CASE EXAMPLE:

Glenn Godfrey, Former Commissioner, Alaska State Troopers

In 2002, 53-year-old Glenn Godfrey was former head of the Alaska State Troopers and had just recently stepped down from his position as Alaska Commissioner of Public Safety. He and his 52-year-old wife, Patricia, shared a home together in Eagle River (see Figure 3-4). However, all was not well. They had separated recently and were in the middle of an attempt at reconciliation.

Their separation had been due in no small part to Mr. Godfrey being in the process of ending an affair with 33-year-old Karen Brand, then vice president of the Alaska State Chamber of Commerce (see Figure 3-5). Ms. Brand did not take former Commissioner Godfrey's decision to end their relationship well. According to published accounts, including an official report by the Alaska Office of Victims' Rights (Branchflower and de Luca, 2002),

Brand entered the Godfreys' Eagle River home on August 2, 2002, while they were away, found Mr. Godfrey's .44 Magnum handgun inside, and waited. When they returned and entered the house, she shot them both. The details of the crime that followed are provided in Mauer (2002):

> Sitting on a pillow in a hallway closet with a protein bar, a bottle of water and a .44 Magnum revolver lifted from the house she'd broken into, Karen Brand apparently passed the time with a Tom Clancy novel. She was awaiting the return of Glenn and Patti Godfrey and, probably more importantly, waiting to hear their reaction to the message she left on their answering machine.

FIGURE 3-4
Glenn Godfrey with his wife, Patricia.

FIGURE 3-5
Karen Brand, Mr. Godfrey's jilted lover.

Continued

CASE EXAMPLE: *CONTINUED*

The message was about her affair with Glenn Godfrey, the retired Alaska public safety commissioner, and it hinted at her growing sense of betrayal.... The crime scene was the Godfreys' 1980s split-level Eagle River home. It was there that the couple had raised four children while Glenn rose through the ranks of the Alaska State Troopers. In June, at age 53, he retired as the state's top cop.

Brand, 33, was vice president of the Alaska State Chamber of Commerce and a former legislative aide who had lived in Juneau. She also was married. Police reports show that days before the shooting, on July 30, a person matching Brand's striking description—nearly 6 feet tall, 135 pounds, blond hair, blue eyes—cut through a nearby yard to the Godfreys' home.

Days later, when police searched Brand's 9-year-old Jeep Cherokee, they found prescription pill bottles for Patti Godfrey. The Godfreys' son Gerad, a private security official, believes Brand entered the house that day and may have stolen the keys to Glenn Godfrey's gun case. Gerad said his father had been searching for the keys for several days. He usually kept them in the door frame above the hallway closet, Gerad said, and with the keys missing—and not wanting to break into the case—he was unarmed on Aug. 3.

Early Friday, Aug. 2, Brand had shown up at the Godfreys'. According to Patti's just-released statement to police, Godfrey told Brand they were planning to take Patti's father to the doctor that day.

The Godfreys actually planned a family outing to Seward. On the drive south, they kept seeing Brand's car trailing them. At a turnout, Godfrey suddenly got off the road and Brand sped by, according to Patti's statement. Brand got behind them once again until they reached Girdwood.

After the shootings, Brand's car was found parked at the dead-end side of a street near the Godfreys'. No one knows how long Brand was in the Godfreys' house. Police found a window ajar. There was a light in the hall closet, and

Brand could have passed the time reading Tom Clancy's "Op-Center" thriller until the Godfreys returned around 11 p.m. Gerad found the book underneath the pillow after police finished their search. A water bottle nearby had Brand's fingerprints.

According to police, Brand left two messages on the answering machine. She talked about having put off buying a house and horse for years at Godfrey's request and suggested Godfrey not keep Patti "in the dark any longer."

She wondered whether he was leading on both women and said she was surprised he lied to her about taking his father-in-law to the doctor that day, because she had thought he never lied to her.

Patti and Glenn moved to the living room, half a flight of steps up from the hall closet, and spent more than an hour talking, she told police. "He admitted he was trying to break off with this person since like January, February."

Patti went to the bathroom. Glenn went downstairs. Patti came back to the couch. She heard two shots. Up the stairs came Brand, who sat down in Patti's pink chair.

"Hello, Patti," Brand said. It was the first time Patti had seen her up close, she told police. Brand had Godfrey's gun in her lap. Patti said Brand was stroking the barrel "like it was a baby or a puppy."

Still believing her husband might be alive, Patti told Brand, "'You just get out of here. Let me go get help for him, please.' She says, 'No.' She says, 'We're all going to burn in hell.'"

As Patti prayed, "she says, 'If I can't have him, nobody can have him.' I'm praying, and she says, 'Hurry up with your prayers.'" After about a minute, Patti decided she'd had enough and rose to call for help. "I'll see you in hell," Brand said, then started shooting, Patti recalled.

After Patti was hit with four shots, the gun stopped firing but Brand kept pulling the trigger. Patti saw Brand reach into her shirt, then watched Brand's expression change dramatically

CASE EXAMPLE: *CONTINUED*

as she picked up the phone. "She's saying: 'No, Patti, no. No, Patti, no.' I totally ignored her."

Patti dialed 911. Brand left in panic. While Patti was talking to police, she heard more shots—several fired into her husband, and then the suicide. When police entered the house about 45 minutes later, the gun was resting on Brand's belly.

Later, during the autopsy, the medical examiner found two unspent rounds in her black sports bra and Patti's credit card in one of her loafers.

(It should also be noted that the autopsy revealed no drugs or alcohol in Brand's system.)

Under most circumstances, calling 911 immediately sets into motion a series of rapidly unfolding events that often can and do save lives. In a case involving someone like Glenn Godfrey, who would be considered law enforcement royalty, one would expect the response to be even more focused, directed, and intense. However, this is not what Patricia Godfrey experienced. As explained in AP Staff (2002), which is corroborated in the official report prepared by Branchflower and de Luca (2002):

> Anchorage police dispatchers disregarded the address Patti Godfrey gave them during a 911 call, relying instead on inadequate computer information, a tape of the call shows.
>
> A badly injured Godfrey waited 48 minutes for help after she reported that she and her husband, retired public safety commissioner Glenn Godfrey, had been shot inside their Eagle River home. Glenn Godfrey had been killed, although Patti Godfrey didn't know it at the time.
>
> Minutes into the 12:30 a.m. call Aug. 3, Patti Godfrey gave dispatchers the name and phone number of her daughter and repeatedly begged them to call her. Dispatchers didn't make that call, and they didn't ask Godfrey for directions to her house until about 40 minutes into the call.... "I've been shot, please," Godfrey, 52, said in her first words to the 911 dispatcher. Dispatcher Billy Miller, one of two who talked to Godfrey during the call, asked who shot her, where Karen was, what Karen looked like, where the gun was.

Less than two minutes later, Godfrey said, "I...she just shot herself, I believe." Godfrey at that point was alert and responsive to questions. She also confirmed the Godfreys' address: 22953 Eagle River Road, at Mile 4.6. But dispatchers did not ask her for directions, which they typically do, Deputy Police Chief Mark Mew said.

Because the address Godfrey gave did not appear in the database, the computer gave similar but incorrect addresses and officers could not find the right house. Several minutes into the call, believing officers were at Godfrey's door, dispatchers assured her help was just outside and told her to hang on.

..."I'm begging," she said. "Save Glenn's life. Save Glenn's life. Lord Jesus, please help us. Save Glenn's life. Give us another chance. Lord Jesus. Please God, help him." She described her injuries in detail. One bullet had ripped through her stomach, another through her leg, and her right arm was nearly severed, she said.

...As officers failed to show up, Godfrey sounded more angry, telling them they weren't helping her and they were lying about officers being just outside the house. Late in the call, Godfrey hung up on the operators. They called her back immediately and heard the sound of dialing. When Godfrey realized she was on the phone with them, she again killed the connection.

When dispatchers successfully got through again, dispatcher Jeri Wallin told Godfrey they needed her to tell them exactly how to get to her home. "We can't find your house!" Wallin said urgently. Godfrey gave broken directions, mumbling. By the time officers arrived, it was nearly 1:19 a.m.

In 2003, Patricia Godfrey filed a claim against the estate of Karen Brand for $2 million. In 2004, the city of Anchorage agreed to pay her $700,000 for physical and psychological damage suffered as a result of 911-related failures (Toomey, 2004). In addition, it was agreed that response procedures would be reviewed and the system properly updated.

SUMMARY

Nine-one-one (911) is the number that people in the United States call to obtain assistance from government-funded agencies that provide police, fire, and emergency medical services. It is a number that is reserved for emergencies only; therefore, it is intended to triage citizen requests for immediate rescue from dire circumstances.

The 911 operators, sometimes referred to as dispatchers, have specific obligations and responsibilities to their callers. Obligations and responsibilities include taking the call, obtaining caller information quickly, triaging the call, summarizing the call, staying on the line, updating information, avoiding nonpertinent details, and maintaining professionalism. The 911 dispatchers have the power to shape all other responding agencies' impressions, conclusions, and attitudes.

There are universal challenges faced by every 911 emergency response system. The top three tend to be personnel, budgets, and false alarms. Consequences include delayed or nonexistent responses, mental health consequences suffered by 911 dispatchers that go unrecognized, and a public loss of confidence in the emergency response system. It is necessary to ensure that emergency response systems are properly funded, staffed, and managed to ensure that calls and cases are resolved swiftly, with the protection of victims in mind.

QUESTIONS

1. List and explain three duties of 911 operators.
2. Explain how 911 dispatchers have the power to shape all other responding agencies' impressions, conclusions, and attitudes.
3. Define *excited utterance*. Explain why the courts generally allow 911 calls to be entered into evidence under the excited evidence exception.
4. List the top three universal challenges experienced by every 911 emergency response system.
5. List three consequences that result from emergency response shortcomings.

REFERENCES

Barmann, T.C., 2008. Is 911 system hurting? The Providence Journal, February 20; http://www.theindustrycouncil.org/publications/Is%20911%20system%20hurting.pdf

Branchflower, S., de Luca, T., 2002. Investigative report regarding the Anchorage Police Department's E-911 emergency response to the Patricia Godfrey residence. Alaska Office of Victims' Rights, OCR Complaint no. 02–004, APD report number 02-039245, November 26.

Greenberg, J., 2004. Decision of interest: 911 call is admissible as trial evidence if it meets 'excited utterance' or other hearsay exceptions. New York Law Journal, April 23, pp. 1–4.

Keefe, B., O'Keefe, P.J., 2013. Is calling 911 in the city of Cincinnati a game of roulette? Kentucky Post, May 22; http://www.wcpo.com/dpp/news/local_news/investigations/i-team-is-911-in-the-city-of-cincinnati-a-game-of-roulette

Lilly, M., Pierce, H., 2012. PTSD and depressive symptoms in 911 telecommunicators: the role of peritraumatic distress and world assumptions in predicting risk. Psychological Trauma: Theory, Research, Practice, and Policy 5 (2), 135–141.

Mauer, R., 2002. 'I'll see you in hell,' Brand told Godfrey. Anchorage Daily News, October 1, http://www.juneauempire.com/stories/100102/sta_godfreyshooting.shtml

Mortenson, E., 2012. Josephine County lives with its decision to vote down law enforcement tax levy. Oregon Live, June 1; http://www.oregonlive.com/news/index.ssf/2012/06/reactionary_josephine_county_l.html

Murphy, V., Ridgway, N., 2002. This is an emergency? Forbes 170 (3), 95–97.

Simpson, C., 2012. Career service rule 16-60 discipline and dismissal memo to Juan Rodriguez. Director of 911, City and County of Denver, Department of Safety, May 15.

Spielman, F., 2013. City implements 911 dispatch changes freeing up officers for response. Chicago Sun-Times, February 2; http://www.suntimes.com/news/cityhall/17955932-418/nothing-but-9-1-1.html

Staff, 2002. Tape of Godfrey's 911 call shows dispatcher's delay. The Associated Press, August 25; Available at: http://www.juneauempire.com/stories/082502/sta_shooting.shtml

Templeton, A., 2013. With no officers to respond to 911 calls, Josephine Co. considers tax levy. Oregon Public Broadcasting, May 15; http://www.opb.org/news/article/josephine-county-tax-levy-would-add-deputies-fund-the-jail/

Toomey, S., 2004. City to pay Godfrey $700,000, Anchorage Daily News, August 14.

Tugman, L., 2013. Teen hides in closet as burglars rob her home. CNN/KGTV, March 22; Available at: http://www.thv11.com/news/article/255986/70/Teen-hides-in-closet-as-burglars-rob-her-home

CHAPTER 4

Constructing a Victim Profile

Brent E. Turvey and Jodi Freeman[1]

KEY TERMS

Confirmation bias A form of observer bias, it is the conscious or unconscious tendency to affirm preexisting theories, opinions, or findings.

Critical thinking Indiscriminately questioning all evidence and assumptions, no matter what their source.

Falsification The act of refuting or disproving a hypothesis or theory. The extent to which any theory is scientific is a function of whether and how attempts at falsification have been made. Theories that have survived repeated vigorous attempts at falsification are considered more scientific and more reliable than those that have not. Falsification is the cornerstone of the scientific method.

Identification (or Classification) The placement of any item into a specific category of items with similar characteristic. Identification does not require or imply uniqueness.

Idiographic study The study of the concrete: examining individuals and their actual qualities. Idiographic study concentrates on specific cases and the unique traits or functioning of individuals.

Individuation The assignment of uniqueness to an item; describing it in such a manner as to separate it from all other items in the universe.

Nomothetic A term that refers to the study of the abstract; examining groups and universal laws.

Nomothetic victim profiles Characteristics developed by studying groups of victims.

Observer effects A form of bias characterized by distortions resulting from the context and mental state of the forensic examiner, to include his or her employer, peer relationships, and subconscious expectations and desires.

Practice standards fundamental rules that set the limits of evidentiary interpretation, offering a standard for evaluating acceptable work habits and application of methods.

Science An orderly body of knowledge with principles that are clearly enunciated and reality oriented, with conclusions that are susceptive to testing.

In the study of crime, criminals, victims, or any subject for that matter, there are two major approaches to the development of knowledge. The first is *nomothetic*, referring to the study of the abstract: examining groups and universal laws.[2] The second is *idiographic*, referring to the study of the concrete: examining individ-

CONTENTS

---

[1]Parts of this chapter have been adapted from material originally published in Turvey, B. (2011).
[2]This should go without saying, but not all knowledge derived nomothetically results in universal laws or even useful generalizations. Occasionally, the best we may hope for is to develop general theories about the group under study. And they may not apply outside the study group. Knowing this, and saying it out loud, are indications of scientific honesty.

Forensic Victimology. http://dx.doi.org/10.1016/B978-0-12-408084-3.00004-1

uals and their actual qualities. Idiographic study concentrates on specific cases and the unique traits or functioning of individuals.

In terms of victimology in general, it is fair to say that there are nomothetic and idiographic methods alike. The primary goal of nomothetic victim studies is to accumulate general, typical, common, or averaged characteristics of victim groups. These characteristics are abstract in the sense that they do not necessarily exist in each individual case; they represent what is theoretically or statistically possible.

Problems arise, however, when nomothetic methods or theories are used inappropriately to make overly confident inferences or conclusive interpretations about individual victims—in other words, applying broad nomothetic knowledge to answer narrow idiographic questions.

At its very best, nomothetic study will yield general knowledge about victim groups that may or may not be applicable to a particular victim in a specific case. This kind of research will certainly assist those who need to discuss and describe group trends. However, in the face of conclusively answering questions about a specific problem or victim separate from the group, nomothetic knowledge falls quite short. In other words, group studies may be used appropriately to help generate theories, but the results are not fit for rendering conclusions that are victim specific.

For example, if we study 20 victims as a group (nomothetically), looking for common or recurrent patterns and characteristics, we will learn little about the uniquely integrated characteristics and expressions of each individual victim. The result of our study will be averaged, diluted, and abstract—with group findings that are true for some victims but not others. Moreover, there is the often-incorrect assumption that victims, crimes, or offenders, are sufficiently similar to be lumped together for aggregate study. When this happens, the resulting nomothetic knowledge is not just average and abstract; it is also inaccurate and ultimately misleading.[3]

Nomothetic victim profiles are, therefore, characteristics developed by studying groups of victims. Furthermore, nomothetic victim profiles are an abstract. That is to say, they do not represent an actual victim that exists in the real world. They represent varying degrees of theory and possibility.

---

[3]The limitations of nomothetic research when applied to individual cases are not completely foreign to the criminological literature. One didactic example is Meloy (1998, p. 8), who was discussing stalkers and threat assessment in specific when he wrote "nomothetic (group) studies on threats and their relationship to behavior are not necessarily helpful in idiographic (single) case research or risk management beyond the making of risk probability statements if the stalker fits closely into the reference groups."

It should be clear from this discussion that if we want to know the actual nature of a thing, we must study it—not just those just those things we suspect may be similar. Unfortunately, the vast majority of victim research is concerned primarily with, or based primarily on, nomothetic study. Consequently, much of the victim research that exists is inappropriate for rendering *conclusions* about individual victims.[4]

However, if we examine the traits and circumstances of an individual victim (idiographically—separate from all others), then we may learn specifics not only about the crimes he or she suffered but also about the person or persons responsible.

Forensic victimology, therefore, is concerned with the investigation and examination of particular victims alleged to have suffered specific crimes—that is to say, idiographic victim study. For our purposes, an *ideographic victim profile* is just what it sounds like: a list of the characteristics possessed by a specific victim. It should include physical, biological, mental, social, educational, occupational, and personality descriptors—among others. It is best conceptualized as open-ended, rather than as confined to a pedantic checklist; the more information and subsequent descriptors available the better.

The purpose of this chapter is to explain the purpose of constructing victim profiles, in concert with the necessary mindset of the forensic victimologist. It also provides general standards of practice for forensic victimologists in the rendering and interpretation of victim profiles. The chapter closes with the basic information that a forensic victimologist must gather and examine to construct an informed profile.

THE PURPOSE OF VICTIM PROFILES

As discussed in the first chapter, forensic victimologists seek to examine, consider, and interpret particular victim evidence in a scientific fashion to help answer investigative and forensic (aka legal) questions. Ultimately, they are truth-seekers. They intend to establish the truth and report it to those who are in positions of authority. Most commonly, forensic victimologists serve investigations and court proceedings in the following ways:

1. Assist in understanding elements of the crime.
2. Assist in developing a timeline.
3. Define the suspect pool.

---

[4]The term *conclusions* has been italicized because this statement does not refer to theories. Nomothetic knowledge, again, is important in the development of theories. It's when these theories are presented as conclusions, and without mention of their limitations, that nomothetic victimologists cross the line.

4. Provide investigative suggestions.
5. Assist with crime reconstruction.
6. Assist with contextualizing allegations of victimization.
7. Assist with the development of offender modus operandi.
8. Assist with the development of offender motive.
9. Assist with case linkage.
10. Assist with public safety response.
11. Educate the court.

Inherent in these considerations are the service of two very separate goals: the *investigative* and the *forensic*. Forensic victimology in the service of investigative goals gathers everything and considers everything. It takes on all information and theories until they are an exhausted possibility. However, as discussed in a later chapter, the court decides actual admissibility of victim evidence (victimology) based on collective issues of precedent, prejudice, and relevance in each case. Part of that equation is the sufficiency and reliability of any expert findings. Forensic victimology in the service of specific forensic (legal) goals must therefore meet a higher standard; victimological conclusions and the evidence upon which they rest must be sufficiently reliable to form the basis of courtroom testimony.

CASE EXAMPLE:

Consider the case of Tamara Anne Moonier (see Figure 4-1). The "victim" evidence in her criminal complaint, specifically video documentation of an alleged gang rape and her conduct, were crucial with respect to establishing whether or not a crime actually occurred. In other words, a video of the incident, documenting everyone's actions and words, helped to refute her allegations of victimization.

Taken from the public record in Moxley (2006):

> You'll never convince six lucky Orange County guys that porn is bad: a single raunchy sex video is keeping them out of prison. Of course, these 20-year-olds couldn't have foreseen this fate when they filmed their wild gangbang after a night of drinking at a Fullerton bar.
>
> This tale begins in the wee hours of June 6, 2004, when a distraught Tamara Anne Moonier entered a Fullerton police station. She said she'd been kidnapped a few hours earlier from a parking lot at Heroes Bar & Grill, hooded and driven to an unknown residence. Moonier, then

28, told police that a group of men brutally raped her at gunpoint for more than an hour, forced her to perform numerous degrading sex acts on film, demanded her silence and then released her.

"She said she feared for her safety," a law-enforcement officer told the *Weekly*.

With money from a victims' assistance program, Moonier immediately moved from her Fullerton apartment to Dana Point. Meanwhile, alarmed police detectives used her descriptions to launch a manhunt. Within about a week of the alleged crime, Moonier had picked one of the suspects out of a photographic lineup. Eventually all of the men were identified.

But Fullerton police refused to file charges. The suspects had voluntarily turned over the sex video Moonier had described. It showed no gun, no threats of violence and no force.

In fact, the woman not only directed action at times but complimented penis sizes, complained about the lighting,

CASE EXAMPLE: *CONTINUED*

FIGURE 4-1

In 2004, Tamara Anne Moonier filed a rape complaint implicating six men in a gang rape. In 2006, she pleaded guilty to felony grand theft, perjury, and presenting a false claim to the state, as well as a misdemeanor count of making a false police report. If any of the accused had been prosecuted and convicted, they faced the possibility of life in prison.

nonchalantly took a cell phone call during the gangbang, yelled, "Get it up!" when some of the men lost their erections, called herself a slut and demanded ejaculations—in her mouth.

She also laughed at least 27 times during the sex, moaned intensely when she wasn't laughing and cheered the men to sexual heroics with, "Yeah! Yeah! Yeah! Yeah!" "I just like sex," Moonier said at one point on the tape. "I can't help it."

Deputy District Attorney Paul J. Chrisopoulos will use the homemade video as Exhibit 1 in his case against Moonier. Last summer, the Orange County grand jury, mostly retired folks, had the thrill (if you want to call it that) of watching the exploits of this petite mother of two children, then toddlers. They indicted her for filing false police reports, committing perjury and stealing funds from a taxpayer-funded victims' program.

If Moonier and her public defender don't gain their senses and seek a plea deal, a judge

and jury will soon view the tape. They'll hear more than the following excerpts:

Male: I took your fucking pants down and started fucking you.

Moonier: You sure did!

Male: You liked it, didn't you?

Moonier: Of course! [Laughs.] Did you?

Male: Fuck, yeah!

Moonier: All right then.

Male: You give good head.

Moonier: Thank you. I told you I've watched lots of movies.

To one guy unable to get an erection, Moonier said, "You're fucking pathetic. You can't get it up. Forget it."

Males: She loves this shit [sex].

Moonier: Yeah, I do. Uhhhhh. Very nice!

When one guy complained that Moonier's teeth hurt his penis during a blowjob, somebody slapped her butt. She responded, "Ouch! Fuck! That's gonna leave a mark. You're gonna kill my game. Now I'm not going to be able to have sex tomorrow night. Damn you." [Laughs.]

Continued

CASE EXAMPLE: *CONTINUED*

Male: How's my dick feeling?

Moonier: Your dick goes great, babe!

During the gangbang, a cell phone rang, and one of the guys answered it and calmly talked to a buddy. While Moonier had sex in the doggie-style position, the guy handed her the phone. She didn't scream for help. She said, "Hello? This is Tammy. Yes. He's fucking me from behind!" The guy took the phone back and gave directions to the residence. Moonier simultaneously complimented one man's penis: "Big and nice!" Later, she said, "How many people are we calling?"

Male: You know I'm a slut?

Moonier: Among other things.

Male: Right.

Moonier: Well, you obviously knew I was!

Male: Fuck, yeah!

Moonier: How could you tell?

During intercourse, Moonier said, "I have some work to do. Shut the fuck up. Shhhhhh. Are you the only one who can perform in front of an audience? The rest of them can't fucking perform. [Moans.] Nice! Much better. Goes in deeper from this angle. [Moans again.]"

A male observer said to the guy having sex, "We can't hear your balls slapping, come on!" [The guy increased the speed of his penetration and Moonier moaned more.] The men cheered their pal on: "Hit harder!" Moonier said, "Shut the fuck up so he can finish. At least somebody will get off tonight."

While performing in the reverse cowgirl position (use your imagination), Moonier turned to the camera and said, "This better not fucking end up on the Internet unless you're gonna give me some of the money!" Minutes later, she yelled at the guys, "Get it up!" And, "That guy can't ejaculate.... Yeah, you fucking gave up on me. ... And this one can't even finish either. I'm getting kind of pissed. I just want somebody to finish."

Male: I want to slap your ass.

Moonier: I don't need any more marks. You know what's gonna happen the next time I hook up with the fucking cops? They're gonna want to know who the fuck I was with. ... I'm fucking three cops!"

Moonier: You gonna finish this time?

Male: I really believe she really wants to swallow [the semen].

Moonier: I always swallow. What's the point? You're gonna get some of it in your mouth anyway. You might as well swallow. I'd be really pissed if somebody was going down on me and fucking turned around to spit. That's just not right. You have to swallow. That's just how it is!"

In November of 2006, Moonier pleaded guilty to felony grand theft, perjury, and presenting a false claim to the state, as well as a misdemeanor count of making a false police report. She accepted a one-year jail sentence. According to "O.C. Woman" (CBS2.com, 2006):

> She told police on June 6, 2004, that she had been kidnapped at gunpoint by one man a few hours earlier outside a Fullerton bar, taken to an unknown location and raped repeatedly by six men. She claimed she had never seen the men prior to the attack but was able to identify them through a photo lineup, Schroeder said.
>
> While the case was under investigation, she received a victim assistance check, signing under penalty of perjury that her claims were true, Schroeder said.
>
> But one of the accused men provided a videotape of the encounter, which showed Moonier actively participating and orchestrating the sexual encounters, and she was indicted by a grand jury, Schroeder said.
>
> "Moonier could have put six innocent men in prison for the rest of their lives for a crime that they did not commit," said Deputy District Attorney Paul Chrisopoulos. "The funds that Ms. Moonier received are reserved for the victims of crimes to be used for emergency relocation, hospital

bills and counseling. When the funds are used fraudulently, it hurts the availability of resources for true victims."

Moonier, who has been diagnosed with bi-polar illness and depression, tearfully apologized to Orange County Judge Carla Singer before the sentencing. "I've changed my life," Moonier said. "I take my medicine. I never believed I had an illness until this happened. I'm very, very sorry."

This graphic case example serves a number of instructive purposes.

First, it demonstrates that without video documentation of complainant conduct, this case would have pitted her word against the words of each accused. Had those accused individuals been arrested, tried, and convicted, they could easily have faced the possibility of life in prison.

Second, and with explicit finality, it dispels any notion that this type of random hook-up and consensual group activity is an unfair consideration. People can and will engage in all manner of consensual sexual encounters. Period. Pretending that it does not happen does not help the cause of justice, and ignorance of such activities among consenting adults is equally unacceptable.

Third, and because of the preceding, forensic victimologists must become accustomed to, and familiar with, accepting that strangers can engage in random sexual activity; that victim evidence is graphic; and that alleged victims will make false statements even when they know evidence exists that can utterly refute their claims. Therefore, basing any conclusion simply on the statements of a complainant, without corroboration, is not a legitimate forensic practice. However, complainant statements are a very reasonable foundation for the development of investigative theory.

STANDARDS OF PRACTICE

In any professional discipline, *practice standards* are the fundamental rules that set the limits of evidentiary interpretation. They offer a mechanism for evaluating acceptable work habits and application of methods. More to the point, professions without clearly delineated practice standards can hardly claim to be professions at all (see generally NAS, 2009).

It should go without saying that all forensic examiners have a duty to strive for objectivity, competence, and professionalism in their work. They should want their findings to be accurate and their methods to be reliable. To that end, practice standards must define a minimum threshold of competency. They must also help define a practitioner's role and outline a mechanism for demonstrating their facility. They are a compass for diligent practitioners to follow and a screen against which those who have lost their way can be delayed and educated.

As this suggests, the purpose of defining practice standards is not only to help professionals achieve a level of competency but also to provide independent reviewers with a basis for checking work that purports to be competent. Practice standards set the bar and are a safeguard against ignorance, incapacity, and incomprehension masquerading as science and reason.

Consistent with general practice standards described in Thornton and Peterson (2007), for all forensic examiners, the practice standards included here are designed to help reduce bias, encourage the employment of analytical logic and the scientific method, and require the formation of hypotheses and conclusions only in accordance with the known evidence.

1.   Forensic Examiners Must Strive Diligently to Avoid Bias

Dr. Paul Kirk wrote of forensic examination, "Physical evidence cannot be wrong; it cannot be perjured; it cannot be wholly absent. *Only in its interpretation can there be error*" (Kirk and Thornton, 1970; p. 4). With this simple observation, Kirk was referring to the influences of examiner ignorance, imprecision, and bias on the reconstruction of physical evidence and its meaning. The evidence is always there, waiting to be understood. The forensic examiner is the imprecise lens through which a form of understanding comes.

Specifically, there are at least two kinds of bias that objective forensic examiners need to be aware of (and strive to mitigate) in their casework: observer effects and confirmation bias.

Observer effects are present when the results of a forensic examination are distorted by the employment context and mental state of forensic examiners, to include subconscious expectations and desires imposed by their employers, supervisors, and workmates (Cooley and Turvey, 2011; Dror, Charlton, and Peron, 2006; and Risinger et al., 2002). Observer effects are governed by fundamental principles of cognitive psychology asserting that subconscious needs and expectations, which are heavily influenced by external pressures and expectations, work to shape both examiner perception and interpretation. As the term *subconscious* implies, this happens without the awareness of the forensic examiner. In the context of a forensic examination, this includes a distortion of what is recognized as evidence, what is collected, what is examined, and how it is interpreted.

Confirmation bias may be described as the conscious or unconscious tendency to affirm particular theories, opinions, or outcomes or findings. It is a specific kind of bias in which information and evidence are screened to include those things that confirm a desired position. At the same time, the examiner actively ignores, does not seek, or undervalues the relevance of anything that contradicts that position. It commonly manifests itself in the form of looking only for particular kinds of evidence that support a desired case theory (i.e., suspect guilt or innocence); and actively explaining away evidence or findings that are undesirable. This includes the selection of evidence to examine by persons advocating a particular theory, or by persons interested in keeping investigative costs low.

CASE EXAMPLE:

For example, consider the case of 30-year-old Brandon Headley out of Prattville, Alabama. Though the victim of a homicidal shooting, questions were raised at trial regarding his culpability. The shooter, Erik Scoggins, claimed that he was acting in self-defense (see Figure 4-2). A determination of this issue rested in no small part on victimology in the form of evidence related to drug use, as reported in Roney (2013):

The victim in an Autauga County homicide case had used marijuana shortly before he was shot in March 2011, documents from the state crime lab showed.

Erik John Scoggins, 30, of Autauga County faces murder charges in the shooting death of Brandon Headley, 30, also of Autauga County. Scoggins has told authorities he was acting in self-defense the night of March 18, 2011, after

FIGURE 4-2

Erik Scoggins was arrested and tried for the shooting death of Brandon Headley in Prattville, Alabama. At trial, the victim's use of marijuana was used to suggest opposing theories by attorneys looking to make their case.

Continued

CASE EXAMPLE: *CONTINUED*

Headley lunged at him while brandishing a large socket wrench.

The trial entered its second day Wednesday. A blood screen performed after Headley's death came back positive for the presence of marijuana, Justin Sanders of the Alabama Department of Forensic Sciences testified. Sanders told the court Headley would have used the marijuana 40 minutes to 4½ hours before his death. On direct examination, Assistant District Attorney Jessica Sanders asked Justin Sanders how marijuana would affect the behavior and mental condition of the user.

Justin Sanders said some people would display a relaxed demeanor and others might show paranoid behavior. Justin Sanders said he could not determine from the blood test whether Headley was under the influence of the drug when he died.

Scoggins admits shooting Headley after he went to Headley's home on Viking Lane about midnight that night to speak with his ex-girlfriend, Rachel Avant.

In a taped interview with sheriff's office investigators played earlier in the day, Scoggins said the men got into a verbal altercation in Headley's yard.

Scoggins told investigators he convinced Avant to leave and go to her home so he could retrieve some of his things from the residence. Scoggins told investigators that when he drove away, Headley followed in his vehicle and Avant followed behind Headley in her vehicle.

As he stopped at the intersection of Autauga County 57, Scoggins said Headley approached his truck holding a wrench. Scoggins said he had stepped out of the truck to wave Avant around, when Headley lunged at him brandishing the bar. That's when Scoggins shot him once in the chest with a 40-caliber handgun, Scoggins told investigators.

In the Headley case, evidence of victim drug use at or near the time of the shooting could be interpreted a number of ways, but the jury is needs to have the information regardless. This helps them to make the most informed decision possible. The prosecution would use this evidence and related testimony to argue that the victim was likely relaxed at the time of the shooting, suggesting that the shooter was the aggressor. The defense would use it to argue that the victim was possibly acting paranoid and erratic, suggesting that the shooter was acting in self-defense. Both sides see the evidence through the lens of their theories and look for that which confirms it. Without further testimony from those familiar with the victim's typical reactions to marijuana, the toxicological information by itself could actually be misleading.

Wrestling with confirmation bias is extremely difficult, often because it is institutional. Many forensic examiners work in systems in which they are rewarded with praise and promotion for successfully advocating their side when true *science* is about anything other than successfully advocating any one side (Turvey, 2013). Consequently, the majority of forensic examiners suffering from confirmation bias has no idea what it is or that it is even a problem.

What all forensic examiners must understand is that their value to the justice system lies in their adherence to the scientific method, and that this demands as much objectivity and intellectual honesty as can be brought to bear. Success in the forensic community must be measured by the diligent elimination of possibilities through the scientific method and peer review, not through securing convictions. In other words, the objective forensic examiner is not out to get the bad guy, or to prove that there is a bad guy, but rather to help determine what actually happened and under what circumstances, using only the most reliable evidence.

Therefore, a strict adherence to scientific methodology is more important than any actual outcome, given that scientific examination seeks reliable knowledge and not merely the confirmation of preconceived ideas. In an objective approach, outcomes are less important than the reliability of the methods of inquiry that are being used.

2. Forensic Examiners Are Responsible for Requesting All Relevant Evidence and Information to Render an Adequate Victim Profile and Form Related Opinions

Forensic examiners must define the scope of evidence and information they need to be able to perform an adequate examination, partial or otherwise, by making a formal request from their client, employer, or the requesting agency. Upon receiving that evidence, they must determine what has been made available and what is missing. This basic task is incumbent upon every forensic examiner.

When they are not able to base their findings on complete information as they define or understand it, this point must be made clear as part of their conclusions. Some lists are provided in the next section of this chapter.

3. Forensic Examiners Are Responsible for Determining Whether the Evidence They Are Examining Is of Sufficient Quality to Provide the Basis for an Adequate Examination

The harsh reality is that crime scene investigation efforts in the United States are often abysmal, if not completely absent, and in need of major reform (see DeForest, 2005). Crime scenes throughout the United States are commonly processed by police-employed technicians or sworn personnel with little or no formal education, to say nothing of having limited training in the forensic sciences and crime scene processing techniques. The in-service forensic training available to law enforcement typically exists in the form of half-day seminars or short courses taught by nonscientists. On their own, such training in no way imparts the discipline and expertise necessary to process crime scenes adequately for the purposes of victimology, crime reconstruction, or crime scene analysis in general (see Turvey, 2011).

In addition, general victim information is often afforded even less attention and consideration. Rather, investigators tend to focus heavily on gathering victim evidence they deem relevant to the crimes they suspect. Anything beyond the charges they are responding to is a luxury item.

Consequently, if the forensic victimologist requests victim information, it may not be immediately available. This should not come as a surprise. However, the mere act of requesting victim information, and explaining why it is important, is in itself a benefit to most investigative efforts.

Once victim information is received, the forensic victimologist must determine whether it comes from a sufficiently reliable source. Is it an objective archive like a security log or is it a subjective opinion by a co-worker? Or is it somewhere in between, containing both objective and subjective information, like an email from the victim written out of anger?

If the forensic victimologist does not receive sufficient victim evidence of sufficient quality, either because it does not exist or it was not gathered, then this also an important finding with a high degree of relevance to the case. The lack of victim evidence will set limits on what may or may not be inferred.

4.   Forensic Examiners Must, Whenever Possible, Visit the Crime Scene

It is highly preferable that any forensic examiner visit the crime scene. The following are examples of the kind of information that may be learned:

- Sights, smells, and sounds of the crime scene, as the victim and the offender may have experienced them.
- Spatial relationships within the scene.
- Direct observation and experience with potential transfer evidence. Vegetation, soil, glass, fibers, and any other material that may have transferred onto the victim or suspects may become evident or may transfer onto the examiner, providing examples of what to look for on victim clothing or in victim vehicles.
- The attentive forensic victimologist may discover items of evidence at the scene previously missed and subsequently uncollected by investigative efforts. This is far more common than many care to admit, and it is one of the most important reasons for visiting the crime scene.

In many cases, it will not be possible for the forensic victimologist to visit the crime scene. This occurs for a variety of practical reasons, including time limitations, budgetary limitations, legal restrictions, the alteration of the scene by forces of nature, or the obliteration of the scene by land or property development. If the forensic victimologist is unable to visit the crime scene for whatever reason, this must be clearly reflected in his or her findings.

It is not disputed that the primary reason for investigating a crime and documenting a crime scene is to provide for later reconstruction and behavioral analysis efforts. Therefore, the inability of the forensic victimologist to visit the scene does not preclude such efforts across the board. Competent crime investigation and scene documentation may be sufficient to address the issues in question, or they may not. Each case is different and must be considered separately and carefully with regard to this issue.

5. Forensic Conclusions and Their Basis Must Be Provided in a Written Format

Dr. Hans Gross, a pioneer in criminal investigation and forensic science, referred to the critical role that exact, deliberate, and patient efforts play in the investigation and resolution of crime. Specifically, he stated that just looking at a crime scene and the evidence is not enough. He argued that there is utility in reducing one's opinions to the form of a report to identify problems in the logic of one's theories (Gross, 1924; p. 439):

> So long as one only looks on the scene, it is impossible, whatever the care, time, and attention bestowed, to detect all the details, and especially note the incongruities: but these strike us at once when we set ourselves to describe the picture on paper as exactly and clearly as possible....
>
> The "defects of the situation" are just those contradictions, those improbabilities, which occur when one desires to represent the situation as something quite different from what it really is, and this with the very best intentions and the purest belief that one has worked with all of the forethought, craft, and consideration imaginable.

Moreover, the forensic examiner, not the recipient of the report (i.e., investigators, attorneys, and the court), bears the burden of ensuring that conclusions are effectively communicated. This means writing them down. This means that the forensic examiner must be competent at intelligible writing, and reports must be comprehensive with regard to examinations performed, findings, and conclusions.

Verbal conclusions should be viewed as a form of substandard work product. They are susceptible to conversions, alterations, and misrepresentations. They may also become lost to time. Written conclusions are fixed in time; easy to reproduce; and less susceptible to accidental or intentional conversion, alteration, and misrepresentation.

Any forensic examiner who prefers verbal conclusions to written ones reveals a preference for conclusive mobility. Apart from their relative permanence, written conclusions also provide the examiner with the best chance to memorialize methods, conclusions, arguments, and the underlying facts of the case. This includes a list of the evidence examined, when it was examined, and under what circumstances. Generally, a written report should include, but need not be limited to, the following information:

- A preliminary background section, describing the examiner's involvement in the case
- A chain of custody section, describing and detailing the evidence that was examined or included
- A descriptive section, in which the examiner thoroughly describes the examinations performed (e.g., forensic analysis, victimology, crime scene analysis), with consideration of the facts and evidence
- A results section, in which the examiner lists any results and conclusions, including their significance and limitations

The intended users of the end result include detectives, judges, and jurors. The report should be worded so that there is no question in the mind of the reader as to what has been found and concluded. If a report cannot be written down in a logical form, easily understood by its intended user, then apart from having no value, it is also probably wrong.

Above all else, the written report should not be rendered in such a manner as to leave a false impression in the mind of anyone who might read it. Not about what was done, when, how, or what it means. It is the responsibility of the forensic examiner to achieve this level of scientific honesty up front, regardless of what questions he or she may or may not be asked by lawyers at some future date.

6. Forensic Examiners Must Demonstrate an Understanding of Behavioral Science, Forensic Science, and the Scientific Method

Victimology is a multidisciplinary field, based on the principles of the forensic and behavioral sciences. Given the advanced level of knowledge required, it is unclear how a forensic victimologist could perform examinations competently without receiving a baseline of formal education and ongoing training in these areas from non-law enforcement forensic and behavioral scientists.

Consequently, any purported expert in the area of forensic victimology should satisfy at least the following minimum criteria:

1. At least an undergraduate education in a behavioral science (psychology, sociology, social work, criminology, etc.). Graduate-level education

in these areas is preferable. This criterion disqualifies those with undergraduate degrees in unrelated areas such as music, police administration, public administration, and education. It should be noted that there are some online university programs that offer graduate degrees in behavioral science-related areas, without an undergraduate degree requirement, without a thesis requirement, and without actual class time. These programs should be considered essentially worthless, as they are designed for professional advancement and resume enhancement as opposed to the discovery of knowledge and actual learning.

2. Advanced study of, and a working knowledge of, the published victimology and criminal profiling literature, to include the areas of behavioral evidence analysis, criminal investigative analysis, and investigative psychology— including the limitations and weaknesses of each.

3. Advanced study of, and a working knowledge of, the published literature in the forensic sciences, specifically those related to evidence analysis and crime reconstruction.

4. Advanced study of, and a working knowledge of, the methods, procedures, and requirements of a criminal investigation.

5. An approach to casework in accordance with objective forensic examination and interpretation, as opposed to a pro-law enforcement or pro-victim mindset.

7. All Conclusions Must Be Based on Established Facts. Facts May Not Be Assumed for the Purpose of Analysis

Many forensic examiners are willing to provide a certain interpretation of offense-related behavior based on experiential comparisons to unnamed cases, factual guesses and assumptions, or nonexistent physical evidence. If the underlying facts have not been established through investigative documentation, crime scene documentation, the examination of physical evidence, or corroborating eyewitness testimony, then any reconstruction of those facts is not a reliable or valid inference of events. This includes hypothetical scenarios.

8. Conclusions Must Be Valid Inferences Based on Logical Arguments and Analytical Reasoning

In the process of establishing the facts that are fit for analysis, facts must be sifted and distinguished from opinions, conjectures, and theories. Inductive hypotheses must further be delineated from deductive conclusions, and conclusions must flow naturally from the facts provided. Furthermore, any opinions or conclusions must be reasonably free from logical fallacies and incorrect statements of fact.

9. Conclusions Must Be Reached with the Assistance of the Scientific Method

The scientific method demands that careful observations of the evidence be made and then hypotheses generated and ultimately tested against all of the known evidence and accepted facts. Subsequently, the forensic examiner must provide not just conclusions but all other postulated theories that have been falsified through examinations, tests, and experiments. *Falsification*, not validation, is the cornerstone of the scientific method. Theories that have not been put to any test or that appear in a report or in courtroom testimony based on rumination and imagination alone (i.e., experience and intuition) should not be considered inherently valid or reliable.

10. Conclusions Must Demonstrate an Understanding of, and Clearly Distinguish between, Individuating Findings and All Others

The concept of identification and individuation is often misunderstood. *Identification* (or *classification*) is the placement of any item into a specific category of items with similar characteristics. Identification does not require or imply uniqueness. *Individuation* is the assignment of uniqueness to an item. To individuate an item, it must be described in such a manner as to separate it from all other items in the universe (Thornton and Peterson, 2007).

In their presentation of findings, forensic examiners will find themselves using statements that suggest varying degrees of confidence. Vague terms or terms of art, such as *probably, likely, identify, match, consistent with,* and *reasonable degree of scientific certainty,* are among those used to qualify the certainty of findings. Unchecked, this language can be misleading to those it is intended to assist. Confidence statements must be qualified and discussed to the point of absolute clarity.

Without clarification, findings may be misunderstood, misrepresented, and misapplied. When the forensic examiner has given findings, there must remain no question as to whether the findings are individuating and no question as to how this was determined. If they provide individuating findings of any sort, the nature of the uniqueness and how it was established must be clearly presented. The purpose of presenting findings is to clarify the evidence, not muddle it.

11. Forensic Examiners Must Demonstrate an Understanding of the Conditions of Transfer (Locard's Exchange Principle and Evidence Dynamics)

It is important to establish the source of any physical evidence relied upon and the conditions under which it was transferred to where it was ultimately found. Forensic examiners must not be quick to oversimplify complex issues, such as the examination and interpretation of physical evidence, or to disregard those circumstances that can move, alter, or obliterate that evidence.

The concepts are discussed further in the next chapter.

12. Any Evidence, Data, or Findings on Which Conclusions Are Based Must Be Made Available through Presentation or Citation

It is not acceptable for the forensic examiner to provide conclusions based on phantom databases, phantom data, phantom research, phantom evidence, or unseen comparisons. Data, research, and evidence must be detailed to the point where others reviewing their work may easily locate or identify them, in the same way we cite the endeavors of others in written work. Data, research, and evidence that cannot be duplicated or identified by the court in some fashion should not find their way into forensic conclusions.

These fundamental practice standards should be applied to the evaluation of any method of forensic examination, both the general and the specialized, to show due diligence. If a forensic examiner is able to meet these standards, then a minimum threshold level of professional competency has indeed been achieved. Subsequently, the recipients of these conclusions may be assured that whatever the findings, they may be independently investigated and reviewed for reliability, accuracy, and validity.

It bears pointing out that forensic examiners who fail to climb even one of the rungs prescribed will not have reached this threshold. In failing, they should have their findings questioned, and their subsequent reports and testimony should be viewed with disfavor. It is also necessary to clarify that these practice standards do not leave anyone behind, but they do require everyone to show his or her work.

Forensic examinations are not easy and must not be rote. Conclusions must be earned, and that means competency must be demonstrated and peer review embraced. Each forensic examiner has a duty to formulate conclusions with the full reach of everything that forensic science, the scientific method, and analytical logic have to offer. Without these tools, forensic examiners are at risk of not being able to recognize forensic and methodological illiteracy in themselves or others.

These practice standards may also raise the ire of some forensic examiners who have been doing the work based on intuition and experience, perhaps for years, and are unaccustomed to explaining themselves or their methods apart from stating their alleged vast experience. If peer review and criticism are not welcome at a conclusion's doorstep, if instead such visitors are met with hostility and derision, then something other than competency dwells within.

To be clearer, the absence of the scientific method and logical inference in any behavioral analysis should not be a point of pride because it is ultimately evidence of ignorance. Any forensic examination conducted in the absence of the scientific method, analytical logic, and *critical thinking* is called a guess. The justice system is no place for ignorance or guessing. Consequently, it is not unreasonable to expect that anyone interpreting evidence in such a manner be prepared to explain why.

VICTIMOLOGY: GENERAL GUIDELINES

Weston and Wells (1974, p. 97) provide a quick checklist of preliminary victimological queries that have been proven to be most useful in eliciting investigative information. This is the kind of information that should be gathered immediately, ideally before the investigator arrives at a given crime scene.

1. Did the victim know the perpetrator?
2. Does the victim suspect any person? Why?
3. Had the victim a history of crime? A history of reporting crimes?
4. Did the victim have a weapon?
5. Had the victim an aggressive personality?
6. Has the victim been the subject of any field [police] reports?

The problem with this checklist is that it may require some misleading assumptions and interpretations prior to the start of the investigation. For example, unless it there is no doubt about the identity of the offender, this is a question to be answered by virtue of an investigation. Also, it presumes that there was actually a crime committed. Not all complaints are founded; not all deaths are homicides. Again, this is something that can be established only by a thorough investigation. The lesson here is that victim information, and victim history, has long been considered essential to professional investigators of fact, to the point of developing these kinds of conceptual checklists.

Gathering this information, along with the careful examination of physical evidence, provides the starting point for investigative activity. Again, no one checklist can suffice; the victimologist must be willing to sift through each victim's history carefully, with no preconceived theories. When one is compiling a forensic victimology, it is important to reference the case material that each piece of information was taken from, ensuring the reader can locate the original document.

The following adapts those victim guidelines into a more cohesive set of objective packages that must be gathered and assessed by the criminal investigator and forensic victimologist alike, as with any intelligence. There can be no mistake as to the importance of this effort and the investigative clarity it will provide. Conversely, the failure to collect these data packages leaves gaping holes in the investigation through which unexamined theories of the crime will most certainly escape.

Again, the gathering and assessment of these packages provide context, and should lead to additional information and evidence. They are not the end of the inquiry but rather the beginning.

Personal Package

1. Sex
2. Race
3. Height
4. Weight
5. Hair color/length/dyed
6. Eyes: color/glasses/contacts
7. Clothing/jewelry
8. Personal items: contents of wallet, purse, handbag, backpack, briefcase, suitcase, or medicine bag
9. Grooming/manner of dress
10. Smoker or nonsmoker
11. Hobbies/skills
12. Routine daily activities and commitments
13. Recently scheduled events
14. Upcoming scheduled events

Digital Package

1. Cell phone: calls, chats, address book, GPS, photos, video
2. Laptop/desktop: email, calls, chats, documents, address books, browser history, photos, video
3. Personal websites: recent browser history, social network and social media activity (e.g., Facebook, Twitter, Tumblr), blogs, dating websites, and other personal subscription websites
4. Financial websites/payment history: stocks, mutual funds/401k, credit cards, and online banking
5. Personal GPS device: recent trips, destinations, bookmarked points of interest

Residence Package

1. Physical home address
2. Location/condition of bedroom
3. Evidence of music/literature/personal interests
4. Personal correspondence
5. Personal sexual items/explicit material

6. Missing items
7. Signs of violence
8. Location/condition of personal vehicle
9. Hard-line phone calls (incoming and outgoing)
10. 911 calls and criminal history of residence

The investigator or profiler should also spend time, when possible, with the victim's personal items, in the personal environments (hangouts, work, school, home/bedroom, etc.). Examine any available photo albums, diaries, or journals. Make note of music and literature preferences. This may be found in hard copy or in the form of digital evidence on the victim's electronic devices. Do this to find out who the victim seemed to believe he or she was, what the victim wanted everyone to perceive, and how the victim seemed to feel about his or her life in general.

Relationship Package
1. Current and previous intimate or marital partner(s)
2. Current and previous family members
3. Current and previous household members
4. Current and previous friends
5. Current and previous co-workers/classmates
6. History of relationship counseling

Employment Package
1. Educational background and history
2. Current occupations/job titles (many people have multiple employers)
3. Place of employment/work schedule/supervisor/co-workers
4. Employment history
5. Work phone: calls, chats, address book, GPS, photos, video
6. Laptop/desktop: email, calls, chats, documents, address books, browser history, photos, video
7. Business GPS device: recent trips, destinations, bookmarked points of interest
8. Business vehicle: logs, travel (times/ destinations), GPS device
9. Business insurance policies

This list can be adapted for students, with the school as the employer, class schedule as work schedule, teachers as supervisors, and classmates as co-workers.

Financial Package
1. Wallet/purse: contents, cards, personal items
2. Credit cards/history
3. Bank accounts/history
4. Property ownership (residences and vehicles)

5. Stocks/mutual funds/401k/retirement benefits
6. Insurance policies

Medical Package

1. Current state of intoxication (alcohol and drug levels)
2. Current medical conditions (physical and mental)
3. History of serious medical conditions
4. Current medications (see purse, desk drawers, and medicine cabinets)
5. Current treatment regimes
6. Current treatment professionals
7. Recent medical appointments
8. Addictions (drugs, alcohol, or obsessive behavior)

Court Package

1. Criminal history (active investigations, protection orders, arrests, warrants, convictions)
2. Civil court history (lawsuits, judgments, and role)
3. Witness history (previous depositions or testimony given in legal proceedings)
4. In-state and out-of-state records
5. Evidence of victim criminal activity during the crime
6. Evidence of ongoing victim criminal activity unrelated to the crime

These packages should be used to complete the following tasks:

1. Compile a list of the victim's daily routines, habits, and activities.
2. Compile a complete list of the victim's family members with contact information.
3. Compile a complete list of the victim's friends with contact information.
4. Compile a complete list of the victim's co-workers/schoolmates with contact information.
5. Create a timeline of events using witness statements, digital evidence, and physical evidence.

Everyone should be interviewed, as people with important information often do not come forward. Many well-meaning witnesses wait for someone to approach them out of ignorance with respect to how the investigative process works. Investigators must be pro-active in this regard.

CREATING A TIMELINE: THE LAST 24 HOURS

The general purpose of creating a timeline is to familiarize forensic victimologists with the last known activities of the victim. Subsequently, they may be able to determine how a given victim got to a place and time where an offender was able to gain access to him or her. The picture needs to be built from the ground up. It is a rewarding and illuminating process that should not be avoided just because it takes some time to accomplish.

A good approach to creating this timeline of locations and events includes at least the following steps:

6. Compile all witness data.
7. Compile all available forensic evidence and findings.
8. Compile all the police/media crime scene photographs and video.
9. Compile all security stills and video covering the crime scene and any paths taken by the victim or offender to or from it.
10. Create a linear timeline of events and locations.
11. Create a map of the victim's route for the 24 hours before the attack, as detailed as possible.
12. Physically walk through the victim's last 24 hours using the map and forensic evidence as a guide.
13. Document expected background elements of the route in terms of vehicles, people, activities, professionals, and so on for the time leading up to, during, and after the victim was acquired. It is possible that the offender is, or was, masquerading as one of those expected elements.

Then attempt to determine the following:

14. The point at which the offender acquired the victim
15. The place where the offender attacked the victim
16. How well the attack location can be seen from any surrounding locations
17. Whether the offender would need to be familiar with the area to know of this specific location or get to it
18. Whether knowledge of the route would require or indicate prior surveillance
19. Whether this route placed the victim at higher or lower exposure to an attack
20. Whether the acquisition of the victim on that route placed the offender at higher or lower exposure to identification or apprehension

The collection and examination of specific victim profile information will provide the victimologist with all the information necessary to perform the assessments discussed in later chapters of this text. It requires a thorough investigation and comprehensive evidence collection and examination efforts. Once complete, it also serves the additional purpose of aiding in case-linkage efforts in relation to serial cases—where multiple victims are being compared to each other across multiple offenses.[5]

---

[5]See Chapter 18, "Victimology at Trial."

SUMMARY

Forensic victimology is concerned with the investigation and examination of particular victims alleged to have suffered specific crimes, which is an idiographic form of knowledge building. It is intended to serve both investigative and forensic goals, which are very different in scope and reliability with respect to findings. To reduce bias and achieve a minimum threshold of reliability, forensic victimologists must request a sufficient amount of victim information, determine its reliability, and perform their examinations in accordance with the practice standards provided. A key feature throughout this effort is an applied understanding of the scientific method, with an emphasis on examiner objectivity and theory falsification.

QUESTIONS

1. Explain the difference between *nomothetic* and *idiographic* study. Which form of knowledge building is forensic victimology concerned with?
2. List three purposes of a victim profile.
3. Define *practice standard*. Name and describe two practice standards for forensic victimologists outlined in this chapter.
4. _____ is the cornerstone of the scientific method.
5. Describe the difference between *identification* and *individuation*.

REFERENCES

Cooley, C.M., Turvey, B.E., 2011. Observer effects and examiner bias: psychological influences on the forensic examiner. In: Chisum, W.J., Turvey, B. (Eds.), Crime Reconstruction, second ed. Elsevier Science, San Diego.

DeForest, P.R., 2005. Crime scene investigation. In: Sullivan, L.E., Rosen, M.S. (Eds.), Encyclopedia of Law Enforcement. Sage Publications, New York, pp. 111–116.

Dror, I., Charlton, D., Peron, A., 2006. Contextual information renders experts vulnerable to making erroneous identifications. Forensic Science International 156, 74–76.

Gross, H., 1924. Criminal Investigation. Sweet & Maxwell, London.

Kirk, P., Thornton, J., 1970. Crime Investigation, second ed. John Wiley & Sons, New York.

Moxley, R.S., February 9, 2006. Great dick, babe: Gang rape or orgy? Let's go to the video. Orange County Weekly, Thursday.

NAS, 2009. On Being a Scientist: A Guide to Responsible Conduct in Research, third ed. National Academy of Sciences Committee on Science, Engineering, and Public Policy, National Academies Press, Washington, DC.

CBS2.com News, 2006 "O.C. woman who lied about rape gets time in jail," CBS2.com News, November 9, 2006; url: http://cbs2.com/local/Dana.Point.Men.2.524133.html

Risinger, D.M., Saks, M.J., Rosenthal, R., Thompson, W.C., 2002. The Daubert/Kumho implications of observer effects in forensic science: hidden problems of expectation and suggestion. California Law Review 90 (1), 1–56.

Thornton, J., Peterson, J., 2007. The general assumptions and rationale of forensic identification. In: Faigman, D., Kaye, D., Saks, M., Sanders, J. (Eds.), Modern Scientific Evidence: The Law and Science of Expert Testimony, vol. 1. West Publishing Group, St. Paul, MN.

Turvey, B., 2011. Criminal Profiling, fourth ed. Elsevier Science, San Diego.

Turvey, B., 2013. Forensic Fraud: Evaluating Law Enforcement and Forensic Science Cultures in the Context of Examiner Misconduct. Elsevier Science, San Diego.

Weston, P., Wells, K., 1974. Criminal Investigation: Basic Perspectives, second ed. Prentice Hall, Englewood Cliffs, NJ.

CHAPTER 5

Forensic Nursing: Objective Victim Examination

Charla M. Jamerson and Brent E. Turvey[1]

KEY TERMS

Colposcope A lighted magnifying instrument used by a gynecologist to examine the tissues of the vagina and the cervix.

Colposcopy The process of using a colposcope during a vaginal and cervical examination.

Contact dermatitis A reaction caused by the skin coming into contact with allergens or irritants (e.g., poison ivy, poison oak, and poison sumac).

Differential diagnosis The possibility that there is more than one cause of any set of injuries, conditions, or symptoms presented by a patient.

Forensic nursing A subspecialty of forensic science and nursing in which the science of nursing is applied to the resolution of legal matters.

Forensic medical examination The entire examination performed by the forensic examiner, including making initial contact, performing an intake assessment, obtaining victim history, performing a physical examination, documenting and collecting evidence, and interpreting findings, including any related treatment.

Medical history Information about a patient gathered by a health care professional for the purposes of making examinations, providing treatment, and rendering a diagnosis.

Negative documentation Recording of areas of the body where there is no evidence of defect, disease, injury, or potential transfer.

Physical examination The act of examination of the body by auscultation, palpation, percussion, inspection, and smelling. Also includes the act of investigating the victim and his or her clothing for signs of defect, disease, injury, and potential transfer evidence from a location, weapon, or suspect.

Seborrhea (also seborrheic dermatitis) A condition commonly known as dandruff, which can present with rashes that itch intensely and become infected due to breaks in the skin.

Urethral meatus The urethra is a tube leading from the bladder that discharges urine outside the body. In females, the urethra is significantly shorter than in males, and the female urethra meatus (or opening) is above the vaginal opening.

Forensic nursing is a subspecialty of forensic science and nursing in which the science of nursing is applied to the resolution of legal matters. It involves patient care in the context of evidence documentation, collection, and preservation

CONTENTS

[1]This chapter is an update to material originally published in Jamerson (2009) and Turvey and Jamerson (2011).

Forensic Victimology. http://dx.doi.org/10.1016/B978-0-12-408084-3.00005-3

efforts. Consequently, *forensic nurses* are registered nurses with additional education and training in forensic science and evidence collection. As explained in Nelson (1998):

> The term forensic nursing was officially coined in 1992 when about 70 nurses gathered in Minneapolis for what was billed as the first national convention for sexual assault nurses. It was thrilling to meet with others doing the same work and enlightening to learn about the issues they were grappling with, [Patty Seneski, ENP, RN, president of the International Association of Forensic Nurses (IAFN)] said. That led to the founding of the IAFN.
>
> Six years later, the New Jersey-based group has 1,500 members, who practice in diverse fields. They range from sexual assault nurse examiners (SANEs)—often an entry point into forensic nursing—to nurses who specialize in such areas as domestic violence, child and elder abuse, and emergency trauma. Forensic nurses may also serve as legal nurse consultants or attorneys, Seneski said.
>
> Forensic nurses' responsibilities vary. For example, they may perform death investigations, work with criminals in prison, or counsel schoolchildren who fire guns, said Seneski, a SANE who works in emergency nursing and does consulting.

Under typical circumstances, a forensic nurse will have only one opportunity to examine a patient, an alleged victim. Often this will occur while law enforcement investigators are waiting in the hallway. Additionally, the more time that passes before the examination, the more likely evidence will be lost or biologically degraded. These circumstances and constraints can put considerable pressure on even the most experienced professionals.

The purpose of this chapter is to discuss the roles and responsibilities of forensic nurses, as well as the rationale behind their methods. At the outset, they are required to understand that the victim's body is a crime scene, that victimity must be established and not assumed, and that time is a limiting factor. They need to develop an appreciation for thoroughness and attention to detail in all aspects of the forensic medical examination.

This chapter was not written for the advanced forensic nurse practitioner. It is, rather, a primer. It is written for students and professionals who need a basic understanding of what forensic nurses do, how they do it, and why.

GETTING TO THE TRUTH

Law enforcement investigators are tasked with investigating complaints of sexual assault to determine what happened and whether a crime actually occurred.

They are meant to be truth-seekers in the criminal justice system. As explained by the Attorney General's Sexual Assault Task Force (SATF), in the State of Oregon (SATF, 2009):

> Law enforcement is responsible for determining whether reports of sexual assault meet the criteria of a criminal offense as determined by the state criminal code. This responsibility includes determining the credibility and, ultimately, the investigative outcome of sexual assault reports.

The criminal investigation of a sexual assault is accomplished by proper crime scene investigation; interviews with complainants, the accused, and any witnesses; and the reconstruction of physical evidence. It is not accomplished by accepting the statements of one party over another without evaluation or by making arrests prior to investigating and establishing the facts (Savino and Turvey, 2011).

The purpose of reconstruction is to establish what did and did not happen during an event by virtue of an objective examination of the physical evidence. This can aid the efforts of law enforcement, and the courts, tremendously. As explained in Boland and colleagues (2007; p. 110):

> The fundamental role of a forensic scientist is to help those who address the burdensome issue of guilt or innocence in a court of law...
>
> A large percentage of crimes against the person, dealt with by forensic science laboratories, are crimes of sexual assault.... In these cases, finding semen and in fact getting a matching DNA profile, may offer no additional evidential value to the case. Other examinations, such as damage interpretation, possibly indicating a struggle or that force was used, may be critical. This analysis may be used to corroborate or refute a particular scenario and indeed, in a small, but significant number of cases, damage interpretation may be critical in preventing false allegations proceeding to prosecution.

Forensic examiners are not allowed to assume facts for the purposes of a reconstruction: facts must be established. This may seem redundant, as facts are generally defined as verifiable and indisputable circumstances or information. However, it is not uncommon for the investigative assumptions and theories generated early in a case to be treated as facts and to remain uninvestigated or unexamined. This is particularly true of witness statements that favor prevailing or expedient investigative theories. The uncritical acceptance of any statement, without an assessment of its internal integrity or evidentiary corroboration, provides an insufficient basis for the reliable reconstruction of events. A scientific examination investigates the evidence to learn the facts, seeking to support or refute the elements of crime-related behavior. It does not assume them.

The forensic nurse is an important part of this overall effort.

FORENSIC NURSE: ROLES AND RESPONSIBILITIES

The role of the forensic nurse is to function as an objective and scientific finder of fact; to utilize scientific principles and methodology in the recognition, documentation, collection, and interpretation of physical evidence related to diseases, injuries, and crimes that may be suffered by all manner of victims. In doing so, the forensic nurse operates with the understanding that those examined in a forensic context are the potential extension of a crime scene. Subsequently, the forensic nurse must serve as a forensic investigator; as an educator to victims and the community; and as an expert witness within the legal system.

Registered nurses (RNs) wishing to practice forensic nursing are generally required to obtain specialty training and certification. This training includes theoretical instruction as well as a clinical component that allows them to work with an experienced forensic nurse on the front lines, examining and providing care for crime victims. The importance of this specialty training, as well as continuing education in the specific area of practice, cannot be emphasized enough. It is critical to have both a solid theoretical and clinical background, as it is this foundation that prepares the forensic nurse to understand and appropriately deal with the victim's body as a crime scene.

Because time, the environment, and individual body chemistry all conspire to degrade the physical evidence, the sooner that a forensic examination can be performed on the victim, the better. In fact, most jurisdictions allow no more than 72 hours between the alleged crime and any evidence collection efforts performed (see Figure 5-1).

FIGURE 5-1

A standard sexual assault evidence collection kit for the preservation of victim evidence. In cases of suspected or alleged sexual assault, a separate suspect kit must also be utilized when a suspect is available.

Consequently, forensic nurses must be available to work when crime occurs and to respond to a case within approximately an hour. This means being on call essentially 24 hours a day, 7 days a week. Occasionally, there will be extenuating circumstances—such as a victim being held in captivity by a perpetrator or delayed reporting under some circumstances—that make a longer interval between crime and examination acceptable. These time constraints vary from state to state and are often determined by the state office of the attorney general.

These concerns are echoed in the National Institute of Justice (NIJ) published guidelines, *A National Protocol for Sexual Assault Medical Forensic Examinations*, 2nd ed. (2013), which offers the following general recommendations regarding evidence collection and its context (p. 73)[2]:

> Recognize the importance of gathering information for the medical forensic history, examining patients, and documenting exam findings, separate from collecting evidence. Examiners should obtain the medical forensic history as appropriate, examine patients, and document findings when patients are willing, whether or not evidence is gathered for the sexual assault evidence collection kit. The history and documentation of exam findings can help in determining if and where there may be evidence to collect and in addressing patients' medical needs. In addition, they can be invaluable in and of themselves to an investigation and prosecution if a report is made. It is also important to document patients' demeanor during the exam process using specific, concrete terms (e.g., crying, shaking) and their statements made related to the assault because if the case is reported, this information could be admitted as evidence at trial. When documenting patient statements, it is important to write down the exact wording of the statement.
>
> Examine patients promptly to minimize the loss of evidence and identify medical needs and concerns. Evidence can be lost from the body and clothing through a number of mechanisms. For example, degradation of some seminal fluid components can occur within body orifices, semen can drain from the vagina or wash from the mouth, sperm can lose motility, bodily fluids can get washed away, and dried secretions and foreign materials can fall from the body and clothing. Prompt examination also helps to quickly identify patients' medical needs and concerns.

---

[2]This second edition is much more victim friendly than the first, which, according to critics, took an improper "prosecutorial tone" (Goode, 2013). It is intended to educate practitioners to engage in practices that do not judge victims, and encourages evidence collection no matter the examiner's personal feelings.

Due to the stability of DNA and sensitivity of tests, advancing DNA technologies also continue to extend time limits. These technologies are even enabling forensic scientists to analyze stored evidence from crimes that occurred years before. Such breakthroughs demonstrate the importance of collecting all possible evidence.

As suggested, forensic nurses are often a "frontline" professional with respect to making victim contact subsequent to the commission of a violent crime. This primarily has to do with the way victims enter the justice system. In many cases, victims will report their assault directly to the police. Or they may show up at a local emergency room or medical clinic seeking treatment. When law enforcement is involved at the outset, officers will take an initial report from victims and then immediately refer victims to a clinic or hospital emergency room that performs forensic examinations.

Bear in mind that not every situation is the same, not all victims are able to move under their own power, and each department may have its own policies and procedures to follow. So not everyone arrives at forensic examination the same way. Subsequent to their initial report to law enforcement or presentation to medical personnel, some victims are transported by the police or emergency medical services; some are transported by friends and family; and some drive themselves.

Once the report to the police has been made and the alleged victim arrives, the forensic nurse should begin the examination. It starts with obtaining consents, biographical intake information, a medical history, and finally a history of events leading up to and surrounding the crime.

CONSENT FORMS

Once the patient arrives at the exam location and the forensic nurse has made his or her introductions, along with any additional staff that may be assisting, it is necessary to obtain the patient's informed consent. Forensic examiners are best off if they begin by explaining the entire forensic medical examination procedure, along with the necessity of evidence collection, to patients, no matter what their age. This will empower patients, involve them in the process, and give them an opportunity to think of and ask questions.

Consent to treat must be obtained before any evidence collection or treatment takes place. This is in keeping with the NIJ (2013), which stipulates the following (p. 5):

Informed consent: Patients should understand the full nature of their consent to each exam procedure. By presenting them with relevant information, in a language they understand, patients are in a position to make an informed decision about whether to accept or decline a procedure. However, they should be aware of the potential impact of declining a particular procedure, as it may negatively affect the quality of care, the usefulness of evidence collection, and, ultimately, any criminal investigation and/or prosecution. They should understand that declining a particular procedure might also be used against them in any justice system proceeding. If a procedure is declined, reasons why should be documented if the patient provides such information....

Recommendations for health care providers and other responders to request patients' consent during the exam process:

- Seek the informed consent of patients as appropriate throughout the exam process.
- Make sure policies exist to guide the process of seeking informed consent from specific populations.

Consent forms may vary from one institution to another, but often include consent to conduct a forensic medical examination, including the collection of evidence, urine specimen with drug testing as needed, collection of blood for lab work as needed, use of a colposcope to assist with injury identification, forensic photography (colposcope and digital photography), use of recording equipment, and consent for emergency contraception. If the victim is a minor, then the parent or guardian will need to sign in his or her place.

This is a good time to take stock of the fact that not every victim will react the same way to the procedures involved in the forensic medical exam, let alone the prospect. As explained in the NIJ (2013), victims' perceptions and reactions may be influenced by a variety of circumstances (p. 30):

Adapt the exam process as needed to address the unique needs and circumstances of each patient. Patients' experiences during the crime and the exam process, as well as their post-assault needs, may be affected by multiple factors, such as:

- Age.
- Gender and/or perceived gender identity/gender expression.
- Physical health history and current status.
- Mental health history and current status.
- Disability.
- Language needs for limited English proficient patients, Deaf and hard-of-hearing individuals, and those with sensory or communication disabilities.
- Ethnic and cultural beliefs and practices.
- Religious and spiritual beliefs and practices.
- Economic status, including homelessness.

- Immigration and refugee status.
- Sexual orientation.
- Military status.
- History of previous victimization.
- Past experience with the criminal justice system.
- Whether the assault involved drugs and/or alcohol.
- Prior relationship with the suspect, if any.
- Whether they were assaulted by an assailant who was in an authority position over them.
- Whether the assault was part of a broader continuum of violence and/or oppression (e.g., intimate partner and family violence, gang violence, hate crimes, war crimes, commercial sexual exploitation, sex and/or labor trafficking).
- Where the assault occurred.
- Whether they sustained physical injuries from the assault and the severity of the injuries.
- Whether they were engaged in illegal activities at the time of the assault (e.g., voluntary use of illegal drugs or underage drinking) or have outstanding criminal charges.
- Whether they were involved in activities prior to the assault that traditionally generate victim blaming or self-blaming (e.g., drinking alcohol prior to the assault or agreeing to go to the assailant's home).
- Whether birth control was used during the assault (e.g., victims may already have been on a form of birth control or the assailant may have used a condom).
- Capacity to cope with trauma and the level of support available from families and friends.
- The importance they place on the needs of their extended families and friends in the aftermath of the assault.
- Whether they have dependents who require care during the exam, were traumatized by the assault, or who may be affected by decisions patients make during the exam process.
- Community/cultural attitudes about sexual assault, its victims, and offenders.
- Frequency of sexual assault and other violence in the community and historical responsiveness of the local justice system, health care systems, and community service agencies.

Clearly, the level of trauma experienced by patients can also influence their initial reactions to an assault and to post-assault needs. While some may suffer physical injuries, contract an STI, or become pregnant as a result of an assault, many others do not. The experience of psychological trauma will be unique to each patient and may be more difficult to recognize than physical trauma. People have their own method of coping with sudden stress. When severely traumatized, they can appear to be calm, indifferent, submissive, jocular, angry, emotionally distraught, or even uncooperative or hostile towards those who are trying to help.

Forensic nurses and other assisting staff are admonished to be sensitive about these factors in the process of obtaining consent, as well as during the exam itself. A judgmental, coercive, or inflexible approach is not advised, nor is it professional.

THE INTAKE FORM

The intake form establishes the informational foundation upon which to start prioritizing different aspects of an eventual forensic medical exam (see Figure 5-2). It also acts as a valuable face sheet, giving case basics at a glance for future reference. Intake information includes biographical data about the patient, those involved in the case, and a thumbnail sketch of the crime and

FIGURE 5-2
Charla Jamerson prepares an intake form and a sexual assault kit for a patient.

the alleged perpetrator. Additional in-depth information is gathered during the forensic interview process or during the medicolegal examination.

Specifically, the intake form establishes the following baseline information:

1. The time and date of the exam.
2. The name of the forensic nurse examiner and anyone who assisted.
3. The patient's name and other identifying information.
4. How to reach the patient if needed, including contact numbers and mailing address.
5. The patient's family and/or guardian information.
6. The patient's insurance information.
7. Date of referral and referral source (e.g., hospital, clinic, law enforcement, or department of health).
8. Collaborating law enforcement agencies responsible for investigating the case.
9. Suspect information; this may or may not be available.
10. Brief history of sexual assault exams; some victims receive more than one medical examination related to their injuries, the forensic medical exam being secondary.

It is also necessary that the intake form document the name of the person providing the patient's history to the examiner, and his or her relationship to the patient (such as a mother or father if the patient is a minor). With this information documented, anyone reviewing the file at a later time will be aware of whether the history came directly from the victim. This may go to the credibility of the information provided at some later date.

These guidelines are consistent with the NIJ (2013), which offers the following guidelines relating to patient intake (pp. 83–84):

> Perform a prompt, competent medical assessment. Then respond to acute injury, the need for trauma care, and safety needs of patients before collecting evidence. In addition to promoting physical health, sensitive and timely medical care can help reduce the likelihood of acute psychological trauma and its aftereffects, support patients' existing and emerging coping skills, and set the tone for patients' resumption of normal functioning.
>
> Acute medical needs take precedence over evidentiary needs. Patients should be instructed to not wash, change clothes, urinate, defecate, smoke, drink, or eat until initially evaluated by examiners, unless necessary for treating acute medical injuries. If alcohol- or drug-facilitated sexual assault is suspected, and patients need to urinate prior to the arrival of examiners, ensure that the urine sample is collected properly while maintaining the chain of custody.

The forensic examiner should be involved in all aspects of the medical forensic examination of the sexual assault patient. As soon as possible after the initial triage, management, and stabilization of acute medical problems and before treating non-acute injuries, the evidentiary exam can be conducted (with patients' permission). In circumstances in which patients are seriously injured or impaired, examiners must be prepared to work alongside other health care providers who are stabilizing and treating them. In such cases, examiners may need to perform exams in settings such as a health care facility's emergency department, an operating room, a recovery room, or an intensive care unit.

Alert examiners of the need for their services. The SART/SARRT, if one exists, can work with exam facilities to identify acceptable time frames to conduct a medical forensic exam after a patient's arrival and medical evaluation, management, and stabilization. If examiners are not based at the site or need to be dispatched, the facility should contact them immediately after identifying a sexual assault patient.

Examiners are often required to arrive at the exam site within a certain period of time (e.g., 30 minutes) after being dispatched.

Contact victim advocates so they can offer services to patients, if not already done....

Assess and respond to safety concerns of victims upon arrival at the exam site, such as threats to patients or staff. The facility should have procedures to assess such safety concerns at the exam site and to respond to such threats or dangerous situations. (For a discussion of this topic, see *A.2. Victim-Centered Care.*) Communicating any information may require a qualified interpreter for victims who are LEP.

Assess patients' needs for immediate medical or mental health intervention prior to the evidentiary exam, following facility policy. Seek informed consent of patients before providing treatment.... Also, inform them that they have a right to receive medical care regardless of whether the assault is reported to law enforcement.

If the information on this form seems overly basic, the reason is that it is intended to be. It is precisely the kind of information that is easily misplaced or forgotten, and can result in hours of wasted time when needed but missing at some later point. Obtaining this information up front saves time and effort, and limits confusion.

There is flexibility in the sequence that historical information may be gathered, but a good place to start after the initial intake information is with the Review of Systems (ROS). As argued in Billings and Stoeckle (1999), the purpose and clinical importance of the ROS protocol is to screen for potential disease processes that have not as yet been discovered. Furthermore, and from a forensic perspective, it's an excellent filter that keys in the examiner to important areas that may need further investigation. Patients are well known for failing to report everything and forgetting to mention even vital details of their medical history. Because the ROS goes over each area of anatomy, it may remind them about current conditions or past ailments. It may even help them recall details involving specific areas of their bodies related to the assault. It is also a formal mechanism that allows the forensic examiner to probe for more information.

When an examiner is eliciting information during the ROS, it is most useful to start with general questions and then move toward the specific. This helps to get patients focused on thinking about their health. Initial questions might include "How is your breathing?" "Are you having any problems with your lungs?" "Have you had any problems with your heart?" "How about your bowels?" It is helpful to proceed with the interview in a head-to-toe format because this approach facilitates a methodical sequence and keeps the interview on track.

THE FORENSIC INTERVIEW, WITH VICTIM HISTORY

Depending on the consideration of multiple and less than constant variables such as state law, institutional policies, the condition of the patient, and the availability of qualified staff, the forensic examiner may choose to conduct either the *forensic interview* or the *forensic medical examination* first. It must be noted, however, that having the intake and history information is necessary to competently inform and prioritize the physical examination. For example, the clinician may obtain information in the history that indicates a physical injury, or source of pain or discomfort, that needs to be assessed right away; in other cases it is appropriate to start the forensic interview first, followed by the physical examination and subsequent evidence collection. Each patient is unique; any treatment and forensic efforts should be individually crafted to his or her particular condition and history.

Medical history[3] is a significant component of the evaluation in the context of any suspected sexual assault, child molestation, or domestic assault. It provides a baseline of information for the examiner so that recent trauma and injury can be discriminated from past conditions and events. Therefore, it must cover all body systems. In this way, the examiner can identify any acute or chronic

---

[3]*Medical history* is the information about a patient gathered by a health care professional for the purposes of making examinations, providing treatment, and rendering a diagnosis. It commonly involves asking patients questions regarding the current and former state of their physical and mental health. Without this background information, examinations, treatments, and diagnoses are at best uninformed, and at worst potentially lethal.

problems, as well as any history of past injury or surgeries. It also informs the nature, extent, and sequence of the forensic medical exam. A failure to document and report medical background information prevents informed medical treatment and leaves the forensic examiner without the proper context for accurate interpretations. Ultimately, conducting an accurate forensic medical examination in the absence of a patient's medical history is not possible.

These recommendations are consistent with the NIJ (2013), which offers the following guidelines regarding medical history (pp. 87–90):

> **Coordinate medical forensic history taking and investigative interviewing.** Examiners typically ask patients to provide a medical forensic history after initial medical care for acute problems and before the examination and evidence collection. This history, obtained by asking patients detailed forensic and medical questions related to the assault, is intended to guide the exam, evidence collection, and crime lab analysis of findings. In cases where the victim reports the assault, law enforcement representatives should also collect information from patients to help in the apprehension of suspects and in case investigation.
>
>   Gathering information from patients often takes place soon after they have experienced the assault. Not only can discussing the assault cause patients to feel re-violated, but their emotional and physical condition may make communication difficult. They may also be uncomfortable discussing personal matters with involved responders. Those seeking information about the assault should work collaboratively to create an information-gathering process that is as respectful to patients as possible and minimizes repetition of questions...
>
>   Use a private and quiet setting for information gathering. Ideally, there should be no interruptions and no time constraints for questioners or for use of the room where the information is being gathered. Although some facilities may lack space, an effort should be made to secure a private and quiet setting for this purpose. In many jurisdictions, history-taking takes place in the exam room prior to the exam.
>
>   **Obtain the medical forensic history.** The specific questions asked of patients by examiners for the medical forensic history vary from one jurisdiction to the next, as do forms used to record the history. However, the following information should be sought routinely from patients:
>
> 1. Date and time of the sexual assault(s): It is essential to know the period of time that has elapsed between the assault and the physical examination/collection of evidence as well as documentation of

injuries. Evidence collection may be influenced by the time interval since the assault as well as the interpretation of both the physical exam and evidence analysis.

2. Pertinent patient medical history: The interpretation of physical findings may be affected by medical data related to menstruation, recent anal-genital injuries, surgeries, or diagnostic procedures, blood-clotting history, and other pertinent medical conditions or treatment.

3. Recent consensual sexual activity: The sensitivity of DNA analysis makes it important to gather information about recent consensual intercourse, whether it was anal, vaginal, and/or oral, and whether a condom was used. A trace amount of semen or other bodily fluid, as well as genital microtrauma, may be identified that is not associated with the crime. Once identified, it may need to be associated with a consensual partner, and then used for elimination purposes to aid in interpreting evidence.

4. Post-assault activities of patients: The quantity and quality of evidence [are] affected both by actions taken by patients and the passage of time. It is critical to know what, if any, activities were performed prior to the examination (e.g., have patients urinated, defecated, had consensual sexual intercourse, wiped genitals or the body, douched, removed/inserted a tampon/sanitary pad/diaphragm, used oral rinse/gargled, washed, brushed teeth, eaten or drank, smoked, used drugs, or changed clothing?).

5. Assault-related patient history: Information such as the location of nongenital injury, tenderness, pain and/or bleeding, and anal-genital injury, pain, and/or bleeding can direct evidence collection and medical care. Patients should also be questioned about strangulation since this type of injury can result in airway obstruction if swelling occurs and strangulation is a very common occurrence in sexual assault cases.

6. Suspect information (if known): Forensic scientists seek evidentiary items that may have had cross-contact or transfer among patients, suspects, and crime scenes. The gender and number of suspects may offer guidance to types and amounts of foreign materials that might be found on patients' bodies and clothing. Suspect information gathered during this history should be limited to that which will guide the exam and forensic evidence collection. Detailed questions about suspects are asked during the investigative interview.

7. Nature of the physical assault(s): Information about the physical surroundings of the assault(s) (e.g., indoors, outdoors, car, alley, room, rug, dirt, mud, or grass) and tactics employed by suspects is crucial to the detection, collection, and analysis of physical evidence. Tactics may include, but are not limited to, use of weapons

(threatened and/or injuries inflicted), physical blows, grabbing, holding, pinching, biting, using physical restraints, strangulation, burns (thermal and/or chemical), threat(s) of harm, and involuntary ingestion of alcohol/drugs. Knowing whether suspects may have been injured during the assault may be useful when recovering evidence from patients (e.g., blood) or from suspects (e.g., bruising, fingernail marks, or bite marks).

8. Detection of alcohol- or drug-facilitated sexual assault: It is critical in these cases to collect information such as whether there was memory loss, lapse of consciousness, or vomiting; whether the patient was given food or drink by the suspect (if the patient knows); or whether the patient voluntarily ingested drugs or alcohol. Collecting toxicology samples within 120 hours of the suspected ingestion is recommended if there was either loss of memory or lapse of consciousness, according to jurisdictional policy.

9. Description of the sexual assault(s): An accurate but brief description is crucial to detecting, collecting, and analyzing physical evidence. The description should include any:

   - Penetration of genitalia (e.g., vulva, hymen, and/or vagina of female patient), however slight, including what was used for penetration (e.g., finger, penis, or other object);
   - Penetration of the anal opening, however slight;
   - Oral contact with genitals (of patients by suspects or of suspects by patients);
   - Other contact with genitals (of patients by suspects or of suspects by patients);
   - Oral contact with the anus (of patients by suspects or of suspects by patients);
   - Nongenital act(s) (e.g., licking, kissing, suction injury, strangulation, and biting);
   - Other act(s) including use of objects;
   - If known, whether ejaculation occurred and location(s) of ejaculation (e.g., mouth, vagina, genitals, anus/rectum, body surface, on clothing, on bedding, or other); and
   - Use of contraception or lubricants.

These questions require specific and sometimes detailed answers. Some may be especially difficult for patients to answer. Examiners should explain that these questions are asked during every sexual assault medical forensic exam. They should also explain why each question is being asked.

This information is essential for the forensic nurse to gather before starting the forensic medical examination, as some preexisting conditions can mimic or be confused for abuse (i.e., skin conditions, nonviolent or sports-related injuries unrelated to assault, etc.) and will need to be clearly differentiated. Also, having an awareness of the medical history guides the clinician in making necessary referrals for other problems that may be assessed during the examination.

Inherent in these guidelines is the understanding that evidence and injury observed in relation to the alleged victim or crime scene may not be the result of criminal activity. Such evidence or injury may, in fact, be the result of some previous and unrelated activity or event. For example, a complainant may present with extensive bruising of the shins and may not clearly recall their origins. Such injuries might be related to a sexual assault, depending on the events described. Alternatively, upon conducting a history, the forensic examiner may learn that the complainant played a soccer game in the days preceding the alleged attack, in which her shins were kicked repeatedly. The forensic examiner interpreting these injuries without the relevant history could improperly make the assumption that they must be related to a sexual assault.

It is also important to note that investigators and forensic examiners will not know what features of complainant history are relevant to an examination until well after they have begun their work (see Figure 5-3). In one case it

FIGURE 5-3

One of the authors (Turvey) worked a sexual assault case in which a female complainant told investigators, and the SANE, that she had not been sexually active for months. However, crime scene photographs told a very different story. This photo in particular, taken in the complainant's bedroom, shows a garbage bag full of empty condom boxes, as well as a recently used condom. This inconsistency was used to undermine her credibility at trial.

may be a question of toxicology. In another it may be which bedroom of the home they occupied. In yet another there may be a question of sexual habits, preferences, or diseases. All of these issues and related details have turned cases, despite seeming irrelevant or minor at the outset. Each victim is different, each case is different, and, therefore, less victim history is not better.

Failure to document history is negligent and potentially dishonest, as it prevents all concerned from learning the relevant facts of the case. Arguing that history is irrelevant to medical and related forensic interpretations is equally negligent and undeniably dishonest. Consequently, such denials have no place in the search for justice.

History of Drug Abuse

It is important to ask the patient if he or she has a history of substance abuse. If the answer is yes, then immediate follow-up questions must include which substances, when was the last use, and how much was taken. Here, it is critical that the forensic examiner explain to the patient the importance of being honest.

The patient needs to fully understand that if he or she has recently ingested a substance such as alcohol, marijuana, cocaine, heroine, methamphetamine—or any other illicit drug—that it will likely show up on the lab tests submitted for analysis. Therefore, it is better for patients' health and overall credibility to be up front about drug use. Patients need to know that if they deny drug use and test "hot" for the presence of something illicit, this will make them look intentionally deceitful, as though they are trying to hide information. The forensic examiner should explain that it is better to establish a pattern of honesty during the forensic medical examination so that any other information provided may be trusted if trust is required.

In cases involving recreational use or abuse of drugs and alcohol by the patient, it may be necessary to obtain collateral descriptions of the patient's typical behavior while under the influence from friends and family members. In this way, the forensic examiner will have a more complete understanding of how particular drugs affect a particular patient to inform subsequent interpretations—though not necessarily his or her own. That is to say, there are happy drunks, loud drunks, "amorous" drunks, forgetful drunks, and angry drunks. It helps to know which the patient is.

Ultimately, toxicology will also be used to inform estimates of the patient's physical and mental capabilities, as well as to assist with addressing the issue of consent. Failure to examine victim toxicology, which is all too common, is negligent. It hides the truth and can result in misinterpretations of related physical and behavioral evidence.

Alcohol: The Real Date Rape Drug

Drug use, most commonly alcohol, is a vital consideration in the interpretation and reconstruction of evidence related to an alleged sexual assault. As such, it is standard forensic protocol to collect blood and/or urine from both complainants and suspects during an investigation. The failure to collect and test toxicological samples is substandard, and in some cases may indicate a desire to protect the complainant from the outcome.

In some instances, drugs are given intentionally yet surreptitiously to a victim by an offender to facilitate rape. There are, in fact, many different kinds of "date rape" drugs, including sedatives, sleeping pills, and, more specifically, Rohypnol. These can each incapacitate victims, induce sleep, and cause memory loss depending on type and dosage.

However, the number one drug associated with sexual assault is alcohol (see Figure 5-4). Research has found that in more than 50% of reported sexual assaults, the victim, the offender, or both had been consuming alcohol (Busch-Armendariz et al., 2010). Along with other well-known side effects, it lowers inhibitions, impairs judgment, and ultimately prevents informed consent (Bates, 2007). As reported in the *Journal of the American Medical Association* (Cole, 2006, p. 504):

> According to a 2003 US Department of Justice (DOJ) report (available at http://www.cops.usdoj. gov/mime/open.pdf), rape is the most common violent crime at US universities. The incidence of rape is estimated to be 35 per 1000 female college students per year in the United States, although less than 5% of these rapes are reported to police. Women may decline to report rape for a variety of reasons, including shame, fear of social isolation from the assailant's friends, and self-reproach for drinking with the assailant before the rape.
>
> Ninety percent of college women who are raped know their assailants, according to the DOJ report. Most rapes occur in social situations, such as at a party or studying together in a dormitory room, and about half of perpetrators and rape survivors are drinking alcohol at the time of the assault, according to a National Institute on Alcohol Abuse and Alcoholism (NIAAA) review of recent studies of alcohol and sexual assault (available at http://pubs.niaaa.nih.gov/ publications/arh25-1/43-51.htm). Henry Wechsler, PhD, of the Harvard School of Public Health, in Boston, who has conducted studies of alcohol use by college students, says that most nonconsensual sex is fueled by alcohol. "Alcohol is the number 1 rape drug," says Wechsler.

This is further supported by findings reported in Cowan (2008, pp. 904–905):

Research has shown that the level of alcohol use in sexual assault cases is alarmingly high. Andrea Finney's 2004 summary of various research studies in this area shows that around 60% of perpetrators have been drinking just prior to the offense of sexual assault. However, statistics on the proportion of victims who have been drinking prior to the offense vary widely and depend partially on the sample—for instance, in student populations, up to 81% of incidents can involve drinking on the part of the victim. There has been no substantive research on intoxication of victims in the U.K. to date and the data referred to by Finney is generated in the U.S. However, more recent research in the U.K. (aimed at analyzing the attrition rate in rape cases rather than the rate of alcohol consumption per se) found that in a sample of 676 cases over eight police force areas, 38% of victims aged 16 and above had been drinking, though not necessarily to the point of intoxication, prior to the assault.

It is important to note that alcohol does not generally require surreptitious delivery; some patients will regularly ingest alcohol to excess and of their own free will. In fact, it is often used precisely because of its narcotic effects, not in spite of them, as a form of recreation. However, this creates an environment of increased risk wherever such activity takes place, especially within large groups.

As explained already, the use of drugs and alcohol in sufficient quantities prevents the user from thinking rationally, and subsequently from being able to form any kind of rational intent (victims and offenders alike). This bears directly on cases of rape involving drug and alcohol use, described in Cowan (2008, pp. 900–901):

> A complainant's intoxication can impact consent in a rape trial in two possible ways. First, the complainant and the defendant could disagree about the fact or level of intoxication, i.e., capacity, so that the defendant claims either that the complainant was not drunk at all, or that she was not drunk to the degree that she was incapable of consenting but merely was disinhibited, and therefore she was in fact capable of, and did, consent. Second, there could be disagreement about whether or not there was consent, i.e., the defendant claims that the complainant gave consent, albeit drunken, and that she was capable even though intoxicated, whereas the complainant states that she cannot remember what happened because she was extremely drunk but that she

JUST BECAUSE YOU HELP HER HOME...

DOESN'T MEAN YOU GET TO HELP YOURSELF.

sex without consent = sexual assault

DON'T BE THAT GUY.

sexualassaultvoices.com

 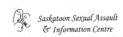 

FIGURE 5-4
One of the posters created for SAVE (Sexual Assault Voices of Edmonton), as part of the "Don't be that guy" campaign in 2012.

Continued

Alcohol: The Real Date Rape Drug *Continued*

knows that she did not want to have sex with the defendant (and she may also claim that she was too drunk to resist). The claim then could be either that she was not intoxicated (enough) and capable, or, that despite a high level of intoxication, she did consent.

Although referring specifically to alcohol intoxication, the issues discussed in Cowan (2008) remain the same with other drugs that cause similar mental defects. This temporary state of being incapable of rationally appraising the nature of one's own conduct is referred to as mental incapacity.

Significantly, research published in Boykins (2005) found that half of the sexual assault victims in her study reported current use of prescription medication, primarily for mental health problems such as depression. This becomes more significant with respect to perception and memory when such medications are mixed with alcohol.

History of Behavioral or Emotional Symptoms, and Menstruation

When an examiner is obtaining history under the behavioral/emotional category, it is important to gather information regarding the patient's mental health, usual sleep patterns, eating patterns, any behavioral problems at school or work, recent mood, as well as any history of sexually transmitted diseases (STDs) and treatment or lack thereof. Most of this information should be easy enough to answer. However, patients may or may not know whether or not they suffer from certain STDs, as more than a few can be present without distinctive or even obvious symptoms.

In addition, it is important to ask about and document the last time the patient had consensual sex. If the patient had consensual sex the same day, or even a few days prior to any reported attack, biological material may still be present. It is therefore necessary to establish the precise nature of the sexual activity, and the potential location of any ejaculate—where it may have landed and where it may have transferred if the patient has continued with his or her daily routine or activities. This can help to explain any mixed samples of biological material that might occur in any subsequent DNA testing of patient samples.

This information may also be important in cases involving older or elderly female patients that have not been sexually active for a number of years. They experience decreased estrogen effect to the vaginal tissue due to menopause and hormonal changes. This is important to establish during the physical examination, and within the context of evidence collection efforts, because oftentimes vaginal tissue that undergoes such changes is more susceptible to injury.

On a related subject, the forensic examiner needs to ask all female patients at what age they started their menstrual cycle; when their last menstrual period was; and what their menstrual cycle is normally like (many females experience irregular bleeding patterns with their menses, and this is important data to collect). The examiner also needs to establish the patients' use of pads, tampons, or both during menses.

Each category within the history is important to ask about and document. The forensic examiner should take care and be cognizant to mark every item in each category as it is accomplished. If something doesn't apply to a particular patient, just mark it as not-applicable (n/a). Then review the form to ensure that nothing has been missed.

The purpose of taking a history is not to help give the forensic nurse excuses to hurry through the forensic medical exam and cut corners because of a subjective victim trait. The purpose is to inform collection efforts and eventual interpretations of findings. As stated in the NIJ (2013), forensic examiners and investigators must do the following (p. 74):

> [A]void basing decisions about whether to collect evidence on how they think patients' characteristics or circumstances will affect the investigation and prosecution. For example, the fact that an adolescent may have lied to her parents about where she was going the night of the assault should in no way influence the decision of the examiner and/or the law enforcement representative to collect evidence.

All these considerations are part of treating the patient's body, including his or her clothing, as a physical extension of a potential crime scene. This are discussed further in subsequent sections.

THE PHYSICAL EXAMINATION

The *physical examination* of the patient is the act of examination of the body by auscultation, palpation, percussion, inspection, and smelling. It also includes the act of investigating the victim and his or her clothing for signs of defect, disease, injury, and potential transfer evidence from a location, weapon, or suspect. The resultant findings (or the absence of findings) are referred to as *physical evidence*. The most informed physical examination follows a process and direction dictated in part by the medical history and forensic interview. According to Giardino and Giardino (2003), the physical examination generally involves the following efforts:

1. Search for and identify any physical injuries or conditions that require treatment.
2. Document physical findings at the time of examination. This may include utilizing photographs, notes, and/or drawings.
3. Obtain laboratory specimens and diagnostic studies when indicated.
4. Collect and preserve forensic evidence.

5. Provide appropriate treatments directed at restoring health when findings or conditions are present.
6. Reassure patient and family of ways to attain or restore health and well-being.
7. Provide appropriate health education and teaching to promote health and wellness.

Each case is different, but most require between two and four hours to complete. However, more complex cases can take six to seven hours, depending on the amount of injury and evidence collection efforts required. A rape case with limited evidence and injury will require less time than a domestic violence case in which there is extensive bruising, scratching, and other injuries that must each be carefully measured, photographed, and examined for potential evidence transfer.

Full Body Photos

It is helpful to begin the physical examination by taking full body photographs of the patient: front, back, and sides. Such documentation is very helpful to have in the patient's chart, or in the patient database, as it provides a pictorial view of the patient's presentation at the time of assessment. It also provides for *negative documentation*—recording of areas of the body where there is no evidence of defect, disease, injury, or potential transfer.

Vital Signs

As with the ROS (Review of Symptoms) at intake, the physical examination is best conducted in a head-to-toe format with the comprehensive investigation and documentation of all systems. At the outset, it is best to obtain a full set of vital signs, which should include the patient's height, weight, body mass index (BMI), blood pressure, pulse, temperature, and respiration. The forensic examiner needs to know the patient's general status and vital signs upon presentation. From this information, she or he can determine if the patient is within normal limits (WNL) and physiologically stable, or if the patient is in distress and needs additional care before or during the forensic evaluation.

Mental Status

Next, the forensic examiner needs to assess and document the patient's mental status: whether the patient is alert and cooperative; lethargic, uncooperative, and irritable; or unconscious. It is also important to document if the patient denies or refuses to have the examination, as well as his or her stated reason for refusal. Such information may become contextually important at a later time, as the reason may be factual or fictitious.

Evidence and Injury

In proceeding with the head-to-toe physical assessment, the next areas to examine are the patient's general appearance, skin, head, face, ears, throat, neck, lymph nodes, chest, lungs, heart, abdomen, breasts, extremities, back, and circulation status.

In each category of a physical examination form, there must be an area that describes findings that are within normal limits (WNL), and another referred to as "specify otherwise" to document findings that are abnormal. In addition to assessing whether each system is within normal limits, the examiner is also focusing on identifying any injuries including bruises, abrasions, lacerations, patterned injuries, burns, and any signs of skeletal trauma and/or head trauma. Each case varies. Some cases involve allegations of domestic or physical abuse, whereas other cases involve allegations of sexual abuse/molestation. However, the head-to-toe physical examination should be conducted in every case.

Specifically, the evaluation of a patient who may have been physically abused or injured also tends to focus on any injuries present. This is best accomplished in a methodical manner so that any external and/or internal injuries consistent with assault or abuse can be identified and thoroughly documented. However, forensic examiners must be mindful not to focus solely on areas of obvious injury. They must be thorough in their search for evidence and documentation of all other areas of the body. As already suggested, forensic evidentiary findings may include biological substances such as saliva, semen, bodily debris, hair, or debris from clothing. It is important to note that in many cases of actual assault there are no physical findings. There may be legitimate reasons for this. For example, the victim may have bathed or taken a shower and washed away vital evidence. In cases involving children, the evidence found greatly depends on the time the child disclosed the suspected abuse versus the time the forensic evaluation takes place. In adult victims, this also depends on whether or not the victim was capable, physically or emotionally, of resisting, as well as other contextual variables.

SEXUAL ASSAULT EXAMINATION

After the head-to-toe portion of the physical examination, the forensic nurse examiner will explain to the patient that it is time to examine the genitalia, or "private parts." It is often helpful to ask the patient what he or she calls those areas of the body, and then refer to those parts with both the patient's terminology and professional terminology. In this way, the forensic examiner provides education by explaining the correct anatomical term, which patients may or may not have heard. However, this approach also works to make patients feel more comfortable by utilizing their language, so as not to speak down to them or appear cold and clinical.

Forensic examiners will need to explain the position they need the patient to be in so that they can examine him or her most effectively. The positioning utilized depends on whether the patient is a child or an adult. Typically, the patient is in one of the following positions:

1. Supine frog-leg (feet and heels together and knees relaxed out and down)
2. Supine/knees to chest or supine with feet in stirrups
3. Prone knee-chest
4. Lateral side lying (lateral decubitus)

Forensic examiners need to be sure to explain that this positioning helps them to see the patient's genital area. They must use terminology that the patient can understand and take the time to explain each part of the exam process. Telling patients what is going on each step of the way educates them and helps them to feel safe. It is also important throughout the exam process to ask patients how they are doing. If they are physically uncomfortable, help them get comfortable; if they are nervous, ask them to explain, and try to help put them at ease.

Once the patient is properly positioned, the clinician can begin a general survey of the genitalia. This includes inspection of the genitalia with the use of a *colposcope*, which is a lighted magnifying instrument used by a gynecologist to examine the tissues of the vagina and the cervix. The process of using a colposcope during a vaginal and cervical examination is called *colposcopy*. A colposcope allows the forensic examiner to assess for, and record, the presence or absence of genital injury. It's like a camera, flashlight, and microscope all in one that allows visualization of genital tissue areas that may be missed with the naked eye or poor lighting. As asserted by Finkel (2002), the colposcope provides not only excellent magnification of the genital tissue, but also an excellent light source that identifies and captures any potential injury or abnormalities on tape or film. Furthermore, it provides a noninvasive method for examining the genitalia—and because the examination is on a screen or monitor, it actually makes the process less intimidating. Patients can observe their own bodies and may even feel more in control.

FALSE POSITIVES: CONDITIONS THAT MIMIC ABUSE

Numerous conditions and circumstances can cause injury consistent with assault or abuse. Therefore, the forensic nurse must be fully aware of the *differential diagnosis*[4] for any finding before making firm conclusions about its origins. This process involves taking into account the possibility that injuries and symptoms may have more than one cause, or a cause unrelated to an assault.

Unfortunately, this basic medical assessment concept can be lost or ignored in a forensic context, where examiners are presented with law enforcement officers or victims insisting that injuries are indeed the result of an assault. The forensic nurse may not make this assumption. Absence of differential diagnosis considerations in any forensic medical exam is the absence of science and the scientific method.

Specific to eliminating false positives in child abuse, but just as important in all other patient examinations, is the advice provided in Burns and Mayer (2000):

> When assessing injuries, the clinician must obtain a complete history, including present illness, review of systems, past medical and psychosocial history, family history (particularly bleeding disorders), and history of injury-related disorders. The caregiver should be permitted to lead the interview with a narrative of the injury. Child abuse should always be suspected when marks or injuries do not match the given history.
>
> Salient clues to child abuse include a history of minor trauma with extensive physical injury, a history of no trauma with evidence of injury, a history of self-inflicted trauma that is incompatible with the child's developmental stage, a history of injury that changes with time, and delays in seeking treatment. Caregivers may blame siblings or playmates for serious injuries. When a third party, especially a sibling, is blamed, the clinician should determine if that sibling is developmentally capable of performing the alleged act. Additionally, the description of the injury mechanism must be consistent with injury type, severity, pain history, and developmental age of the injured child.

Burns and Mayer (2000) specifically discuss the interpretation of *bruises*, which can also mislead the forensic examiner if differentials are not considered:

> Soft tissue trauma, combined with other trauma findings, may be the most common manifestation of physical abuse. Bruises result from blunt force to the skin surface, which disrupts capillaries and other larger blood vessels. The bruise size and depth are indicative of the force of impact, the size of disrupted blood vessels, the vascularity

---

[4]*Differential diagnosis* is strictly defined as the process of weighing the probability of one disease versus that of other diseases possibly accounting for a patient's condition. It considers that symptoms can have multiple causes.

and connective tissue density, and the fragility of blood vessels. For example, the periorbital area is well vascularized and rapidly shows a black-eye syndrome when impacted.

Toddlers and young children may have some minor bruising caused by rough play; however, these frequent and minor injuries usually overlay bony prominences such as shins, knees, elbows, forehead, and the dorsum of the hands. Lacerations and scrapes usually accompany rough-play bruises.

Underlying body organs influence the pattern of the bruise. Flat objects that strike underlying bony processes may leave marks as a result of the underlying soft tissue compressed against the unyielding bone. Therefore, bruises on relatively protected skin sites, such as cheeks, neck, trunk, genitals, and upper legs, should be considered suspicious for abuse.

On a young infant, multiple bruises of different ages, bruises and marks with geometric shapes, or severe bruising are not consistent with any acceptable history. Deep injuries to an area such as the thigh may not be apparent for hours or days. For example, when examining bruises, the caregiver may state that the child fell down the stairs. Common sense indicates that a fall down nonpadded stairs causes a series of bruises the size and shape of the stair edge; however, bruises would rarely exist on one body area.

The clinician should measure the bruise, describe the color, and draw pictures of the injury on the patient's chart. Based on the informed consent protocols of the individual institution, standard or instant photographs are made and labeled for placement in the patient's record. Instant photographs allow the clinician to verify the quality of the photo before the child leaves the office.

Although the color of a bruise changes with time, a definitive means of dating bruises by color does not exist. On impact, a lesion commonly becomes deep red, blue, or purple. Swelling may last for approximately 2 days until the serum is reabsorbed. Localized or diffuse bleeding into tissue creates extensive bruising in children, especially loose tissue with poorly supported blood vessels such as around the periorbital area and genitals. Generally, the color changes from greenish to yellowish-brown before hemoglobin in the clot degenerates and is absorbed.

Apart from misleading injuries, such as old bruises, unintentional burns, and broken bones from known accidents, there are also misleading infections and skin conditions. For example, an adult female patient may reveal during her history that she has suffered from chronic urinary tract infections since the age of 5, due to the fact that she was born with an anatomical abnormality of the *urethral meatus*.[5] A female with a shorter than normal urethral meatus may be prone to a higher incidence of urinary tract infections. The reason is that when the tube leading from the bladder to the opening where urine exits the body (also known as the "pee hole," urethral meatus, urethral opening) is short, general bacteria and bacteria from poor hygiene practices, improper wiping, and feces are more likely to migrate up the tube and cause bladder infections. On the other hand, if the patient reports that she has been experiencing burning upon urination, itching, and discharge only since the alleged assault, then these symptoms are more likely related to the assault.

When the ROS reaches the urogenital and anogenital areas of the body, it is therefore important to inquire if the patient has a history of urinary tract infections. If so, at what age did they start and what was going on during the time of the infection? The history may reveal that the patient has had a series of urinary tract and/or vaginal infections with a pattern that coincides with the history of abuse or assault. Failing to document this history at the time of the forensic medical exam can lead to misinterpretations of findings and the inability to make the appropriate referrals for additional medical care.

Let's consider some further examples to illustrate the importance of obtaining patient history regarding hereditary diseases or existing medical conditions, in the context of considering a differential diagnosis. A patient may reveal in either her medical history or ROS that she has a skin condition known as *contact dermatitis*. This is a reaction caused by the skin coming into contact with allergens or irritants. Examples include poison ivy, poison oak, and poison sumac.

Another example is a skin condition known as *seborrhea*. Also known as seborrheic dermatitis or dandruff, this presents with rashes that can be pruritic (itch intensely) and become infected due to breaks in the skin. Seborrhea in the genital area may be seen more often in infancy, especially in skin folds in the diaper area and between the labia minora and labia majora (Giardino and Giardino, 2003).

Furthermore, a seborrheic lesion in the genitalia often presents itself as raised and erythemic (red in color). It may also display as yellowish, slightly moist greasy scales in the perigenital (around the genitalia) areas. Such findings are not the result of abuse, but may be misinterpreted by examiners without sufficient patient history.

---

[5]The urethra is the tube leading from the bladder that discharges urine outside the body. In females, the urethra is significantly shorter than in males. The female urethral meatus (i.e., opening) is above the vaginal opening.

Another skin condition that must be eliminated as a cause of symptoms is *lichen sclerosus* (LS), which affects the vulva (or penis) and anus. The symptoms of LS include thinning skin, white patches of skin, itching and/or burning, pain during sexual intercourse, and sores or lesions resulting from scratching. However, not all of the symptoms will necessarily be present.

Differential diagnosis considers the possibility that there is more than one cause for any set of injuries, conditions, or symptoms presented by a patient. The objective forensic examiner embraces this medical reality, and works to eliminate causes rather than to prove a relationship between injuries, conditions, and crime. At the very least, this requires the forensic examiner to document each symptom, condition, and injury present with the patient, as well as to establish any specific history that is relevant.

DOCUMENTATION

A few words are necessary on proper documentation. It is advised that the entire physical examination be at the very least audiotaped and transcribed for investigative, reconstructive, and court purposes. After all, this is a forensic procedure, and the resulting findings are intended to be used as evidence. Less information is not better. Additionally, it will protect the forensic examiner should the patient claim to have been mistreated during the examination at some later date.

With respect to photographs, take more not less. But be sensitive and professional. For want of a photo not taken, an entire case may be misinterpreted, or left without resolution.

FINDINGS

As explained in the NIJ (2013) guidelines, forensic nurses must conduct and document every examination they perform thoroughly, as though it will go to trial, even though many will not. This is part of maintaining a forensic mindset. The purpose of any forensic examination is to educate the court system.

Examination reports that do not provide interpretations about whether and how findings may be consistent with sexual assault, abuse, or the patient's account as provided in the forensic interview are unfortunately common. Such reports are, however, unprofessional. Too often they allow forensic examiners latitude in their ultimate interpretations; too often they leave a false or confused impression in the minds of those who read them; and too often they allow attorneys to characterize findings with their own adventitious interpretations.

Additionally, forensic interpretations of exam findings must be made in light of the known victim history and the most current advances in relevant research, methods, and other changes in the field. This places the burden of thorough forensic interviewing squarely on the forensic examiner, as well as the requirement of continuing education. The court should treat forensic interpretations made in the absence of these considerations with skepticism.

To be clear, any forensic report must clearly document what the examiner did, what he or she found, and what it means—not in general, not in part, and not in collusion with a particular side. In other words, the forensic examiner's report should be the truth, the WHOLE truth, and nothing but the truth. Anyone who seeks to contaminate or pervert this creed is not only opposed to good science, but also the oath that the forensic examiner must take before seeking to give expert testimony.

Expert Fraud:

Carolyn Ridling

In the preface to the first edition of this textbook, we discussed the case of *New Hampshire v. Brian Shephard*, involving fraud by Dr. Wendy Gladstone. Readers will recall that she was a forensic nurse who falsified her report to the defense, withheld relevant victim evidence, and saw this as her duty—in violation of her professional ethics and even the law.

As with that case, the false testimony of Carolyn Ridling, a forensic nurse, resulted in another overturned verdict. As reported in *Nguyen v. Texas* (2009):

Joseph Laroche, a child protective services investigator for Grayson County, testified he investigated an allegation of abuse called in by the school counselor. As part of that investigation, he spoke with D.N. at her school. D.N. appeared "very frightened" but told Laroche that appellant "had been licking her boobs and stuff." She also told him he had touched inside her private part with his finger and had put his private part on her private part. She later told Laroche that appellant "had done nothing wrong to her, that this is what you do to people that you love."

Detective Rob Carney testified he works for the Denison Police Department primarily investigating crimes against children. As part of his investigation of this case, he interviewed appellant. Appellant admitted hitting his daughter, D.N., but denied sexually assaulting her. Appellant told Carney D.N. may have "done it herself" because his wife told him D.N. "touched herself" in the vaginal area. Appellant also explained that he bathed D.N. because she did not clean herself well, but denied he touched her in a sexual manner.

Twelve-year-old D.N. testified appellant is her father. When D.N. was ten years old, she was required to come home immediately after school. Her younger brother was in daycare and her parents worked. Her father would come to the house and make sure D.N. had arrived home. When he did so, he would "touch her" on her "boobs and [her] private part." According to D.N., appellant used his hand, his lips, and his tongue to touch her. At trial, D.N. claimed she was clothed when appellant touched her. However, upon further examination, she explained appellant penetrated her vagina with his finger once, after he unzipped her jeans. She also testified that her father helped her younger brother

Continued

Expert Fraud: *Continued*

bathe and clean himself, but she did not "think" he helped her bathe or clean herself.

Carolyn Ridling testified she is a Sexual Assault Nurse Examiner, authorized by the American Nurse Association and by the International Association of Forensic Nursing to perform pediatric sexual assault examinations. Ridling performed such an examination on D.N. According to Ridling, D.N.'s labia were "just stretched out of shape...they were just like they had been used and abused...[t]hey weren't normal. A child shouldn't look like that."

According to Ridling, D.N.'s labia could have been stretched by the "tugging or any sucking" that occurred during oral sex. Ridling also reported D.N. had a well-healed scar on her hymen, indicating there had been penetration of the hymen.

Binh Phan, D.N.'s mother, testified she met appellant in Vietnam and they moved to the United States after they were married. D.N. was six years old at the time. The day appellant slapped D.N., D.N. told Phan he slapped her because "she didn't come home from school. She would stay out late, she went dancing, and...[appellant] was looking all over for her. He was very upset. She gave him dirty look and she talk back so he slap her." Phan also explained that D.N. was not always truthful. For example, D.N. would go out with friends and lie about it. She also lied about what she ate and how often she bathed.

Appellant admitted that he slapped D.N. because he was angry. However, appellant denied sexually assaulting D.N. After hearing this and other evidence, the jury convicted appellant of aggravated sexual assault of a child. After appellant was convicted, appellate counsel filed a motion for new trial, alleging, among other things, that Ridling had given false testimony. After a hearing, the trial court denied appellant's request for a new trial.

Mr. Nguyen's appeal followed and was granted because (*Nguyen v. Texas*, 2009)

> The court abused its discretion by denying a defendant's motion for a new trial after the state's expert witness presented false testimony during the defendant's trial for aggravated sexual assault of a child. The state's witness testified that she was a sexual assault nurse examiner and was authorized to do medical histories and exams for sexual assault victims. At a hearing on the defendant's motion for a new trial, the witness admitted that she was not certified by the state to do sexual assault examinations.

Subsequently, Mr. Nguyen gained his freedom and filed a lawsuit for $18 million against Carolyn Ridling for damages incurred because of her false testimony (Massey, 2011).

SUMMARY

A forensic nurse is a particular kind of forensic examiner who provides patient care in the context of evidence recognition, documentation, collection, and preservation efforts. These nurses are consequently objective and scientific finders of fact, utilizing scientific principles and medical knowledge to discover evidence related to diseases, injuries, and crimes that may be suffered by all manner of victims. Their job is to perform a forensic medical examination of alleged victims, which includes making initial contact, performing an intake assessment, obtaining victim history, performing a physical examination, documenting and collecting evidence, and interpreting findings, including any related treatment.

After obtaining the proper consents from the victim, the forensic nurse collects intake information from her or his patient to govern the nature and sequence of subsequent examination and treatment efforts. Prior to any physical examination or evidence collection efforts, a forensic interview should be conducted to obtain complete victim history information. Conducting an accurate forensic medical examination in the absence of patient medical history is not possible.

Throughout the entire forensic medical examination, forensic nurses must consider and treat the victim's body as a physical extension of the crime scene. They must approach their task methodically and in a thorough, head-to-toe fashion. This will provide the best opportunity for the recognition, documentation, and collection of potential injuries and evidence transfer.

Interpretations by forensic nurses should be grounded in an objective consideration of complete victim history, the results of the physical examination, and the consideration of differential diagnoses. They must also be reported clearly and completely, so as to avoid confusion in the search for the truth.

QUESTIONS

1. Define the term *forensic nursing*.
2. True or False: Forensic nurses typically have only one opportunity to examine a patient.
3. What is the most common drug associated with sexual assault? Explain how this impacts a forensic examination.
4. Explain the importance of negative documentation.
5. Why is it important to properly document a physical examination?

REFERENCES

Billings, J.A., Stoeckle, J., 1999. The Clinical Encounter: A Guide to the Medical Interview and Case Presentation, second ed. Mosby, St. Louis.

Boland, C.A., McDermott, S.C., Ryan, J., 2007. Clothing damage analysis in alleged sexual assaults—The need for a systematic approach. Forensic Science International 167, 110–115.

Boykins, A., 2005. The forensic exam: Assessing health characteristics of adult female victims of recent sexual assault. Journal of Forensic Nursing 1 (4), 166–171.

Burns, P., Mayer, B., 2000. Differential diagnosis of abuse injuries in infants and young children. Nurse Practitioner 25, 15–37.

Busch-Armendariz, N., DiNitto, D., Bell, H., Bohman, T., 2010. Sexual assault perpetrators' alcohol and drug use: The likelihood of concurrent violence and post-sexual assault outcomes for women victims. Journal of Psychoactive Drugs 42 (3), 393–399.

Cole, T., 2006. Rape at US colleges often fueled by alcohol. Journal of American Medical Association, August 2 296 (5), 504–505.

Cowan, S., 2008. The trouble with drink: Intoxication, (in)capacity, and the evaporation of consent to sex. Akron Law Review 41, 899–922.

Finkel, M., 2002. The Evaluation. In: Finkel, M., Giardino, A. (Eds.), Medical Evaluation of Child Sexual Abuse: A Practical Guide, second ed. Sage Publications, Thousand Oaks, CA, pp. 23–37.

Giardino, E.R., Giardino, A.P., 2003. Nursing Approach to the Evaluation of Child Maltreatment. G.W. Publishing, St. Louis, MO.

Goode, E., 2013. New medical exam policy for sexual assault cases. New York Times, April 24; Available at: http://www.nytimes.com/2013/04/25/us/us-issues-guidelines-for-medical-exams-in-sexual-assault-cases.html

Jamerson, C., 2009. Forensic nursing: Approaching the victim as a crime scene. In: Turvey, B., Petherick, W. (Eds.), Forensic Victimology. Elsevier Science, San Diego.

Massey, M., 2011. Exonerated pedophile wants $18 million from nurse who provided false testimony. South Texas Record, July 15; Available at: http://setexasrecord.com/news/234529-exonerated-pedophile-wants-18-million-from-nurse-who-provided-false-testimony

Nelson, V., 1998. Shattering the Myths about Forensic Nursing, Nurseweek, July 13; Availble at : http://www.nurseweek.com/features/98-7/forensic.html

NIJ (National Institute of Justice), 2013. A National Protocol for Sexual Assault Medical Forensic Examinations, second ed. U.S. Department of Justice, Washington, DC Office on Violence Against Women, NCJ 228119, April.

Nguyen v. Texas, 2009. Texas R. App., p. 47, No. 05-07-01775-CR, March 24.

SATF, 2009. False Reports and Case Unfounding: Recommendations for Law Enforcement Response, Attorney General's Sexual Assault Task Force, State of Oregon, January 22.

Savino, J., Turvey, B., 2011. Rape Investigation Handbook, second ed. Elsevier Science, San Diego.

Turvey, B., Jamerson, C., 2011. Sexual assault: Issues in evidence examination and interpretation. In: Chisum, W.J., Turvey, B. (Eds.), Crime Reconstruction, second ed. Elsevier Science, San Diego.

CHAPTER 6

Victim Lifestyle Exposure

Brent E. Turvey and Jodi Freeman[1]

KEY TERMS

Active precipitation Situations in which the victim directly provokes the offender.

Capable guardians Individuals whose presence or proximity discourages offenders from committing crimes. These can be police, security, family members, or regular citizens.

Deification of the victim The tendency to view the victim as lacking flaws. This can happen after a violent crime, when investigators are given reports that victims were saintly in every aspect of their lives.

Extreme-exposure victims Those who are exposed to the possibility of suffering harm or loss every day (e.g., 7 days a week).

High-exposure victims Those who are exposed to the possibility of suffering harm or loss more often than not (e.g., 4–6 days a week).

Lifestyle theory Theory that argues some people are more prone to victimization because their behavior, habits, or customs expose them to a greater frequency of contact with crime and criminals.

Likely offender One who is motivated to offend due to a variety of factors, including availability and vulnerability of victims, fantasy, and so on.

Low-exposure victims Those who are rarely exposed to the possibility of suffering harm or loss (e.g., less than once a week).

Medium-exposure victims Those who are exposed to the possibility of suffering harm or loss less often than not (e.g., 1–3 days a week).

Passive precipitation When a victim exhibits some personal characteristics that unknowingly threaten or encourage the attacker.

Principle of homogamy Theory that suggests individuals are more exposed to the possibility of victimization if they frequently associate, or come into contact with, members of demographic groups containing high numbers of criminals.

Prostitute Any person who engages in sexual activity for payment.

Routine activity theory Examination of victim–offender interaction by considering the spatial and temporal structure of routine legal activities.

Situational exposure Harmful elements experienced by the victim resulting from the environment and personal traits at the time of victimization.

Suitable targets Victims or objects that offenders perceive to be susceptible to their modus operandi.

---

[1]This chapter is an update to, and partial rewrite of, Turvey, Petherick, and Diaz (2008).

Forensic Victimology. http://dx.doi.org/10.1016/B978-0-12-408084-3.00006-5

Victim exposure Amount of contact or vulnerability to harmful elements experienced by a victim in everyday life as a consequence of biological and environmental factors.

Victim precipitation The extent to which a victim plays a role, either knowingly or unknowingly, in his or her own victimization. Precipitation can be passive or active.

Vilification of the victim Viewing or casting certain victim populations as worthless or disposable by their very nature.

By definition, for every crime that has been committed, there must be at least one victim.[2] However, an individual's victimity may not be assumed simply by virtue of his or her proximity to or connection with a crime. There are certainly victims, but there are also offenders and even bystanders. Consequently, once it is evident that a crime has actually been committed, it is necessary to establish which participants are actually victims. As explained by von Hentig (cited in Wolfgang, 1958, p. 245):

> Here are two human beings. As soon as they draw near to one another, male or female, young or old, rich or poor, ugly or attractive—a wide range of interactions, repulsions as well as attractions, is set in motion. What the law does is to watch the one who acts and the one who is acted upon. By this external criterion a subject and object, a perpetrator and a victim are distinguished. In sociological and psychological quality the situation may be completely different. It may happen that the two distinct categories merge. There are cases in which they are reversed and in the long chain of causative forces the victim assumes the role of a determinant.

Though necessary and helpful to both investigative and forensic tasks, deciphering the complex interactions which comprise a victim–offender relationship is not always simple or straightforward. In each case there will be multiple possibilities to consider and eliminate. To make matters worse, dispositive evidence will not always be readily apparent or even available.

Informed analysis requires objective and reliable tools or measures. The author (Turvey) has found that the most objective and reliable measure for examining the victim–offender relationship is the level of *exposure* involved. *Victim exposure* is the amount of contact or vulnerability to harmful elements experienced by the victim (Turvey and Freeman, 2011). Overall victim exposure is determined by examining and considering the separate constructs of *lifestyle exposure* and *situational exposure*. We begin our explicit coverage of this subject by studying the victim's general lifestyle choices.[3]

---

[2]This remains true even in so-called "victimless crimes." This and similar terms are used to describe crimes of vice in which the offender is actually a victim or an addict (e.g., gambling, drug abuse, and prostitution). However, society as a whole suffers because of the violent crimes committed in relation to protecting illegal criminal enterprises.

[3]This coverage continues in Chapter 7, "Victim Situational Exposure."

PURPOSE AND RATIONALE

It is the aim of this chapter to explore how lifestyle factors and choices can influence victim exposure to harm. This, in turn, has an influence on the subsequent dynamics of victimization. The following major section is dedicated to exploring the concept of victim lifestyle exposure—what it is and what it is not. The next major section describes how these lifestyle factors can shape the nature of a criminal offense by reference to certain theoretical criminological constructs. The final section demonstrates how lifestyle exposure is interpreted, with reference to established investigative guidelines. Case studies are provided throughout to illustrate these concepts.

At this point, it is necessary to remind ourselves that studying different aspects of victimology to identify harm and causative influence is not about blaming victims for their suffering. Or more precisely, it is not the explicit purpose of forensic victimology to determine whether victims are necessarily to blame for the crimes that are committed against them. There are two very important reasons for this. First, whether a priest or a prostitute, a victim is not responsible for the decisions of any criminal offenders. Second, from the perspective of forensic victimology, this type of judgment is ultimately a matter for the trier of fact. While the victimologist may assist with this determination by providing relevant information and analysis, it is a judge or jury that decides whether and how a victim may have engaged in some form of contributory negligence.

To be more clear, it is not the place of a forensic victimologist to make personal or moral judgments about any victim—whether positive or negative—nor to put themselves in the victim's place and proclaim what should or should not have been done. This is unprofessional, and ultimately results in an unwarranted projection.

The forensic victimologist seeks to examine the totality of facts and circumstances with objective resolve. This is discussed further at the end of the chapter, in the section regarding victim vilification and deification.

Consequently, the terms and definitions provided in this chapter are designed to help the forensic victimologist with examinations. They are intended to serve as a mechanism for examining and then explaining the relationships between victims, their lifestyles, their environments, and criminal offenders. When examinations are conducted properly, the results of these examinations have tremendous value to investigations and court proceedings alike.

WHAT IS LIFESTYLE EXPOSURE?

As explained in Turvey and Freeman (2011), a victim's *lifestyle exposure* is related to the *frequency* of potentially harmful elements experienced by the victim and resulting from the victim's usual environment and personal traits, as well as

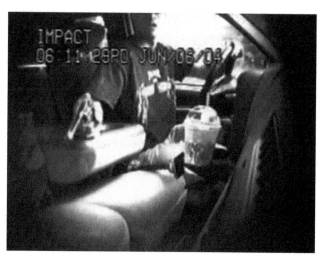

FIGURE 6-1

A car thief in Canada is captured in a police "bait car": first by the hidden camera and then by police as sensors lock the vehicle's door lock and kill the engine. *(Courtesy baitcar.com.)*

past choices. The accurate assessment of lifestyle exposure requires an investigation and examination of a victim's physical condition; his or her mental condition (e.g., enduring personality traits and mental acuity); and his or her personal, professional, and social environments.

A victim's general *lifestyle exposure* to harm or loss must not be confused with his or her *situational exposure,* which refers to harmful elements experienced by the victim resulting from environment and personal disposition *at the time of victimization.* An example that more clearly illustrates these concepts involves car keys (see Figure 6-1).

CASE EXAMPLE:

Car Keys and Car Thieves

Consider the vehicle theft situation on Staten Island, New York, as reported in *Newsday* (2008):

> Lt. John Peruffo of the NYPD's Auto Larceny Unit on Staten Island says more than a third of the vehicles stolen in the borough so far this year had keys in the ignition.
>
> Peruffo says 76 vehicles were reported stolen as of Sunday, 13 more than within the same time frame last year. He says 24 of those had the keys in the ignition.

> Another 10 vehicles were stolen with keys found nearby—in a glovebox, on the ground of a parking lot or discovered inside a jacket left behind at a restaurant.

On Staten Island, and other places with similar crime trends, greater *lifestyle exposure* to vehicle theft would be associated with the general habit of leaving car keys in the vehicle or actually in the ignition. *Incident exposure,* on the other hand, is a question of whether or not the victim actually left the keys in the ignition

CASE EXAMPLE: *CONTINUED*

immediately prior to an actual vehicle theft. In either case, the closer a victim leaves unattended the keys to the vehicle's ignition, the greater that person's exposure to vehicle theft. It is therefore possible for a victim to have a high lifestyle exposure to vehicle theft by virtue of habitually leaving the keys in the ignition with the engine running; and an alternatively low incident exposure by virtue of having his car stolen on a day when it was left secure—with the doors locked and the keys safely in his pocket.

Lifestyle Exposure: A Theoretical Framework

Generally speaking, lifestyle factors can increase the overall possibility of individual harm in three ways: by increasing the victim's proximity to, and interactions with, offenders or those predisposed toward criminality; by fomenting conditions that create a perceived conflict with an offender; and by enhancing an offender's perception of victim vulnerability.

Consider the following criminological theories, which have proven through the author's (Turvey's) casework to be the most useful for identifying and understanding when a victim's lifestyle facilitates victimization.

Victim Precipitation

Victim precipitation theorists argue that the dynamics of criminal acts cannot be fully understood by examining just the characteristics of perpetrators. Specifically, they view criminal acts as relationships that take place between at least two people. Further, they argue that the victim plays a significant role in that relationship which cannot be ignored. As explained in Goetting (1989; p. 348):

> The concept of victim precipitation originated with von Hentig in the 1940s, who observed that "the victim shapes and molds the criminal" and that "the victim assumes the role of a determinant" (von Hentig, 1948: pp. 383–385 cited in Wolfgang, 1958: pp. 245–246). The actual term "victim precipitation" was later coined by Wolfgang (1958: p. 252), and is applied to those offenses in which the victim is the first in the homicide drama to use physical force directed against his subsequent slayer.

This conflicts with the account provided in Rock (2007; p. 42):

> Victim precipitation was propounded first by Mendelsohn, and it alludes to the criminally provocative, collusive or causal impact of the victim in a dyadic relation variously called the 'penal couple' (Mendelsohn, 1963: p. 241); the 'reciprocal action between perpetrator and victim' (von Hentig, 1948, p. 303); the 'duet theory of crime' (von Hentig, 1948, p. 397); a 'situated transaction' (Luckenbill, 1977); 'the

functional responsibility for crime' (Schafer 1968, p. 55), or simply, 'the victim-offender relationship' (Wolfgang, 1957, p. 1).

Rock (2007) goes on to state that (p. 42): "…victim-precipitation portrays crime somewhat neutrally as an interactive process or evolving relation between victim and offender, in which each influences not only the conduct of the other but also the form and content of any crime that may ensue." The major premise of victim precipitation is that victims can knowingly, and unknowingly, contribute to their victimization. According to Siegel (2007), this precipitation can be either *passive* or *active*.

Passive precipitation occurs when a victim exhibits some personal characteristic that unknowingly threatens or encourages the offender. The victim is more exposed to harm because of an offender's perception of conflict during personal interaction. This conflict need not be actual; it may be the result of misperception, misunderstanding, or subconscious influence.

Consider the murder of two patent attorneys and the attempted murder of their paralegal by truck driver Joe Jackson, in Chicago, Illinois. As explained in Maxwell (2006):

> On Friday, consumed by his obsession, Jackson gunned down patent attorney Michael McKenna and two others on the 38th floor of a West Loop high-rise before he was shot and killed by police.
>
> The sad motive behind a seemingly inexplicable tragedy comes clear in Jackson's words.
>
> "I need help because I am very upset," he wrote. "I paid my hard earn money to a unmoral man. Pleased help me. He took this because of greed."
>
> The document, which begins "A portable toilet for truck driver which I am one," says Jackson first met McKenna on Feb. 18, 2002:
>
> "He wrote down every detail and ask me every last question about my project he said cause when he submit it to them patend people he needs to know everything about it…. He told me this was so kind of joke and he told me it would not work or it was already on the market. I told him absolutely not I drive a truck for almost 25 years off and on and it did not exist."
>
> Material provided by Rev. C.L. Sparks, Jackson's pastor at New Pleasant Valley International Cathedral, includes Jackson's handwritten letter documenting his interaction with McKenna as well as a rough sketch—nothing more than a doodle—of the portable truck-cab toilet.

Passive precipitation also includes those situations in which the victim and offender have no prior interaction, yet the offender perceives a conflict because of the victim's association with a particular location, organization, or group.

In such instances, the offender does not care about the specific identity of the victim. Rather, the offender sees the victim as a reasonable object, or target, for his or her retributive acts.

As described in Fletcher (1998), the murder of Dr. Barnett Slepian is a good example of how a victim's professional lifestyle choices can influence exposure to harm through passive precipitation:

> A sniper wielding a high-powered rifle from the cover of darkness shot and killed a well-known abortion doctor Friday night just days after U.S. and Canadian police warned of such an attack, citing four previous shootings against abortion doctors at this time of year in Canada and upstate New York.
>
> Barnett Slepian, 52, was killed by a single shot fired through a window as he stood in the kitchen of his home about 10 p.m. in this Buffalo suburb, police said today. Slepian, for years a defiant target of antiabortion protesters here, had just returned from a synagogue with his wife and four sons, aged seven to 15, Amherst police said.
>
> Police said the fatal shot was fired from a wooded area behind Slepian's home and crashed through a kitchen window before mortally wounding him. His wife called emergency personnel, who took Slepian to nearby Millard Fillmore Suburban Hospital, where he was pronounced dead at 11:30 p.m.
>
> The murder shocked activists on both sides of the volatile abortion issue, not only because of its cold-blooded execution, but also because it bore eerie similarities to a series of sniper attacks that have wounded four abortion doctors here in the border region over the past four years. In each of those cases, the doctors were fired on with high-powered rifles through the windows of their homes at approximately this time of year.

In this case, the doctor chose a medical practice that performed abortions. Subsequently, he was targeted by extremists who view such abortion as murder; consequently immoral; and ironically punishable by death. He did not seek out direct conflict with these extremists, nor was he working at the time of his murder; rather he was executed in his home, in front of his family.

James Kopp, a 48-year-old antiabortion activist, was ultimately convicted of second-degree murder for killing Dr. Slepian (see Figure 6-2). In 2003, he received the maximum sentence: 25 years to life. His conviction was upheld on appeal in 2006.

Active precipitation refers to those situations in which the victim directly provokes the offender. These provocations can range from insults to physical assault. Whatever the case, an actively precipitating victim is one who strikes

FIGURE 6-2
In 2003, James Kopp, a 48-year-old antiabortion activist, was convicted of second-degree murder for killing Dr. Slepian.

first and ultimately loses the most. Active precipitation is more commonly associated with incident exposure, as precipitation is most apparent in cases in which the response toward the victim is immediate. However, it can also be associated with victim lifestyle factors and choices that intentionally seek to trigger a response from a particular group or individual.

Examples of active precipitation may be found in the work of extreme activists who seek out situations in which they can put themselves between the object of their cause and danger. This would include riding an inflatable skiff in the path of a whaling ship, chaining oneself to a tree to prevent it from being cut down, or lying down in front of a tank in an act of protest. This extreme activism may be an ongoing lifestyle choice reflective of a particular kind of character, or a once-in-a-lifetime event in response to unacceptable circumstances.

Lifestyle Theory

Lifestyle theory (Hindelang, Gottfredson, and Farofalo, 1978) argues that some people are more prone to victimization because their behavior, habits, or customs expose them to a greater frequency of contact with crime and criminals. As Siegal (2007, p. 75) explains, "the basis for lifestyle theory is that crime is not a random occurrence but rather a reflection of a person's lifestyle." This thinking is consistent with the *principle of homogamy*, which suggests that individuals are more exposed to the possibility of victimization if they frequently associate with, or come into contact with, members of demographic groups containing a disproportionate number of criminals.

The author (Turvey) agrees that a victim history of interaction or involvement with criminals can increase exposure to certain kinds of harm, and therefore makes harm more likely. For the forensic victimologist, identifying that history

FIGURE 6-3

Hillside disposal scene in the murder of Genna Gamble. Note the drag trail leading up from the river bottoms and the position of the body.

and examining it are necessary parts of any assessment, as doing so may lead to viable suspects. Consider, for example, the homicide of Genna Gamble, originally presented in Turvey (2002; pp. 152–154), provided here in its near entirety. This case thoroughly highlights the need for an extensive investigation into the background of the victim and exemplifies the increased exposure that arises from interaction with offenders:

> In this case, Douglas S. Mouser was tried for the murder of 14-year-old Genna Lynn Gamble, his stepdaughter. Her nude body was found on the hillside along Dry Creek near Waterford, California, on October 14, 1995 [see Figure 6-3]. She had been strangled to death.
>
> The state theorised, based on the speculations of detectives and an FBI trained DOJ criminal profiler, Michael J. Prodan, that Doug Mouser first killed Genna Gamble at their home in Modesto and then drove her body 20–30 minutes away to dispose of it. They felt that this likely occurred during or after she had taken a shower, explaining her nudity.
>
> The criminal profilers in this case were ultimately allowed to testify on several pertinent issues, including victimology. The DOJ criminal profiler testified to the following, as an expert in crime analysis and victimology (this list is not exclusive):
>
> - He is not a forensic scientist, nor does he know what Locard's Exchange Principle is.

- Crime scene evidence and victimology are important parts of crime analysis.
- He did not review much of the available victim information in forming his opinions. He was unaware of the fact that her brother had dealt drugs out of the home, and that she had been spending time with and dating known sex offenders.
- He did not visit the crime scene in forming his opinions.
- He reviewed only 15 of the several hundred crime scene and autopsy photos in forming his opinions.
- He did not review Dr. John Thornton's crime reconstruction of the case in forming his opinions.
- Genna Gamble was a low risk victim.
- Genna Gamble was most likely killed by someone who knew her.
- Genna Gamble likely first encountered her attacker in her home.

No relevant case facts were offered to support any of the opinions provided by Special Agent Prodan. In fact, he admitted, rather surprisingly, to reading very little of the available relevant victimology in the case, blaming detectives for not providing the material to him. Ultimately, the basis for his opinions was stated simply as being derived from his education, training, and experience.

The author then testified to the following, as an expert in crime analysis and victimology, for the defence (this list is not exclusive):

- Examined all the material related to the victim provided by discovery.
- Examined all the forensic examinations and reports generated by both defence and prosecution criminalists.
- Reviewed all of the crime scene and autopsy photographs, as well as the crime scene video.
- Visited the crime scene twice—with Dr. John Thornton.

...

- Genna Gamble was at high risk of being a victim of violent crime, owing to the following:
  1. The victim was diagnosed with Oppositional Defiant Disorder. She was characterised by her therapist as exhibiting behaviour that included the sudden loss of temper, deliberate antagonising of others, refusal to obey parental instruction, and impulsivity.
  2. The victim was known to have a low self-image, which would make her particularly susceptible to the approaches of certain types of sex offenders (those that use a con that involves flattery or the suggestion of acceptance).

3. The victim often spent time at locations socialising with age inappropriate males, unsupervised by adults (Mall, Camelot & Funworks).
4. The victim was known to have socialised with a sex offender whose victim of choice included girls in Genna Gamble's age range, that were acquired at locations similar to the types that Genna Gamble frequented when unsupervised.
5. The victim was thought to have been likely to get into a car with someone that she knew from Camelot.
6. The victim's brother, Gerran Gamble, was known to have been dealing drugs, which he stored at their home.

* There are many unexplained sexual aspects to the circumstances of Genna Gamble's death, and no evidence of profit or anger motivation in the crime scene.

Genna Gamble was a teenage girl who, among other lifestyle factors, lived with a drug dealer and was involved with a convicted sex offender. One was an environmental factor; the other was an ignorant choice. Each of these factors increased her exposure to harm from the dangers of a particular world of criminal activity.

She was also seeking treatment and taking medication for Oppositional Defiant Disorder. She would ignore treatment advice, run away, and discontinue medication when angry—to intentionally create discord with her parents. Whether the actual offender was her stepfather or the sex offender she was seeing, it is hard to image that a harmful synergy between her home life, her mental health, and her self-destructive personal habits played no role in her death.

Routine Activity Theory

In foundational research describing what has come to be known as *routine activity theory* (RAT), criminologists Cohen and Felson (1979) explain (p. 604): "the convergence in time and space of three elements (motivated offenders, suitable targets, and the absence of capable guardians) appears useful for understanding crime rate trends. The lack of any of these elements is sufficient to prevent the occurrence of successful direct-contact predatory crime." In other words, RAT proposes that (Sasse, 2005; p. 547) "victimizations occur when there is a convergence in space and time of a motivated offender, a suitable target, and an absence of a capable guardian."[4]

---

[4]Variations of this theory (e.g., Rational Choice Theory and the theory of crime prevention by environmental design) have been developed by criminologist Ronald Clarke and his colleagues, who have empirically tested its salience under a wide variety of crime-related conditions (see generally Clarke and Felson, 2004; and Clarke, Newman, and Shoham, 1997).

From the forensic victimologist's perspective, a *likely offender* is classified as one who is sufficiently motivated to offend. This motivation may come from a variety of factors, both internal and external. Taken from Turvey (2011; pp. 293–294) those factors that can influence victim selection are all generally related to offender motivation:

> *Victim selection* refers to the process by which an offender chooses or targets a victim. Victim selection can be classified as *targeted* (selected in advance) or *opportunistic*.
>
> **Targeted Victim**
>
> A *targeted victim* is the primary object of the offense, resulting directly from the offender's motive for committing the crime. A targeted victim is selected in advance specifically because of who they are, what they are, what they know, or what they possess. A targeted victim may be in a relationship with the offender (spouse, parents, family member, co-worker, friend, roommate, therapist, teacher, etc.) or may have been in a past relationship with the offender. The offender may also intentionally target a victim because the victim has information, items, or valuables sought by the offender. Examples of targeted victim selection include: administrative homicides that eliminate a witness to a crime; abduction and physical torture of a victim for the purposes of eliciting information; stalking, abducting, and raping a victim as revenge or punishment for a real or perceived wrong; and killing an intimate partner.
>
> **Opportunistic Victim**
>
> An *opportunistic victim* is ancillary to the offense. In such cases, the offender is motivated by a desire to commit the offense and the victim is irrelevant. The victim is selected because of:

> - *Availability*: This refers to a particular victim's accessibility to the offender. It is related to the concept of *offender exposure*.
> - *Vulnerability:* This refers to the offender's perception of how susceptible a particular victim is to the method of approach and attack. It is also related to the concept of *offender exposure*.
> - *Location:* This refers to the victim's particular locality in relation to the offender's. It is often a function of both offender and victim activities and schedules and is also related to the concept of *offender exposure*.

> Opportunistic victims may also be chosen because they fit specific criteria preferred by the offender. These criteria may include:

> - *Fantasy criteria:* Fantasy criteria mean that victims are selected by virtue of having traits that a particular offender views as desirable

or necessary for the satisfaction of a particular fantasy. The nature of these desirable or necessary traits is revealed in the victimology and the offender signature behavior.

- *Symbolic criteria:* Symbolic criteria mean that victims are selected by virtue of sharing the characteristics of others in a relationship with the offender (spouse, parent, family member, co-worker, friend, roommate, therapist, teacher, etc.).

From this list of influences and motivations, it is evident that as a given victim increasingly satisfies a particular offender's criteria, the more likely it becomes that the offender will choose to commit an offense against the victim.

From the offenders' perspective, *suitable targets* are victims or objects that they perceive to be vulnerable (Cohen and Felson, 1979). Vulnerability, as suggested earlier, is the offenders' perception of how susceptible a particular victim is to their modus operandi.[5] An offender's perception that his M.O. is sufficient to successfully complete a particular criminal act results in an increased exposure toward the victim. Suitable targets may be a function of either incident or lifestyle exposure factors. For example, an offender may generally perceive that intoxicated victims are more easily overpowered—and therefore troll related outlets such as bars and nightclubs for targets. However, these victims must actually be intoxicated at the outset of an attack for this perception to be accurate, and the victims must also be a particular kind of drunk. In other words, not the violent kind. So it is possible under such circumstances for an offender to perceive that a particular type of victim is suitable based on general circumstances, while a particular victim in those circumstances is anything but.

Capable guardians are those individuals whose presence or proximity discourages offenders from committing crime. They can take the form of persons, including police officers, private security, family members, or ordinary citizens. They may also take institutional forms, such as proximity of a location to a building that houses capable guardians, including police stations, secured facilities, government offices, or courthouses. Whatever the case, these individuals or institutions must possess the actual ability to respond if criminal behavior is observed.[6] Simply by having capable guardians present, crime may be reduced by discouragement, as there exists a greater chance for outside intervention and ultimate apprehension.

---

[5]*Modus operandi* (M.O.) is a term used to describe any offender actions that are intended to perpetrate a crime successfully. They include actions that protect the offender's identity, ensure criminal success, and/or facilitate escape (Turvey, 2011).

[6]Young children, for example, are not generally considered to be capable guardians because they may fail to intervene against the criminal act and may not be able to get help for the victims. However, inanimate objects such as security cameras can be considered capable guardians because offenders may believe that they are being watched in real time and therefore at risk of both identification and apprehension.

The underlying argument within routine activity theory is that crime generally occurs where there is both the opportunity and ability to commit it. This is dictated by the motivation of the offender, the vulnerability of the victim, and the lack or capable guardians. As these three elements converge, victimization is more likely to occur.

NOTABLE LIFESTYLE FACTORS

Many lifestyle factors are commonly known to increase victim exposure and vulnerability to harm. However, even the most experienced investigators and examiners can fail to consider them in their individual assessments, especially when it suits their purpose. The following is a short list of factors (careers and circumstances) with some discussion of their victimological relevance (see Turvey and Freeman, 2011).

Attorneys

It is true that attorneys do have regular contact with criminals, which provides a high lifestyle exposure to violence and the possibility of retaliation. However, these crimes tend to be underreported by attorneys and the media, leading to a lack of general awareness outside the legal community. This is explained in Kelson (2006; p. 19):

> Aside from the extensively reported acts of violence in Chicago and Atlanta, numerous acts of violence have occurred against the legal profession throughout 2005. For example, in Montezuma County, Colorado, a man with a history of domestic violence burst into his ex-wife's lawyer's office and shot and killed the 62-year-old attorney. In San Fernando, California, a defendant accused of killing two fellow gang members lunged at his defense attorney during his trial, and slashed her right arm with a jail issued razor, requiring five stitches. In Middletown, Connecticut, a former state trooper shot and killed his ex-wife, her attorney, then himself. In Detroit, Michigan, a former client entered his attorney's office building, loitered for fifty minutes on the stairs, and when asked to leave, punched his attorney three times, hit him with a plant stand, and threatened to kill him. Recently, in Provo, Utah, a sex offender was charged for paying an undercover officer to kill the deputy county attorney, prior to his sentencing.
>
> These examples reflect only a sampling of reported incidents of violence against the legal profession in 2005, and represent only a small fraction of those against the legal profession throughout the 2000s. Additionally, numerous incidents of violence regularly occur against the legal profession, but go unnoticed or unreported by the media, or are never disclosed by legal professionals because they do

not take them seriously or consider reporting such events as "bad publicity."

Kelson (2006) goes on to discuss findings from one of the few studies related to violence against attorneys, conducted in 2006 by the Utah Bar Association (p. 20):

> [I]n January and February, 2006, the Utah Bar Association, conducted a survey of its 8,737 members. Although the results of this survey have not yet been published, they present surprising details of violence experienced by the legal profession. In total, 984 members, representing 11.3% of the bar, responded to the survey. 452 or 45.9% of the respondents reported that they had been threatened or physically assaulted at least once. Only 15.7% of those threatened or physically assaulted considered it serious enough to report the incidents to police authorities.
>
> Four hundred and fifty-two incidents of violence reported in the Utah Bar Association survey, 68 incidents were perpetrated against lawyers by their own clients, and 201 incidents of violence were perpetrated against lawyers by the opposing party in a case. Many of these threats and acts of violence include death threats, assaults, and vandalism to the attorney's property. For example, an opposing party in a divorce action pulled papers from the attorney's hands, threw them on the floor then pushed him backwards. Another member of the Utah Bar reported that an opposing party was arrested and subsequently charged for attempting to hire a hitman to kill him. In yet another incident, a client's husband tried to hit her attorney with golf balls while playing golf at a country club. Two hundred and eighty-four respondents identified that they had been threatened more than once. Interestingly enough, the results of the survey also reveal that at least 27 threats and physical assaults were perpetrated by opposing counsel.

The findings here demonstrate that despite an absence of media attention, violence against attorneys is actual, varied, and ongoing. From an investigative standpoint, this means that the suspect pool for crimes against attorneys is often larger than some might understand or perceive.

Law Enforcement

Law enforcement officers have regular contact with a wide variety of criminals and controlled substances. This results in a high lifestyle exposure to violence and the possibility of retaliation for simply showing up to work on any given day. These officers also suffer higher rates of divorce, depression, alcoholism, domestic violence, and suicide than the general public. Law enforcement officers are therefore exposed to dangers on the job, at home, and at every place in between from themselves, from criminal suspects, and from those they love. From an investigative standpoint, the forensic victimologist cannot be shy about investigating and eliminating any of these as contributory factors when dealing with crimes against or involving those employed by a law enforcement agency.

Prostitutes

A *prostitute* is any person who engages in sexual activity for payment. Such activity is often illegal and therefore unregulated. Streetwalkers, for instance, are defined by their willingness to get into vehicles or go into hotel rooms with men they don't know, and perform sex acts in secluded locations, away from witnesses. This increases their exposure to potential assault, rape, robbery, kidnapping, and even homicide. To say nothing of the risks related to drug abuse and venereal disease, both of which form a crime and criminal nexus with prostitution (see Chapter 16, "Sex Trafficking," for more discussion).

CASE EXAMPLE:

Double Exposure

Consider the case of Reema "Nicki" Bajaj. She is a former attorney out of DeKalb, Illinois (see Figure 6-4). She is also a convicted prostitute. As reported in Sarver (2013):

> A local attorney is suing former State's Attorney Clay Campbell and other local lawyers, claiming they circulated nude photos and unflattering news accounts about her, making it difficult for her to find new clients.
>
> The lawsuit, filed Monday in DeKalb County court by Reema "Nicki" Bajaj, 27, alleges that Campbell and local lawyer Timothy W. Johnson, who was acting as her defense attorney, showed nude photographs of her to other lawyers at the DeKalb County Courthouse in June 2011....
>
> Bajaj is seeking more than $50,000 from Campbell, Johnson, and two other unnamed lawyers in the suit for emotional distress and economic damage. Her Maple Park-based legal practice, Bajaj Law Offices, LLC, was dissolved last week, according to the lawsuit....

> Bajaj was charged with three counts of prostitution in May 2011, and hired Johnson to defend her in the case, according to the lawsuit. She pleaded guilty June 20, 2011 to a misdemeanor count of prostitution and was sentenced to court supervision, 50 hours of community service and $2,500 in fines and costs.
>
> According to the lawsuit, in the course of his work as Bajaj's attorney, Johnson received a discovery file from the DeKalb County State's Attorney's office, which included nude photographs of Bajaj. In June 2011, the lawsuit alleges Johnson showed the contents of the discovery file to another attorney in the lawyers' lounge at the DeKalb County Courthouse.

The details made public by Ms. Bajaj's lawsuit reveal what can be described as double exposure to victimization. Not only did her work as an attorney expose her to the criminal element, but her side work as a prostitute made her vulnerable to all manner of violent crime as well as to threats of extortion.

CASE EXAMPLE: *CONTINUED*

FIGURE 6-4
Reema "Nicki" Bajaj was an attorney who also confessed to engaging in prostitution. Both of these professions carry with them inherent dangers that effectively doubled her lifestyle exposure.

Drug Dealers

Drug dealing is among the most violent and dangerous criminal occupations that exists, no matter the community or the culture. It commonly involves the presence of drugs, cash, and firearms—each of which attracts crime and may be used in the perpetuation of violence of just about every kind. It is, as with prostitution, a nexus of crime and criminals (see Figure 6-5).

Alcoholics and Drug Addicts

Drug addiction involves a steady progression of drug use, increased dosages, and decreased dosage intervals. Each drug affects the addict differently, depending on the amount taken, the person's personal chemistry, and the other drugs in his or her system. The one universal consequence of drug use is the inability to think rationally.

Drug addiction can also be associated with progressively violent and criminal drug-seeking behavior. This behavior is characterized by an intense focus on supporting a drug habit regardless of the cost or consequences. Drug addicts

FIGURE 6-5

Typical drug investigation task force seizures commonly include evidence that perfectly characterizes the dangers of the drug-dealing world: drugs, cash, and weapons. Pictured are the fruits of a State Police/New Haven Initiative Task Force Investigation carried out in 2007, including $102,040 in cash; 588 pounds of marijuana (estimated value of $1.8 million); 1.7 grams of cocaine; 13.8 grams of mushrooms; various items of drug paraphernalia; 3 handguns and 1 shotgun; and assorted vehicles (DPS, 2007).

engaged in drug-seeking behavior exist on a continuum that includes falsifying the symptoms of illness to get prescription medications, to stealing medication from neighbors under a false pretext, to stealing items of value for cash to buy drugs, to engaging in prostitution to support a drug habit, to the robbery of a pharmacy. Whatever they believe will get them their drug is what they do. Period. This essentially completes the nexus of crime and criminals associated with drugs and prostitution.

Alcoholism is a particular kind of drug addiction that is not necessarily illegal, although it can result in illegal activity because of the lack of inhibition and absence of rational thought that necessarily result. Additionally, alcoholics may be very difficult to identify if they develop high-functioning coping, rationalization, and concealment skills. This combines to increase their vulnerability to harm from themselves and others with respect to a persistent lack of judgement, memory, and dexterity.

Additionally, consider this list of general traits that can influence a victim lifestyle exposure. This list is not meant to be all-inclusive but rather to provide the forensic victimologist with a starting point (taken from Turvey and Freeman, 2011):

- *Aggressiveness:* People who are more aggressive and confrontational in their behavior are more likely to evoke aggressive behavior in others (see Singer, 1981).
- *Impulsivity:* Impulsive behavior is executed without planning or forethought. As a consequence, impulsive individuals are generally unprepared to meet the challenges that they face, and they fail to consider the actual consequences of their actions.
- *Self-destructive behavior:* Some individuals engage in behavior that routinely puts them in harm's way. Such behaviors exist on a continuum from reckless to overtly self-destructive. The actions can include driving too fast, binge drinking or eating, overmedicating, and even spending beyond one's means.
- *Passivity:* Passive individuals are those who allow or accept the actions and choices of others without question or defiance. This passivity can persist even when they are put in situations that expose them to harm or loss. It is especially problematic if they are known to be passive because others might see them as excellent targets.
- *Low self-esteem:* Those with low self-esteem are more apt to be depressed, to engage in self-destructive behaviors, and to be taken advantage of or otherwise victimized. Low self-esteem can create a strong desire to seek and maintain the approval of others—a tendency that is ripe for abuse by those with bad intentions. Low self-esteem can also foster the belief that one deserves to be victimized, making it difficult to escape a cycle of abuse.
- *Aberrant sexual behavior:* Sexual promiscuity can lead to increased exposure to sexually transmitted disease and the jealousy of possessive lovers. Additionally, extreme sexual behavior can actually be physically dangerous, depending on the types of acts involved (e.g., breath play or choking, extreme bondage, chemical enhancements, and illegal drug use).

It must be understood that any combination of these elements can also have a synergistic effect. In other words, two or more of these factors or similar circumstances, when combined, are likely to enhance the frequency and effects of the others. For example, chronic drug abuse can contribute to and enhance aggressiveness and impulsivity, and a mental disorder can lead to and exacerbate abusive relationships. These circumstances do not typically occur in a vacuum, and those afflicted are rarely able to self-correct.

ASSESSING LIFESTYLE EXPOSURE

The interpretation of a particular victim's lifestyle exposure is not just a function of compiling abstract group statistics for application to non-existent victim stereotypes, although this is an unfortunate victimological tradition. Much more is required to achieve a concrete and actual understanding.

To accurately determine a specific victim's lifestyle exposure, one needs to assess his or her harm in the context of his or her specific lifestyle and personality traits. For investigative purposes, lifestyle factors must be questioned as to how, specifically, they contributed to harm. By utilizing the concept of victim *risk*, one may infer a conclusion based on statistical analyses of the potential to be harmed as being part of a demographic group. These conclusions ignore the specific characteristics of victims and how they uniquely interacted with offenders given their situation. For example, statistics indicate that college students are at higher risk of victimization (Fisher et al., 1998). Therefore, one could assume the mere situation of being a college student increases exposure to harm. This is not necessarily correct; not all college students are identical. Some expose themselves to more harm than others through their drug and alcohol use, routine, sexual activity and a number of other factors. Making conclusions about a victim's level of harm based on statistical analyses or probability estimates of risk do not accurately reflect how a specific victim's lifestyle contributed to his or her harm, nor does it necessarily provide investigative relevance.

By contrast, the concept of *victim exposure* examines how a lifestyle factor specifically increased a victim's contact with harm. Taking Fisher's et al. (1998) example again, an investigator can discover that the victim was a college student and acknowledge that college students are at an increased exposure to harm; however, the specific interaction of *this* college student with his or her environment will dictate the *actual* level of potential for harm. One particular student who does not consume alcohol or drugs, lives at home with her parents, does not engage in high-risk sexual activity, and takes self-defense classes will represent a very different level of exposure than the student who does consume alcohol and drugs, lives in a bad part of town, engages in high-risk sexual practices, and does not take self-defense classes. Certain lifestyle traits such as interacting with potential offenders, drug use, and a high frequency of casual sex with strangers may also increase a victim's exposure to harm. Only by looking at the specific interactions of the variables can one sufficiently argue that a victim was exposed to harm.

It should also be noted that, generally speaking, not all lifestyle factors can be said to have the potential to increase harm to a victim. It cannot be reasonably argued that the habit of collecting baseball cards played a significant role in the sexual assault of a male at a nightclub. Nor can it be easily argued that a victim's depression solely increased her exposure to gang-related homicide. Thus, to argue that a lifestyle factor influenced victim-offender dynamics, it needs to be both potentially harmful, in the sense that its presence could be argued to influence opportunity for harm to occur, and also relevant, within the context of who the particular victim was and the criminal behavior that occurred.

The Victim as a Real Person

Victimology is all about getting to know the victim as a real person. An important facet is realizing that everyone leads multiple lives. At the very least, there is a professional or public life that is shown to all. Then there is the private life that is shared only with close friends and family. There is also a sexual life—a life that each person lives as a function of his or her sexual relationships and related preferences. In all of a person's lives, there will be variations and contradictions. Some will be narrow and focused; others will be broad and scattered. Some will be safe; others will be risky. Some will be open; others will be closed. Unless we know who a victim is, or was, and how the person lived and connected with other people, we cannot say that we truly know the context of the victim's demise or the events leading up to it. And we will most certainly fail to see where the person was exposed to harm.

Unfortunately, the culture within which an investigator or forensic victimologist operates may openly encourage the marginalization, vilification, or deification of a given victim population. *Deification* involves idealizing victims, who are perhaps young schoolchildren, missing adolescents, or those who arrive pre-deified by the press and public opinion. Because of the political or public culture of a certain area or region, certain victim populations tend to be more politically or publicly sympathetic. This view facilitates rationalizations about time expended on the deified case while other investigations suffer, and it does not allow for an unbiased victimology by virtue of depriving the crime and the investigation of true victim context. Deification has the capacity to accomplish the following:

- Cause an incomplete victimology
- Remove good suspects from the suspect pool
- Provide coverage for the false reporter
- Provide coverage for suspects who are family or household members

---

CASE EXAMPLE:

Victim Deification

This case involves the sexual homicide of a blondish white female child victim, the desire to get fast justice for a high-profile crime with horrific and sensational aspects, police refusal to investigate or accept the home as a source of bad things, and the concealment of important victimological information by a zealous prosecutor.

Cynthia Allinger, 9, was last seen on Thursday afternoon, July 4, 1996, near her family's apartment (see Figure 6-6). She was reportedly going to visit some friends who lived nearby. She did not arrive. According to police reports, she was not reported missing to the Pierce County Sheriff's Department until 10:53 p.m. by her mother, Rhonda Plank.

An extensive search began the next day, and police quickly focused their investigation on 30-year-old Guy Rasmussen, a neighborhood man with a past who had been friendly with Cynthia. They put him under surveillance almost immediately to track his movements.

Continued

CASE EXAMPLE: *CONTINUED*

PIERCE COUNTY SHERIFF'S DEPARTMENT
930 Tacoma Avenue South
Tacoma, Washington 98402

SPECIAL BULLETIN

CASE NO. 96-1861378	DATE July 9, 1996	REV. NO.

$5,000.00   REWARD

IS BEING OFFERED FOR INFORMATION LEADING TO THE ARREST AND CONVICTION OF THE PERSON(S) RESPONSIBLE FOR THE ABDUCTION OF CYNTHIA ALLINGER

Cynthia Allinger was last seen on the afternoon of the 4th of July near her home in Lakewood. The neighborhood where she was last seen is known as McChord Gate and is located west of Bridgeport Way S.W. and east of I-5.

Cynthia was last seen wearing the dress shown in the photo to the left. The dress has a wide white lace collar and a pink and green floral design.

Cynthia is 9 years old and is 4' tall. She weighs 50 pounds. She has brown eyes and light brown hair.

If you have *any* information about this case, you are asked to call
THE PIERCE COUNTY SHERIFF'S DEPARTMENT
AT (206) 593-4721
OR
CRIMESTOPPERS
AT (206) 591-5959
All CRIMESTOPPERS calls are confidential

FIGURE 6-6
Nine-year-old Cynthia Allinger was last seen on Thursday afternoon, July 4, 1996, near her family's apartment. Law enforcement immediately distributed this missing person poster. Her body was discovered at an outdoor crime scene on July 17, 1996, at 8:30 p.m., by Detective Robert Floberg of the Pierce County Sheriff's Department.

CASE EXAMPLE: *CONTINUED*

By July 7, search efforts had been exhaustive but fruitless. As Reid and Working (1996) describe:

> As the FBI [Federal Bureau of Investigation] joined the search for a missing Lakewood girl, the Pierce County Sheriff's Department said Saturday it assumes that Cindy Allinger was abducted.
>
> Deputies late Saturday were talking with "a person of interest" in the case.
>
> Because a widespread search has turned up no sign of the 9-year-old, officials doubt she simply got lost when she disappeared Thursday evening, said sheriff's Capt. Nik Dunbar.
>
> "We are assuming she is no longer missing," Dunbar said. "If that were the case, she would've been found. We are assuming there is an abduction that has taken place."
>
> The FBI is helping to draw up a psychological profile of anyone who would commit such a crime, Dunbar said. And the FBI has broad resources to draw on in kidnapping cases....
>
> Deputies late Saturday were interviewing a 30-year-old former neighbor whom they described as a "person of interest" in the case. They found him at a music festival south of Olympia and were bringing him back to Pierce County.
>
> The man was not under arrest.
>
> He had moved out of the girl's neighborhood two weeks ago, Dunbar said.
>
> Cindy had been told to stay away from the man, a drummer, though she might have visited anyway, neighbors have said....
>
> Nearly 70 volunteers fanned out in neighborhoods around her house for a second day Saturday, handing out fliers and looking for signs of her. A Pierce County Explorer Search and Rescue unit went door to door, peering behind fences and under bushes....
>
> Deputies brought in bloodhounds and German shepherds to search for Cindy. German shepherds, often used for sniffing out drugs,

> are trained to smell odors hanging in the air, while bloodhounds are used for tracking after whiffing an article of a person's clothing.
>
> "We're going back to some of the areas that the dogs worked but people were not able to get to because of the brush," Dunbar said. "We're cutting down the brush."
>
> Joe Brentin, an Explorer Scout team leader, led a group through the narrow streets among the apartment buildings that crowd the area. He said his group was not finding much.

On July 14, a week later, authorities made another sweep of the same areas with more dogs and search teams, and still nothing (Dunham and Working, 1996).

Nearly two weeks after extensive search efforts failed to yield any clues in her disappearance, with no arrests having been made, Cynthia's body was finally discovered. As described in Turvey (1998):

> The body of Cynthia Allinger was discovered at an outdoor crime scene on July 17th, 1996 at 8:30pm, by Detective Robert Floberg of the Pierce County Sheriff's Department, in an area of foliage approximately 150 feet behind the unoccupied residence at 4905 SW 123rd Street in Lakewood, WA. It had been placed in a piece of recently discarded carpeting (according to a report by Steven Verhey), beneath a heavy metal water tank, and covered by several layers of older discarded carpeting. This location is approximately 800 yards from her residence, and less than 50 yards from the Bridgeport Way North Interstate 5 onramp.

That her body was found in an area that had been repeatedly searched on previous occasions is interesting, but there's more. The discovery of her body involves the supernatural, apparently. As it turns out, a psychic had written a lengthy letter to a Detective Floberg, detailing her role as a prophet for god, stating the precise location where Cynthia's body could be found. The detective, in an unusual breach of investigative protocol, went out alone on the night of July 17 and found her body. Despite orders and forensic training, he moved the body around quite a bit before anyone else could arrive to document

Continued

CASE EXAMPLE: *CONTINUED*

the scene the next morning. And he didn't make that last fact known until he testified during the trial of Guy Rasmussen, who was subsequently arrested and charged with the crime. As Gillie (1999a) describes:

> No one is sure of exactly where Allinger's body was found because Pierce County detective Robert Floberg never wrote a report noting he moved the body several feet when he discovered it the night of July 17, 1996.
>
> And Floberg is unsure even today how far or in what direction he moved the body before he called in forensic investigators.
>
> The time and place of Allinger's death is critical to the prosecution's case. Prosecutors contend Rasmussen, a former rock band musician, raped and killed Allinger on July 4, 1996. Rasmussen then hid the body under a pile of carpeting near an abandoned Lakewood house, they contend. Defense attorneys contend Allinger died several days later. They say Rasmussen couldn't have murdered her because he was under police surveillance or out of town during the time defense experts say the young girl died.
>
> Defense attorneys Fred Leatherman and Linda Sullivan said they didn't learn that Floberg had moved the body until he testified last month in Rasmussen's murder trial. Deputy prosecutor Barbara Corey-Boulet, however, said the detective disclosed the information at a hearing in January 1998.
>
> Floberg testified last month that, following up on a letter from a psychic, he went to the site late on July 17, smelled the odor of decaying flesh and found Allinger's body covered with carpeting.
>
> Floberg told attorneys recently that he moved the body several feet and might have rotated the pile of carpeting in another direction in the process of discovering the body.

Curiously, the psychic who wrote the letter to Detective Floberg was also the spiritual guide of Gilbert Bauschman—the father of David Bauschman. David Bauschman was Rhonda Plank's live-in boyfriend at the time. Rhonda Plank, of course, was Cynthia Allinger's mother.

To recap—a police detective (not the lead investigator) received a "tip" from a psychic friend of the victim's family. The letter stated precisely where Cynthia's body could be found. The detective went out alone (and against orders) to find it, moved everything around, and didn't tell anybody until he had to on the stand.

If one believes in psychics, then one would not think to investigate this version of events or potential connections back to family or household members. If one does not believe in psychics, however, then one must consider that only the person(s) who killed Cynthia, or those connected to them, would know where to find her body. However, let's be perfectly clear: as explained thoroughly in Turvey (2011), belief in psychic phenomena has no basis in reality, and the vast majority of psychics are criminal frauds.[7]

After Cynthia's body was found, Guy Rasmussen was again questioned about his possible involvement in her death and asked to give a sample of his DNA, which he did. Going on the assumption that the person responsible must be a stranger, Rasmussen was a perfect suspect because of his history and because he apparently fit the FBI's profile. To the authors' knowledge, having carefully examined the investigative record in this case, no effort was made to investigate or eliminate family or household members as suspects, however. "Stranger crime" was the operational assumption from the very beginning. As Albert (1996) describes:

> [Thirty]-year-old [Guy Rasmussen] had been considered a "person of interest" in the case since shortly after the girl's disappearance July 4.
>
> Friday, Pierce County sheriff's detectives received the DNA evidence they had been waiting for since Cindy's body was found July 17.
>
> The evidence matched a blood sample provided by the man, said Curt Benson, sheriff's spokesman.
>
> Friday evening, detectives armed with an arrest warrant took the man into custody at the Java Jump, an all-ages nightspot in Fife where he had been assisting a band.
>
> The man is expected to be arraigned Monday on charges of aggravated first-degree

CASE EXAMPLE: *CONTINUED*

murder, kidnapping in the first degree and rape of a child in the first degree....

Cindy, a slender 4-foot-tall girl who wore a floral-pattern dress, was last seen July 4 when she left her family's home in the Garden Court Apartments near McChord Air Force Base to play outside.

In the following days, hundreds of searchers checked lakes and woods and went door to door, looking for the child. The Federal Bureau of Investigation offered a $5,000 reward and drew a psychological profile.

But Cindy's body was found July 17 in a wooded area near Bridgeport Way Southwest and Interstate 5. The area is just three blocks northeast of Clover Creek, where searchers had concentrated their efforts.

Investigators became interested in the 30-year-old man because witnesses had seen him with the girl the day she vanished. He lived just down the street from her family.

At that time, the man insisted he had nothing to do with the girl's disappearance and was not in the neighborhood July 4.

He claimed detectives were focusing on him only because of his criminal record.

"It's my past coming up to haunt me," the man said last summer.

As a teenager, he was convicted in 1982 in Pierce County of sexual assault against a 16-year-old girl and served five years in prison. In 1990, he served five months after he pleaded guilty to assaulting a 10-year-old Olympia girl.

An important fact to note at this point is that if Guy Rasmussen had killed Cynthia, he would have had to dump her body within a day of her disappearance. If he dumped it anytime after that, the authorities would have seen him do it—because they were already watching him by then. If the evidence demonstrated that her body was dumped after he was put under surveillance, then that would effectively destroy the prosecution's theory of the case.

When the trial started, things went from strange to stranger. The lead prosecutor, Barbara Corey-Boulet, seemed to be under enormous pressure to get a conviction.

She was openly harassing defense experts, jailed a child witness (an 11-year-old honor student) to frighten her into giving prosecution-friendly testimony (Gillie, 1998a), withheld discovery material, and may have been complicit in evidence tampering. All the while, she and her husband Francis were under investigation for charges stemming from theft and fraud at his former place of work.

Eleven-year old Cierra Hull had originally told investigators that she saw Cynthia with Guy Rasmussen on the day that she disappeared. Later, she and her family wanted nothing to do with the case. However, this was a witness that the prosecution desperately needed. Her ordeal is described in Hucks (2003):

> Two Pierce County deputy prosecutors say they had no choice in 1998 but to jail an 11-year-old girl as a witness in a murder trial, and Monday asked a judge to dismiss the girl's family lawsuit against them. Prosecutors Barbara Corey-Boulet and Lisa Wagner said Cierra Hull was vital to the case against child rapist and murderer Guy Rasmussen, but hadn't shown up for a required interview.
>
> Also, they said, her grandmother planned to move her out of state and her family had told police they no longer wanted her involved in the trial....
>
> But attorney Brian Ladenburg, representing Hull's family, said they had been cooperative, and detectives knew by the time they arrested the girl that she simply hadn't had transportation to the missed interview....
>
> On May 28, 1998, after Hull didn't show up for a court-ordered pretrial interview with defense lawyers, Corey-Boulet and Wagner— with the blessing of the prosecutor—asked a judge to detain her as a material witness.
>
> Lawyers for the county and the prosecutors say they had hoped the girl would be held for no more than 12 to 18 hours.
>
> Detectives arrested Hull at Edison Elementary School the next day, just before she was to be named "student of the month."
>
> But Superior Court Judge Karen Strombom wasn't available that Friday afternoon, so Hull spent the weekend at Remann Hall juvenile jail.

Continued

CASE EXAMPLE: *CONTINUED*

"Instead of receiving her student-of-the-month award and being lauded by her peers," Ladenburg said Monday, "she's arrested, thrown in a sheriff's car, taken to Remann Hall for the weekend and then mocked by her peers when she gets out. And she did nothing wrong."

While locked up, Hull was afraid, her lawsuit contends. An older girl spit on her in a fight and she wasn't able to talk to her grandmother as often as she wanted, her lawyer said.

And on that Monday, prosecutors let her go and scheduled the interview for later, he said.

Attorneys for the state and county counter that Hull watched television with the guards and received daily visits from her mother.

Outside the courtroom Monday, attorneys bickered over whether the girl had been unfairly treated. "She came into court in chains," Ladenburg said.

"That's standard procedure" for handling material witnesses, county attorney Dan Hamilton said, noting they feared Hull would flee. "For criminals," Ladenburg shot back.

In an unfortunate decision Hull's lawsuit was dismissed. Her arrest, detention, and placement in jail were determined to be lawful acts by the civil court. Other misconduct and evidence tampering issues in the Rasmussen case are described in Gillie (1998b):

The conduct of prosecutors has been so unethical in the case of a man accused of killing a 9-year-old Lakewood girl that the case should be dismissed, a Seattle defense lawyer claims. In a motion filed in Pierce County Superior Court, Fred Leatherman Jr. contends deputy prosecutors Barbara Corey-Boulet and Lisa Wagner "have intimidated defense witnesses, abused the material witness warrant procedure, hampered the defense investigation, hidden exculpatory evidence, (and) demonized the defendant."…

The Seattle attorney, known for his ardent opposition to the death penalty, listed several specific complaints about the deputy prosecutors' conduct:

The two attorneys used material witness warrants to harass defense witnesses

who could provide an alibi for Rasmussen. Leatherman alleges that the prosecutors had those two witness, one an 11-year-old girl, the other an Idaho construction worker, arrested on suspicion of not cooperating with prosecutors.

But the two witnesses would have willingly talked to investigators if they had only asked, Leatherman said. The girl, who committed no crime, was held over a weekend at Pierce County's juvenile jail at Remann Hall. The man was arrested in Idaho while on a construction job, returned to Pierce County and held in jail for a week, Leatherman claims.

Wagner said the 11-year-old was arrested only after she failed to show up for a court-ordered deposition, and prosecutors had to track the construction worker through several states before finding him.

Leatherman contends the prosecution failed to provide the defense with complete surveillance logs kept by law enforcement officers who followed Rasmussen.

The prosecutors countered they had turned over all existing logs to the defense. Leatherman said the logs are important because they will show Rasmussen couldn't have dumped Allinger's body in a field where she was found.

Wagner posted a caricature of Rasmussen in her office that showed him with horns drawn on his head. Such a caricature prejudiced defense witnesses called to her office, Leatherman claims. Wagner acknowledged she briefly displayed such a picture in her office.

"When I added the horns to the defendant's mug shot, I was exercising my First Amendment right of free expression," she said. She added that no defense witnesses saw the picture.

Leatherman wants the judge to remove Corey-Boulet from the case because she and her husband have been named as defendants in a civil lawsuit over her husband's management of funds at a medical clinic he managed.…

Leatherman contends that if Barbara Corey-Boulet is charged in the clinic investigation, she will have to leave the Rasmussen case, delaying the trial.

CASE EXAMPLE: *CONTINUED*

Furthermore, defense attorneys argued that key evidence linking Rasmussen to the victim's death was likely planted, as described in Gillie (1999b):

> Leatherman also claimed that detectives, desperate to pin charges on Rasmussen, planted DNA evidence on a pair of cutoff shorts and a T-shirt that police seized. That evidence showed blood that matched Allinger's on both pieces of clothing.
>
> Both a specimen of Allinger's spleen and the clothing were stored in a sheriff's property room where detectives could inspect the items unobserved, he said.
>
> He suggested DNA experts in California, who tested the DNA found on the clothing spots, noted a strong odor of chemicals when they opened the bags containing the clothing. Leatherman said that chemical odor came from the preservative used to treat the girl's spleen for storage.

Normally, the author (Turvey) is skeptical of any claims that evidence has been planted. However, in this case, the author finds the theory plausible, given the nature of the evidence, the missing chain of custody for the items involved, and the record of misconduct in the Pierce County prosecutor's office.

At the trial, forensic entomologist Neil Haskell testified that "based on the age and kind of insects present in Allinger's body, she died no earlier than July 7 and as late as July 10, 1996" (Gillie, 1999a). Further still, plant physiologist Dr. Stephen Verhey testified that the body could not have been at the disposal site for more than six days (Gillie, 1999a).

Based on the work of these forensic scientists and others, one of the authors (Turvey) provided a report to the defense that determined the dumpsite was not the location where the victim was killed— as the prosecution contended (Turvey, 1998):

> The physical evidence does not suggest that the location where her body was found is the Primary crime scene, which is a term used to describe a location where an offender engaged in the majority of their attack/assault upon a victim. The reasons for this are as follows:
>
> The entomological evidence provided by Dr. Haskell suggests that the victim's dead body had been in an indoor crime scene at some point.
>
> The entomological evidence provided by Dr. Haskell suggests that death may have occurred between July 7 and July 9, several days after the victim's disappearance.
>
> The entomological evidence provided by Dr. Haskell suggests that the victim's deceased body may have been stored in an intermediate crime scene (a crime scene between the primary scene and the disposal site, where there may be evidence transfer). This location, it is suggested, was more thoroughly protected from insect colonization than the disposal site.
>
> Dr. Vale has opined that the teeth missing from the victim's mouth were dislodged as the result of physical blows. At least two teeth have not yet been accounted for in this investigation. If the tooth associated with the line of fracture was knocked out at the time of that attack, it is reasonable to conclude that this tooth would be found at the primary crime scene. To this examiner's knowledge, this tooth has not been recovered from the location where the victim's body was discovered.
>
> The nature and extent of the behavior that the offender engaged in with the victim, especially on a day where many people would be outside, would have drawn a great deal of attention if done out in the open.

As an adjunct to performing a crime scene analysis, and out of an abundance of suspicion regarding the true context of the murder, the author (Turvey) prepared a written memo requesting victim history, including any reports that might have been prepared by Child Protective Services (CPS). The known victimology made such a request mandatory. The prosecutors met the request with open hostility and denied that CPS reports were relevant to the homicide. In doing so, the prosecutors inadvertently acknowledged that CPS reports existed with respect to the victim and her family in this case.

Continued

CASE EXAMPLE: *CONTINUED*

At the end of the trial, the relationship between David Bauschman and Rhonda Plank unraveled. Bauschman landed in Pierce County Jail on a first-degree assault charge that he beat Plank on January 21, 1999. According to Rhonda Plank, this was not the first time Bauschman had choked and beaten her. Subsequently, Bauschman's lawyer sent a letter to the prosecutors in the Rasmussen case with the revelation that Rhonda Plank killed her own daughter. Bauschman initially told investigators with the prosecutor's office that Plank told him she struck Allinger in the face with a 14-inch-long plywood paddle, which the mother used to discipline her three daughters. Mr. Bauschman further claimed Plank said she stuffed something in the girl's mouth to keep her from crying out. This version of events is consistent with the known facts of the case. It would also explain the psychic's letter. Gillie (1999c) details these revelations:

> The twist involved an 11th-hour allegation—since recanted—that the murder victim, 9-year-old Cynthia Allinger, died at her mother's hand, not Rasmussen's.
>
> The contention came to prosecutors' attention Thursday. A lawyer for the boyfriend of Allinger's mother, Rhonda Plank, sent a letter saying the boyfriend claimed Plank killed the girl. The boyfriend, David Bauschman, is in Pierce County Jail on a first-degree assault charge that he beat [and choked] Plank on Jan. 21.
>
> Prosecutors sent a letter to defense attorneys about the allegations Friday.
>
> Tuesday afternoon, Rasmussen's lead defense counsel asked Pierce County Superior Court Judge Karen Strombom, who has presided over the nearly six-month-long trial, to delay the trial for three weeks while the defense investigates the claims.
>
> But Strombom denied defense attorney Fred Leatherman's motion, saying the allegations weren't relevant in the penalty phase of the trial. Strombom also denied a motion to allow defense lawyers to tell the jury Plank had failed two lie detector tests.
>
> The jury convicted Rasmussen on Jan. 28 of aggravated first-degree murder, kidnapping

and rape and now is charged with deciding how he will be punished: by life imprisonment or by death. Before final arguments began in the penalty phase Tuesday, Leatherman left the courtroom to appeal Strombom's rulings to the Washington State Supreme Court.

> Pierce County deputy prosecutor Lisa Wagner argued Tuesday that Bauschman's allegations had been proved baseless. She said he failed a lie detector test Thursday and the next day admitted he had lied about Allinger's death because he was upset about what Plank was saying about him in the community and in court.
>
> Bauschman initially told investigators with the prosecutor's office that Plank told him she struck Allinger in the face with a 14-inch-long plywood paddle which the mother used to discipline her three daughters. Bauschman claimed Plank said she stuffed cloth in the girl's mouth to keep her from crying out.
>
> Allinger's body was found beneath carpeting near her Lakewood home two weeks after she disappeared July 4, 1996. An autopsy showed she had a broken jaw and a pair of underwear stuffed down her throat. That same autopsy showed vaginal damage but no sperm on her body. Prosecutor Wagner said Plank had taken lie detector tests about the girl's killing, but Wagner contended the test results were invalid.

Not surprisingly, given the tone of previous rulings, the judge in this case agreed with the prosecution. She found that the allegations weren't relevant in the penalty phase of the trial. As Mr. Rasmussen had already been found guilty, this was now a matter to be brought forward in the appeals process—which remain ongoing.

---

[7]The question of psychics and their utility was actually answered four decades ago. In 1979, the Los Angeles Police Department's Behavioral Science Services (BSS; currently responsible for planning, developing, implementing, and administering the department's psychological services program) published a study of the efficacy of using psychics in a police investigation. The results of this study found that psychics often gave unverifiable insights and did no better than chance (or worse) when they offered specific details. The BSS ultimately concluded that psychics were not useful in aiding investigations (Reiser et al., 1979).

Vilification involves viewing or casting certain victim populations as worthless or disposable by their very nature. This view presumes that it is okay, or not as bad, to commit crimes against people of certain lifestyles, races, religions, or creeds. This can include people of a particular ethnic origin, people of a certain social class, prostitutes, drug dealers, drug addicts, and runaways. Ultimately, this thinking tends to be guided by an investigator's subjective sense of personal morality—or that of a like-minded community. Ultimately, it facilitates investigative apathy.

Examples of vilified groups, or groups toward which there is no lack of apathy, commonly include the following:

- The homeless/mentally ill
- Homosexuals
- Minority populations within a particular region, such as immigrants and Native Americans
- Prostitutes
- Drug dealers
- Drug addicts
- Teen runaways who become prostitutes or drug addicts
- Individuals of particular religious beliefs

These groups are marginalized either because of prejudice, because of the fact that they are committing crimes, or because they are viewed as having contributed to their demise in some fashion. An extreme example of this level of investigative apathy, or perhaps outright hostility, can be found in Geberth (1996, p. 850), where he defines the term *misdemeanor murders*:

> A "Geberthism" which suggests that when two "shit-birds" (less than productive citizens) kill each other in some sort of drug-related homicide that the crime might actually be considered less than a felony offense. The author obviously uses the term in a facetious manner.

While this is certainly inappropriate humor as Mr. Geberth admits, Mr. Geberth has put the term in the glossary of a professional textbook. This would suggest that it is a term that he sanctions as appropriate for use by professionals. Ironically, this type of thinking is very much in line with the vilification of victims by some serial murderers.

Detectives and investigators who hold negative views toward certain victim populations may not feel the need to investigate the crimes committed against them thoroughly, if at all. The irony being that, as we've discussed, is some of the most skillful serial offenders exploit these attitudes, which can be prevalent in law enforcement and the media alike. They choose their next victim, in part, based on whether or not the community perceives that person as disposable. And they thrive in environments where such attitudes persist.

The reality is that victims of crime are human beings. They are not the fictional constructs of our prejudices and biases born of our own morality, true crime novels, or films. As we have always secretly feared and must be willing to admit, they are not unlike our own daughters, sons, mothers, fathers, sisters, brothers, wives, husbands, or friends. They are precious, and they are flawed. They are no more or less deserving of our attention because of their lifestyle choices or situations. If we idealize them, or vilify them, we will not learn who they were. We will not have the context for a complete profile and will not be able to provide investigative direction based on victim–victim and victim–offender connections. Subsequently, if we proceed with the mindset that any victims are more or less deserving of our attention, then we do so at the risk of failing to serve justice. And we will most certainly speed ourselves away from the precious flaws in our own humanity.

Categorizing Victim Lifestyle Exposure

Many victimologists have developed typologies that attempt to categorize the characteristics and interactions of the victim with the offender (Barnes and Teeters, 1943; Fattah, 1976; Karmen, 1980; Lamborn, 1968; Mendelsohn, 1963; Schafer, 1968, Sheley, 1979; Silverman, 1974; von Hentig, 1948). This categorization is useful because victim exposure classification provides for more accurate and consistent reporting (and discussion) of victim traits.

The main purpose of classifying victim lifestyle exposure is to arrive at an understanding of the victims' lifestyle and conditions, in order that exposure may be fully understood and described to others. The authors have developed an objective method of classifying the lifestyle exposure level of victims. The categories of exposure used in the method have been adapted from material originally presented in Turvey and Petherick (2009) and Turvey and Freeman (2011). They have also been influenced by similar classifications from Hazel-wood (1995). They include low, medium, high, and extreme lifestyle exposure.

With respect to lifestyle exposure, *extreme-exposure victims* are those who are exposed to the possibility of suffering harm or loss every day (e.g., 7 days a week). The following examples illustrate extreme-exposure victims:

- A prostitute who engages in sexual activity for money on a daily basis
- An alcoholic who is constantly intoxicated
- A prisoner who lives in a confined environment with constant exposure to criminals
- A child who lives in a home where he or she is constantly subjected to physical or sexual abuse

High-exposure victims are those who are exposed to the possibility of suffering harm or loss more often than not (e.g., 4–6 days a week). These victims are frequently exposed to harmful elements; however, the exposure is not constant. For example, a child who lives in an abusive and neglectful environment during the week with his mother but lives in a healthy environment with his father on weekends. This child is exposed to harm or loss during the week but is removed from the harmful environment on the weekend.

Medium-exposure victims are those who are exposed to the possibility of suffering harm or loss less often than not (e.g., 1–3 days a week). An example is a college student who engages in excessive drinking to the point of intoxication every weekend.

Low-exposure victims are those who are rarely exposed to the possibility of suffering harm or loss (e.g., less than once a week). These victims rarely engage in behaviors, or put themselves in positions, that increase their exposure or vulnerability to experiencing harm or loss.

Because lifestyle exposure refers to the *frequency* of exposure, the preceding categories of victim exposure can be defined by time frames. The examiner must acknowledge that not every victim trait or characteristic can be perfectly slotted into one of the preceding categories. For example, a child who accesses the Internet unsupervised on a daily basis is at an increased risk of communicating with online predators, but daily, unsupervised use of the Internet or chat rooms will not necessarily elevate the child's lifestyle exposure to extreme. These categories are merely a guideline to establishing the victim's lifestyle exposure and must be evaluated in the context of the specific victim's lifestyle, personal traits, and choices.

SUMMARY

Victim exposure is the amount of contact or vulnerability to harmful elements experienced by the victim. Overall victim exposure is determined by examining and considering the separate constructs of *lifestyle exposure* and situational exposure. This chapter focuses on *lifestyle exposure*, which is related to the frequency of potentially harmful elements experienced by the victim and resulting from the victim's usual environment and personal traits, as well as past choices.

Lifestyle factors can influence the overall possibility of individual harm in three ways: by increasing the victim's proximity to, and interactions with, offenders or those predisposed toward criminality; by fomenting conditions that create a perceived conflict with an offender; and by enhancing an offender's perception of victim vulnerability. The following criminology theories have proven to be most useful for identifying and understanding when a victim's lifestyle facilitates victimization: victim precipitation, lifestyle theory, and routine activity theory.

Many lifestyle factors are commonly known to increase victim exposure and vulnerability to harm. The following are examples of notable lifestyle factors: attorneys, law enforcement officers, prostitutes, drug dealers, alcoholics, and drug addicts. A number of general traits can also influence a victim's lifestyle exposure.

Victim lifestyle exposure is classified for the purpose of understanding the victim's lifestyle and conditions, in order that exposure may be fully understood and described to others. This chapter categorizes victim lifestyle exposure into *extreme-exposure victims, high-exposure victims, medium-exposure victims,* and *low-exposure victims.* Because lifestyle exposure refers to the frequency of exposure, these categories are defined by time frames.

QUESTIONS

1. What is *lifestyle exposure?* How can lifestyle factors increase the overall possibility of individual harm?
2. List and explain three lifestyle factors that are commonly known to increase victim exposure and vulnerability to harm.
3. List and define the categories of victim lifestyle exposure. Provide one example of each.
4. Describe the difference between *active precipitation* and *passive precipitation.*
5. List two occupations that may increase victim lifestyle exposure.

REFERENCES

Albert, A., 1996. Arrest made in girl's killing: 'person of interest' jailed on DNA evidence. Tacoma News Tribune, November 16; Available at: http://www.corpus-delicti.com/cynthia_allinger_111696.htm

Barnes, H., Teeters, N., 1943. New Horizons in Criminology. Prentice Hall, New York.

Clarke, R., Felson, M., 2004. Routine Activity and Rational Choice: Vol. 5 (Advances in Criminological Theory). Transaction Publishers, Piscataway, NJ.

Clarke, R., Newman, G., Shoham, S., 1997. Rational Choice and Situational Crime Prevention: Theoretical Foundations. Dartmouth Publishing Co, Boston.

Cohen, L., Felson, M., 1979. Social change and crime trends: a routine activity approach. American Sociological Review 44 (4), 588–608.

DPS, 2007. Press Release: "State Police New Haven Initiative task force investigation leads to large drug/weapons/vehicle seizure and 3 arrests in Woodbridge. State of Connecticut, Department of Public Safety, May 18.

Dunham, S., Working, R., 1996. The area briefly—Lakewood: dogs fail to find sign of missing girl, 9. Tacoma News Tribune, July 14; Available at: http://www.corpus-delicti.com/cynthia_allinger_71496.htm

Fattah, E.A., 1976. The use of the victim as an agent of self-legitimization: toward a dynamic explanation of criminal behaviour. In: Viano, E. (Ed.), Victims and Society, Washington DC, Visage, pp. 105–129.

Fisher, B., Sloan, J., Cullen, F., Lu, C., 1998. Crime in the ivory tower: the level and sources of student victimization. Criminology 36, 671–710.

Fletcher, M., 1998. Sniper kills abortion doctor near Buffalo. Oct. 25 [Online], Available at: Washington Post, http://www.washingtonpost.com/wp-srv/national/longterm/abortviolence/stories/sniper.htm (accessed 14.02.08.)

Geberth, V., 1996. Practical Homicide Investigation, third ed. CRC Press, Boca Raton, FL.

Gillie, J., 1998a. 11-year-old murder case witness spent weekend locked up: prosecutors say they feared that her family was leaving the state. Tacoma News Tribune, June 3, p. A1.

Gillie, J., 1998b. Murder suspect's lawyer assails prosecutors: Allinger case attorney alleges unethical conduct, wants charges dropped. Tacoma News Tribune, July 24, p. B3.

Gillie, J., 1999a. Error pivotal in Rasmussen trial: detective's failure to record he moved victim's body used by prosecution to attack defense. Tacoma News Tribune, January 8, p. B1.

Gillie, J., 1999b. Accused's alibi 'airtight,' defense says: jurors in Rasmussen murder trial begin deliberations. Tacoma News Tribune, January 21, p. B1.

Gillie, J., 1999c. Late allegation arises in Rasmussen case: lawyers for man found guilty of killing girl raise questions about her mother's role. Tacoma News Tribune, February 17, p. B1.

Goetting, A., 1989. Patterns of marital homicide: a comparison of husbands and wives. Journal of Comparative Family Studies 20 (3), 341–354.

Hazelwood, R., 1995. Analyzing the Rape and Profiling the Offender. In: Hazelwood, R.R., Burgess, A.W. (Eds.), Practical Aspects of Rape Investigation: A Multidisciplinary Approach, second ed. CRC Press, New York.

Hindelang, M., Gottfredson, M., Farofalo, J., 1978. Victims of Personal Crime: An Empirical Foundation for a Theory of Personal Victimization. Ballinger, Cambridge, MA.

Hucks, K., 2003. Officials defend jailing of 11-year-old. Tacoma News Tribune, April 22; Available at: http://www.corpus-delicti.com/Tribune_042203.html

Karmen, A., 1980. Auto theft: beyond victim blaming. Victimology 5, 161–174.

Kelson, S., 2006. Violence in the legal profession: methods of protection and prevention. Advocate 49, May; pp. 19–22.

Lamborn, L., 1968. Toward a victim orientation in criminal theory. Rutgers Law Review 22, 733–768.

Luckenbill, D.F., 1977. Criminal homicide as a situated transaction. Social Problems 25, 176–186.

Maxwell, T., 2006. Letter reveals shooter's anger. Chicago Tribune, December 12. Available at: http://www.chicagotribune.com/news/local/chi-0612120322dec12, 1, 3695003.story

Mendelsohn, B., 1963. The origin of the doctrine of victimology. Excerpta Criminologica 3, 239–245.

Newsday, One third of stolen vehicles on Staten Island had keys in them. February 28. Available at: http://www.newsday.com/news/local/wire/newyork/ny-bc-ny–autothefts0228feb2820080, 4891329.story

Reid, C., Working, R., 1996. Sheriff's department believes girl abducted; man questioned. Tacoma News Tribune, July 7, p. B1.

Reiser, M., Ludwig, L., Saxe, S., Wagner, C., 1979. An evaluation of the use of psychics in the investigation of major crimes. Journal of Police Science and Administration 7 (1), 18–25.

Rock, P., 2007. Theoretical perspectives on victimization. In: Walklate, S. (Ed.), Handbook on Victims and Victimology, Willian Publishing, Portland, pp. 37–61.

Sarver, F., 2013. Lawsuit: distribution of nude photos hurt Maple Park business. The Daily Chronicle, May 20. Available at: http://www.daily-chronicle.com/2013/05/20/lawsuit-distribution-of-nude-photos-hurt-maple-park-business/ari1tg3/

Sasse, S., 2005. Motivation and routine activities theory. Deviant Behavior 26 (6), 547–570.

Schafer, S., 1968. The Victim and His Criminal: A Study in Functional Responsibility. Random House, New York.

Sheley, J., 1979. Understanding Crime: Concepts, Issues, Decisions. Wadsworth, Belmont, CA.

Siegal, L., 2007. Criminology: Theories Patterns, and Typologies. Thomson Wadsworth, Belmont, CA.

Silverman, R., 1974. Victim precipitation: an examination of the concept. In: Drapkin, I., Viano, E. (Eds.), Victimology: A New Focus, Heath, Lexington, pp. 99–110.

Singer, S., 1981. Homogeneous victim–offender population: a review and some research implications. Journal of Criminal Law and Criminology 72, 779–788.

Turvey, B., 1998. Crime Scene Analysis. Washington v. Guy Rasmussen, October 12.

Turvey, B., 2002. Criminal Profiling: An Introduction to Behavioral Evidence Analysis, second ed. Elsevier Science, London.

Turvey, B., Freeman, J., 2011. Forensic victimology. In: Turvey, B. (Ed.), Criminal Profiling: An Introduction to Behavioral Evidence Analysis, fourth ed. Elsevier Science, San Diego.

Turvey, B., Petherick, W., Diaz, J., 2008. Victim lifestyle exposure. In: Turvey, B., Petherick, W. (Eds.), Forensic Victimology, Elsevier Science, San Diego.

Turvey, B., Petherick, W., 2009. Forensic Victimology. Elsevier Science, San Diego.

von Hentig, H., 1948. The Criminal and His Victim. Archon Books, Hamden, CT.

Wolfgang, M., 1957. Victim precipitated criminal homicide. Journal of Criminal Law, Criminology and Police Science 48 (1).

Wolfgang, M., 1958. Patterns in Criminal Homicide. University of Oxford Press, London.

CHAPTER 7

Victim Situational Exposure

Brent E. Turvey

KEY TERMS

Cherry picking The assignment of greater value to a particular circumstance or finding despite contradictory or equivocal evidence, often because it suits a preferred theory.

Concurrent offender An offender who tracks or pursues two or more victims at the same time.

Concurrent victims Those who have suffered two or more crimes during the same period of time, sometimes during the same incident.

Consecutive victims Those who have suffered multiple incidents of victimization during different time frames.

Consecutive offender A true serial offender who tracks or pursues two or more victims at different times—one right after the other.

Extreme situational exposure The state of being a victim.

High situational exposure victims Those who are routinely exposed to the possibility of suffering harm or loss.

Learned helplessness The psychological condition in which a person comes to believe that he or she has no control over a given situation, and that any effort to change it is futile. The result is often passive, listless behavior, despite suffering continued harm from something that can in fact change.

Low situational exposure victims Those who are exposed to little or no actual harm or loss immediately prior to victimization.

Medium situational exposure victims Those who are somewhat exposed to the possibility of suffering harm or loss immediately prior to victimization.

Victim situational exposure The amount of actual exposure or vulnerability to harm experienced by the victim, resulting from his or her environmental and personal traits, at the time of victimization.

CONTENTS

Before the turn of the twenty-first century, the author was a frequent visitor to the office of Dr. Stephen Pittel in Berkeley, California. Dr. Pittel, a forensic psychologist, specialized in cases that involved interpreting the effects of drugs and alcohol. He was both a friend and trusted colleague. At one point, taped to the wall above his desk, there was a photocopied piece of paper that read:

> Homicide Prevention Guidelines
>   Everyone knows the usual ways to keep yourself from harm in California: stay out of Oakland, Los Angeles, Sacramento, Fresno and Chico, don't work for the postal service, don't drive in rush-hour traffic,

Forensic Victimology. http://dx.doi.org/10.1016/B978-0-12-408084-3.00007-7

don't begin or end intimate relationships, don't make your kids clean their rooms, never leave home, etc.

If you truly value your life, you may also want to observe the following precautions:

1. Don't run out of gas in the foothills.
2. Avoid biker bars.
3. Avoid bikers.
4. Avoid bars.
5. Don't cheat on your Latin lover.
6. Stay out of convenience stores after dark.
7. Don't hire or fire teenagers who wear red, blue, black or white clothing.
8. Avoid men named Billy Joe, Bobby Ray, etc.
9. Beware strangers carrying duct tape.
10. Avoid people who doodle pentagrams or swastikas.

To this list, the author would add the following to prevent homicide and domestic altercations[1]:

11. Avoid people that bring their own drink to a party—from the party they just left.
12. Avoid drinking at parties.
13. Avoid parties.
14. Don't date anyone who praises the virtues of methamphetamine as an aphrodisiac.
15. Don't date anyone who isn't willing to introduce you to his or her parole officer.
16. Don't date anyone who wants to introduce you to his or her parole officer.
17. Don't date anyone who is hiding your relationship from their spouse.
18. Don't date anyone with more than three cellphones.
19. Don't date anyone that you can't tell your spouse or significant other about.
20. Avoid family members with anger issues.
21. Avoid family members with abandonment issues.
22. Avoid family members with financial troubles.
23. Avoid lending money to family members (just give it to them and run).
24. Avoid family members who are inappropriately "grabby." You'll know when this happens.

---

[1]Special thanks to Shawn Mikulay, PhD, for his contributions.

Clearly intended as a form of dark humor, these lists serve as a didactic expression of precisely how one's immediate circumstances can influence direct exposure to harm. Being at the wrong end of a loaded gun exposes one to the harm of being shot; driving anything while intoxicated exposes one to the harm of crashing it; and crossing the street, even while sober, exposes one to the harm of being struck by a motorized vehicle. That is to say, it is reasonable to suggest there are people, places, and circumstances inherently fraught with harm. Some are easily recognized and avoidable. Some are not.

It is the purpose of this chapter to discuss how situational factors can expose individuals to harm. First, we define the concept of *victim situational exposure*. Second, we discuss the more notable or common situational factors that contribute to victim situational exposure—to include people, places, and circumstances that position anyone directly in the path of actual harm. This involves illustrative case examples. Third, and finally, we explain how victim situational exposure is best interpreted in the context of forensic victimology.

WHAT IS SITUATIONAL EXPOSURE?

Victim situational exposure is the amount of actual exposure or vulnerability experienced by the victim to harm, resulting from his or her environment and personal traits, **at the time of victimization**. This is distinct from *lifestyle exposure*, discussed in the preceding chapter, which refers to harmful elements that exist, generally, in a victim's everyday life.

A victim situational exposure can be thought of as an expression of a person's lifestyle exposure within a given environment and set of circumstances. For instance, Joe may be a generally happy person; however, his mood will likely be negative on the day that he loses his job or that his wife divorces him (albeit less negative than someone who is not a generally happy person). Additionally, Jane may normally be a cautious person; however, on the evening she agrees to serve as the designated driver for a group of friends enjoying a night on the town, she experiences *inherited risk* related to their choices and behavior.[2]

Consider the issue of alcohol. Being a person who routinely becomes intoxicated increases one's lifestyle exposure to the many harmful effects of alcohol, which are mentioned shortly. However, unless a victim is actually intoxicated at the time of victimization, alcohol does not necessarily raise his or her

---

[2]*Inherited risk* refers to the likelihood of harm or loss that is accepted or received by virtue or relationships with friends, family members, co-workers, and those in the immediate environment. For example, a person living with a drug a drug dealer inherits the risks associated with drug dealing. In the same way, a sober person in a vehicle with a drunk behind the wheel inherits the risks associated with drunk driving.

situational exposure. It is possible to have a high lifestyle exposure related to alcohol abuse, but a low situational exposure from lack of alcohol use or abuse at the time of victimization. The opposite is also true.

Consider also the issue of firearms. Being a person who does not own a firearm, does not use a firearm, does not have one in his or her home, and does not live with or interact with those who do decreases one's overall lifestyle exposure to their harmful effects. However, if a victim is at a shooting range for the first time and is accidentally shot, it must be recognized that the victim's incident exposure to harm from firearms was quite high at the time of victimization. This is true even if the victim was not participating or holding a gun—given his or her situational proximity to multiple loaded firearms being discharged by multiple persons of varying skill levels.

However, not all immediately harmful exposure is as transparent and easy to recognize from the victim's perspective as these basic examples might suggest. Harmful exposure may not even be apparent to investigators—owing to investigative apathy, or the reliance on false investigative assumptions about who and what was present during the crime. The situational harm coming from persons, environments, and circumstances relating to a particular crime must be thoroughly investigated, carefully established, and never assumed.

NOTABLE SITUATIONAL FACTORS

Many situational factors are commonly understood to increase victim exposure and vulnerability to various forms of harm. The following sections discuss some of these factors and their relevance.

Victim Lifestyle Exposure

Outlined in the preceding chapter, victim lifestyle exposure must be established to help place the crime in context from the victim's perspective. Specifically, it assists with establishing the victim's physical and mental faculties, as well as disposition, coping mechanisms, and perception of reality. Situational exposure is the expression of a particular trait (lifestyle exposure) within a particular incident environment. It is therefore important to understand the mental, social, physical, and pharmacological toolkit that an individual possessed when the incident began. Accordingly, each person's perception of environmental and situational threats will differ along with subsequent response.

Specific circumstances to consider include, but are not limited to the following:

1. *Persons involved in an abusive relationship, i.e. intimate partner violence, physical abuse, or sexual abuse.* This involves shame, self-blame, and social isolation. Individuals trapped in such relationships tend to have low

self-esteem, an inability to invest in genuine trust, social isolation, and they may suffer from *learned helplessness*.[3] This in addition to the physical harm they are suffering on a regular basis.

2. *Multiple sexual partners.* This refers to individuals who engage in multiple individual sexual relationships over the same period of time, or numerous sexual relationships over a brief period of time. Such individuals are often eager to please others and tend to have problems with self-esteem, trust (trusting too much or not enough), emotional commitment, and intimacy. Additionally, there is the issue of venereal disease—which can be transmitted unknowingly, used as a weapon by the infected, and provide victims with a motive for retaliation. As discussed in Pollard (2007; pp.807–808):

> According to the scientific data, a small subgroup of Americans is choosing to engage in promiscuous sexual activity, leading to a sexual disease epidemic that is costing the American public billions of dollars annually. The statistically few persons who choose to have sex with a large number of partners are creating a high risk of serious bodily harm or even death to others that cannot be completely eliminated by exercising reasonable care.

3. All these variables can significantly color a victim's view of other people, the precautions that he or she takes, and his or her understanding of the dangers that might be present in a given situation. Promiscuity compounds these potentials.[4]

4. *Chronic drug and alcohol abuse.* According to Mersy (2003), those engaged in chronic substance abuse often can be identified by red flags such as frequent absences from school or work; a history of frequent trauma or accidental injuries; suffering from depression or anxiety; labile hypertension (blood pressure fluctuations that are sudden and often); gastrointestinal symptoms, such as epigastric distress, diarrhea, or weight changes; sexual dysfunction; and sleep disorders. In short, the body of a substance abuser is in distress, and so is his or her mind—even when not immediately under the influence. This affects not just how the person feels, but how he or she reasons and reacts.

---

[3]*Learned helplessness* refers to perceived powerlessness resulting from extreme trauma or repeated failure, often manifesting itself in submissiveness and depression.

[4]Some investigators hold the unfortunate and erroneous belief that evidence of sexual promiscuity is a sufficient basis to unfound claims of rape (Bryden, 1997). That is not the intended or suggested use of such information as provided in this work, as such behavior in general does not suggest the likelihood of rape in specific. We recommend documenting sexual habits in general, whether a victim is promiscuous or selective, and establishing what that means in context (if anything).

5. *Mental illness.* This refers to individuals who suffer from any disease or condition affecting the brain, influencing the way they think, feel, act, or relate toward others and their environment. Often this involves diminished coping and problem-solving skills, and even altered perceptions of reality. This may be counteracted by medication, however. Therefore, it is important to establish not only the existence of mental illness, but any medications prescribed, and whether or not they were actually taking them.

It should also be noted that any combination of these elements could have a synergistic effect. In other words, two or more of these or similar circumstances are likely to enhance the frequency and impact of the others. Chronic drug abuse can lead to multiple sexual partners; abusive relationships can lead to and exacerbate chronic drug abuse; mental illness can lead to and exacerbate abusive relationships. These types of self-destructive behaviors and circumstances do not typically occur in a vacuum, and those afflicted are not always able to self-correct.

There is, unfortunately, a tendency to rely heavily on crime statistics when considering these issues, encouraged by university culture. This is not entirely wrong, when done properly. Without question, looking at things such as Uniform Crime Report (UCR) data can be helpful and even necessary when contextualizing a given crime event. However, an interpretation of situational exposure is not about the statistics or the math. It is about whether the victim was standing in front of the gun or behind it—so to speak. Either the harm is pointed at the victim, and he or she is in its path, or is not. Learning to examine and interpret this, irrespective of the crime data, is at the heart of understanding situational exposure.

Consecutive and Concurrent Victims

Consecutive victims are those who have suffered multiple incidents of victimization during different time frames. These successive events may or may not be related. One example would be an adult female victim of domestic violence. She is physically beaten for a period of years, and ultimately leaves her husband or boyfriend. Several months later, while living on her own, she is raped and killed. This involves two separate crimes; two separate time frames. The crimes might be connected; only a thorough investigation will reveal which is the case.

It is important for the examiner to look for consecutive victimization and to identify it as such for all to know. However, the examiner must also require that the victimization be investigated to determine what connections exist, if any, to the immediate case. As one example, personality or dispositional issues that may have contributed to the first victimization can help us understand the second. Knowing this and having it available for reference can provide a necessary understanding for the context of victimity that might otherwise be absent.

Concurrent victims are those who have suffered two or more crimes during the same period of time—sometimes during the same incident. This may be at the hands of one or multiple offenders. Although under some circumstances the crimes will be related, it is also possible that they are not. Consider again our adult female victim of domestic violence: only instead of leaving her husband or boyfriend, she stays and remains a constant victim. While still suffering from this crime and its effects on a daily basis, she is raped and killed. Two separate crimes; one time frame. The relationship between them is a possibility to be investigated, not a fact to be assumed.

As with consecutive victimization, it is important for the victimologist to recognize the possibility of concurrent victimization, and to clearly identify it as such when found. The victimologist must also require that it be investigated to establish connections rather than merely assume they exist because of temporal or proximal association. The author has found this practice an all too common vice when evidence of an actual connection is weak or even nonexistent.

To illustrate these concepts, consider the case of a 12-year-old girl from Berkeley, California, who suffered two separate incidents of rape, at two separate schools, in two separate months (May and Lee, 2000; p. A25):

> A 12-year-old Berkeley girl who was sexually assaulted by classmates last month was attacked last week at another Berkeley school where she had transferred after the first assault, police said yesterday.
>
> The girl was moved to Martin Luther King Jr. Middle School after last month's reported attack at Willard Middle School, school officials said. They acknowledged that the girl, who has learning disabilities, received no special protection.
>
> Police said school officials did not tell them that the girl had been transferred until they were called to King after the attack there on Nov. 8, said Berkeley Police Lt. Russ Lopes.
>
> The girl was "conned into going with a young man into a secluded area that she was unfamiliar with—she's not a regular student there, of course—and she was raped by him," Lopes said.
>
> Lopes confirmed last week's reported attack after an anonymous tipster called *The Chronicle* yesterday to report it.
>
> A 13-year-old boy who is a student at King was arrested the day after the incident, on suspicion of rape and penetration with a foreign object, police said. He was released to his parents and has not been charged.
>
> …

Although Lopes said the girl was raped last week, Berkeley Superintendent Jack McLaughlin said yesterday that the King incident was not similar to what happened at Willard last month.

Police say as many as nine boys molested the girl during a five-hour ordeal on Oct. 25 that began at school and continued in a southwest Berkeley backyard, a vacant lot, an abandoned shed, an underground parking garage and seven other locations throughout the city. One of the boys allegedly assaulted the girl the previous day.

Three of the boys were charged this week with oral copulation, false imprisonment, misdemeanor battery and threatening a witness for reportedly telling the girl on Oct. 26 not to tell anyone about the assault.

It was not known whether the 13-year-old boy in the King assault knew the youths involved in the Willard attack, some of whom were part of a group calling itself the "Mini-mob," Lopes said....

The incidents have created ill will between the school district and the Police Department, and each is blaming the other for mishandling the situation.

McLaughlin said police never indicated the girl who was attacked at Willard needed security after she enrolled at King. "We weren't told she was enrolled at King," said Lopes.

After the second attack, police and school officials met and decided the girl must either be schooled at home or attend school with constant supervision from an aide or some type of guard, Lopes said. She is not attending King....

And new details emerged about the Willard incident. A parent volunteer who discovered the girl near the unlocked shed where the assault reportedly began said three to four boys outside the shed ran away when he asked them what they were doing. Several other boys ran out of the shed, he said.

The girl then walked out of the shed, fully clothed, said the parent, Lee Berry. She said she was "just passing by." Berry said he told her, "child, go home," and reported the incident to the vice principal....

A father of one of the seven boys reportedly involved in the Willard attack also apologized for what happened to the girl, but he said the community is unfairly rushing to judgment. The father said his 12-year-old son told him he watched the boys and the girl during the incident but did not have sex with the girl. "He said, 'Daddy, I was scared. I didn't want the other kids to think I was a punk.'"

The victim in this case suffered multiple concurrent attacks during the time frame of the first incident. Subsequently, the victim was moved to a new school and attacked a second time weeks later; this separate incident meets the criteria for consecutive victimization. Some of the constant variables between these incidents at different schools include the victim's learning disability, the failure of each school to adequately provide supervision of their students, and the propensity for young boys at both schools to regard kidnapping, sexual assault, and violence as acceptable expressions of any kind. These constant variables, and others like them, raised this victim's lifestyle exposure and incident exposure in tandem—and her learning disability prevented her from fully recognizing the inherent danger.

It should be noted that these concepts are the flip side of *consecutive* and *concurrent offenders*. The *consecutive offender* is a true serial offender who tracks or pursues two or more victims at different times—one right after the other. The *concurrent offender* is tracking or pursuing two or more victims at the same time.

Time of Occurrence

Certain times of day can result in more exposure to various kinds of harm than others. However, any interpretation of the impact of this factor is highly dependent on the location of occurrence as well as other converging circumstances. It cannot be considered in a vacuum.

Some examples may help to illustrate.

Bank robberies, for instance, occur most frequently between the hours of 9 a.m. and 6 p.m. The reason is primarily that banks are open for business during those hours. When they are closed, banks are more difficult to rob and consequently require a far more developed criminal skill set. It is easier to rob a bank when the front door is unlocked and bank personnel can assist with locating and gathering money.

Similarly, most police officers are killed during felonious attacks between the hours of 10 p.m. and 12 a.m. This is related to the fact that many officers die on patrol while responding to disturbance calls, such as domestic arguments and bar fights. Many others are killed while making arrests or are simply ambushed. These circumstances all trend upwards during that time frame (UCR, 2007).

With respect to sexual assault, the research is very clear that time of day varies as an exposure factor based on the age of the victim. This is detailed in the research conducted by Snyder (2000; p. 7):

> The time of day when sexual assaults occurred was related primarily to the age of the victim.... For adult victims, sexual assaults were most common between midnight and 2 a.m. From morning through 7 p.m. the number of adult sexual assaults committed in each 1-hour period was essentially constant. The number of adult assaults began to increase in the 8 p.m. hour and increased consistently until the peak in the 2 a.m. hour.

The temporal pattern for the sexual assaults of very young victims, children under age 6, was quite different. For these young victims, the temporal distribution appears to be a combination of two separate distributions. The primary temporal pattern for these crimes has a peak in the 3 p.m. hour. This is also the hour other research has found to be the period when juveniles are most likely to be the victims of violent crime in general (Snyder and Sickmund, 1999). This primary temporal pattern shows a consistent increase in the frequency of sexual assaults of very young victims before 3 p.m. and a consistent decline in the hours after 3 p.m. The secondary temporal pattern for the sexual assaults of very young children shows the hours of 8 a.m., noon, and 6 p.m. (traditional meal times) to be periods when the number of sexual assaults of very young victims spike. The temporal patterns of sexual assault of youth ages 6 through 11, and juveniles ages 12 through 17, appear to be a combination of the patterns of the very young, and the adult victims. These temporal distributions combine the after-school and mealtime hour patterns of very young victims and the temporal patterns of sexual assault for adults.

As this research makes clear, time of day is a factor heavily influenced by the regular activities of the victim, their proximity to abusers, and subsequent supervision—all of which is very often a function of victim age.

Location of Occurrence

Location is one of the most important factors to consider in terms of victim situational exposure. Certain environments contain a great deal of criminal activity; others may place a victim outside the immediate reach of assistance; and still others may physically isolate the victim. A starter list of environmental circumstances to be considered in any forensic victimology should include at least the following:

- *Ownership*: Who owns the location, if anyone, and is it insured? Does the victim know this?
- *Relationship to victims*: What is the relationship of the victims to the location? Do they live there, work there, or are they frequent visitors? Establish how they got there, if it was by choice, and why (if they were attacked at a store, what did they go there to buy; if they were attacked on the street, where did they come from and where were they going). Then establish whether or not they were familiar with the location. Could they anticipate changes in the environment and get around in the dark, or would they have needed light to see?
- *Security*: How hard is it to get in and out undetected; what security measures are in place (doors, locks, cameras, roaming patrols); and are

they apparent or concealed? Could security from nearby locations have recorded any crime-related activity? Make a list of security features and their recording capacity, and direct their immediate collection.

- *Ambient lighting*: How much was there, what was its coverage, what was the visibility where the attack occurred, and was it on/available during the attack?
- *Adjacent residences and businesses*: What was the nature of nearby locations? Could the harm from those locations have spilled over into the present location? Make a list of neighboring homes and businesses for interviewing or canvassing.
- *Witnesses*: Which vantage points, if any, provided line of sight to the points of entry, points of exit, and activity in the scene? And by whom? Was it an outdoor scene easily viewed by those walking by, or was it an indoor scene in a soundproofed room with no windows? Make a list of potential witnesses for interviewing or canvassing.
- *Criminal history*: What is the criminal history of the location? If it's a home, get the 911-dispatch history (dates, times, and reasons for any emergency responses to the residence). What are the criminal histories of the residents, friends, and other family members? If it's a business, same thing; and what kind of business? What are the criminal histories of the owners and employees? Has anyone used the location for criminal enterprise, either presently or in the past? Make a list.

In forensic victimology, less information should equate to less certain findings. The inability to account for these or other significant environmental circumstances must be noted in any final report that relies on victimology-related interpretations, and the impact of their absence explained. This provides for changes to interpretations should more information be gathered or otherwise come to light.

Proximity to Criminal Activity

As already suggested, nearness in space, time, or relationship to criminal activity increases one's incident exposure. This can include victim nearness to crime and criminals, or direct victim participation and involvement in criminal activity. The more violence associated with a proximal crime, the greater subsequent victim exposure to harm.

This issue of proximity includes consideration of the victim's profession: drug dealers, drug addicts, and prostitutes are among those with the highest exposure with respect to violent crime proximity. However, and this point is easy to forget, so are those who live with them and those who seek their services. To say nothing of the police who by professional nature will have regular contact with all manner of offenders and offenses. Some profilers have been known to misplace the reality that it is not possible for someone to be a police officer and also have a low lifestyle or incident exposure—unless that person's duties do not bring him or her into contact with criminals of any kind, such as may be found for those officers who work only compiling intelligence reports or others who engage in wholly administrative duties.

CASE EXAMPLE:

Steven Wright—Serial Murderer

Between October and December 2006, former cruise line steward Steven Wright murdered at least five prostitutes and dumped their bodies around Ipswich in the United Kingdom (see Figure 7-1). He was working as a forklift driver at the time of his arrest. He went on trial in January 2008. As detailed in *The Telegraph* (Staff Writers, 2008):

> The bodies of all five women were found dumped in remote locations around Ipswich in Suffolk within 10 days of each other in December 2006, sparking a massive police investigation. [See Figure 7-2.]
>
> Wright, from Ipswich, was arrested on December 19, charged two days later and remanded in custody. He entered five not guilty pleas at Ipswich Crown Court in May 2007.
>
> ...
>
> Detectives in Suffolk launched an inquiry after Miss Nicol vanished on October 30. Just over two weeks later, Miss Adams was reported missing after going to work in Ipswich's red light district.
>
> Her body was discovered in a brook at Hintlesham on December 2, and six days after that Miss Nicol's body was found in water in nearby Copdock.
>
> The body of Miss Alderton, who had not been reported missing, was found in woodland at Nacton on December 10. And on December 12 the bodies of Miss Clennell and Miss Nicholls were found in woods at Levington.
>
> Wright, a former forklift truck driver who will be 50 in April, was arrested seven days later at the home he shared with partner Pam Goodman, a call centre worker.
>
> The charges:
>
> The murder of Gemma Adams, 25, between November 13 and December 3, 2006

> The murder of Tania Nicol, 19, between October 29 and December 9, 2006
>
> The murder of Anneli Alderton, 24, between December 7 and December 11, 2006
>
> The murder of Annette Nicholls, 29, between December 7 and December 13, 2006
>
> The murder of Paula Clennell, 24, between December 9 and December 13, 2006.

Stephen Wright admitted to police that he had known at least four of the victims, and had also visited them on occasion for sex. However, he denied any involvement in their deaths. In February 2008, Stephen Wright was convicted on all five counts listed here. The judge, in deciding his sentence, made specific comments about victim exposure to harm owing to their drug use and chosen profession, as described in BBC (2008a):

> The victims were working as prostitutes when they were murdered and Mr Justice Gross said Wright had targeted vulnerable women. He said: "Drugs and prostitution meant they were at risk. But neither drugs nor prostitution killed them. You did. You killed them, stripped them and left them...why you did it may never be known."
>
> The judge said the case met the legal requirements for a whole life sentence because the murders involved a "substantial degree of pre-meditation and planning."

Further detail is provided in BBC (2008b):

> Wright, 49, of Ipswich, said during his trial that he had had sex with four of the five women, who were working as prostitutes, but denied killing them. Ipswich Crown Court jurors unanimously found him guilty of all five murders and he will be sentenced on Friday.

CASE EXAMPLE: *CONTINUED*

FIGURE 7-1

Stephen Wright was arrested, tried, and convicted for the murders of five prostitutes in Ipswich, UK.

'Crucifix pose'

The trial heard the bodies of Miss Alderton and Miss Nicholls were found arranged with their arms outstretched in a crucifix pose....

Suffolk police began an inquiry after Miss Nicol, 19, vanished in late October 2006.

Two weeks later, Miss Adams, 25, vanished and detectives began a "major inquiry," saying there were "obvious similarities."

This was followed by the disappearance of Miss Alderton, 24, Miss Clennell, 24, and 29-year-old Miss Nicholls.

Their bodies were eventually found in isolated locations around Ipswich.

In 2001, Wright worked as a barman at the Brook Hotel in Felixstowe before being sacked for stealing hundreds of pounds from the till, for which he was ordered to carry out 100 hours community service.

It was a DNA sample taken at the time of that conviction which led to police matching samples taken from the dead women.

He was put under surveillance by police before being arrested on 19 December and charged two days later.

Peter Wright QC, prosecuting, said the decision by the women to turn to prostitution "was ultimately to prove fatal."...

Michael Crimp, from the Crown Prosecution Service, said from outside the court: "Steve Wright is the factor that links all five women."

"He was the last person to see them alive and the scientific evidence proved that he was responsible for their deaths. One telling piece of evidence was a carpet fibre from the footwell of Steve Wright's car found in Tania Nicol's hair. This was despite her body being

Continued

CASE EXAMPLE: *CONTINUED*

FIGURE 7-2
Victims of serial murderer Stephen Wright, start from the top left: Anneli Alderton, Gemma Adams, Tania Nicol, Paula Clennell, and Annette Nicholls. Their nude bodies were dumped in isolated areas around Ipswitch.

found in water. Her killer failed to destroy this significant piece of evidence."...

'Depraved crime'

Robert Sadd, Crown Advocate for the CPS in Suffolk, said Wright's motive for the killing may never be known. "Quite often in a murder case we do not know the motive or understand it if we do. The evidence leads us to who did it, and that's more important."

Scientific evidence was a crucial factor in the case and Home Office Minister Vernon Coaker said it demonstrated the great strides made in DNA profiling. He said: "This was an evil and depraved crime that caused immense suffering to the families and friends of the victims as well as bringing fear to the local community. All of those affected have my deepest sympathy."

Stephen Wright was ultimately given the maximum penalty—life in prison. As of this writing, police are investigating his possible connection to the deaths and disappearances of several other victims in the same area.

Proximity to Criminal, Violent, or Aggressive Individuals

The concept of proximity to criminal, violent, or aggressive individuals is associated with the issue of proximity to criminal behavior. However, it focuses specifically on individuals in the immediate environment, with their particular history of crime, violence, and aggression—or lack thereof. That is to say, one can be around such individuals at a given moment while they are not engaged in violent, aggressive, or criminal activity. Yet the reality of increased victim exposure remains. They have their history of violent associations, associates, and coping mechanisms—all of which they carry around like so much harmful luggage. Proximity of victims to such individuals is one level of exposure; proximity to individuals engaged in criminal activity is another of greater exposure still.

Number of Potential Victims

It is generally true that there is safety in numbers; that is to say, the buddy system can remove one from the path of harm, or speed one from harmful circumstances. Hikers know it, divers know it, and joggers know it. If you get hurt, your buddy can go get help. If you get lost, your buddy can share resources and help find the way home. If you are walking alone at night, however, you are more preferable as a target because there are no witnesses and the odds are even for any offender: 1:1.

This concept tends to be true so long as the people that one is with are not at an increased lifestyle or situational exposure. If your buddy is intoxicated, rather than being an asset, he or she becomes a liability. Same thing if your buddy has a temper, just got in a fight with a significant other and is distressed, or has a mental illness and is not taking his or her medication.

Also, some more competent and confident offenders prefer to select victims in pairs so that they can use one to control the other—such as a mother and child. This would be one of the exceptions that prove the rule. Consider an abusive parent who threatens the life of other family members should anyone tell the police; or the rapist who selects mothers with small children to gain total compliance by threatening harm to the child.

CASE EXAMPLE:

David Welker

Consider the case of 24-year-old David Welker in Orlando, Florida (see Figures 7-3 and 7-4), as described in Prieto (2008):

> The choice was clear: Either she comply or he would shoot her baby girl.

Her attacker already had pulled a gun and forced her back into her car in the nearly deserted Wal-Mart parking lot. He reclined the front passenger seat and ordered her to lie facedown. He then raped her while she looked at her child in the car seat behind her.

Continued

CASE EXAMPLE: *CONTINUED*

FIGURE 7-3
Mug shot of 24-year-old David Welker.

FIGURE 7-4
Welker using the victim's ATM card at a nearby bank to withdraw money.

CASE EXAMPLE: *CONTINUED*

All the while, the victim said, he pressed a .25-caliber pistol against the 15-month-old toddler.

When he was done, he told her to sit in the driver's seat and dump the contents of her purse. He robbed her and ordered her to get into the trunk, leaving her baby alone in the car.

Those details emerged Thursday in an arrest affidavit released by the Orange County Sheriff's Office. Numerous tips and surveillance video led deputies to their suspect, 24-year-old David Welker of Orlando, a felon caught Wednesday afternoon while riding in a car on Orange Center Boulevard.

"It's one of the most heinous rapes I've heard of in a long time," said Carol Wick, chief executive officer of Harbor House, an Orange County domestic-violence agency. "It's horribly traumatic for a woman."

The 35-year-old victim pulled into the Wal-Mart parking lot on South John Young Parkway about 6:15 a.m. Tuesday to pick up milk and supplies for her baby before heading to day care and work, the document said.

She noticed Welker, a skinny man with a long nose and brown hair, waiting near the front door of the store but assumed he was an employee, she told deputies. Security video shows Welker had been loitering there since

5:22 a.m., more than 45 minutes before the attack. He watched others go in and out of the store, the document said.

The victim parked her car and got out, then reached back inside to grab her daughter's sippy cup and pacifier from the center console.

When she turned around, Welker was behind her, ordering her back into the car at gunpoint, the report said. He told her to drive to the back of the store and park.

Fearing for her child's life, she complied, she told detectives.

Taking his time, Welker rummaged through the glove compartment looking for something to steal, according to the affidavit.

Then an unimaginable 20 minutes of terror began. Holding his gun against the toddler, who was awake, Welker began raping the mother, sheriff's reports said.

…

When it was over, the naked woman climbed back into the driver's seat. Welker picked through the contents of her spilled purse, taking her cell phone, a debit card and $70 in cash, the report said.

Before fleeing, Welker made the woman climb inside the trunk but didn't close it all the way because her daughter was still inside the car. When she determined he was gone, she drove away, seeking help.

According to police records, Welker had been arrested at least 27 times prior to this incident. He had also completed a work-release program only a few weeks prior, for convictions relating to illegal possession of firearms and grand-theft. When he was arrested for rape and car-jacking in this case, he had at least $200 in $20 bills on his person, as well as a small amount of marijuana.

Availability of Weapons

Generally speaking, rifles, handguns, knives, saws, rope, screwdrivers, and pantyhose are all tools created to serve a particular function. However, all have been put to service in the crimes of assault, rape, and homicide. The reason is that many criminal cases involve violent decisions made at the last minute affected by a victim or offender using available materials.

The availability of any weapon or material in a given environment increases the likelihood that it will be used in a physical altercation should one ensue. Or that someone will accidentally injure himself or herself or others while handling it for any number of legitimate or illegitimate purposes. The availability of a shotgun in an environment increases victim exposure to shotgun injury or fatality; the availability of knives in an environment increases victim exposure to sharp force injury or fatality; the availability of coat hangers in an environment increases victim exposure to related ligature injury or fatality. However, a weapon's availability does not cause its use.

Care and Supervision

As previously suggested, individuals become more willing to engage in criminal activity when they are not being watched. That is to say, criminal propensity can increase as supervision and accountability decrease. This is why so many offenders choose professions that put them in positions where they are supervising or caring for their preferred victim type (for some, their preferred victim type is teenage boys; for others, it is dollar bills). They want to get their victims alone, they want to have their way, and they want deniability. However, if they are being supervised or monitored to any degree, this may not be possible. They may subsequently move their activities to a location or venue where supervision and personal accountability are diminished or entirely absent.

The advent of the Internet, and a false perception of anonymity by some users, has helped to enable waves of criminal conduct—from those violating copyright to those stealing identities to those soliciting minors for sex in chat rooms. Consider the number of individuals snared in sting operations such as those set up by programs like Dateline NBC's *To Catch a Predator*.[5] First, an adult working with the show poses as an underage teen in an online chat room. Once an adult male has contacted this person for private chat sessions that become sexually explicit, they arrange a meeting at a location that has been surreptitiously rigged with cameras and sound equipment. When the adult male shows up on the premises, having brought items requested by the decoy minor, such as sexual lubricants and alcohol, the police literally rush in and make an arrest. The sheer volume of men routinely operating in a criminal fashion on the Internet with respect to grooming minors for sex, simply because they believe their identities are safe, is telling.

---

[5]See http://www.msnbc.msn.com/id/10912603/.

CASE EXAMPLE:

Rabbi

Consider the representative case of a 56-year-old rabbi from Maryland, who was stung by *To Catch a Predator*, as described in Makron (2006; p. B6):

A Maryland rabbi caught in a television sting operation was sentenced to 6 1/2 years in prison yesterday for trying to solicit sex from a 13-year-old boy over the Internet.

David A. Kaye, 56, told the judge that he traveled to Herndon for what he thought would be sex with a boy "as a cry out for help to fight my personal demons." Sobbing as he acknowledged his father, who sat in the courtroom in a wheelchair, Kaye said his conviction had made him face "the reality of who I am.... I know I need help. I pray that God allows me to get that help."

Kaye's attorney, Peter D. Greenspun, said the rabbi, who was featured last year on the "To Catch a Predator" series on "Dateline NBC," kept his sexuality secret and spent thousands of hours chatting online in search of liaisons.

Kaye thought that he was chatting online with a young adult, Greenspun said. He said Kaye, who is divorced, is in therapy, and he urged a sentence on the low end of federal guidelines, which recommended a term of 63 to 78 months in prison.

"There is a very decent core to this man," Greenspun said.

But U.S. District Judge James C. Cacheris in Alexandria settled on 78 months and said Kaye would then face 10 years of supervised release. The judge said that during that time, Kaye will be forbidden to accept any job involving children, and he ordered him to never be around children younger than 18 without an adult present....

Kaye, of Potomac, is the former vice president of programs at Rockville-based

PANIM: The Institute for Jewish Leaders and Values, an educational foundation that trains Jewish leaders. He resigned last year after informing the organization that he would be on "Dateline."

Kaye was convicted in September after a two-day bench trial in which prosecutors presented evidence of sexually graphic chats between him and the boy. In reality, the boy was a 26-year-old man working for Perverted Justice, a group that tries to expose adults who use the Internet for sexual activity with children.

Perverted Justice was working with "Dateline," which paid the watchdog group to create a pedophile sting that ran as a series of TV reports. When Kaye arrived at the Herndon house that the group had set up, he was confronted on camera by NBC correspondent Chris Hansen.

"You know I'm in trouble. I know I'm in trouble," Kaye told Hansen, according to Cacheris's opinion. The judge convicted Kaye on one count of coercion and enticement and one count of travel with intent to engage in illicit sexual conduct....

During the trial, prosecutors presented outtakes from the NBC show and a log of Kaye's chats with the person posing as a 13-year-old. [See Figure 7-5.] Using the screen name "REDBD," Kaye initiated the chats, Cacheris wrote.

In this particular case, the offender was already in a position of trust within a religious community in Maryland, working for PANIM, which teaches leadership and values to teenagers. However, with the anonymity of the Internet and without the supervision of others, his fantasies found expression. On the day that he was arrested, 18 other men showed up and were arrested as part of the same sting operation.

Continued

CASE EXAMPLE: *CONTINUED*

FIGURE 7-5
Part of one of the nude pictures sent by Rabbi David Kaye to the person he thought was a 13-year-old boy, but was in fact someone working for Perverted Justice.

Victim State of Mind/Perception

Victim state of mind/perception refers to the victim's emotional state before, throughout, and subsequent to an attack (when applicable) as evidenced by convergent patterns of behavior and any reliable witness accounts. An agitated emotional state (e.g., anger, sadness, or panic) may increase victim incident exposure. Additionally, a victim who feels safe in a particular environment or situation will act differently from a victim who does not.

Many variables, including the presence of drugs, alcohol, mental illness, or a heightened emotional state such as anger or sadness, affect this directly.

Drug and Alcohol Use

The use of mind-altering substances may decrease one's physical reaction time, impair one's judgment, and alter one's perception of reality. In either case, victim situational exposure is increased dramatically, even for otherwise low-exposure victims. One thing that a person cannot do under the influence of drugs or alcohol is think rationally. This issue is so pervasive across the spectrum of crime and criminal victimization that it is already a feature of almost every chapter in this text. We do not belabor the point here.

Engaging in Violent or Aggressive Behavior

If the victim engages in violent or aggressive behavior, this can evoke or even provoke a violent response from others. Whether or not this results in legal culpability or diminished culpability is a legal matter for a jury to decide. However, pretending that it doesn't happen can result in victim deification, which prevents getting to the truth.

Violent and aggressive behavior can also remove a victim's attention from matters related to immediate personal safety. For example, if the victim is driving a vehicle while having an argument, he or she could crash; or, if the victim is standing on a boat and yelling at someone on shore or in a nearby craft, he or she can become distracted, lose balance, and fall in. Essentially, the concern is that violent and aggressive behavior affects state of mind, causes a distraction, and accidents are therefore likely to result.

These factors and many others inform the overall context of the crime, and each one on its own has meaning only when placed against the backdrop of the other known facts in a case. The examination of one factor on its own cannot in itself be used to gauge victim situational exposure. Nor is it acceptable to cherry-pick multiple factors out of context and suppress information that might suggest an unpopular or undesirable level of exposure. This point is mentioned again at the end of the chapter.

It must further be explained that the occurrence or existence of any one circumstance by itself is not necessarily enough to cause the tipping point into victim harm, unless direct harm of some kind is inherent (such as with drug and alcohol use, or consecutive and concurrent victimization). Having a gun in a home will not cause someone to use it for violence; having drugs in the home will not make someone use them; leaving a child unsupervised at school will not cause that child to be raped. As we've demonstrated here, it is the synergy of corresponding factors and circumstances that expose victims to ever-increasing levels of harm until their demise becomes almost unavoidable.

INTERPRETING SITUATIONAL EXPOSURE

The interpretation of a particular victim's situational exposure is not just a function of compiling crime stats, comparing it to the victim's presumed state of being when attacked, and making a general risk assessment. Much more is required to achieve a concrete and actual understanding. As discussed, the nature, depth, and character of each victim's harm must be investigated, examined, and explained in its context. This means scrupulous examination of information gathered regarding associated persons and locations. Barring this level of information and effort, the forensic victimologist must have the scientific courage to admit what is known and what is not. That is to say, the victimologist must understand the scope and limits of the evidence. This is not too much to ask of any competent forensic examiner.

Categorizing Victim Situational Exposure

The main purpose of classifying victim incident exposure is, as discussed in the preceding chapter, to understand the victim's lifestyle and circumstances so that exposure may be fully understood. The will allow the examiner to describe it accurately to others. The following categories of victim lifestyle exposure are discussed in Turvey (2011b) and were influenced by similar classifications from Hazelwood (1995).

With respect to incident exposure, the following classifications may be useful:

- *Low situational exposure victims* are those who are exposed to little or no actual harm or loss immediately prior to victimization. For example, an accountant at home, in the middle of the day, in an upper-class neighborhood with low or no crime and a good security system; no alcohol involved and no drugs; no affairs or animosity; and no history of crime, violence or mental illness. A sex offender recently released from prison, visiting a relative who lives nearby, invades the accountant's home and ties him to a chair, hoping to find a female victim in the house. Finding no females, the sex offender becomes enraged, and the accountant is robbed and killed.

- *Medium situational exposure victims* are those who are somewhat exposed to the possibility of suffering harm or loss immediately prior to victimization. For example, the same general situation from the preceding example, except he lives in a middle-class neighborhood with a lot of domestic violence calls and a recent series of break-ins. Also, he's had a few drinks because he's depressed over the fact that his girlfriend won't leave her husband. When he drinks, he gets angry, which is how he lost his first marriage. When the sex offender breaks in, the already agitated accountant attacks him and is killed defending his home and property.

- *High situational exposure victims* are those who are routinely exposed to the possibility of suffering harm or loss. For example, the same general situation from the first example, except the accountant works for an organized crime syndicate and has been embezzling money to support his $5,000 a day cocaine and prostitute habit. He is killed in his bedroom while high on cocaine, and it is staged to look like a burglary gone wrong.

- As discussed in the previous chapter, *extreme lifestyle exposure victims* are those who are exposed to the possibility of suffering harm or loss every day. This concept is specific to lifestyle exposure. With respect to classifying situational exposure, *extreme situational exposure* describes the state of being a victim. For an extreme classification to apply, the victim must have been victimized immediately prior to the event under consideration. Moreover, that prior attack must not be part of the attack being examined. An example would be a prostitute using drugs who is robbed by one client and then raped by the next. Another example might be a child victim who is being trafficked for sexual purposes; the child stays in a locked room and is repeatedly raped by one customer after another, unable to leave or get help.

Cherry Picking

With respect to forensic interpretations, *cherry picking* involves the assignment of greater value to a particular circumstance or finding despite contradictory or equivocal evidence, often because it suits a preferred theory. This can occur because of ignorance, but is most commonly associated with examiner bias (discussed generally in Cooley and Turvey, 2011). Forensic examiners are strongly warned against the practice of cherry picking evidence or results to suit their purposes, and then presenting only those findings that cast themselves, victims, or their clients in the best light. As will be stated again in this text, the forensic examiner's report of findings should be the truth, the WHOLE truth, and nothing but the truth—in strict accordance with the scientific method.

CASE EXAMPLE:

Florida v. Jackson *(2011)*

In 2010, the author was contacted by attorney Raheela Ahmed, Assistant CCRC; Law Office of Capital Collateral for the State of Florida. He was asked to examine the appellate case of *Florida v. Ray J. Jackson* and conduct a crime scene analysis. This case necessarily included a forensic victimological assessment.

Mr. Jackson and his codefendant, Michael Wooten, were tried together and convicted for the kidnapping and first-degree murder of 23-year-old Pallis Paulk. A black female, she was also a drug addict. Police and prosecutors argued that she was murdered after having been kidnapped in retribution for having stolen drugs and money from Jackson.

The State of Florida Supreme Court provided its decision denying the initial appeal based on the following version of events (*Jackson v. Florida*, 2009):

When Pallis Paulk was last seen alive by an acquaintance on November 9, 2004, she was being forced into the trunk of a car by Jackson. Her body was found in a shallow grave several months later. The facts at trial concerning her murder came in through a series of witnesses by which the following factual scenario was presented.

Around 3 a.m. on the morning of November 9th, Paulk arrived at a friend's house, looking for ecstasy pills. Her friend, Curtis Vreen, testified that Paulk arrived in a red hatchback. He noticed that there was someone else in the car, but he could not see the person's face. Vreen gave her half of an ecstasy pill and told her that was all he had.

Continued

CASE EXAMPLE: *CONTINUED*

Later that day, Paulk called her sixteen-year-old cousin, Calvin Morris, and told Morris, "I have a lick for you, Cuz" which meant that she found a person to rob. Morris met Paulk at an apartment in Daytona Beach, and when Morris arrived, he saw Ray Jackson sleeping in bed. Concerned that Jackson might wake up, Morris walked back to the car and waited for his cousin. Paulk arrived at the car, carrying a Sponge Bob bag, which contained about two ounces of cocaine, some marijuana, and approximately $800. She also had men's jewelry and a cell phone that did not belong to her. Together, they drove to pick up Morris's girlfriend in Sanford, Florida, and smoked some of the marijuana. While they were driving, Paulk called Vreen, looking for more ecstasy.

At some point after Paulk left Jackson's apartment, Jackson woke up and realized the theft. Jackson and codefendant Wooten went to Latisha Allen's apartment and asked to speak to Frederick Hunt, who was Vreen's cousin. Based on Jackson's request, Hunt called Vreen to see if he had heard from Paulk. Vreen responded that Paulk had called him and provided the phone number from which Paulk had called Vreen. After Hunt relayed this information to Jackson, Jackson left.

Later in the day, Morris took Paulk to Vreen's house, even though Morris was afraid that Jackson would be there looking for Paulk. Paulk went inside, telling Morris that she would be right back. While Morris was waiting in the car, Wooten came outside and told Morris that Paulk was using the restroom. Jackson and Paulk eventually came out of the house and walked up to Morris's car. Morris saw that Jackson had a gun. Jackson asked, "Where is my stuff at?" Morris immediately gave Jackson his marijuana back. Paulk retrieved some additional items from Morris's car and then left with Jackson.

Morris noticed that Paulk looked upset, like she wanted to cry. According to Morris,

Jackson shoved Paulk into the back of a red hatchback, and Jackson, Wooten, and Paulk drove away. Morris initially followed them, but stopped after Jackson held a gun out of the window. Morris immediately went to his grandmother's house and told her what had happened, but did not go to the police at that time because he had outstanding warrants against him.

Jackson took Paulk to Allen's apartment. Although Hunt, Thomas, and Allen were not there when he first arrived, Jackson had keys to Allen's apartment. Allen and Hunt returned to Allen's apartment and saw a red hatchback parked in front. Jackson was inside, sitting by the hallway that led to the bedrooms. Jackson told Allen that he had been robbed and asked her to go look. Allen went into the bathroom where she saw a woman in her bathtub, dressed but with her hands tied behind her back. [See Figure 7-6.] The woman told Allen that she was fine and that it was her fault. After Allen left the bathroom, Wooten told her not to be "dumb" like the victim or she could end up the same way. Allen asked if Jackson was going to kill the woman, and he nodded yes.[5] Allen left to bail her boyfriend out of jail, but Hunt remained.

Allen also testified that Jackson asked Allen for a douche, so she gave him one. At trial, the State argued that Jackson needed the douche to remove any potential DNA evidence because Paulk and Jackson spent the prior night together and presumably had sex before Paulk stole Jackson's drugs and money.

Although a number of people were in Allen's apartment, Wooten and Jackson were the only people who entered the bathroom after Allen left. Jackson asked if anybody wanted to "have fun" with Paulk, but no one responded. Jackson obtained duct tape and, after putting on some gloves, went into the bathroom with the duct tape.

Once night fell, Jackson had several people serve as lookouts. Jackson then

CASE EXAMPLE: *CONTINUED*

FIGURE 7-6

The place, 208 N. Caroline St., Apt. C-6, where Pallis Paulk was allegedly held in a bathroom bathtub against her will. Investigators documented the exterior of the scene. However, they did not enter it; they did not process it for trace or transfer evidence (including victim and suspect DNA); they did not talk to neighbors; and they did not even seek to confirm whether there was actually a bathtub at all.

retrieved Paulk and carried her over his shoulder to one of his cars, a Oldsmobile Delta 88. As they neared the car, Paulk pleaded with Jackson not to put her in the trunk. Despite her pleas, Jackson forced Paulk into the trunk. Paulk resisted, straightening her legs so the trunk lid would not close. Jackson punched her in the face, Hunt hit Paulk in the back of her legs, and they were finally able to close the trunk. After retrieving his keys, Jackson left. Paulk's friends and family never saw her alive again....

On April 17, 2005, Paulk's body was discovered in a shallow grave. [See Figure 7-7.] There were no visible signs of injury, but her body was severely decomposed. Using dental comparisons, a forensic dentist affirmatively identified the body as Pallis Paulk. The medical examiner opined that the cause of death was homicidal violence of undetermined etiology. Although he was unable to determine the precise method of death, he ruled out a drug overdose after reviewing the toxicology report. Shortly

Continued

CASE EXAMPLE: *CONTINUED*

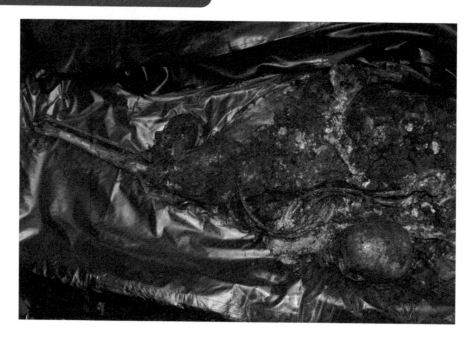

FIGURE 7-7
Pallis Paulk's remains were found in a shallow grave. They were severely decomposed, preventing the ME from determining a precise cause of death.

after Paulk's body was discovered, Hunt and Allen approached the police together, providing information regarding Paulk's disappearance.

At trial, in his defense, Jackson presented Captain Brian Skipper, an officer with the Daytona Beach Police Department, who testified about an alleged serial killer who murdered three women between December 26, 2005, and February 24, 2006. However, on cross-examination, the State demonstrated substantial differences between those crimes and the murder of Paulk.

It bears explaining that this version of events was established almost entirely with witness statements, and without corroboration by any physical evidence (save the medical examiner's and forensic dentist's

testimony, which only established her identity and that she was killed; for cause of death, the ME essentially relied on the theories of law enforcement, which were never investigated beyond witness statements or confirmed with any independent evidence).

With respect to victim exposure, the author testified to the following opinion during an appellate hearing (Turvey, 2011a):

1. The victim in this case, 23-year-old Pallis Paulk, was at extreme risk with respect to her lifestyle exposure, and high risk with respect to her incident exposure. This dramatically increases the number of potential suspects for any harm or loss that she suffered.

    A. As explained in Turvey (2011[b]), *victim exposure* is the amount of contact or vulnerability to harmful elements experienced by the victim. It is determined by evaluating *lifestyle* and *incident* exposure.

CASE EXAMPLE: *CONTINUED*

B. A victim's *lifestyle exposure* is related to the *frequency* of potentially harmful elements experienced by the victim and resulting from the victim's usual environment and personal traits, as well as past choices. *Extreme-exposure victims* are those who are exposed to the possibility of suffering harm or loss almost every day. Factors contributing to this in Ms. Paulk's lifestyle included at least the following:

  i. Ms. Paulk had a documented history of being the victim of domestic violence;

  ii. Ms. Paulk had a documented history of violent outbursts (e.g., punching the walls of her home);

  iii. Ms. Paulk had a documented history of criminal activity relating to forgery and theft;

  iv. Ms. Paulk had a documented history of drug addiction and alcohol abuse.

  v. Ms. Paulk had a documented history of association with those involved drug use, sales, and in violent criminal activity.

C. As explained in Turvey (2011[b]), a victim's *situational* or *incident exposure* refers to the amount of actual exposure or vulnerability to harm resulting from the environment, and the victim's personal traits, *at the time of victimization.* *High-exposure victims* are those who are exposed to harm or loss immediately prior to victimization. These victims are already suffering actual harm or loss prior to the point of victimization. Factors contributing to this in Ms. Paulk's situation, at the time of victimization, included at least the following:

  i. Toxicology results suggest that Ms. Paulk was abusing alcohol, cocaine, and methamphetamine just prior to her death.

  ii. Ms. Paulk had an active warrant out for her arrest at the time of her disappearance.

These factors do not take into account potential but unsubstantiated events from unreliable witness statements. This includes her sleeping with Ray Jackson the night before, her theft of items from Ray Jackson, his waving a gun at Calvin Morris with her in the back seat, her abuse in the bathtub at 208 N. Caroline St., Apt. C-6, and her forcible abduction from that location in the 1978 Oldsmobile Delta 88.

While these events are alleged to have occurred prior to her death, there is no reliable evidence that these events actually occurred.... If proved, they make this finding more likely not less likely. That is to say, the number of potential suspects in her disappearance would increase even further.

It bears mentioning that if the unproved events did occur, then this would have placed the victim at extreme situational risk. The point of this section of the report was to demonstrate that the potential suspects for the apparent murder of Pallis Paulk was actually quite high. More accurately, it was not just limited to the defendants. Given the fact that no physical evidence was found to associate Ms. Paulk with the vehicles or apartment mentioned in this case (and that there should have been), this finding was of particular relevance.

SUMMARY

As the definitions in this and the preceding chapter provide, it is important that lifestyle exposure and incident exposure be assessed independently. The forensic victimologist should avoid blanket characterizations of victim risk or exposure that merely combine an assessment of the two. This practice can lead to and has led to misrepresentation of actual victim exposure, and victim evidence, by virtue of focus on one area or the other. Making a regular habit of examining and characterizing lifestyle and incident exposure as separate features allows for reporting that avoids imprecision, misrepresentation, and eventual misunderstanding.

Additionally, forensic victimologists have a great responsibility to ensure or at least request that victim situational exposure factors be established, in context, before any conclusive interpretations are made. If they are biased in their examinations or report of findings, or if they are incomplete in their methods, then the actual circumstances of a crime will not be revealed. In an investigative context, the suspect pool will not be properly drawn; in a forensic context, the victimology may be misused to support a weak or circumstantial theory. It is the function of forensic victimologists to educate their clients and prevent such abuses by means of thoroughness and objectivity.

QUESTIONS

1. Describe the difference between *situational exposure* and *lifestyle exposure*. Provide one example of each to illustrate the difference.
2. List and describe three notable situational factors.
3. Describe the difference between *consecutive victims* and *concurrent victims*.
4. What is *cherry picking*? Why is it dangerous?
5. Explain what is meant by the term *extreme situational exposure*. How does this differ from *extreme lifestyle exposure*?

REFERENCES

BBC, 2008a. Suffolk killer will die in prison. BBC News, February 22; Available at: http://news.bbc. co.uk/2/hi/uk_news/england/suffolk/7258115.stm

BBC, 2008b. Wright guilty of Suffolk murders. BBC News, February 12; Available at: http://news. bbc.co.uk/1/hi/england/suffolk/7256402.stm

Bryden, D., 1997. Rape in the criminal justice system. Journal of Criminal Law and Criminology 87, Summer; pp. 1194–1384.

Cooley, C., Turvey, B., 2011. Observer effects and examiner bias: psychological influences on the forensic examiner. In: Chisum, W.J., Turvey, B. (Eds.), Crime Reconstruction, second ed. Elsevier Science, San Diego.

Florida v. Ray Jackson, 2009. Supreme Court of Florida, No. SC07–1233, September 24.

Hazelwood, R., 1995. Analyzing the Rape and Profiling the Offender, second ed. In: Burgess, A., Hazelwood, R. (Eds.), Practical Aspects of Rape Investigation: A Multidisciplinary Approach, CRC Press, New York.

Makron, J., 2006. Rabbi sentenced in internet sex sting. Washington Post, Saturday, December 2; p. B03; Available at: http://www.washingtonpost.com/wp-dyn/content/article/2006/12/01/ AR2006120100898.html

May, M., Lee, H., 2000. Sexual assault victim attacked again, police say. San Francisco Chronicle, November 17; p. A25.

Mersy, D., 2003. Recognition of alcohol and substance abuse. American Family Phsyician, April 1; Available at: http://www.aafp.org/afp/20030401/1529.html

Pollard, D., 2007. Sex torts. Minnesota Law Review 91, February; pp.769–824.

Prieto, B., 2008. Man held gun to baby as he raped her mother, Orange Sheriff's Office says. Orlando Sentinel, April 11; Available at: http://www.orlandosentinel.com/orl-rape1108apr11, 0, 7462514.story

Snyder, H., Sickmund, M., 1999. Juvenile Offenders and Victims. National Report 1999, U.S. Department of Justice, Office of Juvenile Justice and Delinquency Prevention, Washington, DC.

Snyder, H., 2000. Sexual assault of young children as reported to law enforcement: victim, incident, and offender characteristics. U.S. Department of Justice, Office of Justice Programs, Bureau of Justice Statistics, NCJ 182990, July.

Staff Writers, 2008. Ipswich prostitutes murder trial: prosecution outlines case against Steve Wright. The Telegraph, UK, January 17 http://www.telegraph.co.uk/news/uknews/1575721/Ipswich-prostitutes-murder-trial-Prosecution-outlines-case-against-Steve-Wright.html

Turvey, B., 2011a. Crime Scene Analysis report. Florida v. Ray J. Jackson Volusia Co. Case No. 05–32590CFAES, Supreme Court Case No. SC07-1233, February 9.

Turvey, B., 2011b. Criminal Profiling: An Introduction to Behavioral Evidence Analysis, fourth ed. Elsevier Science, San Diego.

UCR, 2007. Law enforcement officers killed and assaulted, 2006. U.S. Department of Justice, Federal Bureau of Investigation, Uniform Crime Report, October.

CHAPTER 8

Psychological Aspects of Victimology

Michael McGrath

KEY TERMS

Acute stress disorder (ASD) A diagnosable mental disorder characterized by the emergence of at least three dissociative symptoms within one month of suffering a traumatic event and lasting at least two days.

Battered woman syndrome (BWS) A proposed mental disorder suggested to affect women who have been involved in long-term violent relationships; the victim learns no longer to try to affect the course of the abuse, as she believes it will not change the outcome.

Blaming the victim How some perceive any suggestion that a victim may have contributed to his or her own victimization. It should be noted that pointing out how a victim has exposed himself or herself to being victimized is not the same as claiming that he or she deserved to be victimized.

Collateral victims The spouses, children, other family, and friends of the assaulted individual. They may suffer to varying degrees depending on their insight, age, and relationship to the victim. They may be helpful or unhelpful to the case.

Deification of the victim The tendency to view the victim as lacking flaws. This can happen after a violent crime, when investigators are given reports that victims were saintly in every aspect of their lives.

Hypnosis The art of putting someone in an altered state of consciousness, wherein critical thinking tends to be relaxed and the subject is more suggestible than normal. Those undergoing hypnosis may be susceptible to suggestion made by the hypnotist and may make things up or believe their recalled memories to be more accurate than they actually are.

Post-traumatic stress disorder (PTSD) A mental disorder with symptoms similar to acute stress disorder (ASD) but more chronic.

Rape trauma syndrome (RTS) A syndrome claimed to be developed by victims of rape or attempted rape, which consists of a phase of acute disorganization followed by a phase of long-term reorganization. During both phases, various lifestyle factors may be affected, including physical, psychological, social, and sexual. This syndrome has no criteria for accurate diagnosis other than a person having been subjected to the rape itself.

Stalking A repetitive act usually undertaken to cause distress to the victim; it may be perpetrated both in the real world and in cyberspace. Behaviors can range from unwanted communications with the victim to sexual assault, kidnapping, and homicide.

Stalking trauma syndrome (STS) A syndrome that involves a cycle of crisis, recovery, and anticipation, as the harassment is ongoing.

Victim toxicology The presence or absence of various substances in the system of a victim at a time that is related to the criminal event or the reporting of that event.

CONTENTS

207

Forensic Victimology. http://dx.doi.org/10.1016/B978-0-12-408084-3.00008-9

Victimology is one of the most important aspects of an investigation, following only the physical evidence found at a crime scene. Knowledge of the victim, including his or her habits, vulnerabilities, and strengths, as well as many other facets of his or her life, may offer investigators insight into the offender who acted against the victim. Some crimes are solved quickly, whereas others are not. Failure to adequately delve into the life of the victim of a serious, unsolved crime (such as a homicide) is inexplicable but not uncommon. This should not be surprising, considering that victimology as a field of study and research is rather young, beginning sometime in the 1940s and gaining momentum on the heels of the civil rights movement, the feminist movement, and a general increasing conservatism about crime in general and a fear of being a victim of violent crime in particular (Wallace, 2007).

Having a grasp of the psychological aspects of victimization can be very helpful to the investigator, prosecutor, and defense attorney. Investigators will not only review psychological information related to a deceased victim but also collect information from and interact with live victims. Understanding how the role of victim affects an individual is important, as victims of crime are often victimized twice—once by the offender and again by the criminal justice system. Uncooperative witnesses may be assumed to have filed a false report, when in fact they may be responding to perceived secondary victimization by law enforcement. Very cooperative victims may be perceived as exaggerating the offense because they do not appear to be as affected as expected. Myths regarding victim behavior as well as poorly validated victim "syndromes" add to the problem. This chapter deals with the psychological aspects of victimology, including the victim's response to violent crime, several victim syndromes found in the literature, and *victim toxicology*—the effect of medications and drugs on the victim.

When a violent crime occurs, there is often more than one victim. There is the victim or victims involved in the actual assault. Then there are what is best described as *collateral victims*—the spouses, children, other family, and friends of the assaulted individual. All suffer to varying degrees depending on their insight, age, and relationship. Sometimes they are helpful; sometimes they are not. Some support networks assist the victim in recovering and reintegrating into a former lifestyle, to varying degrees. Other support networks either initially doubt the victim's version of events or at some later time tire of the victim's response and wish that he or she would "just move on." This chapter deals only with the victim who was assaulted, but investigators must keep the collateral victims in mind because they may be interacting with the victim during an investigation. Certain victim populations requiring specialized knowledge are beyond the scope of this chapter. Such populations include children, the developmentally disabled, and the elderly.

CAUTIONARY NOTES

There are two features of victimology that interfere with its function as a body of knowledge and as an investigative tool: "deification of the victim" and fear of being accused of "blaming the victim." Deification of the victim is the tendency to view a victim as lacking flaws. This is sometimes exhibited after a violent crime (often a homicide) has occurred. Investigators are told by family, friends, and colleagues that the victim was essentially a saint and would never have done this or that. Lacking vital victimology information, investigators are unable to adjust the investigative strategy quickly. I recall one investigation in which a 16-year-old female was missing. Her family reported to police that the missing girl had never failed to come home in the past. Later, it was learned that on many occasions the missing teen had stayed away from home overnight, often attending parties where alcohol and sexual activity were commonplace. Apparently, the family was embarrassed that they were unable to control the teen. The inaccurate information delayed law enforcement pursuing appropriate avenues of investigation.

William Ryan (Kennedy and Sacco, 1998; p. 15) is credited with coining the term *blaming the victim*. The term was initially presented in Ryan's book *Blaming the Victim* (Ryan, 1971) as a social construct related to the middle-class blaming the poor for their poverty. The boundaries of blaming the victim expanded, and it has since become a method of attack on anyone who dares to intimate that victims may have in some way cooperated with their victimization or placed themselves in the position of being victimized. Pointing out how victims have exposed themselves to risk is different from implying that the victim "deserved" to be victimized. In fact, unwillingness to identify how victims placed themselves in a vulnerable position does nothing to help a deceased victim and is a disservice to a living victim (and potential future victims) who could be educated as to how to minimize exposure to risk in the future. It is well known that rape victims have often been blamed for being raped and that it has taken much education and social pressure to attempt to reverse this attitude.

In the spring of 2004, a 24-year-old female graduate student was found dead in Brooklyn, New York. She had been sexually assaulted and tortured before being killed. Investigation revealed she had been out drinking with a friend in Lower Manhattan. Her friend wanted to go home, and the victim wanted to stay out. The friend left her in a bar at about 2:30 in the morning. The friend, likely recognizing that the victim was at risk, called her later on her cellphone to check on her. The victim had gone to another bar and stayed until closing at 4:00 a.m. It is believed she was intoxicated when she left, alone. Her body was discovered around 16 hours later in Brooklyn (Wilson, 2006). Did this young woman deserve what happened to her? Of course not. Did she place herself at risk of an assault by being alone and intoxicated in Manhattan at

4:00 in the morning? Absolutely. Yet it was almost verboten for that reality to be mentioned in the media during discussions of the case. My best guess is that the same media commentators who were scrupulously avoiding blaming the victim went home and told their daughters not to go out drinking alone late at night, anywhere, let alone Manhattan.

Unfortunately, several months later, an 18-year-old recent high school graduate out drinking with a friend in Manhattan was murdered when she wandered off by herself, after their car was towed (CBS News, 2006). Again, did this young woman deserve to be killed? Of course not. Did she make choices that placed her at significant risk of assault? Absolutely. Would other potential victims benefit from knowing that being female (or male, for that matter), alone, and intoxicated at 3:00 a.m. in Manhattan is a dangerous situation? Should parents tell their children such things? I would only hope so. Is this blaming the victim? No, but it brings the issue of personal responsibility front and center.

A last note of caution pertains to input from experts. There may be times when obtaining professional input from a psychologist or a psychiatrist could be helpful in addressing victim characteristics and response to crime. However, the clinician would be limited to general commentary, as he or she will likely not have evaluated the victim, in which case confidentiality issues may be present. Occasionally, a psychological autopsy is helpful in assessing victimology, or if a crime has occurred at all. This would be the case when it is uncertain whether a death should be ruled a suicide or accidental death, as opposed to a homicide. It should be highlighted that psychological autopsies should be performed by qualified individuals, that is, forensic psychologists or psychiatrists. Changing the title of a report from a "psychological autopsy" to an "equivocal death analysis" when the review essentially relies on assessing the psychological state of a victim or offender does not relieve the examiner from the need to be qualified.[1]

VICTIM RESPONSE TO VIOLENT CRIME

Victim response to violent crime is highly variable, making any prediction of how a crime victim should behave problematic if not impossible. It is reasonable to frame the general response of a victim into three broad stages or phases: the *impact stage*, the *recoil stage*, and the *reorganization stage* (Wallace, 2007).

---

[1]An excellent example of this is the FBI Equivocal Death Analysis of Clayton Hartwig, accusing him of purposely causing the explosion in the gun turret of the USS Iowa in 1989. The entire botched investigation is described in detail in Thompson (1999). A critique of the FBI's methodology was presented in Otto et al., (1993) and "The U.S.S. Iowa: Guilt by Gestalt" (1991).

The impact stage is the initial response to the assault. The intensity and length will vary according to the intensity of the assault, the level of physical injury, and the perceived threat to life. The event will be filtered through the age, personality, and general mental health and life experience of the victim. Some victims will weather a vicious assault fairly well, whereas others will be functionally paralyzed by seemingly minor assaults.

During the recoil stage, victims attempt to deal with the effect of the crime on themselves and their lives. Emotions will be varied and include sadness, anger, self-pity, fear, and even guilt. At this stage, the victim is attempting to reconstitute his or her former self (Wallace, 2007). Denial often develops, and emotional detachment is sometimes evident. To a degree, this is healthy, allowing the victim time to slowly come to grips with what has happened. The length of time and the psychological depth of this stage will vary depending on the person.

The third phase or stage involves reorganization. The emotional intensity of the recoil stage is expected to lessen, and the victim is more energized to deal with life's daily activities (Wallace, 2007). Some people pass through the three stages fairly quickly, whereas others never finish the process. Completing the three stages does not mean that the victim no longer thinks about the crime or is not at times reminded of it to varying degrees. Depending on the nature and intensity of the assault, some victims never truly get over it.

Just as grief and mourning following the death of a loved one is a natural process, reacting to being a violent crime victim with a disruption of one's usual state of mind and daily function is normal and expected. It is the extent of disorganization and the length of time involved that will alert others to the need for formal intervention. Pathologizing normal reactions of victims by mental health professionals can occur.

Acute Stress Disorder

Acute stress disorder (ASD) is a diagnosable mental disorder that was introduced in the fourth edition of the *Diagnostic and Statistical Manual of Mental Disorders* (DSM-IV, 1994). In the DSM-IV-Text Revision (DSM-IV-TR 2000), the disorder is characterized by the emergence of at least three dissociative[2] symptoms (emotional numbing, feeling "dazed," derealization, depersonalization, dissociative amnesia) within one month after suffering a traumatic event and lasting at least two days. As part of the response to the event, the victim experiences intense fear, helplessness, or horror. The condition resolves within a month,

---

[2]The DSM-IV-TR (2000, p. 822) defines dissociation as a disruption in the usually integrated functions of consciousness, memory, identity, or perception of the environment.

or the diagnosis is changed to reflect the chronicity of symptoms. The traumatic event must be of a severe nature, for example, being exposed to possible death or serious injury, although diagnostic criteria allow for the diagnosis to be made for someone who witnesses such an event or only hears about such an event happening to a loved one or close associate. The traumatic event is persistently re-experienced in some manner, such as in having flashbacks and avoiding reminders of the trauma. There is evidence of hyperarousal or anxiety, and the disorder causes significant distress or interferes with the ability to function (DSM-IV-TR, 2000). A victim of a violent crime may meet criteria for this disorder or may suffer some but not all the necessary criteria. Other victims may suffer depression, anxiety, or both.

ASD was well correlated with the later diagnosis of post-traumatic stress disorder (PTSD) in one prospective study (Brewin et al., 1999), with ASD being diagnosed in 19% of victims of violent crime and PTSD at six months being diagnosed in 20%. This might lead to the question of whether they are really two different disorders. It would appear that there is a high level of overlap. Some researchers (Brewin, Andrews, and Rose, 2003; Marshall, Spitzer, and Liebowitz, 1999) critiqued ASD, questioning the requirement for dissociative symptoms soon after the trauma as a core feature. Theoretically, a person could be diagnosed at day 28 post-trauma with PTSD, but not have met the criteria for ASD during the preceding 28 days. This seems odd. Although the likely goal of the 30-day wait for a PTSD diagnosis is to avoid pathologizing normal reactions to trauma, it seems there should be some leeway to diagnose a post-traumatic stress disorder without dissociative symptoms.

Post-Traumatic Stress Disorder

The most well-known mental disorder related to trauma is *post-traumatic stress disorder (PTSD)*. This is a response very similar to the acute stress disorder but is more chronic. It can be "acute" if less than three months, "chronic" if greater than three months, and "delayed" if the onset is six months or more after the traumatic event. The diagnostic criteria include exposure to a traumatic event with a response including intense fear, helplessness, or horror. The event is re-experienced in a persistent manner in various ways, including one or more of the following: intrusive thoughts of the event; dreams; flashbacks; and psychological and/or physical reactions (rapid heartbeat, sweating) on exposure to cues connected to the event. An example would be a Vietnam veteran having a flashback when hearing something resembling helicopter rotors. In addition, there is emotional numbing and avoidance of stimuli associated with the event, as well as persistent symptoms of arousal, such as poor sleep, anger outbursts, hypervigilance, and an exaggerated startle response (DSM-IV-TR, 2000). The stereotypical example is the war veteran who attacks his wife when she wakes him. A victim of a serious assault, including rape, could develop PTSD.

As military conflict includes much opportunity to engender a stress response, PTSD (although not called that) was first recognized during the Civil War. It was called "shell shock" during World War I and "operational fatigue" and "combat neurosis" during World War II. A similar "concentration camp syndrome" was noted in many Holocaust survivors, highlighting that it was the trauma, not the person, that led to the disorder (Davidson, 1995). When initially formulated, the disorder was conceptualized in the context of the events one endures or witnesses during wartime. It is one of the most politicized diagnoses in the *Diagnostic and Statistical Manual*, being a result (at least to some degree) of the victims' rights movement (Gold, 2004). The present criteria are broader than when the diagnosis first appeared and include many scenarios that would not have qualified in the past. One of the criticisms of the PTSD diagnosis in a forensic context is the subjective nature of the diagnosis; that is, the victim reports the symptoms he or she claims to have (Miller, 2003a). But this critique could be applied to most psychiatric diagnoses. Others claim objective tests, such as the Minnesota Multiphasic Personality Inventory (MMPI), can identify malingerers (Fairbank, McCaffrey, and Keane, 1985) with over 90% accuracy, but not all agree, as one study (Perconte and Goreczney, 1990) found that the MMPI identified malingerers less than half the time.

The diagnosis of PTSD as a sequela of rape varies, with one researcher reporting 94% of rape victims showing symptoms of PTSD within a week of being raped (Rothbaum et al., 1992), although the rate drops as time passes. Rothbaum et al. (1992) included 95 victims of rape or attempted rape (which is arguably two different populations) in their study. As is common in studies of rape, there is no mention of the possibility of false reports. Subjects were recruited from an emergency room, as well as other referrals, and later contacted by researchers for the study. We know nothing of the women who chose not to participate. It is possible that they contained a cohort of women who would not develop PTSD, potentially skewing the sample and therefore the results. Of 95 women who entered the 12-week study, 64 completed. This means one-third did not complete. The researchers assumed, since the non-completers (women who missed at least 2 of the 12 sessions and were dropped from the study) did not appear to differ from completers at the initiation of the study, that it could be inferred they were representative of the entire study. Arguably they could have been more symptomatic or less. At the first session, 94% of the women met the criteria (except the 30-day rule) for PTSD. By the fourth session, 65% of the women met the criteria for PTSD; and at 12 weeks, 47% (p. 463). The study was prospective, had no control group, mixed victims of rape with victims of attempted rape, and was apparently unaware of the occurrence of false allegations of sexual assault.[3]

Regardless of the actual percentages, rape is a horrible thing to experience, and it should not be surprising that victims exhibit PTSD symptomatology to a considerable degree at some point in their recovery. Interestingly, Rothbaum et al. (1992, p. 472) suggest that not all rape victims require treatment because half recover spontaneously. I would argue that timely intervention to support rape victims is crucial in helping to decrease the incidence of psychological sequelae, including PTSD. As Rothbaum et al. (1992, p. 473) note at the end of their paper: "It is clear that PTSD is a prominent response following rape, although not a universal one."

PTSD has the imprimatur of a DSM-IV-TR (2000) diagnostic entity, but it is not without controversy (Faigman et al., 2006). Some (Summerfield, 2001) argue that PTSD is more a social construct than a mental health disorder. Others (Mezey and Robbins, 2001) believe the diagnosis has some validity but needs further refinement. And one group of researchers (Yehuda and McFarlane, 1995) have come to the conclusion that PTSD may be a distinct clinical entity but not for the reasons proffered by psychosocial theory and stress research. One recent study (Bodkin et al., 2006) raises the real possibility that the PTSD symptom picture (ignoring Criterion A, the trauma) is not necessarily trauma related, as there is so much overlap between PTSD symptoms and symptoms of other psychiatric disorders. In the study of 103 patients enrolled in a depression medication trial, the study found that symptomatic criteria, including one-month duration and functional impairment, "occurred commonly, regardless of trauma history" (p. 180).

If one presumes that the DSM is infallible and above politics, only relying on solid science to make its diagnostic category decisions, one would be surprised. We can turn to two examples. Regarding homosexuality, first it was a mental disorder, and then it was not.[4] Regardless of disclaimers, this diagnostic change was in response to pressure from gay rights groups, although the decision is easily supported both socially and medically. Self-defeating personality disorder, which began its life in 1984 as masochistic personality disorder, was introduced as a possible diagnosis. Feminist activists attacked the diagnosis, arguing

---

[3]If the reader thinks false allegations of sexual assault could not possibly skew the findings of such a study, that would be naïve. False allegations of sexual assault vary but can be as high as 50%, depending on the population. False victims included in such a study could be motivated to cooperate with the study to lend validity to their false allegations, reporting expected symptoms to researchers to gain or maintain their victim status.
[4]Currently, unless the subject finds his or her sexual orientation distressing (which may be better seen as a response to a societal expectation, not a criterion of a mental illness), a diagnosis can no longer be made.

it was unscientific and would be used against women (Tavis, 1992), and they were very likely right on both counts. Self-defeating personality disorder cannot be found in the current DSM (DSM-IV-TR, 2000). This commentary is not meant to disparage the DSM to the point of doing away with it, but rather to put the reliability and validity of the DSM in context.

Publication of a new edition of the DSM (DSM-V) is pending at the time of this writing. Expected changes in regard to the PTSD diagnosis are (1) adding "directly" in criterion A1, so that it would read "directly experienced, witnessed or was confronted with"; (2) proposal of PTSD in Preschool Children as a sub-type, instead of a separate diagnosis; (3) proposal of a dissociative symptoms sub-type; and (4) addition of criteria for a trauma- or stressor-related disorder not otherwise specified (APA, 2012).

OTHER TRAUMA SYNDROMES IN THE LITERATURE

Many trauma syndromes have been described that have sparse research to validate their actual diagnostic validity. While literature may exist purporting to support the syndromes, examination of this literature leaves one asking: "Where's the beef?" While PTSD (for better or worse) is the legal gold standard for "proof" that a victim suffered a major trauma, this fails to take into account that victims of violent crime can exhibit symptoms of mental disorders requiring treatment that do not meet criteria for PTSD. Victims can suffer depression, anxiety, dissociative episodes, and other symptoms as independent diagnoses. Obsessive-compulsive traits can emerge or worsen. Avoidance behaviors alone can be debilitative. All deserve attention in the victims of a violent crime. Victims should not be expected to have PTSD as a *sine qua non* of victimization. Also, the fact that a victim has been diagnosed as having PTSD should not be introduced into the courtroom as proof that the subject suffered a particular trauma, as the symptom picture is not trauma specific.

Battered Woman Syndrome

In 1979, Lenore Walker published *The Battered Woman*. After interviewing over 100 women, Walker formulated her theory of the cycle of violence and her adaptation of learned helplessness. Later, she described the *battered woman syndrome (BWS)* in her seminal work *The Battered Woman Syndrome* (1984). This was a study of 435 women who were involved at some point in a relationship that included domestic violence. Walker raised consciousness regarding the problem, confirming that "battered women come from every walk of life and no particular characteristic in a woman leads her to become an abuse victim" (Walker, 2000; p. 17). Regarding one aspect of the research, Walker uses the syndrome to attempt to explain why a woman would remain in a violent relationship, in spite of the physical or psychological violence perpetrated against her. This syndrome has been used at times as a defense after a woman killed her alleged batterer at a time when the victim was not deemed to be in actual peril (e.g., while the batterer was sleeping) or as a reason a woman acted in concert to commit a crime with the alleged batterer.

Walker (1979) described her theory that there was a cycle of violence inherent in domestic violence. There are three phases to the abuse. First, there is a tension-building phase. This is followed by the actual physical assault. The third phase is the loving-contrition phase when the batterer often apologizes, begs forgiveness, and promises not to repeat the abuse. Walker (2000, p. 127) suggests that the third phase "provides the positive reinforcement for remaining in the relationship, for the woman." Walker goes on to state (p. 128) that as the domestic violence progresses, the tension-building phase becomes more common and the loving-contrition phase declines. The cycle theory is helpful in describing domestic violence, but it fails to explain why the battered partner does not end the relationship. Because the loving-contrition phase is the purported reason the woman remains in the relationship, as it dissipates in time and quality, there would appear to be less of an incentive for the battered woman to stay.

Walker introduced the concept of "learned helplessness" to meet that need. Originally conceptualized by Seligman, Maier, and Geer (1968) after Seligman's experiments with dogs, learned helplessness was the result of administering a noxious stimulus with no means of escape. Eventually, the animal stopped trying to evade the stimulus. Walker used this concept for battered women (1979, p. 47):

> Once we believe we cannot control what happens to us, it is difficult to believe we can ever influence it, even if we later experience a favorable outcome. This concept is important for understanding why battered women do not attempt to free themselves from a battering relationship. Once the women are operating from a belief of helplessness, the perception becomes reality and they become passive, submissive, "helpless."

Later, Walker takes pains to explain that "[l]earned helplessness was confused with being helpless, and not its original intended meaning *of having lost the ability to predict that what you do will make a particular outcome occur*" (Walker, 2000; p. 116; emphasis in original).[5] In other words, the victim adopts a mindset in which she no longer tries to affect the course of abuse because it will

---

[5]Dr. Walker's original intent was to portray the battered woman as helpless. This new interpretation adds little if anything. The battered woman has apparently gone from being helpless because she believed she could not control something to being helpless because she cannot predict something.

make no difference in the outcome. Therefore, learned helplessness is not helplessness. But it is the helplessness factor that is presented in court when BWS is presented as a defense or mitigating factor. The revised helplessness in learned helplessness was in response to criticisms of the syndrome, specifically the learned helplessness issue, where some suggested that battered women were masochistic or had personality traits that led them to provoke the violence. Interestingly, while the theory is meant to explain why women remain with their batterers, it does not explain why women leave their batterers.

In addition, while the syndrome has been used as an explanation or defense for women who kill their batterers, it is these very women whose behavior potentially refutes the syndrome. Browne (1987, pp. 128–130) refers to a "turning point" or change in the domestic violence paradigm for a particular couple. As Blackman (1989, p. 188) frames it:

> Thus, they may strike back at times that sound less dangerous than previous episodes of abuse, or that may not sound life-threatening at all. Nonetheless, they may reasonably believe that their lives are at risk because of the changes in the abuser's routine style of assault, or because the abuser says or does something, that in the past, has signaled great danger.

The presence of a "turning point" that causes the battered victim to take a new course of action, that is, kill the batterer when he is not posing an imminent threat, "is arguably incongruous with both a learned helplessness response and Walker's cyclical theory of violence because it involves a diversion from, and not a continuation of, existing cognitive and behavioral patterns" (Craven, 2003). Walker (2000, p. 116) frames criticism of her helplessness paradigm as "a good lesson in battered women's feminist politics." She then advises that (p. 117) "even those colleagues who understood the concept of learned helplessness began to reject it in favor of post-traumatic stress theory."

Walker earlier spelled out the relationship between BWS and PTSD in *Terrifying Love* (1984), Walker's book on battered women who kill, where she advises on how to diagnose BWS ("Making a Diagnosis," pp. 178–179):

> The proper application of Battered Woman Syndrome can make many things clear in cases in which the sanity of a battered woman defendant is in question. Because it is a subcategory of Post-Traumatic Stress Disorder, four specific criteria must be met, clinically measured, and evaluated for Battered Woman Syndrome to be assigned as a psychological diagnosis.

The criteria are the same four criteria for diagnosing PTSD, except the duration of at least one month for meeting the symptom criteria. There is a footnote after the last sentence quoted here, indicating that the authority for the claim that BWS is a sub-category of PTSD is "[a]ccording to section 309.81 of the American Psychiatric Association's *Diagnostic and Statistical Manual of Mental Disorders*, 3rd ed., revised (DSM-III-R)." I was not aware that BWS was a sub-category of PTSD. In reviewing the cited source, I found first that there is no section 309.81.

Presumably, this is a typographical error, as the section for PTSD is 309.89 (DSM-III-TR, 1987; pp. 247–251). Nevertheless, I could not find where in the DSM-III-R Walker reads BWS is a sub-category of PTSD. One would hope that Walker was given enough time to correct this error, but in her second edition of *The Battered Woman Syndrome* (2000, p. 117) Walker writes:

> And while Battered Woman Syndrome has been similarly criticized for making it easier to pathologize battered woman, it is my opinion that as a subcategory of PTSD, it is the most useful diagnostic category to use for battered women when it is necessary to use a diagnostic formulation.

This quote is difficult to interpret as to what is fact and what is opinion. Walker appears to be stating that BWS is a sub-category of PTSD and that it is her opinion a diagnosis of PTSD (with BWS as a sub-category) is most useful for diagnostic purposes. But nowhere in any DSM can one find the term *Battered Woman Syndrome*. As the DSM-III is discussed in relation to "post-traumatic stress theory" in the previous paragraph (Walker 2000, p. 117), a reader would be forgiven if he or she assumed the quote referred to PTSD as defined by the DSM. Not surprisingly, this misinformation is continued (see below) in the third edition of *The Battered Woman Syndrome* (Walker, 2009).

I have two comments regarding this last quote. First, it would appear that Walker is suggesting that if you have identified someone as a battered woman and you need a diagnostic category for her (whether for treatment or for court), then PTSD is the most useful diagnosis. I would suggest that the most useful diagnosis would be the one that best encapsulates the symptoms the person suffers from, be it PTSD, depression, anxiety, and so on.

Second, BWS is not a formal sub-category of PTSD, although some may refer to it as such. These kinds of statements are factually incorrect and misleading to those unfamiliar with the various DSMs. In fact, the DSM-III, DSM-III-R, DSM-IV, and the DSM-IV-TR do not list any sub-categories of PTSD, other than allowing specification of acute, chronic, or delayed onset. While repeated physical, psychological, and/or sexual assault in a domestic violence situation could very well result in diagnosable PTSD in the victim, the diagnosis would be PTSD, not BSW or PTSD-BSW. These types of comments, claiming or inferring that a particular syndrome is a sub-category of PTSD (see below regarding rape trauma syndrome), seem to imply approval of the purported syndrome by the DSM-IV-TR (and by extension the American Psychiatric Association, which publishes the DSM series) when no such approval or endorsement exists. Motor vehicle accidents can lead to PTSD, and the DSM-IV-TR (American Psychiatric Association, 2000, p. 464) notes this, but no one describes a Motor Vehicle Accident (MVA) sub-category of PTSD that can be used as an alternative diagnosis to an MVA Syndrome because no such sub-category exists. The DSM-IV-TR does not have sub-categories related to specific traumas because the symptoms are not trauma specific, despite the wishes of some.

The often-cited[6] four general characteristics of BWS are (1) the woman believes that the violence was her fault; (2) the woman has an inability to place the responsibility for the violence elsewhere; (3) the woman fears for her life and/or her children's lives; and (4) the woman has an irrational belief that the abuser is omnipresent and omniscient. The citation offered in such instances is Walker's *The Battered Woman Syndrome* (1984, pp. 95–97), but no such four characteristics can be found on pages 95, 96, and 97.

Battered woman syndrome testimony has been offered in the courtroom, usually as a way of educating a jury as to why a woman would kill her domestic partner when not actually in imminent danger, or when the credibility of a domestic violence victim has been attacked. For example, in *State v. Haines* (2006) "limited" expert testimony on battered woman syndrome was upheld when it helped the judge or jury determine the victim's state of mind when she returns to or remains in an abusive relationship despite the alleged abuse. In this case, the victim claimed she had endured an 18-day episode of confinement and abuse, yet remained in the relationship and made conflicting statements when finally reporting the events.

Patricia Johnson spent 15 years in prison in California for shooting her husband. Her conviction was overturned in 2004 because the trial judge would not allow expert testimony on BWS. Ms. Johnson had alleged psychological abuse from her husband (Figueroa, 2006). She was convicted again at her second trial. Also in California, Ny Nourn, 18 years old at the time of the crime, was convicted of murder for the December 1993 killing of her boss (Roth, 2003). Her boyfriend had become jealous after finding out that she had had sex with the victim. She was accused of luring him to his death, with her boyfriend committing the actual murder. Several years after the murder, Nourn came forward to authorities, claiming she had been abused by her boyfriend and felt she had to appease him. Her murder conviction was overturned due to her not being able to present battered woman syndrome evidence to the jury.

---

[6]See, for example, http://www.divorcenet.com/states/oregon/or_art02 and http://www.rainn.org/effects-of-rape/battered-woman-syndrome.html.

As of 1996, the National Institute of Justice guidelines regarding expert testimony related to battering and its effects have been admitted to some degree in every state and the District of Columbia, as well as 16 of 19 federal courts that considered the issue. Some courts have allowed testimony on BWS, and some have not. Often a court's review of the situation skirts the issue that the scientific basis for the syndrome is limited.[7] Some states, such as Ohio, allow testimony on BWS as a matter of legislation. This circumvents the court's gatekeeper function regarding the validity of scientific evidence. Faigman et al. (2006, pp. 266–267) comment in a footnote that this sends the wrong message to researchers, among others: "legislation does not solve the problems associated with poor research methodology or advocacy masquerading as science."

There has been significant criticism of BWS, especially in regard to its use in court. Dixon and Dixon (2003) point out that Walker's research has limitations, including the lack of replication by others and lack of control groups. But Walker argues that such criticism is unfair (2000, p. 146):

> In conducting this research design, certain decisions were made that were appropriately influenced by the feminist perspective. For example, given the finite resources available, it was decided to sacrifice the traditional empirical experimental model, with a control group, for the quasiexperimental model using survey-type data collection. It was seen as more important to compare battered women to themselves than to a nonbattered control group. Comparing battered and nonbattered women implies looking for some deficit in the battered group, which can be interpreted as a perpetuation of the victim-blaming model.[8] Our data indicate that the differences within the group of battered women studied ranged across the continuum expected for all women. From this, it is possible to hypothesize that whatever differences exist between groups are so minimal that they serve to confuse rather than gain additional knowledge about spouse abuse.

This explanation of why the study parameters were used appears to be a retrospective justification. Walker, rather than accepting valid criticism of her work, is asking for a scientific pass.[9] McMahon (1999, p. 31) was quite critical of BWS

---

[7]Dixon and Dixon (2003) provide a good critique of gender-based syndromes from both a scientific and a legal perspective.

[8]Note here how "blaming the victim" is used, as anyone who criticizes this research on the lack of control groups runs the risk of being accused of blaming the victim. This line of defense by Dr. Walker would seem to show she is unable to justify her decisions on standard research grounds.

[9]This is reminiscent of the FBI study that resulted in the Organized–Disorganized Dichotomy of serial offenders: [A]n inadequate study design using flawed questionnaire data resulted in a criminal profiling paradigm that was inherently investigatively useless and never validated. Yet to this day the FBI continues to use (with occasional denials) the Organized–Disorganized profiling paradigm.

and the science behind it: "the key empirical basis for battered woman syndrome is…characterized by methodological flaws, conceptual imprecision and internal inconsistency." McMahon (1999) noted that Walker's major research (prior to publication of the third edition of *The Battered Woman Syndrome*) consisted of two self-report studies from a non-random, self-referred sample. Neither study had a control group. To try to overcome this limitation, in one study Walker (1984) used some of the subjects as their own controls, "by obtaining information from them about non-battering relationships in which they had been involved" (McMahon, 1999; p. 31). The two principal studies Walker relies on for BWS were a preliminary study of "more than 120" battered women and a later study of 403 battered women. These samples were from women who sought help of some nature. The larger study sample (p. 31) "was skewed towards professionally employed women who, after experiencing moderate levels of violence, left their abusive partner: 'self-selected survivors' (Walker, 1984; p. 229)." As McMahon (1999, p. 31) points out, there is no way to know how reliable the data is or how representative the sample was of women in general who are battered—a point acknowledged and then dismissed by Walker (1984). The lack of control groups leaves us not knowing "whether levels of depressions and self-esteem reported by Walker's (1984) respondents are significantly different to those of a comparable sample of women in intimate, heterosexual, nonbattering relationships" (McMahon, 1999; p. 31).

McMahon (1999) cites discrepancies in Walker's study data, giving as an example that while Walker reported that the percentage of battered women who were themselves violent toward the abusive partner was "small,"[10] her own data showed almost one-quarter (24%) of women in a violent relationship reported "occasionally" or "frequently" using physical force (p. 174), hardly a "small" proportion. As Walker provides in the appendix to the second edition of *The Battered Woman Syndrome* (2000; Appendix A: Table 13, p. 237), in response to the question, "Did you ever threaten to leave to get something you wanted?" (n = 400), 73% answered occasionally (52%) or frequently (21%) during a violent relationship. It would appear that (at least for this sample) the battered women had little problem threatening to leave as a form of manipulation. As to using actual physical violence to get what they wanted (n = 397), 23% answered occasionally and 1% answered frequently, which is the data noted by McMahon previously. The 1% (2 of 397 subjects) figure for frequent use of violence is simply too low to be believed, and even more so when one realizes that the math is off. Two divided by 397 is 0.5%. While this may be the percentage

---

[10]Walker (1984, p. 150) reports: "Still the percentage was small, with 15% of those in a violent relationship and 5% in a nonbattering relationship reporting the use of violence." This 15% figure is at odds with Walker's Table 13 (p. 174), which give 24% for combined, 23% for occasional, and 1% for frequent use of physical violence.

of battered women who admit in Walker's study to frequently using physical force themselves, it is not likely to be the percentage of battered women who actually engage frequently in physical violence against the batterer.

Compared to other research (Straus, 1999), the finding that women assaulted men in marital, cohabiting, and dating relationships on an almost 50–50 basis as men assault women, the percentage proffered (1%, but corrected to 0.5%) for frequent by the female partner could not be accurate. There has been little interest in exploring violence used by women in general, let alone those involved in domestic violence research, and pursuing such research is often interpreted as anti-feminist (Straus, 1999). One meta-analysis (Archer, 2000) of physical aggression in heterosexual relationships found that men were more likely to inflict an injury and 62% of those injured were women, but the flip side is that 38% of men were injured by the female partner and women were slightly more likely than men to use physical aggression "and to use such acts frequently" (p. 651). Walker should have been alarmed by the low levels of occasional violence and the almost non-existent level of frequent violence suggested by her sample, as an indication that something was seriously amiss with her sample, research methodology, or both.

Additionally, while Walker has described the batterer in her studies, all data on the batterer has been derived from the battered women, a "secondary sampling" approach that tells us about the victim's perceptions of the batterer rather than reliably defining the batterer. Such "secondary sampling" obviously has limited utility.

The Battered Woman (Walker, 1979) and other media chosen by Walker (including one film, four books, and three articles, two authored by Walker [2000, p. 277]) on the subject of battered women were part of the training for the interviewers responsible for day-long interviews and subsequent coding, including coding of subjective data into "usable categories" (Walker, 2000; p. 273). This curriculum on the subject of battered women, which was the basis for the study's hypothesis, ensured that the interviewers were very familiar with not only the area of battered women in general, but Walker's views and theories, specifically the cycle of violence and learned helplessness theory, which was the basis for the research. One cannot help but wonder if bias crept into this study.

Walker identified the issue and then moved past it (2000, p. 280): "Ideally, of course, those who collect data should be unaware of the hypotheses being tested." Since she felt it was unrealistic to find interviewers who had no knowledge of the subject (which may have been a realistic situation), Walker apparently decided to formalize any potential bias (p. 280):

> First, we attempted to "standardize" [quote marks in original] the
> amount of information about battering that each interviewer had, by

making sure they received the same, though minimal, information about the project. Although the specific hypotheses were not discussed, a general outline of some major explanations for battering relationships was given. Aside from this, there was no control over how much information an interviewer obtained.

It could be argued that the curriculum imposed on interviewers was not small, but that may be in the eye of the beholder. Regardless, Walker made sure that her data collectors were very familiar with what she was looking for, even if unwittingly. As noted by McMahon (1999), many of the questions used were open-ended. With the interviewer's familiarity with the research hypotheses (in general, if not specifically), this is cause for concern. One is left wondering if, having recognized the problem of potential interviewer bias, Walker attempted to standardize it or to maximize it.

Further, the "structured" interview changed during the course of the second larger study. McMahon (1999, p. 33) notes that "the format of important items relating to sexual assault were varied from open ended questions to closed questions employing forced-choice response categories during the course of the research study." Faigman (1986) criticized Walker's use of leading questions in her research and the fact that her research does not support her three-stage cycle of violence paradigm. For example, in Walker's data (1984, pp. 96–97), the tension-building phase was present in only 65% of the subject relationships, and only 58% had a contrition phase. Faigman (1986) reviewed Walker's data and determined that only about 38% of her cases would have been likely to have experienced the three stages of the cycle of violence. This means that a little over a third of the affected parties met the criteria for the paradigm that their data was used to create or support. Not surprisingly, there is no good empirical research supporting Walker's cycle of violence or BWS-learned helplessness, no matter what version is offered. Studies finding higher-than-average levels of psychopathology in battered women, such as Gleason (1993), do not correlate this directly with a "battered woman syndrome."

In contrast to helplessness and paralysis, some researchers have viewed battered women as survivors who actively seek help. A Texas study of 6,612 women who entered a shelter for battered women (Gondolf and Fisher, 1988; pp. 91–93), during an 18-month period in 1984–1985, noted:

> The most outstanding of these [the study's] findings is that the battered women are active helpseekers. The woman's helpseeking appears to increase as the batterer becomes more apparently dangerous and incorrigible. The women, in sum, are not the passive victims that notions of learned helplessness would imply. They are in fact "survivors," in that they assertively and persistently attempt to do something about their abuse.

The study also notes that the help sources to which the women turn have limited ability to intervene, which explains to some degree why some battered women stay in an abusive relationship. Even Walker noted (1984, p. 27) that her BWS sample sought help: "As the violence escalated, so did the probability that the battered woman would seek help. While only 14% sought help after the first battering incident, 22% did after the second, 31% after one of the worst, and 49% sought help after the last incident."

Relating the helplessness of BWS to a homicide, Walker was prepared to testify to BWS as a diminished capacity part of a self-defense strategy in a case in which a woman had hired a hit man to kill her husband (Walker, 1989; p. 293). Helen Martin and her husband, Ronald, were separated after five years of an allegedly abusive marriage. The husband did not live with Ms. Martin and had made threats to burn down her house. She hired a man to kill her husband, and in December of 1980 the hit man shot the husband as he left Ms. Martin's house after he had signed some legal papers to avoid foreclosure on the house. The court (*State v. Martin*, 1984; p. 897) quotes her as having said, after the first shot, "He's not dying fast enough—hit him again." Ms. Martin then celebrated a friend's birthday. The next day she reported the husband missing, and the day after that she paid the life insurance premiums for her husband's life insurance policies (pp. 897–898). The trial judge refused to allow Walker to give BWS testimony. Ms. Martin was convicted of murder and appealed, at least in part, on the basis of being denied the opportunity to present BWS testimony to the jury. The Missouri Court of Appeals upheld the trial judge's ruling. Feigman (1986, p. 632) found "Walker's intended role in Martin deeply disturbing. That the leading theoretician of battered woman syndrome would be willing to characterize Martin as a case of legitimate self-defense seems to call into question the credibility of her testimony in other cases."

Other cases in which women hired hit men to kill a spouse and then attempted to use a BWS defense include *State v. Leaphart* (1983), where the testimony was not allowed; *State v. Anderson* (1990); *Anderson* (the same Anderson, now in federal court) *v. Goeke* (1995), where BWS was allowed but a self-defense instruction to the jury was not made; and *People v. Yaklich* (1992), where BWS testimony was allowed but not self-defense instruction.

A neglected topic is malingering, or perhaps more likely, false reporting in total or in part. The subject is usually ignored, yet it exists. In a letter to the editor of the *American Journal of Psychiatry*, Neil Blumberg (1992) mentions that he had identified a woman malingering BWS in his forensic practice. But he takes great pains to indicate that his letter "is not intended to criticize the legitimacy or importance of recognizing the battered woman syndrome" (p. 715). If only the doctor had done his homework, he might not have felt the need to be so cautious.

Walker (2000, p. 161), in describing how one evaluates a battered woman, presents the assumptions she works with: "The first one is to believe a woman when she claims to be battered. It is rare that a woman would make up such ghastly stories." I do not fault Walker for wanting to believe her study subjects; I do, however, fault her for not being realistic regarding the possibility of false reports of victimization in general, and for exaggerating one actor's role while minimizing that of another. Interestingly, Walker further comments (p. 161):

> Many of the new strategies for detecting malingering and deception have not been normed on a population of battered women, who may have self-interest in claiming to be battered when they are not, but also may be telling as much of the truth as they can given their long history of lying and manipulating to cover up for the abuser.

So, according to Walker, we can't use any of the non-battered-women-normed methods of detecting malingering, and we should accept at face value any information presented by Walker to us that is drawn from a population that she advises is skilled in deception.

As Dixon and Dixon (2003, p. 36) point out:

> There is neither scientific evidence that such a distinct syndrome truly exists nor consistency of effects across individuals. In addition, as long as researchers only study pre-identified groups of women who all have a battering history, rates of accuracy and error in diagnosing the syndrome will remain unavailable.... The paucity of research establishing BSW as a bona fide reliable condition egregiously undercuts the claim that the condition exists as a distinct diagnostic entity. Though the battering of women is likely epidemic, experts cannot reliably diagnose a related "Syndrome."

Dutton (1996) critiques BWS with the following points: (1) there is no single profile of a battered woman; (2) the term *battered woman syndrome* is vague; (3) PTSD, compared to other psychological reactions to battering, is not uniquely relevant for understanding legal (or other) domestic violence-related issues; (4) relevant information for expert testimony, advocacy, and treatment involving battered victims extends beyond the psychological effects of battering; and (5) the term *battered woman syndrome* creates an image of pathology. The 1996 National Institute of Justice (p. viii) report on the validity of BWS stated: "The term 'battered woman syndrome' portrays a stereotypic image of battered women as helpless, passive, or psychologically impaired, and battering relationships as matching a single pattern, which might not apply in individual cases."

In Walker's 2002 study (Walker, 2006, p. 148) of 76 battered women, she used the "definition of PTSD plus additional BWS criteria.... The initial results indicate that PTSD does exist in battered women." No one will argue with this statement. The next sentence is: "BWS has been empirically shown to be a subcategory of PTSD" (p. 150). Once again we are presented with a non-randomized, self-selected study (n = "the first 76"), without a control group, that is making unsupportable conclusions. The BWS definition is now (p. 147) PTSD (re-experiencing the event, numbing of responsiveness, hyperarousal) plus three additional "effects": disrupted interpersonal relationships, difficulties with body image/somatic concerns, and sexual and intimacy problems.

It would appear that, as the three additional "effects" are what now separates BWS from non-BWS-PTSD, this is what we will use in the future to make the diagnosis of the purported BSW-PTSD sub-category. But there is nothing to tell us what the prevalence of these three "effects" are in women in general and in women who suffer trauma of types other than domestic violence. There is nothing to convince us that these three "effects" are selective for BWS. Once again, we are left with problematic research defining diagnostic syndromes that may be offered in court as part of a mitigating or self-defense presentation.

The third edition of Dr. Lenore Walker's *The Battered Woman Syndrome* was published in 2009. Although arguably grander in scope, the work suffers from the same research flaws as earlier renditions. While Walker felt it "was time to revisit the information collected in the original study in 1971–1981,"(p. 2) and modify the Battered Woman Syndrome Questionnaire (BWSQ), she still neglects to use appropriate control groups. The new sample group includes women of non-USA nationalities either living elsewhere or in the United States. In an attempt to rehabilitate her learned helplessness prototype of battered women, Walker (p. 8) states: "As we have learned, and these studies confirm, battered women are not helpless at all." But in order to protect the legal prong of BWS, she adds (p. 9): "Sometimes they use force that might seem excessive to a non-battered woman in order to protect themselves and their children."

As an example of Walker's logic when it comes to BWS, she claims that when BWS testimony or information has led to release from prison of women convicted of the murder of a domestic partner (Walker, 2009; p. 32): "The women who have been released have gone on to lead productive lives, *proving* [emphasis added] the testimony that they are not murderers, but rather, killed to save their own or children's lives." How so? Perhaps she is unaware that the recidivism rate for murder is about 1% (U.S. Department of Justice, 2002), which is very low to begin with, and it is likely even lower for those without a criminal record prior to the first homicide.

Once again, Walker misinforms her readers (p. 33): "Meanwhile, the categories of 'Post Traumatic Stress Disorder' (PTSD) and later on, 'Acute Stress Reaction' (ASR) were added to the DSM where it became possible to diagnose women who demonstrated evidence of BWS as having a subcategory of PTSD." Perhaps the devil is in the details. While it is agreed that rape is a trauma that can lead to PTSD, inferring that this then becomes a sub-category of PTSD is not accurate, as there are no sub-categories of PTSD; for good reason, as the symptoms are not trauma specific. While one is free to diagnose PTSD in a battered woman, there is no sub-category for BWS.

The BWSQ #2[11] was developed, and each student interviewer was trained and given a copy of the manual (Walker et al., 2006). "Controls were provided by the groups from the standardized tests" (Walker, 2009; p. 33) It is hard to know what this means, especially when no other explication around control groups is forthcoming. A search of the text only finds references to control groups in relation to other (non-Walker) studies. The research project was still underway at the time of the third edition's publication, and "the data are still being collected and therefore, those that have been evaluated were from a convenience sample without correctional factors…" (p. 48) Walker further notes (p. 52): "These analyses gave some interesting and clarifying information about the development of PTSD, especially since not every woman who is battered will develop it, nor will all battered women, with or without PTSD, develop BWS." It is hard to reconcile this with the assertion that BWS is a sub-category of PTSD.

In attempting to provide empirical data that BWS equates with PTSD, Walker says (2009, p. 64): "There are limitations on generalizing these results. Obviously, this was not a random sample but rather a convenience sample so there may be untold biases that were not controlled for…. However, these women were similar in demographics from the battered women who volunteered to participate in the original study." Walker does not mention that the original study was also a convenience sample (p. 64): "This analysis is a small sample and needs replication with a larger sample…. Nonetheless, it is an important step forward to know that there is some empirical support for the theories that have been around for over 30 years now." This may be a new song, but it is the same old dance. And noting the 30-year history of her theories is an appeal to longevity, not science; astrology has been around much longer, but it is still not science.

Findings inconsistent with BWS are used as evidence for BWS. For example (Walker, 2009; p. 96), "[w]omen still in a violent relationship did not report powerful others as being any more in control of their lives than themselves. Perhaps a battered woman cannot begin to terminate her marriage while there is this lack of realization that her batterer is in control of her everyday activities and of her life." Perhaps, but why does Walker discount what her subjects say only when it does not support BWS? Interestingly, Walker appears to

---

[11]A request to Dr. Walker as to how one might obtain a copy of the manual failed to result in its becoming available.

undermine her whole paradigm describing her cycle of violence. "Once the cost–benefit ratio changes, however, and the rate of reinforcement decreases, then the women may be more inclined to leave the relationship..." (p. 101). "Once the cost of living in a violent relationship begins to escalate, paralleling the seriousness of the abusiveness and injuries, women's help-seeking behavior breaks through the privacy of the home, if they perceive actual help is available" (p. 101). This is not a misunderstanding of her own BWS paradigm, but better seen as damage control, as many have pointed out (see above) that battered women do not appear to fit the BWS exemplar.

According to Walker (see above), BWS is PTSD with several other features that distinguish it further: (1) disruption in interpersonal relationships, (2) difficulties with body image and somatic symptoms, and (3) sexual intimacy issues. Walker's research around body image is presented with percentages (see Walker, 2009; Table 7.4, p. 163), but not the number of subjects. Also, we are not given any data for the alleged control group (see p. 33) or groups referred to. It is not possible to compare the percentage of BWS subjects versus "normal subjects" versus women who have suffered other (non-domestic-violence) trauma. The data is meaningless.

Walker then presents the sexuality issues. She opines that sexual abuse in BWS differs from other types of sexual abuse, with "[p]erhaps the most significant fact was the realization that sexual abuse in intimate relationships is more like incest than stranger rape, which has more physical violence" (Walker, 2009, p. 167). But aren't these male batterers violent? In Table 8.1 (p. 171), the number of subjects responding to questions is given. There are other tables without numbers, only giving percentages. Again, we are left with confusing data, with no way of knowing the relationship to "normal" controls and controls who experienced trauma different from domestic violence. Interestingly, "[f]orty-six percent (46%) of the women said they had stopped having sex with the batterer to get what they wanted from him" (p. 172). How does this equate with a (learned helpless) battered woman as exemplified by BWS? Walker created a scale to measure satisfaction with sexuality (Table 8.2, p. 174). She then subjects her findings to various statistical testing, once again feeling no need to compare anything to controls.

Walker then presents her current research on how BWS affects interpersonal relationships. Not surprisingly (Walker, 2009; p. 205), "our data could not permit determining when attachment difficulties might have begun; either before, during or after the battering relationship (Darby/Nathan, Duros, Tome and Walker, 2007)."[12] Apparently, this is not a problem in determining the effect

---

[12]No further citation is given in *The Battered Woman Syndrome,* 3rd edition. It is not found in the "Reference" section.

of domestic violence on interpersonal relationships. The sample consisted of 32 women. "The majority" were recruited in jail or advertisements.[13] Walker's results "confirm the hypothesis that battered women are at elevated risk for avoidant and/or anxious/ambivalent attachment styles, and less likely to exhibit secure attachment styles" (Walker, 2009; p. 205). Table 9.1 (p. 207) lists the percentage of responses to ten questions designed to measure attachment style. Determining the N for each question should concern the reader because there are three choices: Never, Rarely/Occasionally, and Often/Always. The Rarely/Occasionally and Often/Always are conflated as opposed to the Never category. There is no mention of why this was necessary, although small sample size may have been one reason. The number of subjects who endorsed Often/Always "having difficulty making friends" is four, or 13%. Often/Always "trapped in a relationship" is five subjects (16%). Often/Always "people treat you like a thing" was one subject (3%). The analysis of this could go on, but the point is that (1) it is likely percentages were listed (only) to avoid the reader's being reminded of the very small numbers being relied on to infer support for the hypothesis; (2) there were no controls; and (3) it could be argued the data shows the opposite of Dr. Walker's findings, as most (81%) of the sample do not endorse feeling lonely (versus 9% who do), only 13% endorse difficulty making friends, and only 13% endorse being afraid to form close relationships. And "being treated like a thing" (expected to be high in a battered population) is endorsed by only 3% of the sample with 75% choosing Never or Rarely/Occasionally. The reader may have noticed that 75% plus 3% does not equal 100%. Apparently, a significant portion of the sample is missing from each of the ten questions, leaving (depending on the question) 6% to 40% of the sample either missing, discarded, or unaccounted for without explanation.

The results offered in the third edition (Walker, 2009) do nothing to prove Walker's theories or further the cause of battered women. Critique of the BWS is essentially sidestepped or ignored by Walker.[14]

It is important for the reader and investigator to understand that although I am quite critical of BWS as a "diagnosis" or as a basis for expert testimony, it is my opinion that in individual cases there is room for the expert to evaluate a case and present to a court opinions regarding the state of mind of a victim of domestic violence during the commission of an act, potential reasons for remaining in a violent relationship, and even reasons for participating in a crime. As long as the available evidence warrants the opinions offered, there is no problem. Walker's description of BWS helps describe some victims of domestic violence, but not all, and likely not the majority. Having said this,

---

[13]We have a small sample with problematic pedigree.
[14]See *Psychiatric Times* (2006).

Walker deserves credit for bringing the social problem of domestic violence to public awareness.

Rape Trauma Syndrome

Rape is both a sexual act and a violent act. It is about control and anger. Different rapists have different motivations for the crime, and this will play out with the victim. Some rapists need reassurance of their masculinity and actually fantasize that they and the victim have a relationship, apologizing after the crime, even, incredibly, sometimes contacting the victim after the rape.[15] Others seek to punish the victim and can be unnecessarily brutal during the crime. Different levels of violence will be present from different rapists, and sometimes between different rapes by the same rapist. How victims respond to an assault depends on several factors, including the level of violence, fear for their lives, and whether or not they were able to demonstrate some mastery over the situation, either by thwarting the rape entirely or by controlling the rapist in some manner, such as trying to avoid pregnancy and sexually transmitted diseases by getting the rapist to use a condom (*New York Times*, 1993).

It is hard to imagine another crime that could be expected to damage or destroy someone's sense of personal security and ability to trust others, except, perhaps, prolonged and intense stalking. Rape is a crime that leads to humiliation, shame, self-doubt, distrust, and anger, among other things. As noted, victims' responses to rape will vary. Unfortunately, sexual assault victims often feel retraumatized by the criminal justice response to them (Koss, 2006). Victims of rape or attempted rape can suffer from the same symptoms as victims of violent crime in general, but there is an expectation that on average their course may be more intense and prolonged due to the very nature of the assault, physically as well as culturally.

Rape trauma syndrome (RTS) was first described by Burgess and Holmstrom (1974a). The syndrome reportedly consists of symptoms exhibited by victims of forcible rape or attempted forcible rape. Data was collected from interviews with all women (146) presenting to the emergency room of a Boston hospital from July 1972 to July 1973 who stated that they had been raped, with later follow-up interviews up to six years later (Burgess and Hazelwood, 2001). There was no control group. All the subjects of the study were interviewed either by Burgess or Holmstrom. Burgess and Holmstrom (1974a) correctly noted that while the literature on rape as a crime was "voluminous," it had essentially ignored the victim. They divided the 146 subjects into three groups

---

[15]In one case (Massic, 2002), a victim had given her cellphone to an alleged rapist, advising him that since he knew her number she would not contact the police about the rape. He called her days later and was arrested after arranging a second meeting.

(p. 981): (1) victims of forcible rape or attempted rape, "usually the former"; (2) victims who were an "accessory" due to inability to consent; and (3) "victims of sexually stressful situations," that is, the victim initially consented, but the event went further than she wanted. There is no mention of any attempt to take false allegations of sexual assault into account or even an awareness of their existence. Therefore, it is difficult to know to what extent, if any, the data was in any way affected by this phenomenon.[16]

The syndrome was based on the findings related to the sample cohort (92 women) that reported being forcibly raped (Burgess and Holmstrom, 1974a, p. 1981). RTS is formulated to consist of an acute phase and a long-term reorganization phase (p. 982) "that occurs as a result of forcible rape or attempted forcible rape." It is not clear how the attempted forcible rape cohort factored in, as Burgess and Holmstrom clearly state the syndrome was based on the data from the 92 women who reported forcible rape, not those who reported attempted forcible rape (p. 981). We are not given the number of subjects in any cohort other than the forcible rape group. It would appear, without further explanation from the authors of the study, that they used data from the cohort who suffered the most egregious assault and extrapolated it to a second cohort (attempted forcible rape) that, while certainly at risk for a physical and psychological reaction, clearly underwent a different experience. It would seem obvious that an argument could be made that the attempted forcible rape cohort may be expected to, on average, fare better than those who had been forcibly raped, possibly making the data seem less compelling. Burgess and Holmstrom give no explanation for this decision.

Burgess and Hazelwood (2001, pp. 30–33) describe the acute phase of the syndrome as *disorganization*. This phase consists of an *immediate impact phase* and physical and psychological responses to the assault. In the immediate impact phase the (p. 30) "emotional demeanor of the victim may be one of two types—expressive or guarded." Expressive victims show their emotions, whereas guarded victims do not. There is a further admonition that the victim can change from one type to another and even interchange between the two depending on several parameters. This should alert the reader to the fact that the response of the victim is varied and unpredictable.

Burgess and Hazelwood (2001) and Burgess and Holmstrom (1974a) suggest that the victim will have physical and psychological reactions to the sexual assault. There will be disturbances of sleep and appetite as well as various physical complaints. The victim will suffer feelings of fear, humiliation, shame, guilt, and embarrassment, among others. Intrusive thoughts of the trauma may

---

[16]See Chapter 9 of this text for a discussion of false allegations of crime, including sexual assault.

occur. All of these symptoms are found in conditions other than rape trauma. Burgess and Holmstrom (1974b) state that RTS is further complicated by a "compound reaction," wherein the victim has a recrudescence of prior psychiatric problems, and a "silent reaction," wherein the victim suffers from RTS but has not reported a rape. Both scenarios are known reactions to rape and offer nothing to support the validity of RTS.

The long-term reorganization process (Burgess and Hazelwood, 2001) can take weeks to years and likely never ends. Various lifestyle aspects are affected: physical, psychological, social, and sexual. Resumption of sexual activity after a rape is affected by the victim's pre-trauma sexual framework and by a post-trauma sense of self, as well as partner reactions to the assault, both conscious and unconscious. Some men, as well as some cultures as a whole, view a rape victim as having been sullied and no longer worthwhile or desirable. Some cannot accept that the victim did not invite the attack in some way or should have died rather that give in to the assault.

Although RTS was presented as a newly recognized syndrome, nowhere in the original paper (Burgess and Holmstrom, 1974a) are we given the expected diagnostic criteria to diagnose it. It is surprising to find that a syndrome that has gained significant acceptance in the courts has no criteria for accurate diagnosis other than having been subjected to a specific trauma. It becomes clear that the diagnosis is expected to come from the specific trauma, not from the symptoms. The danger in this is obvious, for if RTS is introduced into a court proceeding as proof that a sexual assault has occurred, the opining expert is indulging in circular reasoning. Also, the acute and long-term phase description of RTS does little, if anything, to differentiate it from other victim responses to violent crime in general, or other catastrophic events that could potentially lead to a diagnosis of PTSD. As Boeschen, Sales, and Koss observe (1998, p 426): "Although still commonly found in the forensic setting, RTS is a phrase no longer used in the clinical setting and thus should no longer be used by a mental health expert." They more forcefully state (p. 428): "Although RTS has historical importance, it makes for confusing and potentially unscientific expert testimony and should no longer be used in the courtroom." They go on to note that PTSD itself is not without problems when brought into the legal arena.

RTS suffers from the same criticism applicable to BWS. Both are gender-specific syndromes based on single or few studies without follow-up validation by others, drawn from a preselected convenience sample (battered women presenting themselves for help for BWS and rape victims who came to an emergency room for RTS) with no control group. The "syndromes" consist of symptoms that are not specific to the syndromes and that are exhibited by people who were never battered or raped. Also, both BWS and RTS have been offered in court as proof that the event (battering or rape) occurred, in spite of the lack of an underlying scientific basis. As Dixon and Dixon note (2003, p. 41): "As with BWS, no evidence exists to differentiate rape victims who develop the syndrome from those who do not develop it, or to differentiate the associated symptoms among women who have and have not experienced rape."

It is hard at times to sort out good science from bad. Cling (2004), a psychologist and lawyer, gives a ringing endorsement to RTS. More than once he offers non-existent proof of the validity and acceptance of RTS using the American Psychiatric Association's endorsement of RTS, because (20):

> Their [Burgess and Holmstrom] formulation [of RTS] was accepted and included in the DSM, published by the American Psychiatric Association. Ultimately…RTS was included as a form of PTSD where the stressor is rape.

One is at a loss to explain how Cling has confused the DSM's listing of rape as a possible trauma leading to PTSD with an endorsement of RTS, yet she goes on (p. 21): "It seems clear…that RTS, as PTSD…is recognized as a verifiable disorder with specific symptomology, which can be distinguished from other disorders and is included in the DSM as a subset of PTSD," including the DSMIV-TR (2000). This was quite a surprise to me. A search of the electronic version (DSM-IV-TR Plus, Version 1.0, 2000) fails to find any mention of RTS, nor can it be found in any prior version of DSM. The word *rape* appears in relation to a trauma that could lead to PTSD, but there is no endorsement (or mention) of RTS, as Cling claims. It is clear that the DSM accepts rape as a trauma that could lead to PTSD. Nowhere does the American Psychiatric Association or the DSM endorse RTS, regardless of Cling's assertions. RTS has no place either in the vocabulary of mental health practitioners or in the opinions of experts.

An attorney (Block, 1990) published an article praising RTS and its utility in the courtroom. He erroneously claimed that (p. 311) "[t]he American Psychiatric Association (1980) recognized rape trauma syndrome as a posttraumatic stress disorder in its *Diagnostic and Statistical Manual of Mental Disorders* (DSM-III)." He also opined that RTS had passed the Frye Test, as he believed its acceptance by the scientific community was evident from inclusion in the DSM, which is not true. That a peer-reviewed clinical journal allowed this misinformation to be published is disconcerting.

When an attempt to introduce expert testimony on RTS is made, it is generally for one of three purposes: to support an opinion that the presence of RTS proves that a rape occurred; to support an opinion that the absence of RTS proves that a rape did not occur; or to explain why a victim behaved in a manner that laymen (jurors) might consider inconsistent with a sexual assault. Often cases involve a consent defense, in which a defendant accused of rape admits sexual activity occurred but was consensual. RTS testimony regarding victim behavior will attempt to shed light on such things as why a victim did not report the rape or delayed reporting, why the victim did not appear upset immediately after the rape, or why the victim let the rapist drive her home, despite the fact that RTS offers nothing to support such testimony.

Consensual defenses were used in *State v. Saldana* and *State v. McGee*, both Minnesota cases appealed in 1982. RTS testimony or testimony that essentially relied on RTS led to the cases being overturned due to the unreliability of such evidence. In *McGee* the Appeals Court found testimony on RTS too prejudicial. Unfortunately, a dissenting justice quoted from the 1974 Burgess and Holmstrom paper as a proffer of reliability for RTS.[17]

In *State v. Marks*, a Kansas case also handed down in 1982, that included a consent defense, one legal issue on appeal was whether RTS testimony invaded the province of the jury by enhancing the credibility of the victim and the guilt of the defendant. The conviction in this case was upheld.

In 1986 in *State v. Allewalt*, a Maryland case, consent was again argued as a defense. The expert psychiatrist testified that the complainant suffered from PTSD, caused by the rape, and that the diagnosis of RTS was made based on the report of the complainant. The expert admitted he had to presume the rape had occurred to make the diagnosis. An appeal was successful in overturning the conviction, but the Special Court of Appeals reinstated. The circular reasoning here should be apparent.

In a 1986 military case that involved a consent defense, *United States v. Carter*, the court held that RTS was admissible when presented by a qualified expert, as long as the jury was also given proper limiting instructions. The psychiatric expert testified she diagnosed RTS as a form of PTSD. She did not testify that the complainant had been raped, but then one would have to be a moron not to connect the dots. The U.S. Military Court of Review decided such testimony was admissible.

In *Commonwealth v. Gallagher*, a 1998 case, the Supreme Court of Pennsylvania reviewed whether RTS testimony admitted trial was admissible. In 1977 an intruder raped the complainant, who was unable to identify the defendant in a photo array or a show-up.[18] Four years later, the complainant picked the defendant from a photo line-up. At trial, there was no question as to the rape, but rather who was the rapist. To address the inability of the complainant to make the identification years earlier, the prosecution presented Dr. Burgess as

---

[17]Parts of this section dealing with legal cases and RTS are adapted from McGrath (2011b).
[18]A one person line-up—i.e., "Is this the guy?"

an expert in RTS. Dr. Burgess examined the complainant, opined she suffered from RTS, and offered testimony also as to how RTS affected the identification process. The court reversed and remanded for a new trial, observing that the only purpose of the expert testimony was to bolster the credibility of the witness regarding her identification of the defendant several years after the crime. It is important to note that RTS has nothing to say regarding eyewitness identification, leading one to question the basis for Dr. Burgess's testimony.[19]

The New York State Court of Appeals[20] in 1990 ruled, in *People v. Taylor/Banks*, that expert testimony on RTS was admissible in New York, unless the only purpose for the testimony was to prove whether a rape had occurred. It could be used to explain "unusual" behavior to a jury unfamiliar with sexual assault victims. In *People v. Bennett* (1992) the Court of Appeals remanded the case back to the trial court for reasons unrelated to RTS. While the case was sent back to trial court on a separate issue, the court indicated that expert testimony to explain the behavior of a rape victim can be admissible. The prosecution expert in this case was Dr. Burgess. She had never met or evaluated the victim, but was asked hypothetical questions to explain a rape victim's behavior. Both post- and pre-assault behavior were considered. The court decided that the previous finding in *Taylor* did not govern this case and if RTS testimony was offered again and objected to, the trial court should determine if the expert's opinion had the necessary scientific foundation, did not unduly prejudice, and did not invade the jury's province to assess witness credibility. It cannot be emphasized enough that RTS itself does not provide the basis for such testimony.

In a 1997 murder case, a 21-year-old female from Brooklyn, New York, with an IQ of 70, was raped. The rapist, her ex-boyfriend, bragged about it, and she confronted him and shot and killed him. At her trial, a psychologist was to testify that the shooting was a product of RTS and PTSD. The judge did not allow the testimony. Her conviction was appealed and confirmed by two appellate courts. In 2003, a federal habeas corpus writ was granted, ordering either retrial or release. The federal judge held that there were significant issues related to the defendant's behavior that needed to be explained to the jury, especially as they were exploited by the prosecution in the absence of RTS testimony (Goodman, 2003).

In New Jersey, during April 2008, a trial court allowed RTS testimony to rebut a defense claim of consent. At the end of a date, Stephen Hernandez, a personal

---

[19]It should also be noted that Dr. Burgess's degree is a DNS, doctor of nursing science. She is not an advanced practice provider (such as a nurse practitioner). While to my knowledge the issue has never been raised, it appears to be outside her scope of practice as a nurse to be diagnosing PTSD or performing any other medical diagnosis.

[20]The equivalent of the supreme court in most other states.

trainer, sexually assaulted a woman. The victim reported she initially resisted but believing rape inevitable became passive and engaged in conversation with Mr. Hernandez. She reported even helping him to put on a condom. After the assault, she attempted to run away but was stopped. She allowed him to drive her to her own vehicle, got out, hugged him, and asked him to call her in a week for another date. As soon as she felt safe, she called the police. At trial, the prosecution presented an expert to testify that the victim's behaviors were consistent with RTS. The jury acquitted on aggravated sexual assault (rape) but convicted on 4th degree sexual contact and simple assault (BenAli, 2008). Hernandez was sentenced to probation. He was rearrested in 2009, charged with kidnapping and sexually assaulting another victim (Chambers, 2009).

It must be remembered that even if RTS was a valid diagnosis, it would not offer a basis to support testimony related to victim behavior during and after a sexual assault. Why is there a need to invoke RTS when victim behavior goes against what a jury might expect? An analogy would be that of a robbery (McGrath, 2011b; p. 261):

> A woman is accosted on the street by someone she has met before. No one is nearby for her to alert. He tells her to get into his car. This is something she would otherwise never do, but under the circumstances she does, fearing physical injury if she does not comply. She is driven to a secluded area and robbed. The robber then engages in casual conversation and the victim comes to believe that a strategy to maintain her safety is to act as if being robbed is not that big a deal and she tries to normalize the situation by acting as if she is not troubled by the criminal act. When the robber offers to drive her back to her car she agrees. In fact, when she gets out of the robber's car, he gets out and she feigns friendship, hugs him and suggests they meet again. As soon as he leaves the victim calls the police and reports the robbery. Whatever anyone thought about the situation, no one would be feeling the need to create a "Robbery Trauma Syndrome" to explain the victim's behavior; it is simply not necessary and adds nothing but a pseudoscientific aura to an easily explained response.

RTS may be offered in civil cases to try to explain victim behavior occurring during and after a rape, as well as to try to prove that a rape occurred. Civil cases can be related to premises liability, negligent hiring and/or supervision, sexual harassment, and other claims. It should be noted that in civil cases, the standard of proof is less than in criminal cases. In civil court, not only can the alleged rapist be sued, but also third parties, such as hotels, apartment buildings, churches, hospitals, prisons, nursing homes, schools, and municipalities. Most civil cases are settled prior to trial. Of those that go to trial, few result in appellate review. This provides a limited opportunity to assess the actual use of RTS testimony in civil cases.

The first mention of RTS in a civil appellate case was in 1979: *White v. Violent Crimes Compensation Board*, out of New Jersey. In that case, a rape victim, White, filed a crime victim's compensation claim past the accepted filing date. The appellate court identified RTS as a reason filing the claim was delayed. In a federal case, *Redmond v. Baxley* (1979), a prison inmate sued the state of Michigan, claiming damages from a prison rape. Expert testimony on the possible sequelae of rape was upheld. The term *rape trauma syndrome* was not used, but language describing trauma resulting from the rape was. In a 1981 Pennsylvania case, *In the Matter of Pittsburgh Action Against Rape*, a defendant in a rape case sued a rape crisis center to gain access to the record of the complainant. The center asked the court to create an absolute privilege for communications between the center and those it counsels. The court said no absolute privilege existed and it would not create one. The lone dissenting judge (Larsen) wrote an opinion citing RTS and argued such a privilege should exist. Cases such as this have served to offer RTS a platform it does not deserve. Justice Larsen's sentiments are appropriate, but his terminology (i.e., RTS) is ill placed and has been cited elsewhere (McCord, 1985), including *State v. Saldana* and *State v. Middleton*.

Stalking

Stalking is a repetitive act usually undertaken to cause distress to the victim. It is often a dysfunctional manner of dealing with anger, designed to harass and a control the object of the anger, which can be a lover who has rejected the stalker or someone the stalker does not even know. There are cases in which the stalker is delusional, believing the victim wants to have a relationship with him or her, and the stalking is an attempt to complete the relationship, but the vast majority of stalking incidents is related to non-psychotic individuals who know the victim and for some reason are angry at the victim and cannot accept that the relationship is over. The style of harassment increases a victim's feelings of impotence and vulnerability, especially when attempts to involve law enforcement are ineffective.

That victims might suffer from psychological symptoms is expected rather than unusual. Anxiety, depression, difficulty sleeping, a heightened startle response, reactive paranoia, and other symptoms or emotions such as anger and rage at the stalker are not uncommon. At times, a victim may meet criteria for PTSD.

Stalking is perpetrated both in the real world and in cyberspace, where some stalkers feel empowered by the false sense of anonymity the Internet engenders (McGrath and Casey, 2002). Regardless of the method of stalking, the behavior takes a toll on the victim. Respondents in one study (Hall, 1998; p. 133) generally described stalking as "akin to psychological terrorism." Yet one person's stalking may be another's dysfunctional courting (Dennison, 2007), with the most common type of stalking due to an obsessional male stalking a female with whom he has had a prior relationship (Meloy, 1998).

A victim's response to the perceived threat can include moving to another city, changing jobs and phone numbers, and taking other measures. Stalkers will sometimes harass victims at work (Logan et al., 2007), affecting job performance and employability, and removing another perceived safe haven.

Rebecca Griego, 26, had ended a relationship with a boyfriend, but he continued to pursue her, causing her to move and change her phone number. She distributed his photo to co-workers and advised them to look out for him. She took out a restraining order in March 2007, after he called her job and threatened to kill her. The only way she was aware he could locate her was at her sister's home or at her job at the University of Washington. In early April 2007, he came to Rebecca's work site, where he shot and killed her and then turned the gun on himself (Frey, McNerthney, and Castro, 2007).

While stalking behaviors can range from annoying up to sexual assault and kidnapping and even homicide, the vast majority of stalking behaviors in Hall's (1998) non-randomized study tended to be unwanted communications (letters, phone calls),[21] with the stalker following the victim at times and driving by his or her home. In domestic violence scenarios, there is a risk that the controlling offender will stalk the spouse or intimate once he or she has finally decided to end the relationship. This must be taken seriously by law enforcement, as victims may be at significant risk of assault if they are confronted by their stalkers and refuse to re-engage in the relationship.

Stalking Trauma Syndrome

Colins and Wilkas (2001, p. 319) proposed a new syndrome, specifically *stalking trauma syndrome (STS)*, to describe what they believe is a diagnosable condition: "STS is a theory that can be related to post-traumatic-stress disorder (PTSD), battered woman syndrome, and rape trauma syndrome; yet STS is a unique condition." They compare and contrast STS to BWS and RTS. Regarding STS, there is actual helplessness (as opposed to learned helplessness), such that the victim is unable to influence the situation. Compared to RTS, STS has an ongoing stressor as opposed to a single incident. While both rape and stalking are about control, the stalker's pursuit of control is ongoing, and, finally, in RTS the syndrome is experienced after the trauma, whereas in STS the victim experiences the syndrome during the trauma (stalking) and afterward (Colins and Wilkas, 2001; pp. 320–321).

Colins and Wilkas (2001, p. 324) present the "Cycle of Crisis" to describe the stalking phenomenon. It consists of three phases: a crisis phase, a recovery phase, and an anticipation phase. Due to the ongoing nature of stalking and

---

[21]The study was done prior to 1998. Today, email communications would be included.

the anticipation of further harassment, the victim is unable to recover. No guidance is offered as to how a victim of STS would differ from a victim of RTS who has anxiety and other symptoms on an ongoing basis, with continued fear of sexual assault, or, for that matter, a battered woman still in a violent relationship. The recovery phase is "brief or nonexistent" (p. 323), so in time we have only the crisis phase and the anticipatory phase.

Colins and Wilkas (2001, p. 324) argue that in the "Cycle of Violence" there are several elements affecting the duration of the stalking: length of stalking, criminal justice system response, victim support system, and the presence of implied and/or direct threats. Their postulation that the length of the stalking episode is related to the length of the cycle of violence is interesting because, first, it is simply circular reasoning. Second, the response of the criminal justice system to the stalking would be expected to usually affect the course of the stalking and therefore its effect on the victim, but this would be true of just about any crime. Colins and Wilkas claim (2001, p. 325) that "[u]nlike other types of crime, it often seems like a victim of stalking assumes the role of proving his/her case against the stalker." While victims of stalking may need to be proactive in building a case against a stalker, there are many crimes (rape, for one) in which a victim sometimes feels the need to prove that a crime has been committed. The claimed exclusivity Colins and Wilkas strive for (presumably to bolster the claim that STS is a unique entity) does not exist.

The victim's support system would be expected to affect the victim's response to the stalking, as it would be expected to affect almost every victim of any crime. It is not clear how this differentiates stalking victims from other victims. The last element in the cycle of violence is the presence of implied versus direct threats, but it is not clear how this affects the length of the cycle of violence, or whether it would shorten or lengthen it.

Colins and Wilkas (2001, p. 326) then list the "most common psychological effects suffered by victims to be helplessness, hopelessness, anxiety, desperation, and loss of control," with helplessness and hopelessness being the "two key elements" of the syndrome. How this differentiates victims of stalking from other victims of crime or even seriously depressed people in general is not explained. Obviously, the fact that the victim was stalked will guide us, but again, this is a so-called syndrome in which the diagnosis is actually the trauma and not the specific symptom set exhibited by the typical stalking victim.

STS is a theory, based on the expectation (unproven) that specific types of trauma lead to specific diagnosable syndromes, either aside from PTSD or as a "sub-category" of PTSD. PTSD allows a broad definition for the instigating trauma, and its diagnosis is made from the symptoms not the trauma. STS suffers from similar problems as BWS and RTS, except that it does not even have a methodologically flawed, non-randomized, non-control group study to support it.

I want to be very clear regarding STS, BWS, and RTS. Although I am critical of the research (or lack of it) supporting these syndromes, this should not be interpreted as dismissing the suffering of the victims of related crimes. Crime victims may suffer many psychological problems and symptoms. When they meet criteria for a DSM-IV diagnosis, they should be diagnosed and treated. Even if they are not suffering from a diagnosable mental condition, they may benefit from support and information. However, attempting to create trauma-specific syndromes does nothing for the victim and entices attorneys and expert witnesses to bring such syndromes into the courtroom, when the bases for the syndromes have more in common with politics than science.

HYPNOSIS

Occasionally, investigators get the idea of using hypnosis to refresh or clarify memories of a crime victim. The use of hypnosis in these cases is to some degree based on the belief that the mind records memories like a camcorder and with help a victim can play back the movie. This memory analogy is faulty, and using hypnosis in this manner has been problematic and is just as likely to hinder an investigation as to help it.

Hypnosis is the art of putting someone in a "trance," which is simply an altered state of consciousness in which the subject will likely be more suggestible than usual, as critical aspects of thinking tend to be relaxed.[22] It is not uncommon for an individual to have the experience of driving somewhere familiar (e.g., home from work) and suddenly realize that he or she is at such and such an intersection but cannot recall driving for the past few minutes. Yet the driving was negotiated safely. The explanation is that the driver was in an altered state of consciousness, a trance state.

Many are surprised to learn, though, that the hypnotic trance is actually a state of focused attention; the subject is focused strongly on something, be it the voice of the hypnotist, or some other stimulus. Hypnosis can be a useful technique in helping someone quit smoking cigarettes or lose weight, or it can simply be a relaxation technique. It is also an amusing entertainment in a variety of settings. But it can be a dangerous modality to use in trying to elicit or "refresh" memories, or to prove a fact, as the whole repressed memory industry has shown.

---

[22]Sadly, I would suggest that critical aspects of thinking tend to be fairly relaxed in many individuals at baseline.

As noted by Webert (2003, p. 1304), there are three general problems with using hypnosis in legal contexts: (1) the subject is more suggestible than he or she would be otherwise, subject to many influences, including verbal and non-verbal cues from the hypnotist and a possible desire to please the hypnotist; (2) the subject may unintentionally confabulate (i.e., make things up) so that the memories presented are more complete and comprehensible; and (3) the subject may have an enhanced belief in the veracity of his or her hypnotically recalled memories, regardless of their actual truthfulness. There is no way to know how accurate hypnotically recalled memories are, unless they can be independently corroborated through other sources.

Interestingly, there is a famous case in which hypnosis resulted in the solving of a crime. In 1976 near Chowchilla, California, three masked men hijacked a school bus full of children and their driver. The victims were left hidden in a moving van buried in a quarry. While the kidnappers were planning ransom demands, the driver and some of the children were able to dig their way out. The driver remembered seeing a license plate from a vehicle used in the hijacking but could not remember the plate number. Under hypnosis, he produced several numbers that led to one of the vehicles used in the crime and broke the case (Turco and Scott, 1982).

Various jurisdictions have taken different approaches to hypnotic testimony, with courts in Illinois, Virginia, California, and the military courts martial system barring testimony from witnesses who have been hypnotized, while courts in Wyoming, Louisiana, North Dakota, and the federal Ninth Circuit have allowed testimony from witnesses who have undergone hypnosis. Some courts, for example, Wisconsin, Colorado, and the federal Fourth and Fifth Circuit, will allow such testimony if it can be shown to be reliable. Other courts in Minnesota, Arizona, Nebraska, New York, North Carolina, Washington, Michigan, Missouri, Massachusetts, Hawaii, Georgia, Alaska, Delaware, and Illinois have allowed witnesses who have been hypnotized to testify to recollections from prior to the hypnosis. The U.S. Supreme Court has held (*Rock v. Arkansas*, 1987) that a defendant[23] who has been hypnotized cannot be barred from testifying on the grounds of the Fifth (self-incrimination), Sixth (compulsory process),[24] and Fourteenth (due process) Amendments (Miller, 2003b). Texas is the only state (Nix, 2009) that mandates testing and certification of police investigators who use hypnosis. One must wonder why police investigators are personally doing forensic hypnosis.

---

[23]It is important to note this applies only to a *defendant* testifying, not another witness.

[24]Compulsory process is the ability of a defendant to force a witness to appear (e.g., by subpoena) who can testify favorably to his or her case. An offshoot of this is that the defendant, as his or her own witness, cannot be barred from testifying on a per se ruling.

Newman and Thompson summarized the status of forensic hypnosis as follows (Newman and Thompson, 2001, pp. 83–84):

> Investigatory forensic hypnosis was based on a well-intentioned but scientifically untenable position: that detailed memories could be accurately retrieved and utilized in criminal investigations. Although anecdotally helpful in some cases, courts recognized the risk hypnotically elicited memories could pose to the rights of a defendant in a criminal case…based on untested theories of repression and misdirected conclusions…. [R]esearchers have identified the pitfalls associated with relying on hypnotically retrieved memories, influencing many courts to follow suit in denying the admissibility of such memories.

Any investigator considering using hypnosis as part of an investigation should check with his or her legal department as to the status of hypnotic testimony in the jurisdiction where the case will be prosecuted. Even in jurisdictions that allow hypnotically refreshed testimony, the court will expect that certain protocols have been followed.

VICTIM TOXICOLOGY

Victim toxicology is an important aspect of any investigation. A victim's ability to accurately recount what occurred during a violent crime can be affected by many factors, including his or her level of fear; whether or not he or she was fully conscious during an attack; whether he or she subsequently was rendered unconscious due to a blunt trauma with potential amnesic effects; and so on.

The reliability of eyewitness[25] memory is notoriously poor in some aspects, as evidenced by many wrongful convictions based on victim eyewitness identification. In addition to potential identification, victims will need to give a detailed account of the crime to assist an investigation. The ability to recall accurately can also be affected by prescribed medications, alcohol, cocaine, and other street drugs. The investigator needs to be aware of this in order to question victims as to medication or drug use.

Consensual alcohol and drug use is a common precursor to rape (Hurley, Parker, and Wells, 2006), and alcohol-related rape is more likely to involve acquaintances and strangers than intimates (Horvath and Brown, 2006). Rape is already a vastly underreported crime. It is very likely that a rape victim who had consensually used drugs or alcohol with the rapist will think twice before going to the police to press a complaint. This is unfortunate because, regardless

---

[25]For a review of problems with eyewitness testimony, see McGrath (2011a).

of how law enforcement will view the victim as a potential witness, a crime has been committed, and the police should have a record of the complaint and an ID of the alleged perpetrator, if possible. Should other victims later make similar complaints, the fact that a pattern has developed implicating a particular individual is important. Some rapists count on a victim's fear of not being believed due to having drunk alcohol with the rapist or having used an illicit drug such as cocaine or ecstasy. While some may infer a victim's use of alcohol implies poor judgment and likely consent, others understand that the same situation makes the victim vulnerable to a sexual assault. Whether or not a victim presents a good case for prosecution, he or she deserves to be treated with dignity and not victimized a second time.

Memory consists of several steps. Described simply, a stimulus (something the victim heard, saw, or felt), such as the sound of a gunshot, must first be perceived by a person. Once perceived, the stimulus can be mentally recorded. Once it is recorded, at some future date a memory of the stimulus can be retrieved. There can be difficulties with any step in the process. It is even possible, under the right conditions, for false memories to be reported, with the reporter not realizing that what he or she is reporting is false. Drugs can potentially affect all three processes, with difficulties in retrieving memories often related to the effects of chronic drug use. Any drug that obtunds a person can affect perception and the "laying down" of the memory. Drugs known to affect memory include alcohol, benzodiazepines, and marijuana, among others.

Alcohol suppresses many activities in the brain. The first thing potentially affected is the perception of a stimulus. Someone who is drinking may not notice something—either because he or she didn't hear it, see it, feel it, or smell it. Obviously, the level of intoxication will dictate the degree of inattention. Even if a stimulus is perceived, alcohol can interfere with the initial recording of the stimulus. It is well known that alcohol can cause a blackout, a period of time for which a person cannot recall anything. This not because the person fell asleep or passed out; in fact, others may be able to tell the drinker what he or she said and did during the period of blackout. It is very possible for others' observations to be that the person who "blacked out" acted normally or fairly normally during the period in question. In less extreme forms of memory impairment, it is common for persons intoxicated on alcohol the night before not to be able to recall accurately what they observed or did, but have a vague recollection, possibly enhanced when given clues (cues). Impairment in laying down new memories accurately can start to occur after relatively low doses of alcohol (Kuhn, Swartzwelder, and Wilson, 2003).

Investigators should also keep in mind that they may be interviewing a victim who is "hung-over" from alcohol or withdrawing from alcohol or some other drug, when faced with poor recollection of facts, irritability, and fatigue in a victim. Long-term effects of regular alcohol abuse can include actual dementia. A known sequela of severe alcohol dependence is a condition known as Korsakoff's psychosis. In this condition, afflicted individuals cannot lay down new memories. They literally cannot remember anything for but a few seconds. Quite notably, such individuals confabulate to cover this deficit. They will make up any response, no matter how bizarre, to attempt to hide the problem. People with Korsakoff's are easily spotted because they cannot recall if they met you even a few moments before.

Marijuana, like alcohol, inhibits new memory formation, probably due to its effect on cells in the hippocampal region of the brain. A victim who was high on marijuana during an assault may have difficulty remembering things. The psychoactive chemical in marijuana is known as THC (delta-9-tetrahydrocannabinol). Due to its affinity for fatty tissues, it can be detected for up to two months in a urine toxicology screen. Therefore, a positive qualitative toxicology screen (indicates if present, not the amount) for marijuana does not necessarily mean that a victim has smoked marijuana in the very recent past.

Benzodiazepines are sedatives and affect memory. Drugs in this class include Valium, Xanax, Ativan, and so on. They are known as sedatives, and it is their sedating effect that interferes with the recording of new memories. Many sleeping pills are benzodiazepines (e.g., Restoril) and can affect memory. Keep in mind that many people dangerously ingest more than one drug, such as Valium and alcohol, to get high, and the effects on memory impairment can be enhanced. Rohypnol, also known as "roofies," is a potent benzodiazepine sometimes used as a "rape drug." It is easily concealed in an alcoholic beverage. However, reports of its widespread use may be exaggerated.

Other sedatives such as GHB (gamma-hydroxybutyrate) are known to inhibit memory formation. This is also known as a "date rape drug" due to its rapid onset, which leads to confusion, obtundation, and recall inhibition. GHB is difficult to detect and can easily be "hidden" in an alcoholic drink. If there is timely suspicion that a victim was subjected to a "rape drug," collection of evidence should be a consideration, including a urine sample and any glass the victim drank from (as well glasses used by the suspect for fingerprints or DNA). Emergency room toxicology testing does not routinely test for GHB, or for hallucinogens such as ketamine ("Special K"), phencyclidine (PCP), LSD, mescaline, Ecstasy, and so on, all of which can affect one's perceptions and level of consciousness. Ecstasy (MDMA) has both stimulant and hallucinogenic effects. While there are no controlled studies in humans regarding the effects of Ecstasy on memory (thank goodness), impaired memory is a frequently noted effect of the drug. In fact, users have coined the term "E-tard" (Kuhn, Swartzwelder, and Wilson, 2003, p. 82) to describe heavy users.

Stimulants, such as cocaine and amphetamine, do not impair memory per se. Use must be considered in the context of dosage level and combination with other drugs. Stimulants actually improve concentration, which is why they work in attention deficit disorders. Use can lead to physiological arousal and even psychosis, so faulty memory related to these drugs is more likely a result of misperception of stimuli, as opposed to inability to record the stimuli. Opiates, such as heroin, are sedative in nature and would be expected to affect the ability to perceive. On the other hand, if a person has become tolerant to opiates, the effect might be minor, if at all. For example, 140 milligrams of methadone may have no demonstrable effect on a person who has taken that daily dose for some time.

Some prescription medications, as mentioned earlier, can affect memory. There are many reports regarding such medications, and it is difficult to know how reliable they are. For example, there are reports that statins (cholesterol-lowering drugs) such as Lipitor affect memory. Sleeping pills, such as Ambien, are known to cause memory impairment. Some anti-depressants, such as Zoloft and other SSRIs (selective serotonin reuptake inhibitors), have a reputation for causing memory problems, but the issue is poorly researched and reliable scientific facts are limited. The number of medications is far too numerous to address here. The side effects of many medications, including some anti-hypertensives and anti-convulsants, list confusion or memory impairment as potential side effects. In fact, there has been some work on using a beta-blocker as a way of blocking the laying down of traumatic memories post-trauma, if given quickly enough (ClinicalTrials.gov, 2007).

It is not possible to predict the level of impairment in a particular person. If an investigator has concerns about a victim's ability to recall events related to a crime, it would be wise to have a full medical history, including any prescribed or illicit medications and drugs and/or alcohol use. While toxicology screens are helpful, it must be kept in mind that they only screen for a limited number of drugs. This information can be assessed by a physician with expertise in pharmacology. It is important to understand that while many things can affect memory, it is quite possible for someone who was intoxicated or affected by a medication to provide accurate information.

Conclusion

Victimology is an important facet of any investigation. Victim response to violent crime is varied. It is not possible to predict how a particular person will respond to a particular traumatic event. Victims of violent crime can benefit from appropriate behavioral health interventions when needed, as well as a supportive network of family, friends, and agencies. Battered woman syndrome and rape trauma syndrome are gender-based paradigms that have failed, despite commentary to the opposite, to meet the requirements of scientific validity and should not be used as a mental health diagnosis or introduced in a courtroom. Stalking trauma syndrome has yet to have even bad science to support it. As can be said about such things, "It's not even wrong." Alcohol, drugs, and prescription medications can affect a victim's ability to recall accurately the details investigators need to further an investigation. This should not be interpreted as meaning that all victims who take medication or have used alcohol or drugs are unreliable witnesses. It is paramount that investigators and examiners are aware of these issues in their preparation of an informed victimology.

SUMMARY

Victim response to violent crime is variable from person to person, making it very difficult if not impossible to predict how a crime victim should or will behave. A victim's response usually involves three stages of recovery: (1) dealing with the initial impact of the attack, (2) attempting to reconstitute his or her former self, and (3) reorganizing himself or herself to attend to life's daily activities.

There have been several attempts to pathologize the normal reactions of victims. The syndromes that have been used to describe these pathologies are acute stress disorder, post-traumatic stress disorder, battered woman syndrome, rape trauma syndrome, and stalking trauma syndrome. Although there is much overlap between these syndromes, the first two (ASD and PTSD) are the only ones that are recognized by the American Psychiatric Association and that have specific diagnostic criteria within the DSM. The remaining three (BWS, RTS, and STS) have been criticized on many levels.

There is limited research to support the validity of RTS and BWS, and what exists suffers from methodological flaws, including lack of control groups, lack of replication, sample selection, etc. There is no literature to support STS. Furthermore, some argue that RTS and BWS are a result of advocacy or political pressures, rather than having a solid scientific basis. Clearly, this would affect the utility of these diagnoses.

These syndromes (BWS, RTS, STS) are often misrepresented as a sub-category of the recognized disorder PTSD. It should be noted that they are not subsets of this syndrome, although the traumatic event involved may very well cause the emergence of PTSD. The difference is that within these claimed syndromes the diagnosis is actually the trauma and not a specified symptom set exhibited by the victim. It should also be noted that although used in court for these purposes, evidence of these so-called mental disorders should not be used as proof that the victim suffered a particular trauma. When presented in court, this argument is not only circular in logic, but also is inherently legally unfair because the syndromes have failed scientific scrutiny and have not been validated.

The ability for victims to recall correctly in a forensics context is affected by hypnosis, medication, alcohol, and street drugs. Investigators need to be aware of the effects these processes and substances may have on the memory of a victim or witness. It is believed that alcohol, benzodiazepines (as well as other sedatives), and marijuana inhibit new memory formation. On the other hand, stimulants such as cocaine and amphetamines are more likely to affect the perception of a stimulus as opposed to the actual memory formation itself. This being said, it is impossible to predict the level of impairment that these factors will cause in any individual.

QUESTIONS

1. The tendency to view a victim as lacking flaws is known as _____.
2. True or False: It is fairly easy for experienced investigators to predict how a specific victim of a violent crime will behave.
3. According to Wallace (2007), there are three broad stages or phases that describe the general response of victims of violent crime. Name and describe all three.
4. Acute stress disorder is characterized by dissociative symptoms such as

   _____.
5. Post-traumatic stress disorder was previously known as _____.
6. Name the two trauma syndromes discussed in this chapter that are legitimate mental disorders recognized by the American Psychological Association and present in the DSM.
7. Describe three weaknesses in battered woman syndrome research.
8. Describe three weaknesses in rape trauma syndrome research.

REFERENCES

American Psychiatric Association, 2000. DSM-IV-TR Plus, Version 1.0, American Psychiatric Publishing Inc, Arlington, VA.

American Psychiatric Association, 2012. Recent Updates to Proposed Revisions for DSM-5. Available at: http://www.dsm5.org/Pages/RecentUpdates.aspx Last (accessed 22.04.13.)

Anderson v. Goeke. (1995) 44 F3rd 675. 8th Cir.

Archer, J., 2000. Sex differences in aggression between heterosexual partners: a meta-analytic review. Psychological Bulletin 126 (no. 5), 651–680.

BenAli, M., 2008, May 2nd. Jury acquits man of most serious charges in date-rape trial. NJ.com, Available at: http://www.nj.com/news/index.ssf/2008/05/jury_acquits_man_of_most_serio. html

Blackman, J., 1989. Intimate Violence. Columbia University Press, New York.

Block, A.P., 1990. Rape trauma syndrome as scientific expert testimony. Archives of Sexual Behavior 19 (4), 309–323.

Blumberg, N., 1992. Letter to the Editor: "Battered Woman Syndrome," American Journal of Psychiatry 149 (no. 5), 714–715.

Bodkin, J.A., Pope, H.G., Detke, M.J., Hudson, M.J., 2006. Is PTSD caused by traumatic stress? Journal of Anxiety Disorders 21 (no. 2), 176–182.

Boeschen, L.E., Sales, B.D., Koss, M., 1998. Rape trauma experts in the courtroom. Psychology, Public Policy and the Law 4 (no. 1/2), 414–432.

Brewin, C.R., Andrews, B., Rose, S., 2003. Diagnostic overlap between acute stress disorder and PTSD in victims of violent crime. American Journal of Psychiatry 160 (no. 4), 783–785.

Brewin, C.R., Andrews, B., Rose, S., Kirk, M., 1999. Acute stress disorder and posttraumatic stress disorder in victims of violent crime. American Journal of Psychiatry 156 (no. 3), 360–366.

Browne, A., 1987. When Battered Women Kill. The Free Press, New York.

Burgess, A., Hazelwood, R., 2001. The victim's perspective. In: Hazelwood, R., Burgess, A. (Eds.), Practical Aspects of Rape Investigation: A Multidisciplinary Approach, third ed. CRC Press, Boca Raton, FL, pp. 29–46.

Burgess, A., Holmstrom, L., 1974a. Rape trauma syndrome. American Journal of Psychiatry 131 (no. 9), 981–986.

Burgess, A., Holmstrom, L., 1974b. Rape: Victims of Crisis. Robert J. Brady, Bowie, MD.

News, C.B.S., 2006. Nightmare murder in Big Apple. July 26. Available at http://www.cbsnews.com/stories/2006/07/28/national/main1844264.shtml

Cling, B.J., 2004. Rape and rape trauma syndrome. In: Cling, B.J. (Ed.), Sexualized Violence against Women and Children, Guilford Press, New York, pp. 13–34.

ClinicalTrials.gov, 2007. Effect of propranolol on preventing post-traumatic stress disorder. U.S. National Institutes of Health, Available at http://clinicaltrials.gov/ct/show/NCT00158262

Chambers, S., 2009. Bergenfield personal trainer charged in second sex assault. NJ.com, March 9. Available at: http://www.nj.com/news/index.ssf/2009/03/bergenfield_personal_trainer_c.html

Colins, M.J., Wilkas, M.B., 2001. Stalking trauma syndrome. In: Davis, J.A. (Ed.), Stalking Crimes and Victim Protection, CRC Press, Boca Raton, pp. 317–334.

Commonwealth v. Gallagher (1988) 519 Pa. 291: 547 A.2d355.

Craven, Z., 2003. Battered woman syndrome. Australian Domestic and Family Violence Clearinghouse, Available at: http://www.austdvclearinghouse.unsw.edu.au/topics/topics_pdf_files/battered %20_woman_syndrome.pdf

Davidson, J.R., 1995. Posttraumatic stress disorder and acute stress disorder. In: Kaplan, H.I., Saddock, B.J. (Eds.), Textbook of Psychiatry, sixth ed. Williams and Wilkins, Philadelphia, pp. 1227–1236.

Dennison, S., 2007. Interpersonal relationships and stalking: identifying when to intervene. Law and Human Behavior 31 (no. 4), 353–367.

Dixon, J.W., Dixon, K.E., 2003. Gender-specific clinical syndromes and their admissibility under the federal rules of evidence. American Journal of Trial Advocacy 27, June, pp. 25–65.

DSM-III-TR, 1987. Diagnostic and Statistical Manual of Mental Disorders, third ed. American Psychiatric Association, Washington, DC. Text Revised.

DSM-IV, 1994. Diagnostic and Statistical Manual of Mental Disorders, fourth ed. American Psychiatric Association, Washington, DC.

DSM-IV-TR, 2000. Diagnostic and Statistical Manual of Mental Disorders, fourth ed. American Psychiatric Association, Washington, DC. Text Revised.

Dutton, M.A., 1996. Critique of the 'battered woman syndrome' model. Applied Research Forum, Available at: http://new.vawnet.org/category/Documents.php?docid=375&category_id=695

Faigman, D.L., 1986. The battered woman syndrome and self-defense: a legal and empirical dissent. Virginia Law Review 72 (no. 3), 619–647.

Faigman, D.L., Kaye, D.H., Saks, M.J., Sanders, J., Cheng, E.K., 2006. Modern Scientific Evidence: The Law and Science of Expert Testimony. vol. 2. Thompson/West, Danvers, MA.

Fairbank, J.A., McCaffrey, R.J., Keane, T.M., 1985. Psychometric detection of fabricated symptoms of PTSD. American Journal of Psychiatry 142 (no. 4), 501–503.

Figueroa, T., 2006. Jury finds wife guilty of second-degree murder. North Country Times, April 12. Available at: http://www.nctimes.com/articles/2006/04/13/news/coastal/15_02_514_12_06.txt

Frey, C., McNerthney, C., Castro, H., 2007. Stalker finds victim at UW, kills her. Seattle.pi.com, April 3. Available at: http://seattlepi.nwsource.com/local/310031_uwshooting03.html

Gleason, W.J., 1993. Mental disorders in battered women: an empirical study. Violence and Victims 8 (no. 1), 53–68.

Gold, L.H., 2004. Sexual Harassment: Psychiatric Assessment in Employment Litigation. American Psychiatric Publishing, Washington, DC.

Gondolf, E.W., Fisher, E.R., 1988. Battered Women as Survivors: An Alternative to Treating Learned Helplessness. Lexington Books, Lexington, MA.

Goodman, E.J., 2003. A case of rape and murder. Gotham Gazette, November 23. Available at: http://www.gothamgazette.com

Hall, D.M., 1998. The victims of stalking. In: Meloy, J.R. (Ed.), The Psychology of Stalking: Clinical and Forensic Perspectives, Academic Press, San Diego, pp. 113–137.

Horvath, M., Brown, J., 2006. The role of drugs and alcohol in rape. Medicine, Science, and the Law 46 (no. 3), 219–228.

Hurley, M., Parker, H., Wells, D., 2006. The epidemiology of drug facilitated sexual assault. Journal of Clinical Forensic Medicine 13 (no. 4), 181–185.

In the Matter of Pittsburgh Action Against Rape, 1981. 494 Pa. 15, 38–43, 428 A.2d 126, 138-40 (Larson, J., dissenting).

Kennedy, L.W., Sacco, V.F., 1998. Crime Victims in Context. Roxbury Publishing, Los Angeles.

Koss, M.P., 2006. Restoring rape survivors: justice, advocacy, and a call to action. Annals of the New York Academy of Sciences 1087 (no. 1), 206–234.

Kuhn, C., Swartzwelder, S., Wilson, W., 2003. Buzzed: The Straight Facts about the Most Used and Abused Drugs, second ed. W.W. Norton, New York.

Logan, T.K., Shannon, L., Cole, J., Swanberg, J., 2007. Partner stalking and implications for women's employment. Journal of Interpersonal Violence 22 (no. 3), 268–291.

Marshall, R.D., Spitzer, R., Liebowitz, M.R., 1999. Review and critique of the new DSM–IV diagnosis of acute stress disorder. American Journal of Psychiatry 156 (no. 11), 1677–1685.

Massic, D., 2002. BU student helps police nab her rapist. The Digital Voice, November 21. Available at: http://media.www.buvoice.com/media/storage/paper227/news/2002/11/21/News/Bu.Student.Helps.Police.Nab.Her.Rapist-330557.shtml

McCord, D., 1985. The admissibility of expert testimony regarding rape trauma syndrome in rape prosecutions. Boston College Law Review 26 (5), 1143–1213, Available at: http://lawdigital-commons.bc.edu/bclr/vol26/iss5/2

McGrath, M., 2011a. Eyewitness reports, identifications, and testimony. In: Turvey, B., Savino, J. (Eds.), Rape Investigation Handbook, second ed. pp. 231–249.

McGrath, M., 2011b. Rape trauma syndrome and investigation of sexual assault. In: Turvey, B., Savino, J. (Eds.), Rape Investigation Handbook, second ed. pp. 251–267.

McGrath, M., Casey, E., 2002. Forensic psychiatry and the internet: practical perspectives on sexual predators and obsessional harassers in cyberspace. Journal of the Academy of Psychiatry and the Law 30 (no. 1), 81–94.

McMahon, M., 1999. Battered women and bad science: the limited validity and utility of battered woman syndrome. Psychiatry, Psychology and Law 6 (no. 1), 23–49.

Meloy, J.R., 1998. The psychology of stalking. In: Meloy, J.R. (Ed.), The Psychology of Stalking: Clinical and Forensic Perspectives, Academic Press, San Diego, pp. 1–23.

Mezey, G., Robbins, I., 2001. Usefulness and validity of post-traumatic stress disorder as a psychiatric category. British Medical Journal 323 (no. 7312), 561–563.

Miller, R.D., 2003a. Novel mental disorders. In: Rosner, R. (Ed.), Principles and Practice of Forensic Psychiatry, second ed. Hodder Arnold, London, pp. 233–238.

Miller, R.D., 2003b. Criminal competence. In: Rosner, R. (Ed.), Principles and Practice of Forensic Psychiatry, second ed. Hodder Arnold, London, p. 212.

National Institute of Justice, 1996. Validity and use of evidence concerning battering and its effects in criminal trials: report responding to Section 40507 of the Violence against Women Act. NCJ 160972. Available at: http://www.ncjrs.gov/App/Publications/abstract.aspx?ID=160972

Newman, A.W., Thompson, J.W., 2001. The rise and fall of forensic hypnosis in criminal investigation. Journal of the American Academy of Psychiatry and the Law 29 (no. 1), 75–81.

New York Times, 1993. Rapist who agreed to use condom gets 40 years. May 15. Available at: http://query.nytimes.com/gst/fullpage.html?res=9F0CE2DF173FF936A25756C0A965958260

Nix, C., 2009. Investigative hypnosis. Telemasp Bulletin 16 (6), 1–7.

Otto, R., Poythress, N., Starr, L., Darkes, 1993. An empirical study of the reports of APA's peer review panel in the Congressional review of the U.S.S. Iowa incident. Journal of Personality Assessment 61 (no. 3), 425–442.

People v. Bennett, 1992. 79 N.Y.2nd 464, 593 N.E.2nd 279.

People v. Taylor/Banks, 1990. 552 NYS 2d 883. Ct App.

People v. Yaklich, 1992. 833 P.2nd, 758. Co. Ct.

Perconte, S.T., Goreczny, A.J., 1990. Failure to detect fabricated PTSD with the use of the MMPI in a clinical population. American Journal of Psychiatry 147 (no. 8), 1057–1060.

Psychiatric Times, 2006. More on battered women syndrome: the debate continues…, October 26. Available at: http://www.psychiatrictimes.com/print/article/10168/1481281

Rock v. Arkansas (1987) 107 S. Ct. 2704.

Roth, A., 2003. Woman convicted in love-triangle murder. Union Tribune, January 28. Available at: http://www.signonsandiego.com/news/metro/20030128-9999_1m28nourn.html

Rothbaum, B.O., Foa, E.B., Murdock, T., Riggs, D.S., Walsh, W., 1992. A prospective examination of posttraumatic stress disorder in rape victims. Journal of Traumatic Stress 5 (no. 3), 455–475.

Ryan, W., 1971. Blaming the Victim. Vintage Books, New York.

Seligman, M.E.P., Maier, S.F., Geer, J., 1968. The alleviation of learned helplessness in dogs. Journal of Abnormal Psychology 73 (no. 3), 256–262.

State v. Allewalt, 1986. 308 Md. 89, 517 A.2d 741.

State v. Anderson, 1990. 785 S.W.2nd 596. Mo. Ct.

State v. Haines, 2006. 112 Ohio St.3d 393, 2006–Ohio–6711. http://www.sconet.state.oh.us/Communications_Office/summaries/2006/1228/050853_050959.asp

State v. Leaphart, 1983. 673 S.W.2nd 870, 872. Tenn. Crim.

State v. Marks, 1982. 231 Kan. 645, 647 P.2nd 1292.

State v. Martin, 1984. 666 S.W.2nd 895. Mo. Ct.

State v. McGee, 1982. 324 N.W.2d 232, 233 (Minn.).

State v. Saldana, 1982. 324 N.W. 277 (Minn.).

Straus, M.A., 1999. The controversy over domestic violence by women: a methodological, theoretical, and sociology of science analysis. In: Arriaga, X.B., Oskamp, S. (Eds.), Violence in Intimate Relationships, Sage, Thousand Oaks, CA, pp. 17–44.

Summerfield, D., 2001. The invention of post-traumatic stress disorder and the social usefulness of a psychiatric category. British Medical Journal 322 (no. 7278), 95–98.

Tavis, C., 1992. Mismeasure of Women. Touchstone, New York.

Thompson, C., 1999. A Glimpse of Hell. W.W. Norton, London.

Turco, R.N., Scott, E.M., 1982. Hypnosis: complications—an illustrative clinical example. International Journal of Offender Therapy and Comparative Criminology 26 (no. 2), 133–137.

The U.S.S. Iowa: Guilt by Gestalt, 1990. Congressional Testimony. Harper's Magazine, March, 24–28.

United States v. Carter, 1986. 22 M.J. 771, 773–774 (C.M.R.).

U.S. Department of Justice, 2002. Recidivism of prisoners released in 1994. Available at: http://bjs.gov/content/pub/pdf/rpr94.pdf

Walker, L.E., 1979. The Battered Woman. Harper Row, New York.

Walker, L.E., 1984. The Battered Woman Syndrome. Springer, New York.

Walker, L.E., 2000. The Battered Woman Syndrome, second ed. Springer, New York.

Walker, L.E., 2006. Battered woman syndrome: empirical findings. Annals of the New York Academy of Science 1087, 142–157.

Walker, L.E., 2009. The Battered Woman Syndrome, third ed. Springer, New York.

Walker, L.E., Arden, H., Tome, A., Bruno, J., Brosch, R., 2006. Battered Woman Questionnaire: Training Manual for Interviewers.

Wallace, H., 2007. Victimology: Legal, Psychological, and Social Perspectives, second ed. Pearson, Boston.

Webert, D.R., 2003. Are the courts in a trance? Approaches to the admissibility of hypnotically enhanced witness testimony in light of empirical evidence. American Criminal Law Review 40, June, pp. 1301–1327.

White v. Violent Crimes Compensation Board, 1979. 90 Mich. App. 727, 282 N.W.2d 10.

Wilson, M., 2006. Being alone raises perils in a night on the town. New York Times, Late Edition, July 28; http://www.nytimes.com/2006/07/28/nyregion/28dead.html

Yehuda, R., McFarlane, A.C., 1995. Conflict between current knowledge about PTSD and its original conceptual basis. American Journal of Psychiatry 152 (no. 12), 1705–1713.

CHAPTER 9

False Allegations of Crime[1]

Brent E. Turvey and Michael McGrath

KEY TERMS

BAFRI (Baeza False Report Index) A list of red flags for false reporting, each indicating the need for further investigation, developed by Det. John J. Baeza of the New York Police Department's Manhattan Special Victim's Squad (sex crimes).

False allegation (aka false report) A false statement, accusation, or complaint to authorities alleging a crime that did not occur. In most jurisdictions, this is itself a crime. In such cases, the alleged victim is actually a criminal offender subject to legal consequences.

Profit Emotional, material, or financial gain.

Revenge The act of inflicting harm on others in return for harm suffered at their hands, direction, or by their complicity.

Having gathered data on the subject of *false allegations* of crime for more than a decade, we have observed that false allegations are not only commonplace but also a significant drain on law enforcement resources. Ignorance on the subject abounds, as does political motivation. Consequently, it remains a tremendous problem that few have sought to define, let alone solve.

There are many reasons for false reports. A partial list of motives would include the desire for financial gain; to garner sympathy; to seek revenge; to cover up another crime; and to excuse behavior, that is, provide an alibi. Mentally ill individuals sometimes make false reports of crime, but these reports are often identified by the fact that they are not reality based. Unfortunately, having a serious mental illness also makes one vulnerable to being victimized. Others make false reports due to underlying (nonpsychotic) psychological needs, and these reports may be harder to ferret out.

While the potential categories of false reports are quite large, this chapter briefly discusses false allegations of abduction and spends the majority of the discussion on false allegations of sexual assault, although the two often overlap. These types of crimes represent the majority of false reports—and are overwhelmingly committed by females.

---

[1]Parts of this chapter have been adapted from material originally published in Baeza and Turvey (2002); McGrath (2000); and McGrath (2005).

Forensic Victimology. http://dx.doi.org/10.1016/B978-0-12-408084-3.00009-0

FALSE ALLEGATIONS OF ABDUCTION

False allegations of abduction serve the same purposes as other false reports, including alibi, sympathy, profit, deflection of responsibility, and others. Consider the following examples, taken from many in just the past few years.

Audrey Seiler

On March 27, 2004, Audrey Seiler, a 20-year-old sophomore at the University of Wisconsin, disappeared from her apartment and was found four days later lying in a marsh (see Figure 9-1). She claimed a man had abducted her at knifepoint. As described in a CNN report (2004a):

> Audrey Seiler, a 20-year-old honor student at the University of Wisconsin in Madison, disappeared early Saturday.
>
> She was found Wednesday about two miles from campus in a marshy area of Madison shortly after someone spotted her and called police, authorities said. Seiler was treated at a hospital and released about five hours later.

FIGURE 9-1
Audrey Seiler, a 20-year-old college student from the University of Wisconsin at Madison, staged her own abduction and falsely reported it to police. She later blamed it on depression.

Blackamore said Seiler told police she was taken at knifepoint and held in captivity, but not harmed. She said she did not know the man....

Seiler described the suspect as a white male in his late 20s or early 30s and about 6 feet tall, police said. He was last seen wearing a black sweatshirt, black hat and jeans, police said.

One of us (Turvey) was asked to examine details of the case for the media. Based on available police reports, there was reason to question Seiler's story despite a national press effort that initially sought to deify her. As Rosario describes (2004):

Brent Turvey, an [Alaskan]-based criminal profiler and forensic scientist with expertise in false reports, said police investigators in Madison will probably wait until the time is appropriate to grill Seiler on specific details on the alleged abduction.

Turvey sees signs of serious doubts in the Seiler case, including the self-reported incident in February in which she claimed she was knocked unconscious and dragged into a bushy area two blocks from her home. There was no evidence that she was robbed or sexually assaulted.

"That's extremely bizarre behavior, whether you live in Madison or L.A.," Turvey said.[2]

Police soon obtained video surveillance tape of Seiler buying the items used to bind her at a store. It appears she was having difficulty in her relationship with her boyfriend and may have staged the abduction for attention. She was charged with two misdemeanor counts of obstructing officers. As explained in a CNN report (2004b):

Seiler said a man had abducted her from her apartment and taken her to the marsh, where he tied her, bound her and forced her to take cold tablets.

The woman's claim that an abductor was lurking nearby led police to initiate a search, which turned up no suspects.

Police decided Seiler's claim was false after they reviewed videotape from a surveillance camera in an area store that showed the woman buying a knife, duct tape, rope and cold medication a day before she was reported missing.

In addition, police interviewed a man who said he had seen the woman in the marsh on days that she was being sought and that she appeared to be alone and unthreatened.

---

[2]This statement refers to the failure of an alleged offender to rape or rob the victim in such a context; to go to all the trouble of acquiring the victim without any evidence of a motive.

Interviewed by police during the search, Heather Thue, the student's roommate, said that Seiler "had been very depressed recently, coming out of her bedroom crying all the time."

Thue said that Seiler "had seemed kind of depressed lately and was 'confused' about her relationship" with her boyfriend, who did not pay as much attention to her as she wanted.

Seiler was given three years' probation after pleading guilty to two misdemeanor counts of obstructing police. She was also ordered to make monthly payments to the Madison Police Department to reimburse their investigative expenses. Their efforts cost about $96,000. She ultimately blamed the entire incident on depression.

Jennifer Wilbanks

Jennifer Wilbanks, a 32-year-old medical assistant (later nicknamed the "runaway bride"), disappeared while out jogging on April 26, 2005, four days before her 600-guest wedding (see Figure 9-2). She was immediately declared missing by her family and fiancé. A national media frenzy ensued, during which some in the psychic community declared her dead or in danger, as described in Radford (2005, p. 7):

> One self-proclaimed psychic in Buffalo, New York, reportedly had a vision that Wilbanks was dead and would be found near some bushes. Another psychic, Christopher Scott, described his involvement in the case at the Blogger News Network Web site: "I am a psychic with experience in this type of investigations [sic] and have offered my help to Duluth police. I left my number two days ago and I haven't heard a word from them. I was involved in the murder of Robert Crane (from *Hogan's Heroes*) many years ago. I have participated in other investigation as well.... I have told police that it's vital that I examine her personal articles before they 'cool down.' I fear Wilbanks is in dire straights [sic].... If her parents can afford to offer $100,000 reward, they can afford to fly me in and at least allow me to examine evidence."

A police investigation revealed that she had bought a bus ticket days before her "disappearance." It turned out that she was overwhelmed with her upcoming wedding and got "cold feet." She traveled to Las Vegas, then to Albuquerque, and then called the police—falsely reporting she had been abducted. Later, after questioning, she admitted she had run away on her own (CNN, 2005). She eventually pleaded guilty to making a false report and was sentenced to probation, community service, and continuation of mental health treatment (*CBS News*, 2005).

FIGURE 9-2
A 2005 billboard in Duluth, Georgia, evidences the dual public perceptions of Jennifer Wilbanks: missing fiancé and "runaway bride."

Sasha Abney and Bryshada Ward

A 17-year-old girl from San Benito, Texas, was charged with filing a false report after claiming she had been abducted from her home, when in fact she had run away. As Abshire (2007) explains:

> The Lampasas County Sheriff's Department issued arrest warrants Thursday for two Terrell women who spun a tale of abduction and returned home three days later to say their disappearance was a hoax.
>
> Sheriff's investigator David Thorp said warrants were issued for both women on charges of making a false report to a peace officer, a Class B misdemeanor punishable by up to six months in jail and a $2,000 fine....

> Sasha Abney and Bryshada Ward showed up at a Central Texas gas station Tuesday night after disappearing Saturday night in Mesquite.
>
> "I'm angry, but I'm glad they're safe," Richard Abney, father of Ms. Abney, 20, and uncle of her 17-year-old cousin Ms. Ward, said at a news conference Wednesday outside Mesquite police headquarters.
>
> "We found out this was a hoax," Mr. Abney said. "They missed their curfew, got in deeper and deeper and decided they were going to drive south. They ran out of money and ran out of gas, and they were afraid to call us. We are apologizing to everyone."
>
> Mr. Abney said Ms. Ward hit his daughter with a shoe to cause a minor injury in an attempt to make the Terrell women's story more believable. As for reports that Ms. Abney was unresponsive when found, that was just an act, he said.

This case not only shows the kinds of motives involved in false abduction reports (curfew violations; fear of parental punishment), but the complexity of evidence that even teenagers are capable of staging evidence to back up their story.

We have observed that there appears to be more community and professional willingness to prosecute false reports of abduction than of rape. This may be due to the nature of the crime of rape, because of the nature of media attention and an angry public that feels it has been duped, or because of the types of victims involved. Specifically, alleged rape victims are often examined less carefully than any other type, because some investigators are unable to accept that false reports of rape are possible, to say nothing of being common. Still other investigators are unwilling to go down that investigative road for fear of political sanctions, inside and outside their department. They may have an activist prosecutor or an intimidating rape advocacy system, for example, that will step in to defend all alleged victims regardless of the evidence. Rape is a sensitive issue for many, and is more likely to get media attention and a community response in favor of the alleged victim up front than any other. All these factors and more come to bear on an investigation, and eventual prosecution, when a rape is reported. This is an area that requires further discussion and study.

FALSE ALLEGATIONS OF SEXUAL ASSAULT

Rape is one of the most ruinous of crimes, potentially destroying a victim's sense of safety and leading to significant psychological and functional sequelae. In the past, unless a woman was significantly injured, claims of rape were often met with distrust. A calm presentation of events was also seen as evidence of a lack of injury, whereas a hysterical presentation of events was seen as lacking credibility (Aiken, Burgess, and Hazelwood, 1995) and more indicative of hypersensitivity than a reaction to a crime. Thus, a victim of rape was in a "no win" situation and was as likely to be victimized by the criminal justice system as by the rapist. Rape is also an underreported crime for many reasons, not the least of which is the victim's fear of not being believed and personal embarrassment. It is subsequently all the more surprising that such a large proportion of reported rapes are false.

Rape myths are varied and far from dead (Johnson, Kuck, and Schander, 1997). As suggested by Herman (1990), one result of the feminist movement has been a redefinition of rape from a crime to a trait of the human male. In this paradigm, all males are rapists, and due to the inherent inequality between the sexes, any sexual interaction between a male and a female is, by definition, rape (Johnson, Kuck, and Schander, 1997). Although this stance is clearly extreme, it has raised consciousness in America related to the crime of rape and the treatment of rape victims. For example, Rape Trauma Syndrome[3] (Burgess and Holmstrom, 1974) and testimony related to it have been both barred and introduced at trial in various states (Block, 1990). Rape Shield Laws have been introduced in an effort to protect the prior sex life of the rape victim from becoming the focus of inquiry at trial (Bryden and Lengnick, 1997). Prior to such statutes, a defense attorney had free rein to delve into the past of the victim. When immaterial to the crime, this information invited a jury to come to the conclusion that because the victim had been, or was currently, sexually active, either she "asked for it," or the damage could not have been too great.

In his seminal work on criminal investigation, in a section dedicated to a discussion of the dangers of preconceived investigative theories, Hans Gross provides one of the earliest and arguably most informed segments on the subject of those who make false allegations of sexual assault (1924, pp. 13–14). His discussion includes topics such as the various motivations for filing false reports, the occurrence of self-injury, and the related responsibilities of the investigating officer. In a more recent text on the history of rape, a discussion of the conceptualization and consequences of such false reports provides little more insight into these and associated problems (Palmer and Thornhill, 2000; pp. 159–161). Here, the topic is couched in a general discussion of deceitfulness and sex differences, with some statistics. Their conclusion is that there are social factors and sex differences that may contribute to a general reluctance to believe female rape allegations (Palmer and Thornhill, 2000; p. 160).

Jonna Spilbor, a prosecutor who became a defense attorney and then a news commentator, had the following to say regarding false allegations of sexual

---

[3]See Chapter 8 for a review of Rape Trauma Syndrome.

assault during a discussion of the rape allegation against popular sports figure Kobe Bryant of the NBA (Spilbor, 2003):

> The statistics on false rape reports in the U.S. are widely divergent, and often too outdated to be meaningful. Not surprisingly, the numbers also depend on whom you ask. Organizations that tout a feminist agenda claim the number of false rape reports to be nearly non-existent—about two percent. But other organizations, taking the side of men, claim that false reports are actually very common—citing numbers ranging from forty-one to sixty percent.
>
> Amid the statistics, the truth is impossible to ascertain—but it's plain that false reports are indeed made, and that they can ruin the life of the accused, whether or not a conviction follows.
>
> Falsely reporting any crime is shameful. Falsely reporting a rape is especially heinous. The liar who files the false claim dishonors—and makes life all the more difficult for—the many true victims who file genuine rape claims because they have been terribly violated, and seek justice for it. At the same time, and perhaps even more seriously, the false report begins to destroy the reputation, and sometimes the life, of the accused from the very moment it is made—a fact of which many accusers are keenly aware.

A point Spilbor (2003) made very strongly is that it is common for the false reporter to suffer no legal consequences from having made a false report. This is reflective of the social and political context of some false allegations, which often includes the agendas of those involved. For example, in Burgess and Hazlewood's *Practical Aspects of Rape Investigation* (2001), one can read the entire chapter "False Rape Allegations" (Burgess, Hazelwood, and Burgess, 2001) and never learn that making a false report of rape to a police officer is a crime, let alone that the false reporter should be held criminally responsible. This would be an example of the politics of victimhood precluding the notion that a "victim" should be held responsible for his or her behavior. This is evident when the chapter ends (p. 195) with the following two sentences:

> Basic principles of police professionalism require that officers who investigate rapes remain objective and compassionate. If they do not, the veracity of the allegation may never be known; and the victim—for she is a victim in either case [i.e., whether the report of sexual assault is true or not]—may never receive the help or support she needs.

There is no mention of what, if anything, should be done for the person (not a victim?) against whom the false allegation was made.

As a counterbalance, we suggest readers consider the representative summary of potential consequences for false allegations provided in Martin (2005, p. 271):

> In Virginia, "[a]ny person fourteen years of age or older who makes or causes to be made a report of child abuse or neglect that he knows to be false shall be guilty of a Class 1 misdemeanor." Washington applies a similar misdemeanor punishment but does not include the age limit, "[a] person who, intentionally and in bad faith or maliciously, knowingly makes a false report of [alleged] abuse or neglect shall be guilty of a misdemeanor."
>
> In Indiana, a person who intentionally makes a false report has committed a Class A misdemeanor which is upgraded to a Class D misdemeanor if they have a prior conviction of false reporting. In addition, they may also be liable in damages to the person accused of abuse.

We would add that while it is true that sometimes people who have made a false report may benefit from some form of mental health intervention, this in no way changes the fact that they have committed a crime.

THE LITERATURE

Every so often false reports will be mentioned in the press, and unofficial false report rates crafted outside the realm of formal scientific research will be disclosed to the public.[4]

However, the professional literature on the subject of false reports remains scarce. There have, for example, been very few scientific studies conducted to ascertain false report rates or percentages. Further still, there is a dearth in the published literature on even the subject of false reports in general. Put another way, those studying rape and sexual assault do not typically discuss false reports, let alone research the issue. This is due in no small part to the fact that many researchers fear being maligned, blacklisted, or threatened with sanctions should their findings not be politically acceptable.[5]

---

[4]An editorial in the *New York Post* on the now-infamous Oliver Jovanovic false report case (Dunleavy, 1999) quoted District Attorney Linda Fairstein from an interview in *Penthouse* magazine where she stated, "There are about 4,000 reports of rape each year in Manhattan, of these half of them didn't happen." In a more recent article, it was stated that out of 2,000 uninvestigated cases in Philadelphia, Pennsylvania, from 1995 to 1997, investigators determined that "600 were false reports or allegations that did not amount to crimes" (Inquirer Staff, 2000).
[5]This opinion is based on discussions with fellow investigators and forensic examiners. It is also based on the fact that a number of the articles reviewed for this paper received scathing commentary from the professional community unrelated to reliability and validity. A common complaint was that the identification and prosecution of false reporters cause legitimate victims to fear reporting their crime to law enforcement. As such, it has been argued that presenting any false report numbers is harmful to victims and casework by preventing legitimate victims from coming forward for fear of not being believed, or even being prosecuted, having reported a crime.

MacDonald

MacDonald (1973) found that, in 1968, the national average for forcible rapes was 18%. He further found that in a one-year period in Denver, Colorado, 25% of all forcible rapes were unfounded. He felt this was a conservative figure, as the police in Denver did not record as false reports any cases in which there was a doubt as to the veracity of the complaint. Referring to the same study, MacDonald (1973) states that 20% of the forcible rape complaints were actually in doubt. MacDonald does not footnote or otherwise reference this information.

2% False Report Rate

There is no shortage of politicians, victim's advocates, and news articles claiming that the nationwide false report rate for rape and sexual assault is almost nonexistent, citing a figure of around 2%. This figure is not accurate, and attempts to find the original source are elusive.

In researching this issue, Haws (1997) prepared a brief but detailed account of his failed attempt to find a legitimate and accurate study supporting the claim that only 2% of reported rapes are false reports:

> If you talk to sexual assault counselors, you'll most likely hear the low figure: that 2 percent of all accusations of sexual assault reported to law enforcement across the country are later found to be false, which, the counselors say, is the same rate as for other crimes. Of all the numbers out there, this has been cited most often, appearing in publications from *The Boston Globe* to the *Houston Chronicle*, *The Christian Science Monitor*, the *Minneapolis Star Tribune*, *Newsweek*, and *Editor and Publisher*.
>
> Sometimes the figure is attributed to a particular source, but that's still no guarantee the numbers can't be challenged. Marcia L. Roth, the author of the 1996 op-ed article in the *Louisville Courier-Journal*, attributed the 2 percent rate to the 1993 book *Rape, the Misunderstood Crime*, by Julie Allison and Lawrence Wrightsman. But Allison and Wrightsman weren't so unequivocal. Noting that the frequency of false rape reports is difficult to assess, they didn't do their own study; instead they looked at a synthesis of research findings from a 1979 book, *Understanding the Rape Victim*, by Sedelle Katz and Mary Ann Mazur. Katz and Mazur, it turns out, had reviewed studies dating back to 1956 that showed the frequency of unfounded and false rape reports ranging from a low of 1 percent to a high of 25 percent. Allison and Wrightsman simply chose the study that showed 2 percent.
>
> Another named source for the 2 percent figure has been *Against Our Will*, the groundbreaking book on sexual violence by Susan

Brownmiller published in 1975. She was reporting on the phenomenon that in New York City, the rate of false accusations dropped "dramatically" to 2 percent as soon as the police began using policewomen instead of men to interview complainants.

Sometimes the 2 percent figure appears without any attribution. It simply floats out there, as in a 1994 article in the *Houston Chronicle* that cites a women's center official as the source for the false-rape-report figure of "between 2 and 3 percent." Period. And sometimes the attribution is vague but credible-sounding, like "federal statistics" or "the FBI." In 1992, *The Boston Globe* reported that a rape counselor stated the 2 percent rate for false reporting of rapes is the same as for false reports of other crimes— "according to the FBI."

But the FBI has been saying since 1991 that the annual rate for the false reporting of forcible sexual assault across the country has been a consistent 8 percent (through 1995, the most recent year available). That's four times higher than the average of the false-reporting rates of the other crimes tracked by the FBI in its *Uniform Crime Report*. The agency's guidelines define a report as false when an investigation determines that no offense occurred. A complainant's failure or refusal to cooperate in the investigation does not, by itself, lead to a finding of false report.

The writings of Susan Brownmiller, published more than three decades ago, stand out on this issue. In her work, *Against Our Will* (1975, p. 435), she argues:

> A decade ago the FBI's *Uniform Crime Reports* noted that 20 percent of all rapes reported to the police "were determined by investigation to be unfounded." By 1973 the figure had dropped to 15 percent, while rape remained, in the FBI's words, "the most underreported crime." A 15 percent figure for false accusations is undeniably high, yet when New York City instituted a special sex crimes analysis squad and put police *women* (instead of men) in charge of interviewing complainants, the number of false charges in New York dropped dramatically to 2 percent, a figure that corresponded exactly to the rate of false reports for other crimes.

First, the statistic cited appears specific to New York City, so its use as a number representing national trends is inappropriate. Second, to support the 2% statistic provided, Brownmiller (1975, p. 373) references the remarks of Lawrence H. Cooke, appellate division justice, before the Association of the Bar of the City of New York, January 16, 1974. In response to criticisms for using this non-peer reviewed remark at a public meeting as the basis for professional arguments and opinions, she wrote this brief response some 20 years later (Brownmiller, 1995):

The cite from the New York City Rape Analysis Squad was reported by Judge Lawrence Cooke to the NY Bar Association in 1974. Cooke was a leading appellate justice at that time. Cooke, the Bar Association, and the NYC Rape Analysis Squad were impeccable sources. The information was fresh and exciting. It had appeared nowhere else. The person who attempted to discount it in the post you reproduced denigrated New York State's leading appellate justice, a city agency, and me.

Ultimately, we are left to conclude that there is no published study or data to support any claim that the national false rape allegation rate is or was ever around 2%, even from those who originally cited that number. Rather, it comes primarily from a judge giving a speech to some attorneys more than 30 years ago whose source has, to date, not been validated.

Unfortunately, the 2% figure has found its way into legitimate research and texts on the subject, inappropriately offered as a national average or as the basis for refuting that false reports happen at all. For example, an otherwise excellent text on the subject of police culture and sexual assault referred to false reports of sexual assault as a "myth" (Gregory and Lees, 1999, p. 90):

> Behind the mutual recriminations about the handling of rape and sexual assault cases, the dominant discourse on male and female sexuality, shared by most police officers, lawyers, magistrates, judges and juries, gives rise to the myth of false allegations and to misunderstandings around the notion of consent.

Consider also the otherwise even-handed discussion in Anderson (2004, pp. 984–986), which concludes with a fair assessment of the current state of the science:

> To be sure, there are personality disorders that might lead a man or woman to lie in any number of outrageous ways, including lodging a false report of a crime. There is, however, no specific empirical research connecting any of these personality disorders with false complaints of rape to the police. In fact, there is no good empirical data on false rape complaints either historically or currently. A debate over the number of false complaints nevertheless continues.
>
> One side of the debate maintains that only two percent of rape complaints made to the police are false. In her popular 1975 book on rape, *Against Our Will*, Susan Brownmiller wrote, "when New York City instituted a special sex crimes analysis squad and put policewomen (instead of men) in charge of interviewing complainants, the number of false charges in New York dropped dramatically to 2 percent, a figure that corresponded exactly to the rate of false reports

for other violent crimes." Over time and perhaps through repetition, this two percent false rate has come to constitute the "conventional scholarly wisdom" on the matter. The United States Justice Department appears to agree, stating that "[f]alse accusations of sexual assault are estimated to occur at the low rate of two percent—similar to the rate of false accusations for other violent crimes."

The other side of the debate claims that eight percent or more of rape complaints made to the police are false, a percentage disproportionate to other crimes. The F.B.I. *Uniform Crime Reports* have in the past indicated that, overall, about eight percent of forcible rape complaints reported to police are "unfounded." The term "unfounded" is misleading, however, because it does not mean "false." Rather, police may code a case "unfounded" when they conclude that it is unverifiable, not serious, or not prosecutable. Various factors can increase a city's percentage of "unfounded" rape complaints, such as police incompetence, bias, or insensitivity to rape victims. As the Department of Justice found, police may think a rape claim is false or unfounded if the victim had a prior relationship with the attacker, used drugs or alcohol at the time of the attack, lacked visible signs of injury, delayed notifying police, did not have a rape exam, blames herself for the rape, or did not immediately conceive of the assault as a rape.

Thus, neither side's numbers in the debate over the rate of false complaints of rape lodged with the police appear to be supported by the kind of empirical evidence upon which one might feel confident. As a scientific matter, the frequency of false rape complaints to police or other legal authorities remains unknown.

It is true that good data on the subject is not available, and good empirical studies have yet to be performed. However, what can be stated with certainty is that the oft-cited 2% has no basis in reality and is not reflective of national crime trends. It is time that we move forward and away from the citation of this figure to newer, more reliable data. Consider the following meta-analysis of available research to date.

McDowell

Charles P. McDowell, a supervisory special agent serving with the U.S. Air Force, studied false reports extensively. Although his study is unpublished, McDowell examined 1,218 cases that were initially reported as rapes. He found that 460 rape allegations were proven, 212 rape allegations were disproved, and 546 rape allegations were unresolved. The total percentage of false reports for all reported rapes was 17.41%, or 212 out of 1,218. The total false report rate for all resolved rape allegations was 31.55%, or 212 out of 672 (McDowell, 1985).

Kanin

Eugene Kanin of Purdue University in Indiana conducted one of the few published studies on false reports. Kanin studied all rapes ($n = 109$) occurring in an unnamed midwestern city with a population of 70,000 from 1978 to 1987. Kanin found a 41% false report rate (Kanin, 1994). It should be noted that in Kanin's study a false report could only be identified by virtue of a confession from the alleged victim. In the same paper, Kanin also discussed the results of an unpublished study he conducted in 1988, which examined all forcible rape complaints during a three-year period on two midwestern college campuses. The false report rate in that study was 50% (1994).

What these numbers combine to suggest is that the rate of false reporting for rape varies from city to city, from state to state, and from region to region. As those of us who work cases know from experience, the numbers can be very high. However, depending on how one approaches the phenomenon to collect and report data, and who is cited as a reference, the numbers can be made to paint a variety of pictures. We strongly urge further research of the matter by those controlling the data rather than burying it, which has too often been the case. The FBI's national average, which includes only reporting police agencies, suggests a false report rate of around 8%. Given other contextual support for higher rates of false reporting throughout the country (see footnote 4), this should be viewed as the most conservative estimate—the lowest possible estimate. It is by no means considered the limit.

Red Flags

When faced with an allegation of sexual assault, an investigator at times walks a fine line between being supportive of a victim and trying to determine if the allegation of sexual assault is a false report. Sex crimes investigators are fully aware that false allegations of sexual assault are common. There are several collections of red flags for false allegations. These flags must be used in a measured manner, as a truthful person can easily raise some red flags.

It is also important to keep in mind that complainants may be telling the complete truth, may be holding back information for a variety of reasons, or may even be misrepresenting only parts of their actual attack. Simply because one has determined that a complainant has lied in one area does not necessarily mean that he or she has lied in all areas or that an attack did not take place. For example, a victim could report a rape, and a review of the alleged crime scene might determine that the report is not corroborated by the condition or evidence at that scene. It could be that the report is unfounded, but it could also be that the victim (for whatever reason) is reluctant to place himself or herself at the true crime scene. It is important to sort out inconsistencies early in the investigation either to identify a false report or to salvage the prosecution of an actual criminal.

Dietz and Hazelwood

During testimony at the Tawana Brawley grand jury, Dr. Park Elliot Dietz, a forensic psychiatrist, proposed 20 false report red flags that he had developed along with retired Supervisory Special Agent Roy Hazelwood of the Federal Bureau of Investigation (*Court TV*, 1997). While under oath, Dietz specifically mentioned the existence of false report red flags and stated that, based on his own research and consultation with Hazelwood, there are 20 characteristics that have appeared in false allegation cases. They are provided here, with commentary as appropriate:

1. *The story tends to be bizarre or sensational.* It is hard to assess this as given. Surely an unusual account will require explanation, but finding something unusual or "bizarre" is subjective to experience. Also, the fact that an account is sensational may or may not be helpful. The fact that some sensational cases are false reports may, in fact, skew our perception. It may be that sensational false reports are the exception, but they are the ones that the media report on. It may be that nonsensational cases are more numerous but receive less media attention.

2. *The pseudo-victim injures himself or herself, sometimes seriously, or simulates injury for the purpose of gaining support.* This cue is difficult to interpret, as it implies the investigator is aware that the injury is self-inflicted or carries secondary gain. If we are that far along, we would submit that we have no further need for additional red flags—we should already be scrutinizing the issue.

3. *The pseudo-victim presents in such a way that people believe no one would do this to himself or herself.* This, also, is difficult to interpret. This may appear obvious until one is presented with a real case. Perhaps a better admonition would be never to assume that people would not go to great lengths to accomplish something when sufficiently motivated. All portions of the complainant's account should be tested to determine whether or not he or she could have been responsible. If the answer is yes, then reality must not be dismissed or explained away.

4. *The pseudo-victim does not initially report the incident to police.* The question begged here is what constitutes a reasonable delay? Does a delay constitute a victim calling a friend before calling 911, or is it a delay if a victim reports the crime three months later? This is a highly subjective criterion that requires more explanation to be useful as a potential indicator. Also, delays in reporting are common in legitimate reports. This criterion has such limited specificity as to border on worthless, especially when relied heavily upon to declare a report false. Perhaps it would be more useful to look for unexplained or unexplainable delays. The unexplained and unexplainable are always red flags to the alert investigator.

5. *A stranger is accused.* Many false reporters will actually name or even provide detailed descriptions of a suspect in their complaint. This may not constitute the majority of false report cases, but there have been far too many to agree that accusing a stranger is a red flag. It begs serious study before more can be inferred from its mere occurrence.

6. *The pseudo-victim claims that overwhelming force was used, or that he or she resisted greatly, or that there were multiple assailants.* Taken out of context, it is hard to imagine how this is helpful. One might argue that it must be taken in context, but there is nothing to indicate this. One might question the credibility of an account in which five assailants assaulted a victim who reported heroic resistance in the absence of any injuries, but this particular red flag does not indicate that and remains uncomfortably vague.

7. *The account is either overly detailed or very vague.* Although "very vague" would likely be easily noted, it is not clear at what point "very vague" morphs into "vague" or even "limited detail." Also, the determination of "overly detailed" would seem to be in the eye of the beholder. While the intent of this red flag seems justified, there is little to allow one to operationalize this criterion. If a complainant avoids giving details that can be verified, that would be a more useful red flag.

8. *The pseudo-victim reports having his or her eyes closed during the attack or was unconscious, or passed out, or has no memory of what happened, or was drugged, and so cannot provide details.* This would serve to avoid giving details that could be followed up on. However, it is only a red flag if the context is sufficient. If these circumstances are reported when the victim has been caught in an inconsistency, or after other scrupulous details have been provided, then there is reason for doubt. This will give investigators something to confirm or refute through the evidence they collected (it is hoped) and preserved during the initial phases of the investigation.

9. *The pseudo-victim is indifferent to his or her injuries.* Apparent indifference to injuries is subjective (per investigator) and may or may not be related to a false report.

10. *The expected laboratory findings are absent.* This needs to be fleshed out further. Certainly if the victim claims that something occurred and laboratory analysis can confirm it—and fails to—then this is a red flag. However, it may only serve to prove that the victim has a poor memory of events.

11. *The pseudo-victim is vague about the location of the assault, or there is no evidence at the scene to corroborate the complaint.* Being vague about the location of the assault may or may not be a red flag. This would depend

on whether the circumstances of the complaint permitted victim memory. For example, a victim who has suffered a head injury, lack of oxygen, been drugged, or used alcohol prior to the alleged attack might be vague about many details. However, absence of corroborating evidence is always a red flag to the alert investigator—unless an absence of evidence is not unexpected.

12. *Damage to the clothing is inconsistent with the injuries.* This would be a useful red flag regarding the truthfulness of statements about injuries but not necessarily proof of a false report.

13. *There are escalating personal problems in the life of the pseudo-victim.* It is hard to assess the significance of this red flag in an individual case, as "escalating personal problems" may conceivably place one at greater risk for assault.

14. *The pseudo-victim has been exposed in the past to accounts of similar things.* It may be hard to apply this, as any American adult or adolescent with access to a television and the Internet would likely meet this criterion. But it is not unreasonable to keep this in mind, as people can model their behavior and report based on either false reports they are aware of, or actual rapes that they have known about. What would be needed is evidence that the complainant could have been exposed to the material (i.e., that it happened prior to the complaint and was widely reported), along with evidence that the complaint is sufficiently similar.

15. *The pseudo-victim's post-assault behavior is inconsistent with the allegations.* The post-assault behaviors need to be spelled out. Are Dietz and Hazelwood referring to the victim laughing, becoming hysterical, crying, and/or not crying at inappropriate moments? Are they referring to the victim going to a party a day or two after the alleged assault? Are they referring to having sexual intercourse the same night as a violent and painful rape was reported? Without some kind of detail and elucidation, this red flag would be difficult to apply to an actual case. This could be important, but can be very subjective and open to misinterpretation. The "gutsy" return to "normalcy" of a rape victim could, or a quick flight back into health could be seen as lack of injury and possible "evidence" of a false report.

16. *The pseudo-victim is uncooperative with the investigation.* This is generally important, absent some explaining variable. But it must be kept in mind that rape victims are entitled to react the way they react, and do not necessarily fit into a mold we expect, including cooperation with law enforcement. If the victim has perceived disinterest or other emotions on the part of investigators, he or she might be less cooperative than expected. Also, there are different levels of cooperation that may be

perceived as uncooperative, when in fact they are simply a reflection of other variables unseen or misperceived by the investigator.

17. *When the pseudo-victim talks to the authorities, he or she tends to steer the conversation away from the specific to the unprovable.* This may be a useful red flag, so long as it is consistent and not a feature of shame or poor memory. This is also similar to a previous red flag (No. 7).

18. *There is writing on the body of the pseudo-victim.* While this occurred in the Tawana Brawley case, it has occurred infrequently in our case experience. If it can be determined through crime reconstruction or wound pattern analysis whether the victim could have made the injury, then this has value to the investigation. If it cannot, merely the existence of such evidence would seem to indicate little. This, too, is a behavior that begs serious study before more can be inferred from its mere occurrence.

19. *There is a history of making other false allegations.* One must be careful with this criterion, but it is clearly something that cannot be ignored. It is potentially a significant red flag, as long as prior allegations were accurately determined to be unfounded. A useful discussion of this issue is provided in Epstein (2006, pp. 657–658):

> In order to be relevant in a criminal proceeding, a false accusation must connote one of three phenomena: a report of forced sexual contact where there was no sexual conduct at all; a claim of forced contact where the actual encounter was consensual; or an accusation of a particular person when the complainant knows that her assailant was someone else. The second guideline should set standards for admissibility. For impeachment purposes, the requirement of "good faith" in posing the question is the requisite standard. As to the admission of false accusation proof as substantive non-character "plan" or "doctrine of chance" evidence, the governing standard must be that used for all "other acts" evidence—whether there is some evidence that would permit the jury to find that a false accusation had occurred, i.e., "such evidence should be admitted if there is sufficient evidence to support a finding by the jury that the defendant committed the similar act." The last guideline should prevent undue prejudice and the harms meant to be protected by Rape Shield Laws. Litigation of a pre-trial motion in limine by the prosecution to ascertain the intended use of "false accusation" evidence will ensure that only proper proof is introduced and proper questioning occurs.

20. Readers are encouraged to give thought to this red flag, and consideration to the admonitions provided.

21. *There is a history of extensive medical care.* As listed, without commentary from Dietz and Hazelwood as to what this means, this may not be as helpful as one might suspect. For example, a history of mental illness may provide evidence that the victim is out of touch with reality, or it may make the victim more vulnerable to assault.

Some of these red flags have investigative value under the right conditions. However, many of them are much too vague and subjective to be of use on their own. We would suggest that the inconsistencies of each case be evaluated in its context, and that the more general red flags be redefined with an eye to greater clarity of context before being applied in actual casework.

Brown, Crowley, Peck, and Slaughter

Brown, Crowley, Peck, and Slaughter (1997) conducted research to address the issue of genital injury in female sexual assault victims. This study examined 311 rape victims who entered San Louis Obispo General Hospital's emergency room in California between January of 1985 and December of 1993. The study also examined a control group of 75 women, from the same location and time period, who had engaged in consensual intercourse. Of those 75 women, 48 had initially been evaluated as victims of rape but later admitted that their encounters had been consensual. Though not conducted to address the issue of false reports specifically, this study ultimately revealed a 13.37% rate of false rape reporters. This study, it should be remembered, involved victims and alleged victims that presented to an emergency room.

Review of Victim Report

The interview with an alleged victim of sexual assault is perhaps the most vital part of a sex crime investigator's effort to establish the facts of a case. Unfortunately, it is common for even seasoned investigators to accept an alleged victim's statement or story without question or suspicion. This uncritical aspect may arise out of a fear of disturbing the alleged victim, being viewed as politically incorrect by victim advocates and colleagues, or a lack of knowledge about the investigation of potential false reports. As explained in Donnelly (2007, p. 898):

> Victim advocates almost always consider accusers to be "victims" even before it is known that a crime has been committed. They also react in horror any time expert investigators suggest that false allegations of sexual assault are common and distinguishable from truthful ones.

An uncritical aspect may also arise out of a common problem that inhabits much of police culture: investigative apathy.[6]

Too many investigators will go to great lengths to explain away factual inconsistencies in an alleged victim's story if it suits them. Inconsistencies that have been explained away in this manner, rather than actually investigated, should be treated as suspect. Whatever the case, there is no legitimate reason to avoid a detailed, frame-by-frame examination of the logic and rationale in any victim's statement. Regardless of the consequences, every alleged victim's statement must be examined thoroughly. If there are breaks in the logic, they must be explained.

False Report Interview Strategy

The literature review just provided demonstrates two things. First, investigators and forensic examiners are very likely to encounter a false report if they work sex crimes. Second, due to the dearth of literature and the limited investigative experience behind it, investigators and forensic examiners will often be unprepared when this happens.

False reporters may report their allegations to the police in the same way that real victims do. The interviewer will want to treat the potential false report case the same as any other, up until the point of the second part of the formal interview, the frame-by-frame analysis. This is where the interviewer should confront the alleged victim with any contradictions between his or her statement and the physical evidence. Any contradiction in the victim's statement needs to be explained by the victim, not the interviewer. The interviewer should never accept contradictory statements in the victim's statement because the victim was upset or experiencing trauma. These contradictions must be explained logically.

At some point during the interview, the interviewer may be convinced that the false reporter is lying. In this case, it is recommended that the investigator inform the false reporter that he or she is now a suspect in a criminal investigation and then read the Miranda warnings. Failing to do so could be problematic for any future prosecution.

---

[6]It is important to note that there are other considerations motivating investigators, forensic examiners, and researchers away from the identification and study of false reports. Aside from apathy, an overall political environment that sanctions such identifications and investigations can promulgate a fearful investigative mindset. This fear of political reprisal routinely provides for the failure to correctly identify and investigate false reports to their fullest conclusion. As discussed in Palmer and Thornhill (2000, p. 160), "To some feminists, the concept of false rape allegation itself constitutes discriminatory harassment." It is not unreasonable in such an environment for investigators and forensic examiners to be concerned that the investigation of a false report, and even the consideration of false reporting as a viable case theory, will result in negative consequences from colleagues, superiors, the media, victim advocates, and the general public.

THE BAFRI

As suggested by the dearth of research in the area of false rape allegations, and the lack of professional awareness and willingness to investigate such instances, the need for tools to assess potential false reports is not being met or even pursued. Baeza (Baeza and Turvey, 2002) offered the *Baeza False Report Index (BAFRI)* as one tool to assess false reports.

The Baeza False Report Index (BAFRI)

The following is a list of false report red flags created by Detective John J. Baeza (retired). Every investigator, victimologist, criminologist, criminal profiler, and attorney should be aware of this index when examining or investigating any case that involves an alleged sex crime.

One or more of the circumstantial red flags described in this index have surfaced in most, if not all, of the false reports investigated by Baeza and Turvey (2002),[7] but they caution investigators against relying blindly on them or placing undue weight on a limited number. These red flags are listed here, with commentary:

1. *A female victim has demanded to speak with a female officer or investigator.* (This excludes those cases in which a male officer or investigator has acted inappropriately toward the female.) As indicated by the disqualifier in parentheses, this must be assessed from the perspective of the victim.
2. *A female victim's husband, boyfriend, or other intimate partner has forced her to report the alleged crime, rather than having reported the crime of her own volition.* This is a major red flag, especially when the allegation provides an alibi for an otherwise unexplainable delay in returning home.
3. *A victim's parents have forced him or her to report the alleged crime, rather than having reported the crime of his or her own volition.* This is essentially a corollary of the preceding flag.
4. *A victim, most often under age (less than 18 years old), has returned home after his or her curfew.* Again, this is a major red flag, especially when the complaint provides an alibi for an otherwise unexplainable delay in returning home.
5. *A victim states that he or she was abducted at a busy intersection (or some other very public location) during the day, and there are no witnesses to the incident.*
6. *A victim states that he or she was attacked by a masked offender in the middle of the day on a busy street.* Although at first glance this red flag appears

---

[7]The value of this list is its identification of areas that require further investigative attention, that is, red flags. They can and will exist in legitimate cases, but when these elements are present, they must be examined, understood, and explained.

similar to Number 5, it actually highlights an important issue—that of paradoxical offender behavior. Descriptions of offender behavior that seem to defy common sense (the mask would seem to draw attention to the offender) should raise some level of suspicion.

7. *A victim is in a drug rehabilitation program and is out past curfew.* This is another alibi flag. Most chemical dependency residential programs have curfews and will discharge residents who do not return by a certain time. Claiming a rape will explain the absence.

8. *A pregnant female victim is forced by a parent or guardian to report the crime to police.*

9. *A victim cannot describe the suspect nor provide details of the crime.* As with the red flag described in the section on Dietz and Hazelwood, the utility of this red flag will depend on the level of vagueness and the overall context.

10. *A victim has previously been charged with falsely reporting an incident.* As previously discussed, one needs to look for a pattern of lying or false representations. This red flag must be taken in context.

11. *A victim has previously reported a similar crime to the police.* The investigators must keep in mind that it is not uncommon for victims to have been assaulted previously—especially if they are medium- or high-exposure victims (see discussions in Chapters 5 and 6).

12. *A victim focuses on relocating to a new home or apartment during the investigation.*

13. *A victim focuses on initiating a lawsuit or on monetary gain during the investigation.*

14. *A victim displays "TV" behavior when initiating a complaint, mimicking the way that stereotypical victims act on television and in film (hysterical, demand female officer, catatonic, etc.).* This may be hard to assess, as the "normal" response to a sexual assault can span the spectrum of behaviors. That said, the basic admonition is well heeded.

15. *A victim cries at crucial points in the interview to avoid answering key questions.* This can be an important flag. The behavior to focus on is avoidance of giving details that can be corroborated, not the crying per se.

16. *A victim has a long psychiatric history.* As discussed previously, this may be a red flag for a false accusation, but it may also be an exposure factor for victimization. Not to be taken out of context.

At this point it must be made absolutely clear that this index (or any other collection of red flags) should be used as a guide only. The items are not foolproof indicators that the victim is falsely reporting a crime. To the sex crimes investigator or forensic examiner, these red flags suggest only the possibility that the allegations may be false and that further investigation is needed.

One of the authors of this chapter (McGrath, 2000) suggests conceptualizing the assessment of a false report as a three-pronged approach, reviewing behavioral, linguistic, and physical evidence in an attempt to determine the credibility of the allegation.[8]

Behavioral red flags would include the presentation of the victim and how cooperative she or he was, among other things. Some examples are as follows (McGrath, 2000):

- Any behavior that functions to interfere with the investigation
- Initiation of a report, or pressure to report, by someone other than the victim, unless the victim is unable to report or is too young to represent himself or herself
- Complainant unable to say where the assault occurred (unless some other aspect of the crime would reasonably preclude knowing where it occurred)
- Vague description of the assailant when descriptions of other facets of the crime are more detailed
- Interest of the complainant more directed to a goal other than the reporting of the crime (e.g., change in housing, disability payments, attention, lawsuit)
- Report of rape serves to provide an alibi

Linguistic assessment would be related to any statements made by the victim and/or suspects that can be examined to help determine credibility and identify areas that warrant further exploration. A properly performed statement analysis can be more helpful than a polygraph examination.[9]

It should be noted that statement analysis is actually a form of behavioral analysis. Since there are multiple ways of saying the same thing, choosing how to say or write something is a behavior that can be analyzed. The pronouns that are used, changes in words denoting certain things or people, and certain wordings can suggest to the investigator areas that require further explication. A detailed discussion of statement analysis is beyond the scope of this chapter.

Physical evidence is often overlooked in investigations on two levels. First, in terms of recognizing and collecting it and, second, in ensuring that the description of a crime (either by a victim or as a result of a confession) matches—to

---

[8]It should be kept in mind that determining the credibility of a witness (which is what the complainant may eventually be) should be an important step in any criminal investigation.
[9]It should be noted that we are not endorsing the polygraph, just commenting on it, as polygraph exams are often used in investigations.

a reasonable extent—the evidence found at the crime scene or as a result of forensic testing. Examples of issues related to physical evidence that should raise concern are as follows (McGrath, 2000):

- Crime scene reconstruction is at odds with the story of the victim.
- Injuries sustained by the victim are consistent with known patterns of self-inflicted injuries, or there is a lack of defensive wounds when a significant struggle is reported.
- Damage to clothing is not consistent with either the account of the assault ("He grabbed my collar and yanked me toward him," yet shirt or blouse is neatly ironed) or wounds.
- Lack of injury to the victim when the account implies significant force was used.

There is no substitute for a thorough investigation. Some red flags are more helpful than others, and some (e.g., delayed reporting) are so unreliable as to be more misleading than useful. We are not aware of any published studies wherein red flags for false allegations have been statistically analyzed for discriminative value, either alone or in groups. Such research may make it easier to assess unfounded or false allegations, although ultimately the final call will remain with the law enforcement investigator.

MOTIVATIONS FOR FALSE REPORTS

As with any list of potential motives for human behavior, there is often no clear delineation, and sometimes motives overlap. Human behavior in general is multidetermined. Some of the more common motivations leading to a false report are provided next. This is not intended to be an exhaustive list.

Revenge

Revenge is the act of inflicting harm on others in return for harm suffered at their hands, direction, or by their complicity. This includes situations in which the reporter is angry at the accused and expresses that anger through a false report. Typically, a prior relationship with the accused is involved. It often occurs in child custody cases and in subordinate relationships. It may also be used as a punishment for perceived infidelity.

Need for Attention

This category may include those who are said to be "crying out for help" as well as those with some degree of personality disorder or mental illness. It can include those who want attention from friends, relatives, spouses, or even wish the attention of the media.

Medical Treatment

Often, medical treatment as motivation is in play when the reporter makes a false complaint to obtain drugs or treatment related to pregnancy, AIDS, or sexually transmitted diseases. For example, one of the authors of this chapter (Turvey) worked a rape case in which the victim claimed to have been attacked by a widely publicized serial rapist. She was an apparent prostitute and represented a general deviation in the victim preference for that particular serial offender. The details of her account were unverifiable, and the alleged assault took place in a location where no corroborating evidence was found. Several months later, she also spontaneously reported being "raped" by possibly the same offender. She reported that this rape occurred prior to the rape she initially reported. However, she stated that the first rape turned from an act of violence into what can only be described as a consensual romantic encounter. The complainant had a history of multiple abortions, and she requested "treatment for morning after pill" during the sexual assault exam, despite no internal ejaculation being reported. These factors and many others led Turvey to strongly suspect that both complaints were, in fact, false reports.

Profit

Profit refers to emotional, material, or financial gain. This may include the reporter filing a lawsuit as well as the desire for new and better housing. For example, crime victims can reap financial reward by suing property owners (and their insurance companies) in what are referred to as premises liability lawsuits. In such a lawsuit, the victim argues that his or her attack could have been foreseen by the property owner and was therefore preventable. Property owners and in some cases landlords are subsequently held financially responsible for criminal attacks on their property, when judgments favor the victim. Judgments in such cases can range into the millions of dollars, which is a powerful financial incentive to make a false report.

Failure of Customer to Pay or Adequately Compensate a Sex Worker

These cases involve prostitutes or other sex/erotic-related workers such as escorts, strippers, or dancers. They may not have received payment or may have been somehow wronged by their customer. They may allege that they were sexually assaulted, raped, or otherwise violated, as a way of retaliating. Ironically, when sex workers are actually raped, they are unlikely to report it. This failure to report can be due to a variety of reasons, including that they consider such attacks part of the cost of doing business; they doubt that they will be believed because of the nature of their work; or because law enforcement officers are regular nonpaying customers, and they don't need the attention that an investigation will bring.

However, sex workers may report a rape if they perceive a continued threat, and if they perceive that law enforcement will do something about it—as in the case of a prostitute in Pomona, California, who reported being raped by a police officer within an hour of being attacked. In that case, the offender turned out to be a man wearing a security guard uniform with a security badge who was pretending to be a police officer in order to coerce sex from those he felt would not report the crime out of fear. He was arrested while picking up another prostitute.

Explanation for Loss of Virginity, Pregnancy, or Sexually Transmitted Disease

The loss of virginity, an unwanted or unexpected pregnancy, or sexually transmitted disease may be explained away by some with a false complaint of rape. This may be related to infidelity, or it may be related to cultural or family expectations regarding sexual activity. Although this type of reporting is more commonly found in juveniles, the same reasoning may motivate adults as well.

Alibi for Inappropriate Absence

Creating an alibi for inappropriate absence is a common motivation for juveniles and adults alike. The false reporter may be so desperate for an alibi to explain his or her absence that he or she will claim that an abduction or rape has occurred. This type of reporting is common among those living in group homes or in treatment programs while under conditions of parole or release, where the consequences for failing to return prior to curfew can be severe. It may also be used by teenagers out past curfew or by an adult to conceal infidelity.

New Housing

A desire for new housing can often motivate individuals to falsely report a rape to authorities. This is especially common in areas where rent-controlled housing is offered by the government. There are long waiting lists to get into the most desirable housing projects. Some residents believe that a way to jump to the front of this list is to claim that a rape or other attack occurred inside their current apartment. It may also be used as a way to get moved to more desirable housing within the same building, as keeping victims of rape in the same unit may be viewed as inappropriate or cruel.

Child Custody

Child custody battles are among the most heated and divisive legal disputes that can occur. When character and parental fitness are at issue, an allegation of sexual assault can be very strategic. These false reports can, and sometimes do, include allegations of rape or sexual abuse of one of the children, made by one side or the other, in an attempt to gain custody of the child in question. Some have merit; some don't. The purpose of an investigation is to find out which is the case. It is hoped that this investigation will take place before things get to a jury.

Attempt to Veil a Reoccurrence of Drug or Alcohol Use

This category includes individuals who have abstained from the use of drugs or alcohol for some period of time and then suddenly relapse, making it necessary for them to develop an excuse for their behavior. They may claim that they were raped and forced to ingest drugs or alcohol against their will. Or, alternately, they may claim that they returned to using drugs or alcohol to deal with the pain of the incident.

Change of Heart after a Consensual Sexual Encounter

Having a change of heart after a consensual sexual encounter is common in juvenile dating situations in which one of the parties of a consensual sexual encounter later feels guilty, angry, or vexed. In order to conceal or explain this behavior to himself or herself or to others and parental figures, he or she falsely claims to have been raped. This type of reporting less commonly involves adults who are trying to explain evidence of sexual behavior to a boyfriend, girlfriend, or spouse.

It will be helpful to present one high-profile false report case, as it highlights several issues: first, that the false reporter usually suffers no legal consequences; second, that the falsely accused suffer greatly; third, that allegations of rape can become political; and finally, that collusion between government agencies (the prosecutor and the laboratory that did the DNA testing) can work to conceal or at least further false accusations.

CASE EXAMPLE:

Duke University Lacrosse Team Case

Duke University lacrosse team players Reade Seligmann, David Evans, and Collin Finnerty were charged with first-degree kidnapping and first-degree sexual offense after an off-campus team party in March 2006. Ultimately dismissed as false, with the North Carolina attorney general declaring the accused were "innocent" (CNN, 2007), the allegations in this case made national news, increased racial tensions, and spanned multiple motives on the part of the accuser, from alleged mental instability to avoiding criminal charges to profit and to revenge.

According to the complaint, Crystal Gail Mangum accused members of the Duke lacrosse team of dragging her into a bathroom at one of their parties, raping her, and shouting racial slurs during an off-campus party in March of 2006 (see Figure 9-3). However, none of this came to light until after she was arrested the same night for public intoxication. And only days after making the complaint she bragged to co-workers about the possibility of filing civil actions against those involved.

Continued

CASE EXAMPLE: *CONTINUED*

FIGURE 9-3

"Exotic dancer" Crystal Gail Mangum. This is a prisoner intake photo from June 2002, when Mangum was arrested by the Durham County Sheriff's Office for charges related to motor vehicle theft.

This case had almost every problem imaginable, and in the absence of public attention it is possible that the accused players, ultimately cleared of all charges, could have been jailed for a very long time. Consider the context: the accuser was a stripper with a criminal history, an alleged mental health history, and a history of unfounded claims of being gang raped. A vocal segment of the African-American community was rallying and demanding swift justice. Racial tensions were, in some circles, rising. The prosecutor was running for reelection, conspiring with forensic personnel to conceal evidence, and openly attacking the defendants in the press. And Duke University was put in the unenviable position of punishing its lacrosse coach and players for crimes that it turns out did not occur.

The following is a timeline of significant events:

- March 13, 2006—Duke University lacrosse players throw a party at an off-campus house, hiring two strippers.
- March 14—One of the dancers tells the police she was forced into a bathroom by three men and beaten, raped, and sodomized.
- March 23—Forty-six of 47 team members comply with the judge's order to provide DNA.

The sole black member is not tested because the accuser said her attackers were white.

- March 28—Duke University suspends the lacrosse team from playing.
- March 29—District Attorney Mike Nifong refers to members of the lacrosse team as "a bunch of hooligans" in the press.
- April 4—The accuser identifies her attackers in a photo lineup.
- April 5—Lacrosse coach Mike Pressler is forced to resign. Duke President Richard Brodhead cancels the rest of the season.
- April 10—Defense attorneys announce DNA tests fail to connect any of the players to the accuser.
- April 17—Grand jury indicts Reade Seligmann and Collin Finnerty on rape and other charges.
- April 25—Granville County authorities confirm the accuser told police 10 years ago that three men raped her when she was 14. None of the men was charged.
- May 15—Grand jury indicts team co-captain David Evans on rape charges. He calls the allegations "fantastic lies."

CASE EXAMPLE: *CONTINUED*

- June 5—Duke University president says the team can resume play in 2007 under close monitoring.
- Nov. 7—DA Mike Nifong wins the election to continue as district attorney.
- Dec. 15—Forensic scientist Brian Meehan, Lab Director of DNA Security, Inc., in an agreement with Nifong, omitted from his report that genetic material from several men—none of them Duke team members—was found in the accuser's underwear and body.[10]
- Dec. 22—Nifong drops the rape charges, saying the woman is no longer certain whether she was penetrated. The players still face charges of kidnapping and sexual offense.
- Dec. 28—North Carolina Bar files ethics charges against Nifong, accusing him of making misleading and inflammatory comments to the media about the athletes. (He is also later accused of withholding evidence and lying to the court.)
- Jan. 3, 2007—Duke invites Seligmann and Finnerty to return to school. (They have not returned.) The accuser gives birth. Both sides later say she was not impregnated at the party.
- Jan. 12—Nifong asks to withdraw from the case because of ethics charges.
- Jan. 13—The North Carolina attorney general's office begins reviewing the case, not only by going over the case to date, but by conducting an independent investigation, including interviewing witnesses.
- Apr. 10—The North Carolina attorney general reports his office's findings. The investigation raised such discrepancies to what the complainant claimed versus the actual evidence that, "Based on the significant inconsistencies between the evidence and the various accounts given by the accusing witness, we believe these three individuals are innocent of these charges" (CNN, 2007).

The attorney general's office investigation was thorough, as noted in the office's April 2007 public statement that included the following (Cooper, 2007):

> During the past 12 weeks, our lawyers and investigators have reviewed the remaining allegations of sexual assault and kidnapping that resulted from a party on March 13, 2006, in Durham, North Carolina. We carefully reviewed the evidence, collected by the Durham County prosecutor's office and the Durham Police Department.
>
> We've also conducted our own interviews and evidence gathering. Our attorneys and [State Bureau of Investigation] agents have interviewed numerous people who were at the party, DNA and other experts, the Durham County district attorney, Durham police officers, defense attorneys, and the accusing witness on several occasions. We have reviewed statements given over the year, photographs, records, and other evidence.
>
> The result of our review and investigation shows clearly that there is insufficient evidence to proceed on any of the charges. Today we are filing notices of dismissal for all charges against Reade Seligmann, Collin Finnerty, and David Evans. The result is that these cases are over, and no more criminal proceedings will occur.
>
> We believe that these cases were the result of a tragic rush to accuse and a failure to verify serious allegations. Based on the significant inconsistencies between the evidence and the various accounts given by the accusing witness, we believe these three individuals are innocent of these charges.
>
> Now, we approached this case with the understanding that rape and sexual assault victims often have some inconsistencies in their account of a traumatic event. However, in this case, the inconsistencies were so significant and so contrary to the evidence that we have no credible evidence that an attack occurred in that house on that night.
>
> Now, the prosecuting witness in this case responded to our questions and offered information. She did want to move forward with the prosecution. However, the contradictions in her many versions of what occurred and the conflicts between what she said occurred and other evidence like photographs and phone records, could not be rectified.

Continued

CASE EXAMPLE: *CONTINUED*

FIGURE 9-4

Reade Seligmann, Collin Finnerty, and David Evans, already cleared of any charges, attend a press conference subsequent to Mike Nifong's disbarment.

Our investigation shows that the eyewitness identification procedures were faulty and unreliable. No DNA confirms the accuser's story. No other witness confirms her story. Other evidence contradicts her story. She contradicts herself....

Now, in this case, with the weight of the state behind him, the Durham district attorney pushed forward unchecked. There were many points in this case where caution would have served justice better than bravado, and in the rush to condemn a community and a state, lost the ability to see clearly....

This case shows the enormous consequences of over-reaching by a prosecutor. What has been learned here is that the internal checks on a criminal charge—sworn statements, reasonable grounds, proper suspect photo lineups, and accurate and fair discovery—all are critically important.

Therefore, I propose a law that the North Carolina Supreme Court have the authority to remove a case from a prosecutor in limited circumstances. This would give the courts a new tool to deal with a prosecutor who needs to step away from a case where justice demands.

In June 2007, Mike Nifong, the prosecutor in the Duke University lacrosse team rape case, was disbarred for unethical conduct related to his actions in that attempted prosecution (see Figures 9-4 and 9-5). The chairman of the disciplinary committee blamed Nifong's "political ambition," a "self-serving agenda," and "self-deception."

The attorneys for each of the exonerated Duke lacrosse team players have promised civil action in an attempt to make their clients whole.

[10]To be perfectly clear, Brian Meehan, Lab Director of DNA Security, Inc., made a conscious decision to assist DA Mike Nifong with the job of hiding exculpatory DNA results in this case (Neff, et al., 2006). For a crime lab of any kind to make an examination of evidence for which there is no report detailing items examined, tests performed, and results achieved is at the least forensically unacceptable and professionally unethical.

CASE EXAMPLE: *CONTINUED*

FIGURE 9-5

A defrocked Mike Nifong listens to the verdict of the North Carolina Bar Association's Ethics Committee. "We are in unanimous agreement that there is no discipline short of disbarment that would be appropriate in this case," said F. Lane Williamson, the committee's chairman. The three-member panel found Nifong guilty of fraud, dishonesty, deceit, or misrepresentation; of making false statements of material fact before a judge; of making false statements of material fact before bar investigators; and of lying about withholding exculpatory DNA evidence.

CONCLUSION

False reports are a problem for all the professional communities that encounter them, and they are more frequent than those with pro-victim political or social agendas would have us believe. The hostility with which inquiry into false reporting has been met has resulted in a standstill with respect to scientific research. As a result, we have no good or even current data on the subject; we only know that lower estimates are continually disproved.

False reporters span all ages, all walks of life, and are capable of staging both injuries and evidence to support their claims. A thorough investigation of the evidence has traditionally been the best way to reveal the false reporter, who is more likely to confess when confronted with logical inconsistencies in his or her statements and behavior. Unfortunately, law enforcement resources are drained away from actual victims by such cases. Innocent citizens are exposed to the possibility of false accusations and damage to their personal and professional lives. Legitimate victims of sexual assault are exposed to the possibility of encountering overtaxed law enforcement resources that are inadequate to the task of investigating their cases thoroughly or competently. Building owners, private companies, and insurance companies are exposed to the threat of costly liability lawsuits. As stated in Gross (1924, p. 14):[11]

> Not only must the self-made victim be exposed, but innocent people who may be suspected must be protected.

Furthermore, research relating to sexual assault, which is often used as the basis for law-enforcement resource and budget allocations, not to mention expert forensic testimony, is necessarily biased or otherwise compromised when such cases go unidentified. This is a problem in both the criminal and civil realms. Hence, the need for more and better research in this area cannot be emphasized too strongly. Nor can the need for objectivity, thorough investigations of each complaint, and strict adherence to the forensic evidence.

SUMMARY

There are many reasons for false reports. False reports may be made out of desire for financial gain, to garner sympathy, for revenge, for crime concealment, to excuse other behavior, and so on. When such false reporting is recognized, it is common for the false reporter to suffer no legal consequences for filing a false report. Despite the many case studies that can be offered, professional literature on the subject remains scarce, as there have been very few scientific studies conducted to date to ascertain false report rates or percentages. The literature that does offer rates and percentages is often unreliable, misrepresented, or inaccurate, as can be seen with the elusive sources for the 2% false report statistic for sexual assault. The actual rates that have been garnered through research vary between 8% and 50% for sexual assault.

When faced with an allegation, investigators walk a fine line between being supportive and compassionate and trying to determine whether the allegation is factual. Several red flags have been offered by various authors as an aid to determine which reports are false. If specific and objective, red flags may have investigative value under the right conditions; however, it is important that each case be evaluated in context to determine whether the red flags apply. These should used with caution because a truthful person can easily raise some red flags, whereas an actual false reporter may show none at all.

Unfortunately, it is not uncommon for even experienced investigators to accept an alleged victim's statement without critical thought or suspicion. This

---

[11]This sentiment is echoed today by former Manhattan Sex Crimes Prosecutor Linda Fairstein, who states, "False reports of rape do occur...[and] have made it difficult for legitimate victims to be taken seriously.... For all prosecutors...it is critical to acknowledge that false accusations of rape are made" (cited in Sarnoff, 1997).

acceptance may be the result of fear of disturbing the alleged victim, or being viewed as politically incorrect by victim advocates and colleagues, or of a lack of knowledge about the investigation of potential false reports.

QUESTIONS

1. What type of crime represents the majority of false reports?
2. Explain why there is a lack of research focusing on false reports of sexual assault.
3. Name and describe two red flags proposed by the BAFRI.
4. True or False: Only 2% of sexual assaults are false reports.
5. Name and describe four general motivations for making a false allegation.

REFERENCES

Abshire, R., 2007. Arrest warrants issued for Terrell cousins after hoax. Dallas Morning News, March 22. www.dallasnews.com/sharedcontent/dws/dn/latestnews/stories/032207dnmetter-rellfound.3291295.html

Anderson, M., 2004. The legacy of the prompt complaint requirement, corroboration requirement, and cautionary instructions on campus sexual assault. Boston University Law Review 84, 945–1022.

Aiken, M., Burgess, A., Hazelwood, R., 1995. False rape allegations. In: Burgess, A., Hazelwood, R. (Eds.), Practical Aspects of Rape Investigation: A Multidisciplinary Approach, CRC Press, Boca Raton, FL.

Baeza, J., Turvey, B., 2002. False reports. In: Turvey, B. (Ed.), Criminal Profiling: An Introduction to Behavioral Evidence Analysis, second ed. Academic Press, London.

Block, A.P., 1990. Rape trauma syndrome as scientific expert testimony. Archives of Sexual Behavior 19 (4), 309–323.

Brown, C., Crowley, S., Peck, R., Slaughter, L., 1997. Patterns of genital injury in female sexual assault victims. American Journal of Obstetrics and Gynecology 176, 609–616.

Brownmiller, S., 1975. Against Our Will: Men, Women, and Rape. Fawcett Columbine, New York.

Brownmiller, S., 1995. Personal e-mail communication to David R. Throop of the Men's Issues Page, June 27. http://www.menweb.org/throop/falsereport/commentary/brownback.html

Bryden, D.P., Lengnick, S., 1997. Rape in the criminal justice system. Journal of Criminal Law and Criminology 87, 1194–1384.

Burgess, A.W., Hazelwood, R.R., Burgess, A.G., 2001. False rape allegations. In: Burgess, A.G., Hazelwood, R.R. (Eds.), Practical Aspects of Rape Investigation: A Multidisciplinary Approach, third ed. CRC Press, Boca Raton, FL.

Burgess, A.W., Holmstrom, L.L., 1974. Rape trauma syndrome. American Journal of Psychiatry 131, 981–986.

CBS News, 2005. Wilbanks: What she was thinking, June 22. Available at: http://www.cbsnews.com/stories/2005/06/22/national/main703401.shtml

CNN, 2004a. Police: student says she was abducted at knifepoint, April 1. Available at: http://www.cnn.com/2004/US/Midwest/03/31/missing.student/index.html?iref=newssearch

CNN, 2004b. Student who faked abduction given probation, April 1. Available at: http://www.cnn.com/2004/LAW/07/01/missing.student.sentence/index.html?iref=newssearch

CNN, 2005. Charges not ruled out for runaway bride, May 2. Available at: http://www.cnn.com/2005/US/05/01/wilbanks.found/index.html

CNN, 2007. N.C. attorney general: Duke players innocent, April 11. Available at: http://www.cnn.com/2007/LAW/04/11/cooper.transcript/index.html

Cooper, R., 2007. Press Release. North Carolina Attorney General's Office. April 11.

Court, T.V., 1997. Report of the grand jury concerning the Tawana Brawley investigation. Online Legal Documents, Available at: http://www.courttv.com/legaldocs/newsmakers/tawana/part3.html#sexual

Donnelly, E., 2007. Constructing the co-ed military. Duke Journal of Gender Law and Policy (14), 815–952.

Dunleavy, S., 1999. Cybersex victim's kin: she's a liar. New York Post, July 26; http://www.nypost.com/p/news/item_GfrL1hoVrxYGciu8wVyBfN

Epstein, J., 2006. True lies: the constitutional and evidentiary bases for admitting prior false accusation evidence in sexual assault prosecutions. Quinnipiac Law Review 24, 609–658.

Gregory, J., Lees, S., 1999. Policing Sexual Assault. Routledge, New York.

Gross, H., 1924. Criminal Investigation, third ed. Sweet and Maxwell, London.

Haws, D., 1997. The elusive numbers on false rape. Columbia Journalism Review, November/December, Available at: http://www.cjr.org/year/97/6/rape.asp

Herman, J.L., 1990. Sex offenders: a feminist perspective. In: Marshall, W.L., Laws, D.R., Barbaree, H.E. (Eds.), Handbook of Sexual Assault: Issues, Theories, and Treatment of the Offender, Plenum Press, New York, pp. 177–193.

Inquirer Staff, 2000. Timoney commends rape-squad reforms. Philadelphia Inquirer, December 13; http://articles.philly.com/2000-12-13/news/25580265_1_investigators-squad-crimes

Johnson, B.E., Kuck, D.L., Schander, P.R., 1997. Rape myth acceptance and sociodemographic characteristics: a multidimensional analysis. Sex Roles: A Journal of Research (36), 693–708.

Kanin, E., 1994. False rape allegations. Archives of Sexual Behavior 23 (no. 1), 81–92.

MacDonald, J., 1973. False accusations of rape. Medical Aspects of Human Sexuality (no. 7), 170–194.

Martin, P., 2005. The sacrifice of a parent: an analysis of parental rights related to false allegations of child sexual abuse. Thomas M. Cooley Journal of Practical and Clinical Law (Hilary Term) 7, 251–283.

McDowell, C., 1985. Chicago Lawyer, June. Available at: http://www.coeffic.demon.co.uk/descrim.htm

McGrath, M., 2000. False allegations of rape and the criminal profiler. Journal of Behavioral Profiling 1 (3).

McGrath, M., 2005. People v. Oliver Jovanovic: from cybersex to sexual assault allegations, Appendix. In: Savino, J., Turvey, B. (Eds.), Rape Investigation Handbook, Academic Press, London.

Neff, J., Niolet, B., Blythe, A., 2006. Head of DNA lab says he and Nifong agreed not to report results. Charlotte News-Observer, December 8; http://www.freerepublic.com/focus/f-news/1754097/posts

Palmer, C., Thornhill, R., 2000. A History of Rape. MIT Press, Cambridge.

Radford, B., 2005. Police, psychics search for 'abducted' runaway bride. Skeptical Inquirer, July 1, Vol. 294, p. 7.

Rosario, R., 2004. Happy ending may obscure disturbing reality. Pioneer Press, April 2, Available at: http://www.twincities.com/mld/twincities/news/8334507.htm

Sarnoff, S., 1997. Assessing the costs of false allegations of child abuse: a prescriptive. Institute for Psychological Therapies Journal 9, Available at: http://www.ipt-forensics.com/journal/volume9/j9_3_2.htm

Spilbor, J.M., 2003. What if Kobe Bryant has been falsely accused? Why the law of acquaintance and date rape should seriously penalize false reports. Findlaw's Writ, August 11, Available at: http://writ.news.findlaw.com/commentary/20030811_spilbor.html

CHAPTER 10

False Confessions

Michael McGrath

KEY TERMS

Coerced-compliant confession A confession to a crime given by an individual who knows he or she is innocent, but due to conditions of the interrogation, says what he or she believes is necessary to placate the interrogator and end the situation.

Coerced-internalized confession A confession to a crime given by an individual who comes to actually believe he or she may have committed the crime.

False confession An involuntary statement of guilt made under duress or as the result of coercion.

Reid Technique A nine-step technique of interviewing and interrogation.

Voluntary false confession A confession to a crime given by an individual who either knows he or she did not commit the crime, but nonetheless has made a decision to confess, or through no pressure from police has come to believe he or she committed the crime to which he or she is confessing.

INTRODUCTION

Why include a chapter on false confessions in a forensic victimology text? The answer is simple: when a false confession is extracted, the confessor has become a victim[1] of the criminal justice system. But what could lead people to confess to a crime they did not commit? Would we have to beat them? Torture them? Would they have to be mentally deficient? What if the crime is of such magnitude that to falsely confess could lead to a long prison sentence or even execution? Surely, such a situation would be rare, if it occurred at all. Yet false confessions are far from rare. Compounding the problem is the blind eye of justice on many levels to the phenomenon, whether it be the law enforcement investigator who continues to pressure a suspect, the overzealous prosecutor who refuses to accept that the confession does not match the facts of the case, the jury member who cannot accept the concept of a false confession, or the appellate judge who does not want to second-guess the trial judge or jury.

---

[1]An exception would be those who falsely confess gain notoriety—for example, John Mark Karr (Golden, 2006).

Forensic Victimology. http://dx.doi.org/10.1016/B978-0-12-408084-3.00010-7

A signed or videotaped confession is powerful evidence of guilt in a courtroom, especially when containing information only the offender should know, such as type of weapon used, specific injuries inflicted, and other pertinent crime scene data, assuming such information has not appeared in the media or was available "on the street." When a false confession is videotaped, the evidence the judge and jury often see is a scripted and limited rendition of the interrogation process giving a false impression of the (pre-interrogation) crime-related knowledge of the defendant, the voluntary nature and sincerity of the confession, and the interrogation conditions. A suspect questioned incessantly for hours might appear on camera after a break to wash up and then (while being videotaped) offered coffee, cigarettes, a sandwich, etc., in a collegial manner by the interrogator(s) to falsely imply that the suspect is not under stress and was not earlier when first confessing. This author refers to these situations as *Confession Theater*. Compounding the problem is the frustrating inertia in all strata of the criminal justice system in admitting that a mistake has been made. It is not unheard of for agents of the criminal justice system to insist on the guilt of a defendant who has had a conviction overturned due to incontrovertible exculpatory evidence (often DNA) and refuse to accept that an error had occurred. And, (some might be surprised to know) even if you never confessed but a police officer says you did, he or she can testify in court that you confessed. The same goes for a "jailhouse snitch." All that is needed is the informant's word under oath—no videotape, no audiotape, no signed confession. Of the 230 persons exonerated by DNA, almost 24% involved a false confession (The Innocence Project, http://www.innocenceproject.org).

The Michael Crowe case is only one example of the incredible hubris shown by some involved in the case. When the abusive interrogation of three teenagers resulted in two confessions, police charged the teens with the murder of Michael's sister. Most egregious, local police, prosecutors, and later the FBI, in order to protect their reputations, were willing to claim at trial that the victim's blood spatter found on the clothing of a transient named Richard Tuite, known to have been knocking on doors nearby, was irrelevant to the case (McCrary, 2009; Sauer, 2004). Apparently locked into protecting the local authorities, the DA refused to prosecute Tuite, and the state had to step in. In 2012 Michael Crowe was declared factually innocent. This followed a $7.25 million civil settlement (Sauer and Sharma, 2011).[2]

One might assume that a false confession could be obtained only when children, adolescents, or mentally ill or developmentally disabled individuals are subjected to the most unethical and horrendous interrogation techniques by rogue law enforcement officials. But this is simply not the case. False confessions

---

[2]Portions of his interrogation can be found on YouTube.com. For example, see http://www.youtube.com/watch?v=WkLHXKHb1Vc&feature=fvw.

can occur when law enforcement agents act in good faith and have no idea they are inducing a false confession. Those most at risk for a false confession share one characteristic: they are naïve to police procedure. The naïveté can be due to chronological age, mental age, or life experience. Some suspects are surprised to learn later that police are allowed to lie to them, even in claiming to have evidence against them that does not exist, or saying an accomplice (who might be someone the suspect does not even know) is implicating them in the crime. Anyone can be induced to give a false confession under the right circumstances. This fact is too uncomfortable for the criminal justice system to accept at face value. The many known false confessions are only a small percentage of those extant. And in cases in which no DNA evidence exists, the convicted innocent is unlikely to ever have his or her case overturned. Even with DNA evidence that would be expected to exonerate a suspect, tunnel vision can still negate the evidence.

A good example of the problem is the notorious Central Park Jogger case (Kassin, 2006), in which black teenagers were played off against each other and led to believe they could go home if they assisted in the investigation. Believing that they were being implicated by their peers, those who confessed to the crime made a rational decision to protect themselves by telling the police what they believed they wanted to hear in a way that limited (in their minds) their legal culpability. There was no need to physically beat anyone. In fact, some of the parents were present during the interrogations, although the investigators often had a parent "step outside" for various periods (Burns, 2012). Not only were false confessions obtained, but the actual offender was a serial rapist operating in the area who went on to commit more crimes, including a murder. When, years later, the true offender confessed to the Central Park Jogger rape and his DNA[3] matched the semen from the case, the NYPD refused to accept they had arrested and prosecuted the wrong people.[4]

While not perfect, one of the most obvious ways to document, if not prevent, a false confession is to videotape all suspect interrogations in their entirety, not the last 20 or so minutes. Yet this simple safeguard has met with varying degrees of acceptance in law enforcement, ranging from horror to acceptance. That an investigator would want to keep out of the public light the method(s) used to obtain a confession is troubling. So far, it appears police departments that have adopted videotaping of suspect interrogations have generally reported positive results and do not feel it has interfered with their ability to conduct an investigation (Sullivan, 2004).

---

[3]Police already had DNA from the offender's arrest in 1989 for a murder and series of rapes.
[4]In all fairness, one can understand the initial reluctance to exclude the defendants from at least participation in the jogger case, but as time has gone on and facts have surfaced, the unwillingness of NYC officials to throw in the towel is sad.

CONFESSION LAW

What safeguards are in place for those questioned or interrogated by the police? To withstand legal scrutiny, confessions are expected to be voluntary and free of "compulsion or inducement" (*Wilson v. US*, 1896). But voluntariness is often in the eye of the beholder. "The use in a state criminal trial of a defendant's confession obtained by coercion—whether physical or mental—is forbidden by the Fourteenth Amendment" (*Leyra v. Denno*, 1954). In 1936, in *Brown v. Mississippi* (the first state court confession case decided by the U.S. Supreme Court), the Court held that convictions resulting solely from confessions obtained through "brutality and violence" violated due process.[5] But the legal onus was on the defendant to be able to prove the confession was extracted through violence.

After two women and three children were killed in a 1988 Chicago fire, Ronald Kitchens and Marvin Reeves had the misfortune to be questioned by detectives working under Jon Burge, a detective commander later convicted of perjury[6] (Associated Press, 2010; Cohen, 2012). Their confessions were introduced at trial, and after conviction, Reeves was sentenced to five life sentences. Kitchens was sentenced to death, although the sentence was later commuted to life (as were other Illinois death row cases) by Governor George Ryan in 2003. The convictions were obtained using physically coerced confessions and a jailhouse snitch[7] (Northwestern Law–Blum Legal Clinic, 2009).

Betty Tyson spent 25 years in a New York state prison after being convicted, along with an alleged accomplice, of the 1973 murder of a Philadelphia businessman in Rochester, New York.[8] Tyson, at the time a 24-year-old street prostitute and heroin addict, was arrested, along with John Duval. Both claimed police beat them to extract confessions. Supporting the confessions was testimony by a (then) 16-year-old who placed Tyson with the victim. Years later, due to dogged journalistic investigation, the witness recanted and claimed that he had been harassed and threatened by law enforcement for months while he was in jail, saying he was told that he would be charged with the murder if he did not cooperate. Once the exoneration case began to gain momentum, witnesses came forward to corroborate Ms. Tyson's claims that she had been beaten in jail. There was no physical evidence tying Tyson

---

[5]So, apparently if a confession is beaten out of a suspect but there is other evidence of guilt, the confession could still be entered at trial?

[6]Burge was convicted after lying during a civil lawsuit to cover up allegations of suspect torture while in police custody.

[7]The author is of the mind that "jailhouse snitch" testimony, absent accompanying audiotapes, ought to be outlawed because it invites abuse and tainted convictions.

[8]Tyson was the longest-imprisoned woman in New York state.

or Duval to the crime. Incredibly (or maybe not) when the then-current (1998) district attorney unearthed the case file, a police report of the initial interview of the 16-year-old witness was found. The witness did not say he had seen Ms. Tyson with the victim. Her murder conviction was overturned in 1998, and as is unfortunately common in these cases, the DA continued to insist he believed that Tyson was guilty, claiming he declined to retry due to the length of time that had passed and the death of some witnesses (Gross, 1998). While those considerations for retrial were no doubt real, one must wonder what it would take to admit that justice has gone wrong? John Duval's conviction was overturned a year later, and he also was not retried.[9]

Although physical coercion (violating the Fourth Amendment) was declared unconstitutional in 1936 (*Brown v. Mississippi*), psychological coercion *per se* was not. *Chambers v. Florida* (1940) and *Ashcraft v. Tennessee* (1944) held confessions obtained through psychological coercion were not admissible. The U.S. Supreme Court in *McNabb v. U.S.* (1943) was unwilling to allow police unlimited leeway in obtaining a confession and said that an arrestee must be taken before a magistrate without undue delay, but there is no clear-cut line between egregious behavior and dogged investigation. The McNabb Rule was reaffirmed in 1957 (*Mallory v. U.S.*)

Other cases touch on various aspects of interrogation. For instance, *Payne v. Arkansas* (1958) 356 U.S. Supreme Court 560 held that keeping a suspect incommunicado is coercive. In 1963 (*Lynum v. Illinois*) the U.S. Supreme Court ruled that threats by the police could make a confession involuntary, as well as inducements by the police to confess (*Haynes v. Washington*, 1963). In 1966, the well-known Miranda Warning was introduced. Police were now expected to advise subjects in police custody[10] that they had a right to an attorney and that they did not have to answer questions and, further, that they had the right not to incriminate themselves; i.e., anything they said could be used against them. Any waiver of these rights had to be intelligent and voluntary (*Miranda v. Arizona* 1966).[11]

---

[9]Duval's situation was complicated by the fact that he eventually "admitted" to the crime in order to be released on parole. He was in the Kafkaesque position of having the opportunity of being eligible for parole in July 1996, but having a chance of being released only if he took responsibility for the crime he did not commit.

[10]The definition of *police custody* is a whole different can of worms.

[11]The Miranda Rights (or Warning) as recited by an arresting officer are as follows: 1. You have the right to remain silent; 2. Anything you say can and will be used against you in a court of law; 3. You have the right to an attorney; 4. If you cannot afford an attorney, one will be appointed for you; It should be noted that after each right/warning is read to subjects, they are expected to verify that they heard the warning and understand it. So, subjects are told they can remain silent but must then talk to show they understand. It is clear a linguist was not consulted.

In 1968, the Omnibus Crime Control and Safe Streets Act was passed to gut the McNabb/Mallory decisions. The Act allowed the admission of a confession at trial as long as it was "voluntary." A delay in bringing the arrestee before a magistrate was now one of many things to consider and not an automatic exclusion.

One issue in interrogations is that courts have held (*Davis v. US*, 1994) that a request for a lawyer must be unambiguous. In the Davis case, the suspect said "maybe" he should talk to a lawyer. The police asked him if he was asking for a lawyer, and he then said no, he was not. While the police in this case were careful to clarify whether or not the suspect was requesting a lawyer, in many cases it is not clear that the suspect was aware he or she was being ambiguous and the police chose not to clarify, allowing the questioning to continue. The legal expectation of "unambiguous" fails to take into account the power differential present in the interrogation scenario and the fact that people often use *pragmatic implication* as a means of communication. When one is in a restaurant and asks a waiter, "May I have a glass of water?" one is asking for water, not permission to have it. And, although the request is phrased as a question, it is actually a demand, although a polite one. Likewise, if a suspect says, "I guess I should have a lawyer," or "I probably should talk to a lawyer," it is very likely he or she is linguistically attempting to convey that he or she wants a lawyer but is uncomfortable stating this fact openly, due to the societal expectations of the police–suspect encounter. Yet such statements are considered legally ambiguous by the courts (*Blakeney v. State*, 2009). Keep in mind that when one is being questioned by police, it is common for it to be explicit or implicit that asking for a lawyer means you have something to hide.

TYPES OF FALSE CONFESSIONS

Kassin and Wrightsman (1985) suggested three types of *false confessions*: (1) voluntary, (2) coerced-compliant and (3) coerced-internalized.

Voluntary

A *voluntary false confession* is a confession to a crime given by an individual who either knows he or she did not commit the crime, but nonetheless has made a decision to confess, or through no pressure from police has come to believe he or she committed the crime to which he or she is confessing. The motive for the decision to confess can vary. For example, one could confess to protect someone else who did commit the crime. Or one could confess to gain notoriety, as happened with John Mark Karr in the Jon Benet Ramsey murder (Golden, 2006). Still stranger, on one's own, one could confess believing he or she committed the crime. The reason for this confession could be the result of a mental illness or merely the end point of misdirected guilt, as appears to have been the case with Chuck Erickson, who was questioned by police after telling friends he might have been involved in a murder (*Forty Eight Hours*, 2013).

Coerced-Compliant

With a *coerced-compliant confession*, the suspect knows he or she is innocent, but due to conditions of the interrogation says what he or she believes is necessary to placate the interrogator and end the situation. One could confess simply to get an interrogation to end. A significant problem is the reporting of false or fabricated evidence that the suspect knows is not possibly true but believes the investigator will eventually come to realize that the "evidence" will exonerate the suspect. For example, imagine a rape without DNA evidence. If told that DNA from a rape will identify him when the results of the test are back, an innocent suspect might be induced to confess, expecting he will later be exonerated by the DNA. Later, the suspect would learn that there was no DNA and now the "evidence" against him is his confession.

Coerced-Internalized Confession

A *coerced-internalized confession* is one in which the suspect comes to actually believe he or she may have committed the crime. Michael Crowe's case had elements of this type of confession when he said maybe he killed his sister, but could not remember—although he continually asserted his innocence by advising his questioner that what he was about to say was a lie. A quite bizarre example of a coerced-internalized false confession is that of Billy Wayne Cope (2013), who confessed to killing his daughter and re-enacted the crime for police, and gave several confessions to the crime, when in fact, it was a serial rapist whose DNA was found at the scene. Cope remains in prison because authorities refuse to believe his confession was false, and in fact tried him as an accomplice of the actual rapist, although the two had never met (Kassin, 2007; http://www.billywaynecope.net).

Ofshe and Leo (1997) make the case that the coerced-internalized false confession is a result of persuasion, not coercion, and relabeled these as *coerced-persuaded* confessions. This author would argue that this label adds little because coercion versus persuasion is in the eye of the beholder. One could design false confession typologies to capture the specifics of a case without adding much practical value.

INTERVIEWING AND INTERROGATION

To grasp just how easy it is to elicit false confessions, one needs to understand police interrogation techniques, designed to elicit confessions once police have decided a suspect is guilty.

Interview and interrogation methods are taught to law enforcement, government agents, and corporate personnel. Many styles of questioning are either directly from, or based to a significant degree, on the *Reid Technique*. At the company website (Reid et al., http://www.reid.com), one can find the following: "Through our training seminars you will learn the Reid Technique of interviewing and interrogation, widely recognized as the most effective means available to exonerate the innocent and identify the guilty." The Reid Technique is described in *Criminal Interrogation and Confessions*, 5th edition (Inbau et al., 2013), hereafter referred to as *CIC5*. Any defense attorney who has not read this book or a prior edition is unprepared to defend clients in criminal cases.

In the introduction, the authors of the CIC5 state

> …we want to make it unmistakably clear that we are unalterably opposed to the so-called third degree, even on suspects whose guilt seems absolutely certain and who remain steadfast in their denials. Moreover, we are opposed to the use of any interrogation tactic or technique that is apt to make an innocent person confess. We are opposed, therefore, to the use of force, threats of force, or promises of leniency. (p. xi)

Inbau et al. further note that "[o]f necessity, therefore, investigators must deal with criminal suspects on a somewhat lower moral plane than that upon which ethical, law-abiding citizens[12] are expected to conduct their everyday affairs. That plane, in the interest of innocent subjects need only be subject to the following restriction: Although both 'fair' and 'unfair' interrogation practices are permissible," the reader is reminded, "nothing should be done or said to the suspect that is apt to make an innocent person confess" (p. xii). Clearly, then, the authors of the CIC5 would be expected to be upset to learn that anyone applying their methodology induced a false confession from an innocent person. Yet this point does not even seem to be entertained, as John Buckley, one of the CIC4 authors, claimed, "[W]e don't interrogate innocent people" (Kassin and Gudjonsson, 2004, p. 36). Richard Leo, an expert in coerced confessions, points out that the criminal justice system often suffers from confirmation bias and tunnel vision:

> Detectives rarely stop to consider the possibility that they are interrogating an innocent person. And that the admissions they are eliciting may be false.…Once interrogators obtain an admission, they treat it as confirmation of their belief in the suspect's guilt rather than a hypothesis to be tested against case evidence. (2008, p. 265)

---

[12]N.B. The very fact a person is being interrogated presumes that person is guilty, therefore allowing interrogators to deal with him or her on a different moral plane.

According to the CIC5 an interview is conducted to obtain information and an interrogation (accusatory) is conducted to "learn the truth." An interview can lead to an interrogation. Mr. Buckley's preceding comment notwithstanding, the CIC5 advises that: "Unfortunately there are occasions when an innocent suspect is interrogated, and only after the suspect has been accused of committing the crime will his or her innocence become apparent" (Inbau et al., 2013, p. 5). But how does one's innocence become apparent?

Chapter 4 of the CIC5 (pp. 35–42) is titled "Initial Precautionary Measures for the Protection of the Innocent."[13] It notes the known problems with eyewitness identifications and cautions the investigator on many areas, but fails to mention possibly one of the most important problems: police contamination of potential eyewitnesses. Repressed memories (p. 37) are discussed, appropriately noting the problems associated with assuming sexual abuse based on symptoms of depression, low self-esteem, etc., without conscious recollection of abuse, as proposed by such books as *Courage to Heal* (Bass and Davis, 1988). But it also advises things such as the following: "A guilty suspect experiences much less internal anxiety when denying broad allegations, such as, 'Did you ever have sexual contact with your step-daughter's vaginal area,' than specifically worded questions such as, 'While giving your step-daughter a bath when she was about five years old, did you put your finger inside her vagina?'" (Inbau, et al., 2013, p. 38). Is this in fact true? Maybe. Maybe not. There is no scientific basis offered for this assumption. But the Reid-trained investigator believes it to be true and will, for better or worse, use it to determine a particular suspect's guilt. What becomes apparent over time is that investigators are taught to rely on behavioral and verbal cues with limited or no scientific validity to make a determination of a suspect's guilt and then proceed to an interrogation to confirm this impression. The book is replete with comments with no basis in reality. Following are some examples:

> Truthful suspects are more comfortable with the silence created by note taking. (p. 60)
>> Innocent suspects are realistic in their assessments of the crime. (p. 110)
>> A telling difference between the innocent and guilty suspect is that the innocent suspect will have given much thought about the guilty person. (p. 110)
>> It is an especially reliable sign of deception when an early response[14] occurs during the middle or end of an interview; by that

---

[13]Using the Reid Technique to protect the innocent is like using gasoline to put out fires.

[14]An early response is when a suspect begins answering before the interrogator finishes asking the question. This makes two assumptions: (1) this unproven premise is correct, and (2) the suspect is no longer nervous, which is highly unlikely if innocent, and any prior denials are stymied.

time, general nervous tension from a truthful subject should have subsided.... (p. 118)

The CIC5 discusses how to conduct interviews and interrogations. One can approach an interview (not an interrogation[15]) with an assumption of guilt, which is designed to catch the subject by surprise; an assumption of innocence; or a neutral stance. With an assumption of guilt, the investigator is supposed to gauge the suspect's behavior against how guilty and innocent people react when treated as if they are guilty. In the fourth edition (Inbau et al., 2001),[16] the reader was advised that a guilty individual will not mind being accused of a crime, while an innocent person will usually express resentment (p. 68). Such simplistic, and unproven, bromides are an invitation to disaster. Couple this with "[a] guilty suspect is also more likely to react nonverbally to the suggestion of guilt," (p. 68) and the wary reader should consider asking for his or her money back.

The investigators have been trained to override denials, likely making the innocent person react both verbally and nonverbally to the accusations, leading to investigators confirming their bias that the subject is guilty. Regardless of the purported approach interviewers take, they will interpret behavior based on what they have been taught, which is fraught with inaccuracy and confirmation bias. For example, investigators are advised to note behaviors during the interview, such as delays in answering, breaks in gaze, direct (or lack of) eye contact, shifting in the chair, crossing of legs, repeating of questions, etc. The interpretations of such behaviors by the investigators will be both codified (as taught in the technique) and subjective. One person's observation of a behavior may be different than another's. None of this has a scientific basis.

Behavior symptom analysis is the subject of Chapter 9 (pp. 101–137). The use of the word *symptom* is an attempt to legitimize or *medicalize* the subject matter.[17] Investigators are advised of the three channels of communication: *verbal* (words chosen to convey a thought), *paralinguistic* (speech characteristics), and *nonverbal* (i.e., body language). These channels are the premise for the "clinical inferences" (p. 101) made. Again, use of such words is an attempt to *medicalize* what is at best speculation, despite this being based "...on our years of observation, as well

---

[15]Interrogations are approached with the presumption of guilt. What is often lost in the shuffle of interview versus interrogation is that the suspect is not (usually) aware of the difference, and which one he or she is being subjected to at the time. That a suspect may react to an interview as if it were an interrogation and display "signs" of guilt is apparently not taken into consideration.
[16]Note that the majority of police were trained on editions preceding the fifth edition.
[17]It should be noted that the original authors of the Reid Technique got their start in interrogations utilizing the polygraph, a device fraught with validity problems and beset with confirmation bias on the part of the polygraphers who use it.

as specific research findings…" (p. 109). The authors advise correctly that *"There are no unique behaviors associated with truthfulness or deception"* (p. 106, italics in original).

The investigators are taught to assess all three channels of communication to see if they are consistent, the presumption being that inconsistencies among the three channels indicate deception and/or guilt. The investigators are advised that their observations of the three communication channels do not specifically correlate to truth or deception, but instead reflect the suspect's inner emotional, physiological and cognitive state. One should look for grouping of inconsistencies, not relying on an isolated sign (for example, poor eye contact) to diagnose deception. But note: "The emotional states most often associated with deception are fear, anger, embarrassment, indignation, or hope (duping)" (p. 106). Says who? These could easily also be emotional states consistent with being questioned by police for something one did not do. Also, regardless of disclaimers offered, they are easily ignored in practice.

Interrogators are advised to consider the three channels simultaneously and be alert for any inconsistency, which is usually subjective and based on nonscientific beliefs regarding how innocent and guilty individuals behave. The investigators are advised to establish a baseline or normal behavioral pattern before judging later behaviors by talking with the subject in a nonthreatening manner for several minutes. Such admonition is arguably helpful but easily misleading. Many people will not feel comfortable talking to the police, especially when aware a crime is being investigated. For investigators to assume they are getting a baseline by chit-chatting with a subject prior to interviewing him or her is problematic and naïve. Deviation from this pseudo-baseline will be seen as indicative of something, regardless of the reason, by investigators predisposed to believe the subject will be lying to them.

Investigators are taught things that increase their belief in their ability to detect deception, when that is not the case. For example, "The deceptive suspect may engage in levity or answer questions inappropriately because he is not paying close attention to the interviewer's questions" (p. 110).[18] A good example of nonsense, wrapped in a veneer of authority is the claim that

> [a] telling difference between the truthful and deceptive suspect is
> that the truthful suspect will have given much thought about the guilty
> person—who that person might be, why and how he committed the

---

[18]The reader should keep in mind that the use of such qualifiers such as "may" often get lost in the shuffle, so that a subject who behaves this way is presumed to be hiding something.

crime; he will express harsh judgments toward the person guilty of committing the crime. The deceptive suspect has not gone through that same thought process. When asked to speculate about the person who committed the crime, the deceptive suspect may simply state that he has not given that issue much thought; he feels uncomfortable providing insight for the crime he committed. For much the same reason he is unlikely to express harsh judgments against the guilty person. (pp. 129–130)

Woe is the suspect who shrugs his shoulders and says "I don't know" when asked what kind of person committed the crime and what should happen to him.

A clearly misleading statement is offered that applies as well to the polygraph as to interview observations: "…lies result in anxiety, and many of the behavior symptoms revealed by a deceptive suspect represent his conscious, or preconscious, efforts to reduce this internal anxiety" (p. 111). Regardless of any possible disclaimers, the message is obvious: anxious people are guilty. "A subject who is properly socialized and mentally healthy will experience anxiety when he lies" (p. 111). A suspect being questioned by the police will likely be anxious, regardless of innocence or guilt, but somehow this is irrelevant. The practiced liar/criminal will be expected to show the expected signs of anxiety. How is this helpful?

Verbal responses (an on-the-fly statement analysis[19]) are assessed for truthfulness, with some patently absurd recommendations; for example, "Whenever a response is predicated on some earlier communication, such as, 'Like I wrote in my statement,' 'As I previously testified…,' 'You already asked me that and I told you before…,' the investigator should suspect lying by referral" (p. 113). An in-depth review of the statement analysis aspects of interrogation are beyond the scope of this chapter. But look at a few examples of what is taught to instill an aura of caution. The interrogators are taught to be alert for "bolstering phrases" (a comment, such as "As God is my witness…") because these are supplied to enhance credibility and could indicate deception. But "[i]t should be noted that bolstering phrases would be appropriate from an innocent suspect who has wrongfully been accused of committing a crime during an interrogation" (p. 116). So how do we know which is which? Consider: *Truthful subjects will offer spontaneous responses; deceptive subjects may offer rehearsed responses*" (p. 116, italics in original).

---

[19]This author is not against statement analysis as a means of assessing credibility but cautions that its use can be problematic.

How is one supposed know what is rehearsed or not? The recommendations given are sprinkled with qualifiers (for example, "may") and are often inherently contradictory.

As far as nonverbal behavior, investigators are advised to assess posture, change in posture, hand movements, other body movements, lack of movement, facial expression, change in expression, eye movement, eye contact, etc. From the fourth edition,

> The authors submit the following, in loosely phrased terminology: A lying suspect's eyes will appear foggy, puzzled, probing, pleading (as though seeking pity), evasive or shifty, cold, hard, strained, or sneaky. A truthful person's eyes will appear clear, bright, alert, warm, direct, easy, soft, and unprobing. (Inbau et al., 2001, p. 152)

There is a disclaimer following that a suspect could look tired because of lack of sleep, which is followed by a disclaimer that a guilty person might have been up all night worrying or rehearsing a story. What is not mentioned is that an individual who is made to feel he or she is under suspicion of committing a serious crime and has had little sleep or has been questioned for a significant period of time could easily exhibit the "symptoms" listed. Frankly, this would all be laughable if it were not for the consequences to an innocent person of being identified as deceptive by "trained" investigators.

The fifth edition of CCI includes the following nonsense (Inbau et al., 2013, p. 121):

- "Inherited behaviors are not restricted to lower animals. Humans also have internal programming that influences nonverbal behaviors. For example, all humans will respond to something that is shocking or unexpected by covering their mouth with a hand." While the first two sentences are true, the third is not.
- "For detection of deception purposes, an investigator is primarily interested in nonverbal behaviors that reflect comfort versus anxiety, confidence versus uncertainty, and a clear conscience versus guilt or shame." Note that the last phrase tells the investigator that anxiety and/ or uncertainty indicate guilt, regardless of the cause, although Reid adherents will point to all the ignored disclaimers as protective of innocent suspects being interrogated. But if you are being interrogated, you are already presumed guilty.
- "After observing a specific nonverbal behavior, the investigator must ask himself, 'Is it appropriate for the suspect to be experiencing, (sic) fear, guilt, or decreased confidence?' When the answer is 'no,' it is suggestive of possible

deception."[20] This determination is made by the person who already has decided the suspect is guilty, as only "guilty" persons are interrogated.

The *Reid Nine Steps of Interrogation* are introduced in Chapter 13 (pp. 185–328). The introduction to the techniques advises "the word guilt, as used in this text, only signifies the investigator's opinion" (p. 185). "These nine steps are presented in the context of the interrogation of suspects whose guilt seems definite or reasonably certain." A footnote to this wording attempts to defuse the obvious implication that by the time someone is interrogated that person is probably guilty. If investigators are so sure of a subject's guilt (presumably from nonconfession evidence), why is there a need to even talk to the suspect? Unfortunately, many investigations essentially consist of an interrogation. The footnote attempts to defect concerns about coerced false confessions: "It has been suggested that the reason for this guideline is because the interrogation techniques are so psychologically sophisticated that they could induce an innocent person to confess (20/20, ABC news, June 18, 1999).[21] This is not the concern. Rather, the guideline is offered to discourage investigators from using accusatory interrogation techniques as the primary means to establish the truthfulness of a suspect. In most situations, a nonaccusatory interview will accomplish that goal" (p. 325). "Regardless of the interrogation approach used, the investigator's goal is to persuade a suspect to tell the truth" (p. 186). This is disingenuous because the purpose of the interrogation is to get the person who has already been assumed to be guilty to confess.

The nine steps (not all used in every interrogation) include

1. a direct positively framed confrontation that the investigator knows the suspect committed the crime in question. Regardless of the suspect's response, the next step
2. is to present the interrogation theme, essentially a theory of why the suspect committed the crime, often allowing the suspect a moral or behavioral out, such as blaming the victim or minimizing the suspect's responsibility.

It is noted that a guilty suspect as well as an innocent one may offer denials.[22] Once the denials start coming, it is the job of the investigator to deal with them (step 3). This step involves interrupting denials, wearing down the suspect and redirecting to step 2, i.e., giving the suspect an out. Incredibly, the CIC5 states

---

[20]Notice the two qualifiers "suggestive" and "possible." This clearly detracts from the force of the statement in print, but likely not in practice.

[21]The 20/20 episode referred to involved interrogation of a 12-year-old using the Reid Techniques.

[22]It is not possible to dissect the entire CIC5 in detail, but hopefully the reader is getting a sense that eventually, despite the aura of methodology and pseudoscientific jargon, the determination of guilt or innocence is made according to the gut feeling of the interrogator.

following: "An innocent person[23] will not allow such denials to be cut off; furthermore he will attempt to more or less 'take over' the situation rather than to submit passively to continued interrogation. A guilty person usually will cease to voice a denial, or else the denials will become weaker, and he will submit to the investigator's return to a theme" (p. 188)—exactly what occurs in a coerced false confession! What does the reader think of the chances of a "take-over" while being interrogated?[24] People need to read this book to see what police are taught and why a false confession is much more easily obtained than might be thought. Earlier in the text, the reader is advised: "One of the greatest fears of an innocent suspect is that his denials of involvement will not be believed. Innocent suspects experience relief when they are convinced of the investigator's objectivity" (p. 79). Hopefully, the reader is realizing how this works. How exactly is the innocent suspect to experience relief? It appears that he or she is expected to be convinced of the interrogator's objectivity. How does that occur? Because at the beginning of questioning, the officer is supposed to tell the suspect that "...*if he is innocent the investigation will indicate that, and, conversely, that if he committed the crime his involvement will be identified*" (p. 79, emphasis in original). So, the innocent suspect is expected to place his confidence in someone who is trained to cut off any attempt to deny guilt. One might expect the suspect to become very anxious (if not already so) at this point. The anxiety will likely leak verbally and physically, all things that the interrogator will interpret as signs of guilt. It should be obvious that this situation is a recipe for disaster, unless, of course, if the goal is a confession regardless of guilt. Reid proponents will say that the technique results in false confessions only when misused. This is the equivalent of "guns don't kill people"; the Reid Technique does not cause false confessions, only interrogators do.

Step 4 involves overcoming a suspect's "secondary line of defense" that follows denials; i.e., reasons why he or she "would not or could not commit the crime" (p. 188). When the suspect's denials meet the immovable wall of the investigator's conviction that the suspect is guilty, the suspect may "mentally withdraw and 'tune out' the investigator's theme," i.e., that the suspect is guilty. The investigator then goes to step 5, which is simply where he or she continues to insist he or she knows the suspect is guilty. The investigator is advised to get physically closer to the suspect and invade his or her personal space. Step 6 allows the investigator to assess the suspect's passive (withdrawn) mood; i.e., is he or she ready to confess? Step 7 is an attempt to get the suspect to incriminate himself or herself by asking the equivalent of a "Did you stop beating your wife?" question.

---

[23]The reader is reminded of Mr. Buckley's admonition that innocent people are not interrogated.
[24]It is suggested the reader watch actual interrogations to see how this actually works when an innocent suspect denies committing a crime. For example, see "Anatomy of a Bad Confession," available online at http://www.wbur.org/2011/12/07/coerced-confession-videos.

Answering either yes or no implies guilt. Step 8 is where the investigator has the suspect say what happened. Step 9 is the conversion of an oral confession to a written confession.

In steps 3, 4, and 5, a suspect essentially is not allowed to deny committing the crime, and any protests of innocence are treated as proof of guilt.[25] If the investigator manages to get the suspect to confess, the next (or at least a subsequent) step would be to check the confession against the facts or evidence of the crime. Unfortunately, this step (step 10?) may never occur, and if it does, there is a risk it will be circular, ignoring data contamination by investigators or others. Discrepancies may be ignored or explained away, and when they cannot be ignored, it is not out of the ordinary to reinterview the suspect and get him or her to change the confession to be more in line with the facts as currently or later known.[26] Even if a suspect refuses to give a written statement, an oral confession can still be admitted at a trial.

The investigator is advised not to put a signature line at the end of a typed confession because it is "connotes too much legalism" and may discourage the suspect from signing, and in the event the suspect refuses to sign, the empty signature line "will look far better without the unused signature line on it" (p. 314). The investigator is also taught to get the suspect to incorporate personal information into the confession, such as where he or she went to high school, so that "the prosecutor may point to it as evidence that the accused actually gave the information contained in the confession and was not merely accommodating the investigator by repeating what he was told to say" (p. 317), when, in fact, getting such information into the confession is exactly a form of the suspect repeating what the investigator wants him or her to say. Following on this, the investigator should include one or two errors on each page of the confession with the goal of getting the suspect to correct the errors in writing so that he or she cannot claim at a later date that her or she didn't read it before signing. Such tactics play well to a jury, whose members are often unaware of this type of strategy, and can cement the fate of someone who signs a coerced confession. The investigator is urged to read the statement aloud while the suspect reads along. If the suspect neglects to point out the errors, the investigator can point them out (p. 317).

Surprisingly, investigators are cautioned that "the more information contained within a confession, the more information a defense counsel has to attack, if some of it turns out to be *slightly*"—emphasis added—"incorrect

---

[25]Even investigators not trained in the full Reid Technique will have learned steps 3, 4, and 5, either formally or informally.

[26]An example of this is the interrogation of Jessie Miskelley, whose first confession didn't correlate with the timeline the West Memphis police needed. See http://www.freewestmemphis3.org/.

(times, sequence of events, nature of conversations, etc.)" (p. 319). That such a recommendation would be made is incredible. We are advised to get a confession but limit the facts? But wait…. Of note: "On those occasions when a written confession is later considered inadequate, such as those lacking in some essential details,[27] the investigator should prepare an entirely new confession rather than one that merely supplements the first confession. This will serve to minimize the controversies and legal difficulties that would otherwise be presented by each document's dependence upon the other for completeness" (p. 319). No direction is given as to what becomes of the first incomplete confession. If it is destroyed and/or kept from the defense, this would be a Brady violation.[28] If it is given to the prosecutor and passed on to the defense, then the goal of "minimizing the controversies and legal difficulties" is negated, so what is really being suggested here is confusing. Clearly, the implication is that if one had to get serial/multiple confessions to be able to include all the known facts of a crime, one would want only a single confession to appear in court. Otherwise, the controversy and legal difficulties would not be minimized.[29] The section on the nine steps ends with the advisement that a confession is not the end of the investigation. If only this were really true!

Chapter 15 of CIC5 deals with distinguishing between true and false confessions (Inbau et al., 2013, pp. 339–377). While noting the problem, this chapter is written in such a manner to minimize the issue and downplay any likely concerns. "[O]ur experience has been that such interrogation techniques, if used in accordance with the guidelines offered in this text, greatly reduce the risk of an innocent suspect confessing. The self-preservation instincts of a suspect during an interrogation, conducted in accordance with the techniques taught in this text, are sufficient to maintain the suspect's stated innocence" (pp. 366–367). After researching the issue of false confessions, one can only ask: Are they serious?

The CIC5 reports that "a false confession should be recognized long before it is entered into evidence against an innocent defendant" (p. 411). Coerced-compliant confessions, voluntary false confessions, and coerced-internalized confessions are described, although their incidence is downplayed, with the CIC5 claiming "[e]ven critics of police interrogations agree

---

[27]Apparently, not the essential details one was just warned could assist defense attorneys.

[28]*Brady v. Maryland*, 373 U.S. 83 (1963): A Brady violation is the withholding of exculpatory or impeachment evidence from the defense.

[29]In a review of CIC5 (or 4), it is difficult to avoid sarcasm. This book is a recipe for confessions, true and false, from suspects naïve to police contact. Hardened criminals will not fall for the techniques taught in these texts. In the author's opinion, the three most dangerous books in the world are the Bible, the Koran, and *Criminal Interrogation and Confessions*.

that most confessions are true" (p. 339). It is not clear what to make of such a statement. It may be linguistically accurate, but what does it mean in absolute terms? If there are 100,000 confessions this year and only 1% are false confessions, that is 1,000 false confessions. Another way to frame the issue is that in a review of 208 DNA exonerations, 16% included a false confession (Garrett, 2007). Regardless of the actual number, it has become obvious that false confessions are far from rare. The examples of false confessions given in CIC5 are banal; one would never know it happened in a rape or a murder case.

The CIC5 offers: "Our long-standing position has been that interrogation incentives that are apt to cause an innocent person to confess are improper" (Inbau et al., 2013, p. 344). But the parameters of such incentives are lacking. Permissible incentives that should not result in false confessions (per the CIC5) are advising of an expectation of decreased guilt feelings, that the suspect will be respected by loved ones for telling the truth, and that the suspect will "learn from his mistake and not commit worse crimes in the future" (p. 345). What is missing from the discussion is that none of this is arguably relevant to an innocent person worn down by a determined investigator convinced the suspect is guilty. None of this occurs in a vacuum. Perhaps the almost complete lack of true psychological insight of the Reid Technique's authors is exemplified by the following statement: "To understand the distinction between messages that are implied versus stated outright, it must be remembered that innocent and guilty suspects have completely different expectations and orientations during an interrogation. Consequently, when they are exposed to the same ambiguous message they will interpret it differently" (p. 346). Why? An innocent person will interpret a suggestion of leniency the same as a guilty person. "An innocent suspect who is told that it is important to explain the reason behind committing the crime will predictably reject the investigator's entire premise and explain that he had no involvement in the crime whatsoever." This statement is startling when one is reminded that the investigator is trained to forcefully squelch any denials immediately.[30] That such commentary is presented in the chapter on how to avoid a false confession should invalidate the entire Reid Technique. Note the following: "When fatigue, withdrawal, hunger, thirst, or a craving for other biological needs serve as the *primary incentive* [emphasis in original] for a confession, duress may be claimed" (p. 347). Note that the wording is *may* be claimed! Apparently, the Reid Technique allows for the fact that fatigue, withdrawal, hunger, thirst, or a craving for other biological needs serving as the *primary incentive* for a confession generally would not be a problem in obtaining a confession.

---

[30]Remember steps 3, 4, and 5.

That this is the *standard of care* in law enforcement should strike fear into the average citizen. We are not talking about hardened criminals staring down inept investigators. We are talking about 16-year-old kids accused of killing their mothers, 25-year-old mothers accused of setting fire to their homes, 50-year-old men whose wives were killed while they were away, and all attempting to tell a seasoned interrogator that they are innocent.

By its very nature, trickery and deceit are part and parcel of police interrogation. The CIC5 naïvely, and likely purposefully, downplays the role such behavior can have on innocent people. "The important question to answer is whether it is human nature to accept responsibility for something we did not do in the face of contrary evidence" (p. 351). The answer to that question is obviously "no." But that is not the question. The proper question is whether it is possible to get an innocent person to confess to a crime. That answer is "absolutely!" Note that "[t]he ordinary citizen is outraged and indignant when presented with supposed 'evidence' of an act he knows he did not commit" (p. 351). But yet any attempts at denial are forcefully cut off if one follows the Reid Technique.

"Consider an innocent rape suspect who is falsely told that DNA evidence positively identifies him as the rapist. Would this false statement cause an innocent person to suddenly shrink in the chair and decide that it would be in his best interest to confess?" (p. 351). Possibly. What of the 16-year-old Hispanic male accused by an 18-year-old girl of raping her at a party a week earlier, when the girl's boyfriend instigated the complaint, not the girl? During the police interrogation, the suspect boy, who never had any physical contact with the girl, was told that (1) there was DNA collected, (2) the girl was not sure she wanted to press charges, and (3) if he confessed, he would be able to go home, at least until the DNA test came back. The youth knew he did not rape the girl. He suspected he had been targeted by the girl, and she had made up a story to garner sympathy because the boyfriend was upset he did not know she was going to a party without him. The suspect youth did not know where the DNA came from, but he knew it was not his. He was confident that when the report came back the police would know he had no sexual contact with girl. So he confessed, having been led to believe he would to be able to go home until the (nonexistent) DNA test came back. After the confession, the youth learned that there was no DNA and the only evidence against him was his confession. Apparently, the Reid Technique was ignored, and the confession ended the investigation. The youth was pressured to plead by his public defender, who did not feel they could overcome the confession, and the boy is now a registered sex offender for a crime that never happened.[31]

---

[31]The author has personal knowledge of this case.

CASE EXAMPLE:

Kevin Fox[32]

Kevin Fox was a 27-year-old father of two: a 6-year-old son, Tyler, and a 3-year-old daughter, Riley. In 2004, while his wife was out of town at a breast cancer benefit march in Chicago, he went to a concert with a brother-in-law. Although they were drinking at the concert, there is no evidence they arrived back in town intoxicated. Kevin picked up his kids from his mother-in-law's house and went home to bed. Because the kids' beds were unmade, his son slept on a chair with an ottoman, and the daughter slept on a couch in the living room. Kevin had a cigarette on the porch and then went to bed around 2:30 a.m.

At 7:50 a.m., Tyler woke up, noticed his sister was gone and went in and woke his father to let him know. Kevin made a quick search of the house, noting the front door was ajar and the screen was cut. He then checked outside for about 40 minutes before calling police on a nonemergency line (i.e., 441, not 911). Later, his wife called him and he told her Riley was missing, causing her to return immediately from Chicago to Wilmington. Riley's body was found at 3:30 p.m. that day in a creek four miles from the Fox home. At the time her body was found, Kevin was at the police station being interviewed by Illinois state police. Although the Wilmington Police initiated the investigation, it was taken over by the Will County Sheriff's Department because the body was found in a county park. The crime scene investigators found no evidence at the Fox home, but did find a pair of sneakers (see below) in the creek downstream from where the young girl's body was found.

Kevin and his wife cooperated fully with police, meeting with investigators and with Kevin giving DNA and the clothes he wore on June 6 and also the day before. Six-year-old Tyler was interviewed by a social worker in what can only be described as child abuse and denied 178 times that his father had taken Riley from the living room. He had indicated that his dad left the home that night.[33] Later, at the Fox home, with no one else present and no recording made, a police officer interviewed Tyler and claimed the child implicated his father, Kevin, in Riley's murder. Saliva taken from Riley's body was sent for DNA testing, and the result

was reported by law enforcement as inconclusive. The saliva evidence was then forwarded to the FBI crime lab, but not tested immediately due to a backlog.

For almost four months, no arrests were made. The investigation was limited: the bridge at the creek was never secured; the public had been allowed to climb/walk on the bridge; people at the crime scene (park) were dispersed instead of questioned; the creek was drained without proper mapping of creek bed; and hooks used to search the creek distorted the crime scene. Witnesses (never interviewed by police) said the body was not in the creek until shortly before it was found, providing an alibi for Kevin, as he was with the police from the time when he called in Riley as missing to when the body was discovered. The coroner reported that death was between 1:30 a.m. and 7:50 a.m., which was likely not accurate. By October 2004, there were no suspects, except the dead girl's father, Kevin.

At the time, there was a hotly contested election for DA nearing. The Fox murder investigation went into overdrive, and police set up a polygraph. On October 26, 2004, Kevin Fox and his wife were called to the police station to find out "something important" and arrived at about 7:00 p.m. Kevin had been up since 4:30 a.m., working all day painting. Once at the police station, the husband and wife were separated. Kevin underwent a 14-hour interrogation. He was not allowed to leave. Several times he asked to speak to his father so that he could get Kevin a lawyer. He was told he did not need a lawyer or his father. Kevin was confronted with Tyler's alleged statements implicating him. He was confronted with supposed surveillance video of his car taken during the night in question,[34] and he made a sarcastic comment that was reframed by police as an alibi attempt. He was offered an accident theme for Riley's death (Reid Technique Step 2) as a way out. Police talked to his wife to convince her that Kevin was guilty so she could ask him to confess.

By midnight, he was told: "We know you killed your daughter." He was offered a way to prove his innocence by taking a polygraph. He was told he failed exam.[35] His wife was told he failed the exam. She met with Kevin

CASE EXAMPLE: *CONTINUED*

but told him she believed him. The police yelled at her, got her out of the room, and continued the interrogation. They invaded Kevin's personal space and told him that now was the time to confess. It was presented as the difference between an accident[36] and first-degree murder, with a possible sentence of 30 years to life or even the death penalty. He was reminded that men get raped in prison. He was shown pictures of his deceased daughter and then told the police could deal with the district attorney, but only if Kevin confessed now. He was led to believe that if he admitted his daughter's death was an accident, he likely could be released on bail,[37] as involuntary manslaughter might carry only a 3- to 5-year sentence.

Everything leading up to the confession was not taped. After Kevin's 14-plus-hour interrogation, with him awake for over 24 hours with little to eat, there was a 20-minute tape[38] (i.e., *Confession Theater*). Kevin confessed, knowing he was innocent, believing he would be out on bond and could then prove his innocence. The DA then announced a major break in the case just before the election, also making a claim there was evidence of sexual abuse of Riley by her father, prior to her death. The DA claimed Riley was alive and struggling when placed in the creek, so he floated the death penalty charge. He lost the election anyway. After Kevin confessed, police called the FBI lab and told them not to process the saliva sample for DNA.[39] When the DNA was eventually tested,[40] it did not match that of Kevin Fox. In an ironic twist, it turned out Wilmington police had spoken to the actual killer the day after the murder, when someone called 911 because he was threatening to harm himself, saying he had done something bad. He denied to police he was a threat to himself, but did ask them if they knew whether they found "the little girl yet?" To add insult to injury, his sneaker was near where the body was discovered.[41] Also, police never processed a nearby crime scene, a park toilet and trash receptacle. It is likely the girl was sexually assaulted in the bathroom and her underwear was thrown in the trash bin. County personnel did enter the bathroom as part of the investigation, noticing the floor had a viscous oily substance on it.[42] Incredibly, the area was

not treated by investigators as part of the crime scene. Canvassing the neighborhood of the Fox residence, police found that a neighbor across the street had had a possible attempted burglary with a cut screen.[43] After a civil suit, Kevin and wife were awarded $12,200,000, later reduced to $8,000,000 (Huffington Post, 2011).

So why did Kevin Fox confess? Actually, understanding why isn't all that hard. Just read the CIC5 (Inbau et al., 2013). Then (1) isolate, (2) invade personal space, (3) don't allow denials, (4) use a polygraph, (5) use false evidence ploys, (6) develop themes, (7) watch Confession Theater. Kevin's decision to confess made sense to him in the context of what was occurring during the interrogation.

Is this okay? Proponents of the Reid Technique will say the program was used improperly. This author would suggest it worked as intended.

---

[32]Information for this case came from the Second Amended Complaint in a lawsuit filed by Kevin Fox (Zellner & Associates) against the Sheriff's Office of Will County and several detectives, and "They promised Kevin Fox they would stop the grilling him—if he'd just say his daughter's death had been an accident," by Brian Smith (2006) and a report commissioned by the Will's County Sheriff (Andrews International, 2010).
[33]This was probably when Kevin went out to the porch for a cigarette before turning in.
[34]There is no proof it was his car in the video. In fact, later independent review of the tape found that to determine the car in the tape was even an SUV was difficult, let alone a Ford Escape. The Fox family's Ford Escape was processed for evidence and nothing was found.
[35]It is common that people who pass a polygraph are told they failed. Reportedly, the exam was inconclusive.
[36]Kevin was given a scenario in which he might have knocked her into a wall or door and injured her head.
[37]Police deny this. This author's money is on Kevin.
[38]The taped confession has never been made available to the public.
[39]The police deny they stopped the testing. The FBI says they did. The Andrews' report classified the situation as a "misunderstanding."
[40]The defense attorney had it tested at a private lab.
[41]Downstream. They later were determined to be prison issue with "EBY" written in them, the name of the actual murderer.
[42]Later determined to be motor oil, used by the murderer with the intent of obscuring any trace evidence.
[43]It was later determined that Riley's killer had burglarized the home before going next to the Fox residence.

CASE EXAMPLE:

Frank Sterling[44,45]

Viola Manville was a 71-year-old grandmother from Hilton, New York. In October 1985, Glen Sterling attempted to sexually assault her by a railroad track she often took as a route on her daily walk. He was convicted and imprisoned for this crime. Several years later, on November 29, 1988, Ms. Manville was found by a hunter walking along an abandoned railroad track bed. She had been murdered in the same general area as the attempted rape. She had been beaten to death and shot twice with a BB gun. Glen Sterling was still in prison at the time of the murder. His brother Frank, though, was not, and he became a suspect with police theorizing Frank had killed Ms. Manville in retaliation for his brother having gone to prison. The day after the murder, Frank voluntarily went to the police station to answer questions. Frank was able to account for his whereabouts on the day of the murder and was not arrested.

The police investigation went nowhere. There was a youth, Mark Kristie, who lived in Hilton. Peers of his told the police he carried a BB gun and bragged about beating and shooting Ms. Manville, and that he frequented the area where her body was found. But police did not consider him a suspect after questioning him. He had an alibi that he was in school and a polygraph exam did not apparently indicate deception. Police reinterviewed Frank about the murder in April 1989. Again, he was released.

In 1991 a cold case review was conducted, and Frank Sterling was once more brought to the police department for questioning at 5:45 p.m. on July 10. He had gone voluntarily to talk and take a polygraph test. Prior to arriving, Frank had been working as a trucker for at least 36 hours with only a few hours' sleep time. He signed a Miranda waiver and a polygraph waiver, and questioning began. The investigators told him his brother, Glen, had been bragging in prison that Frank had killed Ms. Manville as a favor to him. Frank denied involvement in the murder and police accused him of lying.[46] At 9:19 p.m., the polygraph exam started and lasted 45 minutes. Frank was told he was "not being completely honest" about the BB gun. Frank insisted he could not remember the murder and asked to be hypnotized at 11:20 p.m. The polygrapher advised Frank that he could not hypnotize him, but that they could do a relaxation technique. This was at 12:45 a.m.

Frank was asked to "visualize" the crime and then made "implicating statements" to the polygrapher. Then Frank jumped up from the floor and stated, "This is a bunch of bullshit. I didn't do nothing." The polygrapher informed Frank: "I think you killed Manville. I'll be back and I'll prove it." Frank was then given something to eat and showed crime scene photos. Frank reiterated that he could not remember the day of the murder and again asked to be hypnotized. At 2:20 a.m., he underwent another relaxation technique. A police officer massaged his back and shoulders and suggested themes of the crime to Frank.[47] At 2:40 a.m., Frank announced, "I did it and I need help." Frank said he had attacked Viola Manville in anger after coming across her while she was taking her daily walk, but had not intended to kill her. At the time of the confession, Frank had been working for 36 hours with limited sleep, followed by 12 hours of police questioning. At 5:22 a.m., Frank gave a 20-and-a-half minute videotaped confession. The polygrapher worked the video camera. Frank Sterling was arrested and charged with the murder of Viola Manville.

The reader is asked to watch the video of the confession in its entirety[48] and try to imagine the effect it would have if one were a juror in the case. The video can be accessed from many sites online, and is available at http://www.democratandchronicle.com/article/20100509/NEWS01/5090351/Missteps-kept-Frank-Sterling-in-prison.

Frank Sterling's defense team tried to suppress the confession (the only evidence in the case) on the grounds that he had been inducted into a hypnotic state by the interrogators and was therefore very suggestible. The attempt was not successful, and the videotape was played for the jury. On September 22, 1992, Frank Sterling was found guilty at trial of depraved indifference murder. He was subsequently sentenced to 25 years to life in prison.

All Frank Sterling's appeals were denied. In 1994, his defense team requested DNA testing on a hair from the crime scene. The Monroe County DA objected, and the trial judge agreed with the DA. In 2007, the NYS Appellate Court denied testing. Eventually, the DA agreed to test the DNA anyway; it is not clear why.[49] The DNA result created a problem: it did not belong to Frank Sterling.

After the 1992 sentencing, witnesses again came forward related to Mark Christie. Police cleared him again. In 1994, a four-year-old girl went missing in Monroe County, New York, not too far from Hilton. Her body was found in an industrial cooling solution vat at a business,

CASE EXAMPLE: *CONTINUED*

and Mark Christie had access to the site. In 1996, Mark Christie confessed to the young girl's murder. Years later, DNA testing of a hair (see above) linked him to the Viola Manville murder. Staff from the Innocence Project, with the help of an employee of Reid Associates, got Mark Christie to confess to the murder of Viola Manville. Frank Sterling's conviction was vacated April 28, 2000. He had spent 19 years in prison for a crime he did not commit.

The 20-and-a-half minute confession of Frank Sterling is best described as a good example of *Confession Theater*. The 12 hours of questioning, including the polygraph testing and relaxation techniques, were not taped. Interestingly, the confession is notable for what is not there. Frank Sterling never confessed to killing Viola Manville. The reader is asked to watch the confession video in its entirety again, knowing what the reader now knows, reading along with the following transcript.[50] Officer Crough is in a t-shirt. Officer Vasille is wearing a blue short-sleeve shirt, and the polygrapher (acting as videographer and occasional interrogator) is behind the camera and therefore out of frame. The video starts at 5:22 a.m. and lasts 20 minutes and 36 seconds. The transcript is not verbatim where unnecessary. Actual oral statements are in quotation marks. The times noted here are time elapsed during the video, not the time/date stamp from the camera.

0–1:25 Solicitous behaviors: coffee, cream, sugar, stirring coffee, "Be our guest."

1:25 Rights waived, voluntary, "no handcuffs or nothing," "weren't threatened."

2:07 Age: 28, no 27.

2:15 Injection of personal information per Reid Technique.

2:40 Establish Frank speaks English.

2:51 Establishes Frank was allowed to eat, smoke, coffee, pop. "As much as you wanted."

3:04 "Have you been treated good?" Frank answers, "Yes." Investigators begin physical contact, touching his arm.

3:13 Reestablish voluntariness of the situation, begin getting Frank to confess.

3:40 Crough starts directing the confession: "There's been some problems in the past, and it's caused anger and pain for you. Can you just describe to us what it was? And it's OK." Frank parrots the police

theory that he believes his brother is wrongfully in prison. But he fails to continue with the Manville attempted rape connection, so Officer Crough has to redirect him. Crough starts rubbing Frank's arm and shoulder, and Vasille starts on Frank's back.

4:10 "If I'm understanding you correctly, from when we talked earlier, it's because you feel Viola Manville wrongfully pointed him out..." Throughout the video, notice the physical contact between the investigators and the suspect.

4:54 Police lead Frank through the scenario.

5:08 Crough asks Frank to tell them, as best as he can, what happened.

6:13 Vasille asks Frank: "Could you describe a little, Frank, about what happened?"

6:50 Crough gives Frank a cigarette. Frank lights it himself. Keep an eye on the cigarette. Frank never takes a puff.

7:00 Frank describes not knowing Manville and gives that as an explanation for explaining to her why he was upset.

7:16 Frank: "She told me, your brother got what he deserved."

7:45 Frank: "It turned out later she was the one my brother was in prison for." This makes no real sense, since supposedly he attacked her because of who she was.

8:02 Frank: "She said my brother got what he deserved. I hit her." Asked how, with what, "My hand." He then describes a conversation between him and the victim about how he felt she couldn't have been sure in identifying his brother as her attempted rapist. Keep in mind, supposedly he has just struck a 74-year-old woman who is now having a conversation with him, as opposed to screaming and trying to run away.

9:20 Crough has to get back to the beating. "Did you get mad at her again? Did you start hitting her again?" Frank: "Yes." Crough: "What happened then?" Frank says, "She swung back at me several times." Crough realizes a 74-year-old woman wouldn't last long in a boxing match with Frank, so he interjects: "Did she eventually fall down?"

9:32 Frank: "Yes." Crough: "Then what?" Frank: "I started kicking her."

Continued

CASE EXAMPLE: *CONTINUED*

9:40 Viola was beaten to death with a BB gun, but Frank has failed to bring this up. Crough: "Frank, as best as you can remember, and I know this is difficult for you, did something happen with that BB gun?" 9:50 Frank: "I discarded it…." [Discarded? I doubt this is a word Frank used a lot. This is more likely a word used by the interrogators earlier during the untaped questioning.] Crough presses him, much of it inaudible, about where he got rid of the BB gun and Frank ultimately says: 10:10 "I have no idea."

10:20 Frank is apparently not very detail oriented, so Crough asks (instructs?): "In a rage did you take her pants off?" [Why in a rage? Viola was not sexually assaulted, so Crough must supply a reason for Frank to remove her pants.] Frank cries, looks down and says, "Yes." But it is not loud enough, so Crough advises: "I can't hear you," and Frank complies and says "yes" much louder.

10:33 Crough prods: "Did anything happen after that?" Frank says, "No." Crough: "Do you remember what you did with the BB gun?" Frank shakes his head no and says, "Just threw it." [Keep in mind, the BB gun should have been recovered at the crime scene if Frank "just threw it" after he assaulted Viola. Since it was not found…]

10:40 Crough: "Did you throw it in the woods? Or did you throw it in the water?" Frank: "I don't know. I just don't remember. I just gave it a throw." [Recall this is the murder weapon—and Frank cannot remember what he did with it?]

10:55 Crough: "Frank, let me ask you this. Do you feel better now that you've talked to us? Because, we've, from what we talked about earlier, this has been weighing on you for some time." Frank, "Yes." Crough: "Do you feel remorse?" Frank: "Yes."

11:12 Crough: "Can I ask you a question? Answer it if you can. OK. When she fell, did she fall on the (railroad) bed? Or did she fall elsewhere?" Frank: "She fell under the brush." Crough: "And then you kicked her when she was—" Frank: "Yes."

11:29 [This is the first time since lighting the cigarette (at 6:50) that Frank flicks ashes (4 minutes and 39 seconds later), or in any way pays attention to the cigarette in his right hand. He has yet to put the cigarette near his mouth.]

11:40 Vasille: "Is there anything else you might want to add, Frank?" Frank (distraught): "I wish it didn't go that far." This leads to much positive physical reinforcement from the investigators. Note Frank has not said what "that far" is, but the investigators take this as good enough for a confession to murder.

11:55 Crough looks at the camera and the polygrapher whispers: "What year?" Crough: "Do you remember what year this happened?" Frank: "No." Crough: "Would you say it was approximately two years ago?" Frank: "Yes." Crough: "Approximately." Frank: "Approximately." Crough: "Maybe three. Somewhere between two and three years ago." Frank: Yes."

12:15 Vasille: "Do you remember about what time it was during the day, Frank?" [Keep in mind that Frank actually was able to account for his whereabouts when first questioned in 1988.] Crough: "Roughly, Frank. You don't have to be exact. Roughly." Vasille: "Just roughly." 12:20 Frank: "Around one, two." Crough: "Was it before the Chipmunks and the (inaudible) cartoons?" [This is to bypass Frank's 1988 alibi. He had told police he watched cartoons and was able to accurately describe the content.] Frank: "Yes… Yes." Vasille: "You went home and watched TV after…" Frank (distraught): "Yes." Crough: "OK." [Crough starts to rub Frank's neck and shoulder. Note Frank again gets the two-man rubdown, a positive reinforcement for saying what the police want and also for saying it with a distraught demeanor.]

12:23 Crough (and Vasille) again looks to the polygrapher/videographer for either approval or guidance. Nothing is audible, but this author suspects the polygrapher mouthed "BB gun." 12:38 Crough: "About the BB gun…OK and I'm glad, but just one thing…That BB gun, um, had been in the possession of your father, right? He took it away from you for some reasons." Frank: "Yes." [Crough asks about the BB gun to establish that Frank had taken it from his father's bedroom.] Frank says he can't recall, and then says "Yes." Crough: "That's what you told us earlier, is that correct, from what you can recall?" Frank: "Yes." [Since we don't have a video of the entire interrogation, we will never know what Frank told them versus what they got him to say.]

13:05 Crough looks to the polygrapher and then at Frank: "Is there anything you'd like to add?"

CASE EXAMPLE: *CONTINUED*

[Frank interprets this as a request to summarize what he believes the police want to hear.]
13:14 Frank: "Yes. That I didn't intentionally, intentionally used a gun to go after her…." Crough: "Just happen?" Frank: "Took it down there. Just to try to calm myself down, get my mind off it." Vasille: "Did you, did you use the gun there a couple of times (inaudible)…?" Frank: "Yeah."
13:38 Vasille: "Did the gun break when you hit her?" Frank: "Not that I can recall." … Crough: "You were pretty upset anyway." Frank: "Yeah." Crough: "OK."
13:50 Vasille: "Do you remember how many times you shot the gun, the BB gun at (inaudible)?" Frank: "Not offhand." Crough: "Remember what she was wearing Frank?" [Crough is now holding Frank's forearm. This is an important question, as it is allegedly information only the killer would have. But recall, Frank has been shown the crime scene photos.] Frank: "Ah, purple sweatshirt, jacket. Black pants." Crough: "Dark pants." Frank: "Yeah." Crough: "OK." Vasille: "What type of pants were they?"
14:15 Frank: "I believe jeans, (inaudible) or jogging pants." Crough: "Frank, you've demonstrated a lot of courage today…. We know it took a lot for you…to admit to this." [Frank is distraught. Frank gets the two-man rubdown again.]
14:32 Crough: "Frank, one more question. Have you ever told anyone about this?" Frank: "No." Crough: "No one else knows about this?… Your doing this?" Frank: "Just me."
14:41 [Notice that since they've gotten what they believe they need, the investigators now distance themselves from Frank.]
[There is then a break at 5:37 a.m. (14.48) to 5:57 a.m. (14.51). Note, Frank has still not taken a puff from the cigarette he lit 8 minutes before. What occurred during this 20-minute lapse in recording? While Vasille will explain the time lapse, we do not know if anyone has spoken with Frank about anything. But also keep in mind, we do not have a reliable record (i.e., videotape) of the prior 12 or so hours of interrogation.]
15:05 Vasille advises the camera that during the break they showed the "interview" to the district attorney and that the DA has some questions that they will try to clear up: "If that's all right with you." Frank: "OK."
15:20 Vasille: "The first thing is, after this incident occurred, where did you go?" Frank: "Back home."

Vasille: "OK. Um. There was quite a bid of blood involved. OK. Did you get blood on your clothing or anything like that?" Frank: "Um, not that I can recall." Vasille: "How about your boots or your shoes? Or anything like that? Do you remember any of that, that you might have discarded or got rid of, or anything like that? And, it's OK to answer these questions." [Note the word "discarded" used by Frank earlier, could be a word he picked up from Vasille during the prior untaped portions of the interrogation.]
15:44 Frank: "No." [Keep in mind, the police are looking to explain why Frank did not have any blood on him or his clothes when first questioned in 1988.] Crough: "Did you wash anything in particular, like your hands or your arms?" Frank [who already said no to washing blood off himself or anything, picks up on Crough's cue that is not the answer they want and changes his answer]: "Probably just flicked or washed them off in the crick." Crough: "In the crick?" Vasille: "You washed them off in the crick. Did they have blood on them, at the time?… That you remember." [Keep in mind, Frank is not being asked what is factual, but what he remembers.] Frank nods: "That's, yeah."
15:53 Cough: "OK. Did you leave the gun in the creek?" Frank raises hands, palm up: "Umm." Crough: "Did you leave the gun in the creek?" Frank: "Can't remember. I just threw the gun." [This is a problem for the police as the gun should have then been found near the body. See below.]
16:04 Vasille: "Um…what did you do directly after you got home?" Frank is asked a few questions about watching TV.
16:43 Vasille: "Frank, could you explain one more time in your own words, Frank, why this happened to you? Why you were involved in this incident?" [Presumably establishing motive is more important than having evidence.] Frank: "'Cause my brother was in prison…I feel wrongfully." [Keep in mind this is the police theme.] Vasille: "OK. And that Mrs. Manfield (sic) wrongfully accused your brother of something that he didn't do."
16:58 Frank: "Correct." Vasille: "OK. Uh. Do you remember just prior to what happened here, what you were doing, where you were going? I think we talked about you went to the store. And you picked up some frosting for a cake or something." Frank: "Yeah." Vasille: "OK. Can you explain a little bit about that?"

Continued

CASE EXAMPLE: *CONTINUED*

17:20 Frank: "Well, I went to get some frosting for the cake. Down Big M (store). On the way down, didn't see anybody. You know. Just walked down. (Inaudible) to calm myself down. Mom says, we'll need the frosting. That's from what I can recall. You know, I went to the store to get the frosting. I was pretty well upset, so I didn't feel like driving...."

17:51 Vasille: "Sure. Do you remember carrying the pistol with you then?" Frank: "Not offhand. No. Somehow I did have the BB gun with me." Crough: "'Cause this... When did this all happen? When you're coming back from purchasing the frosting—" Frank: "Yes." Crough: "—on the way back home?" Frank: "Yes." Crough: "So you obviously had the pistol (inaudible)?" Frank: "Yes." [Problem solved.] Vasille: "Then, again, you didn't have any blood on your clothing. Just your hands." Frank: "Yes." Vasille: "And you got rid of the pellet, pellet pistol." Frank: "Yeah."

18:20 Crough: "Do you remember what you were wearing, Frank? Like did you have a special jacket on? Or anything? Do you remember exactly what you were wearing? In particular, any jacket, sweater, hat, gloves? Anything in particular that you can remember?" Frank: "Nah, not offhand. Probably just, just jeans, t-shirt probably."

18:40 Vasille: "But you don't remember anything specific articles—" Frank: "Nah." Vasille: "Articles, you don't." Vasille: "OK, one more question, Frank, and I want you to be honest with this question. OK? Somebody didn't put these ideas in your head. You didn't dream up this idea?... You did this. Right?" [This is ironic, as putting the ideas in Frank's head is exactly what has happened. Also, while the police assume "did this" means murdering Viola Manville, asking it like that allows Frank to say yes without confessing to a murder he did not commit.]

19:01 Frank: "From what my memory recalls, yes." [Note: Frank is not saying he believes his statement to be true. He is saying only as his memory recalls it. He does not really remember it.] Vasille: "Did you understand everything that we're doing?" Frank: "Yes." Vasille: "You're not under any influence of any drug or alcohol at this

time." Frank: "Nope." Vasille: "Do you have anything else that you might think about adding, Frank?"

19:22 The polygrapher/videographer: "Frank, I'd like to touch on something if I could? Um, remember you explained to me the next day the issue about the BB gun and with your family? Could you explain that to me?" Frank: "I conferred with Gary (another brother) to find out if he knew what happened to the BB gun." [Conferred? This author doubts this is a word Frank uses regularly.] "He said no. He did not know."

19:43 Polygrapher: "What is it about your father you told me?" After a pause, Crough: "In other words, what we talked about last time. Did your dad and you have an argument relative to you taking the BB gun?" [They are trying to get Frank to make statements related to having a BB gun in his possession on the day of the murder.] Frank: "(Inaudible)" Crough: "Was there a discussion with him about you taking the BB gun when he didn't want you to?"

20:11 Frank: "I told him it's long distance (inaudible) target practice." Crough: "But he was mad, right?" Frank: "Yep." Crough: "And there was a discussion." Frank: "Yes." Crough: "OK."

20:22 Polygrapher: "What day was that?" Frank: "I believe the day after." Vasille: "That's it. Anything else?" Frank: "No." Vasille: "OK."

The reader is reminded that (1) this is a false confession, (2) Frank Sterling never actually said he killed Viola Manville, and (3) no one had to raise a hand to obtain the confession. Also, the actual murderer remained free and was able to later kill a four-year-old child.

---

[44] *Richard Byington, a Reid Technique instructor, has offered the opinion that the interrogation of Frank Sterling did not meet Reid Technique standards.*

[45] *Information related to the Sterling case was taken from Crough and Vasile (1991), Leo (2008), Craig (2010), Habeas Corpus Petition (2004).*

[46] *As per Reid Technique.*

[47] *As per Reid technique.*

[48] *Some websites feature a shorter version.*

[49] *One can only suspect the case was gaining notoriety and to continue to refuse testing was becoming more and more awkward.*

[50] *Although it is proven that the police induced a coerced-compliant confession from Frank Sterling, this author does not believe the investigators realized what they were doing.*

SUMMARY

The fifth edition of *Criminal Interrogation and Confessions* (Inbau et al., 2013) deserves reviewing by all interested in the issue of false confessions, especially defense attorneys, prosecutors, trial judges, and appellate judges. If one has any psychological acumen and familiarity with false confessions, one can only be surprised and at times shocked with the content of this text. Not by the fact that police are taught to deceive a suspect, or that they are taught how to sit or invade a suspect's personal space, or lie about evidence or statements by others. The surprise and shock are that the authors of the Reid Technique purport to present a system of interrogation that would *minimize* false confessions, when it is designed only to get confessions. If one has the opportunity to view police interrogations of false confessors, one will recognize some or all nine Reid steps. Of course, proponents of the method will say that interrogators who get false confessions misused the system, as happened in the Frank Sterling case. If this is so, then what is the vetting process for using this system? You need a license to drive a car. Do you need a license to use the Reid Technique? Regardless, it is this author's contention that it is not necessary to misuse the techniques taught in the Reid Technique to get a false confession.

"Misuse" of the technique can have disastrous consequences for the accused. But the problem goes deeper than the Reid Technique. It includes jurors, judges, and prosecutors unwilling to accept the fact that under the right circumstances just about anyone naïve to the criminal justice system (for whatever reason) can be victimized into a false confession. Police should videotape all criminal interrogations, from beginning to end. There should be a record of the event aside from handwritten notes or recollections. *Confession Theater* should not be allowed in a courtroom.

It is not the author's intention to broadly disparage law enforcement. Many who induce a false confession are unaware of what they have done. Unfortunately, that does not undo the damage. My praise does go out to those in the criminal justice system who fight to right a wrong once it is recognized.

QUESTIONS

1. True or False: The one characteristic that increases the risk for a false confession is age.
2. List the three types of false confessions.
3. Define the term *coerced-internalized confession*. Provide a case example.
4. List three steps of the Reid Technique of interviewing and interrogation.
5. True or False: The Reid Technique minimizes false confessions.

REFERENCES

Andrews International, 2010, December 16. Comprehensive Operational Assessment, Criminal Investigative Unit, Sheriff's Office, Will County, Illinois. Available online at: http://www.scribd.com/full/47496706?access_key=key-d7dvwhg1k4m4ipsr1oi

Ashcraft v. Tennessee, 322 U.S. 143 (1944).

Associated Press, 2010, May 6. Potential jurors answering questionnaire for police torture trial. http://www.chicagotribune.com/news/local/sns-ap-il–policetorture, 0, 4257896.story?obref=obnetwork, (accessed 07.05.10.)

Bass, E., Davis, L., 1988. Courage to Heal: A Guide for Women Survivors of Childhood Sexual Abuse. Harper Row, New York.

Billy Wayne Cope—The Truth. Available online at: http://www.billywaynecope.net (accessed 25.03.13.)

Blakeney v State, 29 So. 3rd 46 (Miss. App. 2009).

Brown v. Mississippi, 297 US 278 (1936).

Burns, S., 2012. The Central Park Five: The Untold Story Behind One of New York City's Most Infamous Crimes. Anchor Books, New York.

Chambers v. Florida, (1940) 309 U.S. 227.

Cohen, S., 2012, January 29. Jon Burge Case: Final judgment in a notorious police abuse scandal. Huffington Post. Available online at: http://www.huffingtonpost.com/2011/01/29/jon-burge-case-final-judg_n_815793.html

Craig, G., 2010, May 9. Missteps kept Frank Sterling in prison. Democrat and Chronicle. Available online at: http://www.democratandchronicle.com/article/20100509/NEWS01/5090351/Missteps-kept-Frank-Sterling-in-prison, (accessed 17.10.12.)

Crough and Vasile, Investigators, 1991, July 10. Arrest report on Frank Sterling.

Davis v. US, 512 US 452 (1994).

Forty Eight Hours, Ryan Ferguson's fight for freedom. CBSNews.com. Available online at: http://www.cbsnews.com/8301-18559_162-57570827/ryan-fergusons-fight-for-freedom/2013, February 23

Garrett, B.L., 2007. Judging Innocence. Columbia Law Review, 101–190. Available at: http://graphics8.nytimes.com/packages/pdf/national/Garrettjudginginnocence.pdf, (accessed 13.05.10.)

Golden, J., 2006, October 20. Looking inside the mind of John Mark Karr. ABCNews. Available online at: http://abcnews.go.com/US/LegalCenter/story?id=2589251&page=1

Habeas Corpus Petition, 2004, April 19. Frank Sterling v. George Bartlett. US District Court/Western District, NY 96-CV-6135 (Fe).

Gross, J., 1998, May 29. A conviction ruled unjust leads to a redemption. New York Times. http://www.nytimes.com/1998/05/29/nyregion/a-conviction-ruled-unjust-leads-to-a-redemption.html?pagewanted=print, (accessed 09.05.10.)

Haynes v. Washington, 373 U.S. 503 (1963).

Huffington Post, 2011, May 25. Kevin Fox receives $8 million in damages; wrongly accused of raping and murdering daughter. Available online at: http://www.huffingtonpost.com/2010/04/08/kevin-fox-receives-8-mill_n_530272.html

Inbau, F.E., Reid, J.E., Buckley, J.P., Jayne, B.C., 2001. Criminal Interrogation and Confessions, fourth ed. Aspen Publishers. Inc, Gathersburg, MD.

Inbau, F.E., Reid, J.E., Buckley, J.P., Jayne, B.C., 2013. Criminal Interrogation and Confessions, fifth ed. Jones and Bartlett Learning, LLC, Burlington, MA.

The Innocence Project, Available online at: http://www.innocenceproject.org/understand/False-Confessions.php (accessed 01.04.13.)

Kassin, S.M., 2006. A critical appraisal of modern police interrogations. In: Williamson, T. (Ed.), Investigative Interviewing: Rights, Research, Regulation, Willan Publishing, Devon, UK, pp. 207–228.

Kassin, S.M., 2007. Internalized false confessions. In: Toglia, M., Read, J., Ross, D., Lindsay, R. (Eds.), Handbook of Eyewitness Psychology: Volume 1, Memory for Events, Mahwah, NJ: Wiley, pp. 175–192.

Kassin, S.M., Gudjonsson, G.H., 2004. The psychology of confessions evidence: A review of the literature and issues. Psychological Science in the Public Interest 5, 33–67.

Kassin, S.M., Wrightsman, L.S., 1985. Confession evidence. In: Kassin, S., Wrightsman, L. (Eds.), The Psychology of Evidence and Trial Procedure, Sage, Beverly Hills, CA, pp. 67–94.

Leyra v. Denno, 347 U.S. 556 (1954).

Leo, R.A., 2008. Police Interrogation and American Justice. Harvard University Press, Cambridge, MA.

Lynum v. Illinois, 372 U.S. 528 (1963).

McNabb v. U.S., 318 U.S. 332 (1943).

McCrary, G., 2009. Who killed Stephanie Crowe? In: Rossmo, D.K. (Ed.), Criminal Investigative Failures, CRC Press, Boca Raton, FL, pp. 143–178.

Mallory v. United States, 354 U.S. 449 (1957).

Miranda v. Arizona 384 U.S. 436 (1966).

Northwestern Law–Blum Legal Clinic, 2009. Burge victim Ronald Kitchen latest Illinois death row exoneree. Available at: http://www.law.northwestern.edu/wrongfulconvictions/exonerations/ilKitchenRSummary.html (accessed 07.05.10.)

Ofshe, R., Leo, R., 1997. The social psychology of police interrogation: The theory and classification of true and false confessions. Studies in Law, Politics and Society 16, 189–251.

Omnibus Crime Control and Safe Streets Act (42 USC § 3701 et seq.)

Reid et al., Website. Available online at: http://www.reid.com (accessed 26.03.13.)

Sauer, M., 2004, May 28. Tuite trial jury's road to verdict revealed. San Diego Union Tribune, p. B1. Available online at: http://legacy.utsandiego.com/news/metro/crowe/20040528-9999-1mi28tuite.html

Sauer, M., Sharma, A., 2011, October 22. $7.25 million settlement reached in Stephanie Crowe murder case. KPBS News. Available online at: http://www.kpbs.org/news/2011/oct/21/7-million-settlement-reached-stephanie-crowe-murde/

Smith, B., 2006. They promised Kevin Fox they would stop grilling him—if he'd just say his daughter's death had been an accident. Adapted from *Chicago* magazine, July 2006. Available online at: http://www.law.northwestern.edu/wrongfulconvictions/issues/causesandremedies/falseconfessions/KevinFox.pdf

Sullivan, T.P., 2004. Police experiences with recording custodial interrogations. Special Report of Northwestern University School of Law Center on Wrongful Convictions. Available online at: http://mcadams.posc.mu.edu/Recording_Interrogations.pdf

Zellner, T., and Associates. Second Amended Complaint. 2006 - court filing in Kevin Fox v. OFFICE OF THE SHERIFF OF WILL COUNTY, et al. Available online at: https://antipolygraph.org/cgi-bin/forums/YaBB.pl?num=1146566231

Wilson v. US, 162 U.S. 613, (1896).

CHAPTER 11

Intimate Violence

Brent E. Turvey

KEY TERMS

Domestic homicide A type of homicide that occurs when one family member, household member, or intimate kills another.

Domestic violence A general term that may be used to describe physical aggression between family members, household members, or intimates.

Intimate terrorism A type of intimate personal violence in which violence is one tactic in a larger pattern of power and control. It involves more frequent per-couple incidents, more severe violence, and results in more serious injury.

Intimate violence A particular type of domestic violence that occurs when a current or former intimate relationship partner becomes physically violent toward the other.

Situational couple violence A type of violence that occurs in the context of a specific disagreement that spirals into a violent incident. It is an isolated reaction to conflict and does not involve a larger pattern of power and control.

Violent resistance Situation in which a female victim defends herself against her aggressive male partner.

Domestic violence is a general term that may be used to describe physical aggression between family members, household members, or intimates. Accordingly, *intimate violence* is a particular type of domestic violence that occurs when a current or former intimate relationship partner becomes physically violent toward the other. It does not necessarily involve people who live together, but those involved must be or have been involved in a deep personal relationship of some kind. Often it is a sexual or romantic relationship, although it can involve non-sexual relationships. In cases of intimate violence, barring mental disorder or defect, the motivation is almost exclusively about power, anger/revenge, profit, or some combination.

This chapter discusses the dynamics of abuse in intimate relationships. It also discusses some of the major risk factors associated with intimate violence, dispelling certain myths along the way. The chapter closes with a focus on law enforcement-involved intimate homicide, using this particular sub-type to provide a contrast with the many others that the victimologist may encounter. Case examples and research findings are adduced as needed.

319

Forensic Victimology. http://dx.doi.org/10.1016/B978-0-12-408084-3.00011-9

THE DYNAMICS OF INTIMATE VIOLENCE

The dynamics of intimate violence—the way it begins, expresses, and evolves—are complex. Yet they are driven by a sense of overall powerlessness experienced on the part of the aggressor. This powerlessness is expressed by the assertion of power and control over the victim. As explained in Burke (2007; p. 555): "Outside the realm of criminal law, social scientists almost universally describe domestic violence as an ongoing pattern of conduct motivated by the batterer's desire for power and control over the victim." Burke then goes on to explain more precisely why domestic violence is different from other forms of interpersonal violence, with respect to qualitative and quantitative features (pp. 567–569):

A. Quantitative Factors: Frequency and Duration

Compared to assaults between strangers or nonintimate acquaintances, violence between intimates is more likely to involve repeated assaults over a period of time, rather than a one-time incident of violence. One quantitative aspect of domestic violence is its frequency. One expert estimates that sixty-three percent of men who assault their wives repeat the behavior. That estimate is consistent with the results of the National Violence Against Women Survey, which found that more than sixty-five percent of the women who reported being physically assaulted by an intimate partner said they were victimized multiple times by that same person. Nearly twenty percent of the assaulted women recalled ten or more incidents, and the average number of assaults by the same partner was nearly seven. Domestic violence is quantitatively distinct from nonintimate violence not only in its frequency, but also in its duration. The same survey found that nearly seventy percent of women who had been assaulted by an intimate partner reported that their victimization lasted more than one year. For more than a quarter of the women, the victimization occurred over more than five years, and the average duration of the violence was four and a half years. Indeed, even the language used to describe the experience of domestic violence reflects its frequent and prolonged character. We say that a woman who has been assaulted by her husband is "battered" or "beaten," or has been subjected to "domestic violence," suggesting a general status or a continued phenomenon. In contrast, when a person has been assaulted by a stranger or casual acquaintance, we say he has been "attacked" or "assaulted," or has gotten into a "fight," suggesting a one-time act of violence, not violence more generally.

B. Qualitative Factors: Power and Control

The frequency and duration of domestic violence distinguish it quantitatively from other examples of criminal violence, but they also give rise to a qualitative distinction. Social scientists universally speak of domestic violence in terms that transcend the physical injuries from individual incidents of assault. Instead, they speak of domestic violence as a pattern of conduct that uses physical battering as just one method of inflicting emotional trauma.

Although social scientists caution that there is no singular profile of a domestic abuser's psychology, they commonly use a framework of power and control to explain the coercive nature of domestic violence, emphasizing that the intended harm goes beyond physical injury. Empirical evidence supports the theory that domestic violence is often driven by a desire to control. For example, men who are jealous, controlling, or verbally abusive are statistically more likely to assault, rape, or stalk their partners. Many domestic violence offenders suffer from low self-esteem and little self-control, and may physically retaliate against exercises of independence by their intimate partners.

In a discussion of the contradictions found in domestic violence research, specifically regarding the issue of male versus female victims,[1] Ver Steegh (2005) ultimately refers to a useful domestic violence typology that may be of some assistance (pp. 1382–1384):

> Disquieting inconsistencies [in domestic violence research], as well as major contradictions, are either ignored or become the subject of rancorous cross-professional debate. For example, for the past twenty-five years, researchers have engaged in an intense debate concerning how often assaults occur and whether men and women are equally violent. The controversy stems from the contradictory findings of various studies. Epidemiological "family conflict" studies show higher overall assault rates with nearly equal rates of assault by men and women. In contrast, so-called "crime" studies and police call data show lower overall annual assault rates and much higher rates of assault by men than by women.
>
> The "family conflict" studies have been criticized by service providers and some feminist scholars who challenge the methodology of the studies, particularly the use of reliance on the Conflict Tactics Scale. These critics believe that the studies focus too heavily on specific acts of aggression and too little on resulting injury and the context of the behavior. "However, both groups of researchers agree that women are ten times as likely as men to be injured as a result of

---

[1]There is a great deal of literature out there on the subject of female victims of domestic abuse. The author agrees that women are far more often the victims of domestic abuse. According to Rennison (2003), 85% of intimate partner violence victims were, in fact, women. However, the author also agrees that men may be victims as well. This is discussed further. Bearing that in mind, the generic term *victims* is far more appropriate for use in objective victimology.

domestic violence." Differences also stem from definitional issues. The family conflict researchers define domestic violence narrowly in terms of physical assault, while service providers and clinical researchers define it broadly to include all types of maltreatment.

In the final analysis, despite the high level of acrimony, these studies may not actually contradict each other. As Murray Straus explains, researchers may in fact be observing and measuring different phenomena. He asserts that both groups of researchers are correct. They are merely studying different populations experiencing different types of violence. He speculates that, "these two types of violence probably have different etiologies and probably require different types of intervention."

Researcher Michael P. Johnson has taken the process of integrating competing studies to its conclusion by developing a comprehensive typology that accounts for contradictory research and connects contrasting perspectives. Based on his analysis of the "family conflict" and the "feminist" studies discussed above, he concludes that women's advocates and service providers are primarily observing one type of domestic violence, Intimate Terrorism, while family conflict researchers are predominantly measuring another type of violence, Situational Couple Violence.

The Johnson Typology of Intimate Personal Violence (IPV) provides four discrete categories that are meant take an offender's use of threats, economic control, privilege and punishment, children, isolation, emotional abuse, and sexual control into account. These are *intimate terrorism* (IT), *violent resistance* (VR), *situational couple violence* (SCV), and *mutual violent control* (MVC). They are determined based on offender motivation and the overall pattern of offense behavior. According to Johnson (2006; pp. 1009–1010):

> "[I]ntimate terrorism[...]" refers to relationships in which only one of the spouses is violent and controlling. The other spouse is either nonviolent or has used violence but is not controlling.... [Then there are] cases in which the focal spouse is violent but not controlling, and his or her partner is violent and controlling. I call it *violent resistance*, and it is almost entirely a woman's type of violence in this sample of heterosexual relationships. Of course, that is because in these marriages almost all of the intimate terrorism is perpetrated by men, and in some cases the wives do respond with violence, although rarely are they also controlling.... "[S]ituational couple violence[...]" [refers to] individual noncontrolling violence in a dyadic context in which neither of the spouses is violent and controlling.... "[M]utual violent control[...]" refers to controlling violence in a relationship in which both spouses are violent and controlling.

Ver Steegh (2005) actually provides a more useful discussion of the Johnson IPV Typology for our purposes. Of *intimate terrorism,* she writes (pp. 1387–1390):

1. Intimate Terrorism
   a. The Johnson Typology: Intimate Terrorism

   Intimate Terrorism (IT) is the type of violence observed in battered women's shelters and measured by crime and clinical studies. In Intimate Terrorism, violence is one tactic in a larger pattern of power and control. Control is exerted by making threats, wielding economic control, applying privilege and punishment, manipulating and threatening children, isolating the victim, and inflicting emotional and sexual abuse. As compared with other types of violence, Intimate Terrorism involves more frequent per couple incidents, more severe violence, and results in more serious injury. This type of violence is quite likely to escalate over time.

   Intimate Terrorism is nearly always perpetrated by men upon women, and female victims are more likely to suffer from Post Traumatic Stress Syndrome (PTSD), depression, and poor health. These women actively seek formal help and are likely to leave the abuser. Intimate Terrorism accounts for somewhere between eleven percent and thirty-five percent of domestic violence situations....

   i. Victims of Intimate Terrorism

   While most research regarding victims of domestic violence does not explicitly distinguish between Intimate Terrorism and Situational Couple Violence, much of the research seems focused on female victims of Intimate Terrorism. The most commonly held view of "battered women" is based on "the traumatization model" which includes themes such as "learned helplessness" and "battered women's syndrome." Some women who are victims of Intimate Terrorism suffer from Post Traumatic Stress Disorder as a result of the abuse. Victims experience painful and serious physical injuries, as well as depression, PTSD, suicide attempts, and substance abuse. Victimization is also related to difficulty maintaining employment and a permanent residence.

   However, contrary to popular belief, many victims of domestic violence leave the violent relationship. In fact, Richard Gelles reports that women who experience the most frequent and severe violence (arguably victims of Intimate Terrorism) are more likely to leave. This is consistent with research demonstrating victims' use of a "vast array of personal strategies and help resources." For example, in one study, researcher Lee Bowker found that women used seven personal strategies (such as talking to or avoiding their partner, hiding or running away, threatening to call police or file divorce, or fighting back physically) to end the abuse, after which they accessed informal and formal resources (including police, clergy, physicians, and lawyers). Victims, therefore, are not necessarily passive but may be active survivors of abuse.

Of *situational couple violence,* she writes (pp. 1394–1396):

2. Situational Couple Violence
   a. The Johnson Typology: Situational Couple Violence
   Situational Couple Violence (SCV) occurs in the context of a specific disagreement that spirals into a violent incident; it is an isolated reaction to conflict and does not involve a larger pattern of power and control. Situational Couple Violence generally involves fewer per couple incidents than Intimate Terrorism, and the violence is generally less severe and less likely to result in injury. It is important to note, however, that Situational Couple Violence is not simply a milder form of Intimate Terrorism. Situational Couple Violence can involve severe violence; however, the violence is not part of a larger pattern of control.
   Situational Couple Violence is the type of domestic violence measured in the epidemiological "family conflict" studies, and it is initiated nearly equally by men and women. However, there is evidence that men and women are differently motivated and that women suffer more injury and negative consequences resulting from the violence. These consequences include higher levels of depression, low self-esteem, and substance abuse. This type of violence usually does not escalate and may in fact de-escalate or stop altogether. Situational Couple Violence is the most common form of domestic violence accounting for an estimated fifty-one percent of cases....
   i. Victims of Situational Couple Violence
   There is a common assumption that all victims of domestic violence should want to leave their relationships. Obviously, many should and do leave, including some victims of Situational Couple Violence. However, others want to live safely in their current relationships, seeking only an end to the violence. As compared to victims of Intimate Terrorism, victims of Situational Couple Violence are more likely to voluntarily choose to work on the relationship rather than leave it. Campbell, Rose, Kub, and Nedd suggest that victims engage in "a process of achieving nonviolence," which includes negotiating with the partner and implementing strategies to end the violence; this research is likely to apply to victims of Situational Couple Violence. Similarly, Campbell, Miller, Cardwell, and Belknap found that after two and one-half years, only twenty-five percent of battered women were still being abused. Forty-seven percent were in a relationship with no violence (half were in new relationships and half in the same

relationship, but violence free for one year), and twenty percent had left the abuser but not entered into another relationship. One might speculate that victims in relationships that became free of violence for at least one year were more likely to have been victims of Situational Couple Violence.

Relatively fewer services are available to victims who choose to stay in their relationships. However, these couples could benefit from monitoring and enhancement of their conflict resolution skills. Such support would also be beneficial to Situational Couple Violence victims who decide to leave the relationship. Thought should also be given to the reality that some of the victims of Situational Couple Violence are men. Even though female victims of Situational Couple Violence are more likely to experience injury and other detrimental effects than are male victims, some male victims might seek supportive services.

Of *violent resistance,* she writes (p. 1398):

iv. Violent Resistance

Violent Resistance involves situations where a female victim defends herself against her aggressive male partner. In one study, researchers found that victims who resist violence, either physically or verbally, were twice as likely to be injured.

While some perpetrators of Situational Couple Violence are female, they must be carefully distinguished from women who are violent resisters of Intimate Terrorism. Confusing a woman defending herself from Intimate Terrorism with a woman perpetrator of Situational Couple Violence could be a deadly mistake for her and her children. A woman resisting Intimate Terrorism (and her children) needs immediate protection, not anger management techniques. The possibility of such a mistake illustrates a danger inherent in the creation and use of typologies. At the same time, "a monolithic etiological model of marital aggression is inadequate to capture the diversity of relationship and individual dynamics in physically aggressive marriages."

Ver Steegh's discussion of the Johnson IPV Typology ends here with an important caveat about the limitations of any typology. General categories can be a useful theoretical lens at the outset of any victimology; however, they are invariably limited for meaningful application in a particular case. The reason is that individual cases may involve multiple categories of violence at different times. Also, there are many specific dynamic variables to consider that a general typology will not anticipate—such as drugs, alcohol, or mental illness, to name but a few. Therefore, it is important for victimologists to understand how individual relationship dynamics can be perceived and communicated, to investigate and grasp what precisely motivates them, and to assess the subsequent risk and actual exposure involved. According to Mills (1999), a good way to consistently describe the different kinds of abuse dynamics that can occur in a relationship is via the behavior motivational typology presented next. The caution is that, as with any behavioral motivational typology, the categories are not exclusive. The following has been adapted from Mills (1999), with the sex-specific term *woman* replaced with the generic term *victim*:

1. *Rejection:* This includes criticizing, punishing, or judging the victim, refusing to help the person, and routinely discounting the victim's opinion.
2. *Degradation:* This includes verbally abusing and physically humiliating the victim.
3. *Terrorization:* This involves threatening to harm the victim or the victim's loved ones and punishing the victim by playing on his or her fears. It can include behaviors such as setting unrealistic expectations with threat of loss and harm if they are not met.
4. *Social isolation:* This involves preventing the victim from engaging in normal social activities and other interactions with people.
5. *Missocialization:* This involves corrupting the victim by encouraging the victim to engage in criminal or delinquent behavior.
6. *Exploitation:* This involves using the victim to support the abuser and his or her abusive lifestyle.
7. *Emotional unresponsiveness:* This includes showing detachment and lack of involvement with the victim and interacting only if absolutely necessary. It also includes failure to express affection, caring, and love toward the victim.
8. *Close confinement:* This includes restricting the victim's movement, even to the point of imprisonment.

RISK AND EXPOSURE

It is generally well known that drugs and alcohol play a significant role in domestic violence. Some studies have shown that as many as 92% of domestic batterers used alcohol or drugs before domestic assaults (Brookoff et al., 1997), and that the use of alcohol or drugs is one of the most significant risk factors for domestic violence (Bennett et al., 1994). Whatever the current or local numbers surrounding the student, it is enough to know that the association between substance abuse and domestic violence will make itself clear in criminal casework to the point of exhaustion. It is, however, a mistake to assume that this association is necessarily causal. In some cases, substance abuse may be symptomatic of other issues (i.e., as a self-medicating/coping mechanism for a mental defect or disorder) as opposed to being the explicit reason for subsequent violence.

Less well known is the fact that many domestic abuse and neglect deaths fail to be counted as domestic homicides. For example, a study conducted by Johnson, Lutz, and Websdale (2000) revealed that, in Florida, the FDLE itemized 230 domestic homicides for 1994. Researchers went on to discover that there were actually 319 domestic homicides, roughly a third more than had been officially counted. In 1995, the FDLE list itemized 195 domestic homicides, and the final total was 295. One of the other reasons cited for this consistent misclassification was the fact that the law enforcement agencies did not code boyfriend/girlfriend homicides as domestic when the two people did not officially live together. Consequently, as bad as the problem of intimate homicide appears when one examines the statistics, it is actually much worse.

According to the research presented in Johnson et al. (2000), a number of circumstances increase one's risk of domestic homicide (written from the perspective of female victims). The high-risk factors are as follows:

1. Prior history of domestic violence
   - Escalation of violence
   - Past homicide attempts, choking
   - Rape and sexual violence
   - Violence toward pets
   - Violence during pregnancy
2. Escaping violent relationships
   - Marital estrangement
3. Obsessive-possessiveness
   - Extreme jealousy
   - Stalking
   - Obsessiveness about the relationship
   - Suicide attempts or threats
4. Prior police involvement
5. Prior criminal history of the perpetrator
6. Threats to kill
7. Alcohol/drug problems
8. Protection orders
9. Acute perceptions of betrayal
10. Child custody disputes
    - Past attempts to kill or abduct children
    - Severe abuse of children
    - Sexual abuse of children

11. Mental illness of perpetrator (paranoia, schizophrenia, depression)
    - Severe abuse as child
12. Hostage-taking
13. Children are hers not his
14. Change in circumstances
    - Unemployment
15. Her fear!

Depending on the facts and the victim's perceptions in the particular case, whether the research is deemed to suggest a greater degree of risk or a risk of death is far less important to the court than is the court's per se heightened vigilance when confronted with any number of these factors.

Victimologists must look for and consider these factors in the preparation of *any* victimology. The existence of any one or more of them (aside from risk factors 13 and 14) should be enough to place a person in the medium- to high-exposure category for being the victim of violence, if not homicide. Sources of information that can have a direct bearing on these factors include medical records, court records, mental health records, phone records, email records, prescriptions on hand, personal toxicology, and personal diaries. Failure to gather this kind of information in this or any case leaves the analyst in the dark with respect to the actual risks and exposures of a particular victim.

DOMESTIC HOMICIDE

Domestic homicide occurs when one family member, household member, or intimate kills another. It is often the result of accumulated as opposed to situational rage, and therefore it is often the culmination of long-term fighting, abuse, or betrayal. It also frequently occurs in association with drug and alcohol use. Subsequently, it can involve some of the more violent and aberrant behaviors that investigators will encounter.

It is well known that domestic homicide is a regular occurrence in the United States, to say nothing of the rest of the world. In the United States alone, more than three women are murdered by an intimate partner every day (Bureau of Justice Statistics [BJS], 2003). According to FBI statistics, domestic homicide is more than twice as likely to involve in the killing of a female victim (NIJ, 1996) and regularly results in the death of more than one person at the hands of the offender, as well as the offender's own death.[2]

---

[2]According to a Florida study conducted in 1994 (Task Force, 1997), 38% of domestic homicides involve multiple victims, usually combining a spouse homicide and suicide or child homicide. According to a San Francisco study from 1995 to 1996, 43% of the male murders in domestic homicides killed themselves after killing the woman (Hallinan, 1997).

With intimate homicides, it is particularly vital to establish the context of any violent behavior. Given that exposure to domestic violence and abuse increases the risk of domestic homicide, those risk factors must be considered as well. As Wilson (2005) observes, these include the age of the woman, being a mother of children not related to the male aggressor, and making threats to leave or actually leaving the male. She also notes with respect to domestic homicide, "there does seem to be a tendency for men who kill their female intimates to do so when the women are in their child-bearing years." Wilson goes on to discuss the issue of threats to leave or actual departure as a major precipitating event, citing some fairly alarming research (pp. 307–309):

> Perhaps the largest single trigger for male violence is a woman's threat or attempt to leave her partner. Ironically, where domestic violence is already a problem, the very act that is undertaken in order to assure survival often ends up activating a dose of lethal violence.
>
> The evidence that women are at a particularly high risk of violence of homicide when they are poised to leave or recently have left a relationship is overwhelming. Three quarters of homicide victims and eighty-five percent of victims of severe (but non-fatal) abuse had tried to leave the relationship within the past year. In situations where abuse is ongoing, leaving can end the violence, but when it does not, the abuse often becomes more extreme.
>
> According to one report, an attempt to leave was the precipitating factor in forty-five percent of femicides. In another study by Brewer and Paulsen, while female-initiated separation was a motivating factor in fifty-six percent of the cases of wife-killing, this trend was not found in situations where men initiated the separation. In a study of 293 women killed by intimates in North Carolina from 1991 to 1993, Beth Moracco and her colleagues at the University of North Carolina School for Public Health found that forty-two percent had been killed after they threatened to separate, tried to separate, or had recently separated from their partners.
>
> Women are at particularly high risk in the two months after the separation. The proximity in time of the deadly attack to the separation is not a coincidence. In cases in which the husband's abuse does turn deadly, it is often clear that the event that precipitated the lethal attack was her departure. In the aftermath of uxoricide, it is often noted that husbands did precisely what they threatened to do, and husbands often admit that their spouse's desertion was the cause of the deadly violence. Hence, there is rarely any question as to what motivated the murder—in these cases, the women who died were attempting to leave their killers.

Just as lethal assaults increase when a wife threatens to leave, so do non-lethal assaults. As Wilson and Daly point out, "[a] credible threat of violent death can very effectively control people, and the...evidence on risks to estranged wives suggests that such threats by husbands are often sincere." This remark underscores the proprietary aspect of this type of violence. In fact, sexual jealousy and fear of desertion both elicit similar aggressive reactions. Clearly, killing a wife is not utilitarian if the goal is to assure access for future procreation. Ironically, what motivates this type of homicide is clearly not a desire to be free of the woman. Were that the case, presumably the man would allow her to leave. Instead, Wilson, Johnson, and Daily propose that uxoricide occurs when male proprietariness gets carried to an extreme. In many cases, the male may have used the threat of lethal violence in the past in a less counterproductive way to successfully prevent his wife from leaving. Proprietary uxoricide may occur in cases where men use more force than intended, attempting to intimidate their wives into staying. Equally likely, however, is the possibility that the man was simply carrying out a promise he made the woman before she left, adopting the attitude, "If I can't have her, then no one shall."

In such cases, homicide can be a proprietary expression. Arguably, this may be associated with historical or cultural views of certain groups of people as property, reinforced by criminal law that has been drafted and interpreted accordingly. As will be shown in Chapter 17, regarding offender perspectives, related practices and traditions have been used to rationalize horrific acts of sexual violence.

PREGNANCY AS A RISK FACTOR

The previous section begs the question of pregnancy as a risk factor. In recent years, there has been considerable media coverage of intimate homicides involving pregnant women. Headlines, copy, and pundits have repeatedly and incorrectly affirmed that homicide is *the* leading cause or *a* leading cause of death for pregnant women. Much of the related reporting has been biased, inflammatory, or just plain uninformed. This circumstance has been made worse by reporters and criminal profilers citing incorrect or non-existent data and research to support their particular view.

The actual study at the heart of these numbers, published in the *American Journal of Public Health* (Chang et al., 2005), reports that 31% of all pregnancy-related deaths that were also injury-related deaths between 1991 and 1999 were the result of homicide. Specifically, they found that homicide was not the leading cause of death for pregnant women as many in the media have been eagerly reporting:

> For the years 1991 through 1999, 7342 deaths were reported to the PMSS [Pregnancy Mortality Surveillance System]. A majority of the reported deaths (n = 4200 [57.2%]) were pregnancy-related (e.g., they occurred during or within 1 year of pregnancy and were causally related to pregnancy).* A total of 1993 deaths (27.1%) were pregnancy associated and injury related.
>
> The remaining 1149 (15.7%) deaths included those that were pregnancy associated but not caused by injuries or pregnancy complications and those that were not pregnancy associated (e.g., the time interval between the end of pregnancy and maternal death exceeded 1 year).
>
> Of all pregnancy-associated injury deaths (n = 1993), 617 (31.0%) women died as a result of homicide, ranking homicide as the second leading cause of total reported injury deaths among pregnant women and postpartum women, following deaths caused by motor vehicle accidents (44.1%). The rest of the pregnancy-associated injury deaths were attributed to unintentional injuries (12.7%), suicide (10.3%), and other (2.0%)....
>
> When interpreting this report's finding that homicide is the second leading cause of injury related death among pregnant and postpartum women, it is important to note that our findings regarding homicides involving pregnant and postpartum women are similar to national statistics on homicide among all women of reproductive age (regardless of whether they are pregnant or not).
>
> *Chang J, Elam-Evans LD, Berg CJ, et al. Pregnancy related mortality surveillance: United States, 1991–1999. *MMWR Surveill Summ.* 2003;52:1–8.

According to the study, there were 4,200 pregnancy-related deaths between 1991 and 1999; these were deaths that occurred during or within one year of pregnancy and were causally related to pregnancy. Note that 1,993 (47.5%) of these pregnancy-related deaths were also injury related; 613 (14.6%) of pregnancy-related deaths were the result of homicide. So homicide is not, in fact, the leading cause of death among pregnant women, nor is it even the leading cause of death among all pregnancy-associated injury deaths. This matters because certain profilers have no difficulty going on television and stating the opposite—and the media is quick to repeat it, and the public is very quick to believe.

Certainly, any victim's pregnancy is a potential motive for any violence she might suffer. It must be considered when preparing a victimology. However, as with all factors, it must be considered in its particular context, and its value must not be overstated simply because it makes a good sound bite. This is one of those areas where experts can do the most good by educating themselves so that they may subsequently educate the public in an honest and informed fashion when asked to do so.

ORDERS OF PROTECTION AND SEPARATION ASSAULT

One of the risk/exposure factors mentioned previously is the issuance of a protective order by the court—barring the offender from contact with the victim. The issue of "Orders of Protection" or "Restraining Orders" is deceptively complex. On the face of things, it seems reasonable that all victims of domestic violence should want or should have protection orders in place, both to notify law enforcement of their situation and to provide a solid foundation for law enforcement or legal actions in the future. However, as explained in Tarr (2007; pp. 388–390):

> Not all women should get an Order for Protection. As a threshold matter, women do not easily define themselves as "victims of domestic violence" because, as with many social ills in our society, denial serves as a psychological means of surviving. For decades, social service providers, religious leaders and the justice system ignored domestic violence or blamed the victim, resulting in a disincentive to self-identify.
>
> A woman may decide that she should NOT get an Order for Protection to escape a physically dangerous situation because the period when a woman decides to leave is the time she is most vulnerable. Martha Mahoney coined the term "separation assault" to capture this moment of extreme danger. Women in these situations may appear to be clueless to outsiders, but they are often able to read when the violence is going to escalate and thus know when the time is right to escape. Getting an Order for Protection is only getting a piece of paper, a court order that says to "stay away"; it does not give the woman a personal bodyguard. In most jurisdictions, the police will serve the perpetrator and assist the victim at the moment that the perpetrator is required to move out of any shared premises or pick up personal property. However, after that, it is a piece of paper and only the beginning of the story.
>
> If a batterer is accustomed to flouting the law, the Order may be useless. One of my clients had an Order for Protection and her estranged husband came to her home and shot her. In less extreme cases, the batterer will try to test the boundaries of the Order, and

often harassment on the phone and in person at the workplace is part of the game. At what point does she call the police to have him arrested for violating the order? Would an employer assess her as being hysterical or whiney for calling the police over what is viewed as a "trivial matter," or suggest that she has been too passive for waiting too long to call?

Depending on the jurisdiction, the police may or may not arrest the batterer when he violates the Order, and each time he gets away without consequence, he feels more empowered. Many jurisdictions have "mandatory arrest" laws that require arrest if the officer has probable cause to believe a violation has taken place. Although it may be a means of asserting some strength for the victim, the arrest can cause economic and emotional discord for children. Research indicates that despite the arrests, only a small portion of domestic violence cases are prosecuted; thus, some locales have adopted "no drop" policies that range from eliminating all prosecutorial discretion so that all cases are prosecuted, to less rigid assumptions of prosecution.

A key element in the "no drop" policies is the elimination of the victim's participation in the decision to prosecute, though she may be subpoenaed to testify regardless of the consequences. Therefore, the employer who sees an Order for Protection and subsequent invocation of the criminal justice system as a means of gaining a reliable employee is ignoring the reality of what may come in terms of lost time on the job and emotional turmoil in the employee's life. Even if arrested, even if prosecuted, even if tried, and even if convicted, there is a high likelihood that the perpetrator will not serve time, will not be physically removed from the vicinity of the victim, or will not even be deterred by the process.

The decision to get a protection order is an individual one. In some instances, it is a reasonable precaution that will have a specific and reliable result. For others, it may be irrelevant or actually make matters worse. Therefore, the failure to seek and receive a protection order is not in itself evidence that a complainant feels safe. In fact, precisely the opposite may be true.

This issue also relates to studies which have demonstrated that a woman's perception of the likelihood that she will suffer future violence is a reliable predictor of an actual future assault (Harding and Helweg-Larsen, 2009; Heckert and Gondolf, 2004; see also Cattaneo, Bell, Goodman, and Dutton, 2007). As reported in Harding and Helweg-Larsen (2009; p. 75):

Every year in the United States approximately 1.5 million women experience a physical or sexual assault from a current or former intimate partner. Nationwide, approximately 25% of all women have experienced a physical or sexual assault by a current or former intimate partner or date at some point in their lifetime. Because victimized women are often assaulted on multiple occasions, national prevalence rates of intimate partner violence (IPV) and sexual assaults amount to roughly 4.8 million incidents per year....

Not surprisingly, female victims also seek mental health services and utilize medical care (e.g., emergency medical services, hospital, or physician visits) at disproportionately greater rates than male victims (Arias and Corso 2005). Severe IPV not only carries the risk of serious physical and psychological injury, but is also a significant predictor of future victimization for women (Cattaneo and Goodman 2005; Krause et al. 2006). Given the associated risk of future abuse for victims of severe IPV, it is important to examine how women perceive their risk for re-abuse in their relationships.

The Harding and Helweg-Larsen (2009) study concluded (p. 84): "Women's risk perceptions are often accurate and, as supported by the current findings, related to intended relationship behavior"; and therefore personal "[r]isk perceptions remain a vital consideration when helping women to maximize their safety and research should continue to explore the correlates and potential consequences of perceived risk in a condition-specific manner."

In short, when victims of domestic violence are to the point where they are making reports to police, filing restraining orders with the court, or seeking refuge in a woman's shelter, then it is likely that their fears of being victimized are well founded. These fears are also more likely than not to become a reality. By taking any of these steps, they risk their safety and that of any children in their care, which is why evidence of these must be given the proper weight in any victimological assessment.

Though it is uncertain precisely what was in the petition, and whether the order was properly denied by the judge or not, it is clear that the future danger perceived by the victim was very real.

CASE EXAMPLE:

Naomie Breton

Consider the case of Naomie Breton of Lantana, Florida. In 2012, she petitioned a restraining order against her estranged boyfriend, Roosevelt Mondesir (see Figure 11-1). As reported in Skrzypek (2012):

> Despite her efforts to protect herself, the Lantana woman who was set on fire on Monday had filed a restraining order against her alleged attacker.
>
> Less than two weeks before her estranged boyfriend Roosevelt Mondesir allegedly assaulted her, Naomie Breton detailed their rocky and sometimes abusive relationship in a petition for a restraining order.

CASE EXAMPLE: *CONTINUED*

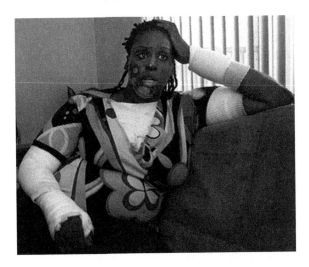

FIGURE 11-1

In 2012, Naomie Breton petitioned for a restraining order against her estranged boyfriend. A judge denied it. Less than two weeks later, he set her on fire at a gas station.

"I need to file this. I need to keep him away from me, so I did," said Breton.

An hour after filing the order, a judge denied the restraining order citing what he termed as a lack of supporting facts.

"I felt let down by the state of Florida and I felt, what do I have to, what am I suppose to do?" said Breton. Out of choices, Breton said she tried to fix the problem on her own deciding to meet Mondesir that morning at the gas station. "If I had that restraining order, I wouldn't feel fear or pressure," said Breton.

When a victim of domestic violence files for a restraining order at the Palm Beach County Courthouse only to find their petition is denied, advocates for abuse victims say they should come to places like the YWCA for help and advice.

"Maybe whatever was in that restraining order did not detail the history that existed.

That's why we're always trying to reach out to victims," said Mary Cauthen, a YWCA advocate....

One of the biggest hurdles the YWCA said victims face is what needs to be included in a restraining order.

"It can't be something that happened six months ago and you've been back with a person who you were afraid of, that isn't imminent fear," said Palm Beach County family division Judge Jack Cox. While Judge Cox did not make the decision in the Breton case, he explained judges can only base their rulings on what is provided by victims.

Though it is uncertain precisely what was in the petition, and whether the order was properly denied by the judge or not, it is clear that the future danger perceived by the victim was very real.

THE PERFECT VICTIM: INTIMATE VIOLENCE BY LAW ENFORCEMENT[3]

Most law enforcement officers have been trained to understand that domestic violence is a serious crime that can result in serious injury or death.[4] They have also likely been trained to understand that domestic violence happens regardless of socio-economic status, race, ethnicity, age, education, employment status, or marital status. They have further likely been trained or experienced that domestic batterers use emotional, psychological, economic, and physical abuse as a way of controlling their intimate partners. In extreme cases, this control is far reaching, involving such things as screening the victim's phone calls, alienating family members, forbidding long-time friends from visiting the residence, preventing the development of new friends, and constantly monitoring the victim's conversations and whereabouts. Even in the absence of formal training, certainly most law enforcement officers have responded to a domestic violence call and handed a domestic violence informational pamphlet to a victim that contains at least some of these facts. This knowledge and training may be ignored, however, when the accused is one of their own.

The Numbers and "Professional Courtesy"

Research has shown that police families are more likely to experience domestic violence than others. This may be due to the nature of the work and the personality of those who are attracted to it. According to one source, citing two different studies (Davidow and Teichroeb, 2003):

> Police officers may be more prone to mistreating their families than others, partly because some attracted to such work are more authoritarian and liable to misuse their training, experts say. Although more in-depth research is needed, two informal studies report rates of physical violence in law-enforcement homes of up to 40 percent. One study was done by Arizona State University family-studies professor Leanor Boulin Johnson in the late 1980s, while the other was published in the Police Studies journal in 1992.

According to another source (Brannan, 2003):

> Domestic violence is 2 to 4 times more common in police families than in the general population. In two separate studies, 40% of police

---

[3]Portions of this section were previously published in Turvey (2003) and Turvey (2013).
[4]In 1993, 2,289 men and women were killed by an intimate partner. This toll accounted for 32.2% of all murders committed during that year. In the year 2000, the total number of men and women killed by an intimate partner dropped to 1,687. However, this new toll accounted for 37.2% of all murders committed during that year (Rennison, 2003). The numbers dropped, but the proportions increased. Subsequently, intimate partner homicides remain a significant issue for law enforcement, currently filling more than a third of the national homicide caseload.

officers self-report that they have used violence against their domestic partners within the last year. In the general population, it's estimated that domestic violence occurs in about 10% of families.

Other estimates suggest that as many 15% of U.S. families experience domestic violence ("Facts…", 2003). This figure remains less than half of the self-reported numbers for law enforcement families.

Law enforcement officers are trained to take control of any situation in conflict and remain in control as the undisputed authority until that conflict has been resolved. Any challenge or perceived challenge to that authority necessitates a response, and the use of force, or violence, is one available option. For a particular percentage of officers, the temptation to use force to resolve every conflict, on and off the job, is regularly indulged.

Despite the increased occurrence of domestic violence within the ranks, it has too often been the practice of police officers to ignore their training and experience when dealing with other officers of the law. That is to say, for some law enforcement officers and supervisors, the first instinct is to protect their brother officers, preserve the departmental image, or work to limit the liability of the city government; this as opposed to investigating or supporting domestic violence allegations against one of their own.

This is often done under the guise of extending what is referred to in law enforcement as "professional courtesy," whereby laws are selectively enforced when fellow officers may have broken them. In this way, one officer is preserved from having to go up against another. Also in this way, conflict is avoided within and between departments. According to Captain Dottie Davis, Director of the Fort Wayne, Indiana, police academy and a specialist in police abuse (Davidow and Teichroeb, 2003):

> "Rather than protecting our own, we need to do a better job of weeding them out…. Most (departments) would rather keep their heads in the sand."

Anne O'Dell, a retired San Diego Police Sergeant and domestic violence coordinator, suggests that police departments have ignored the problem of domestic violence within the ranks because (Kauffman, 2003):

> "There's still that belief [within law enforcement] that our own guys would not do that. Our own guys are the good guys. This is a guy who backs me up. This is a guy I trust with my life. Certainly he isn't doing this. SHE must be the problem."

Another possibility includes the fear of being ostracized by the law enforcement community as an informer or a whistleblower. Those who inform cannot be trusted, and trust is essential between officers expected to protect each other in potentially life-threatening circumstances. Either of these reasons can be enough to keep officers from thinking objectively and performing their sworn duty.

The Culture of Victim Fear

The immediate consequences of ignoring or failing to thoroughly investigate police-involved domestic violence allegations are incurred primarily by the victim. Being a victim of domestic violence is bad enough because it wears on one's sense of personal safety, emotional and financial security, and self-worth. It can take a lot of time and lot of mistakes before any victim of domestic violence has the emotional ability to call 911 for help. Then there is the shame, the social stigma, and the self-doubt. But they can overcome. As found in one study of 389 women of intimate violence in Chicago (Johnson et al., 2007; p. 436):

> Women who experience partner violence of any kind are not passive victims but rather actively cope with the violence. In fact, 81% of all women in this study sought some form of help. The more potent finding, however, is that violence type predicted different help-seeking patterns. Women subjected to [Intimate Terrorism] rely more heavily on social institutions, whereas [Situational Couple Violence] victims rely more on friends or neighbors.

The study goes on to explain (p. 438)

> [T]he help-seeking differences between IT and SCV victims are apparent and likely reflect differences in victims' needs. The fundamental implication of these findings is that the dominating context that defines IT combined with the more severe physical violence and consequences forces its victims to seek help from multiple social institutions at a higher rate than victims of SCV.

Victims of domestic violence by a police officer face not only traditional barriers, but others as well. The biggest hurdle for this particular victim population, permeating their fears, is what has been referred to within the law enforcement community as the "Brotherhood in Blue" (Davidow and Teichroeb, 2003):

> Police officers can be among the most sophisticated, manipulative batterers, armed with an insider's knowledge of the legal system.
> They know how to restrain and intimidate without leaving marks, experts say. They undermine the credibility of their victims, portraying them as mentally unstable and vindictive. They call 911 first and claim to be the victim. They know what to say on the witness stand.
> Fellow officers may gather incomplete evidence at the scene by failing to take photos or witness statements, or by writing up an

incident as "mutual combat" rather than determining the primary aggressor, said [Captain Dottie] Davis, the Indiana expert.

"They can control the investigation the whole way through the system," she said.

And they can often count on other officers to back them up. Victims of abusive cops say the "Brotherhood in Blue" is one more reason to be afraid.

First, victims may not feel safe because their abuser has, at the very least, a government-issued firearm. The existence of that firearm represents an extreme choice that may be made by the abuser at any time. The victims must live with the constant fear that their abuser may make that choice at any time. They may even live with threats involving the firearm, whether direct or veiled.

Second, victims may not feel safe because their abuser has a police badge and all the authority that comes with it. Law enforcement officers have a tremendous amount of power, authority, discretion, and influence. They also have greater ability and resources to track down people. There are few places to run that a law enforcement officer cannot find given enough time and motivation. The fear of suffering the full weight of this authority and ability is daunting to even the most law-abiding citizen.

Third, victims may not feel safe calling the police because their abuser is the police, and may have relationships with potential responding officers (i.e., friend, colleague, supervisor). If such a relationship does not exist at the outset, general law enforcement camaraderie may develop quickly once the abuser's badge is shown. The abuser, after all, speaks the language and knows how to handle fellow officers. The abuser may even be extended "professional courtesy," as previously discussed. In the worst cases, other law enforcement officers may pose a threat to victim safety because of their willingness and ability to assist the abuser with intimidating, harassing, and monitoring the victim.

Fourth, victims may not feel safe going to a domestic violence shelter because their abuser likely knows where all the shelters are; it will not be a protected sanctuary at an unknown location. Additionally, their abuser may have relationships with those working at the shelters, professional or otherwise. If not, again, the abuser can easily cultivate such a relationship.

Fifth, victims run the risk of not being believed by anyone, including law enforcement responders, victim's advocates, and the prosecutor's office, because they are accusing a law enforcement officer. It will be the victim's word against the word of someone who testifies in court, under oath, on a regular basis. Further still, from an administrative or supervisory point of view, if the officer's word is no good, then all his cases are compromised. If the victim's word is no good, then none of the law enforcement officer's cases are compromised. The choice for some may be that simple.

Sixth, victims may fear that mandatory arrest laws for domestic violence cases, and the office of the prosecutor, will not protect them should they decide to call 911 and seek to press charges. Mandatory arrest laws exist to prevent law enforcement from making subjective determinations regarding arrest during a domestic violence call. They are meant to prevent police apathy, abuser likeability, personal relationships, and other personal bias from influencing the decision to arrest. Ultimately, they are meant to prevent the primary aggressor in such cases from further injuring or killing the victim after law enforcement has departed the residence. Many states have these kinds of laws. However, the reality is that individual departments maintain broad discretion, and can find reasons not to arrest if they work hard enough and refrain from investigating too thoroughly. As discussed in Durant (2003):

> Changes in law…do not necessarily change officers' behavior; studies and anecdotal reports suggest that many officers still do not arrest in response to a report of domestic violence. …
>
> Although most states now mandate or encourage arrest when there is probable cause that a domestic violence incident has occurred, police still retain discretion to determine, under a mandatory regime, when probable cause exists and, under a pro-arrest regime, whether or not to arrest at all.

The decision not to arrest despite mandatory arrest laws may have something to do with the issues already discussed. However, it may also have to do with law enforcement perceiving a lack of support from prosecutors. The local district attorney may not prosecute domestic violence crimes against police officers with the same zeal for justice as others. According to one study (Brannan, 2003):

> In San Diego, a national model in domestic violence prosecution, the City Attorney typically prosecutes 92% of referred domestic violence cases, but only 42% of cases where the batterer is a cop.

When a prosecutor cannot or will not put a case on, this often goes right back to the quality of the investigation that was performed. A case that has not been properly put together by law enforcement in the first place cannot and likely will not see a trial. In such ways, law enforcement has tremendous influence over whether a case can be brought to trial, whether or not the district attorney is willing.

In this culture of fear, it is not difficult to appreciate that victims of domestic violence by law enforcement intimates must overcome significant barriers to ask for any kind of help. It is also not difficult to appreciate their silence once these fears are realized by a failure to investigate or a failure to protect. It is in this fashion that those who are meant to help victims become what they were intended to shield, and are subsequently unworthy of service.

Tacit Approval

The victim fears as discussed in the preceding sections are not unreasonable, nor are they unjustified. First, the motive for officer misconduct in such cases is self-evident. Many officers value their career above all else. Consider that merely an allegation of abuse is serious. Before there is even an investigation, it can temporarily cost an officer his current assignment or, worse, his badge and gun—the symbols of law enforcement authority, culture, and identity.

Second, the failure to investigate or protect is not isolated to the actions of one officer engaged in abusive conduct and another officer willing to extend "professional courtesy" by ignoring department policy and the law. The problem is systemic and cannot survive without at least the tacit approval of law enforcement administrators and prosecutors. For example, one independent investigation revealed that over a five-year period 41 officers in King County and Pierce County, Washington, were accused of assaulting, stalking, threatening, or harassing their wives, girlfriends, or children. However, only half of those officers faced charges (Davidow and Teichroeb, 2003). This same investigation found further evidence of disparity between domestic violence complaints that involve police officers and those that do not, including that police departments were (Davidow and Teichroeb, 2003):

- Creating a double standard by not immediately arresting officers accused of domestic violence. Ordinary citizens facing such allegations are routinely jailed.
- Putting victims at greater risk by not taking away the officers' guns. During the investigation, officers suspected of abuse should be taken off patrol and not allowed to carry weapons, according to model policies drafted by national experts.
- Failing to conduct thorough internal investigations of the incidents—or, in some cases, not bothering with any review. That's how officers escape disciplinary action, experts say.
- Rarely determining there was wrongdoing in domestic violence complaints against officers, and meting out minimal discipline in the vast majority of those cases.
- Lacking specific policies on how to deal with officers accused of abuse.

Also of great concern was the fact that only one of these cases resulted in a conviction. The patrol officer in that case had made harassing phone calls to his former wife. However, he kept his badge, gun, and authority despite earning a criminal conviction (Davidow and Teichroeb, 2003). That a criminal conviction against a police officer does not result in immediate termination is unfathomable. Then King County Sheriff Dave Reichert stated (Davidow and Teichroeb, 2003) "domestic violence is a 'firing offense' for any officer, regardless of whether the accused is found guilty in the courts."

The author agrees, as the hypocrisy of a convict charged with protecting the citizenry, armed with a badge and a gun, is of the worst sort. But not every law enforcement agency agrees. This was inadvertently revealed at the turn of this century, on the cusp of a new federal law prohibiting those convicted of certain domestic violence crimes from carrying a firearm (Rodriquez, 1997):

> A new federal law that makes it illegal for anyone convicted of domestic violence to carry a gun is threatening the jobs of dozens of police officers around the country.
>
> Officers in Texas, Colorado, California, Minnesota and Michigan have been re-assigned or put on administrative leave as a result of their past arrests. The numbers are growing, and those affected are claiming the law is unfair and even unconstitutional.

It should go without saying that a criminal is unfit for police service. As argued by Dallas Police Chief Ben Click (Rodriquez, 1997), "I don't want people on this police department that don't have the maturity or self-control that is necessary to do this job." Subsequently, the retention of such an officer speaks to a negligent administrator and a disregard for the safety of the community.

As already implied, this is where law enforcement management and leadership play the greatest role. Their example and their absolute intolerance of any acts of domestic violence by subordinate officers can create the right environment for reducing its existence. This kind of management and leadership is not common, and requires unflinching links in the chain of accountability.

CASE EXAMPLE:

U.S. v. Hayes (2009)

Consider the case of *U.S. v. Hayes* (2009). This litigation arose from federal legislation enacted in 1996: Possession of Firearm After Conviction of Misdemeanor *Crime of Domestic Violence*, 18 U.S.C. §922(g)(9): "As of September 30, 1996, it is illegal to possess a firearm after conviction of a misdemeanor crime of domestic violence. This prohibition applies to persons convicted of such misdemeanors at any time, even if the conviction occurred prior to the new law's effective date. A qualifying misdemeanor domestic violence crime must have as an element the use or attempted use of physical force or the threatened use of a deadly weapon." Some in law enforcement have expressed gratitude that the existence of convicted domestic violence offenders among the ranks of law enforcement has been made an issue by such legislation, considering these violations a firing offense (Davidow and Teichroeb, 2003).

Since 1996, however, many law enforcement defendants have attempted to get around the consequences of this legislation by pleading "down to a plain simple assault not *called* domestic violence" (Rider, 2010), when charged with offenses that might cause them to lose their right to carry a firearm—and any related employment. A simple assault, for example, is a criminal charge without the

CASE EXAMPLE: *CONTINUED*

predicate "domestic" descriptor. This is essentially the type of situation described in *U.S. v. Hayes* (2009):

In 2004, law enforcement officers in Marion County, West Virginia, came to the home of Randy Edward Hayes in response to a 911 call reporting domestic violence. Hayes consented to a search of his home, and the officers discovered a rifle. Further investigation revealed that Hayes had recently possessed several other firearms as well. Based on this evidence, a federal grand jury returned an indictment in 2005, charging Hayes, under §§922(g)(9) and 924(a)(2), with three counts of possessing firearms after having been convicted of a misdemeanor crime of domestic violence.

The indictment identified Hayes's predicate misdemeanor crime of domestic violence as a 1994 conviction for battery in violation of West Virginia law. The victim of that battery, the indictment alleged, was Hayes's then wife—a person who "shared a child in common" with Hayes and "who was cohabiting with...him as a spouse." App. 3. Asserting that his 1994 West Virginia battery conviction did not qualify as a predicate offense under §922(g)(9), Hayes moved to dismiss the indictment. Section 922(g (9), Hayes maintained, applies only to persons previously convicted of an offense that has as an element a domestic relationship between aggressor and victim. The West Virginia statute under which he was convicted in 1994, Hayes observed, was a generic battery proscription, not a law designating a domestic relationship between offender and victim as an element of the offense. The United States District Court for the Northern District of West Virginia rejected Hayes's argument and denied his motion to dismiss the indictment. 377 F. Supp. 2d 540, 541–542 (2005). Hayes then entered a conditional guilty plea and appealed.

In a 2-to-1 decision, the United States Court of Appeals for the Fourth Circuit reversed. A §922(g)(9) predicate offense, the Court of Appeals held, must "have as an element a domestic relationship between the offender and the victim." 482 F. 3d 749, 751 (2007). In so ruling, the Fourth Circuit created a split between itself and the nine other Courts of Appeals that had previously published opinions deciding the same question. According to those courts, §922(g)(9) does not require that the offense predicate to the defendant's firearm possession conviction have as an element a domestic relationship between offender and victim. We granted certiorari, 552 U. S. ___ (2008), to resolve this conflict.

Though *Hayes* did not involve a law enforcement officer, the Supreme Court ruling affects quite a few of them.

A percentage of law enforcement officers and other government employees faced the possibility of retroactively losing their guns and jobs in the resulting fallout from the 1996 legislation. These were individuals who had been convicted of violent offenses against their intimate partners, but not subsequently terminated by their law enforcement employers (May, 2005). *Hayes* makes their termination or reassignment a legal necessity.

In any case, *Hayes* closes any perceptual loophole: it holds that a domestic relationship need not be a consideration in the specific criminal conviction; only the actual relationship between the victim and the offender matters. If anyone is convicted of any crime that involves violence against a domestic partner, whether it is a misdemeanor or a felony, that person is banned from carrying a firearm by federal law. If one's profession requires carrying a firearm, then one must find other employment if so convicted. It remains to be seen whether law enforcement agencies will find a new loophole in this recent ruling to further retain those personnel with related convictions.

In the experience of this author, there is a chain of accountability for law enforcement that breaks down at the same point in many cities, providing for law enforcement officers and agencies to act almost independent of any external supervision or review. A supervisor, usually a sergeant, reviews the work (the reports) of each officer or investigator. Sergeants report to lieutenants. In larger departments, lieutenants may report to captains or even precinct commanders. They, in turn, report to chiefs of police. The communication disconnect tends to occur at the point where sworn law enforcement administrators report to

Continued

CASE EXAMPLE: *CONTINUED*

(or fail to report to) civilian law enforcement administrators. Chiefs of police (or the equivalent form of law enforcement administrator) are supposed to report to a city manager or to an elected city assembly, counsel, or commission of some kind. In other words, law enforcement oversight is ultimately the responsibility of an appointed civilian administrator or an elected body of civilians. That is how the law is written, but that is not how it works in practice.

In practice, sworn law enforcement administrators do not necessarily discuss the day-to-day operations of the police department, let alone internal investigations, with civilian law enforcement administrators. In fact, they may rarely meet to discuss anything with them at all. Or when they do meet, it is to discuss the police department budget or topical public safety issues. In any case, there is not necessarily any oversight regarding the investigation of, or discipline of, law enforcement personnel; allegations of police misconduct are handled internally and may not ever be passed up to civilian law enforcement administrators for explanation or review. This practice may be mandated by official policy. Or it may be a result of the very real consideration that law enforcement officers are inherently intimidating to civilians, and those civilians are sometimes less willing to hold them accountable, even when it is their job. Regardless, the net result is that sworn law enforcement administrators may have little if any oversight and subsequently may suffer very little real accountability.

Given the existence of this disconnect in communication between sworn and civilian law enforcement administrators, it is clear how domestic violence complaints against officers may occur yet remain obscured from view. However, it is also clear that for this to continue requires civilian law enforcement administrators who are unwilling or unable to supervise their sworn employees.

If an investigation into police-involved domestic violence does occur, the facts as they are revealed may expose the municipality to greater and greater liability. There may have been a concealed or uninvestigated history of domestic violence, harassment, or threats by the officer involved, or within the ranks of the department. This could involve failure to investigate, witness tampering, collusion, evidence destruction, false reporting, abuses of office, and other criminal and administrative misconduct. Some of those in positions of authority may even have been aware of these and other circumstances, and ignored or helped to actively conceal them.[5]

---

[5]*These are only some of the possibilities. A deceptive police officer is a liability from a casework standpoint because law enforcement duties regularly require sworn courtroom testimony. In some cases, the outcome of hearing or a trial will hinge on the character and reliability of an officer. If officers have any history of deception in their casework, it diminishes their credibility. It would be foolish to put such officers on the witness stand. Consequently, it is not uncommon for various levels of misconduct to go undocumented, ignored, or to receive an application of whitewash—for purely political reasons.*

CASE EXAMPLE:

Intimate Murder-Suicide, The Shooting Death of Crystal Brame

In February of 2003, Crystal Brame of Tacoma, Washington, filed for divorce from her husband of 12 years, Tacoma Police Chief David Brame (see Figure 11-2). In divorce papers filed with the report, she alleged a history of physical and emotional abuse, including death threats. Subsequently, local newspapers reported on the divorce and her allegations. Human resource officials recommended suspending Chief Brame, taking away his badge and gun. Ray Corpuz, the city administrator, ignored that advice and stated that the city should not investigate the case

because it was a "private matter." Both the mayor of Tacoma and its city administrator were in agreement, as was reported to the press on April 26, 2003.

That same day, just after 3 p.m., Crystal Brame and David Brame met by chance at a parking lot in Gig Harbor. He had picked up their two children from day care earlier, and they were with him in his car. An altercation ensued, during which he shot Crystal Brame in the head with his service weapon, and then turned it on himself (see Figure 11-3). He died later that day, and she died the next week on May 3.

FIGURE 11-2
David Brame, Chief of Police in Tacoma, Washington, attends a press conference in early 2003.

FIGURE 11-3
David Brame's police issued Glock handgun was recovered at the scene.

Red Flags

Quite a number of red flags went up regarding Chief Brame prior to the murder-suicide in which he killed his estranged wife. Had those in positions in law enforcement administration responded to one or more of them, David Brame may have been neutralized in some fashion, and Crystal Brame may not have been killed or victimized at all. Consider the following:

■ In 1981, two police psychologists recommended that David Brame not be hired as a police officer by the City of Tacoma. He was reported to have failed the behavioral portion of one evaluation, in which the psychologist determined that "[i]t appears Mr. Brame is a marginal police officer applicant and the prognosis for his developing into an above average officer is judged poor at this time." It was also determined that David

Continued

CASE EXAMPLE: *CONTINUED*

Brame had a "tendency to exaggerate his potential to the point of being deceptive" (Barker and Skolnik, 2003).

- In 1989, while working as a patrol officer, David Brame was accused of raping a woman he had dated once 15 months previously. According to sworn testimony by retired Capt. David Olsen who had investigated the rape claim, "both he and another detective believed Brame was guilty of raping the woman" (Barker and Skolnik, 2003). According to reports (*Estate of Crystal Brame v. City of Tacoma* et al., 2003), Brame confessed to detectives, who then handed the case file over to their chief for review. Then Chief Ray Fjetland determined that the allegation could not be sustained because of witness reluctance and the passage of time.

- According to reports (*Estate of Crystal Brame v. City of Tacoma* et al., 2003), David Brame was accused of sexual harassment toward fellow Tacoma police officers and "alleged promises of promotion in exchange for sex."

- In his application for the chief's position in December 2001, David Brame gave references that should have raised red flags and disqualified him for the position. According to published reports (Hagey and Modeen, 2003):

  The job references David Brame supplied when he was a candidate for Tacoma's police chief in December 2001 should have been enough, on their own, to eliminate him as a finalist for the post, human resources specialists in and outside the city say.

  Nearly half his references—six of 13 people—could not be reached for comment by human resources officials. Three of those who did speak made vague references to something in Brame's past that would embarrass him or the city if made public.

  And several key people who logically would have been listed as references—including two former police chiefs, his current boss and two peers—were omitted.

  Human resources officials contacted some of those people—including Brame's then-boss, Chief James Hairston, and two assistant chiefs—but they flatly refused to talk about Brame.

"That would have been a huge red flag," said Dawn MacNab, principal with Waldron & Co., a Seattle firm that specializes in executive job searches for government agencies and nonprofit organizations.

Mary Brown, assistant director of Tacoma's human resources department, identified these red flags to Tacoma City Manager Ray Corpuz in a written note and followed that up with a verbal briefing (Hagey and Modeen, 2003). Rather than investigate these issues further, Corpuz ultimately hired Brame to become chief of police.

- According to documents filed within the Brame's divorce case, there was a history of domestic violence. They report that (Police Chief, 2003) "Crystal accused her husband of pointing his gun at her, trying to choke her in November and saying he 'could snap my neck if he wanted to.'"

- According to reports, Crystal Brame disclosed David Brame's violent and aberrant behavior to her family after they were divorced in February of 2003. This included that he had "choked her four times the previous year, shoved her in a closet and pointed a gun at her head. Each time he would send her flowers to apologize. She also told her psychologist that David Brame was pressing her to have group sex" (Teichroeb, 2003).

The Administrative Response

The response of police administrators in this case included initial public support for Chief Brame and then the issuance of misleading public statements about who knew what and when. It also included officers being placed on leave and at least one resignation:

- David Brame's close friend and second in command, Catherine Woodard, took command of the Tacoma Police Department after the murder-suicide (see Figure 11-4). When it was learned that she had accompanied him to divorce-related hearings and to help retrieve his children while in uniform, further intimidating Crystal Brame, she was placed on paid administrative leave by city administrator Ray Corpuz pending an investigation into "possible criminal misconduct."

CASE EXAMPLE: *CONTINUED*

FIGURE 11-4
Then acting Chief Catherine Woodard, who took command of the Tacoma Police Department after the murder-suicide, stated that Chief Brame had been outspoken on the subject of domestic violence; that he was intolerant of it; and that he showed no clear warnings signs that he might kill himself or anyone else. Such assertions do not comport with the public record, and are of concern given Woodard's personal relationship with Chief Brame in the months immediately prior his death.

■ During her four days as acting chief of police, Catherine Woodward placed officer Patrick Frantz, president of police union Local 6, on paid administrative leave pending an investigation into a threatening email he allegedly sent to the journalist who had first reported on the Brame divorce.

■ City administrator Ray Corpuz subsequently placed himself on paid administrative leave and then announced he would resign after the Brame investigation concluded.

The estate of Crystal Brame subsequently filed a lawsuit against the City of Tacoma for $75 million, seeking financial damages for the "harassment, domestic violence against, and, ultimately, the fatal shooting of Crystal Brame" (*Brame v. City of Tacoma* et al., 2003). In 2005, Crystal Brame-Judson's family settled for $12 million and the promise of certain reforms regarding better domestic violence training for law enforcement, domestic violence legislation, and increased oversight in relation to complaints against police officers.

SUMMARY

Domestic violence is more than physical injuries from individual incidents of assault. It is a pattern of conduct that uses physical battering as just one method of inflicting emotional trauma. In this chapter, we discussed the Johnson Typology of Intimate Personal Violence, which provides four categories that are meant to take an offender's use of threats, economic control, privilege and punishment, children, isolation, emotional abuse, and sexual control into account. Moreover, the Mills behavior motivation typology was presented, which discusses eight types of abuse dynamics, including rejection, degradation, terrorization, social isolation, missocialization, exploitation, emotional unresponsiveness, and close confinement, that often happen in intimate violence situations.

Risk factors for domestic homicide were discussed, including pregnancy, attempting to leave the relationship, and so on. Further, issues with reporting and presenting statistics of domestic homicide and violence were discussed in some detail, with a focus on the media's misrepresentation of research surrounding pregnant women becoming victims. The problem with protective orders and the culture of secrecy within law enforcement were also examined in some details.

It should now be clear that the ways intimate violence begins, expresses, and evolves are quite complex. They are often driven by an overall sense of powerlessness experienced on the part of the aggressor, and may present in various ways, depending on the context of the situation, the people involved, and any precipitating factors.

QUESTIONS

1. List and describe the four discrete categories of the Johnson Typology of Intimate Personal Violence (IPV).
2. Name and describe three of the different types of abuse dynamics discussed in Mills (1999).
3. Define *domestic homicide*. List three risk factors.
4. What is one of the most significant risk factors for domestic violence?
5. True or False: Domestic violence describes the physical injuries from individual incidents of assault.

REFERENCES

Arias, I., Corso, P., 2005. Average cost per person victimized by an intimate partner of the opposite gender: a comparison of men and women. Violence and Victims 20, 379–391. doi:10.1891/vivi.2005.20.4.379.

Barker, J., Skolnik, S., 2003. Tacoma police knew Brame had been accused of rape. Seattle Post-Intelligencer, May 10; Available at: http://seattlepi.nwsource.com/local/121446_tacoma10.html

Bennett, L.W., Tolman, R.M., Rogalski, C.J., Srinivasaraghavan, J., 1994. Domestic abuse by male alcohol and drug addicts. Violence and Victims 9 (4), 359–368.

Brookoff, D., O'Brien, K., Cook, C.S., Thompson, T.D., Williams, C., 1997. Characteristics of participants in domestic violence. Journal of the American Medical Association 277, 1369–1373.

Burke, A., 2007. Domestic violence as a crime of pattern and intent: an alternative reconceptualization. George Washington Law Review 75, April; pp. 552–612.

Brannan, T., 2003. Domestic violence in police families. Purple Berets, June, Available at: http://www.purpleberets.org/violence_police_families.html

BJS (Bureau of Justice Statistics). Crime Data Brief, 2003. Intimate Partner Violence, 1993–2001, February.

Cattaneo, L., Bell, M.E., Goodman, L.A., Dutton, M.A., 2007. Intimate partner violence victims' accuracy in assessing their risk of re-abuse. Journal of Family Violence 22, 429–440.

Cattaneo, L., Goodman, L., 2005. Risk factors for re-abuse in intimate partner violence: a cross disciplinary critical review. Trauma, Violence and Abuse: A Review Journal 6, 141–175.

Chang, J., Berg, C., Saltzman, L., Herndon, J., 2005. Homicide: a leading cause of injury deaths among pregnant and postpartum women in the United States, 1991–1999. American Journal of Public Health 95 (3), 471–477.

Chang, J., Elam-Evans, L.D., Berg, C.J., et al., 2003. Pregnancy related mortality surveillance: United States, 1991–1999. MMWR Surveill Summ. 52, 1–8.

Davidow, J., Teichroeb, R., 2003. Cops who abuse their wives rarely pay the price. Seattle Post-Intelligencer, July 23; Available at: http://seattlepi.nwsource.com/local/131879_cops23.html

Durant, C., 2003. When to arrest: what influences police determination to arrest when there is a report of domestic violence? Southern California Review of Law and Women's Studies, Spring, 301–340.

Estate of Crystal Brame v. City of Tacoma, et al., 2003. Claim for damages and offer for settlement. August 22.

Facts about domestic violence, 2003. Seattle Post-Intelligencer. , July 23, Available at: http://seattlepi.nwsource.com/local/131932_dvfacts23.html

Hagey, J., Modeen, M., 2003. References should have eliminated Brame, officials say. Tacoma News Tribune, May 11; Available at: http://dwb.thenewstribune.com/news/projects/david_brame/police/story/3856110p-3455288c.html

Hallinan, T., 1997. Domestic terror: family and domestic violence homicide cases in San Francisco 1993–1994. San Francisco Family Violence Project, San Francisco District Attorney's Office, March 31.

Harding, H., Helweg-Larsen, M., 2009. Perceived risk for future intimate partner violence among women in a domestic violence shelter. Journal of Family Violence 24, 75–85.

Heckert, D.A., Gondolf, E.W., 2004. Battered women's perceptions of risk versus risk factors and instruments in predicting repeat assault. Journal of Interpersonal Violence 19, 778–799.

Johnson, M., 2006. Conflict and control: gender symmetry and asymmetry in domestic violence. Violence Against Women, vol. 12 (11), November; pp. 1003–1018.

Johnson, M., Leone, J., Cohan, C., 2007. Victim help seeking: differences between intimate terrorism and situational couple violence. Family Relations 56, December, pp. 427–439.

Johnson, J., Lutz, V., Websdale, N., 2000. Death by intimacy: risk factors for domestic violence. Pace Law Review, Spring, vol. 20, pp. 1101–1134.

Kauffman, H., 2003. Husband, Cop and Enemy. CBS News, July 21; Available at: http://www.cbsnews.com/stories/2003/07/21/earlyshow/living/main564202.shtml

Krause, E.D., Kaltman, S., Goodman, L.A., Dutton, M.A., 2006. Role of distinct PTSD symptoms in intimate partner reabuse: a prospective study. Journal of Traumatic Stress 19, 507–516. doi:10.1002/jts.20136

Mills, L., 1999. Killing her softly: intimate abuse and the violence of state intervention. Harvard Law Review, December 113 (2), 550–613.

National Institute of Justice, 1996. Domestic Violence, Stalking, and Antistalking Legislation: An Annual Report to Congress under the Violence Against Women Act. April; http://www.ncjrs.gov/pdffiles/stlkbook.pdf

Police chief had sought help for stress, 2003. CNN, April 28; Available at: http://www.cnn.com/2003/US/West/04/27/police.shooting.ap/

Rennison, C., 2003. Intimate partner violence, 1993–2001. U.S. Department of Justice, Bureau of Justice Statistics, February.

Rider, R., 2010. United States v. Hayes: Retroactive removal of your ability to be a police officer, at Officer.com, Available at: http://www.officer.com/article/10232309/united-states-v-hayes

Rodriquez, R., 1997. Some police say domestic violence law a threat to their jobs. CNN, January 6; http://www.cnn.com/US/9701/06/domestic.abuse.cops/

Skrzypek, J., 2012. Lantana woman set on fire frustrated by judge denying restraining order filed prior to attack. WPTV-News Channel 5, June 15; http://www.wptv.com/dpp/news/region_c_palm_beach_county/lantana/lantana-woman-set-on-fire-filed-restraining-order-prior-to-attack-judge-denied

Tarr, N., 2007. Employment and economic security for victims of domestic abuse. Southern California Review of Law and Social Justice, vol. 16, Spring, 2007; pp. 371–427.

Teichroeb, R., 2003. Why rein in the police? 5-year-old David Brame Jr. knows. Seattle Post-Intelligencer, July 25, Available at http://seattlepi.nwsource.com/local/132287_dvbrame25.html

Task Force, 1997. Florida governor's task force on domestic and sexual violence. Florida Mortality Review Project, p. 45, table 12.

Turvey, B., 2003. The reality of police-involved domestic violence: lessons for law enforcement administrators. Illinois Law Enforcement Executive Forum, November, 3(5), 51–64.

Turvey, B., 2013. Forensic Fraud: Evaluating Law Enforcement and Forensic Science Cultures in the Context of Examiner Misconduct. Elsevier Science, San Diego.

U.S. v. Hayes, 2009. Supreme Court of the United States. No. 07–608. February 24.

Ver Steegh, N., 2005. Differentiating Types of Domestic Violence: Implications For Child Custody. Louisiana Law Review, Summer, 65, 1379–1429.

Wilson, M.J., 2005. An evolutionary perspective on male domestic violence: practical and policy implications. American Journal of Criminal Law, Summer, 291–323.

CHAPTER 12

Workplace Violence

Brent E. Turvey and Shawn Mikulay[1]

KEY TERMS

Anger-retaliatory motives Crime scene behaviors that indicate a great deal of rage, either toward a specific person, group, or institution, or a symbol of any of these.

Collateral victims Those who are attacked and injured unintentionally, because of their proximity to a primary or secondary target within a given environment.

Idiographic victim analysis The study of the concrete; examining individual victims and their actual qualities.

Intent The specific aim that guides behavior.

Motive The emotional, psychological, and material needs that impel and are satisfied by behavior.

Nomothetic victim study The examination of grouped victim data, as opposed to individual victim case information.

Primary target One who is of the greatest importance to the offender; dictates the location and timing of any attack.

Profit motives Motives that service material or personal gain. These can be found in all types of homicides, robberies, burglaries, muggings, arsons, bombings, kidnappings, most forms of white-collar crime, and so on.

Secondary target One who is of lesser importance to the offender.

Victim selection The process used by an offender to choose his or her intended victim or victims.

Violence Acts that involve force, harm, or threat of harm by one person against another.

Workplace violence Violence or the threat of violence against workers.

Violence refers to acts that involve force, harm, or threat of harm by one person against another. *Workplace violence* is defined by OSHA as "violence or the threat of violence against workers" (OSHA, 2002; p. 1). It could also be more broadly defined as "violent acts against a person at work or on duty, including physical assaults (rape and sexual assault and aggravated and simple assault) and robbery" (Warchol, 1998).

Because of sensational coverage by the popular media, public perceptions regarding the frequency of workplace-related violence, such as homicide, are likely to be greatly distorted.[2] When one watches the evening news, it is not

---

[1]This chapter is an update to, and partial rewrite of, Turvey and Petherick (2008).

[2]This is owing to the *availability heuristic*. As explained in Chapter 2, this in play when judgments are made based on what one can remember rather than on complete or actual information. We use it for judging the commonality, frequency, or likelihood of events when assessing subjects that we have very little actual knowledge of.

Forensic Victimology. http://dx.doi.org/10.1016/B978-0-12-408084-3.00012-0

difficult to understand why. In our present culture, in which sexuality, violence, and fear are valuable retail commodities, the workplace is routinely characterized with one or more of these when given airtime or column space. Stories without such marketable traits are seldom featured.

This problem and others are encapsulated in a summary of workplace violence cause-and-effect issues prepared by Riley (2003; pp. 2–3):

> While incidents of workplace violence do not appear to be on the rise, society is paying greater attention to the problem. Increasing awareness of workplace violence is due, in part, to the media's sensationalism of acts of violence in the workplace. However, the significant toll exerted by workplace violence cannot be understated, and the statistics are alarming. One out of every four employees will be a victim of workplace violence during their life. One out of every six violent crimes occurs in the workplace. As an occupational hazard, homicide is the second leading cause of death, accounting for one sixth of all occupational fatalities. Every year 1,000 people are murdered in the workplace; another 1.5 to 2 million people are victims of assault, rape, or robbery. Offenders use various means to disrupt the workplace. For example, everyday 16,400 threats are made, 723 workers are attacked and 43,800 workers are harassed.
>
> Workplace violence also has a ripple effect, affecting not only the targeted victim, but everyone associated with the workplace. Violence in the workplace may inflict irreparable psychological harm. One report concludes that "negative publicity drives customers away, valued employees leave the company and new hires are harder to attract." Workplace violence also imposes substantial financial costs. Experts estimate the total economic loss to be around $4.2 billion a year. Given the frequency and severity of workplace violence, it is not surprising that for the last three years, workplace violence has been employers' greatest concern.

As professionals, forensic victimologists are required to have insight into the actual nature and occurrence of a particular type of crime before offering related interpretations and opinions. We need to know more than what is being reported on the nightly news or in the crime section of the daily paper. And we need real tools with which to approach and analyze the evidence that presents in casework. Unfortunately, there is no shortage of "professionals" operating in precisely the opposite fashion.

The goals of this chapter are then twofold: to dispel any myths regarding workplace violence perpetuated by the media and to provide forensic victimologists with some language and lenses through which to perceive workplace violence more objectively.

NOMOTHETICALLY SPEAKING: THE AGGREGATE

Nomothetic victim study is the examination of grouped victim data, as opposed to individual victim case information. Such study is useful in theory generation, and also in providing context. However, it is not often useful for rendering final conclusions about the evidence of a particular case. With that in mind, it is necessary to review the nomothetic basics regarding workplace violence.

As reported in Harrell (2011; p. 1): "In 2009, approximately 572,000 nonfatal violent crimes (rape/sexual assault, robbery, and aggravated and simple assault) occurred against persons age 16 or older while they were at work or on duty." Moreover, this overall rate has been on the decline since 1993. With respect to workplace homicides in 2009, at least "521 persons age 16 or older were victims of homicide in the workplace."

The most recent "highlights" are reported in Harrell (2011; p. 1):

- Between 2002 to 2009, the rate of nonfatal workplace violence declined by 35%, slowing from a 62% decline in the rate between 1993 to 2002.
- From 2005 to 2009, law enforcement officers, security guards, and bartenders had the highest rates of nonfatal workplace violence.
- With respect to homicides in the workplace between 2005 and 2009, about 28% of victims were in sales and related occupations, while about 17% of victims were in protective service occupations.
- From 2005 to 2009, approximately 70% of homicides in the workplace were committed by robbers and other attackers; however about 21% were committed by workplace "associates."
- From 2005 [to] 2009, firearms were used in 5% of nonfatal workplace violence. However, shootings accounted for 80% of homicides in the workplace; and stabbings accounted for another 8.1%.

Statistics related to the most high-risk professions include the following (Harrell, 2011; pp. 4–5):

> From 2005 through 2009 persons working in law enforcement experienced about 19% of workplace violence while accounting for 2% of employed persons
>
> Among the occupations measured, persons in law enforcement experienced the highest proportion (19%) of workplace violence.... Persons in retail sales occupations experienced about 13% of workplace violence while accounting for about 9% of employed persons. About 10% of victims of workplace violence worked in medical occupations.
>
> Law enforcement officers, security guards, and bartenders had the highest rate of workplace violence.

From 2005 through 2009, of the occupational groups examined, law enforcement occupations had the highest average annual rate of workplace violence (48 violent crimes per 1,000 employed persons age 16 or older), followed by mental health occupations (21 per 1,000). Among the individual occupations examined, no occupation had workplace violence rates higher than those for law enforcement officers, security guards, and bartenders.

Bartenders (80 per 1,000) had the highest workplace violence rate of all retail sales occupations. Persons working in all mental health occupations had a similar rate of workplace violence. Among teaching occupations, no occupation had a higher rate of workplace violence than persons working in technical or industrial schools. All transportation occupations had a similar rate of workplace violence.

Alternatively, data from low-risk professions is also revealing. Convenience and liquor store clerks displayed a relatively low risk of violence (0.7% of all workplace violence). This level of risk was fairly close to that found with gas station attendants (0.8% of all workplace violence). Physicians accounted for 1.1% of all victims of workplace violence (a rate of 10.1 per 1,000 workers) while nurses accounted for 3.9% of all victims of workplace violence (a rate of 8.1 per 1,000 workers). Those employed specifically in the mental health field also experienced 3.9% of all acts of workplace violence which leads to a substantially higher rate of 20.5.

Educators are also represented in the most recent data. Preschool teachers received both the lowest rate of violence per 1,000 workers (0.09) and the lowest total incidence of workplace violence (0.01% of all incidences). Rates of workplace violence increased through K–12 with high school teachers accounting for approximately 2.5% of all incidences, although the existence of ten times as many high school teachers as bartenders means that teachers experience a far lower rate of victimization than bartenders. Special education teachers do experience a slightly higher rate of violence (17.8 vs. 13.5), but the rarity of special education teachers as opposed to K–12 teachers means that even a small increase in total number of violent encounters will translate into a magnified rate of incidence. The rate of workplace violence for college and university instructors drops by approximately 90% from high school teachers to be lower even than that of elementary but not preschool teachers (Harrell, 2011).

In terms of the victim–offender relationship, strangers committed more workplace violence by a narrow majority (Harrell, 2011; p. 6):

Strangers committed the greatest proportion of workplace violence
From 2005 through 2009, strangers committed about 53% of workplace violence against males and about 41% against females. Similar

proportions of males and females were victims of intimate partner violence in the workplace. About a quarter (26%) of workplace violence against males and about a third against females were committed by someone with whom the victim had a work relationship[1]. Among the work relationships examined, coworkers were the most likely to attack persons in the workplace. Current or former coworkers committed 16% of workplace violence against males and about 14% against females. Patients committed a higher percentage of workplace violence against females than males.

[fn. 1] Work relationships include offenders who were customers, clients, patients, and current or former supervisors, employees, or coworkers of the victim.

Other notable findings related to offender traits and modus operandi from data reported between 2005 and 2009 include the following:

- "Workplace violence was less likely to involve an offender under the influence of alcohol or drugs than nonworkplace violence" (Harrell, 2011; p. 7).
- "Firearms were less likely to be present in workplace violence than nonworkplace violence" (Harrell, 2011; p. 7).
- "Workplace violence was slightly less likely than nonworkplace violence to be reported to police" (Harrell, 2011; p. 8).
- "The most common reasons for reporting workplace violence to the police were to stop or prevent an incident from happening (31%), prevent future incidents (21%), and stop attacker (20%)" (Harrell, 2011; p. 9).
- Interestingly, 60.4% of victims resisted their attackers by yelling, arguing, or running. Only 2.3% of victims of workplace violence responded by threatening or attacking with a weapon. This contradicts sworn testimony by FBI profilers regarding their expectations of a "normal" victim response to armed attackers in their home (e.g., that they would most likely go for a weapon to protect themselves or loved ones).[3]

All these contextual victim statistics and likelihoods are interesting, and even important, for developing case theories and establishing risk or exposure factors in some instances. However, one must bear in mind that grouped and averaged victim data is also abstract. It does not represent particular victims that exist in the real world. It represents increased or decreased possibility, not actuality. This limitation is important to understand and must be incorporated into subsequent findings regarding case-specific interpretations and assessments.

---

[3]See testimony of Mark Safarik in *California v. Jennifer and Matt Fletcher* (2004).

DOMESTIC VIOLENCE

As already suggested in Chapter 9, domestic violence in its many incarnations is perhaps one of the greatest threats to public health in the United States. It can bruise, crush, and ultimately destroy the physical, mental, and economical well-being of any of its victims. It provides for unsafe homes, unsafe communities, and even unsafe work environments. None among these are immune. As explained in Tarr (2007; pp. 376–377):

> The issue of domestic violence is relevant in the employment context because its consequences impact every aspect of the victim's life. Domestic violence can cause victims to be absent or late for work, interfere with their ability to perform on the job, result in termination of their employment, or force them to quit their jobs to escape the violence. Their abusers stalk them at work, make harassing phone calls to their place of employment, prevent them from going to work because of abuse or other interfering behavior, and call supervisors to get the victims in trouble. At the most extreme, victims of domestic violence are murdered by their abusive partners.

Victimologists may be confronted with cases in which domestic abuse is suspected but not yet confirmed. There are circumstances highly indicative of domestic abuse, and some may be apparent to those in the workplace. Questions to ask co-workers include the following:

1. Did the victim report being threatened or injured by a domestic partner?
2. Did the victim show feelings of fear and social withdrawal?
3. Did the victim evidence bruises or physical complaints that have been the result of an assault?
4. Did the victim engage in intermittent crying or outbursts of anger while talking with a domestic partner at the workplace, either on the telephone or in person?
5. Did the victim suffer from frequent or prolonged periods of depression, irritability, anxiety, and apathetic withdrawal?
6. Did the victim suffer from a lack of concentration?
7. Did the victim suffer from increased absenteeism or reduced productivity?
8. Did the victim's spouse or partner make disruptive visits to the workplace?
9. Did the victim's spouse or partner call the workplace repeatedly to check up on her or him?
10. Did the victim's spouse or partner become hostile with or threaten to harm anyone at the workplace?

More insidious, and given the persistence of these types of circumstances, domestic violence also creates particular challenges for employers with respect to employee safety and any related liability (Matejkovic, 2004; pp. 311–312):

While workplace violence from any source is obviously a concern for employers, the issues presented when acts of domestic violence spill into the workplace are particularly thorny, as employers face exposure to liability claims based upon a variety of sources and theories. It is apparent that when domestic violence spills into the workplace, the victims include not only the individuals involved, but also the victim's employer, which must deal with the adverse publicity and often claims made by the individual victims, and too often innocent bystanders, including co-workers, who also may suffer injuries in any violent act.

What this means is that some employers may feel compelled to act in a way that protects their businesses and other employees at the expense of a domestic violence victim who brings danger to the doorstep. Kennedy (2005) provides a reasonable discussion of workplace violence in general as it relates to employer liability (p. 1777):

> Employers can sometimes find themselves liable in tort for those instances of workplace violence which were "substantially certain" to befall their employees and where no preventive action was taken to protect these employees. Causes of action such as negligent hiring, negligent retention, negligent supervision, and negligent entrustment have been successfully brought against employers by injured employees who are not barred by workers compensation laws from bringing suit. To avoid such litigation, to prevent other financial losses, and to fulfill their moral duty to their employees, many employers are adopting "zero tolerance" policies toward aggressive behavior on the part of their employees. Security surveys are being conducted to identify threats to employee safety. Employee Assistance Programs are becoming responsive to victimization prevention needs, and company leaders are forming threat assessment teams to evaluate developing situations that may prove a threat to employee safety.

Of course, not every employer has the foresight or the economic means to respond pro-actively to workplace violence, let alone attend to the needs of specific employees.

Many employers see victims of domestic violence as a liability and act accordingly. In some cases, at-risk employees may simply be terminated. In others, where the employees enjoy protection from arbitrary termination, employers may simply start building a file—actively soliciting complaints and documenting absences and errors. The smallest issue becomes another immovable stone as the employee-victim is walled off from the rest of the workplace until his or her termination becomes inevitable.

Even when the victim or employer does everything right, however, there remains the possibility of tragedy.

CASE EXAMPLE:

Cindy Bischof

Consider the case of 43-year-old real estate broker Cindy Bischof, in Elmhurst, Illinois (see Figure 12-1). She was shot to death in the parking lot of her workplace, Darwin Realty, by a former boyfriend. He then shot himself. Both died later at Elmhurst Memorial Hospital. As explained in Twohey and Ford (2008):

> Cindy Bischof thought her breakup with a longtime boyfriend would go smoothly after he agreed to move out of her house. But Michael Giroux quickly turned hostile, writing up a plan to destroy her home and following through with it.

Terrified after Giroux, 60, spray-painted every wall and piece of furniture in her Arlington Heights home last spring, the 43-year-old real estate broker moved swiftly to secure a protective order from a Cook County judge that prohibited him from contacting her.

When he violated the order on two occasions, including an attempt to hang himself on her patio, she didn't hesitate to press charges that landed him in jail for two months followed by home confinement.

FIGURE 12-1
Cindy L. Bischof was a successful real estate agent and had won a number of awards for her work. She did everything she could to keep her co-workers safe by confronting the problem with her ex-boyfriend head on and following the law. He was, in the end, undeterred.

CASE EXAMPLE: *CONTINUED*

To relatives and prosecutors, it appeared that Bischof was taking all the necessary steps to stay safe and that the legal system was delivering protection.

But after Giroux was released from home confinement this month, he showed up at Bischof's office in Elmhurst armed with a .38-caliber revolver. When she tried to get into her car, he shot her repeatedly then turned the gun on himself.

...A woman's risk of being seriously injured or killed by an intimate partner increases when she breaks off the relationship. In certain cases, a protective court order is not enough and the only viable option is for a woman to either enter a shelter or relocate, experts say.

...Research has identified danger signs—such as suicide attempts and losing interest in work, both of which Giroux displayed—that point to an increased likelihood of murder. ...

But as Giroux demonstrated, some people are not deterred by aggressive prosecution. ...

Today, the Illinois Domestic Violence Act is seen as one of the strongest laws of its kind in the country, said Dawn Dalton, executive director of the Chicago Metropolitan Battered Women's Network. Still, victims and their advocates see flaws in the legal system. If someone violates an order of protection, the person is supposed to face legal consequences, in some cases jail.

But some police officers, prosecutors and judges can be dismissive of violations, allowing harassment, stalking and other abusive behavior to continue, said Jennifer Greene, director of legal advocacy at Family Rescue, an organization that helps victims of domestic abuse in Cook County.

That was not the case with Bischof, who secured a two-year order of protection against Giroux last June after he vandalized her house. After pleading guilty to vandalism, he was ordered to serve time in Cook County Jail and underwent a psychiatric evaluation.

When Bischof reported that he had called and threatened to kill her family during the 4th of July weekend, he was charged with violating the protection order. Police re-arrested him in early September after he showed up at Bischof's house and placed a rope around his neck in an apparent suicide attempt, records show.

The judge set bond at $75,000 and ordered Giroux to undergo another mental health evaluation.

He pleaded guilty in November to violating the order of protection and was sentenced to 63 days in jail followed by 60 days of home confinement and two years of intensive probation.

For several months, Bischof heard nothing from Giroux and thought the danger might have passed, said her mother, Barbara Bischof.

In a brief voice-mail message about 10 days before the slaying, he apologized for everything he had done. It seemed harmless, so Bischof didn't report it, her mother said.

But Giroux's behavior mirrored warning signs of a harasser bent on violence, according to advocates and legal authorities.

Studies of women killed by an intimate partner have identified common traits among the perpetrators. Among them: access to a gun, previous threat with a weapon, estrangement from the partner, stalking, forced sex, abuse during pregnancy, drug abuse and unemployment.

Giroux did not have a Firearm Owners Identification Card, which Illinois requires to buy guns. Elmhurst police say they are working with federal officials to determine how he got the pistol used to kill Bischof.

Giroux had financial troubles for years before he and Bischof started dating, and his fortunes seemed to decline during their three-year relationship, according to relatives and court records. Records show he was unemployed for at least part of the time and that he had declared bankruptcy in 2002.

Continued

CASE EXAMPLE: *CONTINUED*

"When individuals are unemployed or they start spiraling downward...then that's a huge, huge red flag," said Pam Paziotopoulos, a former head of the Cook County state's attorney's domestic violence division.

Quite different from the victim who stays with an abuser and enables him to continue perpetuating abuse,

Cindy Bischof actually confronted her ex-boyfriend's abuse and reported him to law enforcement when appropriate. She saw the danger, reported it, and tried to remove it from her life. Unfortunately, these actions along with other converging problems in his life caused him to fixate on her further, and ultimately to seek her destruction along with his own.

IDIOGRAPHIC VICTIM ANALYSIS

As explained in Chapter 4, *idiographic victim analysis* involves the study of the concrete: examining individual victims and their actual qualities. It focuses on specific cases and the unique traits or functioning of the individuals involved. In the following sections, we discuss certain basic idiographic considerations with respect to workplace violence and adduce illustrative examples as necessary.[4]

Targets

Every offender has particular victim or target criteria that satisfies his or her needs—no matter how general or specific. Offenders may want to hit a thousand targets or just one. They may want to destroy everything they hit or inflict tactical damage. *Victim selection* refers to the process that is used by offenders to choose their intended victim or victims (Turvey, 2011). Depending on the tactical capabilities of the offender, this process may be passive or active.

The authors note that Holmes and Holmes (2000) refer to this process as *victim selectivity*. However, the term *selectivity* implies particular criteria that are actively sought by the offender. This describes only some offenders.

In some cases, as with Cindy Bischof, a particular victim will be the entire reason for the commission of an offense. In other cases, the victim can be a function of ease and opportunity—someone that the offender can expediently acquire for his or her intended purposes. And in still other cases, the victim may be representative of a group. This all depends on the intent of the offender.

---

[4]Law enforcement-oriented examples are used more often than not in this chapter for two very specific reasons: first, law enforcement-related workplace violence is the most common and therefore the most likely to be encountered by the forensic victimologist; and second, law enforcement investigators represent an overwhelming number of practicing victimologists.

There are essentially three kinds of targets: primary, secondary, and collateral.

Primary Targets

A *primary target* is one that is of the greatest importance to the offender. It dictates the location and timing of any attack. Often, the offender will have planned out and intend to hit that victim at the risk of forgoing any or all other targets in the environment. In some cases, there will be more than one primary target.

In workplace violence cases, the primary target (victim) will be known to the offender; the connection between them will be personal. This remains true whether the primary target is a specific person, a specific cluster of persons, or the workplace itself.

Secondary Targets

A *secondary target* is one that is of lesser importance to the offender. It will not dictate the location and timing of an attack. However, it will be a conscious choice based on the availability within environmental and temporal constraints dictated by primary targets. Not all offenders will take the time to deliberate over the possibility of achieving secondary targets, and some offenders might have the intent but not the opportunity to acquire secondary targets.

In workplace violence cases, secondary targets will be representative of the primary targets—someone who is associated with them, immediately subordinate to them, or superior to them. Or something that they control or own. Instead of a supervisor—their secretary; instead of a co-worker—their partner, friend, or intimate (if available); and instead of a person—their office, belongings, or vehicle.

Collateral Victims

A *collateral victim* is one who is attacked and injured unintentionally because of proximity to a primary or secondary target within a given environment. His or her injury is completely uncalculated, and incidental to the intended outcome. A collateral victim is, in fact, not a target. It is important to distinguish between secondary targets and collateral victims—the key difference being intent.

In workplace violence cases, collateral victims will be hit because they are simply in the way. They are in the wrong place at the wrong time. The person who is hit by a bullet that comes through a wall; people killed in a fire set to damage a building; an explosion intended to blow up a person in a room that hits a gas main and takes out an entire city block.

The Victim–Offender Relationship

In each case, the relationship between the victim and the offender should be established. However, before we dive in and commence sorting, let us take a moment and embrace the cautionary offered in Kennedy (2005; p. 1776), which states

> Because the circumstances and targets of workplace violence vary widely, so, too, will the motivations of various perpetrators. Due to the wide range of workplace violence incident types, no single etiological theory will generalize broadly enough to be universally applicable.

The importance of these words will become clear as we discuss specific examples subsequent to the typology.

According to Loveless (2001), there are essentially four types of workplace violence offenders with respect to their relationship to the workplace itself: *Criminal Intent* (e.g., stranger theft); *Customer/Client*; *Worker-on-Worker* (e.g., co-worker, former employee); and *Personal Relationship* (e.g., intimate, spouse, friend, or relative of an employee) (p. 4):

Criminal Intent (Type I): The perpetrator has no legitimate relationship to the business or its employees, and is usually committing a crime in conjunction with the violence. These crimes can include robbery, shoplifting, and trespassing. The vast majority of workplace homicides (85%) fall into this category.[5]

Customer/Client (Type II): The perpetrator has a legitimate relationship with the business and becomes violent while being served by the business. This category includes customers, clients, patients, students, inmates, and any other group for which the business provides services. It is believed that a large proportion of customer/client incidents occur in the health care industry, in settings such as nursing homes or psychiatric facilities; the victims are often patient caregivers. Police officers, prison staff, flight attendants, and teachers are some other examples of workers who may be exposed to this kind of workplace violence.[6]

Worker-on-Worker (Type III): The perpetrator is an employee or past employee of the business who attacks or threatens another

---

[5]In this category, 52.9% of male victims of non-fatal attacks did not know their attacker; 40.9% of female victims did not know their attacker; and 70.3% of homicide victims were killed by a robber or other assailants (Harrell, 2011).

[6]In this category, 5.4% of male victims of non-fatal attacks had a customer/client relationship with their attacker; 12.5% of female victims of non-fatal attacks had a customer/client relationship with their attacker; and 10% of homicide victims were killed by a customer or client (Harrell, 2011).

employee(s) or past employee(s) in the workplace. Worker-on-worker fatalities account for approximately 7% of all workplace violence homicides.[7]

   Personal Relationship (Type IV): The perpetrator usually does not have a relationship with the business but has a personal relationship with the intended victim. This category includes victims of domestic violence assaulted or threatened while at work.[8]

There is the suggestion that these are discrete relationship types, with each useful as a broad descriptive category for a particular case. However, as with most nomothetic classification systems, this does not bear out in actual casework. In application, these categories are oversimplified, and a single incident may contain more than one relationship, especially when multiple victims are involved.

When workplace violence stems from abusive domestic relationships (Type IV), victims experience a compounded form of suffering. For example, the *Illinois Department of Labor Victims' Economic Security and Safety Act of 2003* (VESSA) states that employees who have been victims of domestic violence, dating violence, sexual assault, or stalking too often suffer adverse consequences in the workplace as a result of their victimization. For example, victims of domestic violence, dating violence, sexual assault, and stalking face the threat of job loss and loss of health insurance as a result of the illegal acts of the perpetrators of violence.

In a related concern, women who have experienced domestic violence or dating violence are more likely than other women to be unemployed, to suffer from health problems that can affect employability and job performance, to report lower personal income, and to rely on welfare. These problems are compounded by abusers who frequently seek to control their partners. They often do so by actively interfering with their ability to work, including preventing victims from going to work, harassing them at work, limiting their access to cash or transportation, and sabotaging child care arrangements.

Case Examples

To illustrate victim–offender relationships in an applied fashion, the following actual case examples are provided with discussion.

---

[7]In this category, 20.1% of male victims of non-fatal attacks had a workplace relationship with their attacker; 19.3% of female victims of non-fatal attacks had a workplace relationship with their attacker; and 11.4% of homicide victims were killed by someone who worked or had worked with them (Harrell, 2011).

[8]In this category, 13.1% of male victims of non-fatal attacks had a personal relationship (partner, relative, acquaintance) with their attacker; 21.3% of female victims of non-fatal attacks had a personal relationship with their attacker; and 8.3% of homicide victims were killed by an intimate (Harrell, 2011).

CASE EXAMPLE:

Customer/Client and Worker-on-Worker

Consider the case of Michael Burgess, Sheriff in Custer County, Oklahoma, since 1994 (see Figure 12-2). He surrendered to agents of the Oklahoma Bureau of Investigation in April of 2008, facing 35 felony charges, including multiple counts of rape, forcible oral sodomy, bribery by a public official, and perjury. As detailed in Schoetz (2008):

> The charges were announced by James Boring, a district attorney in Texas County, Okla., who took control of the Burgess investigation in May 2007 after prosecutors in Custer County cited a conflict of interest in the case and the state attorney general requested Boring's involvement.
>
> Information presented in court documents filed in Custer County District Court Wednesday signed by Boring and an agent for the Oklahoma State Bureau of Investigation lay out a pattern of alleged criminal behavior from 2005 to 2007. Burgess allegedly used his power as sheriff repeatedly to pressure a female employee, inmates and members of his county's drug court program to pleasure him in exchange for special treatment.
>
> Burgess offered his official resignation Wednesday, effective immediately. He was released on $50,000 bond under the condition that he has no direct or indirect contact with any of the prosecution's 33 witnesses. ...
>
> The documents paint a predatory profile of a sheriff who authorities say would force inmates under his supervision to perform oral, vaginal and anal sex in his office, his official sheriff's vehicle, local motels and hotels, a truck stop, and houses belonging to inmates and friends.
>
> The four women named in the court documents who were either inmates or members of the county's drug program all were promised some type of leniency or preferential treatment in return for their sexual favors.
>
> The alleged sexual liaisons took place between February 2006 and April 2007, according to court documents. One of the women even traveled with the sheriff to Oklahoma City in April 2006 to take part in a "legislative" initiative relating to drug court programs across the state.
>
> "During the night of their stay at the Biltmore Hotel, Sheriff [Burgess] directed

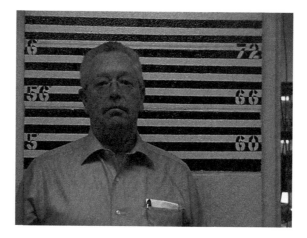

FIGURE 12-2
Booking photo of former Custer County Sheriff Michael Burgess.

CASE EXAMPLE: *CONTINUED*

and required that [the woman] stay with him at the hotel rather than go with other participants and their counselor for dinner," according to the probable cause affidavit for the sheriff's arrest. "Sheriff [Burgess] took [the woman] to his room at the Biltmore Hotel where he engaged in multiple acts of sexual intercourse with [the woman] during the night."

On May 21, 2007, however, that same woman failed a drug test that was required as part of her release from jail. "When she failed the drug screen, she disclosed that she had been having sex with Sheriff [Burgess] and that he had promised her that he would protect her and keep her from going back to jail," the documents stated.

In the hours after the woman told of her sexual history with the sheriff, authorities say Burgess contacted the woman's cousin, a female who was also part of the drug court program and asked her to remove any DNA evidence, such as a condom, from the woman's house that might incriminate him. Burgess allegedly promised to have her bother released from jail in exchange for helping cover up the sexual tryst. It was the statement by the woman who failed the drug test that triggered the state's involvement.

Another allegation involves a former sheriff's office employee who accused Burgess of inappropriately touching her at a restaurant, in a courtroom and while she tried on her sheriff's office uniform.

A federal lawsuit was filed in October after Boring's investigation began. In the suit, 12 former inmates alleged that the sheriff's employees had them engage in wet T-shirt contests and offered cigarettes to women who exposed their breasts.

Burgess, a former police officer and state government investigator, was appointed sheriff in 1994 when his predecessor died. He was elected to the position in 1996 and re-elected in 2000 and 2004. ...

The daily population at Custer County Detention and Law Enforcement Center is about 80 inmates, according to the sheriff's office Web site. The sheriff oversaw a staff that included an undersheriff, 10 deputies, 11 jailers, seven dispatchers and an administrative assistant.

In 2009, former Sheriff Burgess was convicted of charges related to these allegations and sentenced to 79 years in prison.

This case represent workplace violence of a sexual nature by the sheriff toward a co-worker (Type III) who is also a subordinate. This because he alleged to have touched her inappropriately on multiple occasions in work-related contexts, and because he is her supervisor. There is also very little argument to be made that unwanted sexual contact is not also coercive in the context provided.

This case also reveals that perhaps special subcategories of the Type III relationship are warranted, given that when victim and offender are not equals at work, this can alter any subsequent relationship dynamic: Type IIIa, Supervisor to Subordinate; Type IIIb, Subordinate to Supervisor; and Type IIIc, Workplace Neutrals. Any descriptors will do, so long as the power relationship is made clear, especially in cases involving sexual violence.

This case also represents a *Customer/Client (Type II)* relationship. There can be no question that, if true, these allegations amount to numerous instances of coerced sex acts and sexual performance inflicted against prisoners in the sheriff's custody. The citizens within that sheriff's jurisdiction are his customers, as they pay for his services, even when they are being detained by lawful arrest.

Again, this relationship type as defined does not make the power structure or relationship victim and offender all that clear when applied to a specific case. In fact, it seems to assume that the violence is one way—originating from the client or customer. As such, special subcategories of the Type II relationship are warranted to delineate the origin of the violence and whether or not the "client" is actually a ward of some kind.

CASE EXAMPLE:

Customer/Client, Worker-on-Worker, and Possible Criminal Intent

The case of police officer Jay Dailey in Duluth, Georgia, brings attention to the "always armed; always on-duty" policy that is a common law enforcement practice in the United States—requiring off-duty officers to carry their weapons. It makes every place that police officers go in the community, whether on duty or off, an extension of their workplace.

The facts in the case are not generally disputed. In February of 2008, Officer Dailey assaulted a female motorist and damaged her vehicle after feigning injury to gain her trust; then he opened fire on a responding officer. The known facts are provided in Simmons (2008):

> Fulton officer Paul Phillips returned only four rounds, said Gwinnett County police Detective Shelly Millsap, who testified in a preliminary hearing.
>
> The shootout left Dailey and Phillips wounded on a two-lane road and culminated [in] a bizarre series of events in the small town of Sugar Hill. Dailey's memory appeared disjointed when detectives questioned him at the hospital, Millsaps said. Dailey allegedly admitted he had been drinking, remembered wrecking his car and thought he recalled shooting a police officer. "He made a motion as if pulling a trigger and said his finger was tired," Millsap said.
>
> When he was arrested, Dailey had a handgun tucked into the rear of his waistband and another stashed in his front pocket.
>
> Detectives eventually pieced together what happened that day after talking to the victims and witnesses. Millsap, the only witness at the preliminary hearing, gave this account of the shootout on Level Creek Road:
>
> Dailey was off duty when he flagged down a female motorist, who said she'd never met him before. He slumped over and grabbed his stomach, claiming he was injured. The officer wore jeans, a green knit shirt and a bulletproof vest and flashed a police badge.
>
> When the woman started to call 911 on her cell phone, Dailey grew agitated and sprayed her with pepper spray. He reached through the car window, struggled with her over the phone and threatened to kill her, saying "you're ruining my life now."
>
> Dailey is also accused of pointing a gun at two passing motorists. One of the motorists continued down the street and signaled to Phillips, a Fulton officer who was off-duty and driving home from a part-time job. Phillips wore a uniform and drove a marked patrol car.
>
> When Philips got out of the car, Dailey allegedly drew his gun. Phillips raised his hand to say "hold on" and was shot by Dailey.
>
> After the two officers exchanged gunfire, Phillips retreated to his car for cover. Dailey came around to the driver's side and fired several more shots at Phillips, two of which pierced the windshield of the patrol car. Phillips told detectives that Dailey was still pulling the trigger after he ran out of bullets. Other police arrived and arrested Dailey.
>
> Both officers were injured. Phillips, 37, is still recovering from a gunshot wound to the arm at Gwinnett Medical Center. Dailey was shot in the hand and wore a bandage in court on Tuesday. Dailey appeared fidgety and wiped away tears at several times during the testimony. …
>
> Duluth police spokesman Maj. Don Woodruff said Dailey was fired last week. He has until Feb. 15 to appeal.

Officer Dailey was ultimately convicted and sentenced to 60 years in prison for his crimes. His attorney blamed a family history of alcoholism. Dailey was also sued by one of his victims for damages.

In this case, there are multiple attacks on multiple victims with multiple weapons by a single and admittedly intoxicated police officer (see Figures 12-3 and 12-4).

At the outset, this case may involve a *Criminal Intent (Type I)* relationship. To determine this, we need to know precisely what officer Dailey intended to accomplish by stopping the female motorist. We do know that it resulted in her being assaulted with pepper spray, and her car window was broken after his arm got stuck in it. What we do not know is why he wrecked his own

CASE EXAMPLE: *CONTINUED*

car, the injuries he sustained prior to the shooting, and whether there were any influences on his state of mind other than alcohol. Did he intend to steal or "commandeer" her vehicle? Did he intend to sexually assault her? Was his request for help legitimate in his mind at the time? These are all possibilities, some of which are consistent with a criminal intent relationship. Also, and to be very clear, the possibility of this being a legitimate car-stop gone wrong is removed by the fact that Dailey did not have a vehicle of his own, was not on duty, and opened fire on a fellow officer.

This case certainly involves a *Customer/ Client (Type II)* relationship, as the citizen who was attacked is a client of law enforcement. Again, a mechanism for identifying the power disparity here is needed because this relationship is not on par with someone buying a pack of cigarettes and being pepper sprayed by the clerk.

This case also certainly involves a *Worker-on-Worker (Type III)* relationship because one of the victims was also employed as a police officer, with equitable firepower and authority, although they worked for different agencies and had no prior relationship.

FIGURE 12-3
The scene of the shooting between officers Jay Dailey and Paul Phillips after responders arrived. Officer Phillips's marked vehicle is on the right, door still open.

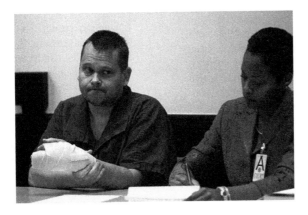

FIGURE 12-4
Former Duluth Police Officer Jay Dailey sits in court, still wearing bandages over an injured hand. He is seated next to his attorney, Theresa Hood.

Motivational Events and Circumstances

A great deal has been written about the particular motivations of individuals who have perpetrated acts of workplace violence—much of it sensational, generalized, and wrong. Moreover, what is referred to as a motivation is often a description of the progression of events and circumstances that led to violence. An example would be stating that a given employee was fired, or in a dispute with his supervisor, and then "went postal"—arriving at work with a firearm and shooting everyone who showed up, starting with the supervisor. The actual motive in such a case would, in fact, be anger or revenge.

As explained in Turvey (2011), *motive* is composed of the emotional, psychological, and material needs that impel and are satisfied by behavior, while *intent* is the specific aim that guides behavior. The available motives for workplace violence are no different than for any other type of violence. They include the service of profit, anger, power, and sadism, with no bright yellow line between them.

Also, bear in mind that motive is relative. What might enrage one person in a set of personal circumstances (and toxicology) might just as easily be ignored by someone else; what precisely constitutes a lot of money (an amount worth killing for or stealing) is often a function of individual wealth; and what is unacceptable violent behavior in one employment setting is par for the course in another.

CASE EXAMPLE:

In Custody Assault/Anger Motivated

As explained in Turvey (2011): *Anger-retaliatory motives* are evidenced by crime scene behaviors that suggest rage, either toward a specific person, group, institution, or a symbol of either. Such behaviors are commonly found in stranger-to-stranger sexual assaults, domestic homicides, work-related homicides, and those crimes committed by political or religious terrorists. This could also be seen in a revenge orientation for perceived slights/injustices by co-workers and/or managers—perhaps by a worker who was skipped for promotion and/or promised raises.

Consider the 2007 case of a former police officer, now a part-time jail officer, in Homer, Alaska. A prisoner who was in the process of being taken into custody spat in his face at the police station while a state trooper was attempting to remove the prisoner's handcuffs. The jail officer responded by choking the still cuffed prisoner with his bare hands and ramming him into the wall. The state trooper was knocked to the ground. The details,

taken directly from the Alaska Bureau of Investigation's report on the incident, are provided in Armstrong (2008):

> During processing of a prisoner arrested last May, an Alaska State Trooper and two Homer Police officers had to separate a jail guard from the prisoner, an Alaska State Trooper investigator wrote in a report released last week by the Alaska Department of Public Safety. The trooper report said the guard choked the prisoner while he was being booked on a charge of disorderly conduct and resisting arrest at the Homer Jail.
>
> Homer Police Chief Mark Robl confirmed the incident happened, but, citing department policy, declined to identify the jail officer or the suspect or say if any disciplinary action was taken against the jailer.

CASE EXAMPLE: *CONTINUED*

The city of Homer conducted its own internal investigation and determined the jailer violated the Homer Police Use of Force Policy. Serious disciplinary action was taken against the jailer, said Homer City Manager Walt Wrede, but he did not specify the action. ...

Investigator Mark Granda of the Alaska Bureau of Investigations, the author of the report, forwarded the case to the Alaska Office of Special Prosecutions and Appeals for review of a charge of assault in the third degree, a class C felony. No charges were returned against the guard. Robl said the jail officer still works as a guard for Homer Police.

The trooper report said the city suspended the jailer the night of the incident and while troopers did their investigation.

The incident came to the attention of the Homer News when an anonymous caller last month reported the alleged assault. The Department of Public Safety provided the Homer News with a redacted copy of its report after the paper filed an Open Records Request. The report identifies Granda, Trooper Derek Loop, the arresting officer, and Robl, but no other parties were named.

In the trooper report, Robl describes the jail guard as a former Homer Police officer with 22 years' experience who retired in 1999. The officer has been working as a part-time jail guard since 2007. ...

Based on interviews with the trooper who arrested the suspect, the suspect, another trooper at the jail, a dispatcher, a Homer Police officer, a police sergeant and the jail officer, ABI Investigator Granda gives this account:

At about 12:55 a.m. on May 28, Trooper Derek Loop took an Anchor Point man to the Homer Jail after arresting him for disorderly conduct and resisting arrest. The report identified Loop as the arresting officer, but did not name other police or troopers involved. Troopers arrested the man while investigating a 911 call and hang up made from his Anchor Point home. Troopers found no emergency, but when the man became belligerent, they arrested him.

The disorderly conduct charge was later dismissed, and the Anchor Point man pleaded no contest to resisting arrest and served 10 days in jail.

Loop told Granda he dropped off the suspect in the police booking room and left the room. While he stood in the hallway outside the booking room, a dispatcher on duty told him to get into the booking room. Loop went into the room and saw the jailer with both hands around the suspect's neck. He said the suspect's neck and face were turning red. Loop said the suspect blew and spat in the jailer's face, and the jailer said, "Nobody does that to me."

A police officer told Granda a similar story. He said the jailer had both arms straightened out and pushed against the suspect's throat. He said the suspect was still handcuffed. He said this was the first time he saw the jailer act like that. After thinking about the incident, he said he felt the jailer's use of force was inappropriate.

Another trooper at the jail said he had just finished booking another person for a driving under the influence charge. He heard from the jailer that Loop was bringing in a suspect who would take several people to handle. The trooper recognized the suspect from earlier arrests for domestic violence assault, resisting arrest and eluding police. He helped the jailer book the suspect.

The trooper said the suspect mouthed off when he was brought into the booking area. He said the jailer took off the right handcuff, but couldn't get the left handcuff off because of a piece of metal stuck in the keyhole. The trooper used a Leatherman tool to remove the metal.

Continued

CASE EXAMPLE: *CONTINUED*

He was still working on the handcuff when the jailer grabbed the suspect's neck with both hands and shoved him against the wall. The jailer, the trooper and the suspect were all standing.

The trooper said he either stepped away or was pushed, and then yelled to the jailer, "Let him go, let him go." He said the suspect did not fight back, that he turned a dark purple-blue color, made a raspy sound and his tongue stuck out of his mouth. The suspect was put on a bench and handcuffed to a rail on the wall above it.

The trooper later called the Kenai District Attorney's office about the incident and was advised to report the incident to his supervisor.

A police officer at the station that night came into the booking room after the alleged assault. He told Granda he called a trooper sergeant about the incident.

Granda's report noted the booking room had videotape cameras, but no one had put a tape in the camera and recorded the incident. Police and troopers also did not have audio tape recorders running during the incident, although they turned on the recorders after the incident.

In an interview with Granda, the jailer said he did not feel he did anything wrong. He said when the trooper had trouble with the left handcuff, he kept a hold on the handcuffs so the suspect wouldn't use the handcuffs as a weapon. The suspect tried to pull his hand away from the jailer. When the suspect blew in his face, the jailer said he pushed him away at arm's length. After the suspect spat on him, the jailer said he reached up with his left hand to hold the suspect's neck and pushed him against the wall.

Robl told Granda Homer has a Use of Force policy that prohibits choke holds. Robl said when the jailer started working, he read the police department's jail and department policy manuals and signed a statement that

he read the jail policy. Robl said the jailer was supposed to have sent Robl an email saying he'd reviewed the department policy manual, but Robl could not find a copy of that email.

The jailer told Granda he had reviewed the police department's policy and jail policy manual. He said he knows choke holds are not allowed, but said he did not do a choke hold on the suspect. The jailer defined a choke hold as getting behind the suspect and putting his neck between your arm and chest. The jailer told Granda he believed the suspect assaulted him and his use of force was justified.

The jailer told Granda he used force against the suspect because he spat in his face. "My intent was not to be spit on again and to make sure he didn't get loose," the jailer told Granda.

In this case the assault of the suspect in custody by the jail officer was viewed by all as a violation of the Homer Police Department's use of force policies. However, the incident did not come to light until reported by a witness from an outside agency. Additionally, the incident details and suspect information were withheld from the public by the Homer Police Department, to say nothing of the lack of an arrest. This is precisely the opposite of what happens when regular citizens admit to the commission of a crime.

It should also be noted that the jail officer was not terminated for committing the prisoner assault when officers throughout Alaska have been fired for precisely the same conduct, and even far less. The Homer Police Department has consequently exposed itself to incredible liability with respect to the foreseeability of future incidents. They have also sent a clear message to the community that it will work hard to protect its own, and to keep police crime and misconduct in house. There are fewer practices more corrosive to the public's trust of law enforcement.

With respect to motive, the jail officer felt he had been disrespected and responded to a non-lethal gesture with potentially lethal force. Such context, intent, and subsequent over-the-top responses are the very essence of anger-retaliatory behavior. The jail officer became instantly enraged by the suspect's actions, wanted to teach him a lesson, and did.

CASE EXAMPLE:

Debt, Divorce, and Termination/Profit and Anger Motivated

As explained in Turvey (2011), *profit motives* involve *profit-oriented* behaviors [that] result in material or financial gain. Examples of these behaviors can include torturing victims for money or information, theft of valuables, and drug-seeking behaviors associated with addition, such as theft or prostitution.

Consider the 2007 case of 38-year-old Anthony LaCalamita, an auditor with Gordon Advisers PC, an accounting firm in Troy, Michigan. In the space of a month, all of his problems converged and his life essentially collapsed. This culminated in a workplace shooting incident that took the life of one co-worker and wounded two others. As explained in Snell (2007):

> [LaCalamita] had been losing money in his real estate investments. Three weeks ago, he and his wife separated. Last week, he was fired from his job as an auditor at a Troy accounting firm.
>
> On Monday morning, according to police and witnesses, LaCalamita burst into the offices of his former employer and opened fire with a shotgun, killing one employee and wounding two others.
>
> By Monday night, he was in the custody of the Troy Police Department.
>
> Troubles for LaCalamita, 38, started mounting in 2006 when he began unloading properties at a loss in one of the country's worst housing markets. In one transaction, he sold a Plymouth home in October for $100,000 less than he owed on the mortgage, property records show.
>
> He also owed more than $100,000 on two loans obtained last year for a multi-unit building in Detroit.
>
> The deals were partially offset in February 2006 when he sold a Garden City home for $32,000 more than the amount he paid a year earlier, property records show. … The real estate losses followed a few profitable investments. From 2004 to 2005, LaCalamita made about $140,000 profit selling three homes in Livonia and Canton Township.
>
> Police: Couple separated

> Three weeks ago, LaCalamita and wife Michele separated, police said.
>
> He moved to Troy into the Kirts Village apartments, a two-story brick building with mustard-colored siding located east of Crooks, where police tape blocked the entrance Monday night as officers combed for clues. His wife apparently is living in Novi's Whispering Meadows subdivision, in a $263,000 tan-brick home with manicured hedges, purchased a year ago.

According to testimony from one of the victims, LaCalamita was fired for not putting in the required time and effort at his job. After his termination, he went to a shooting range for practice and then purchased a shotgun. Detailed in Brasier (2008):

> Three days before he went on a shooting spree at the Troy office building where he had been fired, Anthony LaCalamita went target practicing at a local gun range, using a Remington shotgun, the kind of gun he then bought and used to shoot three of his former colleagues.
>
> "He was normal customer, a nice guy, nothing out of the ordinary," said Roy Jihad, manager of Target Sports, a Royal Oak gun shop and range told jurors in the second day of LaCalamita's murder trial. LaCalamita arrived at the gun shop on April 6, 2007, the morning after he was fired from Gordon Advisers PC, asking to buy a gun.
>
> He paid $48 for a half hour of target practice in the range at the back of the building, located on Woodward, then purchased a Remington shot gun, and four boxes of ammunition. He also apparently lied on the application to purchase the gun, saying he had never been committed to a mental hospital. Records show he was twice admitted after suicide attempts.

On the day of the shooting, LaCalamita appeared to have specific targets in mind when he entered his former place of employment (see Figures 12-5 and 12-6). As explained in Aguilar (2007):

Continued

CASE EXAMPLE: *CONTINUED*

FIGURE 12-5
Thirty-eight-year-old Anthony LaCalamita is arrested and given a GunShot Residue test after eluding police on the day of the shooting.

FIGURE 12-6
A shackled LaCalamita hangs his head as a sheriff's deputy in court assists him.

CASE EXAMPLE: *CONTINUED*

Ninety minutes after reporting to work, Jean Larson heard what turned out to be deadly gunfire inside her office building—then "all hell broke loose."

Police say Anthony LaCalamita III, an accounting firm employee fired from his job last week, returned Monday to the building where he previously worked and shot three people, killing one. Two of the victims were apparently targeted, police said.

"We heard pop, pop, pop," smelled gunpowder and heard co-workers yelling, said Larson, 48, a staff accountant for G&C, a subsidiary of Gordon Advisors. "I heard one employee screaming, 'He's got a gun. He's got a gun.' ... It was a panic. No one knew what to do. No one knew where to go."

The gunman then left the office complex and headed north, where he was spotted hours later by a motorist 50 miles north of Detroit. He was taken into custody after leading officers on a 30-mile highway chase that reached speeds up to 120 mph.

LaCalamita, 38, said nothing after officers surrounded him, Genesee County Sheriff Robert J. Pickell said. Officers subdued him and found a 12-gauge pump-action shotgun and three live shells in the vehicle, the sheriff said.

Madeline Kafoury, 63, was killed, the company said.

LaCalamita was being held on charges of fleeing and eluding police. Police investigators met Tuesday with Oakland County prosecutors to decide charges in the shootings, and LaCalamita was to be arraigned Wednesday, Troy Police Lt. Gerry Scherlinck said.

...

"We are especially devastated by the death of Madeline Kafoury and our hearts go out to her family. Maddie was revered by clients, employees and owners alike," the statement said. Larson said Kafoury was well-known and well-liked. She said Kafoury retired last year after tax season ended, but returned part-time this year after her successor quit.

Scherlinck identified the other victims as a 47-year-old man and a 48-year-old man. He said the men were in management positions, and the gunman may have also been seeking another man who wasn't at the office at the time. "It appears that he was especially targeting those two males," Scherlinck said.

Frank DeArmas, whose wife works part-time in the office, said two partners in the firm, Paul Riva, 47, of Sterling Heights, and Alan Steinberg, 48, of Bruce Township, were still being treated Tuesday at a local hospital. ...

Witnesses told police that when the gunman walked into the office on the building's second floor around 10 a.m. Monday, he looked as if he was trying to hide something, Craft said.

Police couldn't say how many shots were fired.

After briefly assembling in the employee lunchroom, some employees opted to hole up inside individual offices. Larson joined two female co-workers, barricading the locked door with chairs, turning off the lights and silencing their cellphones.

Beneath a desk, the three curled up and kept quiet. "I was just so scared," Larson said. "I just kept thinking, 'This can't be happening.'"

In this case, there is not one specific event or circumstance that can be considered the sole reason for the shootings. Certainly, LaCalamita externalized more blame to his supervisors, but without the other combined financial and personal losses, his employment might not have been an issue. Add to these proximate circumstances the pathological debt and mental health issues related to prior suicide attempts and the tipping point was apparently reached. Given the high-speed chase that followed the shooting, one is left to wonder where LaCalamita was headed and how much more planning was actually involved—if any.

SUMMARY

Workplace violence takes many forms, affecting employees and employers alike. However, some professions are more susceptible than others. Moreover, the power dynamics between individuals involved are not always equitable. This needs to be investigated and established in every case.

It would be a mistake to conclude that there is one lens (e.g., typology, classification system) through which to view a particular case involving workplace violence. It is characterized by the same behaviors and motivations evident in other forms of violent crime—because it involves most of them. Therefore, one approach won't cover it.

The greatest mistake that a victimologist can make when analyzing these kinds of cases is to apply nomothetic workplace victim research as a conclusive absolute when it is, in fact, an abstract theory. Each offender chooses his or her own targets. Each offender incurs his or her own collaterals. Each offender has his or her own motivations and underlying circumstances. It is the job of the forensic victimologist to investigate these and render them out.

QUESTIONS

1. Name the four types of workplace violence offenders according to Loveless (2001).
2. True or False: *Nomothetic victim study* refers to the study of the concrete; examining individual victims and their actual qualities.
3. Explain the difference between *motive* and *intent*.
4. True or False: Profit motives are evident specifically in robberies and muggings.
5. What is the greatest mistake that a victimologist can make when analyzing cases of workplace violence? Explain.

REFERENCES

Armstrong, M., 2008. Homer jail guard investigated: jailer choked suspect, report says; no charges filed. Homer News, April 24; Available at: http://www.homernews.com/stories/042408/news_1_003.shtml

Brasier, L.L., 2008. LaCalamita practiced at gun range before rampage, owner testifies. Detroit Free Press, April 22; Available at: http://www.freep.com/apps/pbcs.dll/article?AID=/20080422/NEWS03/80422041/1005/news

California v. Jennifer and Matt Fletcher, 2004. Superior Court, Case No. PA 040748-01. Los Angeles County, CA.

Harrell, E., 2011. Workplace Violence, 1993–2009: National Crime Victimization Survey and the Census of Fatal Occupational Injuries. U.S. Department of Justice, Washington, DC.

Holmes, R., Holmes, S., 2000. Mass Murder in the United States. Prentice Hall, Upper Saddle River, NJ.

Kennedy, D., 2005. Workplace violence. In: Miller, J., Wright, R. (Eds.), Encyclopedia of Criminology, Vol. III, Routledge, New York, pp. 1775–1777.

Loveless, L., 2001. Workplace Violence: A Report to the Nation. Injury Prevention Research Center, The University of Iowa, Iowa City, IA, February; Available at: http://www.public-health.uiowa.edu/IPRC/NATION.pdf

Matejkovic, J., 2004. Which suit would you like? The employer's dilemma in dealing with domestic violence. Capital University Law Review, vol. 33, Winter; pp. 309–346.

OSHA, 2002. Workplace Violence—OSHA Fact Sheet. U.S. Department of Labor, Occupational Safety and Health Administration, Washington, DC.

Riley, K., 2003. Employer TROs are all the rage: a new approach to workplace violence. Nevada Law Journal, vol. 4, Fall; pp. 1–34.

Schoetz, D., 2008. Sheriff embroiled in inmate sex scandal. ABCNews.com, April 18; Available at: http://abcnews.go.com/print?id=4674575

Simmons, A., 2008. Duluth cop admits drinking before shooting another cop. The Atlanta Journal-Constitution, February 12; Available at: http://www.ajc.com/metro/content/metro/gwinnett/stories/2008/02/12/dailey_0213.html

Snell, R., 2007. How auditor's life unraveled. The Detroit News, Tuesday, April 10; Available at: http://www.detnews.com/apps/pbcs.dll/article?AID=/20070410/METRO/704100359

Tarr, N., 2007. Employment and economic security for victims of domestic abuse. Southern California Review of Law & Social Justice, Spring 16, 371–427.

Turvey, B., 2011. Criminal Profiling: An Introduction to Behavioral Evidence Analysis, fourth ed. Elsevier Science, San Diego.

Turvey, B., Petherick, W., 2008. Workplace violence. In: Turvey, B., Petherick, W. (Eds.), Forensic Victimology, Elsevier Science, San Diego.

Twohey, M., Ford, L., 2008. The law didn't save her. Chicago Tribune, March 16; Available at: www.chicagotribune.com/news/chi-domestic-violence_bd16mar16,0,6195124.story

Warchol, G., 1998. Workplace Violence, 1992–96. Bureau of Justice Statistics Special Report, July, Washington, DC.

CHAPTER 13

School Shootings

Brent E. Turvey[1]

KEY TERMS

Collateral victims Those who are attacked and injured unintentionally because of their proximity to a primary or secondary target within a given environment.

Familial problems Problems that might expose students to violent behavior or cause them to act violently, such as exposure to or suffering as a victim of family violence.

Internal problems Problems that might expose students to violent behavior or cause them to act violently, such as chemical, biological, or psychological problems.

Peer relationship problems Problems that might expose students to violent behavior or cause them to act violently, such as lack of parental guidance, support, and attachment, and a subsequent inability to resist or cope with peers.

Primary targets Those who are of greatest importance to the offender; they dictate the location and timing of the attack.

School shootings A particular form of workplace violence that occurs when anyone enters a campus and begins firing a weapon, such as a rifle, shotgun, or handgun.

Secondary targets Those who are of lesser importance to the offender; they will not dictate the location and timing of an attack.

Social and environmental factors Those factors that might expose students to violent behavior or cause them to act violently, such as routine exposure to violence as a component of fantasy or entertainment.

CONTENTS

As with any attack that occurs at an educational facility—to include grade schools, colleges, and universities—*school shootings* are a subtype of workplace violence. The relationships are fairly straightforward in this regard. Instructors, administrators, and support staff are employed and work on site, while the students are essentially clients.[2] There are also visitors, such as contracting service professionals, visiting sports teams, student parents, and student guests. Violent attacks on school campuses can occur between or within any of these groups.[3]

---

[1]This chapter is an update to, and partial rewrite of, Turvey and Petherick (2008).

[2]This is similar to the custodial relationship that exists between a hospital and its patients, or a prison and its inmates—with the exception that in some cases the clients are, in fact, minors.

[3]It is acknowledged here that the preceding chapter noted university lecturers are among the lowest risk groups for workplace violence; however, despite their infrequency, they do exist, and they need to be discussed.

Forensic Victimology. http://dx.doi.org/10.1016/B978-0-12-408084-3.00013-2

A *school shooting* occurs when anyone enters a campus and begins firing a projectile weapon such as a rifle, shotgun, handgun, or a crossbow. The specific target is irrelevant to this definition. Only the location and the use of a projectile weapon are relevant. There is no one profile that exists which accurately describes the typical school shooter, no checklist of red flags that will predict the shooter's behavior, no single overriding motive, and no preferred victim type.

School shootings remain horrific events, ripe for real-time 24-7 media coverage and related exploitation by those who would seek to benefit from it. When such an event happens, everyone becomes an expert, and everyone seeks to assign blame, often before the shooter is identified or apprehended. This chapter is intended to dispel common myths regarding school shootings perpetuated by the political agendas and sensational news coverage that tend to surround them. It also provides forensic victimologists with some language and lenses through which to perceive and assess such incidents more objectively.

NOMOTHETICALLY SPEAKING: THE AGGREGATE

There is wide agreement among researchers that no consistent school shooter profile exists. However, according to one study, some interesting themes emerge in such cases—if one considers only incidents with student offenders. As described in Angel (2001; pp. 486–487):

> All of these cases involved students bringing firearms to their schools and killing and wounding multiple victims. I will refer to these as "the school shooter cases." All the multiple shot, multiple victim school shooters have been white male adolescents who went to school with firearms and the intent to kill, and then killed. In a shockingly large percentage of these cases, they killed or wounded girls that they claimed to have "loved." Girls they harassed and stalked. Girls they believed had rejected them. Girls they killed in juvenile separation attacks.
>
> The pattern to all of the school shooter cases is that the killers were white boys who saw themselves as rejected by a girl or woman and/or who had their "manhood" threatened by bullying and, often, by being called gay. They all had access to firearms—rifles, shot guns, and pistols. All of the school shooters left clear indicators that they were about to commit mass violence. An extremely high number of them attempted, threatened, or actually committed suicide or died during or after their attacks.

This research was not as directed toward illuminating the characteristics of school shooter attacks by students as it was on finding a relationship between violence and gender stereotypes—which it did. It also draws deeply from the well of school shooter archetypes—namely, the lovelorn and bullied white male adolescent. Not to say that this isn't a persistent theme, but rather that the weakness of any generalization is that it tends to be a generalization.

The findings reported in Vossekuil et al. (2002), however, are more detailed. This study was conducted by the United States Secret Service in conjunction with the Department of Education. Researchers (p. 8) "identified 37 incidents of targeted school violence involving 41 attackers that occurred in the United States from 1974, the year in which the earliest incident identified took place, through June 2000, when data collection for the study was completed."

Again, a specific profile did not emerge in this study. Tendencies surfaced. Predispositions became evident. However, the only concrete and universal trait shared by school shooters in the study is the fact that 100% of them were male. With respect to incident characteristics, they found the following (pp. 15–16):

- In almost three-quarters of the incidents, the attacker killed one or more students, faculty or others at the school (73 percent, n = 2716). In the remaining incidents, the attackers used a weapon to injure at least one person at school (24 percent, n = 9). In one incident, a student killed his family and then held his class hostage with a weapon.
- More than one-half of the attacks occurred during the school day (59 percent, n = 22), with fewer occurring before school (22 percent, n = 8) or after school (16 percent, n = 6).
- Almost all of the attackers were current students at the school where they carried out their attacks (95 percent, n = 39). Only two attackers were former students of the school where they carried out their attacks at the time of those attacks (5 percent, n = 2).
- All of the incidents of targeted school violence examined in the Safe School Initiative were committed by boys or young men (100 percent, n = 41).
- In most of the incidents, the attackers carried out the attack alone (81 percent, n = 30). In four of the incidents, the attacker engaged in the attack on his own but had assistance in planning the attack (11 percent, n = 4). In three incidents, two or more attackers carried out the attack together (8 percent, n = 3).
- Most attackers used some type of gun as their primary weapon, with over half of the attackers using handguns (61 percent, n = 25), and nearly half of them using rifles or shotguns (49 percent, n = 20). Three-quarters of the attackers used only one weapon (76 percent, n = 31) to harm their victims, although almost half of the attackers had more than one weapon with them at the time of the attack (46 percent, n = 19).

With respect to victim and targeting characteristics, they found that planning and forethought were typical (p. 16):

- Perpetrators of incidents of targeted school violence chose a range of targets for their attacks, including fellow students, faculty and staff, and the school itself. These incidents were usually planned in advance and for [the] most part included intent to harm a specific, pre-selected target, whether or not the attacker's execution of the incident, in fact, resulted in harm to the target....
- In over half of the incidents (54 percent, n = 22), the attacker had selected at least one school administrator, faculty member or staff member as a target. Students were chosen as targets in fewer than half of the incidents (41 percent, n = 15).
- In nearly half of the incidents, the attackers were known to have chosen more than one target prior to their attack (44 percent, n = 16).
- Most attackers had a grievance against at least one of their targets prior to the attack (73 percent, n = 30).
- In almost half of the incidents (46 percent, n = 17), individuals who were targeted prior to the attack also became victims (i.e., individuals actually harmed in the attack). However, other individuals at the school, who were not identified as original targets of the attack, were injured or killed as well.
- Among these non-targeted individuals, over half were other students (57 percent, n = 21) and over one-third (39 percent, n = 16) were school administrators, faculty or staff.

Ultimately, these researchers focused on 10 findings from their study that beg further investigation and research, most of which will frontload any effort with an overwhelming sense of helplessness and despair (p. 31):

The 10 key findings that the authors believe may have implications for the development of strategies to address the problem of targeted school violence are as follows:

- Incidents of targeted violence at school rarely are sudden, impulsive acts.
- Prior to most incidents, other people knew about the attacker's idea and/or plan to attack.
- Most attackers did not threaten their targets directly prior to advancing the attack.
- There is no accurate or useful profile of students who engaged in targeted school violence.
- Most attackers engaged in some behavior prior to the incident that caused others concern or indicated a need for help.

- Most attackers had difficulty coping with significant losses or personal failures. Moreover, many had considered or attempted suicide.
- Many attackers felt bullied, persecuted or injured by others prior to the attack.
- Most attackers had access to and had used weapons prior to the attack.
- In many cases, other students were involved in some capacity.
- Despite prompt law enforcement responses, most shooting incidents were stopped by means other than law enforcement intervention.

In line with the preceding research of Vossekuil et al., a number of checklists are available for the purpose of identifying potential school shooters. They are essentially an aggregate of previous high-profile incidents, offering a snapshot of common characteristics. Interestingly, most also identify the problem with the predictive validity of the checklist, suggest it is a starting point only. This is a caution that we wholly endorse. Consider the following from the National School Safety Center (1998):

> The National School Safety Center offers the following checklist derived from tracking school-associated violent deaths in the United States from July 1992 to the present.... After studying common characteristics of youngsters who have caused such deaths, NSSC has identified the following behaviors, which could indicate a youth's potential for harming him/herself or others.
>
> Accounts of these tragic incidents repeatedly indicate that in most cases, a troubled youth has demonstrated or has talked to others about problems with bullying and feelings of isolation, anger, depression and frustration. While there is no foolproof system for identifying potentially dangerous students who may harm themselves and/or others, this checklist provides a starting point.
>
> These characteristics should serve to alert school administrators, teachers and support staff to address needs of troubled students through meetings with parents, provision of school counseling, guidance and mentoring services, as well as referrals to appropriate community health/social services and law enforcement personnel. Further, such behavior should also provide an early warning signal that safe school plans and crisis prevention/intervention procedures must be in place to protect the health and safety of all school students and staff members so that schools remain safe havens for learning.

- Has a history of tantrums and uncontrollable angry outbursts.
- Characteristically resorts to name calling, cursing or abusive language.

- Habitually makes violent threats when angry.
- Has previously brought a weapon to school.
- Has a background of serious disciplinary problems at school and in the community.
- Has a background of drug, alcohol or other substance abuse or dependency.
- Is on the fringe of his/her peer group with few or no close friends.
- Is preoccupied with weapons, explosives or other incendiary devices.
- Has previously been truant, suspended or expelled from school.
- Displays cruelty to animals.
- Has little or no supervision and support from parents or a caring adult.
- Has witnessed or been a victim of abuse or neglect in the home.
- Has been bullied and/or bullies or intimidates peers or younger children.
- Tends to blame others for difficulties and problems s/he causes her/himself.
- Consistently prefers TV shows, movies or music expressing violent themes and acts.
- Prefers reading materials dealing with violent themes, rituals and abuse.
- Reflects anger, frustration and the dark side of life in school essays or writing projects.
- Is involved with a gang or an antisocial group on the fringe of peer acceptance.
- Is often depressed and/or has significant mood swings.
- Has threatened or attempted suicide.

Unfortunately, many of these characteristics will not become known until after a full examination of the background characteristics of the offender can be conducted—by which time it is too late. They can assist with determining why a shooting incident occurred, but reveal precious little about how to identify troubled or at-risk persons. The reason is that many of these characteristics are quite prevalent in student groups across the board; specifically, teenage angst, largely reflected herein, does not necessarily reflect violent and destructive tendencies.

In a move away from these limited studies reports, psychological assessment tools are meant to provide a more rigorous and empirically sound approach to risk assessment. However, research in the area has cast a somewhat gloomy light on the efficacy of these models as well. Let's consider three of the more common tools for this purpose: the PCL-R, the Violence Risk Appraisal Guide (VRAG), and the Static-99.

Freedman (2001) provides a fairly critical commentary on the use of the PCL-R as a tool for predicting the propensity to commit violence, as well as being incorporated into other risk assessment tools such as the VRAG. Rightly stated within this critique is that the uncritical reliance on such tools promotes the unjustified incarcerations of people who would not otherwise have posed a risk, perhaps because of the propensity of mental health professionals to favor assessments of risk over none, resulting in a large number of false positives.

This problem has been canvassed by Ogloff and Davis (2005, p. 311), with their second critique relating directly to the use of such checklists as described previously:

> It was found, perhaps not surprisingly, that psychiatrists, psychologists, and release decision-makers tended to make conservative decisions that suggested that people were are risk for dangerousness or violence when, in fact, they were not....
>
> At least three problems led to false positive errors made in predicting risk for violence. First, research had not identified empirically supported risk factors associated with violence. As such, many myths existed about the factors that indicated that one was at risk for being violent. The so-called "triad" is a good example. For many years it was incorrectly believed that if one child had been prone to encopresis, fire setting, and harming animals as a child, one would be at risk for violence.
>
> Second, in addition to failing to identify the correct factors that increased one's level of risk for violence, even when some valid factors were identified, it was difficult for clinicians to systematically assess them or to understand how they went together. For example, if we know that mental illness and substance abuse are two risk factors, what would we consider one's level of risk to be if one had a mental illness but not a substance abuse problem (or vice versa), or if one had both a mental illness and substance abuse problem contemporaneously?
>
> Finally, and perhaps most insidious, is the fact that the base rate for violence in many populations is generally so low that it is difficult to accurately predict whether one will be violent in the future.

These concerns can be easily juxtaposed onto those of Freedman (2001, p. 91), especially point two and three above, regarding the use of the PCL-R for violence prediction:

> The research that has been conducted thus far shows that the use of the PCL-R to predict violent behavior involves substantial and unacceptable rates of error. Although the PCL-R has been used to differentiate between psychopaths and non-psychopaths, the more

important concern is within-group statistics. As discussed previously, because the research has artificially increased the number of people claimed to score high by lowering the cutting scores, the proper analysis of the reliability and validity of the instrument must start with intragroup assessment of the high-scoring group.

The evidence of intragroup statistics indicates poor prediction capacity concerning violence. The rate of false-positives associated with use of the PCL-R, although often unreported in favor of inter-group data, is strikingly consistent and very high, worse than a coin toss in predictive validity.

The Violence Risk Appraisal Guide (VRAG) and the Static-99 are another two, and among the most popular two, Actuarial Risk Assessment Instruments (ARAIs). Both have also been critiqued fairly heavily by Litwack (2001) and Hart, Michie, and Cooke (2007). The study by Litwack is not chronicled here further. Suffice it to say that it is a very comprehensive meta-analysis of the literature surrounding risk assessment and a must-read for any student or practitioner with more than a passing interest in the area.

Hart and colleagues examined the efficacy of both the VRAG and the Static-99. For the VRAG, the precision of the instrument was assessed for violent recidivism over a 10-year period. For the Static-99, the precision of the instrument was assessed for sexually violent recidivism over a 15-year period. For each instrument, a 95% confidence interval was employed to determine the accuracy of prediction. Without needing to dig deeper into the results of the study, one can well make the point simply by restating the discussion section (Hart, Michie, and Cooke, 2007; p. 63, below). However, the reader is advised to consult the paper for a full and complete discussion of their findings.

Our analyses indicated that two popular ARAIs used in risk assessment have poor precision. The margins of error for risk estimates made using the tests were substantial, even at the group level. At the individual level, the margins of error were so high as to render the test results virtually meaningless. Our findings are consistent with Bohr's conclusion that predicting the future is very difficult.

Our findings likely come as no surprise to many people. The difficulties in predicting the outcomes for groups versus individuals—whether in the context of games of chance or of violence risk assessments—are intuitively obvious.

By now, the point should be fairly clear: the nomothetic average as found in an empirical study may apply to a given case, or it may not; there may be factors in an individual's background that contribute to his or her propensity for violence, or there may not. However, until a full analysis of a case can be conducted, the existence of these factors might remain unseen and therefore unknown. Additionally, a full analysis is generally not possible until often long after the trigger has been pulled. Consequently, using empirical research to predict whether a particular individual will start shooting people at a school is likely to be underinformed and overall misleading.

CASE EXAMPLE:

Louisiana Technical College

On February 8, 2008, at 8:35 a.m., Latina Williams, 23, killed herself and two other nursing students in a second-floor classroom at Louisiana Technical College in Baton Rouge, Louisiana (see Figure 13-1). She fired six shots from a .357-caliber revolver into Karsheika Graves, 21, and Taneshia Butler, 26. Then she reloaded and shot herself in the head (Smith and Vetter, 2008).

The 911 call details were published in Smith (2008):

Calls started pouring into 911 dispatch after shots rang out inside Louisiana Technical College on Feb. 8. The Baton Rouge Police Department released tapes of the calls Friday....

"Has anybody been shot?" dispatch asked the first caller, who dialed 911 at 8:35 a.m.

"I don't know, I'm in the office right now. I heard a shooting in the hallway and I hear screaming," she said.

Less than two minutes later, a woman called from an upstairs nursing classroom, near the shooting. "We're locked in the room and we've turned the light off," the woman said.

She added that she did not know who the shooter was, but heard shouts of, "Get down, hurry, run," from the hallway.

A minute later, a sister of someone inside the school called 911 to relay her sister's message at 8:38 a.m.

"I was calling to report a shooting at LTC. My sister just called me and told me that they are shooting inside the building," she says calmly.

A particularly harried caller phoned at 8:40 a.m., after police had arrived at the scene.

"Come on help!" she screams as dispatch answers.

FIGURE 13-1

In 2008, 23-year-old nursing student Latina Williams killed herself and two others with a handgun in a classroom at Louisiana Technical College in Baton Rouge.

Continued

CASE EXAMPLE: *CONTINUED*

"Yes? Can I help you?" the dispatcher replies.

"The school!" she says.

"Where? Which school?" the dispatcher asks.

"She shot several times! I don't know who was shot or how many shots, times," the caller replies, out of breath.

The caller said she ran out of the building to get her phone after the shots rang out.

Dispatchers helped assure those who were locked down in classrooms before police reached them. One caller phoned at 8:41 a.m. from the second floor near the crime scene, saying that the school is under lockdown.

"They have police on scene and they have EMS up there, OK?" the dispatcher assured the caller.

The final caller in the tapes had barricaded herself in a bathroom at the school. "Are they gonna let us know when it's safe to come out of the bathroom at Louisiana Technical College?" she asked.

Janes (2008), quoting directly from public statements made by the Baton Rouge Police, provides insight into Williams' state of mind prior to the attack. They are reminiscent of reported findings from the white male school shooter population.

Latina Williams had been living in a car and showing signs of paranoia before she went to a New Orleans pawnshop where she bought the .357-caliber revolver she used the next day to fatally shoot two classmates and then herself, police said Monday.

Williams, 23, kept the weapon concealed in her purse as she opened fire Friday at her Louisiana Technical College nursing classmates before stopping to reload, Baton Rouge Police Department spokesman Sgt. Don Kelly said.

["]Don't worry, I'm not mad at y'all,["] Williams told those in the classroom before turning the gun on herself, witnesses said.

Police believe that shortly before the morning onslaught Williams anonymously called a crisis counselor, indicating she planned to take her own life, Kelly said. The alarmed counselor contacted authorities to tell them about the nameless call around the time Williams was opening fire inside her classroom....

Williams had no permanent residence and was apparently living out of her car, Kelly said in a written release. She was estranged from her family in Mississippi and had sparingly spoken with them in the past two years....

Kelly also said Latina Williams had displayed signs of paranoia, though he declined to elaborate further on her mental state....

The day before the shooting, Williams purchased a .357-caliber revolver and a box of ammunition from a New Orleans pawn shop, Kelly said. He would not release the name of the pawn shop, but he did say some of the money used in the purchase came from the sale of some of Williams' possessions.

Police will complete their investigation sometime next week, Kelly said.

Investigators have not found any connection between Williams and her victims, Graves and Butler, to explain why or if they were targeted, Kelly said. Authorities have not been able to determine if Williams left a suicide note.

At a memorial service Sunday night, classmates of Graves and Butler said they did not believe the shooting was provoked, only that their proximity to Williams when she entered the classroom led to their deaths.

Possible red flags

Williams' homelessness estrangement from her family, paranoid behavior and the call to the counselor were all indicators of a risk for violence, said Kathy Seifert, a Maryland-based psychologist with an expertise in youth and family violence....

CASE EXAMPLE: *CONTINUED*

You can look at these risk factors and can see there's going to be a bad outcome if there is no treatment, said Seifert, who has written the book *How Children Become Violent* and said she is researching another about women and violence.

Seifert said there were basic similarities between Williams and Cho Seung-Hui, the gunman who opened fire in a Virginia Tech building and murdered 32 people before killing himself.

Cho kept to himself, did not interact with other students and had a psychiatric problem that had not been addressed when he moved from secondary school to college.

Williams' classmates said she stuck to herself and ate alone at lunch. In a class photo, Williams is barely visible, hiding her face behind other students.

Seifert said Williams' homelessness was likely one of the stressors that could have contributed to the violence that ended her life and took two others.

Anybody can come unglued if the stressors they are under exceeds their resources, Seifert said. She had risk factors for violence, suicide.

It could have been mental breakdown. When you see somebody with all these risk factors, there is a need to assess this person so the inevitable outcome doesn't happen.

This example essentially contradicts major inviolate findings in published school shooting research: the offender was not only black, but was also a female. Another issue is Williams' connection with the two victims and how they were targeted. If indeed no personal connection is evident (police claimed that she exhibited signs of detachment from reality prior to the shooting), then the context becomes all-important. Her primary target may have been herself, and she may have simply wanted everyone to see and to remember her destruction.

More interesting than her race and sex (these barriers were bound to be broken) is the issue of her overall comportment. The absence of outward rage (other than the big gun and the killing) and the reported apologetic nature of Williams' demeanor are not evident in the literature to date. In fact, quite the opposite. School shooters are known for their angry or vacant expressions, their ruthless and purposeful victim selection, and their recriminating taunts toward victims. No matter how you approach it, using the existing literature as a guide to the Williams case, one becomes immediately lost.

Given this example, the cautionary refrain from previous chapters remains relevant and bears repeating. Contextual data is interesting, and even important for developing case theories and establishing risk or exposure factors in some instances. However, grouped and averaged victim data is also abstract. It does not represent particular victims that exist in the real world. It represents possibility, not actuality. And that possibility is limited by what has been recognized and studied. In actual casework, one is bound to encounter circumstances that have not been previously documented, let alone studied. This limitation is important to understand, and must be incorporated into subsequent findings regarding case-specific interpretations.

To be clear, it is fair to say that we won't really know what is present in a case until it is established by the evidence. Prediction is often inaccurate and therefore rarely responsible. Nomothetic information is useful for forming possible theories and avenues of investigation, but these theories need to be tested against the real-world circumstances of a particular case. Then, and only then, can the full universe of the case be known, and the nomothetic theories that exist be established as relevant to *this* victim, *this* offender, and *this* crime.

IDIOGRAPHIC ANALYSIS

In the following sections, we discuss certain basic idiographic considerations with respect to school shootings and adduce illustrative examples as necessary.

Targets

As explained in the preceding chapter, every offender has particular victim or target criteria that satisfies his or her needs—no matter how general or specific. There are essentially three kinds of targets: primary, secondary, and collateral.

Primary Targets

Primary targets are those that are of the greatest importance to the offender. They dictate the location and timing of any attack. Often, the offender will have planned out and intend to hit that victim at the risk of forgoing any or all other targets in the environment. In some cases, there will be more than one primary target.

In school shootings, the student shooter may target a classmate who has made fun of him or her in the past, a romantic interest that has left him or her feeling scorned (whether this be real or perceived), a teacher who gave an unfavorable mark, or an administrator who gave an unfavorable punishment. The student may also target the school in general, seeking the greatest destruction and body count in his or her efforts.

Secondary Targets

Secondary targets are those who are of lesser importance to the offender. They will not dictate the location and timing of an attack. However, they will be a conscious choice based on the availability within environmental and temporal constraints dictated by primary targets. Not all offenders will take the time to deliberate over the possibility of achieving secondary targets.

In school shootings, secondary targets will be representative of the primary targets. Someone or something that is associated with them. Instead of a teacher—the principal; instead of a classmate—their friends or intimates (if available); and instead of a principal—their office, belongings, or vehicle.

Collateral Victims

Collateral victims are those who is attacked and injured unintentionally because of their proximity to a primary or secondary target within a given environment. Their injury is completely uncalculated and incidental to the intended outcome. Collateral victims are, in fact, not targets. It is important to distinguish between secondary targets and collateral victims—the key difference being intent.

In school shootings, collateral victims will be hit because they are in the way. They are in the wrong place at the wrong time. The student who is hit by a bullet that comes through a wall; the teacher hit by a shotgun blast meant for the student standing next to him or her; or the principal who is shot while trying to get a primary target to safety. Many collateral victims are simply in the field of fire.

Exposure Factors

Rather than try to create a new breed of criminal in which to cast the school shooter, the authors take the approach that perhaps a step back is necessary. To understand school shootings, and because they can originate from other forms of school violence, we recommend a general approach. Lintott (2004) breaks down the general factors that influence school violence of all kinds into four general areas: internal problems, familial problems, peer relationship problems, and social/environmental factors.

Internal Problems

Students with *internal problems* that may expose them to violent behavior or cause them to act violently include those with chemical, biological, or psychological predispositions. This is explained thoroughly in Lintott (2004; pp. 556–557):

> Some students may have disabilities so severe that they need an intensely therapeutic environment, one that is not practical in a traditional school setting. Not every student, however, that has a mild chemical imbalance needs to be removed from a public school setting....
>
> One problem associated with student violence is a neurological chemical imbalance. When a student feels threatened, the body produces noradrenaline, the "alarm hormone" that produces the instinct to fight or flee. At the same time, high amounts of stress may decrease serotonin, the "feel-good hormone," which reduces the effects of noradrenaline. This chemical imbalance may create a stressful situation where a child is more likely to interpret neutral behavior as aggressive and react violently. Thus, some students may be chemically prone to violence, making it difficult for schools to anticipate and understand the student's violent reactions and to respond appropriately.
>
> Other problems associated with student violence and biological disorders are hyperactivity and attention deficit disorder. These

students lack problem-solving capabilities and have difficulty controlling their emotions. Students with these problems may not be able to distinguish between non-violent situations and those conflicts that could result in violence. While some of this behavior may be curbed by medication, not all children have adequate healthcare. Furthermore, some parents refuse to medicate their children because the medication causes a change in the child's personality, or the parents do not want the stigma of having a "medicated child." This problem may be compounded if the student has an improper diet. Studies have shown that a diet high in sugar may increase aggressive behavior. It is the complexity of factors in dealing with these students that requires a school system to expend a great deal of attention to behavior and aggression.

Students with learning disabilities are also more likely to be involved in violence. Learning-disabled children experience daily failure and frustration, leading to a negative self-image that is often reinforced by teachers and peers. This negative self-image may result in an attempt to gain recognition through delinquent behavior, some of which may be in the form of aggressive actions. Therefore, violent reactions to conflict may be a natural reaction to an internal, medical disability.

The predispositions discussed here can cause students, or other shooters, to act in a way that might appear to come from nowhere when, in reality, clear symptoms are missed due to the absence of proper staff training, student screening, and related funding.

Familial Problems

Students with *familial problems* that may expose them to violent behavior or cause them to act violently include those who have been exposed to, or suffered as a victim of, domestic violence and abuse. As explained in Lintott (2004; pp. 557–558):

A predominate theme is that family violence in the home is often associated with student violence. Researchers have proposed that a child who is a victim of family violence may be responding to this traumatic experience through disruptive or violent classroom behavior. This is due to the abused child's heightened levels of anxiety even when in a non-abusive environment, and they "express their anger and hurt through antisocial behaviors." This trend in violent behavior has been observed increasingly in very young students.

Another problem associated with school violence is parental acceptance of violent responses to conflict. When the child is taught to solve conflict with violence by his family, but is taught to resolve the conflict nonviolently by the school, the child becomes confused. This student needs constant affirmation that there are non-violent ways to deal with conflicts, and that these are appropriate while in school. Without a significant support system, however, practitioners find that it is unlikely that the student will reject the violent influence of his family or guardians.

When violence is learned at home as an acceptable tool for problem solving, this can become the tool of choice when dealing with problems outside the home. This is learned not just from the example set by parents and guardians, but also siblings and extended family members.

Peer Relationship Problems

Students with *peer relationship problems* that may expose them to violent behavior or cause them to act violently include those who do not have parental guidance, support, or attachment. Subsequently, they are unable to resist or cope with the demands of their peers. As explained in Lintott (2004; pp. 558–559):

> Students' relationships with peers are very important in predicting school performance and delinquent behavior. Students who do not have "parental support and attachment are less equipped to deal with school demands and the resulting frustration of school failure." These students are "more vulnerable to the temptations and pressures they experience from their peers, and many youth turn to disruptive and delinquent behavior in schools."
>
> A compounding problem affecting peer relationships in urban schools today is the presence of gangs. Twenty-nine percent of urban students reported that street gangs were present in their schools. These gangs can range from national organizations involved in organized crime, to cliques of students who have "gang signs" or "gang colors," but may not be considered a "gang" under all definitions. These groups can provide its members a sense of identity and belonging, increasing that member's self-esteem. Unfortunately, this makes those students who are doing poorly in school and not involved in school activities the most likely students to join gangs. Violence among gangs can stem from issues such as status, reputation, or "turf," and a substantial amount of gang violence can permeate into school. When violence is gang related, traditional mechanisms that a school uses to curb violence may not have an impact. In these situations, the pressure from the gang to commit violence may overwhelm the influence of a school to dissuade violence.

Concerns regarding peer group criminality are related to what criminologists refer to as *Differential Association Theory* (DAT; aka Differential

Association-Reinforcement). This theory of crime was first published in 1947 by Edwin Sutherland, a sociological criminologist, as a means to (Vold and Bernard, 1988; p. 210) "organize the many diverse facts known about criminal behavior into some logical arrangement," or as Cressey (1953) explains, to provide (p. 43) "a general theory of crime causation."

DAT, in association with *Social Learning Theory*,[4] proposes that criminal behaviors, crime-specific techniques, criminal motives, and corresponding rationalizations for violating the law are not genetic; that they are learned through direct social interaction with others; and that criminal values vary, depending on an individual's perception of related social, cultural, and peer attitudes (Jeffery, 1965; Matsueda, 2006; Reid, 2003; Sutherland, 1947; and Vold and Bernard, 1986). As explained in Cressey (1953), DAT provides that (p. 43) "persons acquire patterns of criminal behavior in the same way they acquire patterns of lawful behavior—through learning in interaction with other persons." As an adjunct to this theory, the propensity for criminal behavior is maintained by material and social consequences, or their absence (Jeffery, 1965).

Other Social and Environmental Factors

Students with *social and environmental factors* that may expose them to violent behavior, or cause them to act violently, include those who are routinely exposed to violence as a component of the media or personal entertainment choices. However, such factors are not enough to impel any-one toward an act of violence. It is commonly understood that most people who watch violent movies, play violent video games, or listen to music with violent lyrics do not necessarily commit violent crime. In fact, the opposite is most certainly true. For violence to result, there must be something else present—some other compounding factor. As explained in Lintott (2004; pp. 559):

> Many practitioners today feel that the increase in school violence can be attributed to increased violence in popular culture. Media outlets such as television and the internet are commonly blamed for the increase of school violence. According to the American Psychological Association, "children watch an average of 8,000 murders and 100,000 other violent acts on television before finishing elementary school."...

---

[4]An extension of Differential Association, *Social Learning Theory* holds that "peer associations, attitudes, reinforcement, and modeling are predictors of delinquency and crime in general" (Chappell and Piquero, 2004; p. 89).

While the extent to which violent images can encourage actual violence is beyond the scope of this note, it is important to note that this violent environment may affect those students who are more prone to violence due to other factors.

Finally...violence may be increased in our schools because of administrators' responses to school violence. One study found that excessive discipline for misbehaving students often increases violent behavior in students. In 1984, the National School Boards Association warned that "traditional approaches—such as punishment, removing troublemakers, and similar measures—often harden delinquent behavior patterns, alienate troubled youths from the schools, and foster distrust."

The author includes these general factors influencing school violence because it is necessary to appreciate the extent to which the school shooter may, in fact, be born of victimization. Many—pushed down by successive failure, an inability to cope, a lack of support, or even bullying—are simply coming back over the top with a response that they believe is acceptable. Many (and certainly not all) believe that they have been victimized, and they believe that they are justified in fighting back—whether or not their victimization is, in fact, real.

Motivational Events and Circumstances

The motivations for school shootings have traditionally focused on anger, retaliation, and rage. School shooters are, in this regard, perceived as a form of urban terrorist. This is an oversimplification that comes from our first response to the notion of a school shooting: we aren't safe; our children aren't safe; and our communities are not safe. We are filled with terror and we are not wrong to feel terrorized.

However, terrorization may not have been the intent of a given school shooter. True enough that it is the intent for some. But not all are angry, not all want a high body count, and not all are interested in evoking terror. Some are mentally ill or otherwise distressed, and then they don't want anything else ever again.

Case Examples

Consider the following cases, all of which go against the published research. The first involves an Asian male with narcissistic motives that evoking terror (and the accompanying air-time) will satisfy. The second involves a non-student shooter with an obvious sexual motive who chose victims beyond the media's immediate reach.

CASE EXAMPLE:

Virginia Tech

Because of available cellphone and Internet technology and the competitive nature of the 24-hour news cycle, the relationship between violent crime and the media is rapidly approaching a critical mass. Victims and offenders alike are communicating directly with news outlets before, during, and after the commission of crimes. It's a matter of narcissism, supply, and demand. Certain offenders want to be seen, the media outlets want to make money, and the public wants to see offenders commit crime as well as any related victim suffering.

In April 2007, 23-year-old Virginia Tech student Cho Seung-Hui, a senior and English major, committed a mass homicide with the highest body count in the history of U.S. school shootings. Though his background and mental state are similar to many school shooters, his Asian descent is not (Flannery, 2008; pp. 287–289):

> Seung Hui Cho was an angry and disturbed college student. During his tenure at Virginia Tech, Cho showed himself to be a loner who was withdrawn from those around him. Cho was also the type of person who had had suicidal and homicidal ideations as early as the eighth grade and who stabbed at the carpet in a female student's room in the presence of his college suitemates. In addition, Cho also took inappropriate pictures of his female college classmates from a camera under his desk, wrote poetry that was all about violence, and thus was individually counseled, and identified as a Virginia Tech student with problems. In response to being asked to cease his conduct, Cho emailed a suitemate stating that "I might as well kill myself now."…
>
> Virginia Tech conducted an assessment and pre-screen interview of Cho at 8:15 p.m. on December 13, 2005. A licensed clinical social worker for New River Valley Community Services Board (CSB) interviewed Cho and a police officer, as well as Cho's roommate and his suitemate. The social worker found that Cho was "mentally ill," was an imminent danger to himself or others, and was not willing to be treated voluntarily. She recommended

> involuntary hospitalization and indicated that the CSB could assist with treatment. The social worker then located a psychiatric bed, as required by state law, at St. Albans Behavioral Health Center at the Carilion New River Valley Medical Center. When Cho was admitted to this hospital overnight, he denied that he was violent but admitted that he did have access to a firearm.
>
> The hearing concerning Cho's psychological condition was held on December 14, 2005 before Special Justice Paul M. Barnett of the Montgomery County General District Court. The Justice considered various source materials and heard from Cho himself. He concluded that Cho "presents an imminent danger to himself as a result of mental illness" and ordered "O-P [outpatient treatment] to follow all recommended treatments."
>
> After these events, the warning signs kept piling up. Cho subsequently wrote a paper for his creative writing class about "a young man who hated the students at his school and planned to kill them and himself," saying, among other things, "I hate my life…. This is it…. This is when you die with me." Another professor alerted a dean about Cho's distressing conduct but nothing happened, not even the counseling that the professor recommended.

Numerous precursors and warning signs were evident. Everyone knew that he was getting worse, from the courts to the counselors. However, no action was taken. Details of the shootings, and a timeline, are provided from Flannery (2008; pp. 292–294):

> On April 16, 2007, at about 7:15 a.m. at the West Ambler Johnston residential hall, Cho shot and killed Emily Hilscher and Ryan Christopher Clark [see Figure 13-2]. The police responded to the scene, but no one was taken into custody. At 9:26 a.m., two hours and fifteen minutes after the first shooting, the Virginia Tech Administration sent an email

CASE EXAMPLE: *CONTINUED*

FIGURE 13-2
Emily Hilscher and Ryan Clark were the first victims killed by Cho Seung-Hui.

to staff, faculty and students about the first shooting.

About two-and-a-half hours after the first shooting, and about ten minutes after the email was circulated, Cho started shooting in Room 206 in Norris Hall killing nine and wounding three of the thirteen students in that room. Cho then went across the hall and entered Room 207, a German class. Cho shot the teacher, as well as the students near the front of the classroom, and then started walking down the aisle shooting other students.

Cho then left the classroom and walked into the hallway. In the meantime, students in Room 205 heard gunshots and barricaded the door. Cho fired through the door.

As the tragic event unfolded further, in Room 211, the teacher asked a student to call 911 on her cell phone.

The students shoved a desk in front of the door but Cho pushed past it. Cho then walked down the row of desks shooting people. The student with the cell phone was shot in the leg. Another student picked up the cell phone and begged the police to hurry. Cho heard her speak and shot her, grazing her head twice. She played dead while holding the phone under her head with the line open.

Three of the students pretended to be dead and managed to survive. Meanwhile, police outside tried but failed to shoot open the locks that Cho affixed to the three doors at Norris Hall.

Cho then went back to room 207, the German class, where two injured students and two that were not injured managed to hold the door shut with their feet and hands. In response, Cho returned to the French class and opened fire on the students there again.

At about 9:45 a.m., five minutes into the siege, a janitor saw Cho loading his gun and thus was able to escape....

Continued

CASE EXAMPLE: *CONTINUED*

Cho also tried to enter Room 204, where an engineering professor braced his body against the door, taking Cho's shots himself and losing his life, while saving many students who had time to escape through the window.

Tragically, two students did not escape the carnage and were shot by Cho....

Cho then returned to Room 206 to shoot the survivors. At that time, the police finally used a shotgun to break the locks and stormed the second floor [see Figure 13-3].

At 9:50 a.m., the administration sent a second email warning the campus: "A gunman is loose on campus. Stay in buildings until further notice. Stay away from all windows." Four loudspeakers blasted this same message.

At 9:51 a.m., Cho shot himself in the head.

In keeping with the new relationship between the media and mass murder, and the narcissism at work behind this particular crime, Cho Seung-Hui mailed photographs, video, and writings to NBC News that chronicled his motives and state of mind. NBC aired it, and the public consumed it without hesitation.

As per Cho's intent, international mass media coverage and infamy followed. This was all much to the distress of the victims, their families, and the Virginia Tech community in general.

FIGURE 13-3
Law enforcement and other first responders work to retrieve those injured occupants of Norris Hall at Virginia Tech, where the shooter, Cho Seung-Hui, killed nine and wounded three.

CASE EXAMPLE:

Nickel Mines, Amish School Shooting

As we've made clear throughout this text, it is a mistake to practice as though prior case experience will allow us to generalize accurately regarding present offenses. Not every school shooting is the work of a disenfranchised white student with an ax to grind against a particular student or school. Nor is technology always present. Nor is every school shooting about present anger or wrongs. Sometimes the shooter is an outsider, sometimes technology is literally absent, and sometimes the motive comes from the past. Consider the case of

CASE EXAMPLE: *CONTINUED*

Charles Carl Roberts IV. On October 2, 2006, he defied all school shooter archetypes to date (Holusha, 2006):

A lone gunman walked into a one-room schoolhouse in a largely Amish community in southeastern Pennsylvania today and shot as many as 10 girls, killing three immediately before turning the gun on himself and dying at the scene, according to the state police [see Figure 13-4].

The school is just outside Nickel Mines, a tiny village about 55 miles west of Philadelphia.

The man, identified as Charles Carl Roberts IV, 32, who lived in the area, was evidently nursing a long-ago grievance expressed in notes left for his wife and children, said Jeffrey Miller, commissioner of the state police.

He said the gunman lined the girls against the blackboard, bound their feet and shot them execution-style in the head. "He split them up, males and females," Commissioner Miller said. "He let the males go, some of the adults go. He bound the females at the blackboard, and apparently executed them."

Three of the girls were dead at the scene in Nickel Mines, Pa., and seven others were rushed to nearby hospitals, some of them severely wounded. An earlier Associated Press report quoted a local coroner as saying there were six people dead, but the coroner later said he was unsure.

The A.P. said…"There was some issue in the past" that had left the gunman with a desire to harm female students, Commissioner Miller said. He said that the murders were premeditated and that the gunman had called his wife—without telling her he was holding hostages in a school—that he would not be coming home.

Commissioner Miller said Mr. Roberts called his wife from a cell phone, saying he was "acting out in revenge for something that happened 20 years ago." "It seems as though he wanted to attack young, female victims," he said, according to The Associated Press.

The gunman released about 16 boys in the class, a pregnant teacher's aide and three women with small children before the shooting

FIGURE 13-4

Members of the Amish community stand outside law enforcement barrier tape at the scene of the school shooting in Bart Township, Pennsylvania.

Continued

CASE EXAMPLE: *CONTINUED*

began, Commissioner Miller said. The principal teacher escaped at that time and ran to a nearby property to call 911.

The gunman, who was not Amish, evidently chose the small, private Amish school in Lancaster County about 55 miles west of Philadelphia because the security would be lax, Commissioner Miller said. He said when police tried to talk to the gunman over loudspeakers to begin negotiations, Mr. Roberts made a cell phone call from inside the building threatening to start shooting unless police pulled back.

He was armed with an automatic pistol and a shotgun and had barricaded the doors to the school with structural lumber to slow down the police, who tried to charge in once the shooting started.

Police said the gunman worked as a truck driver who collected milk from nearby farms for processing and sale. Police said he walked his own children at a nearby bus stop before borrowing a relative's pick-up truck and heading for the Amish school.

Commissioner Miller of the State Police said the gunman was not wanted for any crimes and apparently did not have a criminal record.

Far from being revenge oriented as suggested by some, the motive behind the Amish Schoolhouse takeover appears to be a sex crime that ended in suicide. This is detailed in Knight (2006):

"He wasn't agitated, he wasn't screaming, he was just taking control," said Commissioner Jeffrey Miller, of the Pennsylvania Police, as he recounted the last moments of Charles Carl Roberts IV, a milk lorry driver, who shot ten Amish schoolgirls at close range yesterday morning.

In the first insight into the possible motives of Roberts, a respected and well-liked father of three, Mr. Miller said that the gunman had called his wife, Marie, on a mobile phone soon after taking the schoolgirls hostage and said he had attacked two young relatives as a 12-year-old.

"I'm not coming home, the police are here," he is reported to have said before directing her to suicide notes in which Roberts said he had been assailed by dreams of assaulting young people again.

Police said today that Roberts had panicked when ten state troopers surrounded the one-room Georgetown Amish School in the tiny village of Nickel Mines, Pennsylvania, and started "executing" the schoolgirls rather than following what appeared to be a plan "to victimize them in many ways."

Three girls died instantly when Roberts shot them in the back of the head and two more succumbed to their injuries overnight. Five others remain in hospital after being shot in the head and back. All of the victims were students. The dead girls were named today as Naomi Rose Edersol, 7, Anna Mae Stolzfus, 12, Marian Fischer, 13, and sisters Lina and Mary Liz Miller, aged 7 and 8.

Roberts then killed himself as police broke through the windows of the school. Officers had to free the dead and wounded from wires that bound their ankles.

Roberts had nailed closed the side door of the school and blocked the main entrance with a piece of wood and desks. As well as equipping himself with 600 rounds of ammunition and a change of clothes, he also brought plastic handcuffs, planks of wood mounted with ten pairs of hooks, apparently to restrain his victims, and KY jelly, a sexual lubricant.

At a news conference this afternoon, Mr. Miller said that rambling suicide notes left for Roberts's wife, Marie, and his three children, suggested that the gunman, a home-schooled Christian, acted out of grief for a daughter who died nine years ago and as a furious reaction to his alleged attack on two relatives as young as 3 when he was just 12 years old. [See Figure 13-5.]

Mr. Miller said that Roberts's confession had come as a complete surprise to his wife

CASE EXAMPLE: *CONTINUED*

FIGURE 13-5

A family photo of Marie and Charles Roberts IV, and their daughter Abigail (provided to the media by the family).

and that interviews with his family, although ongoing, had yet to corroborate any wrongdoing. "They have no knowledge of any molestation of family members or anyone else," he said.

Although it is unclear what, if any, crime Robert committed as a young boy, his assault, America's third fatal school shooting incident in the last week, was meticulously planned. Mr. Miller said today that Roberts parked his milk lorry outside the Nickel Mines Auction House, just yards from the school, after every shift and that the unprotected building represented "a target of opportunity."

Based on his phone call and suicide letters, investigators believed he wanted to attack girls of a certain age rather than members of the Amish community.

Police discovered a checklist and receipts that showed Roberts was buying equipment for the attack up to six days ago. A handwritten list in a notebook read: "Tape. Eyebolts. Tools. Nails. Hoes. KY. Bullets. Guns. Binoculars. Earplugs. Batteries. Flashlight. Candle. Wood."

CASE EXAMPLE:

Sandy Hook Elementary, Newtown, Connecticut

On December 14, 2012, classes began at 9:30 a.m. as per usual at Sandy Hook Elementary School in Newtown, Connecticut (see Figure 13-6). Shortly afterward, police began receiving 911 calls reporting a masked man in the school building with multiple weapons, firing on staff and students alike. By 9:45 a.m., SWAT teams were on scene conducting an active shooter search of the school building. Within an hour, it was announced that the shooter was dead at the scene—by his own hand.

An investigation ultimately revealed that the shooter, 20-year-old Adam Lanza, had first killed his mother at the home they shared prior to driving to Sandy Hook Elementary that day. She was a noted gun enthusiast, had purchased firearms for Adam, and also taught him how to shoot. As reported in Lysiak and McShane (2013):

> Adam Lanza, wearing a bullet-proof vest and carrying an assault rifle, drove his dead mother's car to the elementary school where he mercilessly killed 20 students and six staffers.
>
> The mother and son shared a Newtown home where they were armed to the teeth, with rifles, knives, Samurai swords, a 7-foot spear and more than 1,600 rounds of ammunition.

> Investigators found a Sandy Hook report card inside the house—along with a holiday gift card from mother to son with a check for him to buy a new gun.

The shooting scene was emotionally disturbing to all responders, including those from the medical examiner's office, as reported in Dunavin (2013):

> Responding to difficult questions posed by a national media corps that descended just one day earlier on this normally quiet town about 60 miles northeast of New York City, the Connecticut chief medical examiner described how and where the bullets entered the children, what the kids were wearing and how he felt about what he'd seen inside Sandy Hook Elementary School.
>
> "This probably is the worst I have seen or the worst that I know any of my colleagues having seen," said Dr. H. Wayne Carver II of the Office of the Chief Medical Examiner, where he's been working for 31 years including 26 as chief.[5]

FIGURE 13-6
The exterior of Sandy Hook Elementary School in Newtown, Connecticut.

CASE EXAMPLE: *CONTINUED*

Carver said he saw no difference in the pattern of shooting deaths between children and adults inside the school.

The weapon used primarily in the shootings was a long rifle, Carver said, and victims young and old were shot "all over" with some at close range and some not. "I only did seven of the autopsies, the victims I had ranged from three to 11 wounds apiece and I only saw two of them with close range shooting," Carver said.

The shooter who wielded that gun—discovered dead inside the building Friday with a rifle and two smaller guns near his body, police have said—has been widely reported to be Adam Lanza, 20. His motives remain unclear; state police are investigating.

Carver said he would complete autopsies on the shooter and the shooter's mother, widely reported to be Nancy Lanza of Sandy Hook, on Sunday morning.

All bodies were removed from the school before dawn Saturday and transported to the medical examiner's base in Farmington—about 40 miles away. The children's autopsies were performed first so that their bodies could be made available to funeral directors "for obvious reasons," Carver said.

Asked whether the shooting victims at the school suffered, Carver responded: "To [the] best of my ability to answer that question, which is always less than perfect: If so, not for very long."

Family members have since come forward to report that Adam Lanza may have suffered physical abuse, perhaps as the result of bullying, when he was a student at Sandy Hook, and that his mother had considered filing a lawsuit for related staff negligence at the time (Lysiak and McShane, 2013). It has also been reported that he may have suffered from other mental disturbances, such as Asperger's Syndrome. These reports, though from the family, are as of yet unconfirmed.

The 20 child victims of Adam Lanza were all ages 6 and 7. This school shooting incident so shocked the conscience of the nation that the gun control debate took center stage for several months afterward. However, while the debate continues in the media and the Newtown massacre has become a lightning rod issue, no specific legislation has resulted.[6] Ironically, out of concern over potential bans, gun and ammunition sales across the United States soared during the post-shooting interval.

A major lesson to be learned from the Adam Lanza case is that victim targeting is often a function of the location of the attack—period. Certainly, the current staff and children could have done nothing to provoke any rational person to a violent breaking point, let alone mass homicide. What Adam Lanza perceived were his emotions, cumulative and isolated from the emotions or reactions of others, in relation to his perceived experiences with the school. Ultimately, they were directed at the school in general and suffered by its specific occupants in what could be described as a tragedy of timing. That is to say, this assault on the school could easily have happened a year or two prior; it could have happened a year or two later; or under certain conditions it might not have happened at all. Only a full investigation of Adam Lanza's pathology might begin to answer these questions.

---

[5]The author was fortunate enough to be a student of Dr. Carver's at the University of New Haven, where he taught a course on Medicolegal Death Investigation.
[6]The author has nothing to add to the debate other than the fact that school violence takes many forms, including beatings, rapes, stabbings, and even bombings. This would suggest that debating gun control is debating only one of the symptoms related to school violence, and not the cause of it.

SUMMARY

School shootings are a particular form of workplace violence that defies profiles and predictions. Despite sensational coverage by the popular media, they vary with respect to victim–offender relationships, victim targeting, and offender motivation. The archetypical angry white male student shooter image is slowly eroding, and the other races and sexes are emerging. Rather than seeing school shooters as an isolated construct, one may find it more useful to view them in the overall context of school violence—as both a cause and consequence—in order that more informed analysis of individual cases may be possible.

QUESTIONS

1. True or False: School shootings are a form of workplace violence.
2. List and describe the three kinds of targets.
3. True or False: Motivations for school shootings typically focus on power.
4. Name five characteristics often displayed in potentially dangerous students.
5. List and describe four general factors that influence school violence according to Lintott (2004).

REFERENCES

Angel, M., 2001. The school shooters: surprise! boys are far more violent than girls and gender stereotypes underlie school violence. Ohio Northern University Law Review 27, 485–516.

Chappell, A., Piquero, A., 2004. Applying social learning theory to police misconduct. Deviant Behavior 25, 89–108.

Cressey, D., 1953/1973. Other People's Money, Reprint edition. Wadsworth, Belmont, CA.

Dunavin, D., 2013. Medical examiner: Newtown shooting victims suffered 'devastating set of injuries.' Newtown Patch, January 24; Available at: http://newtown.patch.com/groups/police-and-fire/p/police-no-motive-emerging-in-newtown-school-shooting

Flannery, J., 2008. Students died at Virginia Tech because our government failed to act! George Mason University Civil Rights Law Journal vol. 18, Spring; pp. 285–304.

Freedman, D., 2001. False prediction of future dangerousness: error rates and psychopathy check-list-revised. Journal of the American Academy of Psychiatry and Law 29 (1), 89–95.

Hart, S.D., Michie, C., Cooke, D.J., 2007. Precision of actuarial risk assessment instruments. British Journal of Psychiatry 190 (49), 60–65.

Holusha, J., 2006. Students killed by gunman at Amish schoolhouse. New York Times, October 2; http://www.nytimes.com/2006/10/02/us/03amishcnd.html

Janes, J., 2008. Killer acted paranoid *** Woman lived in car, believed suicidal before shootings. The Baton Rouge Advocate, April 12, p. 1A.

Jeffery, C., 1965. Criminal behavior and learning theory. Journal of Criminal Law, Criminology, and Police Science 56 (3), 294–300.

Knight, S., 2006. Amish school shooter's sex crime secret. The Age, October 4; http://www.theaustralian.com.au/news/world/amish-school-shooters-sex-crime-secret/story-e6frg6so-1111112308021

Lintott, J., 2004. Teaching and learning in the face of school violence. Georgetown Journal on Poverty Law and Policy 11, Fall, pp. 553–580.

Litwack, T.R., 2001. Actuarial versus clinical assessments of dangerousness. Psychology, Public Policy, and Law 7 (2), 409–443.

Lysiak, M., McShane, L., 2013. Newtown shooter Adam Lanza taunted and beaten by fellow students when he attended Sandy Hook Elementary School, relative reveals. New York Daily News, April 13; Available at: http://www.nydailynews.com/news/national/exclusive-lanza-mom-mulled-lawsuit-article-1.1315985

Matsueda, R., 2006. Differential social organization, collective action, and crime. Crime, Law and Social Change 46 (1–2), 3–33.

Ogloff, J.P.R., Davis, M., 2005. Assessing risk for violence in the Australian context. In: Chappell, D., Wilson, P. (Eds.), Issues in Australian Crime and Criminal Justice, LexisNexis Butterworths, Sydney.

Reid, S., 2003. Crime and Criminology, tenth ed. McGraw-Hill, Boston.

Smith, S., 2008. First 911 caller asked: 'Anybody been shot?' The Baton Rouge Advocate, April 5; p. 4A.

Smith, S., Vetter, K., 2008. 911 tapes reveal chaos at LTC / Woman killed 2, self in February shootings. The Baton Rouge Advocate, April 5; p. 1A.

Turvey, B., Petherick, W., 2008. School shootings. In: Turvey, B., Petherick, W. (Eds.), Forensic Victimology, Elsevier Science, San Diego.

Vold, G., Bernard, T., 1986. Theoretical Criminology, third ed. Oxford University Press, New York.

Vossekuil, B., Fein, R., Reddy, M., Borum, R., Modzeleski, W., 2002. The Final Report and Findings of the Safe School Initiative: Implications for the Prevention of School Attacks in the United States. U.S. Secret Service and U.S. Department of Education, Washington, DC, May.

CHAPTER 14

Stranger Violence

Brent E. Turvey[1]

KEY TERMS

Collateral victims Those who are attacked and injured unintentionally because of their proximity to a primary or secondary target within a given environment.

Convenience offenders Those who select victims who can easily learn their identity, the locations they frequent, and the circumstances that will be more likely to result in their later identification and apprehension.

Displaced anger Anger directed at someone or something other than the original investigator of that feeling; it is directed at a representative or proxy.

Homicide Death at the hands of another, regardless of intent.

Precautionary offenders Those who select victims whom they do not know, locations they do not frequent, and circumstances that will be less likely to result in their later identification and apprehension.

Primary targets Those who are of greatest importance to the offender; they dictate the location and timing of the attack.

Secondary targets Those who are of lesser importance to the offender; they will not dictate the location and timing of an attack.

Stranger violence Violence that occurs when an offender attacks a victim whom he or she does not know; someone who is not part of the family, not a friend or co-worker, and not an acquaintance of any kind.

A stranger is someone who is unknown or foreign. *Stranger violence* occurs when an offender attacks a victim that he or she does not know. This refers to a victim who is not a part of the offender's family, not a friend or co-worker, and not an acquaintance of any kind. Though generally less common than violence suffered at the hands of friends, family, and acquaintances, stranger violence enjoys a great deal more of our attention.

The goals of this chapter are to dispel prevailing myths and rhetoric connected with stranger violence perpetuated by sensational media coverage of such incidents, and to provide forensic victimologists with some language and lenses through which to perceive stranger violence more objectively.

---

[1]This chapter is an update to, and partial rewrite of, Turvey and Petherick (2008).

Forensic Victimology. http://dx.doi.org/10.1016/B978-0-12-408084-3.00014-4

"STRANGER DANGER"—AN OVERVALUED CONCEPT

There is a false belief held by some that strangers represent the greatest danger to our personal safety. This perception endures because of the way the media reports and portrays crime. News, film, television, mystery novels and true crime books supply us with a constant barrage of stories and imagery depicting the perils of stranger crime. Consequently, the general public cannot help but be limited by what is available to them from these sources when conceptualizing the threats in their environment (see the *availability heuristic*, discussed in Chapter 2).

However, it is not just the public who are at risk of being biased and forming preconceptions; investigators and other criminal justice professionals can also be influenced. Consider, for instance, a situation in which a victim is unable to identify his or her attacker—either because the victim did not see the attacker, cannot recall what he or she saw, or because the victim actually died as a result of the attack. In such instances, there are some investigators who prefer to advance and maintain only those case theories that do not implicate a victim's friends or family. This can occur for many reasons: partly because of the availability heuristic, partly because of investigative politics, partly because of preconceived bias, and partly because of desire to avoid direct contact with the victim and his or her loved ones.

This preference is endemic to criminal justice professionals suffering from inadequate education, training, and experience, as well as those with victim–family *embroilment*.[2] Under these circumstances, those responsible for establishing the facts of a case may not consider the involvement of those in the victim's immediate home environment to be viable suspects. They may cling to a misplaced belief that stranger crime is the first, best, or most likely (or most preferable) theory. Consequently, they may not give sufficient effort and consideration to the elimination of family and household members with respect to possible involvement.

The reality is that criminal investigation requires, in most cases, the development and elimination of suspects associated with the crime scene and the

---

[2]Discussed in Crowder and Turvey (2013), *embroilment* refers to the abandonment of objective and professional responsibilities because of personal feelings. In the case of investigators and forensic examiners, it can occur when one's professional roles and obligations are compromised by over-involvement or over-identification with a victim or his or her family members. Embroilment is a risk for every investigator and every examiner in every case. The determining factor is whether the investigator changes his or her behavior, or abandons professional obligations, because of his or her personal feelings. This is very common, for example, in cases involving the abuse, sexual assault, or murder of children. Or in domestic violence and sexual cases in which the investigator is attracted to the victim.

victim (e.g., friends, family members, household members, and co-workers)—particularly in cases that involve children. This must be a primary consideration. Failure to develop and eliminate these specific suspect pools represents an investigative failure at the most fundamental level—unless the identity of the offender can be unequivocally established by some other means.

CASE EXAMPLE:

Ariel Castro, Cleveland, Ohio

Consider the case of Ariel Castro, the 52-year-old former school bus driver in Ohio that, as of this writing, stands accused of abducting three women, holding them captive in his home for around a decade (see Figure 14-1), sexually assaulting them, impregnating them, and killing almost all the children that resulted (he reportedly induced abortions in his captives by means of physical assault). The abductions of the three women, which police claimed to have been investigating for years, were high profile in the community: Amanda Berry, Gina DeJesus, and Michelle Knight. Amanda Berry was reported to have escaped with a six-year-old daughter fathered by Castro. As reported in Barr and Sheeran (2013):

> Police say the women were apparently bound by ropes and chains at times and were kept in different rooms. They suffered prolonged

sexual and psychological abuse and had miscarriages, according to a city official briefed on the case.

Castro has been charged with four counts of kidnapping—covering the captives and the daughter born to one of them—and three counts of rape, against all three women....

The women, now in their 20s and 30s, vanished separately between 2002 and 2004. At the time, they were 14, 16 and 20 years old....

They never saw a chance to escape over the last 10 years until this week when Amanda Berry broke through a door and ran to freedom, alerting police who rescued the other two women while Castro was away from the house.

FIGURE 14-1
Police crime scene technicians remove evidence from 2207 Seymour Avenue, where Castro is reported to have held Amanda Berry, Gina DeJesus, and Michelle Knight captive for around ten years.

Continued

CASE EXAMPLE: *CONTINUED*

In newly released police audio tapes, a 911 dispatcher notifies officers on Monday that she's just spoken to a woman who "says her name is Amanda Berry and that she had been kidnapped 10 years ago." An officer on the recorded call says, "This might be for real."

After police arrive at the house, women can be heard crying in the background. Then an officer tells the dispatcher: "We found 'em. We found 'em." ...

Police investigators were evidently treating these abductions as either runaways or stranger crimes. Had a proper victimology been done by those responsible, it is likely that they would eventually have found Castro's connection to at least two of the victims through his own daughter. As reported in Muskal (2013):

One of the daughters of the man accused of holding three women prisoner for about a decade in Cleveland says her father preyed on her friends.

Two of the women held prisoner went to school with two daughters of Ariel Castro, the former school bus driver charged with kidnapping and rape in the case, according to the suspect's daughter Emily....

"It couldn't be coincidence," said Emily Castro, now serving a 25-year prison sentence for stabbing her daughter in 2011. The two Castro daughters, Emily and Arlene, were friendly with Gina DeJesus and Amanda Berry, two of the women police say were kidnapped and held in the house at 2207 Seymour Ave., owned by Ariel Castro, 52. Berry lived near the Castro girls, who were living with their mother and stepfather, Emily said.

Arlene Castro was the last to see DeJesus before she disappeared in 2004, police have already said.

Emily Castro said she was bothered that her father allegedly used her and her sister to look for victims on their street where they lived and played. "He would come to his own kids' neighborhood, not his own. I'm not saying he should have done it [at] all. I'm saying he didn't consider anything about us being his kids. He didn't consider that he's not only doing [kidnapping children] but he's hurting us," Castro said, according to ABC News....

The three women were held for about a decade until Berry broke through a screen door on May 6. With the help of neighbors, she escaped and called police who freed the women and the child. [See Figure 14-2.]

FIGURE 14-2

A missing poster for Amanda Berry outside her family home. Note the balloons and banner in the background on her porch which reads "Welcome Home Amanda!".

CASE EXAMPLE: *CONTINUED*

Had a proper victimology been done (e.g., a timeline, a friends and family list), and had the last person to see Ms. DeJesus alive been properly investigated, law enforcement would also have learned of Castro's connection. They would also have discovered his propensity for domestic violence and for abducting his own children. That is, if after that connection was identified, a basic background investigation had been conducted.[3] However, as more

information comes out, it becomes clear that the focus in these missing person cases was on stranger crime, or that no active investigation was being conducted at all.

---

[3]*Reported in Barr and Sheeran (2013), Castro's deceased wife had filed an order of protection against him after reporting multiple instances of domestic violence, threats to kill her and her daughters, and frequent abduction of her daughters to keep her from them.*

This overvalued concept also has implications with respect to social policy and legislation. As explained in (Maguire and Singer, 2011; pp. 310–311):

> Current sex offender legislation assumes that sex offenders go to schools or parks to connect with their victims and that they have a pattern of offending against strangers. Victim choice is one of the defining differences between child molesters and rapists. However, these differences are not accounted for in sex offender legislation. Rapists, who do not generally choose child victims, also cannot live near a park or a school or a place where children regularly gather.
>
> It is reasonable to be afraid of the notion of a stranger violating one's personal space or body or one's child, and it is this fear that is fueled to drive present day sex offender legislation. However, the assumptions (that unknown offenders will connect with our children at a school yard or park) of the sex offender legislation are not supported by empirical evidence. When legislation does not target the correct behaviors, it is less likely to make the community safe....
>
> While sex offenders can be dangerous, just as armed robbers and homicidal neighbors are dangerous, much of the policy that governs the life of the sex offender after prison is a result of socially constructed fear perpetuated by the media. The general lack of public understanding of sex offenders makes them easy to sensationalize by short media blitzes.

Similar influences can take hold over criminologists, or be inherited by them from the fruits of inadequate investigations. Given that a majority of crime researchers lack direct access to specific case data beyond media accounts, too many are left to study its narrow and heavily filtered leavings. As with the public, they may fall prey to specific types of sensationalized imagery that, in the absence of case experience, may infect their methods and findings. This is to say nothing of their emotions, which can be equally distorting.

It is far more interesting, and marketable, for the criminologist to study strangers who lurk in dark alleys than it is to study the extent to which friends and family members victimize each other. After all, if the greatest danger comes from inside our homes and the narrow circle of friends we draw around ourselves, then we can never truly be safe; that which we cling to for protection, and for comfort, is also our greatest liability. Examining the horror of the situation only makes it that much more horrible. As explained in Collins (2007), there is a resulting dissonance between perception and reality with respect to stranger crime (p. 133):

> In 2002, approximately sixty-five percent of all murder victims under the age of thirteen were killed by a family member. Yet these crimes are not ordinarily the ones that capture public attention; instead, we reserve our greatest outrage for those relatively rare cases where a child is murdered or sexually molested by a sexual-predator stranger. As a result, we have a tremendous mismatch between perception and reality: we think we are tough on crimes committed against children by passing statutes like Megan's Law, but in practice, we are overlooking the reality that children face the most danger from family members rather than from strangers. As one reporter for the *Washington Post* recently wrote "People think child homicide is big news, like Adam Walsh or JonBenet Ramsey[,]…but they're wrong. Six or seven infants, toddlers or children under the age of 10 are killed by adults in the District [of Columbia] each year, about 1,500 across the country. Most of them, if they make the news at all, are dispatched with paragraphs as short as their lives." Equally troubling, these cases often do not result in a perpetrator being held accountable by the criminal justice system, particularly when that perpetrator is a parent.

Further still, Collins (2007) argues that culturally we have romanticized family relationships—specifically parent–child relationships, to the point of denial about what is going on in our homes right in front of us (p. 134):

> [W]e struggle with holding some parents accountable for the harm they do to their children, […] because of our tendency to romanticize the parent–child relationship. This romanticization phenomenon has several core components. First, we continue to believe that love, not law, is sufficient to protect our children, even in situations where love is clearly not enough. In other words, we engage in denial; we want to believe that parents will do the right thing by their children without the intervention of the criminal justice system. As a result, we tend to focus on therapeutic approaches to address violence committed against children, without grappling sufficiently with difficult questions about whether the criminal justice system can also play an appropriate

role. In contrast, reformers working in the spousal-abuse area have been far more willing to consider utilizing a criminal approach. The second component is minimization: when violence does occur, we tend to downplay it. This phenomenon is reflected both in statutes that treat intrafamilial and extrafamilial offenders differently and in the difficulties prosecutors face in securing criminal convictions against parents.

These cultural tendencies and professional failings have had specific consequences across the criminal justice spectra, as discussed in Dawson (2006; pp. 1418–1419):

> The degree of intimacy that exists between victims and defendants has traditionally been seen as a major explanatory variable in determining criminal justice outcomes in cases of violent crime. Typically, it is argued that intimate violence and, in particular, violence between intimate partners, is treated more leniently by the courts than crimes between those who share more distant relationships. Even though numerous legislative and policy changes have occurred in recent decades to respond to intimate violence, it is still commonly assumed that these acts are treated more leniently than non-intimate violence by criminal justice actors. This belief has persisted despite the lack of consistent empirical support for an association between intimacy and law. As a result, one might argue, as Hagan and O'Donnel have with respect to gender and sentencing, that the perceived criminal justice leniency toward intimate violence has become part of conventional criminological and sociological wisdom. In other words, it may be that sociologists and citizens alike assume that those who victimize intimates are less cold-blooded, less rational, less dangerous, and, in sum, less blameworthy, for example, than those who victimize non-intimates. These assumptions may also lead one to believe that defendants who victimize intimates are, and should be, treated more leniently by the courts than those who share more distant relationships with their victims. This may also explain the lack of systematic and empirical research that has focused on the association between intimacy and law, compared to the abundance of research that has examined the effect of other variables on criminal justice outcomes such as gender, race and age.

To make a competent study of the victim, the forensic victimologist must examine the victim's friends, family, and household members in a manner that is guaranteed to upset pretty much everyone when problems are found to exist. Invariably, family problems and relationship discord are found, as familiarity often breeds contempt. The issues in a victim's personal life can be minor, such as getting bad grades at school, having arguments over financial concerns, and dealing with issues of personal jealousy. Or they can be toxic and traumatic, such as alcoholism, physical abuse, drug abuse, or sexual abuse. Whatever the case, the forensic victimologist must pry deeply because even small things can have big consequences.

Because of these existent problems, even when unrelated to the crime at hand, the victim's family and household members tend not to embrace scrutiny that might require the airing of dirty laundry. They are therefore likely to minimize them, conceal them, or otherwise block their discovery for any number of reasons—harmful and benign alike. They may also cry, act in an avoidant manner, or become enraged.

As a result of these realities, inexperienced and improperly trained investigators tend not to scrutinize victims or their statements with sufficient care. To do so, they are required to deal directly with victims, their family and household members, and any relationship partners. This generally occurs face to face, or over the phone, and can be very uncomfortable if not completely upsetting. An investigator's unwillingness to fully investigate victims and their home life, whatever the excuse, places a veil over their case that can have disastrous consequences. The least of which is that the investigator is willfully blinded to a victim's true circumstances; the worst of which is the conviction of an innocent while a criminal goes free.

Forensic victimologists must navigate these concerns with great care and yet remain apart from them. They must work to be insulated from criticism by objectivity, scientific methodology, and an accelerated understanding of how and why their role is necessary to the investigation of fact. They must understand that stranger violence is common, and therefore a reasonable consideration in suspect development in many unsolved cases. However, the prevalence of intimate violence demands that they must also be fearless in their efforts to help to eliminate friends, family, and other household members as suspects. This can only be accomplished with thorough investigative and forensic efforts.

Media Distortion of Public Perception

Most people do not work in the criminal justice system. Consequently, most people do not have direct and unfiltered access to actual accounts of crime. Even those who do tend to know only what occurs within their experiential bandwidth—with respect to a specific region, jurisdiction, and occupation. Unless one works cases in multiple regions of varying social contrast, overall perceptions about crime and related trends come primarily from one source: the media.

There is a specific relationship between the media and public fear. People fear the unknown. They tend to shy away from unfamiliar environments and individuals. They tend to embrace the emotional safety of the usual, the customary, and the routine.

Those in the media are fully aware of what frightens the public, but they are also aware of something else. Fear from a distance is a form of entertainment. The more fear a story evokes in the viewership or readership, the more marketable. This becomes more important when we consider that fear of stranger crime, in specific, represents the ultimate fear of the unknown.

For those who did not know, media outlets are businesses. They are also less and less concerned with delivering accurate information to consumers—especially in the news. Newspapers and newscasts are about delivering market share to advertisers and turning a profit. As explained in Buckler (2005), they do so based on various criteria unrelated to rendering a fair or balanced perspective (pp. 2–3):

> Communication scholars and criminologists have provided theoretical commentary about the particular factors that influenced journalist and news editor assessment of the newsworthiness of crime stories based on market-driven criteria. Chermak (1995) argued that the staff of news organizations assessed newsworthiness of a crime occurrence on the basis of five criteria: (a) the violent or heinous nature of the offense, (b) demographic factors of the victim and offender (age, race, gender, income, and socioeconomic status), (c) characteristics of the incident producers (the news agency), (d) the uniqueness of the event, and (e) event salience (e.g., is the offense a local event?). Prichard and Hughes (1997) similarly argued that the important determinants of news organization assessment of newsworthiness included such factors as how unusual the criminal event was relative to characteristics of more typically occurring offenses, the qualities of the parties involved, and the extent to which the behavior violated formally and informally established cultural norms and expectations.
>
> Practicing journalists have also acknowledged that there are certain criteria that are used to judge the marketability of crime news events. One such set of criteria was recognized by Pat Doyle in 1976 and has been referred to as the "Doyle criteria," (Johnstone, Hawkins, and Michener, 1994). The pursuit of stories that are marketable is best conceptualized as an organizational pressure that is placed upon journalists and news editors that influence their decisions in how they cover the news. In this regard, journalists and news editors, in making their news coverage decisions, act as agents of the news organization and vicariously make day-to-day decisions that support the market-driven approach of the news organization.

In a 1976 interview of Pat Doyle of the *New York Daily News*, he described four elements of a human interest story that Johnstone et al. (1994) have referred to as the "Doyle criteria." According to Doyle, a human interest story is one that either (a) involves a socially "prominent" or "respectable" citizen who is involved as either an offender or as a victim; (b) the victim is an innocent or an overmatched target; (c) the murder was either shocking or brutal, involved multiple victims and/or offenders, or in which a particularly brutal method of killing was employed; or (d) the narrative generates mystery suspense, or drama.

What this tells us is that the more extreme elements in a story, the more violent, and the more sensational—the more likely it is that the media will fixate on it.[4] This because it will be entertaining, consequently more people will watch it, and more ad revenue may be commanded from advertisers. The extreme case or circumstance is therefore the media norm. This also tells us that if we rely on the news as our primary source regarding general perceptions of crime, we are literally being sold a bill of goods. Our perception of crime becomes a reflection of the extreme rather than the usual.

Fear is a form of entertainment for many—sometimes healthy and sometimes not. Fear of stranger violence, however, is the ultimate fear of the unknown. Our resulting preoccupation with it has created a media marketplace rich with memorable examples to populate our availability heuristics. The result is a distorted perception that affects the way crime is reported, investigated, studied, adjudicated, and reported all over again.

Nomothetically Speaking: The Aggregate

Because the media damages our perspective of crime so thoroughly and on such a regular basis, it is vital that we ground ourselves with some actual data. As with previous chapters, the warning regarding nomothetic study remains: group data tells us about groups, not individuals.

Homicide refers to death at the hands of another, regardless of intent. There are many different kinds of homicide; however, they are commonly grouped (sometimes improperly) for study. Consider the most recent statistics at the time of this writing, reported by the U.S. Department of Justice, Bureau of Justice Statistics.

With respect to non-fatal violence[5] (Harrell, 2012; p. 1): "Violent victimizations committed by strangers accounted for about 38% of all non-fatal violence in

---

[4]Hence, the unfortunate journalistic expression, "If it bleeds, it leads."
[5]Non-fatal violence refers to crime such as rape/sexual assault, robbery, and aggravated assault.

2010. Simple assault made up the majority (60%) of victimizations committed by strangers during the year, followed by aggravated assault (20%), robbery (17%), and rape or sexual assault (2%)." This indicates that strangers generally account for a little over a third of all non-fatal violence.

However, it was found that overall, between 2005 and 2010, more than half (52%) of reported robberies were committed by strangers. So the one-third generalization does not hold up for every type of non-violent crime.

With respect to homicidal violence (Harrell, 2012; p. 1): "From 1993 to 2008, among homicides reported to the FBI for which the victim–offender relationship was known, between 21% and 27% of homicides were committed by strangers and between 73% and 79% were committed by offenders known to the victims." This indicates that strangers generally account for less than a quarter of all homicides.

Also, Harrell (2012) found that from 2005 to 2008, around 43% of homicides determined to have been committed by a stranger occurred during the commission of a robbery or during an argument.

With respect to the actual crime scene, Harrell (2012) found that between 2005 and 2010, only about 9% of violent victimizations that occurred in victims' homes were determined to be committed by strangers; and during the same time frame (p. 1): "among violence committed by strangers more than half (51%) of the victimizations occurred in public places, including in commercial locations (14%), parking lots or garages (9%), and on streets, public transportation and other open areas (such as public parks) (27%)." This means that stranger violence typically occurs in public, and that intimate violence tends to occur in the home.

These statistics provide an interesting theoretical starting point for investigators without a strong suspect. But they also remind us that when the offender is unknown, both stranger and non-stranger theories should be considered viable.

Consider a snapshot from the northwest region of the United States, provided from police reports in Bruder (2007; p. 10):

> The 10 people who died by homicide in Clackamas County in 2006 ranged in age from 19 months to 85 years old.
>
> The youngest was crushed under a chair by his 4-year-old sister while their father slept nearby. The oldest, a woman suffering from advanced Parkinson's disease, was shot by her husband, who then killed himself.
>
> Police believed most of the victims knew their killers but said one man was killed by a stranger who hit him with a car and stabbed him

as he was on his way home from a Milwaukie bar. Clackamas County sheriff's detectives consider two of the homicides unsolved. They are still searching for the killers of Meghan Flynn Kohl, the 21-year-old daughter of a Washington County Circuit Court judge, and Andrew William Corpe, 44, a transient. Last year, officers shot and killed four people. This year, no one was fatally shot by police....

* Marrissa Lynne Boros, 24, was fatally shot by her boyfriend during a Jan. 11 altercation in her Clackamas home. Police responding to an anonymous call found Boros dead in her home in the 7600 block of Southeast Overland Street, and her two boys, ages 4 and 5, unattended. Her boyfriend, Keith James Bryant, 27, an ex-convict with an extensive and violent criminal history, was arrested in Portland a few hours later on a parole violation.

In December, Bryant pleaded guilty to killing Boros. Bryant was also convicted of attempted murder and assault with a firearm in other incidents that included shooting at a Milwaukie man. He received consecutive sentences totaling at least 22 1/2 years in prison.

* Juan Gabriel Perez Solis, 36, was fatally shot by his wife on Jan. 19 at their Milwaukie home.

Prosecutors did not bring charges against Rose Perez, 50, after a seven-month investigation suggested Juan Perez was beating her with a stick when she shot him in the chest with a rifle.

Responding to a call from a neighbor, Milwaukie police found Juan Perez dead in the kitchen of the couple's home in the 10900 block of Southeast Myrtle Street. He was holding a wooden stick, and Rose Perez's hair was intertwined in his fingers as though he'd pulled it from her head, prosecutors said.

Rose Perez told investigators that she and her husband had been arguing because he said he was going to move in with their daughter-in-law, who she said was pregnant with Juan Perez's child.

* Tyler Scott Watson, 42, of Gladstone was killed on March 27 by a homeless friend who was staying at his apartment in the 200 block of West Arlington Street. Jason Arthur Brown, 37, gouged him with a knife near his Adam's apple, slashed his scalp and strangled him with a stereo cord. Brown pleaded guilty to murder in May and was sentenced to life in prison with possibility of parole after 25 years.

Brown and Watson lived across the street from each other in Gladstone as children and re-established their friendship in 1997, said Watson's brother, Timothy. Brown was homeless and had a criminal record that included convictions for first-degree burglary, drunken driving and assault. Tyler Watson would let Brown sleep on the couch of his one-bedroom apartment for stretches of time, Timothy Watson said, and sometimes Brown refused to leave....

* Timmie Laurel Stumpf, 55, and her husband, Craig Stephen Stumpf, 60, were found dead in their home in the Charbonneau district of Wilsonville on April 7, after friends and relatives failed in attempts to contact them. Both had been stabbed several times.

Police soon arrested Timmie Stumpf's son, Joseph Ray O'Neil, 26, of Southeast Portland in connection with the killings. O'Neil has been charged with two counts of aggravated murder and is being held without bail in the Clackamas County Jail.

A trial date has not yet been set. O'Neil, described by police as a drifter, also has been accused of menacing his former girlfriend and stabbing her dog.

* Meghan Flynn Kohl, 21, was found dead at home July 21 by two roommates who shared her Gladstone apartment in the 200 block of West Arlington Street. An autopsy confirmed that she died of homicidal violence, but police did not specify how she was killed. She lived in the same small apartment complex where Tyler Scott Watson had been murdered four months earlier. Kohl was the daughter of Washington County Circuit Judge Thomas W. Kohl....

* Beverly Liberto, 85, a Clackamas woman suffering from advanced Parkinson's disease, was fatally shot Aug. 21 by her husband, Anthony Liberto, 91, who then killed himself, according to police.

Before the shootings, Anthony Liberto had spoken with his wife's in-home caregiver and was despondent at the prospect of his wife entering a nursing home, said Detective Jim Strovink, spokesman for the Clackamas County Sheriff's Office.

Parkinson's disease left Beverly Liberto unable to feed or care for herself. She had been admitted to a care facility earlier this year, Strovink said, but after 10 hours Anthony Liberto took her home. After his wife's caregiver left about 4 p.m., Anthony Liberto tidied their house in a manufactured-home park off Southeast 122nd Avenue, Strovink said. He left a note, then shot his wife with a handgun, activated her medical alert bracelet, and shot himself.

* Anthony Vaughn, who was 19 months old, died Sept. 9 when his sister crushed him under a chair in the family's Milwaukie apartment. Investigators determined that Anthony died after his 4-year-old sister repeatedly jumped on the footrest of a recliner, collapsing the boy's chest and cutting off circulation to the heart....

* Andrew William Corpe, 44, was found shot to death Oct. 20 in Johnson Creek near Southeast Johnson Creek Boulevard and Bell Avenue. A passing bicyclist discovered his body floating in the creek, which runs along the popular Springwater Corridor Trail.

Corpe was a transient who had been arrested 24 times in Oregon, according to the Clackamas County Sheriff's Office. The arrests include accusations of burglary, theft, assaulting a public safety officer and driving under the influence of intoxicants….

* Darrell Wyant, 64, of Milwaukie was fatally stabbed while walking home from a bar early Dec. 3. Hours after the incident, Jeremy C. Metelak, 27, also of Milwaukie, turned himself in to authorities. He was later charged with aggravated murder, felony hit and run, and possession of methamphetamine.

Investigators said Metelak was outside his house at about 3 a.m. when Darrell Wyant, who had just left Bo's Pub on Southeast McLoughlin Boulevard, walked past. The two men, who apparently did not know each other, got into an argument before Metelak drove into Wyant on Southeast Hull Avenue and then stabbed him, police said.

Note how intimate homicides contextualize the infrequency of stranger homicides in this area, and how this equates to a decreased solvability. This is consistent with overall findings evident in Turvey (2006; p. 45):

> This preliminary review of rape and murder clearance rates, in combination with investigative realities and solvability factors, strongly suggests that investigative and forensic skill, ability and attentiveness are not being brought to bear in the majority of these cases. As a result, the vast majority of cases are being cleared because the victim–offender relationship is already known, and the investigation may focus on developing that presumed connection. In other words, criminal investigation is at this point reactive.

This gets back to an issue raised at the beginning of this chapter: investigative bias and presumption related to the victim–offender relationship. Intimate homicides are the easiest to solve because they do not involve criminal investigation with respect to suspect development—the responsible party is often standing over the body, weapon in hand. However, a theory of intimate homicide may in some cases be politically inexpedient: the family may be wealthy or influential, the investigator may be or become emotionally involved with the family, or public sentiment may hamper efforts to investigate intimate suspects. Whatever the case, investigators must refrain from following the path of least effort and least resistance in their casework. It is not their job to make friends. Rather, they must investigate the evidence, following it scrupulously to its actual end.

Unfortunately, stranger crime numbers just aren't getting through to the public, from which our professional castes are drawn. The perception remains among the uninitiated that stranger violence is the greater likelihood and subsequent threat. Consider the perspective offered in Gruenberg (2008):

> In my nine years of working with survivors of sexual assault in the Boulder area as well as the Roaring Fork Valley, I have found that

society as a whole has a very conflicted and often ill-informed view of both the crime and the nature of the victim. Ask the average individual to describe the mental picture that they have of what a "rape" looks like and you will invariably be painted the picture of an unknown male assailant hiding behind a Dumpster in a dark alley that attacks a female victim. The sexual acts are then forcibly attained through physical violence possibly including the use of a weapon. This is what I refer to as one of the myths of rape.

The truth however, is that most woman are sexually assaulted by someone that they know: a boyfriend, a date, a husband, a parent or family member, a friend, a teacher or coach. The sobering statistic is that 80 percent of sexual assault victims know their assailant.[6] In addition, most sexual assaults include no physical force. Instead the perpetrator utilizes threats, intimidation, manipulation, verbal and emotional pressure, an imbalance of power and control, and of course substances that can affect a victim's ability to give consent, the most pervasive and accessible being alcohol.

Consistent with Dawson (2006), cited previously, consequences within the criminal justice system related to this ignorant view are further discussed in Hessick (2007; pp. 345–346):

> The specter of violence at the hands of a stranger dominates the modern construction of crime. Despite the higher rate of non-stranger violence, respondents to a recent poll indicated a belief that they were significantly more likely to be shot or badly hurt by a stranger than hit by their spouse or partner. Criminal law commentators have long remarked that violent crimes committed by strangers are more likely to lead to an arrest, result in a conviction, and garner a longer sentence than comparable crimes committed by family or acquaintances. Well-publicized studies of capital sentencing decisions have consistently demonstrated that offenders who murder strangers are significantly more likely to receive the death penalty than offenders who murder people they already know. The idea that crimes between strangers are more serious than crimes between those who already know each other has been repeated so often that it has become the conventional wisdom in criminal law.

It is consequently the burden of forensic victimologists to use this information in at least three ways: first, as a shield to the barrage of stranger crime imagery that can distort their availability heuristic; second, as a contextual case note, to

---

[6]This is actually not consistent with the national percentage of non-stranger sexual assaults provided in Catalano (2006) at 64%. However, Gruenberg may have been speaking locally or experientially.

help structure the initial viability of case theories; and third, as an educational mandate, to help fight the battle against ignorance that persists in investigative and forensic contexts.

Idiographic Analysis

In the following sections, we discuss certain basic idiographic considerations with respect to stranger violence and adduce illustrative examples as necessary.

Targets

Every offender has particular victim or target criteria that satisfy his or her needs—no matter how general or specific. As with intimate crime, there are essentially three kinds of targets: primary, secondary, and collateral. However, a general question is raised at the outset: why target a stranger?

The first reason implies a level of planning and forethought that is simply not present in the vast majority of crime: *to avoid detection*. This is a particular feature of unimpaired serial offenders.[7] Those who select victims that they don't know, locations where they don't frequent, and circumstances that will be less likely to result in their later identification and apprehension may be referred to generally as *precautionary offenders*. Their victims are the product of a conscious set of criteria, no matter how indefinite. Victims are chosen because they satisfy a need, and these offenders take time to seek them out where they may be found.

The second reason is precisely the opposite of the first, requiring little or no planning and forethought, and also the most common: *opportunity*. This is a particular feature of impaired and inexperienced offenders. Those who select victims that can easily learn their identity, locations where they frequent, and circumstances that will be more likely to result in their later identification and apprehension may be referred to generally as *convenience offenders*. Their victims are not the product of reflection and care, but rather of proximity. They are chosen simply because they are within easy reach and involve little effort to acquire.

Primary Targets

A *primary target* is one that is of the greatest importance to the offender. It dictates the location and timing of any attack. Often, the offender will have planned out and intend to hit that victim at the risk of forgoing any or all other targets in the environment. In some cases, there will be more than one primary target.

---

[7]*Unimpaired* refers to those who are not under the influence of drugs, alcohol, intense mood swings, or the delusions that can accompany mental illness.

In cases of stranger violence, these offenders may target a person met at a bar, a jogger running in a public park, or a home in a conveniently located neighborhood. Their targeting of primary victims is dictated by what they want from the victims, and whether the attack is planned or unplanned. If planned, these offenders go where their preferred victim type can be found; if unplanned, they target those in their immediate environment.

CASE EXAMPLE:

Jason Higgins, Ogden, Utah

Consider the case of Jason Higgins, a serial rapist who operated in Ogden, Utah, just before the turn of this century (see Figure 14-3). In 1998, Higgins was convicted for nine rapes and sexual assaults of girls or women; he was convicted of multiple concurrent sentences, resulting in an overall 30 years to life sentence for his crimes. In 2012, he came up for parole, as reported in Reavy (2012):

> One of Ogden's most notorious serial rapists apologized Tuesday to the eight teen girls and adult women he raped 15 years ago. "I am so sorry for the pain and torment I put you through," Jason Brett Higgins said, calling his actions "cowardly, disgusting and violent."
>
> But Rebecca Mills, who had barely turned 16 when she was raped by Higgins at knife point in October 1996, beginning what would become a string of abductions, rapes and sexual assaults that would terrorize the Ogden and Roy area for five months, said she didn't believe his apology was completely sincere....
>
> Between October 1996 and March 1997, Higgins grabbed young girls and adult women who were walking or jogging alone and raped or sexually assaulted them. Many of his victims were between the ages of 14 and 16.
>
> Higgins was convicted in 1998 for nine rapes or sexual assaults of eight girls or women. He was given several one-to-15-years and 15-years-to-life sentences to run concurrently and consecutively. A judge

FIGURE 14-3
Between October 1996 and March 1997, Jason Higgins (pictured in the foreground) attacked "young girls and adult women who were walking or jogging alone and raped or sexually assaulted them" (Reavy, 2012). Most of his victims were between 14 and 16 years old. Only one showed up to his hearing; she is pictured, distraught, in the background.

Continued

CASE EXAMPLE: *CONTINUED*

ordered two of those 15-to-life sentences to run consecutively, essentially giving him a 30-years-to-life sentence.

[Don Blanchard, a part-time hearing officer and former longtime member of the Board of Pardons and Parole] described how Higgins, typically after he got off work or early in the morning, would spot females walking or jogging alone, wait until they were in an area with no one else around, and then grabbed them from behind and raped them. In some cases he punched his victims in the mouth before raping them and in others he threatened to harm them if they shouted.

Note that Jason Higgins targeted female victims, walking or jogging alone in the early hours of the morning, for the purposes of sexual assault. This is an extremely common serial rapist modus operandi.

Secondary Targets

A *secondary target* is one that is of lesser importance to the offender. It will not dictate the location and timing of an attack. However, it will be a conscious choice based on the availability within environmental and temporal constraints dictated by primary targets. Not all offenders will take the time to deliberate over the possibility of achieving secondary targets.

In cases of stranger violence, secondary targets will often be those who are incidentally discovered with the primary target. They are targets of intentional opportunity. Examples include an unknown roommate found with an intended rape victim who is then also raped, people standing in line at a bank who are forced to give up valuables by bank robbers, someone who witnesses a crime and is eliminated on the spot to prevent his or her testimony, or friends who attempt to defend a victim being assaulted in a pub fight.

CASE EXAMPLE:

Jerry Active, Anchorage, Alaska

Consider the case of 24-year-old Jerry Active of Anchorage, Alaska (see Figure 14-4). In 2009, he pled guilty to breaking into a home in Dillingham and sexually assaulting a child and other residents (see Figure 14-5). He was sentenced to 7 years, but was released early for unknown reasons on Saturday, May 25, 2013, at around 8:00 a.m. About 12 hours later, he apparently killed an elderly couple and raped their 2-year-old great-grandchild. As reported in Reuters (2013):

A 24-year-old man charged with killing an elderly couple and raping their 2-year-old great-grandchild had been released early from prison just hours before the attacks, state officials said on Tuesday. Jerry Active was arrested on Saturday by police and has been charged in the murders of Sorn Sreap, 71, and her husband, Touch Chea, 73, and the rape of the toddler they were babysitting that night. Active is also charged with raping Sreap.

The elderly victims' bodies had signs of blunt-force trauma, but autopsies will determine the cause of death, the Anchorage Police Department said in a statement....

CASE EXAMPLE: *CONTINUED*

FIGURE 14-4
Jerry Active is arraigned for charges related to the murder of a elderly couple, and the rapes of both the elderly woman and the couple's 2-year-old great-grandchild.

FIGURE 14-5
An exterior of the child's home where the great-grandparents were babysitting while the parents went to a movie.

The toddler's parents returned home from a movie and found the suspect naked in a bedroom with the child and the great-grandparents dead, said the Anchorage police statement. The parents confronted the suspect, but he escaped, police said....

Active has a lengthy court record, with several misdemeanor arrests prior to the 2009 felony case. He was first released on the Dillingham case on October 2, 2011, but violated probation and was sent back to prison two days later, according to records Schroeder

Continued

CASE EXAMPLE: *CONTINUED*

released. Since then he has been in and out of prison after committing other probation violations....

In this case, the elderly victims did not live at the home. Therefore, their presence could not have been anticipated by a stranger offender. Especially one

that had just been released from prison that morning. Clearly, the primary target in this case was the child: this is clear from the fact that the great-grandparents were both killed in order to allow for time spent in bed with the child who was kept alive. This means that the great-grandparents were secondary targets.

Collateral Victims

A *collateral victim* is one that is attacked and injured unintentionally, because of his or her proximity to a primary or secondary target within a given environment. The victim's injury is completely uncalculated and incidental to the intended outcome. A collateral victim is, in fact, not a target. It is important to distinguish between secondary targets and collateral victims—the key difference being intent.

In cases of stranger violence, collateral victims will, again, be hit because they are in the way. They are in the wrong place at the wrong time. However, collateral stranger victims are unique because they may be harmed in the course of non-stranger violence. Examples include a child left in a car seat by a parent forced from a vehicle in a car-jacking, a bystander killed by stray gunfire related to a non-stranger shooting, and a bomb intended for one mailbox that is accidentally placed and goes off in another.

Intrinsic Motivation

The motivations involved with stranger violence differ from those related to intimate violence only in that they tend to be intrinsic rather than extrinsic. That is to say, the motives in stranger violence tend to come from within the offender, without deliberation about, or ongoing reinforcement by, the eventual stranger victim. The offender brings the need for violent expression with him or her to the circumstance. The victim is selected because he or she can satisfy the motive at reduced risk, or because he or she is convenient when the motive engages.

For example, if a person gets angry with someone he has just met, to the point of violence, that emotion reflects more about the problems that exist in his own life. His anger is likely to be *displaced*—a result of his particular history and circumstances.[8] In contrast, violence between two people who know each other

---

[8]Displaced anger is anger directed at someone or something other than the original instigator of that feeling. Displaced anger is directed at a representative or proxy.

is more likely to be cumulative, with a mutual history of interactions to feed the flames. Additionally, drugs, alcohol, or mental illness may cause, enable, or lead to a mood or misunderstanding that results in a physical altercation. These, again, are intrinsic circumstances that have less to do with the ultimate victim.

CASE EXAMPLE:

Adam Lane, North Carolina

Adam Leroy Lane was a 43-year-old truck driver from North Carolina (see Figure 14-6). The facts and circumstances surrounding his crimes suggest that he would be best referred to as a precautionary offender with a power motivation, with respect to his reasons for targeting stranger victims.

On July 30, 2007, Lane broke into the home of Jean and Kevin McDonough. He was dressed in black, wore a mask and gloves, and carried a choke wire and a belt with Chinese throwing stars. Once inside the home, he attempted to rape their 15-year-old daughter at knifepoint. Described in Ellement (2007):

> The girl screamed, and her parents came running. The mother fought with Lane, who slashed her hands, police said. The father put Lane in a headlock, and the girl called 911.

Once New Jersey authorities learned of the case, they charged Lane with killing 38-year-old Monica Massaro less than 24 hours before he allegedly attacked the Chelmsford family. In both cases, authorities in both states said, Lane drove into a truck stop and then drifted into neighboring towns, searching for victims.

Details relating to the homicides are provided in Hepp (2007):

> The truck driver charged with murdering a New Jersey woman and trying to rape a Massachusetts teenager is now being investigated by authorities in Pennsylvania as a possible suspect in the stabbing death of one woman and the slashing of another.
>
> In each of the four cases the victim was attacked late at night, while at home but not

FIGURE 14-6
Adam Leroy Lane is led by authorities to his arraignment.

CASE EXAMPLE: *CONTINUED*

behind locked doors, and was stabbed, cut, or threatened with a knife.

Police in Pennsylvania confirmed Friday they are investigating Adam Leroy Lane in connection with the July 13 stabbing death of Darlene Ewalt in a Harrisburg suburb, and the wounding of a woman in her home near York on July 17.

The attacks occurred about two weeks before Lane, a 43-year-old trucker from Jonesboro, N.C., is accused of killing 38-year-old Monica Massaro in her Hunterdon County home. Investigators have said Lane parked his rig at a truck stop just off Interstate 78 in the early morning of July 29 and walked the streets of Bloomsbury trying several doors before finding the door to Massaro's Main Street duplex unlocked. She was found the following day, stabbed repeatedly in the head, neck and chest.

Lane then drove to the Boston suburb of Chelmsford, where police said he parked his rig at an Interstate highway truck stop and walked to a nearby residential area. Again finding an unlocked door, Lane entered a home just before 4 a.m. on July 30 and tried to rape a 15-year-old girl at knifepoint before her father grabbed him and held him for police, authorities said.

Lane ultimately pleaded guilty in the McDonough case to home invasion, armed assault in a dwelling, assault with intent to commit murder, and assault and battery with a dangerous weapon. He was subsequently sentenced to 25 to 30 years in Lowell Superior Court. As of this writing, the investigation into Lane's involvement with other crimes in other states is ongoing.

SUMMARY

Stranger violence is a very real concern with motives and means similar to those found in non-stranger violence. However, motives in stranger violence tend to be intrinsic to the offender, and victim targeting tends to be more dependent upon offender planning with respect to precautionary intent. Despite the fact that there are fewer stranger crimes than not, the media reports them with greater frequency. This creates a false impression in the minds of the public and can also have a negative impact on the criminal justice system.

In unsolved cases, determining whether a victim suffered his or her attack at the hands of a stranger is a crucial yet too often political consideration. It dictates the nature and extent of investigative direction and the ultimate suspect pool. Forensic victimologists must remain objective in their analysis despite these pressures and be willing to follow the evidence to its actual rather than expeditious end.

QUESTIONS

1. True or False: Strangers represent the greatest danger to our personal safety.
2. Describe the difference between a *convenience offender* and a *precautionary offender*.

3. A _____ is one that is attacked and injured unintentionally, because of his or her proximity to a primary or secondary target within a given environment.

4. Describe the difference between the motivations involved with stranger violence compared to those related to intimate violence.

REFERENCES

Barr, M., Sheeran, T., 2013. Women held captive in Ohio endured lonely, dark lives; kidnap suspect due in court Thursday. The Star-Tribune, May 9; Available at: http://www.startribune.com/206564831.html

Bruder, J., 2007. Motives and circumstances of 2006 homicides vary widely. The Oregonian, January 4; p. 10.

Buckler, K., 2005. Assessing the newsworthiness of homicide events: an analysis of coverage in the Houston Chronicle. Journal of Criminal Justice and Popular Culture 12 (1), 1–25.

Catalano, S., 2006. National Crime Victimization Survey: Criminal Victimization, U.S. Department of Justice, Office of Justice Programs, Bureau of Justice Statistics Bulletin, Washington, DC. NCJ 214644, September 2005.

Chermak, S., 1995. Victims in the news: Crime and the American news media. Westview Press, Boulder, CO.

Collins, J., 2007. Lady Madonna, children at your feet: the criminal justice system's romanticization of the parent—child relationship. Iowa Law Review 93, November, pp. 131–184.

Crowder, S., Turvey, B., 2013. Ethical Justice: Applied Issues for Criminal Justice Students and Professionals. Elsevier Science, San Diego.

Dawson, M., 2006. Intimacy and violence: exploring the role of victim-defendant relationship in criminal law. Journal of Criminal Law and Criminology, vol. 96, Summer; pp. 1417–1449.

Ellement, J., 2007. Victims face alleged intruder in court: Trucker is held without bail. The Boston Globe, September 13; Available at: http://www.boston.com/news/local/articles/2007/09/13/victims_face_alleged_intruder_in_court

Gruenberg, J., 2008. Exposing the myths of rape. The Aspen Times, April 13; Available at: http://www.aspentimes.com/article/20080413/COLUMN/471926728/0/FRONTPAGE

Harrell, E., 2012. Violent Victimization Committed by Strangers, 1993–2010. U.S. Department of Justice, Office of Justice Programs, Bureau of Justice Statistics Bulletin, Washington, DC, NCJ 239424, December

Hepp, R., 2007. Suspect in Hunterdon murder investigated in two Pa. attacks. N.J. Star-Ledger, Saturday, September 1; Available at: http://www.nj.com/news/index.ssf/2007/09/suspect_in_hunterdon_murder_in.html

Hessick, C., 2007. Violence between lovers, strangers, and friends. Washington University Law Review 85, 343–407.

Johnstone, J.W.C., Hawkins, D.F., Michener, A., 1994. Homicide reporting in Chicago dailies. Journalism Quarterly 71, 860–872.

Maguire, M., Singer, J., 2011. A false sense of security: moral panic driven sex offender legislation. Critical Criminology 19, 301–312.

Muskal, M., 2013. Daughter of Cleveland suspect Ariel Castro: He preyed on my friends. Los Angeles Times, May 17; Available at: http://articles.latimes.com/2013/may/17/nation/la-na-nn-cleveland-kidnapping-ariel-castro-reportedly-preyed-on-daughters-friends-20130517

Prichard, D., Hughes, K., 1997. Patterns of deviance in crime news. Journal of Communication 47, 49–67.

Reavy, P., 2012. Serial rapist apologizes to victims at parole hearing. KSL News Radio, Utah, May 27; Available at: http://www.ksl.com/index.php?sid=19753904&nid=481

Reuters, 2013. Alaska man who killed couple, raped tot released early from prison hours before: cops. New York Daily News, May 29; Available at: http://www.nydailynews.com/news/national/alaskan-rapist-spung-early-jail-cops-article-1.1357247

Turvey, B.E., 2006. Beneath the numbers: rape and homicide clearance rates in the United States. Journal of Behavioral Profiling 6 (1), May;36–47.

Turvey, B., Petherick, W., 2008. Stranger violence. In: Turvey, B., Petherick, W. (Eds.), Forensic Victimology, Elsevier Science, San Diego.

CHAPTER 15

Forensic Victimology and Civil Remedy in Premises Liability Cases

Brent E. Turvey[1]

Lawsuits are a vital complement to the criminal justice system because civil litigation offers more options for redress, lower standards of proof, and greater opportunities for survivors to steer their litigation. Even the U.S. Department of Justice—hardly a shill for the plaintiffs' bar—distributes a publication that "encourages victim consideration of civil remedies."

> —Tom Lininger, Associate Professor of Law, University of Oregon (2008; p. 1560)

CONTENTS

KEY TERMS

Balancing Test A legal test which provides that property owners need to scale their security efforts to meet known threats based on the potential for harm, and within reason.

Deterrent "[A]nything which impedes or has a tendency to prevent" (Black, 1990, p. 450).

Expressive offender An offender who is defined by heightened emotional state; his or her motive is personal, being associated with jealousy, anger, power, or even sexual desire.

Foreseeability "[T]he ability to see or know in advance; e.g., the reasonable anticipation that harm or injury is a likely result from certain acts or omissions" (Black, 1990, p. 649).

Imminent harm test (aka *specific harm test*) A test which "requires the plaintiff to show that a landlord was aware that a specific individual was acting in such a manner as to pose a clear threat to the safety of an identifiable target" (Kennedy, 2006, p. 124).

Instrumental offender An offender who is defined by the desire to achieve a specific end, usually financial or materially oriented. Such offenders are deliberate, planful, and engage in acts of precaution to limit their exposure to being apprehended and identified.

Premises liability The civil responsibility incurred by property owners who fail to provide reasonable and adequate security to their lessees, customers, and other invited patrons or guests while on their property, to include the structures within.

Prior similar acts test A test which is based on the premise that the past is in fact the best indication of the future.

---

[1]This chapter is an update of the original presented in Turvey and Petherick (2010).

Forensic Victimology. http://dx.doi.org/10.1016/B978-0-12-408084-3.00015-6

Reasonableness In legal terms, a reference to what a rationally thinking layperson would think or do under a particular set of circumstances. Highly subjective.

Tort A civil wrong for which the plaintiff hopes to receive compensation (Kennedy, 2006).

Totality of the circumstances test The determination of foreseeability by virtue of examining the social and environmental factors related to a particular type of crime.

Forensic victimology is not limited only to use in criminal investigations and the resulting criminal trials.[2] It also serves an important role in civil litigation. When someone is harmed because of a crime or an act of negligence, the state may be able to pursue criminal charges against those responsible. Or there may be no criminal charges involved. In either case, a victim does not automatically get restitution from his or her offender. In order to be made whole, the victim will likely need to take civil action.

Civil litigation is initiated by victim-plaintiffs as a consequence of defendant liability for harm caused during criminal acts or acts that involve defendant negligence (Voigt and Thornton, 1996). In civil law, that harm is referred to as a *tort*. Kennedy (2006) provides a useful explanation, writing that (p. 122)

> A tort is a civil wrong for which the plaintiff hopes to receive compensation. In order to prove his or her case, the plaintiff must establish by a preponderance of the evidence that the defendant (1) owed the plaintiff a *duty* to act in a certain way, that (2) the defendant *breached* his or her duty by failing to act as the duty required, and that this (3) *caused* some (4) *harm* to the plaintiff.

Despite misplaced beliefs to the contrary, negligence lawsuits are not necessarily a function of victim litigiousness and greed. As explained in Lininger (2008), the criminal justice system serves primarily to punish criminals; victims are a secondary concern and will generally be left to move forward on their own. Though referencing sex crimes in specific, we will learn that these comments may be generalized to just about any type of violent crime (pp. 1559–1560):

> The last few years have seen a tremendous increase in lawsuits alleging rape or sexual assault. Not only has the number of plaintiffs grown, but claimants are recovering larger awards. In particular, 2007 was a record year for such suits. According to one scholar, the recent success of civil claims for sexual abuse proves the symbiosis of tort law and criminal law.
>
> There are many reasons for this burgeoning civil litigation. Broader insurance coverage, better organization among the plaintiffs' bar,

---

[2]Forensic victimology, it must be remembered, is one of the many sub-disciplines of forensic criminology (Turvey, Petherick, and Ferguson, 2010).

innovative theories of third-party liability, feminist support for civil remedies, the success of civil claimants in high-profile cases—all have played a role in expanding civil litigation by survivors of rape.

One important change in the last decade is the government's endorsement of civil litigation as a remedy for rape victims. At both the federal and local level, agencies are urging survivors of rape to consider civil recourse. These agencies recognize that criminal prosecutions cannot make victims whole.

This chapter is aimed at educating the reader regarding the contributions that forensic criminology and victimology can make in civil litigation. Specifically, it focuses on negligent security issues and premises liability, as these are most commonly associated with violent crime victims seeking compensation. Case examples are provided as needed.

PREMISES LIABILITY

Premises liability is the civil responsibility incurred by property owners who fail to provide reasonable and adequate security to their lessees, customers, and other invited patrons or guests while on their property, to include the structures within. This includes harm caused by third parties engaged in the commission of criminal acts. As explained in Voigt and Thornton (1996; p. 167):

> When a property owner fails to provide a reasonably safe environment to patrons and, as a result, an invited individual suffers a criminal victimization such as a rape, armed robbery, or assault by a third party, the property owner may be liable under civil jurisdiction for losses the patron incurs. Relatives of patrons who are murdered on premises are, likewise, subject to civil remedy associated with the loss of a loved one. Losses may include costs associated with physical injury, psychological trauma leading to inability to enjoy life or earn a living, and future income foregone as a result of victimization.

Kennedy (2006) offers further elucidation of those crimes and circumstances that commonly result in premises liability related negligence suits (p. 120):

> [L]andowners and landlords of all stripes may be legally liable should a passenger, customer, client, tenant, guest, or other category of visitor to the premises be assaulted while on property under their control. For example, merchants may be sued by a customer attacked in a store's restroom or car park. A hotel guest sexually assaulted in her room by a nighttime intruder may have a cause of action against hotel management. Students at a university, visitors to a corporate headquarters, and passengers of common carriers are increasingly looking to the courts to order compensation from the owners and

managers of the property whereupon their injures were sustained (Michael and Ellis, 2003). The actual perpetrators of these acts are unlikely targets of such lawsuits since their identities often remain unknown or they themselves are simply uncollectible. This leaves, of course, the third-party corporate entity which is often looked upon as a 'deep pockets' defendant.

Not only might a commercial enterprise be sued for a criminal act occurring on its property, a lawsuit might arise out of the actions of its own employees. Should a salesperson assault a customer, or a contract security officer wrongfully detain a suspected shoplifter, liability may attach. In addition to crimes by employees, modern organizations must be concerned about crimes *against* employees. Traditionally, business entities had been relatively immune from lawsuits instituted against them by their own employees for injuries sustained while at work because in many jurisdictions workers' compensation was their exclusive remedy. Even this barrier, however, is beginning to erode as more and more courts are carving out exceptions to workers' compensation laws and allowing increasing numbers of employees or their heirs to successfully sue employers for crime-related injuries sustained while on the job (Sakis and Kennedy, 2002).

Ultimately, premises liability comes down to responsibility. Much like vehicle owners are responsible for any accidents or damage that they cause while driving, so too are employers and property owners. Employers have a duty to hire and retain only qualified and responsible individuals; they also have a duty to make sure that the workplace is safe and that those entering the workplace are made aware of safety issues. Similarly, property owners have a duty to make sure that their visitors are safe. Failure can incur liability.

Consider Yale University. It is both an employer and a property owner. In 2013, Yale University was fined $165,000 by the U.S. Department of Education (DOE) for failing to accurately report the number of sexual crimes on campus. This fine was related to publishing false crime statistics, failing to report sexual assaults, and creating a hostile environment for survivors of sexual assault in general, as reported in Adkins (2013):

> DOE initiated its investigation in 2004, after its Alumni Magazine's July–August edition published an article, 'Lux, Veritas and Sexual Trespass,' that elaborated on the mishandled sexual assault cases.
>
> Upon reading the article, S. Daniel Carter, who was the then senior vice president of the non-profit Clery Center for Security On Campus, filed the original complaint with the DOE regarding the university's negligence of campus security requirements.

The immediate probe revealed that the university undocumented four cases of sex crimes on its campus in 2001 and 2002.

Yale is being penalized $27,500 for each of the unrecorded offenses. Plus, two additional fines have been slapped for not including crime figures from Yale–New Haven Hospital in the University's annual report and neglecting to include required policy statements in its 2004 assessment.

"This is a serious violation because current and prospective students/employees must be able to rely on accurate and complete crime information," Mary Gust, the director of the Department of Education's Administrative Actions and Appeals Service Group, said. "Yale's correction of the crime statistics only after the department alerted the University of its Obligations in 2004 does not excuse its earlier failure to comply with its legal obligations."

By under-reporting rape cases, the university violated [the] Clery Act, which requires colleges to release the exact crime statistics to the U.S. government.

By publishing inaccurate crime statistics, Yale University was able to create a false impression regarding overall campus safety. Obviously, lower crime stats can positively impact student enrollments and general public perception. However, they also have an impact on students, employees, and visitors to campus who rely on those statistics when making decisions regarding personal safety concerns.

For example, consider the case of 24-year-old Annie Le. She was a Yale University doctoral candidate in pharmacology who was killed by a lab technician where she conducted research (see Figure 15-1). Raymond Clark, who was in charge of taking care of the lab animals, committed the attack just before Le's wedding day.

Ms. Le's family filed a negligence suit against Yale University as a result, as reported in Griffin (2011):

The family of a Yale University student murdered by a co-worker in a campus research facility two years ago filed a wrongful death lawsuit on Tuesday against the university, accusing Yale of failing to protect women and tolerating aggressive male behavior.

The 10-page lawsuit, filed at Superior Court in New Haven by the administrator of the estate of slain student Annie Le, says: "Yale had long taken inadequate steps to ensure the safety and security of women on its campus."

The lawsuit alleges that "sexual attacks on and harassment of women at Yale had been a well-documented and long-standing problem, and there was a widespread belief that Yale repeatedly failed to impose meaningful discipline on offenders."

$10,000 Reward
Missing Person

Photo 1   Photo 2   Photo 3

Annie Le

Age: 24 years old, 07/03/1985

Race: Asian female

Hair: Straight brown shoulder length

Eye color: Brown

Height: 4'11

Weight: 90lbs

Missing From: New Haven, CT since the morning of 09/08/2009

Details: Annie Le is a Yale School of Medicine graduate student who has not been seen or heard from by family, co-workers and friends since 09/08/2009. Annie Le's purse containing her cell phone, credit cards and money was left in her office on the morning of 09/08/2009. She was last seen at 10 Amistad Street wearing a knee length brown skirt, bright green short sleeved tee-shirt, brown shoes, and a brown necklace; photo #2 depicts Annie Le entering 10 Amistad the morning of her disappearance. She does not have access to a vehicle. There are no apparent medical issues.

Anyone with information on Annie Le's whereabouts is asked to contact the 24 hour FBI tip-line at

1-877-503-1950

Yale University Police Department
101 Ashmun St
New Haven, CT 06511

Phone: 203-432-4400
Fax: 203-432-4416

FIGURE 15-1

In the days after Annie Le's disappearance, the Yale University Police Department circulated these fliers with her description and a contact number for anyone with information to call. Her body was found in the wall of the lab where she worked; she had been beaten, sexually assaulted, and strangled to death.

The lawsuit also accuses Yale of being slow to respond to concerns that Le was missing.

Although Yale was aware that Le did not return home on the night of Sept. 8, 2009, the university "did not investigate her absence in earnest until the following morning," the lawsuit states.

A Superior Court judge in June sentenced Raymond Clark III to 44 years in prison for the slaying of Le, a third-year doctoral student in pharmacology and bride-to-be from Placerville, Calif. She was reported missing Sept. 8, 2009, shortly before her wedding.... Clark worked as a lab technician at the center, and Le did research there.

Police found Le's body stuffed inside the wall of the lab on Sept. 13, the day that Le, 24, was to be married. The state medical examiner said that Le was strangled and her body was badly beaten. Many of her bones were broken in the attack.

Yale University and the Yale School of Medicine are named in the lawsuit, which seeks unspecified compensatory damages.

Attorneys Paul Slager of Stamford and Joseph Tacopina of New York, who represent Le's family, said in a statement that Yale had "long taken inadequate steps to ensure the safety and security of women on its campus. Yale's persistent tolerance of sexual harassment and sexual assaults on campus caused students to file a Title IX Complaint against Yale University. And, just five days before she was to be married, Annie Le was a victim of that environment."

The lawsuit says that Yale knew or should have known that Clark posed a potential threat to the safety of Le, claiming that Clark "previously demonstrated aggressive behavior and a violent propensity towards women."...

"Based on Yale's negligence in, among other things, hiring, retaining and supervising Clark, and providing a safe and secure environment for Annie Le, Ms. Le endured a brutal physical and sexual attack, resulting in significant conscious suffering before her death, for which Yale is liable," the attorneys said in their statement.

Litigation in this case remains ongoing, as of this writing. Whether or not the lawsuit is ultimately successful, the allegations are consistent with the kinds of premises liability and negligence issues raised in similar legal actions.

THE DUTY TO PROTECT

In a negligence case, the court will rule on whether or not the defendants owed an alleged victim a duty of care—from a legal standpoint. Kennedy (2006) describes the two cases in the United States that are regarded as the "forerunners of third-party litigation against landlords, businesses, and corporate entities": *Kline v. 1500 Massachusetts Avenue Apartment Corporation* and *Garzilli v. Howard Johnson's Motor Lodges, Inc.* (p. 122):

> In the 1970 case of *Kline v. 1500 Massachusetts Avenue Apartment Corporation*, a tenant sued her landlord for allowing the apartment building's security to deteriorate after she had moved in. Ms Kline was subsequently assaulted and robbed. Ultimately, the appeals court ruled the landlord had a duty to take steps to protect Ms. Kline since only the landlord had sufficient control of the premises to do so. The court ruled the landlord–tenant contract required the landlord to provide those protective measures which are within his reasonable capacity. It also noted that the relationship of the modern apartment house dweller to a landlord is akin to that of innkeeper and guest, and, therefore, a duty similar to that imposed on innkeepers would apply (Carrington and Rapp, 1991).
>
> The Garzilli case, also known as the 'Connie Francis' case, has given great impetus to victims' rights litigation. In *Garzilli v. Howard Johnson's Motor Lodges, Inc.*, the internationally known recording artist was assaulted in 1974 while in her motel suite. The unit's sliding glass doors gave the appearance of being locked, but the faulty latches were easily defeated by an intruder. The property manager had known the locks were defective but had not yet provided for secondary-locking devices. The notoriety of the Connie Francis case came because of her star status and because the jury initially awarded her over two million dollars in compensatory damages (Carrington and Rapp, 1991). Thereafter, crime victims were more inclined to pursue redress through the civil courts and soon found their pleas resonating with plaintiffs' attorneys, juries, and the judiciary as well.

Both cases involve clearly defined circumstances where there is a special relationship binding the plaintiff (the victim) to the defendant (the property owner).

Generally speaking, there is no duty of care owed to any victim "unless there is a special relationship between the two parties such as that of merchant–invitee, landlord–tenant, innkeeper–guest, public carrier–passenger or the like" (Kennedy, 2006; p. 122). As explained in Driscoll (2006), those who are invited onto a property (aka invitees), or have some other right to be there, are ostensibly under the supervision and guardianship of those holding ownership (p. 883):

> The owner owes the highest duty of care to the invitee. There is some disagreement in the literature about what exactly defines an invitee: some argue that if the land has been held open to the public in such a way as to imply an invitation, then anyone entering becomes an

invitee; whereas others argue that the concept of an invitee only encompasses business relationships. This ambiguity is reflected in the Restatement (Second) of Torts which defines an invitee as not only one who enters the land "for a purpose for which the land is held open to the public," but also as a "business visitor" who comes upon the land for a purpose connected in some way with "business dealings with the possessor of the land." Since the invitee has been invited onto the land by the landowner, whether implicitly or explicitly, the landowner has a duty of "reasonable care for his safety." Thus, he must not only warn the invitee of conditions which may exist and cause harm, but also protect him against those dangers of which the invitee "knows or has reason to know, where it may reasonably be expected that he will fail to protect himself notwithstanding his knowledge."

Conversely, trespassers enter a property with no rights and no special relationship, accepting the risk of whatever they encounter. There are exceptions to this, including "situations in which the landowner knows or has reason to know that members of the public constantly trespass, knows or has reason to know of a specific trespasser on the land, or with trespassers who are children" (p. 885). Barring these exceptions, owners need only refrain from intentional and unprovoked acts against trespassers to avoid this kind of premises liability. Despite what is often seen in films and on television, property owners may not set traps for, or deliberately shoot at, those who are simply trespassing on their land or in their structures.

Once a duty of care is established by virtue of a special relationship, the question will arise as to what precisely that duty is, and whether or not the defendant breached it. This is where the forensic criminologist comes in. As explained in Kennedy (2006; p. 129):

> [L]itigants will often introduce evidence purporting to establish certain standards of care against which a defendant's conduct is to be compared. Theoretically, a jury's job would be much easier if it could simply assess a defendant's behavior and then compare it to a known, descriptive standard specifying what the behavior should have been. The problem, of course, is identifying just what the standard of care is for a given set of circumstances. Not only will knowledgeable people disagree as to the nature of the appropriate standard, debates over the meaning of related concepts such as 'guidelines' or 'best practices' are likely to ensue. In order for the forensic security specialist to navigate in the legal arena, it is important for him or her to understand the sources of various standards of care pertaining to security.

As this suggests, standards of care vary from case to case, depending on the region, community, and professionals involved. The standards of care at a hospital, for example, are radically different from the standards of care that govern hotels or even schools.

Kennedy (2008) suggests that best practice, or the community standard of care, may be determined by referencing the following sources (p. 5):

1. Statutes and ordinances
2. National consensus standards
3. Community practices
4. Organizational policies and procedures
5. Learned treatises, association literature, and expert opinions
6. Reasonableness

Reasonableness is the most subjective of these, referring to what a reasonable person would do. However, this is intended to be distinct from personal standards of care offered *ipse dixit*.[3] This is warned against as being essentially self-interested and contrary to those adopted by a community or a group of professionals. The absence of a consensus regarding practice standards in a particular professional community or discipline may therefore be used to argue negligence, because those involved may not have pulled it together enough to bother defining best professional practice. In such cases, those with a duty of care may be acting without an informed and appraisable professional compass despite the need for one.

FORESEEABILITY

Foreseeability refers to "the ability to see or know in advance; e.g. the reasonable anticipation that harm or injury is a likely result from certain acts or omissions" (Black, 1990; p. 649). As explained in Huber (1988; p. 58): "Foreseeing the future depends largely on remembering the past. This means that an accident involving bizarre behavior becomes foreseeable as soon as it has happened." Easily confused with concrete prediction, assessing foreseeability is actually about determining whether the occurrence of a particular crime was more likely than not. This is done by examining the current case and its circumstances in light of the past.

To determine the foreseeability of a particular crime and subsequent harm within the facts of a given case, Voigt and Thornton (1996) suggest the employment of an overall "crime foreseeability model" (p. 171). This mandates an in-depth analysis of prior similar and other interpersonal crimes; incident reports and supplemental crime data related to the offense; other types of

---

[3]Latin phrase meaning "he himself said it." This refers generally to statements that are asserted solely on the basis of faith in an expert or authority, without proofs or critiques.

crime at the location (e.g., property crimes, burglaries); the level of physical security at the location, including the security plan and philosophy (if any); relevant and applicable industry standards as set forth by related professional organizations; the social, economic, and demographic characteristics of the area surrounding the location; the nature and profile of the offender; and the nature and profile of the victim. The presence of synergistic factors from this evidence and material can be used to effectively argue the likelihood of a particular crime and the harm it caused, so long as the forensic criminologist is familiar with the data and published research related to each.

Kennedy (2006), on the other hand, provides that "foreseeability should be assessed on a continuum from not foreseeable to highly foreseeable" (p. 123), explaining that there are at least four tests being used in different legal jurisdictions: the imminent or specific harm test, the prior similar acts test, the totality of the circumstances test, and the balancing test. These should, in some fashion, incorporate the analyses didactically suggested in Voigt and Thornton (1996).

The *imminent harm test*, aka the specific harm test, "requires the plaintiff to show that a landlord was aware that a specific individual was acting in such a manner as to pose a clear threat to the safety of an identifiable target. Given the large size of much commercial property open for business to the public, it is unlikely that landlords or their agents will be physically present at many emergent situations, thus effectively absolving them of liability" (p. 124).

The *prior similar acts test* is based on the premise that the past is in fact the best indication of the future. As explained in Kennedy (2006; p. 124): "It is almost axiomatic in forensic criminology and psychology that the best predictor of future behavior is past behavior." Contrary to the adage that lightning doesn't strike twice in the same place, it is an empirical reality that once a particular crime has occurred at a given location, its reoccurrence becomes more likely as "hot spots" develop. Moreover, the same is true of offenders; once they have committed a particular type of crime, the likelihood that they will commit it again goes up (p. 124):

> Empirical research involving the course of crime at 'hot spots' has shown, for example, that in one major city, each location had initially only an 8 percent chance of suffering a predatory offense. Once such an offense occurred, however, the chance of a second increased to 26 percent. After a third offense, the risk of a fourth within the year exceeded 50 percent (Sherman, Gartin, and Buerger, 1989). Should a burglary take place at a residential location, the likelihood it will be reburglarized may increase up to fourfold (Weisel, 2002). Similar patterns may be applied to individuals. Criminal recidivism rates often reach 60 to 70 percent (Austin and Irwin, 2001). The more

crimes an individual has committed in the past, the more crimes he is likely to commit in the future. This is particularly true of early-onset delinquents and psychopaths (Lykken, 1995; Piquero and Mazerolle, 2001). Given the importance of past history in attempting to forecast future events, the forensic security expert should immediately acquaint himself with the history of a property either to be protected or which has already become the subject of litigation. Jurisdictions will vary as to whether prior crime must be substantially similar to the litigated crime or whether, for example, as in Georgia, crimes against property may also make crimes against persons foreseeable (Gorby, 1998).

This makes clear the need for not only educating oneself regarding the recidivism literature related to offenses in particular regions as they bear on specific types of crime, but also the need for staying current as crime trends evolve. What may have been true for one type of crime in a particular region five years ago may not hold true today.

The *totality of the circumstances test* refers to the determination of foreseeability by virtue of examining the social and environmental factors related to a particular type of crime (Kennedy, 2006). Certain demographic characteristics are associated with increased crime in urban areas, such as proximity to criminal activities, criminal populations, the poverty level, and population mobility. Additionally, certain locations are known to attract or generate criminal activity. They are explained in Kennedy (2006; p. 127):

> Further related to land use, an interesting distinction can be made between properties described as crime 'attractors' and those described as crime 'generators' (Brantingham and Brantingham, 1995). The former tend to experience more crime than other locations simply because there are more potential victims from which criminals may choose although the level of risk per individual may not be heightened. Crime generators, on the other hand, foretell more crime because of the illicit nature of activities on the premises, such as illegal gambling, prostitution, and drug trafficking. Since the association between drug use, drug trafficking, and crime is so well established (Goldstein, 1985), security managers must take action to both prevent and aggressively respond to any such activities occurring on the properties for which they are responsible.

Criminologists must gather as much contextual information as is available when applying this particular test, as less information about social and demographic characteristics is not better.

The *balancing test* is a compromise used in legal jurisdictions where the prior similar incidents test is seen to overly favor the landowner, and the totality of circumstances test is seen to overly favor the victim. It provides that property owners need to scale their security efforts to meet known threats based on the potential for harm, and within reason. That is to say, they need not engage in extravagant security efforts. Moreover, as "the gravity of the possible harm increases, the likelihood of its occurrence needs to be correspondingly less in order to trigger the implementation of appropriate security measures" (Kennedy, 2006; p. 127). A specific recommendation regarding the prongs of this test to be employed by forensic criminologists is provided in Kennedy (p. 127):

> The three prongs of this test are: (1) the level of crime foreseeability, (2) the likelihood a given combination of security measures will prevent future harm, and (3) the burden of taking such precautions.

As a consequence of jurisdictional inconsistency regarding legal standards of proof on the issue of foreseeability, forensic examiners must take care to learn those in use by the presiding court when accepting a premises liability case. This will dictate the nature, scope, and admissibility of their expert opinions. However, they should still fall back on the recommended "crime foreseeability model" as a basis for any findings, because criminological assessments are to be conducted outside the influence of the court. Recall that the court may rule on what is admissible, but it may not dictate the limits of good science or best practice.

As pointed out by Kennedy (2006), unless the foreseeability of harm can first be established, there is no duty to protect. If the forensic examiner determines that a crime was not foreseeable, then this may be used by the defense to argue that no duty existed in the case at hand. Consequently, while the court may determine that a defendant has a clear duty of care, the issue of foreseeability can be used to remove it. If we think back to our Yale University example, involving suppressed sexual assault data, it is not difficult to see another motive for the manipulation of local crime data by reporting agencies: increased crime leads to increased foreseeability and therefore potentially increased liability.

OFFENSE AND OFFENDER DETERRABILITY

Once the issue of foreseeability has been assessed, the forensic examiner may reassess the same evidence to determine whether the offense would have been preventable and the offender deterrable.

In this context, a *deterrent* is "anything which impedes or has a tendency to prevent" (Black, 1990; p. 450). This refers to specific security measures that may be taken by property owners to impede different types of crime. Some measures work, and some don't. As explained in Kennedy (2006; p. 134):

> [L]ighting is not the automatic crime deterrent it is thought to be by so many laymen (Farrington and Welsh, 2002; Marchant, 2004) nor does CCTV function universally to deter crimes against the person (Gill and

Loveday, 2003; Painter and Tilley, 1999; Welsh and Farrington, 2003; Welsh and Farrington, 2004). Just as random police patrol is losing ground to directed patrol, security managers may need to rethink standard security officer deployment practices based on the best empirical evidence available (e.g., Sherman, Gottfredson, MacKenzie, Eck, Reuter and Bushway, 1997).

The forensic implications of these critical evaluations are obvious: improved lighting may not have prevented an attack in a parking lot so there may be no obvious causal relationship between a defendant's lighting levels and the crime. If CCTV does not prevent violent crimes in convenience stores, how can failure to install CCTV at a given location be the cause of a clerk's attack? On the other hand, lighting and CCTV may manifest preventive benefits in certain circumstances involving certain perpetrators. Lighting, for example, seems to be the catalyst which provides for the synergy of several security measures working together to more effectively harden a target. Hence, the liability implications of conventional security measures still need to be sorted out on a case-by-case basis. Lighting, CCTV, and preventive patrol are mentioned only as examples of popular security practices which need to be evaluated for the purposes of each particular property. Other security measures should also be realistically assessed before implementation so that a false sense of security is not generated.

This is simply to say that every security measure has an appropriate aim and context; some are capable of deterring only certain offenders from specific offenses, whereas others may actually encourage them by recording it. And not every security measure seeks to deter but rather may only provide for the later identification of suspects, as with CCTV cameras, providing they are of sufficient quality and are actually turned on (the author has worked cases in which such cameras are only for show, without connection to a power source or a recording device).

However, Voigt and Thornton (1996) argue that certain offenses cannot be predicted, and certain offenders cannot be deterred (p. 186):

> Certain types of particularly heinous or dangerous offenders who have severe character disorders or mental illnesses (e.g., antisocial personality, conduct disorders, or psychoses) or who otherwise commit bizarre, one-of-a-kind types of offenses (e.g., rampage or mass murders) present threats to public or private establishments that cannot be reasonably predicted or deterred by usual security methods.

While this may be true in specific cases, the authors would disagree with the generalization that all offenders with mental health issues or illnesses are necessarily undeterrable, or that all rampages and mass murders are unpredictable. Each case must be assessed on its own merits. For example, prior threats of mass murder by an employee or a student make the anticipation of a shooting spree fairly reasonable in the right context, and certain mental disorders can make offenders very predictable with respect to their propensity for irrationality and level of violence, depending on their individual affliction. So although we agree with the spirit of Voigt and Thornton (1996) that some offenders and offenses cannot be predicted or deterred, we also agree that this must be assessed on a case-by-case basis and without blanket generalizations.

Of concern are those offenders with distorted perceptions of reality owing to specific types of mental illness or substance abuse. They are unpredictable and often unaffected by traditional security measures for failure to perceive them at all, let alone perceive them as a threat to safety, identification, and capture. Particularly of interest are those with psychopathic traits. Psychopathic offenders are impulsive, unpredictable, and they do not experience fear as the rest of us do (Hare, 1993). They are therefore more apt to be undeterred by security measures that might cause more deliberate offenders to rethink their plans.

Another useful measure is whether offenders are instrumental or expressive in the commission of their crimes. *Instrumental offenders* are defined by their desire to achieve a specific end, usually financial or materially oriented. They are deliberate, planful, and engage in acts of precaution to limit their exposure of being discovered, identified, and apprehended. *Expressive offenders* are defined by their heightened emotional state; their motive is personal, being associated with jealousy, anger, power, or even sexual desire. As discussed in Kennedy (2006; p. 135):

> As a practical matter, criminologists have generally found the criminal who acts instrumentally to be more deterrable (or displaceable) than one whose crimes tend to be expressive in nature (cf. Nettler, 1989). Thus, a professional criminal who tends to choose a lucrative target carefully might be more sensitive to security measures than a morbidly jealous man who charges into his girlfriend's place of work and shoots her in front of many witnesses because he had recently heard rumors of her infidelity.

The highly variable nature of offense and offender deterrability, again, speaks to the need for forensic criminologists to make a deliberate assessment of the facts and circumstances on a case-by-case basis, not blanket generalizations about security efforts and offender types.

THE IMPORTANCE OF VICTIMOLOGY

Equally important to the assessment of offenders in a premises liability case are similar assessments that must be conducted of the victims. It is accepted in civil litigation that the victims may have engaged in contributory negligence with respect to the harm that has befallen them. In other words, they may be partially, if not completely, responsible for their own suffering or loss. In civil actions arising out of criminal acts, this is far less likely, but it can be a legitimate defense against all or part of a property owner's liability.

Victims may be in a vulnerable state: whether intoxicated, using a controlled substance, or in an agitated mental state (e.g., angry or excited). Or they may possess personal or lifestyle traits that increase their vulnerability, such as old age, mental illness, or mental or physical disability. Whatever the circumstance, forensic criminologists must conduct a victimology to determine whether and how enduring victim traits and temporary circumstances played a role in their victimity. As discussed in Voigt and Thornton (1996), the questions to resolve when assessing victims revolve around establishing their responsibility for the crime, and the nature of their vulnerability to crime (p. 187):

> Using these two variables (responsibility and risk), criminologists attempt to explain the dynamic and varied relationship between the criminal and the victim....
>
> Complete innocence is the most commonly accepted category of victimization. It includes people who did nothing that conceivably could have elicited criminal action. They have no culpability for the crime. Unintentional facilitation is unwittingly, carelessly, or negligently making it easier for a crime to occur, such as leaving car keys in the ignition of a car or leaving a door to an apartment unlocked....
>
> Victim precipitation, on the other hand, occurs when a person willfully initiates the encounter with the eventual offender, directly enticing, challenging, insulting, provoking, or even initially assaulting the person.

It should be noted that victim responsibility and risk are not either–or propositions as this passage might tend to suggest; it's not a binary state in which one is either completely innocent or completely precipitant. Rather, responsibility and risk exist on a continuum that must be assessed on a case-by-case basis. Most victims are not going to be completely innocent, but that does not necessarily remove or even diminish the liability of property owners. The degree to which this holds true will be determined by the trier of fact. It is the place of the forensic criminologist to ensure that, when making these determinations, the trier is given the most complete and accurate picture of related events.

ASSESSMENT RECOMMENDATIONS

Beyond the assessment recommendations already provided, the authors strongly encourage forensic examiners to consider the following additional measures:

1. Before setting to the task of assessing the crime, the victim, or the offender, attempt to exclude the possibility of a false report with an equivocal forensic analysis of the underlying case facts.

2. Don't be afraid to consider and assess the strengths and weaknesses of opposing counsel's theory of liability as it relates to criminological issues. This is useful for both reasons of objectivity and full disclosure. An attorney–client will be glad to know from where the swords may fall, and you may identify facts and information that would otherwise be left without consideration.

3. If opposing counsel appoints an expert with an alternate view, make certain to study his or her notes and reports carefully to determine whether and how your findings differ and why.

4. On the same note, take care to scrutinize any opposing experts by diligently checking out their resume for errors, omissions, exaggerations, and falsifications. Be certain that all qualifications ring true, and that they are actually related to the area of expertise being proffered.

5. Interviewing the offender is optional, as that is more aligned with psychological assessments than criminological ones. Moreover, any interview conducted at this stage is not going to be proximate to the offense. Reading offender interviews or statements from the police file and examining case facts closer in time to events will provide better insight in motive and intent. That is, unless there are specific questions that may benefit from an answer despite the passage of time.

Consider the following case example.

CASE EXAMPLE:

Estate of Elizabeth Garcia v. Allsup's Convenience Stores, Inc. *(2008)*

This case involves the abduction, rape, and murder of 26-year-old Elizabeth Ann Garcia, in the early morning hours of January 16, 2002, from her place of work at Allsup's Convenience Store located at 5312 North Lovington Highway, Hobbs, New Mexico (see Figure 15-2). She was working alone when she was abducted, and her body was found later that day in a field, with evidence of sexual assault and having suffered 57 stab wounds. The cause of death was provided as "multiple stab wounds of head, neck and torso." Paul Lovett was arrested for Elizabeth Garcia's murder in 2003, after he was first connected to the murder of another woman almost a year later (35-year-old Patty Simon). He has been convicted of both homicides.

The family of Elizabeth Garcia filed a lawsuit against the convenience store chain that she had worked for, alleging the chain's negligence contributed to her death. The defense hired retired FBI Profiler Gregg O. McCrary as a security expert to evaluate the offender behavior, and the offense, in the light of those claims.

Mr. McCrary testified pretrial that Elizabeth Garcia was preselected as a target by Paul Lovett, and therefore undeterrable by any security measures. This despite the fact that they did not know each other, had never met, and did not have a pre-existing relationship. In his deposition, McCrary also strayed wildly into profiling related areas while claiming that he wasn't, and claimed expertise that he does not actually possess.

Mr. McCrary also failed to give his clients damaging impeachment information regarding prior cases in which his testimony had been excluded; that he fabricated a degree on his resume (not for the first time); and that he generally misrepresented his education, training, and experience under oath.

Continued

CASE EXAMPLE: *CONTINUED*

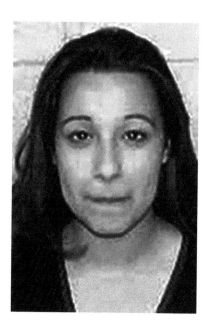

FIGURE 15-2
Elizabeth Garcia, a 26-year-old student at New Mexico Junior College, was found dead in a field approximately 12 hours after she disappeared from her new job at an Allsup's convenience store. It was her third day, and the cause of death was multiple stab wounds to the upper body (Kitchen, 2002).

The plaintiff in this case retained the services of the author (Turvey), and these facts were brought to light in a subsequent expert declaration. As provided in an excerpt from that declaration (Turvey, 2008):

8. I [Brent E. Turvey] have been asked by Allegra C. Carpenter, an attorney for The Estate of Elizabeth Garcia, to examine the deposition testimony of Gregg O. McCrary in *Estate of Elizabeth Garcia v. Allsup's Convenience Stores, Inc.* I was asked to evaluate soundness of his methodology and findings with respect to the current state of forensic practice and literature.

9. This case involves the abduction, rape, and murder of 26-year-old Elizabeth Ann Garcia, in the early morning hours of January 16, 2002, from her place of work at Allsup's Convenience Store located at 5312 N. Lovington Hwy, Hobbs, NM. She was working alone when she was abducted, and her body was found later that day in a field, with evidence of sexual assault and having suffered 57 stab wounds. Cause of death was provided as "multiple stab wounds of head, neck and torso." Paul Lovett was arrested for Garcia's murder in 2003, after he was first connected to the murder of another woman almost a year later, 35-year-old Patty Simon. He has been convicted of both homicides.

10. In rendering my opinions, I have examined the transcript of Mr. McCrary's deposition (Second Judicial District Court, County of Santa Fe, State of New Mexico, No. D-0101-CV-2005-00045, December 12, 2007), and reviewed CV that he provided in this case. I have also examined the autopsy report of Elizabeth Garcia by Ross Zumwalt, MD (Feb. 12, 2002) and related reports documentation, to include trauma-grams, notes, toxicology report, and investigative notes and reports.

CASE EXAMPLE: *CONTINUED*

FINDINGS

11. Mr. McCrary has provided false information on his CV in this case. The undated McCrary CV provided to this examiner, which appears to have been updated through at least July 2006, provides on page 1 under EDUCATION "Master of Arts in Psychology, Marymount University Arlington, VA 1992." This would suggest that Mr. McCrary holds a graduate degree in psychology from Marymount University through their school of psychology, received in 1992. This is false information. As provided to Ms. Carpenter, this examiner has examined this issue with respect to Mr. McCrary on a previous occasion, as a consultant to the defense in *U.S. v. O.C. Smith* (2005). Consistent with a previous version of Mr. McCrary's CV obtained by this examiner when consulting on the *Estate of Sam Sheppard v. Ohio* (2000), Mr. McCrary actually holds a Master of Arts in Professional Psychological Services from Marymount University—obtained through their school of education. In *U.S. v. O.C. Smith*, Mr. McCrary provided a similar false CV to the court and was removed as an expert witness from the case by the prosecution when this information was disclosed to them. That Mr. McCrary has continued to provide this same false information on his CV subsequent to the Smith case removes the possibility of it being a typo, or similar error.

12. Mr. McCrary has offered himself as an expert in behavioral science without demonstrable behavioral science qualifications (e.g., deposition testimony at p. 7 "deterrability occurs in only one place, and that is in the mind of a would-be offender"). His undergraduate degrees are in music and criminal justice, and his graduate degree is related to guidance counseling. One could argue that as an FBI agent he accrued knowledge in the behavioral sciences, but there is no evidence of this. His experience and training appears to be that of an analyst or investigator preparing investigative findings—not forensic ones—without completing formal education in any of the behavioral sciences (psychology, sociology, criminology or even anthropology). Moreover, his CV provides no peer reviewed research or publications in this subject area. On his CV, there are three publications listed.

The first involves his contributor status to the Crime Classification Manual—as one of more than a hundred law enforcement contributors with no specific showing of his contribution to the text; the second involves a five page paper on stalking (*Journal of Interpersonal Violence*, Vol. 11, No. 4, pp. 487–502, 1996) with five other contributors; and the final publication is a co-authored, true crime, trade oriented, memoir style book of no professional merit or value. This lack of demonstrable expertise in the behavioral sciences may explain why false information is provided on the CV.

13. Mr. McCrary did not prepare written findings in this case. As provided in Chisum and Turvey's *Crime Reconstruction* (2007; pp. 120–121), the employment of verbal opinions alone is a substandard practice: Hans Gross referred to the critical role that exact, deliberate, and patient efforts at crime reconstruction can play in the investigation and resolution of crime. Specifically, he stated that just looking at a crime scene is not enough. He argued that there is utility in reducing one's opinions regarding the reconstruction to the form of a report in order to identify problems in the logic of one's theories (Gross, 1924, p. 439):

> So long as one only looks on the scene, it is impossible, whatever the care, time, and attention bestowed, to detect all the details, and especially note the incongruities: but these strike us at once when we set ourselves to describe the picture on paper as exactly and clearly as possible…. The "defects of the situation" are just those contradictions, those improbabilities, which occur when one desires to represent the situation as something quite different from what it really is, and this with the very best intentions and the purest belief that one has worked with all of the forethought, craft, and consideration imaginable.

> Moreover, the reconstructionist, not the recipient of the reconstructionist's opinions (i.e., investigators, attorneys, and the court), bears the burden of ensuring that her conclusions are effectively communicated. This means writing them down. This means that the reconstructionist must be competent

Continued

CASE EXAMPLE: *CONTINUED*

at intelligible writing, and her reports must be comprehensive with regard to examinations performed, findings, and conclusions.

Verbal conclusions should be viewed as a form of substandard work product. They are susceptible to conversions, alterations, and misrepresentations. They may also become lost to time. Written conclusions are fixed in time, easy to reproduce, and are less susceptible to accidental or intentional conversion, alteration, and misrepresentation. An analyst who prefers verbal conclusions as opposed to written conclusions reveals his preference for conclusive mobility.

Though speaking of reconstructionists specifically in this section, the authors were referring to forensic examiners in general when rendering these practice standards from the available literature.

14. On p. 56 of his deposition, Mr. McCrary testifies regarding deterrability: "That is the humbling reality of violent crime, is that, like I say, not all crime is evenly distributed by place—type of crime or place of occurrence. And we don't really know why that is. There are lots of theories about this. Criminologists have a lot of theories. Law enforcement has theories. We try different things. Some things seem to work better than other things. In the long run, sometimes we find out, well, it was just a coincidence that that worked. It really didn't have any—you know, it was a correlation rather than a causation, so bottom line is, we really don't know why that is." This position would seem to preclude offering opinions about what may or may not deter any criminal from committing any given offense. However, Mr. McCrary has given the opinion that Mr. Lovett was not deterrable because he went to the convenience store for the specific purpose of killing the victim, making the crime "target-oriented."

15. Mr. McCrary has provided no research or authority, other than his own unqualified experience, that "target-oriented" offenders are any more or less deterrable than other offenders. When asked directly he evades the issue and argues experience—of which he has none as it relates to convenience

store crime. Experience is not meant to be a shield. As explained by Dr. John I. Thornton, the dishonest forensic examiner exploits the ignorance of their audience by citing experience rather that demonstrating knowledge. Taken from Thornton, John I. (1997) "The General Assumptions and Rationale of Forensic Identification," In David L. Faigman, David H. Kaye, Michael J. Saks, and Joseph Sanders, (Eds.), *Modern Scientific Evidence: The Law and Science of Expert Testimony*, Volume 2:

Experience is neither a liability nor an enemy of the truth; it is a valuable commodity, but it should not be used as a mask to deflect legitimate scientific scrutiny, the sort of scrutiny that customarily is leveled at scientific evidence of all sorts. To do so is professionally bankrupt and devoid of scientific legitimacy, and courts would do well to disallow testimony of this sort. Experience ought to be used to enable the expert to remember the when and the how, why, who, and what. Experience should not make the expert less responsible, but rather more responsible for justifying an opinion with defensible scientific facts.

Equally important are the words of Dr. Paul L. Kirk from his text *Crime Investigation* (1953; pp. 17–18):

The question of what constitutes adequate experience for the expert witness is a critical one in court procedures, and appears to be poorly understood in many quarters. It is quite common for the witness to be interrogated as to the number of years during which he has worked in a field, and the number of cases he has handled, the number of pieces of evidence he has examined, and similar quantitative matters. It must be apparent that the amount of his experience is not important beside the question of what he has learned from it.

The summoning of experience in this context is a red herring that moves attention away from matters of science, objectivity, and sound methodology. This is not a legitimate forensic practice.

CASE EXAMPLE: *CONTINUED*

16. When pressed, Mr. McCrary concedes his opinion that the offender is "target-oriented" is actually based on one of several possible scenarios—none of which he has investigated or reliably established. As shown in the exchange on p. 158 "A: Well, he certainly could have stumbled into her. He could have wanted to kill her and then just stumbled into her. That is a possibility. But I think it's more likely that he went there with the intention of killing her and did. Q: Even though you have no evidence that he knew she was working there? A: That never came out. That wasn't an issue in the criminal trial that I could see." See also p. 185 "I have no evidence that she knew him. I have no evidence that she did not know him. I have no evidence one way or the other." This testimony suggests that Mr. McCrary has assumed knowledge of the victim by the offender for the purpose of his analysis. This is not a legitimate forensic practice.

17. On p. 112 of his deposition, Mr. McCrary testifies that part of his opinion regarding Paul Lovett's individual deterrability is that "there is profound pathology here." Presumably, this refers to some disease on the part of Mr. Lovett. Mr. McCrary is not a mental health professional, nor a behavioral scientist, nor has he interviewed and evaluated Mr. Lovett. Furthermore, I could find no evidence that Mr. Lovett had been examined in a forensic context, or diagnosed with any mental disorders. This inference by Mr. McCrary seems to overstep his expertise by a wide margin, as well as not being based on any known mental health evidence.

18. Based on his deposition, Mr. McCrary's opinions in this case are not based on the necessary victimological information required to make assessments about victim–offender interactions, and whether or not the offense could have been planned (e.g., p. 157–159; McCrary concedes not gathering information relating to victim's work habits, schedule, and other related information—he did not know which stores she worked at, when, who had knowledge of this schedule, or if the offender actually knew the victim or her schedule). As explained in Mr. McCrary's own text on the subject (*Crime Classification Manual*, Burgess et al., 1992; p. 7) "Victimology is often one of the most

beneficial investigative tools in classifying and solving violent crime. It is also a crucial part of crime analysis. Through it, the investigator tries to evaluate why this particular person was targeted for a violent crime." Failure to perform a complete victimology before offering an opinion about whether or not the victim was targeted is not a legitimate forensic practice.

19. Mr. McCrary testified that he is an expert in general security, and therefore to a degree in convenience store security, despite no experience working or researching cases involving convenience stores. (See p. 56 "Q: You're not an expert in convenience store security, are you? A: I think security, in general, and to the degree it carries over to a convenience store, I would say, yes. Q: Yes, you are an expert in convenience store security? A: Security, in general. And, certainly, security at a convenience store would be the same security issue you face in any workplace. Q: Yes, sir. You have never done an analysis of any convenience store chain? A: No.") Suggesting that general knowledge is equal to specialized knowledge is a non-sequitor. Moreover, that Mr. McCrary believes convenience store security involves the same issues as any workplace belies his expertise on this subject. That he does not know enough to know that he is inexpert on this issue, given the facts and circumstances of this particular case, is problematic at best.

20. Mr. McCrary came to his opinions in this case without having read the whole law enforcement investigative file. (See p. 61 "A: Well, again, I don't know exactly what the police did. I have some idea from reading the trial transcript of what the investigation was, but, you know, I haven't seen the whole investigative file.") The investigative file often contains victimological detail, forensic information, and behavioral indicators about the crime that are not available elsewhere. Failing to avail oneself to this prior to rendering court-worthy behaviorally oriented conclusions is not a legitimate forensic practice.

21. P.188–194 of Mr. McCrary's deposition involves an exchange regarding Mr. McCrary's known error rates. He testifies that he and other FBI profilers were routinely "tested" while at the FBI, and that he is or has been in charge of testing analysts for the IACIAF.

Continued

CASE EXAMPLE: *CONTINUED*

However, paradoxically, he claims to be unaware of his error rate, and then claims that there is no way to really know whether or not conclusions are truly accurate. This testimony does not seem consistent.

22. Mr. McCrary's testimony in this case regarding his error rates may be at odds with his previous testimony in *Estate of Sam Sheppard v. Ohio* (2000). As reported in McKnight, K., "Expert's Opinion Challenged," *Ohio Beacon Journal*, April 1, 2000:

An ex-FBI agent who said he hasn't been wrong yet in his analyses of crime scenes, was prepared to testify for the state yesterday that the long-debated 1954 bludgeoning death of Marilyn Sheppard was the result of a "staged domestic homicide."

But ready or not, Gregg O. McCrary—like many of the state's witnesses in the Dr. Sam Sheppard wrongful imprisonment civil trial—spent the bulk of the day being challenged by Sheppard attorney Terry Gilbert over whether he was enough of an expert to make such a determination.

Though I have not read the transcript, my information from counsel Terry Gilbert is this characterization of his testimony is accurate.

23. One test of FBI profiling methods that may cast some light on the error rate issue is provided by Howard Teten (the very first FBI profiler). In an FBI study of 192 cases where profiling was performed, 88 cases were solved. Of those 88 cases, the profile helped with the identification of the suspect only 17% of the time (15 cases). So the known efficacy rate for FBI profilers (using criminal investigative analysis) is 15 out 192. Taken from Teten, H. "Offender profiling" in Bailey, W. (Ed.) (1995) *The Encyclopedia of Police Science*; p. 45.

Subsequent to the disclosure of findings by the author, the plaintiffs in this case filed a motion to exclude the testimony of Mr. McCrary. Upon consideration of these findings, incorporated into the motion and cross-examination of Mr. McCrary in a hearing, the judge issued the following order (*Garcia et al v. Allsup's Convenience Stores Inc.*, 2008):

ORDER

THIS MATTER having come before the Court on the Plaintiffs Daubert/Alberico Motion to Exclude Defense Expert Gregg McCrary and the Court having reviewed the briefing, heard the arguments of counsel and the testimony of Mr. McCrary and Dr. Ross Zumwalt on February 13, 2007,

FINDS, as follows:

1. Crime scene analysis and criminal profiling related to the motives of a killer do not meet the standards for expert testimony in Daubert v. Merrell Dow Pharmaceuticals or State v. Alberico;

2. The methodology used by Mr. McCrary is:

a. Not able to be tested by experiments, research or otherwise;

b. Not based upon or is not capable of scientific analysis;

c. Not reproducible;

d. Not reviewable for any rate of error.

3. The opinions of Mr. McCrary related to the motives of Paul Lovett, whether described as "victim-targeted" behavior, deterrability or foreseeability, are not reliable;

-P.2-

4. The opinions of Mr. McCrary related to "crime scene analysis" whether described as "victim-targeted" behavior, deterrability or foreseeability, do not comply with New Mexico Rule of Evidence 11-702 in that they will not materially assist the trier of fact to determine facts in issue in this case.

IT IS ORDERED:

1. The testimony of Gregg McCrary on crime scene analysis and any issue related to the motives of Paul Lovett, whether described as "victim-targeted" behavior, deterrability, foreseeability or some other heading, is excluded at trial;

2. Based on his law enforcement background, Mr. McCrary may testify about the best practices to prevent crime and the adequacy of security at this Allsup's store, provided he does the following:

CASE EXAMPLE: *CONTINUED*

a. Within 10 days of the date of the hearing (by February 23, 2009), Mr. McCrary produces to the plaintiff all documents, studies, training materials, guidelines and other materials he has used or uses when providing security advice to other companies; and

b. Mr. McCrary makes himself available for deposition at least 20 days before trial.

RAYMOND Z. ORTIZ
DISTRICT JUDGE RAYMOND Z. ORTIZ
Approved as to Form:
Randi McGinn
MCML, p. A.
Attorneys for the Plaintiff
Approved Telephonically 2/19/08
Tom Outler
RODEY, DICKASON, SLOAN, AKTN & ROBB, p. A.
Phil Krehbiel
Chris Key
Attorneys for the Defendant

Subsequent to this decision by Judge Ortiz, Mr. McCrary was not called to testify when the case went to trial. Instead, the defense relied on the testimony of Dr. Merlyn Moore.[4] Dr. Moore is a former Naval Intelligence officer with a strong academic background, and a Professor in the College of Criminal Justice at Sam Houston State University. As reported in Sharpe (2008a):

> The defense called security expert Merlyn Moore, who said having two clerks on duty could increase the potential for an injury because the clerks might confront a robber. Bullet-proof enclosures, he said, suggest a high-crime area, inhibit communication between clerks and customers, and even cause criminals to turn on customers. Moore said alarms can endanger clerks if a robber sees them activating one. "It might be valuable as a last resort if someone is forcing you out of the store," he added. He said video surveillance can assist police after the fact, but "I don't know if it would have deterred Paul Lovett."

The jury did not agree with Dr. Moore's assertions. The case ultimately settled for an undisclosed amount during jury deliberations, just as a verdict was about to be returned. As reported in (Sharpe, 2008b):

> Lawyers in the case of an Allsup's clerk murdered during her graveyard shift settled her estate's wrongful-death lawsuit Tuesday, minutes before a Santa Fe jury was to return a $51.2 million verdict.
>
> Jury forewoman Jean Lehman said jurors had decided to assess Allsup's Enterprises $21.2 million in compensatory damages and $30 million in punitive damages.
>
> But when they told the bailiff they were ready to deliver a verdict about 4:30 p.m., she said, the bailiff told them they were to return to court, where state District Judge Raymond Ortiz informed them the case had been settled.
>
> Allegra Carpenter, one of three Albuquerque lawyers representing the three minor children of Elizabeth Garcia, 26—who was abducted from an Allsup's in Hobbs, raped and stabbed to death Jan. 16, 2002, on just her fourth day on the job—said she could not reveal the amount of the monetary settlement. During closing arguments Monday, plaintiffs' lawyers suggested jurors award the estate $60 million.
>
> Carpenter said the settlement includes a promise from Allsup's that it will never again challenge state regulations requiring convenience stores open between 11 p.m. and 7 a.m. to put at least two clerks on duty, station a guard with one clerk or put clerks in bulletproof enclosures.
>
> Garcia's death spurred efforts to boost security at convenience stores, and Carpenter said Allsup's lobbyists or the Petroleum Marketers Association, to which Allsup's belongs, have challenged the rules every year since they were passed. A jury verdict could not have included such an assurance, and the settlement would not have been possible if not for the pressure of the lawsuit, she said.

Continued

CASE EXAMPLE: *CONTINUED*

"There was a little bit of talk (with lawyers for Allsup's) back and forth, but none of it was very serious until today," Carpenter said.

Lehman, a real-estate agent, said jurors were heavily influenced toward the plaintiff when they learned Allsup's successfully sued its previous insurance company over how to make its stores safer, yet never implemented any of the suggestions. "That was a huge inconsistency," she said.

Lehman said jurors also were curious why so little information was provided about Paul Lovett, the man convicted of abducting, raping and killing Garcia. Last year, Lovett was sentenced to life in prison for murdering Garcia and another woman. Although defense attorneys called Lovett's ex-wife and her father, they did not call Lovett or present a deposition from him during the two-week trial. Lehman and another juror, Elaine Lucero, said it seemed Allsup's provided little information on past crimes at its stores. Attorneys for Garcia's estate said they had to do much of their own research to prove, for example, that 12 Allsup's clerks have been murdered in 30 years, making the near-minimum-wage jobs the most dangerous in the state.

This case illustrates not only the seriousness of premises liability lawsuits and the types of violent crimes they can encompass, but also the tremendous stakes involved for both sides. Additionally, it demonstrates the fact that it is not always merely about seeking and receiving financial gain, although this can be an effective lesson for the negligent. Liability actions of all kinds can also be about leveraging much needed reform, confirming their value to the justice system. Finally, this case serves to illustrate how victim selection, which is useful when developing investigative strategy, can also become a central issue in civil litigation.

---

[4]Dr. Moore holds a PhD from Michigan State University in Criminal Justice and Criminology; an MS in Criminal Justice; and a BA in Police Administration, both from Indiana University.

SUMMARY

As a result of ever-increasing civil litigation initiated by victim-plaintiffs related to liability for the harm caused during criminal acts, forensic criminologists may now be heavily involved with educating the court on issues of standards of care, foreseeability, deterrability, and the like.

Each of these issues varies from cases to case, depending on the region, community, and professionals involved. For example, the standards of care at a hospital are radically different from the standards of care that govern hotels or even schools.

Foreseeability is perhaps the most important issue for criminologists because unless the foreseeability of harm can first be established, there is no duty to protect. If a forensic criminologist determines that a crime was not foreseeable, then this may be used by defense to argue that no duty existed in the case at hand. Consequently, while the court may determine that a defendant has a clear duty of care, the issue of foreseeability can be used to remove it. Once the issue of foreseeability has been assessed, the forensic criminologist may examine the same evidence to determine whether the offense would have been preventable and the offender deterrable.

The highly variable nature of offense and offender deterrability, again, speaks to the need for forensic criminologists to make a deliberate assessment of the facts and circumstances on a case-by-case basis, not blanket generalizations about security efforts and offender types. It is only when all this is considered that forensic criminologists are able to advise the court on these and related issues.

QUESTIONS

1. True or False: *Duty of care* is established by virtue of a special relationship.
2. Are property owners liable for trespassers who enter their property? Explain.
3. What is *deterrability*? How does it relate to premises liability?
4. Describe the difference between an *instrumental* offender and an *expressive* offender.
5. How should forensic criminologists go about assessing premises liability cases?
6. Describe the importance of a thorough victimology in premises liability cases.

REFERENCES

Adkins, S., 2013. Yale fined $165,000 for inadequate reporting of campus crime statistics. University Herald, May 18; Available at: http://www.universityherald.com/articles/3254/20130518/yale-fined-165-000-inadequate-reporting-campus-crime-statistics.htm

Austin, J., Irwin, J., 2001. It's About Time, third ed. Wadsworth, Belmont, CA.

Black, H.C., 1990. Black's Law Dictionary, sixth ed. West Publishing Co, St. Paul, MN.

Brantingham, P., Brantingham, P., 1995. Criminality of place: crime generators and crime attractors. European Journal on Criminal Policy and Research 3 (1), 5–26.

Burgess, A.N., Burgess, A.W., Douglas, J., Ressler, R., 1992. Crime Classification Manual. Lexington Books, New York.

Carrington, F., Rapp, J., 1991. Victims' Rights: Law and Litigation. Matthew Bender, New York.

Chisum, W.J., Turvey, B., 2007. Crime Reconstruction. Elsevier Science, Boston.

Driscoll, R., 2006. The law of premises liability in America: its past, present, and some considerations for its future. Notre Dame Law Review 82, December; pp. 881–909.

Estate of Elizabeth Garcia et al, Plaintiffs v. Allsup's Convenience Stores Inc., Defendant (2008) Case No. D -010 1-CV-20050 0045, First Judicial District Court, County of Santa Fe, State of New Mexico, Order dated February 22.

Farrington, D., Welsh, B., 2002. Improved street lighting and crime prevention. Justice Quarterly 19 (2), 313–342.

Gill, M., Loveday, K., 2003. What do offenders think about CCTV? Crime Prevention and Community Safety 5 (3), 17–25.

Goldstein, p, 1985. The drugs/violence nexus: a tripartite conceptual approach. Journal of Drug Issues 15 (1), 493–506.

Gorby, M., 1998. Premises Liability in Georgia. The Harrison Company, Norcross, GA.

Griffin, A., 2011. Annie Le's family sues, saying Yale failed to protect women on campus. The Hartford Courant, September 6.

Gross, H., 1924. Criminal Investigation. Sweet & Maxwell, London.

Hare, R., 1993. Without Conscience: The Disturbing World of the Psychopaths Among Us. The Guilford Press, New York.

Huber, P., 1988. Liability: The Legal Revolution and Its Consequences. Basic Books, Inc, New York.

Kennedy, D., 2006. Forensic Security and the Law. In: Gill, M. (Ed.), The Handbook of Security. Palgrave MacMillan, New York.

Kennedy, D., 2008. Colloquium: Criminologists in the Courtroom: Consulting and Forensic Criminology. School of Criminal Justice, Michigan State University, February 25.

Kirk, P., 1953. Crime Investigation. Interscience, New York.

Kitchen, S., 2002. Authorities probe death of store clerk. Lubbock Avalanche-Journal, January 19; Available at: http://lubbockonline.com/stories/011902/reg_0119020089.shtml

Lininger, T., 2008. Is it wrong to sue for rape? Duke Law Journal 57, April; 1557–1640.

Lykken, D., 1995. The Antisocial Personalities. Lawrence Erlbaum, Hillsdale, NJ.

Marchant, P., 2004. A demonstration that the claim that brighter lighting reduces crime is unfounded. British Journal of Criminology 44 (3), 441–447.

McKnight, K., 2000. Expert's opinion challenged. Ohio Beacon Journal, April 1; http://www.corpus-delicti.com/sheppard_ohiobj_040100.html

Michael, K., Ellis, Z., 2003. Avoiding Liability in Premises Security, fifth ed. Strafford Publications, Atlanta.

Nettler, G., 1989. Criminology Lessons. Anderson, Cincinnati.

Painter, K., Tilley, N., 1999. Surveillance of Public Space: CCTV, Street Lighting and Crime Prevention. Criminal Justice Press, Monsey, NY.

Piquero, A., Mazerolle, P., 2001. Life-Course Criminology: Contemporary and Classic Readings. Wadsworth, Belmont, CA.

Sakis, J., Kennedy, D., 2002. Violence at work. Trial 38 (12), 32–36.

Sharpe, T., 2008a. S.F. jurors weighing Allsup's culpability in worker's rape, slaying. The New Mexican, April 7.

Sharpe, T., 2008b. Allsup's settles with family of slain clerk: jurors say they were ready to award estate $51.2 million. The New Mexican, April 8; (a) http://www.m2mevolution.com/news/2008/04/08/3377054.htm, (b) http://www.m2mevolution.com/news/2008/04/09/3377054.htm

Sherman, L., Gartin, P., Buerger, M., 1989. Hot spots of predatory crime: routine activities and the criminology of place. Criminology 27 (1), 27–55.

Sherman, L., Gottfredson, D., MacKenzie, D., Eck, J., Reuter, P., Bushway, S., 1997. Preventing Crime: What Works, What Doesn't and What's Promising. U.S. Department of Justice, Washington, DC.

Teten, H., 1995. Offender profiling. In: Bailey, W. (Ed.), The Encyclopedia of Police Science, Garland Publishing, New York.

Thornton, J.I., 1997. The general assumptions and rationale of forensic identification. In: Faigman, D., Kaye, D., Saks, M., Sanders, J. (Eds.), Modern Scientific Evidence: The Law and Science of Expert Testimony, vol. 2. West, St. Paul, MN.

Turvey, B., 2008. Expert declaration in Estate of Elizabeth Garcia v. Allsup's Convenience Stores, Inc. January 9.

Turvey, B., Petherick, W., 2010. Premises liability. In: Turvey, B., Petherick, W., Ferguson, C. (Eds.), Forensic Criminology, Elsevier Science, San Diego.

Turvey, B., Petherick, W., Ferguson, C., 2010. Forensic Criminology, Elsevier Science, San Diego.

Voigt, L., Thornton, W., 1996. Sociology and negligent security: premises liability and crime prevention. In: Jenkins, P.J., Kroll-Smith, S. (Eds.), Witnessing for Sociology: Sociologists in Court, Praeger, Westport, CT.

Welsh, B., Farrington, D., 2003. Effects of closed-circuit television on crime. Annals of the American Academy of Political and Social Science 587, May, 110–135.

Welsh, B., Farrington, D., 2004. Surveillance for crime prevention in public space: results and policy choices in Britain and America. Criminology and Public Policy 3 (3), 497–525.

Weisel, D., 2002. Burglary of Single Family Houses. U.S. Department of Justice, Washington, DC.

CHAPTER 16

Sex Trafficking

John O. Savino and Brent E. Turvey

CONTENTS

KEY TERMS

Cycle of dependence The pattern of coercion, abuse, addiction, and emotional and financial dependence that can bind a sex worker to a trafficker.

Indentured servant A person with limited means who is transported to a new location, presumably for better opportunities, and works off the cost of transportation, food, clothing, lodging, and any other necessities during the term of indenture.

Recruitment The means by which sex traffickers acquire sex workers.

Sex trafficking Inducing a sex act for profit by force, fraud, or coercion, or in which the person induced to perform the act is under 18 years of age.

Sex worker Anyone who works in the sex industry, performing sexual acts for money.

For the majority of people, sex trafficking is a hidden crime. They don't know anything about it. They don't know or care about the victims, they don't know the offenders, and they don't know all the other crimes generally associated with it. Nor are they aware of its origins and realities. This prevents them from recognizing it, even when it is right in front of them. It also causes them to proceed with all manner of false assumptions about sex trafficking and sex workers, often to the point of making some extremely uninformed judgments.

This kind of ignorance creates problems—even more so when the ignorant work in the criminal justice system, in law enforcement, or specifically as sex crimes investigators. The purpose of this chapter is to introduce readers to the concept of sex trafficking, dispel some of the uninformed notions about who is involved and why, and help in understanding the broad spectrum of sexual assault victimization that it creates. To be clear, the culture of sex trafficking is, in part, created by sexual assault, thrives on sexual assault as a commodity and a weapon, and ensures the continued sexual assault of those coerced into servitude.

DEFINITIONS

The U.S. federal government formally recognized human trafficking as a growing global problem, often found in association with other forms of organized

Forensic Victimology. http://dx.doi.org/10.1016/B978-0-12-408084-3.00016-8

crime, during the 1990s. This acknowledgment resulted in the Trafficking Victims Protection Act of 2000 (a.k.a. the TVPA; Wagner, 2010). The TVPA criminalized coerced labor of any kind, defining it as follows (Kim, 2011, p. 437):

(A) sex trafficking in which a commercial sex act is induced by force, fraud, or coercion, or in which the person induced to perform such act has not attained 18 years of age; or

(B) the recruitment, harboring, transportation, provision, or obtaining of a person for labor or services, through the use of force, fraud, or coercion for the purpose of subjection to involuntary servitude, peonage, debt bondage, or slavery.

Sex trafficking, then, involves a sex act for profit induced by force, fraud, or coercion or in which the person induced to perform the act is under 18 years of age. Some might not believe this definition applies to most *sex workers*.[1] First, they may wrongly assume that the majority of sex workers have given their explicit consent to work in the conditions where they are found. Second, they may reason that when sex workers accept payment, this amounts to implied consent for anything that happens on the job—even when they are under age. Finally, they may wrongly assume that this definition requires the crossing of borders. Kim (2011) explains how any consent that might have been given is irrelevant when obtained by deception or force, and that trafficking does not require crossing borders (p. 438):

> In addition to "force" and "fraud," the definition explicitly includes "coercion" as one of the means by which an individual may be trafficked into sex or labor exploitation. Moreover, any initial consent to the work situation that a trafficked individual may have given is rendered immaterial due to the trafficker's forceful, deceptive, or coercive conduct and subsequent exploitation. Finally, while migration across international borders is often a characteristic of human trafficking, the TVPA's definition makes clear that any "recruitment, harboring, transportation, provision, or obtaining" of an individual for the purpose of involuntary labor qualifies as human trafficking. Thus, cross-border movement is not a requirement to meet the legal definition of human trafficking.

As we will discover in this chapter, sex worker consent is often coerced, and payment is often minimal or withheld entirely. It is important to note that coercion, in this context, need not be physical. It can also be a pattern of violence, threats, or psychological abuse that creates an "environment of fear and

---

[1]A *sex worker* is anyone who works in the sex industry, performing sexual acts for money. Not all sex work is criminalized, and not all sex workers are being "trafficked."

intimidation that may prevent a worker from leaving an exploitive work situation" (Kim, 2011, p. 438). *Coercion* is explicitly defined in the TVPA as follows
(Kim, 2011, p. 439):

(A) threats of serious harm to or physical restraint against any person;
(B) any scheme, plan, or pattern intended to cause a person to believe that
failure to perform an act would result in serious harm to or physical
restraint against any person; or
(C) the abuse or threatened abuse of the legal process.

This will become particularly important when we discuss why victims of sex
trafficking don't often leave their "pimps," even when they are physically able
to do so.

TYPES OF SEX WORKERS

It is important to understand that there are many different kinds of sex workers.
The economic continuum is extreme among sex workers, as is their continuum
of risk. It is also important to remember that not all of these sex workers are
necessarily being trafficked, although many are. And this is by no means an
exhaustive list of their circumstances.

Brothel: A brothel is a house of prostitution. In the United States, brothels are
legal only in the state of Nevada, and then only in counties with a smaller
population. Prostitutes who work in a legal brothel are generally required
to give a percentage of their earnings to the house. They must also register
with law enforcement and receive regular medical examinations. There are, of
course, illegal brothels where disease is rampant and the conditions are akin
to slavery.

Escorts/call girls: Escorts are prostitutes who may work for an agency, for pimps,
or for themselves. They advertise their "companionship" services openly in
phone directories and on the Internet. They travel to meet their "clients" at
their homes (outcall), or they rent an apartment or a hotel room and arrange
for "clients" to meet them there (incall). Some escorts are very expensive and
service high-end clients for large sums of money, from upwards of $5,500 an
hour. At the other end of the escort spectrum are drug-addicted prostitutes who
rent cheap hotel rooms by the day; they will service "clients" in house, taking
whatever cash is offered.

Strollers: These are prostitutes who work the corners and walk the street, also
referred to as "the track" or "the stroll." They wait to be approached by customers either on foot or in vehicles. Then they engage in sex for money in
semisecluded public areas (e.g., an alley, between two cars in a parking lot),
in vehicles, or in inexpensive nearby hotels. These prostitutes may work for

a pimp who controls their money or for themselves. In some cases, the pimp may be someone who has multiple girls in his "stable" or may simply be the prostitute's spouse, boyfriend, or even a family member (e.g., mother, step-father). Strollers working the street are those most likely to be suffering from drug addiction (crack, crystal meth, or heroin, depending on the region), which their sex work pays for.

Escorts and strollers can be found working in proximity to particular locations or major events as well, such as

- Airports
- Hotels
- Casinos
- Truck stops
- Military bases
- Major sporting events (e.g., the playoffs, the Super Bowl, the Olympics)

Strip clubs: These clubs are a gray area, as some are associated with drugs and prostitution, whereas others are not. This depends entirely on the club owners and the region.

In any case, there are many other kinds of sex workers (e.g., adult film actresses, adult models, phone sex operators, cam girls, and "bottle girls"). These are gen-erally not individuals who are being trafficked; most are well compensated for their time and can leave their work circumstances whenever they choose. This chapter focuses on those sex worker populations associated most commonly with sex trafficking in the United States.

STATISTICS

The U.S. Department of Justice reports the following regarding incidents of trafficking reported by various task forces in the United States, taken from Kyckelhahn and colleagues (2009):

- 83% of human trafficking involves sex trafficking
- 48.5% involves forced prostitution
- 32% involves child sex trafficking

Regarding *suspects* in confirmed human trafficking incidents, while males were dominant, they were by no means exclusive. Also, most were not white; they were predominantly black or Hispanic:

- *Sex*: 74.3% were males; 25.7% were females
- *Race*: 38.6% Hispanic; 32.9% black; 12.9% Asian; and 10% white
- *Age*: 57.2% were between the ages of 18 and 34; 38.2% were 35 or older

Regarding *victims* in confirmed human trafficking incidents, females were by far more common than males. Also, most were either Hispanic or white and the majority were over 17 years of age.

- *Sex*: 94.4% were females; 5.6% were males
- *Race*: 61.7% Hispanic; 19.5% white; 9.2% Asian; and 6.9% black
- *Age*: 22.5% were 17 or less; 34.1% were 18–24; 33% were 25–34; and 10.5% were 35 or older

Victim age is of particular concern, as many prostitutes start work at a young age. As explained in Reid (2010, pp. 148–149):

> No child seems too young: the falling age of children being lured into sex trafficking is distressing. The demand for "virgins" (i.e., prepubescent children) has increased due to the rising fear of contracting AIDS or other sexually transmitted infections (Fang 2005; Hanna 2002; Hughes 2005; Kreston 2000, 2005). The average age of entry into prostitution for girls in the United States is 12 to 14, with boys entering at even younger ages (Estes and Weiner 2001).

With respect to these underage victims, according to statistics gathered by Radio (2010a): 55% of girls living on the streets in the United States engaged in prostitution; 75% of the girls engaged in prostitution work for a pimp; 76% of the transactions for sex with underage girls are conducted over the Internet; and the average pimp can make between $150,000 and $200,000 per year from each girl.

PREDISPOSITIONS

Being the child victim of abuse or sexual assault pushes kids out of their homes early and into sex work. Some run away from their homes or from foster care, whereas others are simply kicked out by a parent who no longer wants to care for them. In many ways, it can be argued that the wrong family life and the wrong kind of parenting prepare some children for both street life and prostitution quite early on, as reported in Sullivan (1999):

> The very existence of the street kids...sends a subversive message: Bad things happen to young people. Those bad things almost always begin at home. At New Avenues for Youth, a social-services agency downtown [Portland, OR], the staff files child-abuse reports on eighty percent of the kids who are in their clinical programs, a figure that is fairly consistent with what social workers are seeing all across the country.
>
> "We deal with kids who have been shot by their parents, kids who've been stuffed in closets or tied to beds for days and days," said

Daniel Pitasky, who serves as associate director at New Avenues. "And with a lot of kids who've been molested on a daily basis since they were very young. So to say, 'I'm not gonna take this any more' and leave home is a survival choice for the vast majority of them."

Once they hit the streets, though, adolescents on their own face a profusion of dangers. Portland, which offers more services to street kids than most U.S. cities, currently has just fifty-five shelter beds for homeless youth. Those who have no place to stay can only rely on the kindness of strangers in figuring out where to go and what to do. And many strangers are not all that kind.

"A lot of times, what happens is a kid meets an older person at, say, a dance club," explained Cecelia Carlson of the Salvation Army Greenhouse, a drop-in center for street kids in downtown Portland. "The adult says, 'Where are you staying? You can sleep on my couch. I'll buy you a meal.' Then it's, 'Would you like a beer? Would you like to smoke some pot?' A lot of kids might feel that giving somebody a blow job at that point is not such a big deal, because they've been nice. Then maybe this person has some friends who can help the kid pick up some extra money. He's not pimping you; he's trying to help you out."

Many homeless teens have been prepared for careers in prostitution by their own parents. In Portland, girls living on the street who will admit to having been sexually molested say that their abuse began, on average, at age seven. For boys, it's age eleven. The rate of HIV infection among homeless teens has been estimated to be ten times that of the general population.

"Most of us just can't comprehend how powerful it is for an abused kid who has never been told by his family that they care about him to hear it from someone he meets downtown," observed Pitasky. The concept of "street families" has been around since at least the Sixties, but it really became the codified social unit of homeless youth during the early Eighties, when veterans of life on the street began hanging out with the kids and taking on the roles of street moms and street dads.

"For most of these kids, their street families provide not only a place and a purpose," said Carlson, "but also protection and instruction in the skills you need to survive."

As an example, one of the authors (Turvey) worked on a serial murder case involving female prostitutes in Portland, Oregon, during the late 1990s. Along with other private forensic scientists, the author examined and evaluated physical evidence and victimology for the defense. One of the victims was an underage girl named Alex Ison (Figure 16-1), whose mother, Susan, was both a former prostitute and a drug addict. As reported in Sullivan (1999):

FIGURE 16-1
One of the last photographs taken of Alex Ison before her death in 1999.

Susan Ison doesn't like looking back any more than her daughter did, and that's understandable. Her own childhood, spent mostly in a small town about twenty miles from Gainesville, Florida, was like a nightmare from which she didn't wake until she was thirty-six years old. Susan's mother, who suffered from major depression, was in and out of mental institutions, often leaving her daughter for months at a time with a stepfather who began sexually assaulting her when she was three.

"I just sort of slid into prostitution," she said. "I got into drugs so I could do the prostitution. Then pretty soon I was doing the prostitution so I could get the drugs."

Susan was twenty-five before she discovered heroin— "the love of my life" —and had been working as a prostitute for more than a dozen years when her second child was born, in 1982.

Alex spent a lot of time alone in her crib as a baby. "While I was out hustling money, her biological father was supposedly watching her," Susan explained. "He was my dope connection and a violent person who threatened to kill me every time I tried to leave him. I hate to think what he might have done to her when I was gone."

Alex was barely a year old when her father beat her half-brother, Sean, nearly to death, and Susan had the man arrested. "That was one of the first times I was ever able to draw a line," Susan said. Charged with first-degree criminal mischief, the man came looking for Susan as soon as he got out of jail. "The last time I saw him, he had a knife at my throat," she said. "I moved us all into a motel, and after that I never wanted Alex to have any contact with him. That's why I put Sean's father on her birth certificate."

Her son's father was a heroin addict, too, but more pitiful than dangerous, Susan said. His best quality was his absence; the man had just begun serving a fifteen-year prison sentence.

Alex was two in April 1984 when her mother shot up with a friend one evening, passed out, then came to the next morning to discover her companion dead from an overdose. "Because it happened in my apartment, they took my kids away," Susan said. "I was devastated. I really didn't believe I deserved that. I was so strung out that I had no idea what effect my life was having on my kids."

She realized how bad it was when a pair of social workers came for Alex: "I will never, ever forget the look on her face when they took her. It was relief."

Susan went straight into a treatment program but relapsed all through that summer and into the fall. "I stopped using heroin in September," she remembered, "but I still had a gram of cocaine that I couldn't bear to throw away, so on Halloween of 1984, I did it—the last drug I ever used."

Sean was returned to his mother after a year and a half in foster care. One month later, Susan gave birth to a third child, Ryan, who had been fathered by a man she met in her outpatient program. She was living on welfare when five-year-old Alex was returned to her in May 1986.

"Bright as she was, Alex already had a lot of problems," her mother recalled. "It was a struggle for both of us."

Shortly after beginning her first term of college, Susan became pregnant with her fourth child, Catie. By 1990, when Alex turned eight, her mother had graduated with honors and was working full time as a counselor in the chemical-dependency program at Mount Hood Medical Center. That same year, though, Susan made another misstep, marrying a man who ran a group home for adolescent boys. "Mainly, I had three young children that had no business being around those boys," Susan said.

During the year they lived in the group home, Alex was sexually assaulted by a fifteen-year-old boy. "Alex was filled with rage," Susan said. "She never stopped being angry about it inside."

The girl's fury only increased when she learned the identity of her real father. "I felt like I couldn't keep lying to Alex, so I told her," Susan said. "And she never forgave me for that."

Susan tried to compensate by acquiring what she considered to be the ultimate emblem of straight citizenship in December 1993, when she purchased a little house in southeast Portland. "It seemed like things were finally getting better for all of us," she said, "except that Alex was having trouble in school. She was extremely hyper, and they diagnosed her with attention-deficit disorder. But I know in my heart that the molestation changed her."...

Eleven-year-old Alex found friends in her new neighborhood right away. Sarah Walker was one year younger and had just moved into the house next door. "It was Christmastime, and I got an Easy-Bake Oven and all this little-girl stuff," Sarah said. "Alex was not into that at all. She's like, 'Hide that. I'm too old to even look at it.'"

Alex told Sarah on the day they met that she had quit school. "She was Miss Sophisticated," Sarah remembered, "telling me about having sex and smoking pot. I was like, 'How old are you?' And she said, 'Almost twelve.'"

Shortly after Alex and Sarah met, the two girls introduced themselves to red-haired Bob Holly, who was twelve and had lived in the neighborhood most of his life. "Alex and I were in my yard," Sarah said. "Bob came walkin' by, and Alex was like, 'Hey!' I hid behind some bushes, but Alex just said, 'You wanna come inside?'"

Bob, it turned out, was one of a number of kids in the Isons' new neighborhood who were being raised by drug addicts....

To twelve-year-old Alex, he was a hero. "After my dad killed himself, Alex always wanted to hang around me," Bob recalled. "She was really drawn."

The first time Bob and Alex stayed out all night, they slept in the bleachers at nearby Centennial High School. "If I couldn't stay with friends, I'd mostly just fall asleep on school playgrounds or in parking lots," Bob said. "I'd nod off and wake up two hours later, freezin' on the cement."

"Me and Alex, we'd maybe find some little spot next to a school building. But I wouldn't touch her. I'd be in my little corner and she'd be in hers. And she couldn't stand that. She was always tellin' me that we could get warm if we had sex."

Sarah said she and Bob knew that "something sexual" had happened to Alex when she was young but that she refused either to say what it was or to admit that it bothered her. "She always said how great sex was," Sarah said. "She talked about being a stripper someday. She'd say things to guys like, 'You can rape me if you want.' I guess she was trying to take a bad thing that happened to her and make it good."

When Bob stayed outside overnight with Alex, he woke up several times to find her hands down his pants. "Or if I was going to the bathroom, she'd climb up on the sink to watch me," Bob said. "I'd call her perverted, but Alex didn't care."...

Alex was smoking pot and drinking alcohol, as well, but what most frightened her mother was that the girl had started cutting herself, using razor blades or broken glass to slash the inside of her forearms, between the wrist and the elbow. "And these were deep cuts," Susan said. "I read some of her writings where she said that was her God for a while, the pain she felt when she cut herself."

Around the same time that she started cutting herself, Alex began to take her vanishing act to a new level. "She'd just disappear on impulse," Susan said. "One night we drove home, and as we were getting out of the car I saw Bob Holly standing outside, and by the time I turned around Alex was gone. It was that quick."

"At first she wouldn't come back for a couple of days," Susan said. "But pretty soon it was a week. I could usually find her at the beginning, because she stayed in this general area. But once she started going downtown, she was harder to find."

"She thought the people downtown were just so cool," Sarah remembered. "She'd tell me about these friends who were older and took her places and taught her stuff."

"What it was," Bob explained, "Alex found a bunch of people on the streets that were just like her. They were the family she wanted."

Alex Ison wound up in downtown Portland, addicted to heroin, and working as a prostitute on the steps of the Multnomah County Library by the time she was 16. With a long and troubled history of sexual abuse, drug abuse, and running away, she was ultimately picked up, raped, and murdered by Todd Alan Reed [Figure 16-2]. Reed eventually made a plea deal, confessing to the sexual murders of three Portland area prostitutes: Lilla Faye Moler, 28; Stephanie Lynn Russell, 26; and Alexandria Nicole Ison, 17. He was given three consecutive life sentences without the possibility of parole.

Again, a history of abuse leads to a predisposition to become victimized by sex traffickers. This is consistent with data provided in Radio (2010a):

According to a recent survey of social service providers in Oakland and the rest of the county, 61 percent of the teen prostitutes they see say they were raped as children.

That's what happened to Brittney. She says she was raped by her stepfather and years later by her trafficker. Brittney tries to understand how she kept going back to her pimp. "I knew what he was capable of," she says. "He'd beat me and he'd rape me, he'd beat me and he'd rape me, and I just kept going back until I ended up being pregnant by him. And he beat me so bad that I ended up having a miscarriage."

FIGURE 16-2

Todd Alan Reed, 32, appears Tuesday, July 20, 1999, in Multnomah County Circuit Court. Reed had a history of burglary and violent sexual assault. DNA linked him to the murders of three Portland area prostitutes: Lilla Faye Moler, 28; Stephanie Lynn Russell, 26; and Alexandria Nicole Ison, 17 (see Figure 16-1). He dumped their bodies in Forest Park. In February 2001, Reed agreed to a plea bargain and was sentenced to three consecutive terms of life in prison without the possibility of parole.

This is also similar to the detailed account provided in McBride (2011):

Prostitution is not an easy subject to talk about, especially for those who have engaged in it—but Heather McMenamin-Bozart, a recovering drug addict who spent 10 years enslaved to a sex trafficker named Don Webster, wants to change that.

McMenamin-Bozart was one of 40 witnesses who put Webster behind bars in February 2008. Webster was convicted of exploiting women and girls between the ages of 13 and 30.

McMenamin-Bozart believes childhood trauma made it easy for Webster to lure her into the sex trade.

Presented with a pile of stones alongside a backpack on a table and asked to think of each one as a bad experience growing up, she quickly began to list a litany of woes. "Growing up without a father," McMenamin-Bozart said, putting the first stone into the backpack. She said the next stone she put in represented child molestation; then she picked up another, and another.

"The drugs and alcohol inside my family," McMenamin-Bozart said. "Feeling like an outcast at home. Or not having any food or clothing or being picked up at school."

Before long, the backpack was filled with about 20 stones. "It just becomes one big bag," she said as she tried to lift it up. "That's what you're carrying around on you. It's a lot of weight, a lot of weight on a child's shoulder."

When McMenamin-Bozart first crossed paths with Webster, she was 22. When they met at an Anchorage strip club, she believes he instantly recognized that she had grown up emotionally needy. At that time, she says Webster went by the name of Jerry Starr. "(He) portrayed himself as a man who was interested in meeting me as a boyfriend," she said. "He introduced me to crack cocaine and he got me hooked that way."

She was soon to discover that she wasn't alone, that she was one of many girls Starr had seduced with drugs and charm. "He could have sold you ocean-front property in Arizona," McMenamin-Bozart said. "He was that good."

As part of his prostitution ring, Starr maintained several houses of women, hooked on drugs and turning tricks. "It was a smooth operation, if you want to look at it that way," McMenamin-Bozart said. Several of his houses were in middle-class neighborhoods, where McMenamin-Bozart was also was expected to help groom younger girls to work in the trade. "When the young girls are first introduced to this, they latch on—they'll find one of the older girls to latch onto, kind of maybe a big sister role, or a mother role," she said.

Starr wanted the women to think of him as the family patriarch. "He would have us call him Daddy. So he was like our lover, our father, our supporter, our everything," McMenamin-Bozart said.

She says Starr was always on the look-out for broken girls. "Then he builds them up by lavishing them with gifts, telling them how much he wants to take care of them, putting them in nice places and giving them nice homes and clothes," McMenamin-Bozart said.

Starr also treated girls to getting their hair and nails done—but he expected the girls to turn over every dollar they earned, and if he felt he was being shorted he would turn violent. "We had what we call the box," McMenamin-Bozart said. Starr would punish his girls by locking them up in small spaces. In the house McMenamin-Bozart stayed at in East Anchorage, Starr used a crawl space under the house to punish her. "There was a time I got locked into the box and I was stripped down naked, hog-tied and thrown into the box and held down there for three days," she said.

The FBI salvaged a closet from a trailer that Starr used to house another group of prostitutes. It was used in his trial as evidence of his cruelty. "He had a box no matter where he went; that was his punishment," McMenamin-Bozart said. "There was never lights. We never had lights in them." When girls were released from the box, Starr would tell them that their Daddy still loved them.

The FBI and the Anchorage Police Department say Starr typified an underground culture of pimping. Like other prostitution kingpins, he would take away driver's licenses and other forms of identification from his women, to break their connection to the outside world and increase their dependence on him.

Special Agent Jolene Goeden says Starr would form what is called a "trauma bond" with his women, similar to the Stockholm Syndrome in which hostages become emotionally attached to their captors. "Breaking them down, building them back up: that loyalty is created out of that, because that young girl or young woman becomes so dependent on him, they think he literally controls their lives," Goeden said.

Starr liked young girls because they were easier to control. "Their minds are more moldable, like Play-Doh," McMenamin-Bozart said.

Starr would often cruise Spenard or troll the People Mover bus service's Downtown Transit Center, keeping an eye out for broken girls.

The attitude of the child victim who leaves home to escape sexual abuse can become one of simple economics: "if I'm going to be having sex, I'm going to get paid for it." They may come to view males as either users or abusers, sex as a commodity, and themselves as an object with a price tag. Sex traffickers learn to read the signs of a broken or angry girl—the facial expressions, the body language, and the manner of dress. They know what to do, what to say, and how to gain their confidence in order to recruit them effectively. Once caught up in the *cycle of dependence*, it becomes almost impossible to break free.

RECRUITMENT

Recruitment refers to the means by which sex traffickers acquire sex workers. As described in the preceding section, this is not something that happens by accident. It is generally the result of a planned con, fraud, or even kidnapping. In the United States, as reported in Albanese (2007, p. 3):

> Pimps scout bus stations, arcades, and malls, focusing on girls who appear to be runaways without money or job skills. Pimps, or their procurers, befriend the children by showing affection and buying them meals, clothes, jewelry, or video games in exchange for sex.

The method of recruitment is dictated by the vulnerability of the victim and the capabilities of the trafficker.

The Con

Traffickers who con their victims do so in a variety of ways that have remained unchanged over generations. They may send a girl in to befriend the target victims and recruit them or they may coerce or reward the girls in their "stable" for recruiting "straight" girlfriends. However, the sex trafficker may also acquire their targets as a "Romeo pimp." Consider, for example, the case of Darlene, reported in Radio (2010a):

> Darlene, whose name has been changed as well, came into "the game" a different way. She entered her teens around the same time [that] her native Oakland, as part of the San Francisco Bay Area, was named by the FBI as one of the 13 national hot spots for child prostitution.
>
> Classmates talked about their boyfriends who had lots of money, and—like most kids in the Bay Area—she listened to music by Oakland rappers, whose lyrics about pimping glamorized "the game."
>
> "A lot of it is glorified," says Darlene. "Oh, you're from Oakland. Everybody has dreads; everybody goes dumb; we pop pills, smoke a lot of weed; parties, sideshows and hos."
>
> If you're not part of the scene, it's hard to believe that prostitution has become normal for so many in Oakland and other cities. But many see it as an alternative to desperate home lives, friends getting shot, no food on the table and absent parents. And pimps take advantage of that.
>
> Darlene became a prostitute at the hands of what Oakland police call a "Romeo pimp." Now 18, she moved in with her boyfriend when she was 14, after she was kicked out of the house. "On my 15th birthday, he was like, 'Well, you know, since you'll be staying with me, we need more food. We need to find a way to get some money,'" says Darlene. "He's the one that, like, introduced me to prostitution, and I didn't see anything wrong with it."
>
> Darlene says she later found out her then-18-year-old boyfriend had pimped other girls before. When he became her pimp, Darlene says, he told her what to do to make money. "This is how you look at the guys; this is what you tell them; these are what cars to stay away from; this is how much you charge."

Another con involves false advertisements for "modeling" work. Target victims (usually young females) are lured to hotel rooms or apartments with the promise of easy money, posing for pictures. When they arrive, they are slowly encouraged to take increasingly revealing photos until compromising images are obtained. The trafficker can then use these photos to blackmail the victim into sexual servitude.

The problem of sex trafficking has increased in the United States, particularly in Alaska, where sexual molestation in Native communities drives young women to Anchorage, almost directly into the clutches of highly organized sex traffickers. As reported in Hopkins (2010), underage Native girls, looking to escape alcoholism and all manner of abuse at home, are often easy to con or convince:

A disproportionate number of women working in the Anchorage sex trade are Alaska Native and pimps and sex traffickers are pursuing Native girls at events like AFN, police warned tribes and villagers today.

"There have been traffickers and pimps who specifically target Native girls because they feel that they're versatile and they can post them (online) as Hawaiian, as Native, as Asian, as you name it," said Jolene Goeden, a special agent for the FBI in Anchorage.

Far from home and surrounded by strangers, girls from remote villages are particularly vulnerable to sex-trade recruiters said Goeden and Sgt. Kathy Lacey, supervisor for the Anchorage police vice unit. The investigators delivered a kind of "Prostitution 101" to people from villages across the state at an annual Bureau of Indian Affairs conference, telling community leaders and health workers to be on the lookout for pimps preying on Alaska Native women and girls.

The pair gave a similar, shorter talk in October in Bethel. For some, the stories were personal. "We don't think that this is happening in our in small villages. It happens. It happened to my baby sister," said a woman from a rural hub city, who said her sister was 14 years old when she disappeared while visiting the Alaska Federation of Natives convention in Anchorage about four years ago.

Her family tracked the girl down at a downtown shelter for homeless teens, her body surging with drugs, said the woman, who I'm not identifying because it would also identify her sister. "That really ruined her life," the woman said sharply. "I can't get my sister back the way she...." Her voiced trailed off before a shell-shocked crowd of about 200 at the Egan Civic and Convention Center.

Sex traffickers use a combination of mind games and beatings, promises and drugs to control girls, authorities said.

Alaska Native girls are commonly lured from their hometowns by friends or relatives who are already working as prostitutes. They invite the girl to come hang out and go shopping rent free. Others are recruited while visiting the city. About one-third of the women arrested this year for prostitution in Anchorage are Alaska Native, according to Lacey's figures. It's unclear how many under-age Native girls are the victims of pimps or sex traffickers.

Four Anchorage residents charged last year with running a sex-trafficking ring got at least some of their "stable" of prostitutes from

Alaska Native villages, prowling the AFN convention and streets surrounding the Covenant House shelter.

It was an Alaska Native girl who moved to Anchorage to stay with family at the age of 12 who helped point investigators toward another prostitution kingpin: Don Webster, also known as Jerry Starr, Goeden said. Webster, who was sentenced to 30 years in prison in 2008, had tried to recruit the girl, Goeden said.

The FBI agent got to know the teen during visits to a youth jail. The pair talked about how the girl ended up selling her body at age 14 in Anchorage. "Her response to me was, 'I could be back home in the village where I could be having sex with my grandpa for free, or I could be here getting paid for me,'" Goeden said. "I didn't know what to say. I had no idea how to respond to this little girl."

Regardless of where they're from, many prostitutes are former sexual abuse victims, Lacey told the crowd. Many are addicted to drugs, Lacey said. "It used to be every prostitute we patted down had a crack pipe on them. Not any more, the drug of choice is heroin," she said after today's meeting.

Many are runaways. Under-age kids can't rent cars or rent hotel rooms, after all, and they have to get money somehow. "(That) especially holds true when you get young girls from the villages that come in here and they come in to visit an auntie or whoever they're going to visit and they decide that they're going to run away," Lacey said. Very quickly they're propositioned by someone trying to lead them on a path toward prostitution, she said....

People always ask why the girls don't leave pimps or sex traffickers on their own, the investigators told the crowd. Some feel so bad about themselves they don't believe they deserve anything better, they said. Others don't know who to ask for help or are afraid of violent reprisals.

Some, particularly those from small communities, don't want their friends or family to know what's happening to them. "These girls typically, almost always, do not see themselves as a victim," Goeden said

In most cases, law enforcement officers familiar with the realities of sex trafficking are sympathetic to the victims and want to help them escape their situation if possible. In extreme cases, however, law enforcement officers have been known to approach prostitutes and offer them protection from other pimps, and safety from arrest, in exchange for sex and a cut of their earnings. They have also been known to run, or work as "security" for, illegal brothels in their jurisdiction, as reported in Hauser (2007):

A former city police officer admitted on Thursday that he took favors and money from a Queens brothel as part of a protection scheme that helped shut down its competitors.

The former officer, Dennis Kim, 31, pleaded guilty in United States District Court in Brooklyn to a federal charge of conspiracy to commit extortion in his capacity as a police officer. The plea enables him to avoid a trial and the prospect of a lengthy jail sentence.

Mr. Kim, who resigned from the Police Department on Monday, admitted that he and a partner accepted money from the owners of the brothel, who supplied information that was then used in raids that closed their rivals. Mr. Kim also said that his partner would receive sexual services from the brothel's prostitutes for his role in the scheme.

In March 2006, law enforcement authorities arrested Mr. Kim and the partner, Jerry Svoronos, now 32, along with the man and woman who ran the brothel. Immigration took into custody 16 women believed to have worked there as prostitutes. The case was one of the city's largest sex-and-bribes protection scandals since more than a dozen officers were implicated a decade ago for protecting a brothel on the West Side of Manhattan....

Mr. Kim's lawyer, Maurice H. Sercarz, said his client had been a capable and aggressive police officer, and now wanted to put the ordeal behind him. "That and a feeling he let down people close to him," Mr. Sercarz said....

The arrests followed a 10-month investigation by the Federal Bureau of Investigation, the Police Department, the United States attorney's office in Brooklyn, and Immigration and Customs Enforcement. According to court documents, the brothel took in more than $1 million a year, and the information supplied by the brothel owners enabled the officers to make career-advancing arrests.

In other jurisdictions, officers have also been found doing such things and running escort services with underaged girls out of their homes with their wives, providing secure transportation of prostitutes from one jurisdiction to another.

Indentured Servitude

An *indentured servant* is a person with limited means who is transported to a new location, presumably for better opportunities, and works off the cost of his or her transportation, food, clothing, lodging, and any other necessities during the term of his or her indenture. This is how many international sex traffickers acquire their target victims, including those from Mexico, Asia, and eastern Europe. Torgoley (2006) reports on the international recruitment of women who are often brought to the United States (pp. 561–562):

Recruiters can be anyone from a family friend, an employment agency, or even reputable individuals within the community. Such individuals frequently use deception as a tactic to lure "willing" women to gainful "work" abroad. A common example in China involves the promise to rural women of factory jobs elsewhere, when in reality they are trafficked into prostitution....

Recruitment of women for trafficking and prostitution comes in many forms. Patterns of slavery generally involve drawing people in from poor areas and introducing them into slavery or selling them to wealthy individuals for labor or sexual servitude. Many victims are unwilling participants in the act of trafficking to begin with. In this context, traffickers procure or abduct outright victims from their nations of origin.

Other times traffickers secure the complicit transportation of victims through false promises of job opportunities and desirable lifestyles. For young women, especially, promises made to their families by traffickers help ease concerns about sending the girls to far off nations.

As further reported in Albanese (2007, p. 4):

Traffickers also recruit children by convincing families—through "success" stories—that their children will be safer, better taken care of, and taught a useful skill or trade. Cash may be paid to families, to be "repaid" through their child's earnings. (Sometimes a "contract" is created that implies a legal indebtedness, which provides even more leverage to force a child into prostitution.)

In the beginning of this chapter, we provided statistics showing that the most common victims of sex trafficking are young Hispanic females. These victims are commonly brought into the United States illegally from Mexico, with the promise of a new life, but also without any support, and a heavy debt to repay. Consider Rosa's story, from Torgoley (2006, pp. 555–556):

Rosa's story: When I was 14, a man came to my parents' house in Veracruz, Mexico and asked me if I was interested in making money in the United States. He said I could make many times as much money doing the same things that I was doing in Mexico. At the time, I was working in a hotel cleaning rooms and I also helped around my house by watching my brothers and sisters. He said I would be in good hands and would meet many other Mexican girls who had taken advantage of this great opportunity. My parents didn't want me to go but I persuaded them.

A week later, I was smuggled into the United States through Mexico to Orlando, Florida. It was then the men—it was then when the men told me my employment would consist of having sex with men for money. I had never had sex before and I had never imagined selling my body. And so my nightmare began.

Because I was a virgin, the men decided to initiate me by raping me again and again to teach me how to have sex. Over the next three months, I was taken to a different trailer every 15 days. Every night, I had to sleep in the same bed in which I had been forced to service customers all day.

I couldn't do anything to stop it. I wasn't allowed to go outside without a guard. Many of the bosses had guns. I was constantly afraid. One of the bosses carried me off to a hotel one night where he raped me. I could do nothing to stop him.

Because I was so young, I was always in demand with the customers. It was awful. Although the men were supposed to wear condoms, sometimes they didn't. So eventually, I became pregnant and was forced to have an abortion. They sent me back to the brothel almost immediately.

I cannot forget what has happened. I can't put it behind me. I find it nearly impossible to trust people. I still feel shame. I was a decent girl in Mexico. I used to go to church with my family. I only wish none of this ever happened.

This recruitment tactic exploits the impoverished and the ignorant. It can also play on the target victims' sense of hope, fear, shame, and responsibility to repay their debt, or the debts of their family.

Kidnapping

In cases in which less confrontational methods of recruitment may not be successful and sex traffickers are sufficiently motivated, they may target, con, and kidnap their victims. This happens everywhere, from eastern Europe to the United States, as explained in Torgoley (2006, p. 562):

If traditional methods of luring do not work, which is often the case where victims are uncooperative, outright kidnapping occurs as a method of obtaining women. In Albania, for example, the abduction of girls from school by traffickers has become such a problem that many Albanian families simply do not send their children to school.

Consider the case of Lorenzo Calvin (Figure 16-3), a pimp from Stockton, California, as reported in Staff (2006):

A man suspected of kidnapping a 17-year-old Lathrop girl and forcing her into prostitution was arrested Thursday in Manteca after prostitutes he sent to pick up his impounded vehicle unknowingly led investigators to him, police said.

Lorenzo Arthur Calvin, 29, was arrested in the 1400 block of South Airport Way and was booked into San Joaquin County Jail on suspicion of kidnapping, forced oral copulation, and pimping and pandering of a minor.

FIGURE 16-3

Lorenzo Calvin was arrested for prostituting an underaged girl using the Internet during a Milpitas police raid of a prostitution ring operating out of the Executive Inn Hotel in Milpitas, California.

According to the Sheriff's Office, the Lathrop girl was reported as a runaway Oct. 16. She was found Nov. 18 during a Milpitas police raid of a prostitution ring at the Executive Inn Hotel, a three-star hotel in Milpitas.

The girl told Milpitas police that she had been held against her will and forced to have sex with about seven men each day....

According to a Sheriff's Office report, Calvin and several prostitutes had worked out of two adjoining rooms at the Milpitas hotel raided last month. In one room, police found a computer with a Web site advertising the prostitutes.

According to the report, friends of the girl identified Calvin as the last person seen with her before she ran away. They told police she had called several times but had to hang up quickly.

The girl told police she tried to run away from Calvin once, but he found her and allegedly beat her. On another occasion, he had forced her to perform oral sex on him, a report said. Deputies followed suspected prostitutes who picked up a vehicle belonging to Calvin from an impound lot Thursday and followed the vehicle to Calvin.

This case is instructive because it typifies a method of operating common to sex traffickers: befriend a young girl (perhaps a runaway), kidnap her to large metro area, rent a hotel room, put up some online ads, take the calls, make the appointments, and collect the money. As mentioned, this can be a very lucrative venture in a very short period of time, especially if the pimp is able to run multiple girls.

RETENTION

Invariably, the question arises as to why victims of sex traffickers stay with them, even when they have the opportunity to leave. The answer is a cycle of dependence that, once initiated, is hard to break free from. The primary element in this cycle of dependence is fear: fear of being hurt, fear of being alone, fear of harm to their family, or fear that their family will learn what they have been doing and will reject them. The sex trafficker knows these fears well, and knows how to use them. It is both an emotional and a financial connection, as reported in Albanese (2007, p. 3):

> Eventually, pimps use the children's emotional and financial dependency to coerce them into selling sex for money that is turned over to the pimp. In time, the relationship becomes less emotional and more "contractual" as the pimp sets a minimum on the child's earnings.

Once caught up in this cycle, the victim becomes easy to control, as explained in Torgoley (2006, p. 562):

> Traffickers use various methods to solicit the compliance of their victims. Once the victims are away from home and in the control of traffickers, further cooperation is coerced. Often traffickers achieve victim compliance by threats to harm the victim, threats to turn them over to officials for deportation, physical abuse, torture, rape, confinement, seclusion, and even threats to the victim's family in the nation of origin. Families of the victims are often helpless to intervene, especially when the traffickers are members of organized crime, wanton criminals, or government agencies. However, in most cases families simply do not know the condition of their family member victim.

Other tools of the sex trafficker, with respect to controlling their victims, include extortion, threats of violence, physical abuse, and drugs. Consider this case reported in Albanese (2007), involving a typical combination of these (pp. 2–3):

> In one case, for example, a pimp recruited girls from Vancouver, British Columbia, and took them to Hawaii, withholding their papers so they could not leave. The girls were drugged, handcuffed, and told that if they did not comply, photographs of them engaging in sex would be sent to magazines or to their families.

Drug addiction is also a major aspect in the cycle of dependence. The addiction provides a powerful mechanism for controlling trafficked victims, physically and emotionally. Physically, it binds them to their trafficker—to ensure the proximity of their next fix. Emotionally, it provides the only escape from their depressed situation, and allows them to endure or tune out whatever the day brings them. Once the victims are addicted to drugs, whether it is crack, methamphetamine, or heroin, the trafficker has a nearly unbreakable grip on the victims that will cause them to "consent" to just about anything.

CASE EXAMPLE:

Underage Trafficking

Meth and Porn

Fifty-year-old Douglas Winberry was arrested in Prosser, Washington, while Colby Watson, 36, and Lindsey McKeehan, 23, were arrested in Meridian, Idaho (Figures 16-4a–16-4c). Watson and McKeehan, both from Boise, were in an ongoing intimate relationship; they became friends with Winberry. At some point, they became involved with minor teen girls, giving them meth in exchange for sex and selling their sexual services over the Internet using the popular website Craigslist. A tip to the police led them to Winberry's home, where they initially found a CD of sexually exploitative images of a female under age 18. As provided in an official press release from the Ada county prosecuting attorney's office (Bower, 2008):

> On July 22, 2008, an Ada County Grand Jury indicted three co-defendants in multiple acts of Lewd Conduct, Sexual Abuse of a Child and Felony Injury to Child involving two minor fifteen year old girls. Douglas Winberry, Lindsey McKeehan and Colby Watson were all indicted after the Grand Jury heard evidence from a number of witnesses involved in the

investigation stemming from the Meridian Police Department's investigation in June and July 2008. Winberry is charged with sexually molesting two adolescent girls while McKeehan and Watson are charged with sexually molesting one adolescent girl.

Originally charged with various counts of Child Exploitation and Inducing Child Prostitution, the Ada County Prosecutor's Office elected to charge acts of lewd conduct, sexual abuse and injury to a child. The charges involve sexual acts by all three individuals, taking of photographs and/or videos of the minor adolescents, and supplying the minor adolescents with methamphetamine in exchange for sexual acts.

McKeehan subsequently took a plea deal from the Ada county prosecutor in exchange for her testimony against Watson, her former boyfriend, and their associate Winberry. Both men eventually pled guilty, making their own deals with the Ada county prosecutor to avoid trial (Staff, 2009).

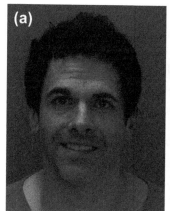 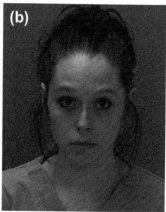 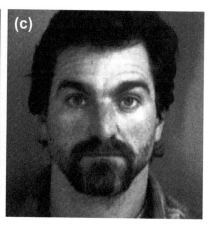

FIGURE 16-4

Pictured left to right: Colby Watson (a), Linsey McKeehan (b), and Douglas Winberry (c). All three pled guilty to charges stemming from their arrest and indictment for multiple acts of lewd conduct, sexual abuse of a child, and felony injury to a child. They had been trading meth for sex with minor teen girls and prostituting them via the Internet using Craigslist.

CASE EXAMPLE:

Underage Trafficking

The threat of being assaulted or hunted down should they try to escape is very real for most victims of sexual trafficking. Consider the case of Joey Wayne Simpson, Jr. (Figure 16-5), reported in Pavuk (2011):

> An Orlando prostitute was burned with a metal mallet and beaten by her pimp after she tried to flee to her home in Ohio, an Orange County Sheriff's Office report said.
>
> The man alleged to be the pimp, 27-year-old Joey Wayne Simpson Jr., was arrested Tuesday on charges that include aggravated battery, kidnapping and sex trafficking.
>
> According to the sheriff's report, Orlando police and Orange County deputies learned about the attack when another woman called 911 on Monday to report that she was punched in the mouth and jumped out of a moving vehicle.
>
> That woman told deputies she moved to Orlando from Ohio and met Simpson through a friend, whose identity was marked out in the Sheriff's Office report, and that Simpson and other people tried to convince her to become a prostitute.
>
> The woman told deputies Simpson protects prostitutes and handles their money. The woman, who denied engaging in prostitution, told deputies that on Sunday, she went to an apartment on South Texas Avenue where she met the victim.

This threat is corroborated in Albanese (2007), which explains the mechanisms of achieving and maintaining control over trafficked victims recruited in Tijuana, Mexico—just over the border from the United States (p. 4):

> One Mexican study revealed that, upon arriving in Tijuana, 14- to 17-year-old girls were recruited by "middlemen" (local exploiters), beaten, and threatened that their families would be harmed. Other means of maintaining control over the prostituted children included giving them drugs and keeping them in forced isolation. In addition to their sexual exploitation in brothels and on the streets, the girls in this study were forced to work in hotels, boarding houses, parks, bus stations, bars, nightclubs, beauty and massage parlors, modeling and escort agencies, and spas. Adults seeking sex with children obtained referrals from waiters,

FIGURE 16-5

Joey Wayne Simpson, Jr. —arrested for aggravated battery, kidnapping, and sex trafficking—allegedly protects prostitutes and handles their money.

Continued

CASE EXAMPLE: *CONTINUED*

doormen, taxi drivers, receptionists, nightclub security guards, valet parking attendants, and street vendors.

This speaks to a high level of organization: a network of "local exploiters" working to identify potential targets for recruitment, a series of safe locations for the victims to work once they are acquired, and a referral system to route "clients." In short, there must be an entire community of people working very hard to make this happen, profiting substantially from this culture of rape.

SEX WORKERS AND SEXUAL ASSAULT

The relationship between trafficked sex workers and sexual assault should be clear at this point. They are victims of rape. And their victimization is essentially unending, as long as they are unable to escape their situation.

First, there is often a personal history involved. Many of these girls will have been raped as children, possibly by members of their own family. This is related to their reasons for leaving home early in the first place—to escape abuse.

Second, many of these girls will have been raped by their traffickers. This is, in fact, a common method of induction into the world of prostitution. The trafficker will rape his new girls to establish ownership and dominance or to break them in if they are virgins.

Third, violent rape will often be used as a punishment. If the girl disobeys the trafficker or tries to escape, he may reassert his ownership and dominance. Again, this is accomplished by repeating the initiation rape she was forced to endure when she first started working. This time, however, there will be less concern for inflicting damage and more focus on teaching her a lesson.

Finally, rape is an occupational hazard for trafficked sex workers. Every new "client" is a potential rapist. In fact, those familiar with prostitutes can tell you that they are generally raped on average about once a month—and that's in a slow month.

EASY PREY

The sex crime investigator must remember that, as a direct result of the illicit nature of the sex trade, sex offenders frequently target those who work in it. They are easy prey for both sophisticated and inexperienced offenders alike. Both types consider illegal sex workers far less likely to report any attack to police due to their complicity in criminal activity (e.g., prostitution, drugs). Sex workers are also targeted because of the vulnerabilities and inherent things they are willing to do with any potential customers: without knowing anything about the customers, and with only the promise of few dollars, sex workers will meet with "clients" anywhere; they will go with them anywhere, including isolated locations; they will take off their clothes without coercion; and they will submit to defenseless situations. All of this makes these sex workers extremely vulnerable. The authors have investigated many cases in which serial offenders targeted sex workers specifically because of these traits.

VOLUNTARY SEX WORKERS: AN INVESTIGATIVE RESOURCE

As explained already, there are many adult sex workers who participate in the sex trade voluntarily. They arrive from every conceivable background: they can be drug addicts, survivors of incest, college students, or mentally ill; they can be all of these things and more. Some work for a pimp; some work for themselves. All of them have a story, and all of them have a reason.

Most of these voluntary sex workers will not be convinced to leave the sex trade until they are ready, if ever. This means that they will be out there, plying their illicit trade with all of the risk that it entails, no matter what efforts are made on their behalf. Often, it is money and/or an addiction that keeps them in place; they can make in one evening what a straight girl makes in two weeks or a month. Returning to straight life is, therefore, not an option for them.

Consequently, the sex crimes investigator will encounter the same sex workers over and over—sometimes while they are being arrested, and sometimes while they are filing a police report. There are two things to remember about voluntary sex workers: they must be taken seriously when reporting a sex crime and are an invaluable source of "street" intelligence. But this is only true when they are afforded respect and treated with dignity.

Sex Workers and False Reports

If a sex worker, such as a prostitute, takes the time to report a sexual assault, investigators should not be dismissive. Remember that the sex worker is taking time out of his or her day, time that he or she could be making money, to file that complaint. As readers will learn, the complaint process involves extensive interviews and physical examinations, all of which can take several hours. Most sex workers are well aware of this reality. A false report is generally going to be a waste of their time and will incur the wrath of any pimp they are accountable to. They must be highly motivated to lose that much money and to risk any punishment that they might receive for being "short" in their earnings. By taking the reports of sex workers seriously and investigating them with the same professionalism as any other report, the sex crimes investigator can show respect and gain an invaluable source of intelligence.

Sex Workers as a Source of Intelligence

The women in the sex trade, and even their pimps, should not be forgotten as potential sources of information when conducting criminal investigations.

These people exist in a secret underground world. They often have volumes of information to share, should they be inclined to do so. If the sex crimes investigator has earned their respect during prior contacts and treated them with dignity, they may be receptive to providing assistance when asked.

Consider the following two examples. These cases are significant because they involve two innocent victims. These were not willing participants; they were not involved in the sex trade business; they had family and friends who were missing them; they had regular jobs; and they had regular lives. Although they were lured with the promise of illicit drugs, they did not agree to become prostitutes or sex slaves. This lesson must be remembered when dealing with any victims involved in the sex trade: the investigator's involvement may save their life. This requires not taking things at face value and looking beneath the surface in every case to learn the truth.

CASE EXAMPLE:

"The Village Voice"

In April 2006, two young Asian females were selling their services out of a small apartment in an affluent neighborhood in Manhattan's Upper East Side. Their services had been advertised in the "Escort" section of a local NYC newspaper, the *Village Voice*.

Shortly before 9:00 p.m., one of the females received a telephone call from an individual who wanted to arrange a "date" for himself and two of his friends. The female gave them the address of the building where they were located, with instructions to call when they arrived. About an hour later, the male called back and indicated he and his friends were outside. One of the females went downstairs to meet the men; this was their practice to make sure the police were not raiding them.

The men were brought into the apartment where they exchanged small talk. They also provided a cash payment to the only female who spoke English. One of the females was going to be servicing all three of these men. That female and one of the men went into a back bedroom. Once inside, the female undressed and got into bed. It was at this point the man with her displayed a handgun and sexually assaulted her. After the sexual assault, the attacker took back the money she had been given and demanded she hand over any other cash that she had. The victim was then forced back into the common area of the apartment at gunpoint.

Then the other woman was forced into the bedroom at gunpoint by one of the other men, where she was sexually assaulted. The third male raped the first female in the living room. After the sexual assaults had been completed, they ransacked the apartment looking for additional money.

The victims eventually called the police. Uniformed officers responded and established a crime scene. They also had the victims taken to a hospital for examination.

This investigation was somewhat easy to solve, using phone records. We were able to identify the owner of the phone used to make the appointment and quickly identified a possible suspect. We also discovered that the victim's first call after the assault was not to 911, but rather to an individual who later turned out to be the "manager"/"pimp."

The real difficulty in this case came in gaining the trust and cooperation of both victims and their "manager"/"pimp." This is where the sex crime investigator needs to establish trust with all of those involved in making the complaint. Investigators need to make it clear, so everyone understands, that the investigation is about the sexual assault. The investigation is not about the illegal activity they were engaged in (e.g., prostitution, illegal drug use).

This situation becomes even more complicated when the "manager"/"pimp" is concerned primarily about protecting himself from any culpability. He might do everything in his power to keep the victims from cooperating, even moving them to another city. The "manager"/"pimp" may believe that he will become a target of the investigation. The investigator must

CASE EXAMPLE: *CONTINUED*

do his or her best to alleviate these concerns; at least until the sexual assault suspects are apprehended.

In this case, we were able to convince the "manager" to cooperate along with the victims. As a result, we were able to positively identify one of the suspects using photo identification. In the meantime, searches were conducted using various databases, and we were able to locate several similar cases involving robberies of "Asian escorts" who had advertised in the *Village Voice*. Those instances were in other areas of New York City and had not involved sexual assaults.

Using the suspect's phone records, we were also able to identify his associates. We quickly obtained a positive identification of the two other males involved in the sexual assaults. Because of the relationship we established originally with the victims and their "manager"/"pimp," they were extremely cooperative. They viewed photos when we needed them, they met with the prosecutor when they had to, and they viewed line-ups when they were arranged. They all understood that we were not investigating them. We did not make an issue of their illegal status in the country, and we did not make an issue of the illegal activity that they were engaged in.

Our focus was on the three individuals who sexually assaulted and robbed them, and they knew that.

When the first suspect was arrested, he confessed quickly and provided additional information on the other suspects involved, as well as information regarding several other crimes they had committed. Using the call detail information from the suspects' phones, we were further able to identify several phone numbers from advertisements for escort services in the *Village Voice*, as well as similar ads in several "sex trade" papers in the NYC area. This allowed us to identify other crimes and to receive the cooperation of other victims. In the end, the apprehension and arrest of these three suspects helped us close out numerous other unsolved cases, identifying a sexual assault pattern that had been completely hidden inside the criminal world.

In this case we were able to avoid a common problem that arises when investigating women involved in organized prostitution—they are frequently moved to different cities and across the country. The sex crime investigator must anticipate this reality and be willing to provide both transportation and lodging for the victims should they be needed at trial. In this case, both victims testified at the trial, and all three individuals received a lengthy jail sentence.

John O. Savino

CASE EXAMPLE:

Harold Nelson

In September 1992, a 20-year-old female reported she had been at a New York City nightclub and met an individual who offered her drugs. He lured the victim to an apartment on the East Side of Manhattan, where the drugs were said to be located. Once at the apartment, the man beat and raped her. The victim was held against her will for 18 days. During her captivity, the man forced her to ingest large quantities of narcotics and alcohol. He beat and raped her at least twice a day, every day.

While the victim was in captivity, the rapist introduced her to six other females. These women also beat her and forced her to engage in several acts of prostitution inside the apartment. Their goal was to get her to "willingly" join the suspect's "stable" of girls. Although beaten and brutalized every day, she resisted and would not give in.

After 18 days of repeated sexual assaults, the rapist had grown tired of trying to break her down. He forced her into a drug-induced stupor and told her that she was being sent to California. He warned that she better not say anything to anyone or ever return to New York City. The victim was placed on a Greyhound bus bound for California.

When the bus made its first stop in Philadelphia, the victim became somewhat lucid and told the bus driver what had happened. The local police became involved, along with the FBI. They relayed the information to the New York City Police Department. It was discovered that this victim had been reported missing by her parents to the local police in Connecticut. She lived with them there, and they made the report when she failed to return home from NYC one evening.

Continued

CASE EXAMPLE: *CONTINUED*

The victim was willing to meet with me. However, when I interviewed her, she did not provide enough information to identify a suspect. At the time, she felt that she was not physically or emotionally capable of returning to NYC to cooperate with any further investigation.

In October 1992, a second female was lured to an apartment on East 24th Street. Again, the attacker was a man who met the victim in a Manhattan nightclub and lured her away with the promise of drugs. Once at the apartment, the victim was beaten and raped. During her captivity, she was also forced into several acts of prostitution. This victim eventually decided that the only way she was going to get out of the apartment was to act as if she were cooperating with the rapist. She eventually convinced him that she had to return to her own apartment in order to feed her cat, who must have gone hungry in her absence.

On her fifth day of captivity, the rapist agreed to bring her home in order to feed the cat. While at the victim's apartment, and after feeding the cat, he felt comfortable enough to leave her alone. He walked to a nearby store. While he was out of the apartment, she was able to call 911. When the rapist returned, she stalled their departure until the police arrived. Uniformed officers took the man into custody.

I conducted the preliminary interview with this victim. Within a few minutes of questioning, it became clear that this case more than likely involved the same man who had lured and attacked the victim from Connecticut in the month prior. I arrested the man with her at the time, Harold Nelson, and charged him with rape, sodomy, and kidnapping (Figure 16-6).

After interviewing the victim, we obtained search warrants for the four different apartments that Nelson operated inside the same building on East 24th Street. By the time we got there, the other women had fled.

I also went back to speak with the first victim. This time I was able to get her cooperation. I was then able to return and arrest Nelson a second time for kidnapping and sexual assault.

Harold Nelson had previously been arrested and convicted in 1984 for running a sex-slavery ring. In that case, he had abducted young women and forced them to engage in prostitution. Nelson pled guilty in 1993 to kidnapping, rape, and sodomy. He was sentenced to 25 years to life in prison.

John O. Savino

Harold Nelson

FIGURE 16-6

Harold Nelson had previous convictions for running a sex-slavery ring when he was arrested by one of the authors (Savino) for kidnapping young girls, and doing essentially the same thing, 10 years later.

THE LAW ENFORCEMENT RESPONSE

The law enforcement response to sex trafficking has been, generally, to focus on efforts to arrest the trafficked victims. As explained in Radio (2010b), the reason is that it's easier than arresting customers or traffickers:

Though they arrest few pimps and prosecute even fewer, Oakland police say that arresting the girls is a necessary first step toward shutting down sex trafficking. But many children's advocates disagree.

Nola Brantley, who was trafficked as a teenager, now runs MISSSEY, a program that helps girls get out of the sex trade.

"The reason why we arrest them is because they are the easiest person to arrest," Brantley says. "It's hard to arrest the johns, and they represent many different facets of society and life. It's hard to arrest the exploiters because of the amount of evidence necessary. So, the easiest person to arrest is the child."

Brantley says these children are not really prostitutes. "Every act of what's called… 'prostitution' with these children is actually a form of child sexual abuse—and to take it further, child rape," she says. "So I don't think children who are raped should be criminalized, no I don't."

Alameda County Assistant District Attorney Sharmin Bock counters that arresting the girls is actually a way to save them—it gives the county a way to introduce victimized girls to social services. "Having a court involved with a case hanging over your head provides that added incentive to stay in a program, at the end of which a great likelihood exists that you will in fact recognize that you were in fact exploited," she says.

And, Bock says, the logistics of going after the men are daunting. "It's very hard to get a hold of those johns. Because by the time you hear about it, they're just a number. It's the child telling you, 'I had sex with 15 different men yesterday.' They're long gone."

As explained in Lodge (2011), when law enforcement arrests the prostitute and does not investigate the flow of money up to the top, the conditions that create organized trafficking are essentially ignored (p. 1B):

Theresa Flores, who helps exploited teens at a safe house in Dublin, Ohio, also told members of the Human Trafficking Task Force for the Middle District of Louisiana that children increasingly are victims of the monstrous business.

Worldwide, Flores said, sex slavery pours $32 billion into the pockets of criminals each year.…

She said children forced into prostitution sometimes are branded as criminals for their inability to escape the adults who are torturing them. "We're arresting teenagers for this," Flores said. "We're arresting the wrong people."…

Today, approximately 20,000 sex slaves are brought into the U.S. annually, Flores noted. But more than 3,500 children born in this country go missing or become runaways each day. She said many of those children become sex slaves. Flores said 77 percent of adult prostitutes in this country were trafficked as children.

The result of arresting trafficked sex workers can be secondary victimization; they may learn that the system does not recognize them as a victim and that their trafficker has both power and immunity. This is especially true when arrests are not part of an overall effort to intervene and provide mental health and social services they may need to escape the cycle that they are in.

Even worse are some of the attorneys who are meant to represent victims of sex trafficking. If you ask prostitutes, many will tell you that some defense attorneys are just as bad as the "police officer pimps" they learn to endure on the streets. Quality legal services are provided, in some cases, only on the condition that the victim repay the counselor in trade.

The lesson for readers is, again: the culture of sex trafficking is born out of sexual assault, thrives on sexual assault, and ensures the continued sexual assault of those coerced into servitude. When, in the course of an investigation, a sex worker is encountered, consider that you are very likely dealing with someone whose life is caught up in this cycle. Consider that for her or him the trauma of a past sexual assault, and the fear of sexual assault in the future, is likely a constant. Consider also that the sex worker may be a willing participant in the sex trade and may therefore be an invaluable source of investigative information. In either case, treating this person with some respect is the first and only place to start. From there, an investigation of the facts can begin and the truth of the circumstances learned. Regardless, nobody deserves to be sexually assaulted, no matter who she or he is or what she or he does.

SUMMARY

Sex trafficking involves a sex act for profit induced by force, fraud, or coercion or in which the person induced to perform the act is under 18 years of age. This definition applies to most *sex workers*—anyone who works in the sex industry, performing sexual acts for money. It is important to understand that there are many different kinds of sex workers. Not all sex workers are necessarily being trafficked, although many are. This chapter discussed brothels, escorts/call girls, strollers, and strip clubs.

Recruitment refers to the means by which sex traffickers acquire sex workers. This is not something that happens by accident. It is generally the result of a planned con, fraud, or even kidnapping. The cycle of dependence retains victims, even when they have the opportunity to leave. The primary element in this cycle is fear and, once initiated, it is hard to break free. Other tools of sex traffickers, with respect to controlling their victims, include extortion, threats of violence, physical abuse, and drugs.

This chapter clarified the relationship between trafficked sex workers and sexual assault. They are victims of rape. And their victimization is essentially unending, as long as they are unable to escape their situation. The law enforcement response to sex trafficking has been, generally, to focus on efforts to arrest the trafficked victims. The result of arresting trafficked sex workers can be secondary victimization; they may learn that the system does not recognize them as a victim and that their trafficker has both power and immunity. When, in the course of an investigation, a sex worker is encountered, the reader should consider that he or she is very likely dealing with someone whose life is caught up in this cycle. Treating sex workers with respect is the first and only place to start. From there, an investigation of the facts can begin and the truth of their circumstances learned. Regardless, nobody deserves to be sexually assaulted, no matter who she or he is or what she or he does.

QUESTIONS

1. True or False: All sex workers are "trafficked."
2. Explain one recruitment strategy for sex traffickers.
3. True or False: Suspects in confirmed human trafficking incidents are mostly white.
4. Explain the power of drug addiction in the cycle of dependence.
5. Explain the relationship between sex workers and sexual assault.

REFERENCES

Albanese, J., 2007. Commercial Sexual Exploitation of Children: What Do We Know and What Do We Do About It? NCJ 215733. U.S. Department of Justice, December, Washington, DC.

Bower, G., 2008. Press release. Ada County Prosecuting Attorney, July 22.

Hauser, C., 2007. Officer admits he helped thwart a brothel's rivals. New York Times, December 28; http://www.nytimes.com/2007/12/28/nyregion/28plea.html

Hopkins, K., 2010. I can't get my sister back: Investigators warn of sex traffickers targeting Natives. Anchorage Daily News, December 2; http://community.adn.com/adn/node/154636

Kim, K., 2011. The coercion of trafficked workers. Iowa Law Review 96, 409–474.

Kyckelhahn, T., Beck, A., Cohen, T., 2009. Characteristics of Suspected Human Trafficking Incidents, 2007–08. NCJ 224526. U.S. Department of Justice, Bureau of Justice Statistics, January, Washington, DC.

Lodge, B., 2011. Escaped victim, officials target sex slavery in state. The Baton Rouge Advocate, January 27; p. 1B.

McBride, R., 2011. Stones in the backpack: The burden of teen prostitution part 1. KTUU.com, February 28; http://www.ktuu.com/news/ktuu-prostitution-in-alaska-how-it-happens-20110228, 0, 7992068.story

Pavuk, A., 2011. Sex-trafficking victim: I was burned, beaten after trying to flee. Orlando Sentinel, March 1; http://articles.orlandosentinel.com/2011-03-01/news/os-sex-trafficking-beating-20110301_1_prostituting-orange-county-deputies-orlando-police

Reid, J., 2010. Doors wide shut: Barriers to the successful delivery of victim services for domestically trafficked minors in a southern U.S. metropolitan area. Women & Criminal Justice 20, 147–166.

Radio, Y., 2010a. Trafficked teen girls describe life in "the game." NPR.org, December 6; http://www.npr.org/2010/12/06/131757019/youth-radio-trafficked-teen-girls-describe-life-in-the-game

Radio, Y., 2010b. Arresting youth in sex trafficking raises debate. NPR.org, December 7; http://www.npr.org/2010/12/07/131757175/arresting-youth-in-sex-trafficking-raises-debate

Staff, 2006. Man accused of forcing kidnapped teen into prostitution. The Stockton Record, December 23; http://www.recordnet.com/apps/pbcs.dll/article?AID=/20061223/A_NEWS/612230319

Staff, 2009. Woman pleads guilty in Craigslist prostitution. KTVB.com, August 15; http://www.ktvb.com/news/local/64171552.html

Sullivan, R., 1999. Requiem for tomorrow. Rolling Stone (824), October 28; 76–89.

Torgoley, S., 2006. Trafficking and forced prostitution: A manifestation of modern slavery. Tulane Journal of International and Comparative Law 14, 553–578, Spring.

Wagner, J., 2010. Serving California's human trafficking victims and refugees. Policy & Practice, December; 14–17.

CHAPTER 17

Sexual Offenders and their Victims

Angela N. Torres and Angela van der Walt[1]

KEY TERMS

Child molestation Any sexual contact with a child or adolescent below the age of consent.

Child pornography Any picture or video depicting a child in a sexual manner.

Date rape Non-violent rape between acquaintances that is not accompanied by any assault or battery except for the unwanted sexual touching and overpowerment inherent in a non-consensual sexual act.

Exhibitionism In a criminal context, non-contact sexual assault in which offenders expose themselves to others.

Fetish When an individual becomes sexually aroused by an object.

Fixed victim profile selection A type of victim selection in which offenders have specific characteristics they are attracted to and wait to come across people who possess these qualities.

Gang rape Two or more males having sex with a non-consenting female or male.

Grooming/Victim set-up What a sex offender does in order to commit a sexual assault and to reduce the chance of being caught.

Hebephilia Recurrent, intense, sexual arousal and behaviors involving postpubescent adolescents.

Noncontact sexual assault Any sexual crime in which the perpetrator does not physically touch the victim.

Opportunistic victim selection A type of victim selection in which offenders choose victims based on their access and availability.

Partner rape Forcing of sex on another person with whom someone is in a significant relationship, such as a wife, girlfriend, boyfriend, or fiancée.

Pedophilia A recurrent, intense, sexually arousing fantasy, sexual urge, or behavior involving prepubescent children.

Planful victim selection A type of victim selection in which time is taken to select victims and plan how the sexual assault will be accomplished.

Rapist Anyone who has physical sexual contact with a non-consenting individual.

Sexual offender A heterogeneous term to describe anyone who has been convicted of a sex crime of any type.

Sexual offense Any time a person forces a sexual act upon another without his or her consent.

Sodomy Any sexual act that does not involve a penis penetrating a vagina. It can include behaviors such as manual stimulation of a partner, oral sex, anal sex, and the use of sexual toys.

---

[1] Angela van der Walt, PsyD, has worked in sex-offender therapy for several years, in both group and individual contexts. Angela Torres, PhD, has interviewed many sexual offenders in the context of a lengthy sex-offender–risk research study. Both authors have conducted sexual-offender risk assessment evaluations. This chapter is subsequently a blend of the authors' scholarly research and direct experience working with sex offenders.

489

Forensic Victimology. http://dx.doi.org/10.1016/B978-0-12-408084-3.00017-X

Statutory rape Crime of sex between a person who is below the legal age of consent with someone who is above the legal age to consent. Legally, the term refers to acts that are both consensual and non-consensual. The age of consent differs depending on jurisdiction.

Voyeurism Act in which a person becomes sexually aroused by watching the private activity of others, especially when it involves nudity or sexual behavior. Perpetrators are commonly referred to as "peeping Toms."

Sexual offenses are considered among the most heinous crimes that can be committed by one person against another. Frequently conjured images of the sexual offender include the stranger rapist who lies in wait, ready to spring out and abduct the weak, the young, or the innocent.[2] They also include the trolling child molester who kidnaps victims from public parks or as they walk home alone from school—perhaps with the aid of candy or tales of a lost puppy. These and other traditional images of sexual offenders, regularly depicted in books, films, and television, are as frightening as they are lasting. They color how people feel about and react to sex offenders in general, and how professionals treat them in specific.[3]

However, it is often the case that these stereotypes are the exception instead of the rule. As explained in Peters-Baker (1998, p. 629), there is no one definitive profile:

> What is your image of a sex offender? Is he the dirty old man reading erotica material in the back of the bookstore, a stranger in dark clothing lurking behind the bushes, a respected priest, a decorated scout leader? The truth about sex offenders is that each of these individuals fits the profile of a sex offender.

Whatever we believe, the reality is that sexual offenders are not just socially displaced strangers; they are more commonly our teachers, our bankers, our fathers, our sisters, our children, and our friends.[4]

The purpose of this chapter is to move readers toward a deeper understanding of sexual offenders and their victims—beyond the stereotypical and purely theoretical. First, we outline what sexual offending is, and the legal history of managing, containing, and punishing sexual offenders. Then, we describe

---

[2]It is understood that sexual offenders can be male or female, and victims can be of either sex; however, throughout this chapter, offenders will be referred to as male, while victims will be referred to as female, unless otherwise noted.

[3]See Griffin and West (2006, p. 143): "Sex offenders are treated as the outcasts of our communities. They are stigmatized and exiled by the community, law enforcement, media, other offenders, and professionals in the field of sex research, psychology, and criminology. They are demonized through general discussion, crime reports, research focus, and paper titles."

[4]See Fenton (2001, p. 45): "These predators can operate in any social classification or situation." See also Nagayama-Hall (1996, p. 3): "Often the perpetrators are pillars of society, including clergy, police, teachers, and physicians."

typologies of sexual offenders. Typologies are useful because different types of sexual offenders have different victim populations, with different levels of risk for sexual offending in the future. Next, we share some of the justifications sexual offenders commonly use to explain their behavior. Rationales for sexually offending are often a blend of denial, manipulation, and bizarre cognitive distortions. Finally, we review different victim types and what sexual offenders seek in victims of sexual assault.

A BRIEF LEGAL AND CULTURAL HISTORY OF SEXUAL OFFENDING

The contemporary view is that whenever someone forces a sexual act upon another without his or her consent, such an act is a *sexual offense*. The person who forced the act is a *sexual offender*, and the person forced into the act is a victim of a sexual assault. However, this has not always been the case.

Sex Crimes as Property Crimes

Interestingly, it is property law that has shaped and defined who can be a victim of a criminal sexual act. Historically, children, slaves, animals, and other similarly classed groups have been considered the property of white, land-owning men.[5]

Until fairly recently, women in particular were viewed as the property of their fathers and subsequently of their husbands after marriage. Such beliefs are the basis for modern marriage traditions, such as the father "giving away the bride" at her wedding. In a legal sense, this often exempted husbands from being charged with rape related to any sexual acts they committed with their wives, whether she agreed to them or not. As provided in Woolley (2007, pp. 275–277):

> Under traditional property theories, women were considered the property of their husbands, or fathers if unmarried. First, the concept of marital rape was a legal nullity analogous to the inability to steal what one already owns. "The rape of a married woman by her husband himself was not a transgression at all because a man was allowed to treat his chattel as he deemed appropriate." Thus women who were

---

[5]As one example, consider Pokorak (2006, p. 1): "For most of this nation's history, raping a Black woman was simply not a crime. First, laws prevented the prosecution of any offender for the rape of a slave woman. At the same time, the rape of a White woman by a Black man was treated with especial violence. The Thirteenth and Fourteenth Amendments were proposed and ratified as vehicles to ensure the equal protection of the laws. After their enactment, although the de jure prohibition on prosecuting the rape of Black women ended, de facto barriers to prosecution remained."

forced to have sex in their marriage did not even have the option of seeking criminal prosecution.

Second, the marital rape exemption was defended under the assertion that a husband and wife acted in concert and the wife had no separate rights apart from her husband. The husband was legally responsible for his wife's conduct…. This doctrine of coverture gave husbands physical and legal control over their wives. Once married, women lacked legal standing apart from their husbands to enter into contracts, own their own property, or defend themselves in court. Consequently, a husband would be unlikely to go to court on behalf of his wife to allege he had raped her.

The third justification for the marital rape exemption is that the courts and police are often reluctant to pierce the veil of privacy regarding sexual matters as they are seen as at the heart of marital and familial relations. Kapila Juthani, a scholar and researcher on police treatment of domestic violence, argued that domestic violence is "largely unacknowledged by the public or legal system due in part to the lingering beliefs that the husband and wife become legally one upon marriage…the law did not reach domestic violence largely because it occurred in the private sphere."

…

The fourth (and perhaps most popular) justification for the marital rape exemption was the notion that a woman's marriage vows provided ongoing consent to her husband's sexual demands.

Even though major legal progress had already been achieved with fashioning rights for children, slaves, and animals, it was not until 1993 that marital rape became illegal in all 50 of the United States (Woolley, 2007).[6]

Marriage and Sexual Control

Despite a long history of arranged marriages and marriages of convenience,[7] modern Western law and culture tend toward the belief that people may choose their sexual and marriage partners freely. However, in Western and non-Western cultures alike, there are those who seek to maintain control over the sexuality of women.[8]

---

[6]According to Woolley (2007, p. 269): "Although marital rape has been a pervasive socio-cultural problem for centuries, most activity involving the recognition, criminalization, and reform of marital rape laws has occurred in the past few decades."

[7]See generally Adams (2007), Jackson (2007), and Torgoley (2006).

[8]Adams (2007) provides an international (non-U.S.) overview of historical and contemporary intimate violence against women to include sexual assault. It describes how men control women, physically, sexually, and financially—with the legal protection of male-dominated courts that often purport to know better on paper.

In such cases, the institution of marriage is or provides a mechanism for sexual control. It can be seen in the tradition of fathers arranging marriages between their daughters and sons in order to capitalize political power, for financial well-being, to formulate alliances, and to move up the social hierarchy.[9] Or it can be more violent, involving control over female sexuality with long-standing traditions such as "honor killings,"[10] female circumcision,[11] and forced prostitution. As explained in Jackson (2007, p. 897), this last form of

---

[9]In many cultures, contemporary attitudes regarding arranged marriages still reflect the historical tradition of sexual control and ownership rather than the letter of any written law. Recently this has proven to be true in the United States with the case of polygamist Warren S. Jeffs, the president of the Fundamentalist Church of Jesus Christ of Latter Day Saints. In 2007, he was tried and convicted for sex crimes related to his performance of forced child bride marriages in Utah—originally evading arrest with the assistance of local law enforcement (Turvey, 2008; p. xxxi). While a rarity in the United States, arranged marriages are still common in other cultures. For example, consider the issue of dowry deaths—a major social problem in the Indian subcontinent. A dowry is money or property brought by a bride (or her family) to pay the bride's future husband to marry her. Dowry deaths involve the killing of a bride by her husband or his family for failure to provide sufficient dowry—reflecting the view of marriage as a property-oriented or financial transaction. With a long history, the dowry institution and related violence persist, as explained in Bhave (2007, pp. 292–293): In 1961, India enacted the Dowry Prohibition Act, its most important legislation aimed at curbing the problems dowry provokes. The Indian Parliament later amended its national penal code in 1983, and again in 1986, to proscribe the offense of dowry death. The government's attempt to cure the problem through criminal legislation, however, has been futile. While some courts have upheld dowry death convictions, the government generally has not enforced the criminal laws and has failed to investigate potential dowry deaths properly. Further, the Indian Supreme Court ruled recently that India's penal code does not permit courts to compel dowry death perpetrators to pay compensation as a form of criminal punishment to their victims.

[10]So-called "honor killings" often take place in Muslim cultures. A common scenario involves a family that perceives a loss of honor due to some type of "sexual immodesty" by a female family member. She is then killed by a family member as a way of reinstating honor in the eyes of the community. In some instances, a woman who has been raped is then murdered by her family for bringing shame upon them as a victim of rape. As explained in Asamoah-Wade (2000, p. 21): "Hundreds of women are killed around the world every year on the basis of accusations of infidelity. These murders can occur as a result of mere suspicions of infidelity, a woman's attempt to marry a man of her choice, or as a result of promiscuous behavior."

[11]Female circumcision, also known as female genital mutilation (FGM), is the practice, mostly occurring in Africa, of removing the clitoris and/or outer genitalia of a young girl. This is often done without anesthesia by family members or community leaders with crude materials and no medical training. It is done out of religious practice and as a cultural milestone in a young woman's life. As described in Collopy (2007, pp. 470–471): FGM is a series of procedures involving the removal of all or part of the external genitalia. The procedure is performed on approximately two million females each year in Africa, Asia, and the Middle East. An estimated total of 80 to 110 million women and girls already have undergone FGM. The procedure is "extremely painful.… It permanently disfigures the female genitalia [and] exposes the girl or woman to the risk of serious, potentially life-threatening complications… [including,] among others, bleeding, infection, urine retention, stress, shock, psychological trauma, and damage to the urethra and anus." It is "a form of 'sexual oppression' that is 'based on the manipulation of women's sexuality in order to assure male dominance and exploitation.'" For these reasons, the United Nations, Amnesty International, and other international human rights organizations condemn FGM as a human rights violation. Many countries, including the United States, have criminalized FGM.

sexual control is still suffered by women all over the world, irrespective of culture or religion:

> In China, decades of abortion and infanticide favoring male children has left fewer women available for marriage, impelling "bride trafficking" where men purchase women and girls outright for purposes of forced marriage. In the United States, one small study of forty women in prostitution found that almost 30 percent of the U.S.-born women were prostituted by husbands or boyfriends. Across the world, husbands use physical abuse to extract sexual and domestic services from their wives, even prostituting them for profit or selling them outright to brothels or agents.
>
>   Brokers conduct some of this marriage-based slave trade in public; for example, one Taiwanese publication recently advertised nearly thirty Vietnamese women for sale as brides at a price of about $6,000 apiece.

Thus, even where there are now laws on the books to prevent the sexual control of wives and daughters, overt cultural attitudes and practices that maintain women as a sexual commodity or property can still be found.

Sex Crimes and the Age of Consent

In contrast to those who seek to achieve or maintain sexual control over women, we have found that many men became entangled in *statutory rape* charges. These are crimes of "consensual" sex between a person (most often the female) who is below the legal age of consent with someone (most often the male) who is of legal age of consent to sex. As explained in Oglebsy (2007, pp. 1069–1071):

> The crime of statutory rape appears in substance as far back in time as the 4,000-year-old Code of Hammurabi, which provided that a man be seized and slain if he raped a betrothed virgin, whom the law considered to be an innocent victim. It was not until 1275 A.D. that the Statutes of Westminster established the first known English definition of the offense of statutory rape, making it illegal to "ravish" a female under the age of twelve years; English law lowered the age at which a female could legally consent to sexual relations to ten years old in 1576 A.D.
>
>   In the early years of the development of the American system, statutory rape laws were absorbed into the legal landscape via the English common law. American case law has even specifically held that the definitive English statute from 1576 was part of the common law originally imported into the United States. This trend in American case law signifies basic agreement with the legislative

purpose and intent behind the original English statutes. Such agreement has allowed the courts to interpret American statutory rape laws by relying upon long-standing historical reasoning to bolster the majority trend of classifying statutory rape as a strict liability crime with no availability of affirmative defenses, such as mistake of age of one's sexual partner. Because of this method of judicial interpretation, such strict liability criminal statutes continue to thrive in the modern era, causing unfair, unjust, and possibly even unconstitutional outcomes in statutory rape prosecutions around the country today.

English and Teare (2001, pp. 830–831) go further, explaining:

> "Statutory rape" itself is a somewhat imprecise term, and not one that usually appears in state criminal codes. It is often loosely used to describe sex between adults and minors, even in circumstances when that description does not correspond to any specific legal crime or classification.... From a legal perspective, the concept of statutory rape (rather than the term itself) usually refers to sexual intercourse that involves at least one minor and is prohibited in a state's criminal code because the minor is below what is commonly referred to as the "age of consent." Thus, legally the term may be used to cover both consensual and non-consensual acts.

Consider, for example, that the age of consent for sexual behaviors in the state of California is 18 years old (California Penal Code, Section 261-269). As a strict matter of law, a 16-year-old female who is dating her 19-year-old boyfriend and then has sex with him is the victim of sexual assault—no matter what the circumstances. Many citizens of California would not consider her a victim, or the young man a sexual offender. However, it is the law that defines who is and is not the victim of sexual assault, and the law varies widely from state to state.

Additionally, each state defines what is appropriate for the prosecution in such cases. As a practical matter, many district attorneys choose not to prosecute some statutory rape cases based on a variety of factors, including age difference. For example, some states will not prosecute if the "victim" is 15 or older (even though the law states consent is an older age), or unless the "perpetrator" is in a position of trust such as a teacher or coach.[12]

---

[12]In Minnesota, sexual acts with someone under 16 years of age can be illegal if the victim is 13 years of age or less. However, sexual abuse is defined in the statute "to only include those acts perpetrated by a person responsible for the child's care, someone living in the same house as the child or related to the child, or someone in a position of authority" (Gardiner, Glosser, and Fishman, 2004; pp. 67–68).

In Texas, for example, the act is not prosecuted unless there is a significant age difference, as explained in Gardiner, Glosser, and Fishman (2004, p. 110).

> Children less than 14 years of age are unable to consent to sexual acts regardless of the age of the defendant. Sexual acts with children less than 17 years of age and at least 14 years of age are illegal if the defendant is more than 3 years older than the victim.

So the issue of whether or not someone is a sexual offender may not only be a function of the age of the victim, but the laws of state where the victim lives and the attitudes of the local prosecutor.

Sodomy Decriminalized

The law not only defines who can be a "victim" of sexual assault, but also which specific sexual behaviors can be criminalized, even between consenting adults. The clearest examples of this are so-called anti-sodomy laws. *Sodomy* may be defined as any sexual act that does not involve a penis penetrating a vagina. It can include behaviors such as manual stimulation of a partner (e.g., mutual masturbation), oral sex, anal sex, and the use of sexual toys (e.g., vibrators, dildos). Anti-sodomy laws originally served to punish people for engaging in sexual behavior for the sake of pleasure only, that is, sexual behavior that does not lead to the potential conception of a child. More recently, sodomy laws were used to criminalize acts between consenting gay and lesbian people. As explained in Hough (2004, pp. 105–106):

> References to sodomy can be traced back to biblical times. Historically, the definition of sodomy has often been confusing, but the courts have almost always defined sodomy as an act done by men. In fact, in the late twentieth century, courts and theorists found sodomy between women to be a legal impossibility. Today sodomy is defined as "oral or anal copulation between humans, especially those of the same sex."
>
> Sodomy is an example of a private act that does not harm the actors or others, but has been prohibited on the basis of moral arguments. Sodomy laws were not originally created to regulate homosexual sex; in fact, they were originally applied to almost all sexual activity outside of marital procreative sex. These laws did not classify people as homosexual and were not applied to gay and lesbian people as a class. It was only when society began to recognize homosexuals as an identifiable group of people and began to identify homosexual people with sodomitical acts that sodomy laws were targeted toward a specific group in society.

In colonial times, laws against sodomy were often not directed at homosexual conduct, but were focused on sexual acts between men and children, men raping women, or men engaging in bestiality. These laws were created on the grounds that sodomy was immoral and unchristian.

It has only been in recent history that sodomy has been attached to a certain type of person, rather than just to a particular sexual activity. In today's society, sodomy laws have defined the place of gay people in American society. Even in cases where sodomy is referred to in a gender-neutral way, the assumption is that it refers to homosexual acts only, not to sodomy in other contexts. The existence of sodomy laws has limited homosexuals to a second-class position in society, whether or not the laws have actually been enforced. This second-class status is reflected in derogatory synonyms for sodomy such as: unnatural offense, abominable and detestable crime against nature, and buggery. Until the Supreme Court's landmark decision in *Lawrence v. Texas*, states were allowed to prohibit sodomy and prosecute homosexual couples who engaged in consensual sexual acts.

Sodomy was essentially decriminalized by the U.S. Supreme Court in *Lawrence v. Texas*, 539 U.S. 558 (2003).[13]

Like some statutory rape cases, the impetus for prosecuting sodomy as a crime was related to a moral imperative rather than actual harm suffered by a coerced victim. These and related issues become important when considering the different types of sex offenders that inhabit the penal system.

SEX OFFENDER TYPES

The term *sex offender* refers generally to anyone who has been convicted of a sex crime. The heterogeneity of what we call sexual offending makes the term almost meaningless and even misleading. Consider, for example, that both the man convicted for indecent exposure while peeing on the side of the road and the sadistic rapist may be categorized as sex offenders. We need to be careful when we use this term and when we are interpreting its use by others.

---

[13]Even though Justice Clarence Thomas (*Lawrence v. Texas*, 2003) dissented with the majority decision in Lawrence on the strict face of the law, he wrote that the anti-sodomy laws in Texas were "uncommonly silly," and "[p]unishing someone for expressing his sexual preference through noncommercial consensual conduct with another adult does not appear to be a worthy way to expend valuable law enforcement resources."

As already mentioned, sexual offending crosses the barriers of gender, race, socioeconomic status, age, religion, and sexual orientation.[14] There is no typical offender and no typical victim. Subsequently, no one is immune to the devastating impact that sex crimes can inflict, and most of us know someone who is a victim of sexual assault.

Again, for the purposes of this chapter, we are going to focus the majority of our attention on adult male sex offenders. This subset contains the highest number of perpetrators and is the most routinely researched group of sex offenders. It also makes up the majority of our research.

Sexual offenders often commit multiple assaults ranging across a variety of sexually deviant behavior before they are identified in the criminal justice system (English, 1998). Abel and Rouleau (1990) collected self-reports from convicted sex offenders and found that 51% had sexually abused victims from multiple age groups, 20% had abused both male and female victims, and 23% of offenders convicted of abusing family members had also molested children outside the family. Additionally, they found that sexually deviant behavior often begins early in life, for some as early as ten years of age (Abel and Rouleau, 1990). This suggests that the sexually deviant behavior of these offenders is likely integrated and ingrained into their lifestyle (English, 1998).

As a whole, male sex offenders are more dissimilar than similar.[15] However, some similarities appear to exist. Based on our collective experiences, male sex offenders commonly have inappropriate anger management skills, increased levels of anxiety, and a higher prevalence of mood dysregulation. They are also likely to display antisocial behavior, such as making verbal and physical threats; perpetrating violence toward self, others, and property; engaging in inappropriate behavior; having a lack of consideration for others; and instigating confrontation with others. Their cognitions (mental

---

[14]As explained in Baerga-Buffler and Johnson (2006, p. 14): Pedophiles, rapists, child molesters, child traffickers, and Internet child pornographers are all classified as sex offenders. The reality is that sex offenders are not a homogeneous group. On the contrary, they are a very heterogeneous group who come from all walks of life, professions, and lifestyles. They range from the "dirty old man hiding in alley ways," to the highly educated professor, law enforcement officer, and teacher. Physically, sex offenders are indistinguishable from you or me—which is essentially why it is critical for probation and pre-trial services officers to be aware of who these sex offenders are and, just as important, the potential risk they pose to the community.

[15]Interestingly, according to Baker (1997, p. 577): Numerous studies have also found that men who rape are "normal" to the extent that psychologists fail to find evidence of abnormality. Male levels of sexual aggression do not correlate with elevated scores on the Psychopathic Deviate scale. One well-cited study found that 35 percent of college men indicated a likelihood to rape if they were sure that they could get away with it. Psychologists working with rapists in prison report that the incident of mental illness among rapists varies from only 2 to 20 percent. Researchers have consistently failed to find significant psychological differences between the rapist and nonrapist populations. There is simply no evidence, save the rape itself, suggesting that all or even most rapists are objectively depraved.

processes and understandings) often follow themes of criminal and sexual deviance as well as paranoia toward others. Adult male sex offenders tend to have difficulty regulating impulses, most apparently their sexual impulses. They have a propensity to complain about others, blame others, refuse to engage in therapeutic services, and often refuse medications. Sexual offenders also often have histories of substance abuse or dependence. In addition, they tend to have difficulty establishing and sustaining relationships. Our experience as therapists is consistent with research cited in Fabian (2005, pp. 130–131):

> [R]esearchers found that sexual recidivists were likely to have poor social supports, attitudes tolerant of sexual assault, antisocial lifestyles, poor self-management strategies, and difficulties cooperating with supervision. The recidivists showed increased anger and subjective distress just before reoffending. Sex offenders are more likely to sexually reoffend if they experience sexual energy aroused by many circumstances, including negative affect, and if they feel deprived or frustrated when they are unable to pacify their sexual urges. They often experience stress, depression, loneliness, fear of intimacy and rejection, often leading to feelings of hostility and anger. Sex offenders may deal with these affective states through deviant sexual fantasy and masturbatory practices. Ultimately, these factors may impede their ability to control their urge to engage in offending behaviors.

Hanson and Harris developed the Sex Offender Need Assessment Rating (SONAR), a method for measuring change in risk levels. The authors note that sex offenders may have problems with emotional or sexual regulation, general self-regulation, and impulse control problems, such as using drugs, quitting jobs or school, and having multiple short-term sexual relationships.

As previously discussed, criminal sexual acts are defined by a conviction in a court of law as opposed to the persistence of some discernible mental illness.[16] Criminal sexual acts are consequently many and varied across each jurisdiction—to include anything from prostitution to pedophilia to voyeurism. Individual sex crimes can involve varying levels of violence, manipulation, and/or seduction. For the purposes of this shorter treatment, we have chosen to focus our discussion on the more common forms of sex crimes that

---

[16]This remains true unless there is some underlying psychopathology, such as pedophilia or sadism, which is uncommon. However, as explained in Prentky et al. (2006, p. 366): "Although pedophilia, unquestionably, is a diagnosis that, in appropriate cases, can satisfy the required elements for a mental disorder, the universal application of the diagnosis of pedophilia for all child molesters fails to differentiate among them, producing one highly heterogeneous group, all classified as pedophiles."

we encounter in our forensic assessments: child molestation, rape, and non-contact sexual assault.

Child Molestation

Child molestation, as a category, covers a wide range of criminal acts from incest to pedophilia. These sex offenders are those who have sexual contact with any child or adolescent below the age of consent. Offenders may be strangers, acquaintances, or family members. Child molesters make up the largest portion of convicted sex offenders (Lindsay et al., 2004).

More often than not, the sexual abuse of children occurs in their own homes (Marshall, Serran, and Cortoni, 2000). These children are often abused by someone within their immediate or extended family. This can take the form of incest, a biological relative having sexual contact with a child, or a step-parent, step-sibling, or pseudo-parent.[17]

These children are often chosen because of the perpetrators' access and opportunity to be alone with them. They are extremely vulnerable and have limited resources to report the abuse. Owing to the ease with which they are accessed by known offenders, child victims often suffer longstanding abuse that becomes increasingly intrusive. These types of offenses have an enormous impact on their victims, as the psychological damage and confusion caused by being harmed by a person who is supposed to care for you is difficult to comprehend and overcome.

According to the *Diagnostic and Statistical Manual of Mental Disorders,* 4th Edition, Text Revision (DSM-IV-TR 2000,), *pedophilia* is a recurrent, intense, sexually arousing fantasy, sexual urge, or behavior involving prepubescent children. Pedophiles can be either of the exclusive type, only sexually aroused by prepubescent children, or non-exclusive type, aroused by both adults and prepubescent children. Their sexual arousal can be toward girls, boys, or both. Pedophilia becomes a criminal act when the arousal is acted upon. For example, one pedophile was a missionary on the African continent, who sexually abused hundreds of African boys during his 40-plus years of missionary service. His sexual abuse never came to light until he returned to the United States and sexually abused his grandsons. It is likely that due to his high status within the community he worked in overseas, his sexual molestation was never reported.

Many pedophiles seek out positions of trust to get near children, such as working at a swimming pool or dating a woman with young children. A position of trust is one in which an adult is in a care-giving role with a child or adolescent. A case example illustrating this involved a teenage boy who started a

---

[17]A pseudo-parent is a non-biological, non-legal parental figure.

babysitting business. He promoted his babysitting services with the clear intention of seeking sexual contact with children. Once he gained access to these children, he began showing them pornography, touching them inappropriately, and becoming physically and emotionally abusive toward them. Due to the nature and severity of his offenses, he was tried and sentenced as an adult.

Hebephilia involves recurrent, intense, sexual arousal and behaviors involving postpubescent adolescents. Just like pedophiles, hebephiles can be of an exclusive or a non-exclusive type. These individuals seek out sexual relationships with postpubescent adolescent boys and/or girls who are still under the age of consent. A famous line from the movie *Dazed and Confused* perfectly depicts a hebephile: "I keep getting older, but they stay the same age" (referring to high school girls). These offenses can take the form of statutory rape (which will be discussed in further detail in the next section, on rape), position of trust hebephilia, or stranger hebephilia.

A position of trust would include a teacher, coach, step-parent, or religious leader who engages in sexual contact with an adolescent under the age of 18. Due to the nature of his role with the adolescent, such a caregiver can be prosecuted for sexual assault even if the adolescent is above the age of consent but under the age of 18. A stranger hebephile attempts to seduce adolescents below the age of consent. Since the introduction of the Internet, this has frequently occurred online. An adult will seek out minors in chat rooms or other Internet locations with the intention of soliciting sexual contact. Due to the frequency of this behavior, many law enforcement agencies have set up "sting" operations online using officers or volunteers of legal age posing as those beneath the age of consent. Although this is common knowledge, thanks to the popularity of shows such as NBC's *To Catch a Predator*, they continue to make arrests on a regular basis.

Rape

The second subgroup of our discussion are *rapists*—those who have physical sexual contact with a non-consenting individual. These offenders include stranger rapists, date rapists, gang rapists, statutory rapists, and partner rapists.

Stranger rapists are the least common yet the most feared sexual predators. These individuals are the stalkers, the guys in the bushes, the repairmen you let into the house, and the thieves who happen to find a woman home alone. These rapists can be planful, carefully selecting their victims, or they can be opportunistic, happening upon a vulnerable woman during the course of another crime. Some rapists will have a certain victim preference, such as women with straight blond hair of medium build, while more opportunistic rapists may only care that the victim is a woman. The commonality among these perpetrators is that they are unknown to the victim. In fact, they often thrive off the anonymity they have and the fear they instill in their victims. In this respect, rape is actually a form of terrorism.

Baker (2004, p. 179) defines *date rape* as "'nonviolent' rape between acquaintances...that is not accompanied by any assault or battery except the battery implicit in unwanted sexual touching and the assault implicit in the ability of someone bigger and stronger to overpower someone smaller and weaker." These rapists are often familiar with their victims. Their victims often consent to spending time with them and sometimes consent to some sexual contact. However, when the victim decides to stop the sexual contact or turns down a proposal for sexual contact and the offender continues to have sexual contact, it becomes rape.[18]

These rapists often deflect responsibility for the assault, claiming it was consensual or that they were unable to stop. Date rapists also tend to have multiple victims and are at times encouraged by their male peers. As explained in Baker (2004, p. 180):

> Date rape happens, in large part, because some men want or need sex so much that the question of consent becomes irrelevant. These men need sex so much because, for them, the greater the number of sexual encounters they have, the more they demonstrate their masculinity to other men. Their desire for sex exists completely apart from its consensual nature, and it is integrally linked to the cultural construct of masculinity.

A common example would be a 20-year-old female college student attending a fraternity party. The female becomes intoxicated and agrees to go to a bedroom with a frat boy. They begin having sexual contact, and then the female attempts to end the contact. She is met with pleading, coercion, force, or violence, as the perpetrator continues to have intercourse with her.

Gang rape, although infrequent, is on the rise (Ullman, 1999). This offense consists of two or more males having sex with a non-consenting female or male. These rapists often instigate additional men to participate in the act and cheer them on, as if it is a game. This was accurately depicted in the movie *The Accused*, starring Jodie Foster. Her character, Sarah Tobias, went out to a bar and became intoxicated. She was dancing and flirting with several men when two of them began to rape her. This occurred in the

---

[18]Date rape is often one of the most difficult types of sexual offenses to prosecute because it becomes a "he said, she said" type of scenario. Such cases are particularly difficult to prosecute when the victim initially consents to a sexual act or when the victim and/or perpetrator is intoxicated. Alcohol and drug use by the victim can make her question if a rape took place or fear that she will not be believed. This may also contribute to not reporting the rape.

presence of many other patrons who only hooted and hollered while she was assaulted.

Gang rape is also found in association with street gang activities (e.g., the Crips or Bloods). Many female gang members, for example, are initiated into the gang by having sex with multiple male gang members.[19] However, sex with multiple simultaneous partners can also be a rite of passage for some groups of males, whether organized as a gang or not. As described in Baker (2004, pp. 186–188):

> For these men, sex is often a means of gaining the esteem of their peers. 'Scoring' is seen as an individual accomplishment for which one earns prestige. Many young men are eager to have sex because they want to think of themselves and to have others think of them as men worthy of esteem.
>
> Sometimes these esteem systems are explicit. The infamous Spur Posse gang of adolescent boys in Southern California devised a game in which each boy got a point for every girl (most of them were between 13 and 16 years old) he had sex with. The winner was he who had the most points. Arguably, the Spur Posse story got so much attention in the press and in the rape literature not because it was so outrageous, but because the Posse point system made so perfectly explicit that which we know happens every day anyway. Anyone familiar with locker room or fraternity banter knows that an affirmative answer to the question 'did you score?' entitles one to the respect of one's peers....
>
> Peer support also explains numerous gang rape stories with which we are now, sadly, familiar. Consider the comments of Nathan McCall when he joined the 'train' his gang was running on a 13 year old girl: "All the fellas were there and everybody was anxious to show everybody else how cool and worldly he was." Or consider the behavior of the men who stood by and cheered as their friends raped a woman at a bar in New Bedford, Massachusetts, a scene depicted in the movie *The Accused*. The more they "performed," the more praise they received from their peers.

A horrific gang rape offense that has remained vivid to the authors involved a 13-year-old girl. She grew up in the inner city, and like many others, she was fascinated by the gang lifestyle. She decided to join a gang and was told she would have to pull a "train"[20] with seven gang members as her initiation into the gang.

---

[19]The process of being initiated into a gang through gang rape is called being "sexed in."
[20]A "train" is when a person, often a woman, has sex with several men, one right after the other without any rest or break between sexual acts.

She agreed and had sex with seven men in an abandoned house. One of the gang members found a metal pipe and convinced the girl to masturbate with it while the members watched. As she was masturbating with the pipe, another member kicked the pipe inside her. When she pulled it out, tissue from her body was stuck to the pipe. The gang members fled from the house, leaving her there alone. She was found later that night crawling out of the house. In order to save this young girl's life, doctors were forced to perform a hysterectomy on her.

As already discussed, statutory rapists are defined differently by each state. Each state has identified an age of consent: the age in which a teenager is legally allowed to give consent to sexual contact with an adult. If an adult has intercourse with a post-pubescent teenager below the legally defined age of consent, he (or she) can be criminally charged with a sex crime. Some states have set the age of consent at 15, while others hold it at 18. Some state laws maintain that in order for adults to be charged with rape, they must be 10 years older than the victim, while others identify anyone over the age of 18 as potential offenders. This grouping of rapists tends to be the most controversial, as societal opinions regarding statutory rape being a criminal act varies. It was not that long ago that men routinely married 12- or 13-year-old girls, and in some cultures around the world this continues to be an acceptable way of life. However, in the United States, our laws clearly state that teenagers are not able to give consent for sex until they reach a certain age.

Partner rape is the forcing of sex on another person with whom one is in a significant relationship, such as a wife, girlfriend, boyfriend, or fiancée. Partner rape often occurs within the context of other forms of domestic violence, such as physical or emotional abuse. This is one of the most difficult crimes to prosecute, as it is extremely difficult for a victim to report and prove the sex was not consenting beyond a reasonable doubt.

Included within the subcategory of rapists are the deviant sexual acts that most communities condemn. Some of these acts include fetishes, whereas others are identified as unacceptable sexual behaviors in society. A *fetish* is when an individual becomes sexually aroused by an object (DSM-IV-TR, 2000). For example, necrophilia is having sexual contact with dead people. Another fetish is zoophilia, having sexual contact with animals, which is sometimes referred to as bestiality. Other more common fetishes include arousal by a specific part of a body or clothing typically worn by someone, such as feet or underwear.

Unacceptable sexual behavior in society is any sexual act that the overwhelming majority of society would describe as deplorable and intolerable. An example would be frottage, the act of touching a stranger's breast, buttock, or genital area without their consent. Another example of an unacceptable sexual behavior is illustrated in the following offense. A Caucasian male portrayed himself as an African-American female online and lured men to his home. He set up a scenario in which the men come into his home, go into the bathroom, blind-fold themselves, and get into the shower. When the men arrive at his home, they see photos of an African-American woman, because the perpetrator's wife happens to be African American. The men assume this is the woman they are about to have a sexual encounter with at the house. Once these men got into the shower, the perpetrator performed oral sex on them. Since these men have obviously not consented to have sex with a male partner, this sexual act constitutes a crime.

Often victims of rape are blamed for the assaults they endure. They hear, "If only you had not been wearing that short skirt"; "You should never have let him into your home"; "A wife is supposed to satisfy her husband's sexual needs"; "How did you get yourself into that situation"; and "You must have been asking for it." Although more and more rapists are now being held responsible for their offenses, blaming the victim still occurs. The victims of rape are sometimes physically injured, and they are always emotionally scarred.

Noncontact Sexual Assault

Noncontact sexual assault is any sexual crime in which the perpetrator does not physically touch the victim. These crimes consist of anything from looking at child pornography to peeping on someone changing through a window. The commission of these acts is for the sexual gratification of the perpetrator.

As mentioned previously, fetishes with non-consenting individuals can become sexual offenses. A non-contact sexual assault fetish includes crimes such as the theft of another's underwear. A specific example involved a young man who lived in an apartment building with public laundry facilities. When women in the building washed their clothing, he would sneak over, steal their underwear, and masturbate with the underwear.

Another non-contact sexual assault is *exhibitionism*. Exhibitionists are offenders who expose themselves to others, typically a stranger and usually in a public place. These offenses could involve anything from a "trench coat flasher" to a male wearing short shorts that allows for his penis to be partially exposed. In the case of the "trench coat flasher," surprise on the victim's face is not interpreted as disgust or shock at the act; instead, it is sometimes interpreted by the offender as surprise about the enormous size of his penis. These perpetrators tend to commit the largest number of offenses. It is not unusual for these sex offenders to report more than 500 past offenses. A woman in her 50s once confided that she had hired an interior house painter and returned home to find him painting her home in the nude. This is a clear, yet unusual, example of an exhibitionist.

Public masturbation is also considered a non-contact sexual offense. Just as one would imagine, these individuals masturbate in public places. A common modus operandi for these perpetrators is to masturbate in their cars where others can easily see them, such as at a park or a parking lot. These individuals are aroused by the possibility that others will see them masturbating. One sexual offender stated that he would drive around town in his pickup truck until he saw a woman or small group of women walking. He would see the women and begin masturbating. He would then open the truck door to expose himself masturbating to the victims. He said that most of the time this behavior resulted in a shocked expression and some choice comments from the women. He also claimed that sometimes a woman would come to the truck and perform oral sex on him once she saw him masturbate; however, the truthfulness of his claims is very suspect.

The next subcategory is *voyeurism*. These sex offenders are commonly referred to as "peeping Toms." Voyeuristic offenses consist of a variety of offenses. Some of the most common include perpetrators looking through windows with the hope of seeing people in various states of undress; taking pictures of others in bathrooms; and viewing others in dressing rooms without their knowledge. A specific example involved a manager at a health club. He drilled holes into the women's locker room so he could view women changing and showering. These offenders often escalate in risk level, as barely avoiding detection is part of their arousal.

Another set of non-contact sexual offenders are those responsible for sexual harassment. This can include sexually explicit phone callers and Internet communicators. These individuals will call or email strangers or people they know and make sexually inappropriate comments. A second type of sexual harasser makes sexual comments or gestures to another during face-to-face contact. This can occur in the workplace or any other public domain.

Child pornography is an additional non-contact sexual offense. This includes any picture or video depicting a child in a sexual manner. Child pornography has been difficult to define, as it can include fully clothed children positioned in provocative poses. Professionals often state, "I know it when I see it," when asked to define what constitutes child pornography. However, a picture of a child in a bathing suit can be a sweet memory of a fun summer day for one person, and used by another for sexual gratification. It is illegal to produce, view, or sell sexual images of children. Child pornography has increased significantly since the introduction of the Internet, as it has become much easier to access and exchange these images. It is also a criminal offense to show a child pictures or videos of adult pornography. An offender who distributed and possessed volumes of child pornography stated that his distribution crime was not egregious because he never touched a child. He failed to recognize or admit that a child at some point was assaulted for the pornography, and his purchases propagated this sexual abuse.

OFFENDER JUSTIFICATIONS FOR SEX OFFENDING

Sex offenders must overcome their knowledge that sexual abuse is both wrong and criminal in order to commit a sexual assault. They come up with a variety of ways to justify their sexually abusive behaviors and make it acceptable to themselves. The following sections present the most common justifications for sex offending.

"I'm a Victim of Sex Abuse"

Childhood sexual abuse is a devastating problem throughout the world (Beitchman et al., 1992). Of the great many children who become victims of sexual abuse, the majority neither abuse nor neglect their own or other children (Herman, 1992). However, of the subset that does go on to commit sexual abuse on children, many have experienced sexual abuse during their own childhoods (Marshall, Serran, and Cortoni, 2000). Studies differ in the statistics they offer regarding male sexual offenders who have themselves been victims of childhood sexual abuse. Ryan (1989) found that as many as 70% to 80% of adult sex offenders were themselves victims, whereas Simons, Wurtele, and Heil (2002) reported that 25% to 70% of all adult male sexual perpetrators report a history of childhood sexual abuse. While the statistics show discrepancies in the number of convicted sexual offenders who have been victims, the conclusions are consistent: a statistically large portion of convicted sexual offenders have been perpetrated against sexually as children.

The reason why some children who are sexually abused grow up to become perpetrators while others do not is unclear. Several possible theories have been developed to try to answer this question (Bagley, Wood, and Young, 1994). They include the following: the child develops an impulse to overcome victimization by identifying with the perpetrator; the child's arousal becomes fixated on the sexual abuse; the child develops addicted sexual behaviors; the child develops cognitive distortions that prevent the development of empathy; the child becomes victim to intergeneration transmission of deviant behaviors; the child develops a pattern of violent offending of which sexual abuse becomes a part; and the child has socially learned sexually abusive behaviors. Of these competing theories, none has been successful at breaking this cycle (Bagley, Wood, and Young, 1994).

Even though it is a fact that many sex offenders are victims of childhood sexual abuse, using this as a justification to abuse other children is unacceptable. These offenders, more than others, know firsthand the devastating impact that sexual abuse has on a child. This is a commonly used yet disgusting example of an offender's justification of sexual abuse.

"She was Asking for it"

Common justifications that fall under this category are offenders who say, "She came onto me," or that the victim "wanted it," or that the victim was sexually precocious. Some adult males will state that the victim was the sexual aggressor and actually enticed them into a sexual act. Most disturbingly, we hear this justification used by child molesters. For example, an adult male convicted of sexual assault against a minor told one of us that the three-year-old female victim "came onto him" and was the sexual aggressor in the scenario. A little child who sits on the lap of an adult, wears short shorts, or runs around naked after a bath is interpreted as flirting by child molesters who use this excuse. Child victims of offenders who use this excuse are sometimes viewed by the offenders as sexually precocious and old beyond their years in regard to sexual matters.

In terms of acquaintance rape, the justification used was "she wanted it." This is not a misperception of sexual cues; rather, these offenders use this justification as a means of forcing sex on their victim.

"I am not a Bad Guy"

We have confronted many offenders who felt they were not a "bad guy" and instead were doing the victim a service or favor. For instance, a common justification is that the offender was "teaching" the victim about sex. Offenders who molest children often use this rationale. The sexual offenders see themselves as teachers and mentors for the sexual development of their child victims. Some of the offenders we spoke to stated that the children were going to learn about sex anyway and should learn from someone who was "caring" and could tutor them.

A sexual offender one of us interviewed used another version of the "I'm a good guy" rationale. He told about how he and his friend discovered a man and woman in their car. The offenders took the young couple and beat the male almost to death. Then they took turns repeatedly raping the woman. Afterward, they forced her to walk through the field with them, naked and beaten. When the three of them reached a barbed wire fence, the friend of the offender relaying the tale wanted to force the young woman to crawl through the barbed wire as another way to humiliate and torture her. However, the offender being interviewed stated he thought that was "too much." Because he was a "nice guy," he took the effort to pick her up and throw her over the fence. It mattered to him to be seen as a "good guy" even in a scenario in which he described raping and terrorizing a young woman and almost murdering a young man.

Another way offenders minimize their sexual offenses is by highlighting all the good that they have done in other areas of their life. The pedophile mentioned earlier, who molested hundreds of young boys while a missionary in Africa, justified his offenses because of all the other good he was contributing to the community in which he was offending.

A rare instance of this is the delusional romantic. Some sexual offenders will use the excuse that the sex took place within the context of a romantic relationship. The most famous example of this is the teacher–student sexual relationships. A young adult female becomes enamored with a young teenage boy, believing that she is in a romantic relationship with him even though he is a child. A more extreme version of this is the rapist who kisses the victim, demanding that she tell him that she loves him or likes what he is doing to her.

"We were Just having a Little Fun"

Another common justification we have heard is that the offense was not a crime or not as horrible as the victim said. The rapist will say that he and the victim were having "a little fun" or that he vaginally raped the victim but will deny beating or anally raping the victim. A variation of this justification is that the rape did not hurt the victim. Some rapists will tell the victim that they will not hurt her. Then the offender will command the victim to take her clothes off and rape her. He does not see the act of rape as being as "harmful" as beating her.

"I'm Addicted to Sex"

Stating that sex is an addiction is another justification for sexual offending that we have heard. Rapists and other sexual offenders will state that sex is an addiction, likening their offending to heroin dependence or alcoholism. By saying that sexual offending is like an addiction, the offender tries to minimize the context and blame a "disease" instead of taking responsibility for his behavior.

"I was Drunk"; "I was on Drugs"

Another common excuse we hear as offenders attempt to minimize their responsibility for a sexual offense was alcohol or drug use. Offenders will often use this excuse, as if they can be absolved from all responsibility. However, when you ask them about the hours or days precipitating the offense, the offenders' use of alcohol and drugs is somewhat calculated. For example, one child molester said he was not fully responsible for his actions because he was drunk at the time of his numerous offenses, elaborating that he would never have committed the offenses if he were sober. However, after questioning, it was clear that the offender intentionally became intoxicated before he was placed into a situation in which he would be alone with children: he would drink before he babysat his grandchildren. This was his way of "allowing" himself to engage in this behavior.

Another similar excuse for behavior is that pornography is the reason they offend. Most famously, serial killer Ted Bundy provided the excuse that pornography caused him to rape and murder. Again, the offender uses pornography as a means of excusing his sexual violence.

"I was Just Bored and Curious"

An interesting justification we heard from those who viewed, produced, and distributed child pornography was that they viewed the pornography out of curiosity. One offender, who was convicted of possession of child pornography, informed one of us that he had the child pornography not because it was sexually arousing to him, but because he was drawn to the "rarity" of it. He likened childhood pornography to rare B-side tracks by musicians and to Hungarian folklore. Another offender who was convicted of possession and distribution of child pornography stated that he was not aroused by the child pornography; rather, he knew that child pornography was rare and marketable to a certain set of people. He said he distributed child pornography to make money to support his drug habit.

A similar justification is that the offender engaged in criminally deviant sexual acts because he became "bored with vanilla sex."

VICTIM SELECTION

In our experience, the majority of sex offenders can be categorized into three subtypes related to how they select their victims. The first is *opportunistic*. These perpetrators choose their victims based on access and availability. An example would be a babysitter who becomes sexually aroused and molests the child he or she is babysitting, not because of an attraction to the child, but because the child is there.

The second type of sex offender is *planful*. These offenders take time to choose who their victim will be and plan out how they will accomplish the sexual assault. For instance, this type of sex offender could be a stalker who carefully selects a woman, learns her schedule and common travel routes, and sets up a situation to rape her.

The final type is a sex offender with a *fixed victim profile*. These offenders have very specific qualities they are attracted to and wait to come across people who possess these characteristics. An example is a pedophile who only molests blond-haired, blue-eyed, outgoing, five-year-old girls.

During our interviews with various sexual offenders, offenders have shared what they looked for in their adult and child victims. Child molesters look for children who are less likely to tell another adult that they are being abused due to low self-esteem, poor parent–child relationships, and their own desire for attention, even if it's negative attention. They look for children who do not have a lot of parental involvement. Distracted, poor, single mothers with children whom the mothers perceive to be in need of a father figure for their children are often targets of child molesters. Some will engage in "romantic" relationships with these women in order to have access to the children.

Other offenders will enter into positions of trust such as a coach. They will offer to bring the child to and from practices and games, and offer extra attention with coaching. The parents will often feel thankful for this other adult's interest in their child and their ability to give attention and provide certain things for their children. It is not until the child reveals the abuse to the parent that the abuse comes to light. Sometimes this does not happen until many years after the abuse. Even though the child does not like the sexual abuse, he or she is often confused and enjoys the attention and gifts. It is often after the child "ages out" of the preferred victim age or body characteristics the pedophile desires that the abuse ceases. When the child is no longer abused or receives other types of "attention," the child then reports the abuse. Children with a strong sense of self, strong familial ties, parental involvement, and resources such as transportation and money are less likely to be victims of abuse.

Many adults have been victims of some type of sexual assault. Because there are so many types of sexual offenders, it's difficult to name a specific adult victim profile. For example, opportunistic rapists may choose victims who appear to be unaware of their surroundings, have poor self-esteem, be under the influence of alcohol or drugs, or be alone. Another interesting phenomenon we observed in our work with perpetrators and victims of sexual assault is that people who have been victimized before are sometimes victimized again.

Grooming/Victim Set-Up

Grooming or *victim set-up* refers to what a sex offender does in order to commit the sexual assault and to reduce the chance of being caught. A common way this is accomplished is through *quid pro quo* or indebting. A sex offender may do something for the victim in order for the victim to feel obligated to do something for the perpetrator. An example would be a stepfather lying to the child's mother to keep the child from getting in trouble and then using this against the child. "If you don't give me a blow job, I will tell your mother that you are failing your math class."

Another frequently used grooming technique is flattery. A sex offender may compliment a child with poor self-esteem in order to coax her into having sexual contact. For instance, a sex offender may tell an emotionally abused child that she is smart, pretty, and special. These may be the only positive remarks she has ever received, and it feels good. The perpetrator will then use this as reinforcement for the child having sexual contact with him.

Physical or emotional abuse is another way to set up a victim while protecting the offender. When a person is harmed, he or she will become fearful of the person causing the harm. The perpetrator is then able to control the victim. In this manner a sex offender may threaten the victim with physical harm if he or she does not participate in the sexual contact or may use violence within the commission of the sexual assault. When a victim is fearful of the offender, it is much more difficult for him or her to report the sex abuse.

A fourth grooming behavior is inoculation, which is when an offender sets up the circumstances so another caregiver is unalarmed when a child presents with alarming behavior. An example that comes to mind involved divorced parents with joint custody of a child. Prior to the father beginning to sexually abuse his three-year-old daughter, he began making complaints to the mother that the child was scratching and rubbing herself. He accused the mother of not properly cleaning the daughter's vaginal area. Soon thereafter, he began sexually assaulting the child. He believed that if the child complained, the mother would think it was an ongoing problem for her daughter and would not suspect the father was sexually abusing the child.

The use of substances can be employed either as a way to break down the barriers of a victim or an excuse for sexually abusive behaviors. An offender may give a potential victim alcohol or rohypnol (date rape drug) to intoxicate and reduce the chance of resistance from a victim. In addition, if a victim does not remember or only vaguely remembers, it becomes more difficult for her to report the assault. Offenders may also drink or use drugs as a way not to be held responsible for their abusive behavior. They have often made statements to their victims such as "I would never hurt you, but the alcohol made me do it." This also increases the likelihood that the victim will not report the sexual assault.

As mentioned earlier in this chapter, religious figures often hold a position of trust and access with respect to various victim populations. Additionally, religion itself has also been used as a way to groom or set up victims. Perpetrators have been known to tell their victims, "God said it was okay," or "God wants me to teach you this." The perpetrators who use this technique often have some type of religious role with the victim, whether it be a formal teaching position or a parent instructing the child's religious development.

Preying on the naïve or friendly nature of a child, or the vulnerable, is a common grooming technique for sex offenders. This is how many stranger perpetrators lure their victims into cars, their homes, or other secluded areas. An offender may tell a child that her mother has been in a car accident and he is supposed to take her to a hospital in order to get the child in the car with him. Another example would be an offender asking a mentally retarded woman to help him find his lost puppy.

Another frequently used grooming technique is pornography. Offenders use pornography as a way to normalize sexual activity. Some perpetrators will intentionally display pornography and then attempt to make it accidental and embarrassing when the victim sees it. They often will use it as a progression toward a hands-on sexual assault. If the child does not tell about viewing the pornography, the offender will watch it with the child, then ask the child if he wants to try what was viewed, and so on. This has been a very effective way for perpetrators to set up their victims.

The last method to groom and set up a victim that we discuss is taking on a position of trust. Priests, teachers, coaches, foster parents, babysitters, and other care-giving positions exist with inherent power over numerous potential victims. It is not only difficult for others to believe that these caring people would harm a child, but is also hard for a child to recognize the perpetration as abuse. It is common for pedophiles or hebephiles to obtain positions of trust as a way to be near children and adolescents. They use their position to build further trust in the children and adults with whom they work. Only after this trust has been developed will these offenders abuse their victims. A case that illustrates this behavior involved a Christian youth leader who volunteered his time to the community. He gained the trust of the children and their parents. He then chose the most vulnerable children to abuse: those with poor self-esteem and little parental supervision. After the first accusations were made, many of the parents came to the defense of the youth leader. It was not until after he admitted the sexual abuse that they acknowledged he was a sex offender.

SUMMARY

The popular portrayal of the sexual offender often includes the creepy stranger waiting in a dark parking lot or the scheming child molester using a puppy to lure innocent children. However, the frightening reality is that a sexual offender is more likely to be a person of trust from among your family, friends, or community.

The sexual behaviors that have been criminalized, as well as who may be considered a victim of a sexual crime, have been shaped by many factors. These factors include property law, religion, and culture. A myriad of different sexual behaviors may be categorized as sexual offenses. They range from the relatively benign, in the case of public urination, to the horrific serial sadistic rapist. Just as varied as their behaviors, sexual offenders are an extremely heterogeneous group. Therefore, the term *sexual offender* is fairly useless as a construct. Instead, describing offenders by their type of offense (e.g., rapist, child molester, exhibitionist) is more useful to understand victim selection and management of these offenders. There are some commonalities between sexual offenders, including poor anger management, anxiety, mood deregulation, antisocial behavior, and poor impulse control.

Sex offender attitudes toward their victims appear to have been shaped by the same influences just described—property law, religion, and culture. This may be found in the kind of value they place on women that exists beneath the surface of their justifications and rationalizations for offending. In our collective experience as researchers and therapists, we have found that many different sexual offenders use similar justifications when discussing their offenses. These include but are not limited to "I was a victim of sexual abuse"; "She was asking for it"; "I'm not a bad guy"; "We were just having a little fun"; "I'm addicted to sex"; "I was drunk/on drugs"; and "I was bored or curious." There are also different types of victim selection: some offenders are more opportunistic, whereas others are more planful in their behaviors or have a fixed victim profile. Offenders will use similar techniques to gain access to victims, often through the process of grooming. These methods include indebting, flattery, abuse, inoculation, substance abuse, religion, preying, pornography, and exploiting positions of trust.

QUESTIONS

1. True or False: Sexual offenders often commit multiple assaults ranging across a variety of sexually deviant behaviors before they are identified in the criminal justice system.
2. True or False: *Sodomy* is a term used to refer to anal sex.
3. Child molesters make up the (largest/smallest) portion of sex offenders.
4. Name and describe the two types of pedophilia.
5. True or False: Stranger rape is the most common type of rape.
6. True or False: The frequency of gang rape is increasing.
7. A statistically (large/small) portion of convicted sexual offenders were the victims of sexual assault as children.

REFERENCES

Abel, G.G., Rouleau, J.L., 1990. The nature and extent of sexual assault. In: Marshall, W.L., Laws, D.R., Barbaree, H.E. (Eds.), Handbook of Sexual Assault: Issues, Theories and Treatment of the Offender, Plenum Press, New York, pp. 9–20.

Adams, R., 2007. Violence against women and international law: the fundamental right to state protection from domestic violence. New York International Law Review 20, 57–129.

Asamoah-Wade, Y., 2000. Women's human rights and 'honor killings' in Islamic cultures. Buffalo Women's Law Journal 8, 21–23.

Bagley, C., Wood, M., Young, L., 1994. Victim to abuser: mental health and behavioral sequels of child sexual abuse in a community survey of young adult males. Child Abuse and Neglect 188, 683–697.

Baker, K., 1997. Once a rapist? Motivational evidence and relevancy in rape law. Harvard Law Review 110, 563–624.

Barker, K., 2004. Sex, rape, and shame. DePaul Journal of Health Care Law 8, 179–236.

Baerga-Buffler, M., Johnson, J., 2006. Sex offender management in the federal probation and pretrial services system. Federal Probation 70, 13–17.

Beitchman, J.H., Zucker, K.J., Hood, J.E., daCosta, G.A., Akman, D., Cassavia, E., 1992. A review of the long-term effects of child sexual abuse. Child Abuse and Neglect 16, 101–118.

Bhave, S., 2007. Deterring dowry deaths in India: applying tort law to reverse the economic incentives that fuel the dowry market. Suffolk University Law Review 40, 291–313.

Collopy, D., 2007. Incorporating a hardship factor in asylum claims based on female genital mutilation: a legislative solution to protect the best interests of children. Georgetown Immigration Law Journal 21, 469–503.

DSM-IV-TR, 2000. Diagnostic and Statistical Manual of Mental Disorders, fourth ed. American Psychiatric Association, Washington, DC, text revised.

English, K., 1998. The containment approach: an aggressive strategy for the community management of adult sex offenders. Psychology, Public Policy, and Law 4 (1/2), 218–235.

English, A., Teare, C., 2001. Statutory rape enforcement and child abuse reporting: effects on health care access for adolescents. DePaul Law Review 50, 827–864.

Fabian, J., 2005. The risky business of conducting risk assessments for those already civilly committed as sexually violent predators. William Mitchell Law Review 32, 81–159.

Fenton, Z., 2001. Faith in justice: fiduciaries, malpractice and sexual abuse by clergy. Michigan Journal of Gender and Law 8, 45–96.

Gardiner, K., Glosser, A., Fishman, M., 2004. Statutory Rape: A Guide to State Laws and Reporting Requirements, December 15, Office of the Assistant Secretary for Planning and Evaluation, U.S. Department of Health and Human Services. Available at: http://www.lewin.com/Lewin_Publications/Human_Services/StateLawsReport.htm

Griffin, M., West, D., 2006. The lowest of the low? Addressing the disparity between community view, public policy, and treatment effectiveness for sex offenders. Law and Psychology Review 30, 149–163.

Herman, J.L., 1992. Trauma and Recovery. Basic Books, New York.

Hough, N.A., 2004. Sodomy and prostitution: Laws protecting the 'fabric of society.' Pierce Law Review 3, 101–124.

Jackson, S., 2007. Marriages of convenience: international marriage brokers, mail-order brides, and domestic servitude. University of Toledo Law Review 38, 895–922.

Lawrence, Garner v. Texas, 2003. Supreme Court of the United States No. 02–102 (539 U.S. 558). Decided June 26, 2003.

Lindsay, W.R., Murphy, L., Smith, G., Murphy, D., Edwards, Z., Chittock, C., Grieve, A., Young, S.J., 2004. The dynamic risk assessment and management system: an assessment of immediate risk of violence for individuals with offending and challenging behavior. Journal of Applied Research in Intellectual Disabilities 17, 267–274.

Marshall, W.L., Serran, G.A., Cortoni, F.A., 2000. Childhood attachments, sexual abuse, and their relationship to adult coping in child molesters. Sexual Abuse: A Journal of Research and Treatment 12 (1), 17–26.

Nagayama-Hall, G., 1996. Theory-Based Assessment, Treatment, and Prevention of Sexual Aggression. Oxford University Press, New York.

Oglebsy, A., 2007. Eliminating Injustice: Revising Mississippi's Statutory Rape Laws. Mississippi Law Journal 6 (4), 1067–1100.

Peters-Baker, J., 1998. Challenging traditional notions of managing sex offenders: prognosis is lifetime management. UMKC Law Review 66, 629–679.

Pokorak, J., 2006. Rape as a badge of slavery: the legal history of, and remedies for, prosecutorial race-of-victim charging disparities. Nevada Law Journal 7, 1–54.

Prentky, R., Janus, E., Barbaree, H., Schwartz, B., Kafka, M., 2006. Sexually violent predators in the courtroom. Psychology, Public Policy, and Law 12, 357–386.

Ryan, G., 1989. Victim to victimizer: rethinking victim treatment. Journal of Interpersonal Violence 4 (3), 325–341.

Simons, D., Wurtele, S.K., Heil, P., 2002. Childhood victimization and lack of empathy as predictors of sexual offending against women and children. Journal of Interpersonal Violence 17 (12), 1291–1307.

Torgoley, S., 2006. Trafficking and forced prostitution: a manifestation of modern slavery. Tulane Journal of International and Comparative Law 14, 553–578.

Turvey, B., 2008. Criminal Profiling, third ed. Elsevier Science, Boston.

Ullman, S.E., 1999. A comparison of gang and individual rape incidents. Violence Victims 14 (2), 123–133.

Woolley, M., 2007. Marital rape: a unique blend of domestic violence and non-marital rape issues. Hastings Women's Law Journal 18, 269–293.

CHAPTER 18

Forensic Victimology on Trial

Brent E. Turvey[1]

KEY TERMS

Daubert v. Merrell Dow Pharmaceuticals, Inc. The 1993 Supreme Court ruling superseding *Frye*, which holds that expert testimony may be admitted if it is both relevant and reliable.

Exclusionary rules Rules used in a court of law to ensure that evidence deemed relevant and admissible is not confusing, misleading, or otherwise a distraction from the task at hand.

Forensic criminologists Those who study, examine, and interpret the biological, social, behavioral, and/or cognitive aspects of crime and criminality and testify about it in a court of law.

Forensic pathologists Those charged with determining cause and manner in cases of violent or unexpected death.

Forensic toxicologists Criminalists trained to identify and establish the level of particular drugs, alcohol, or toxins in the human body.

Frye v. United States The 1923 decision in which the court of appeals required a showing that methodology be generally accepted in the scientific community for admissibility.

Observer effects A form of bias characterized by distortions resulting from the context and mental state of the forensic examiner, to include his or her employer, peer relationships, and subconscious expectations and desires.

Rape shield laws Laws designed to protect victims from humiliation and harassment in the courtroom by limiting the introduction of evidence pertaining to a victim's sexual history.

Relevance Any victim information that is deemed relevant may be admissible in court, where relevance refers to whether or not the victim information serves to prove or disprove a fact in question.

Victim impact statements (VIS) Accounts by victims or their families designed to inform the judge, jury, and parole boards of the impact the crime has had on their lives.

CONTENTS

Victimology—that is, information about the victim, his or her background, actions, and injuries—is a regular feature of civil and criminal trials. In cases involving victim death, evidence about the victim may be presented by fact witnesses such as family members and investigators; or by expert witnesses such as medical examiners, forensic nurses, mental health experts, forensic criminologists, and other qualified professionals. In cases that involve a living victim, that victim may testify to these things in person along with corroborating details from fact witnesses (e.g., family members, friends, and co-workers), or even medical and mental health professionals (e.g., emergency room personnel and therapists).

---

[1]This chapter is an update of text originally presented in Turvey and Ferguson (2010).

Forensic Victimology. http://dx.doi.org/10.1016/B978-0-12-408084-3.00018-1

It is fair to say that, in a criminal matter, there can be no charges, no arrest, and no trial without evidence and testimony related to the victim and the harms that he or she has suffered. In civil matters, there is a similar burden that requires even more victim detail; specific injuries must be assessed, and harms explicitly detailed, in order to calculate the dollar value for damages being sought. Therefore, the suggestion that a victim and his or her history can be excluded from either of these types of legal proceedings is misguided and even perhaps reckless. Such notions stem from a misunderstanding of what victimology is, the shapes it can take, and what the law requires.

However, when information about a victim is presented in court, there are many potential motivations behind it—and not all of them oriented toward fact or truth. Motivational considerations can hinge on who is offering the information, who that person works for, and what he or she believes. All of this influences what is at stake for that person, be it his or her personal or professional reputation; his or her relationship with the victim or accused (and perceptions about that relationship); or his or her personal, political, and/or professional goals.

CASE EXAMPLE:

Jodi Arias and Travis Alexander

Jodi Arias was charged with first degree murder in the killing of her ex-boyfriend, Travis Alexander (see Figures 18-1 through 18-3). The killing took place at his home in Mesa, Arizona, in June 2008. Ms. Arias claimed she killed Mr. Alexander in self-defense. As part of her defense, she asserted that Mr. Alexander had become increasingly violent and more sexually demanding in the months before the confrontation that led to his death. She also claimed he was sexually interested in young boys. The prosecution, however, claimed that Ms. Arias killed him in a jealous rage, stabbing him at least 27 times.

As part of her defense, explicit details regarding Ms. Arias' sexual relationship with the victim were a constant feature of courtroom testimony. As reported in Curry (2013):

> Though accused murderer Jodi Arias said she sometimes felt "like a prostitute" at the hands of her ex-boyfriend, Travis Alexander, she admitted today that she often enjoyed their sex life and even suggested sex acts they could try.
>
> Prosecutor Juan Martinez, after a day of aggressive questioning and bickering with

Arias, asked her about her own suggestions for her sex life with Alexander, including a phone conversation in which she suggested using sexual lubricant.

> Arias, 32, is accused of killing Alexander, but claims it was in self-defense. "You introduced KY Jelly into the relationship to make it more sexually enjoyable, right? When we're talking about the level of experimentation, it looks like both of you were experimenting together sexually. So when we hear things like, 'I felt like a prostitute,' that's not exactly true, is it?" Martinez said.
>
> "It was often mutual," Arias said. "I didn't feel like a prostitute during, just after."
>
> Martinez showed the jury a text message Arias sent offering to perform oral sex on Alexander, comparing it to a statement she made on direct testimony saying that she once felt like a prostitute when Alexander tossed a piece of chocolate at her and walked

CASE EXAMPLE: *CONTINUED*

FIGURE 18-1
Jodi Arias was charged with killing her ex-boyfriend, Travis Alexander, at his home in Mesa, Arizona.

FIGURE 18-2
Photos introduced into evidence include those from both the victim's and the defendant's MySpace pages, and intimate photos of both recovered from cameras found at the death scene.

away without a word after she performed oral sex. "How is it you can say you 'felt like a prostitute' when you're moving the relationship ahead like this?" Martinez asked. "The act itself is the same thing, and here you're requesting it. The geography is different, but that aside, isn't it the same act? And you're requesting it?

"When he (ejaculated) and left afterward I felt like a prostitute. When we mutually went through things together I didn't," she said.

Arias also admitted that she sent Alexander a topless photo of herself after he sent her photos of his penis, and that she only did it after she had her breasts enhanced surgically.

Continued

CASE EXAMPLE: *CONTINUED*

FIGURE 18-3
Recovered photos included those of the victim in the shower, taken by Arias, just before she killed him.

The testimony came as Martinez continued his efforts to discredit Arias' testimony on the stand, including her statements that she often succumbed to Alexander's sexual fantasies so she wouldn't hurt his feelings. Martinez has focused on portraying Arias as a liar for much of his direct examination.

Jodi Arias was ultimately convicted of first degree murder in the shooting and stabbing death of Travis Alexander in May 2013, and as of this writing faces the death penalty.

This case demonstrates a number of the many ways that even the most private victim history can become relevant and admissible during a criminal trial. It also demonstrates the variety of sources for that information—including photos taken for distribution via social media accounts, and any photos taken of the victim or the crime scene that exist on cameras found as the result of investigative efforts.

This chapter discusses the nature and purpose of forensic victimology in court proceedings. The first part reviews the victim's role at trial and admissibility issues related to victim information. The second part discusses issues related to forensic examiners who might give victimology evidence, such as expert admissibility and bias. This chapter concludes with a discussion of the different types of forensic examiners who traditionally give victimology evidence at trial and the relevance of each with appropriate examples. Although the primary focus is criminal trials, related concepts in civil matters are not entirely ignored.

THE VICTIM AT TRIAL

According to the United States Bureau of Justice Statistics (Reaves, 2006), the vast majority of cases brought against criminal defendants never go to trial.[2] A number of circumstances can cause this result. Sometimes the prosecutor finds there is a lack of evidence to proceed; sometimes the judge finds there is a lack of evidence to proceed; sometimes the accused pleads guilty and a trial is unnecessary; and sometimes the accused makes a deal, pleading guilty to lesser charges for a reduced sentence.

In each case that lands on a prosecutor's desk, he or she must determine which of these courses to pursue: to go to court or take another path. When there is less evidence or less certainty as to guilt, taking a case to trial is referred to as "rolling the dice"—because it is difficult on even the best days to accurately predict what juries will do. The decision to go to court is by no means final. As a case moves forward and new information is revealed, the decision to prosecute, drop, or plea the case may be revisited. This can happen on the eve of trial or during it.

Victimology, to include victims, the harm and loss they suffered, their present character, and their background, can play a key role in this decision-making process. However, forget everything that films and television have portrayed about police and prosecutors working hand in hand with victims or their families. Such involvements are not the norm. The tenuous and sometimes misleading relationship between victims of crime and the prosecution is characterized in Pokorak (2007; pp. 697–699):

> Each lawyer, judge and second year law student understands that the prosecution's "client" is the state. The core roles of the prosecutor are to represent the interests of the government and the interests of citizens as a whole. In its most blunt incarnation, the specific victim of a crime is relevant to a prosecutor only as a witness and a symbol of the threat a defendant poses to society. Because of this professional distance from individual victims, chief prosecutors in most jurisdictions are elected, and the chief prosecutors in the federal system are appointed by the President in power.
>
> This representational and political aspect of the prosecutor's role, however, is in part responsible for the confusion about the prosecutor's duty to individual victims. While arguing for voter support in the political arena, most prosecutorial candidates prefer to speechify about representing victims rather than talk about representing a political subdivision. It is simply much more powerful to talk about vindicating a specific victim's harm than to more accurately discuss the abstract harm to the society as a whole. Likewise, it is easier to display pictures

---

[2]As explained in Reaves (2006; p. 7), who studied the conviction data related to violent felons in large urban cities: "Eighty-eight percent of violent felons were convicted through a guilty plea and 12% at trial."

of an individual's wounds than to try to describe the damage done to a community.

Add to this political reality the very important movement by victims to seek respect and dignity in the courts—particularly the criminal courts. Victims have seen judges as too indifferent to their concerns, defendants as too powerful in the balance of power inside the courts, and prosecutors as too insensitive to their needs. Currently, the victim's movement attempts to educate judges and limit defendants' rights, while supporting prosecutors and increased budgets for their offices.

This latter alliance is not surprising, as victims have generally seen the prosecutor as the most directly accessible player in the criminal justice system. However, this alliance of convenience is now starting to fray as victims are beginning to understand that their real interests are too often subjugated to the prosecutor's legal and ethical duties as imposed by the role of public prosecution.

Perhaps the largest reason for the reassessment of this relationship of convenience is the conflicted way prosecutors relate to victims. Although they portray themselves as the champions of victims, prosecutors are too often forced to be the primary messengers, if not agents, of victim disappointment in the criminal justice system. For example, when cases fall apart and are dismissed, it is the prosecutor who is responsible for dealing with the victim. If a victim's legal interests diverge from that of the prosecutor, her special status as complaining witness is often abandoned, and she is then treated as a "mere witness." Any time victims provide exculpatory information regarding the crime, prosecutors are legally and ethically bound to disclose that information to the defendant. Whenever a victim's presence is needed at a hearing, either to supply testimony or for simple emotional impact, prosecutors generally issue a subpoena to guarantee her presence. And, though a victim may be consulted when a prosecutor assesses the correct plea to offer, her opinion is often necessarily second to the prosecutor's independent case assessment. In short, it is the very powers granted to the prosecution because of its unique public purpose that give rise to the conflicts with individual victims.

These scenarios pose difficult challenges that are a constant reality in the most scrupulous public prosecution offices. The problems caused by these situations are exacerbated when victims are led to believe, either overtly or by compassionate promises, that the prosecutor represents them—that the prosecutor is their personal attorney in the upcoming criminal proceedings. Although, as mentioned above, this message may be generally suggested in the political contests for election, the direct representation concept is thoroughly reinforced by statutory obligations of prosecutors vis-à-vis victims in pre-trial proceedings and sentencing hearings. Additionally, victims cannot be faulted in their well-founded belief that the prosecutor is their personal attorney in light of the words and common practices of police, victim witness advocates, and paralegals who are employed by prosecutorial offices.

In short, victims soon find their role at trial is not one of partnership with the prosecutor but one of performance for the judge and jury. They must either perform the role of victim to gain sympathy or that of pure fact witness to make a particular record of events. Sometimes—in fact, much of the time—they will be asked to do both. For many victims, this means a simple change in their normal mode of dress or demeanor; for others, it means attempting to withhold certain kinds of details about their personal life to maintain credibility; and for still others, it means trying to keep the court from learning that they smoked marijuana to calm down before going under oath.[3] This is true under even the best circumstances, when the facts and evidence are on their side.

The general role of victims in legal proceedings is described bluntly from the perspective of a public defender in Gruber (2003; pp. 654–657):

> The role of the victim in the legal process starts at the beginning of a criminal case. Prosecutors generally take into consideration whether or not the victim desires to "press charges," although they do not do so in every case and in fact cannot in some arenas like domestic violence. Prosecutors, as a matter of course, take the victim's wishes into consideration during the plea negotiation process. For example, as a public defender, I often encountered rejections of plea suggestions on the ground that "the victim would never accept such a plea agreement." Indeed, some jurisdictions require prosecutors to consult the victim during plea bargaining.
>
> Turning to the trial phase of the prosecution, the victim participates in the trial most importantly as an essential witness. Victims' rights advocates have successfully persuaded legislatures to exempt victims from rules that prohibit testifying witnesses from observing the trial. Indeed, some victims' rights advocates argue that the victim (or victim's family) should have an absolute right to testify during the guilt as well as sentencing phase of a trial, even if the testimony has little probative value and tends to prejudice the defendant.

---

[3]The author worked a civil case in which the complainant was required to admit, under oath, that immediately prior to her deposition she had illegally smoked a "joint" to calm her nerves. Whenever someone gives a statement under oath, that person may be asked whether he or she is under the influence of any illegal drugs, alcohol, or prescription medications—as investigators the court, and the trier of fact have a right to know this information and weigh it appropriately. However, it should be understood that many victims use mind-altering drugs subsequent to injury and traumatization as part of a medical treatment regimen or perhaps as a personal coping mechanism. When they lie about it, that's when it can become a problem.

Ultimately, from the view of the prosecution, the role of the victim is to help establish that the prosecution's theory of the crime is correct. Victims are meant to assist in demonstrating that events unfolded in a particular way, causing a particular type of harm. Also, and sometimes unfairly, victims (and their various representative witnesses) must establish that they are being truthful or that they did not contribute to the harm that was caused. The more any victim fails at these tasks, the more difficult it is to secure a conviction (or a judgment) at the ceiling of the charges made by the prosecution (or the allegations made by the plaintiff). The victim's place, then, is to "watch from the sidelines and testify when called upon" without losing the case through his or her poor choices, bad character, or ongoing bad conduct (Simmons, 2007; fn 315).[4]

Once a conviction (or a judgment) has been secured, the victim or his or her family may take on a more emotional role during the penalty phase of the trial; the victim may be allowed to provide a victim impact statement. This is discussed later in the chapter.

EVIDENTIARY AND ADMISSIBILITY ISSUES

The question of whether or not a certain piece of evidence or information should be admissible in any court is really a question of "[s]hould the fact finder be exposed to [this information or evidence], and thus permitted to take [this information or evidence] into account in arriving at a verdict" (Roberts and Zuckerman, 2004; p. 96). It is the role of the judge to act as a filter for the information that both prosecution and defense hope to use in support of their version of events. Put simply, they do this by determining what is relevant to the specific issues at hand and what is not.

Theoretically, any victim information that is deemed relevant and does not also fall within any of the *exclusionary rules*[5] present is admissible at trial. When proposing a working definition for what is meant by the term *relevant*, Keane (2006, p. 22) suggests that "the relevant fact need only make the matter requiring proof more (or less) probable." That is, a piece of evidence or information may be deemed sufficiently relevant by the presiding judge if that judge believes that a fact in issue will be proven or disproved to be more or less probable based on that piece of evidence. Roberts and Zuckerman (2004; p. 98) explain *relevance* simply as "x is relevant to y for our purposes if x contributes towards proving or disproving y." The judge has wide discretion in determining

---

[4]This sentiment reflects the cold reality of trial, not the author's personal views about what should actually happen in court.
[5]An *exclusionary rule* is one that forbids the use or introduction of a particular type of evidence at trial.

whether or not certain information and evidence will be relevant to the jury. Issues with this discretion are addressed shortly.

As already mentioned, judges must adhere to certain rules that theoretically exclude certain types of evidence in every case (Keane, 2006; Murphy, 2008; Roberts and Zuckerman, 2004). These are called *exclusionary rules*, and they are designed to ensure that evidence which is deemed relevant is not also confusing, misleading, or otherwise a distraction from the task at hand (Keane, 2006; Roberts and Zuckerman, 2004). Many exclusionary rules may be argued for various types of evidence; however, the one most relevant to this discussion of forensic victimology is the rule pertaining to privilege.

According to Roberts and Zuckerman (2004: p. 97), "[r]ules of privilege protect relationships founded on mutual reliance and confidentiality, such as the bond of trust between husband and wife, or between the client and legal advisor, at the cost of depriving the fact-finder of relevant information." Rules of privilege can result in the trier being denied access to pertinent information relating to the victim. For example, it is recognized that doctors, mental health professionals, spouses, legal professionals, and victims themselves may be privy to important victimological evidence that is crucial to the case. However, these individuals may be exempt from giving evidence of certain facts or from giving evidence at all based on these privileges.

When we address the question of which victim information will be admissible in court, it is important to remember that regardless of country or jurisdiction, adversarial systems in general provide that judges maintain a large amount of discretion (Murphy, 2008). In criminal cases, it is the duty of the judge to ensure that the accused receives a fair trial. To fulfill this duty, the judge maintains the power to exclude any evidence he or she sees fit based on a balance between its *probative*[6] value and any foreseeable prejudice (Crowder and Turvey, 2013). As explained in Murphy (2008; p. 47), "the judge should consider the probative value of the evidence, the likely extent of the unfair prejudice, and the circumstances of the trial as a whole, and in a necessarily subjective manner, do what appears necessary in those circumstances to secure a fair trial."

Unfortunately, this level of consideration does not always occur, as cognitive research has found that judges are just as prone to bias and error as anyone else. For example, as found in Guthrie (2007; pp. 455–456):

> [G]ood judges, who make up the vast majority of the trial bench, are prone to predictable blinders that can lead them to misjudge.

---

[6] *Probative* refers to evidence that tends to prove or disprove a particular fact that is relevant at trial.

> To say that judges misjudge is to say simply that they are human, and that their decision making, though often quite good and arguably better than that of many other expert and novice decision makers, is subject to error. The problem with flawed judicial decisions—in contrast to the bad decisions the rest of us make—is that they shape the lives of untold numbers of disputants.

Additionally, as determined in Guthrie, Rachlinski, and Wistrich (2007; p. 43), judges tend to make decisions based on intuitive systems of cognition rather than deliberate ones:[7]

> We believe that most judges attempt to "reach their decisions utilizing facts, evidence, and highly constrained legal criteria, while putting aside personal biases, attitudes, emotions, and other individuating factors." Despite their best efforts, however, judges, like everyone else, have two cognitive systems for making judgments—the intuitive and the deliberative—and the intuitive system appears to have a powerful effect on judges' decision making. The intuitive approach might work well in some cases, but it can lead to erroneous and unjust outcomes in others. The justice system should take what steps it can to increase the likelihood that judges will decide cases in a predominately deliberative, rather than a predominately intuitive, way.

This empirical reality may begin to explain why the admissibility of victimological evidence varies so greatly within states, counties, and even courthouses. When intuition (i.e., instinct informed by subconscious reasoning) is at the helm, we are at the mercy of our subconscious biases and prejudices.

Shield Laws

Shield laws come in a variety of forms; however, *rape shield laws* are the focus of the current discussion because they are most commonly at issue with respect to forensic victimology.

Originally, rape shield laws were developed as a way to protect victims from fear of humiliation and harassment in the courtroom regarding their sexual history. In the simplest definition, shield laws are meant to do just that—to *shield* the victim from being further victimized by the system (Berger, 1977). As explained in Flowe, Ebbesen, and Putcha-Bhagavatula (Flowe et al., 2007; pp. 159–160):

> The legal system has historically treated claims of rape with skepticism. Many states, for example, once had cautionary instructions

---

[7]As explained in Guthrie, Rachlinski, and Wistrich (2007; fn28), "the term *deliberate system* is meant to encompass all processes that require effort, that is, attention and deliberation."

to the jury warning of women's propensity to make false charges of rape. Moreover, evidence of promiscuity was routinely admitted at trial to undermine the credibility of a complainant and to demonstrate to the jury that in all likelihood she consented on the occasion in question (Anderson, 2002). Since the 1970s, however, all state legislatures have passed changes in rape statutes. One major change was the enactment of so-called rape shield laws, which limit the introduction of evidence at trial concerning the complainant's sexual history. Congress (Fed. R. Evid. 412), the military (Mil. R. Evid. 412), and all of the states (Miller, 1997) have implemented rape shield laws. Similar to federal and military rape shield laws, almost half of the states generally exclude all sexual history evidence unless it (1) relates to the complainant's sexual conduct with the defendant, or (2) provides information regarding pregnancy, disease, or the source of semen. In the remaining states, sexual history evidence is generally allowed for proving consent, for impeaching the complainant's credibility, or when a trial judge agrees that it is relevant (Anderson, 2002, for a historical review of the chastity requirement in rape law, and Price, 1996, for a review of rape shield laws by state). Rape shield provisions attempt to balance protecting the complainant from potentially capricious invasions of privacy, and the defendant's rights to confront and cross-examine witnesses about potentially probative information (Galvin, 1986; Herman, 1976–1977; Lowery, 1992; Price, 1996). As such, sexual history evidence can still be admitted despite rape shield provisions if the defendant is able to successfully demonstrate that it is relevant in establishing his innocence.

In the past, accused rapists could mount a fairly convincing argument for consent if they were able to prove that a female complainant had a history of sexual promiscuity, or any sexual activity at all for that matter. This was based on traditionally held notions that (adapted from Berger, 1977)

- Women who do not value chastity are immoral and therefore cannot be trusted as witnesses; and
- Women who have had consensual sex previously are more likely to agree to have sex again, and therefore, proving past sexual experience lends to consent.

Rape shield laws were designed to prevent the defense from simply arguing that a victim did not value chastity and would therefore consent to the advances of the accused just so long as they could demonstrate she had some sort of sexual history. According to Berger (1977), shield laws were not only designed to alleviate re-victimization in the courtroom, but "in line with these goals they encourage the victim to report the assault and assist in bringing the offender to justice by testifying against him in court. In so far as the laws in fact increase the number of prosecutions, they support the government's aim of deterring would be rapists as well as its interest in going after actual suspects" (p. 54). These goals are undoubtedly good ones, and it would be difficult to find anyone who would not support compassion toward actual victims.

However, there are problems. First, these laws have further endorsed the notion that rape victims should be unequivocally believed and supported—regardless of any weaknesses in the evidence against the accused. Moreover, failure to project an uncritical pro-victim attitude is often perceived as politically incorrect or unnecessarily cold. After all, who would lie about being the victim of something so heinous as a rape, and what kind of monster would doubt the victim's story? Finally, rape shield laws have the potential to make it easier for prosecutors to make their case—especially when there is unsympathetic victim history that might be relevant to the facts at hand. As explained in Pokorak (2007; pp. 726–728):

> [T]he rape shield laws that were enacted to exclude extraneous and irrelevant evidence of past sexual activity by the victim are universally seen as protecting that victim from inappropriate attacks on her character at trial and before a jury. Indeed, the federal rape shield rule was specifically enacted to protect the privacy of victims. The federal rape shield evidentiary rule bans the trial use of any evidence of prior sexual conduct or sexual predisposition on the part of the victim unless that evidence fits into specifically listed exceptions.
>
> There are basically four different types of rape shield statutes: the federal model, the "Michigan" model, full discretion for the trial court, and the "consent and credibility" test. Each of these models focuses on the exclusion of evidence that directly implicates the victim's most private and personal information—her past sexual conduct. The fact that exclusion of this evidence makes the prosecutor's case easier to prove is secondary to the statutory intent of keeping rape victims free from vicious intrusion.

As is evident in Chapter 9 on false allegations, as well as the preface to the first edition of this text, there are many who are motivated by various reasons to feign or fabricate the elements of victimization. The endorsement of blind victim advocacy through shield laws may assist these false reporters to slip through the cracks of the justice system. Forensic examiners understand that it is important to encourage victims of rape to come forward and to testify against their attackers in court. However, they also understand that this encouragement cannot come at the cost of a loss of freedom for anyone who is being falsely accused. All statements must be investigated—victim and suspect alike—before the truth can be established.

Admissibility, therefore, is not the primary concern of ethical or scientific forensic examiners. Theirs is a search for truth, and that search requires the consideration of all victim history and information, not just that which supports a particular side of a legal argument. As discussed in Chapter 5 on forensic nursing, forensic professionals must gather and consider victim history and circumstances to conduct competent assessments. Blinding oneself to such information results in incompetent practice and conclusions, and pretending that such information is not relevant to investigative and forensic efforts is dishonest. The legal admissibility of such evidence will be decided on a case-by-case basis, and that cannot be a deciding factor in the search for the truth.

Consider the case of Vincent J. Montoya out of Sante Fe, New Mexico. His case is challenging that state's rape shield law all the way to the New Mexico Supreme Court, as reported in Simonich (2013):

> She was only 15. Her boyfriend, Vincent J. Montoya, was two years older.
>
> By Montoya's account and that of his lawyers, he and the girl had been having sex long before a night of violence that led to his being charged with kidnapping and other crimes.
>
> Tried as an adult, Montoya was acquitted by a Bernalillo County jury in 2010 of attempted criminal penetration of the girl. Jurors, though, convicted him of kidnapping her. He went to prison.
>
> Now on parole, Montoya says New Mexico's rape-shield law for victims buried the truth by depriving him of his right to confront his accuser about her past. Montoya lost in the state Court of Appeals, but the New Mexico Supreme Court has agreed to hear his case on May 15.
>
> The implications are enormous. New Mexico has had a rape-shield law since 1975 that now is under attack.
>
> Montoya is asking the Supreme Court to reverse his kidnapping conviction and give him a new trial, one where the girl now a woman of 21 would have to answer a cross-examiner's questions about her sexual history.
>
> This story, unpublicized until now, says more about the world we live in than about the working of our courts.
>
> For one, if there was any doubt about the challenges that schoolteachers face each day, Montoya's case erases them. Secondly, if anyone believed that parents always control kids, Montoya's court pleadings should disabuse them of that notion.
>
> Montoya and his girlfriend were teenagers when the case began, but they were living dangerous lives.
>
> The state attorney general's staff, in a brief to the Supreme Court, said the jury did not learn much about Montoya because the trial judge bottled up the sordid parts of his life.

At trial, prosecutors said, they could not mention evidence that Montoya was a gang member, that he bit the girl on her inner thigh or that he supposedly answered his door that night with a gun in his hand....

Montoya and the girl began the night with an argument. She was angry because another girl had called him. Strangely enough, both sides agree on most of what happened.

Montoya pushed the girl into a bedroom of his grandmother's house, where he stayed and where his girlfriend had arrived to visit him. He pinned the girl on the bed. When she fought him and tried to call her mother on her cellphone, Montoya grabbed it and threw it to the floor. He broke the zipper on the girl's pants as he pressured her.

Montoya's defense is one sometimes used in allegations of acquaintance rape. He said he and the girl often had "makeup sex" after arguments.

But, his appeals lawyer said, the jury did not receive the full context of their relationship because the judge blocked that information from coming out. "For all the jury knew, this was the first and only sexual encounter," the defense said in its brief. "In fact, however, the girl and Montoya had a long sexual history.... Through no fault of her own, the girl did not tell the whole truth."

The trial judge, M. Monica Zamora, would not allow his lawyers to cross-examine the girl in a way that would elicit that history....

Investigators and forensic examiners alike have an obligation to establish whether a crime actually occurred, and if so, whether the victim is telling whole truth about it. This requires the collection and examination of complete victim information and history (Chisum and Turvey, 2011; Savino and Turvey, 2011).[8] By fulfilling these threshold duties early on, they help determine whether there will be criminal charges levied against a defendant, or civil ones, and whether a trial is even going to be necessary. Anything less subverts the cause of justice, and risks deceiving the court (Crowder and Turvey, 2013).[9]

---

[8]Law enforcement agencies have a duty to investigate criminal complaints, establish the facts, and determine whether a crime has actually been committed (Bopp and Schultz, 1972; Kappeler, 2006; and SATF, 2009). When their agents believe that a crime has been committed, they also have a related obligation to eliminate, identify, and apprehend any suspects (Bopp and Schultz, 1972; Kleinig, 1996). As explained in Sullivan (1977, p. 149): "It is the job of the police to enforce the law. Thus, officers must remember that they are primarily fact-finders for their department and have no authority or control over the judicial or legislative branches of government."

[9]*Justice* requires fair and impartial treatment during the resolution of conflict. Moreover, "*Legal justice* is the result of forging the rights of individuals with the government's corresponding duty to ensure and protect those rights" and "is intended to be the proper administration of due process and the law, with the fair and impartial treatment of all individuals by agents of the justice system" (Crowder and Turvey, 2013; p. 7). This means victims and defendants alike. Anyone who disagrees with these sentiments has no business working in the justice system.

Victim Impact Statements

Victim impact statements (VIS) are accounts by victims or their family members designed to inform the judge, jury, and/or parole boards of the impact that the crime has had on their lives. This can take the form of physical, financial, psychological, and emotional harm. VIS are presented to the court prior to sentencing but after a conviction has been made, or during parole hearings. They allow victims to explicitly detail in their own words how the convicted criminal's actions have affected their lives (Wallace, 1998).

Living victims of crime have reported suffering from post-traumatic stress disorder, depression, sleep disturbances, feelings of alienation and helplessness, fear, anger, and lack of control (Williams, 1999). Moreover, families living in the wake of a violent or unexpected death may suffer emotionally and financially. These consequences of crime are not always clear in the courtroom for a variety of reasons, or they may not be given a clear face during the trial. Subsequently, some courts recognize the explicit need for the trier to be made aware of these effects. A useful discussion is provided in Myers and Greene (2004; pp. 492–493):

> Victim impact statements are presented to jurors, judges, or parole officers. They generally concern the impact of the defendant's crime on the victim (i.e., primary victim) or, in the case of a capital crime, the victim's surviving relatives (i.e., related victim). Although the particulars of VIS may vary from one jurisdiction to another, they typically contain information that (a) identifies the offender, (b) indicates financial losses suffered by the victim, (c) lists physical injuries suffered by the victim including seriousness and permanence, (d) describes changes to the victim's personal welfare or familial relationships, (e) identifies requests for psychological services initiated by the victim or the victim's surviving family, and (f) contains other information related to the impact of the offense on the victim or the victim's family (*Booth v. Maryland*, 1987, p. 2531).
>
> The current practice of allowing the introduction of VIS during sentencing is the result of a slow evolution in the role of the victim in judicial proceedings. Leaders of various victims' rights organizations have called for greater involvement by victims in the criminal justice process. This concern for victims' rights was initiated in the 1940s and intensified in the 1970s. It coincided with increasing acceptance of conservative views regarding the "crime control" model of criminal justice that emphasizes efficiency over due process concerns (Henderson, 1985). Heightened attention to the role of crime victims in judicial proceedings is probably driven by multiple factors: public dissatisfaction with the treatment of victims by the criminal justice

system, prosecutors' beliefs about the benefits of cooperation from victims in securing convictions, and politicians' desires to portray themselves as tough on criminals and sympathetic toward victims.

Those who advocate the use of VIS during sentencing cite numerous advantages including psychological benefits to the victim and fairer sentencing decisions (Kilpatrick and Otto, 1987). Providing the jury with information about the harm suffered by victims is believed to enhance the chances that sentencing will be consistent with the principle of proportionality (Erez, 1990). Additionally, proponents argue that fairness requires that victims have the same opportunities as perpetrators to speak before the jury and share their personal qualities and character traits (Erez, 1994; Sumner, 1987). The use of VIS may also promote improved attitudes among victims with regard to the criminal justice process (Kelly, 1984) and could result in a greater willingness on the part of victims to participate in the prosecution of crimes.

To sum up the perceived benefits of VIS: they can give a face and a voice to those who have suffered a loss; they can be empowering and potentially healing; and they may even promote a positive environment for victim cooperation at trial (as opposed to victim hostility and mistrust toward the prosecutor and the court, which are all too common).

VIS: Admissibility

Some courts have been alert enough to recognize that VIS are often used not as a form of relevant victim expression and empowerment, but rather as a tool for the prosecutor to introduce irrelevant and inflammatory details to play on the emotions of jurors or other triers of fact. Hence, there have been significant re-interpretations of the legitimate role that VIS may play at trial, starting with *Booth v. Maryland* (1987). A history of VIS admissibility in the United States is provided in Kuhn (2006; pp. 254–259):

> In *Booth [v. Maryland, 1987]*, the United States Supreme Court invalidated a Maryland statute that required consideration of victim impact statements during the sentencing phase of capital murder trials. The Court found that the statute violated the Eighth Amendment. In 1983, John Booth and an accomplice robbed and murdered an elderly couple in the couple's West Baltimore home. Booth was the couple's neighbor, and he knew that they would be able to identify him to police so he "bound and gagged [them] and then stabbed [them] repeatedly in the chest with a kitchen knife."
>
> The victim impact evidence in Booth's trial was comprised of information gathered from the victims' children and grandchildren. That evidence did not compare the value of the defendant's and

victims' lives, but did describe the emotional trauma suffered by the victims' family, as well as the victims' personal characteristics. For example, the jury was told that the victims' daughter suffered from a lack of sleep, withdrawal, distrust, and could no longer look at kitchen knives or watch violent movies without being reminded of her parents' murders. The victims' son reported that he suffered from lack of sleep and depression. He also characterized his parents as loving parents and grandparents, "amazing people who attended the senior citizens' center and made many devout friends...." and said that "[t]heir funeral was the largest in the history of the...[f]uneral [h]ome." The victims' granddaughter explained how the murders ruined a family wedding that took place days after the killings.

The family members also offered their "opinions and characterizations of the crimes." For example, the victims' son stated that he believed that his parents were "butchered like animals." Additionally, the victims' daughter stated that she would never be able to forgive the defendant and that she believed such a murderer could never "be rehabilitated."

The Supreme Court's majority opinion, delivered by Justice Powell, held that the statements detailing the family's grief caused by the murders "serve[d] no other purpose than to inflame the jury and divert it from deciding the case on the relevant evidence concerning the crime and the defendant." The Court reasoned that admitting such "emotionally charged opinions as to what conclusions the jury should draw" is contrary to the "reasoned decision-making" required in capital cases. Justice Powell's opinion also held that victim impact evidence presenting the family's emotional distress and the victims' characteristics was not appropriate for a capital sentencing hearing. The Court explained that such evidence may be completely unrelated to the defendant's "blameworthiness," and that it may result in a sentence based on factors unknown to, nor considered by the defendant when he made the decision to kill. The Court also cited inequality in different families' abilities to be "articulate and persuasive" resulting in a possible variation in the effect of victim impact evidence from case to case. The Court also could not justify allowing a sentencing decision to turn on whether a victim was a "sterling member of the community," or one of "questionable character." Powell also cited the difficulty the defense would have in rebutting this type of victim impact evidence without shifting the focus away from the defendant and onto a "mini-trial" of the victim's character. This type of "mini-trial" would distract the jury from determining the appropriateness of the death penalty in light of the defendant's background and the circumstances of the crime.

The Court did state, however, that there might be times during a capital trial when information that would have been used as victim impact evidence may be relevant. For example, similar types of evidence might be admitted to illustrate the circumstances of the crime or to rebut arguments offered by the defense.

In [*South Carolina v.*] *Gathers* [(1989)], the Supreme Court did not overturn *Booth*, but held that its opinion in *Booth* did not preclude the admissibility of all information common to victim impact evidence if the information "relate[d] directly to the circumstances of the crime." *Gathers* involved the brutal murder of Richard Haynes, who referred to himself as "Reverend Minister" and considered himself a preacher. Haynes was a thirty-one-year-old man who had a history of mental illness and typically carried with him religious articles including two Bibles, rosary beads, religious tracts, and a plastic angel. Haynes's mother testified that he often preached to others about his religious beliefs. One evening, Demetrius Gathers and three companions approached Haynes, who had been sitting alone on a park bench. Gathers tried to strike up a conversation with Haynes, but Haynes snubbed this attempt. Gathers and his friends then severely beat Haynes and smashed a bottle over his head. Then, Gathers beat Haynes with an umbrella and forced the umbrella into his anus. At some point later in the night, Gathers returned to the scene and stabbed Haynes to death.

The prosecutor used victim impact evidence during his closing statement, which, in part, described the religious items Haynes carried that Gathers found when rifling through Haynes's pockets. The prosecutor proposed that Gathers saw a voter registration card, and a religious tract called the "Game Guy's Prayer" before murdering Haynes. The prosecutor read aloud the "Game Guy's Prayer" during the closing argument. The Supreme Court affirmed the South Carolina Supreme Court in finding that the prosecutor's "'extensive comments to the jury regarding the victim's character were unnecessary for an understanding of the circumstances of the crime'...." Justice Brennan, writing for the Court, declared that "[the defendant's] punishment must be tailored to his personal responsibility and moral guilt."

In *Payne* [*v. Tennessee*, (1991)], Charisse Christopher and her two toddlers, Lacie and Nicholas, were stabbed repeatedly in their home by Pervis Tyrone Payne. The mother and one child bled to death, while the other child, who had been viciously stabbed and left for dead, survived. The prosecution used victim impact evidence in its closing argument to relay to the jury the effect that the murders had on the surviving child who witnessed his mother's and sister's slayings. During the sentencing phase of the trial, Charisse's mother testified that, "[Nicholas] cries for his mom. He doesn't seem to understand why she doesn't come home. And he cries for his sister Lacie. He comes to me many times during the week, and asks me, Grandmama, do you miss my Lacie[?]... I'm worried about my Lacie." The prosecutor also commented on the effect the crimes had on Nicholas:

But we know that Nicholas was alive. And Nicholas was in the same room. Nicholas was still conscious. His eyes were open.... He was able to follow [the paramedics'] directions. He was able to hold his intestines in as he was carried to the ambulance. So he knew what happened to his mother and baby sister.... But there is something that you can do for Nicholas. Somewhere down the road Nicholas is going to grow up, hopefully. He's going to want to know what happened. And he is going to know what happened to his baby sister and his mother. He is going to want to know what type of justice was done.... With your verdict, you will provide the answer.

The Supreme Court revisited the issue of victim impact statements and held that the Eighth Amendment is not a bar to the use of victim impact evidence in the sentencing phase of a capital trial if a state chooses to permit the admission of such evidence. The Court decided that a state might introduce evidence during the sentencing phase about the specific harm caused by the defendant, so that the jury can assess the defendant's moral culpability and blameworthiness. Additionally, a state may introduce information about the victim and the impact of the murder on the victim's family, so that the jury can decide whether to impose the death penalty. The Court did state, however, that if evidence "is so unduly prejudicial that it renders the trial fundamentally unfair, [then]...the Fourteenth Amendment provides a mechanism for relief."

In *Payne*, the Supreme Court did not explicitly rule on the constitutionality of victim impact statements that compare the value of the life of the defendant to the value of the life of the victim. The Court did address the issue of juries potentially finding that defendants whose victims contributed to their communities deserve punishment more than those whose victims are regarded as "less worthy." The Court asserted, however, that victim impact evidence is not generally offered to "encourage comparative judgments of this kind." Instead, the Court stressed that victim impact evidence is designed to display to the jury a victim's "uniqueness as an individual human being," leaving it to the jury to decide what the resultant loss to the community might be.

As this provides, the U.S. Supreme Court holds that VIS are properly admissible so long as they are not unduly prejudicial, to the point of being fundamentally unfair to the defendant. This means that trial court judges may exercise their discretion, but they have a related obligation to intervene when things get out of hand.

VIS: The Debate

The use of VIS has led to many debates between victim and offender advocates. It is believed by some that victim participation will lead to dignity for victims, regaining of some control, and greater satisfaction in the justice system (Kilpatrick and Otto, 1987). Advocates of offender rights hold that the allowance of victim input into sentencing can undermine the objective nature of a judge's ruling, allowing a source of inconsistency which has no place in a court of law (Grabosky, 1987). Generally, the debate about the use of VIS centers around the notion that sentences may be increased when victim input is admitted, that the process of composing VIS may or may not be therapeutic in and of itself, and that victims may feel more or less satisfaction with the legal system depending on how their statements are used.

Psychologists studying the issue from an empirical and cognitive standpoint have made it clear that while victims need to have a voice in the justice system, VIS as they are currently used can have an improper and inflammatory effect on jurors. Consequently, these psychologists hold that reform is necessary to make the process more even handed. As explained in Myers and Greene (2004; p. 511):

> So what *is* the proper role of VIS in capital trials, and should their use be prohibited or welcomed? One might argue, based on the body of empirical research that we recounted, that jurors are *improperly* affected by VIS. Support for this notion comes from studies showing that mock jurors' sentencing sentiments are influenced by the extent to which victims' survivors have suffered, the social value of the victim, and the highly emotional content of the VIS-issues that have little *legal* relevance to the sentencing decision. Others might argue, though, that VIS are indeed relevant to the ultimate judgment precisely because jurors pay attention to them and are affected by them. This notion, more commonsensical than legal (see, e.g., Finkel, 1995), leads to the conclusion that VIS may provide legitimate and, indeed, desired input to the sentencer.
>
> Can we reconcile these opposing perspectives? Probably not without giving a great deal more thought to the disjunction between legal standards that define capital sentencing (inconsistent and haphazardly drawn as they are across jurisdictions) and jurors' notions of what is important and useful information for them to have when sentencing a capital offender.
>
> But even without that undertaking, we feel strongly that victim impact evidence that distracts jurors' attention from considerations

that are clearly relevant to the sentencing decision—namely, the circumstances of the crime and the background and character of the defendant—should be disallowed or limited. We acknowledge that the determination of when VIS are useful to jurors and when they distract may be impossible to know ahead of time. That is, judges are probably ill-equipped to forecast how juries would make use of victim impact evidence. But we already have some examples of situations in which judges have limited or regulated the extent of the VIS. We think that these were the proper decisions.

The author agrees that not only are VIS reforms and limits necessary to maintain an objective stream of information directed toward the trier of fact, but also that forensic experts should refrain from reliance on such information should they encounter it in their examinations. Information compiled by investigators for investigative and forensic purposes is significantly different from that compiled by the victims or their families to achieve an emotional impact. Failure to properly screen this information can result in biased examinations and conclusions.

EXPERT TESTIMONY

When a forensic examiner testifies at trial, he or she will do so as an expert witness. In the United States, under Article VII, Rule 702 of the Federal Rules of Evidence (FRE), the court may permit a witness qualified as an expert to provide an opinion regarding "scientific, technical, or other specialized knowledge" if such testimony "will assist the trier of fact." The two key criteria for admission of expert testimony under FRE 702 are a qualified witness and helpful testimony. However, some courts go further in their assessment of expert testimony, applying either the *Frye* test or the *Daubert* test to determine admissibility. As explained in Saks et al., (2004; p. 4), "[u]nder virtually all evidence codes, trial courts must evaluate the admissibility of proffered expert testimony. The manner in which they accomplish this task, however, varies greatly among jurisdictions." The different admissibility issues are explained in Cooley (2011; pp. 568–569):

> In *Frye v. United States* [293 F. 1013 (D.C. Cir. 1923)], the Court of Appeals for the District of Columbia affirmed the exclusion of a psychologist's finding, based on blood pressure measurements, that the defendant was being truthful when he denied committing a murder. The *Frye* Court required a showing that the psychologist's novel scientific test for deception be generally accepted by the relevant scientific community.
>
> …Although many courts throughout the United States embraced *Frye*'s general acceptance standard [see *United States v. Addison*,

498 F. 2d. 741 (D.C. Cir. 1974); *Reed v. State*, 391 A.2d 364 (Md. 1978); and *People v. Kelly*, 549 P.2d 1240 (Cal. 1976)], it still had numerous admitted shortcomings (Giannelli, 1980). In 1975, the Federal Rules of Evidence were signed into law. Rule 702 revolutionized expert testimony by sweeping away the restrictive doctrine that curtailed expert testimony under the common law. Rule 702 employed a "helpfulness" test that departed from the common law's more strict standard requiring an expert's testimony to be "beyond the ken" of an ordinary trier of fact.

...Legal scholars and courts characterized this rule as a "relevancy test" (Giannelli, 1994). As applied, this test often meant that once a court qualified a witness, so too was his or her technique automatically qualified (Giannelli and Imwinkelried, 1999). Ironically, neither the advisory committee's commentary nor Rule 702 mentioned *Frye*. The failure to clarify whether Rule 702 superseded *Frye* produced confusion among federal (and even state courts) during the 1970s and 1980s.

In *Daubert v. Merrell Dow Pharmaceuticals, Inc.* (509 U.S. 579, 1993), the Supreme Court held that Rule 702 superseded *Frye*. *Daubert* stressed that trial judges were obligated to utilize their "gatekeeping" capacities when screening expert testimony to make certain that it is "not only relevant, but reliable" (509 U.S. 589). In carrying out their gatekeeping responsibilities, the Supreme Court instructed trial judges to assess not merely whether a technique or theory was generally accepted but also whether it was testable, falsifiable, and whether it possessed an identifiable error rate and had undergone the rigors of peer review (509 U.S. 589).

...*Daubert*, nevertheless, left open the question of whether "technical" and "specialized knowledge," the two other forms of expert testimony identified in Rule 702, fell within the parameters of *Daubert*'s reliability standard.

In *Kumho Tire Co. v. Carmichael* (526 U.S. 137, 1999), the Supreme Court held that *Daubert* "applies not only to testimony based on 'scientific' knowledge, but also to testimony based on 'technical' and 'other specialized' knowledge" (526 U.S. 141). The Supreme Court believed it would be an administrative nightmare if trial judges were required to apply different admissibility standards to areas of knowledge where "there is no clear line that divides...one from the other" (526 U.S. 148). *Kumho Tire* put forth another significant, although less overt, principle that the gatekeeping decision must focus on the "task at hand" and not the standard reliability of a generally and broadly defined vicinity of expertise (Risinger, 2000).

Rule 702 was amended in 2000. The amendment codified the Supreme Court's decisions in *Daubert*, *Kumho Tire*, and *General*

Electric Co. v. Joiner (522 U.S. 136, 1997, holding that abuse of discretion is the proper standard of review for district court evidentiary rulings). Rule 702 now reads:

If scientific, technical, or other specialized knowledge will assist the trier of fact to understand the evidence or to determine a fact in issue, a witness qualified as an expert by knowledge, skill, experience, training, or education, may testify thereto in the form of an opinion or otherwise, if (1) the testimony is based upon sufficient facts or data, (2) the testimony is the product of reliable principles and methods, and (3) the witness has applied the principles and methods reliably to the facts of the case.

Like *Daubert* and its progeny, newly amended FRE 702 forces courts to question the empirical underpinnings of all expert testimony and to exclude those opinions that are "connected to existing data only by the *ipse dixit* of the expert" (*General Elec. Co. v. Joiner*, 522 U.S. 136, 146, 1997). Since *Daubert* was handed down, courts and legal observers have expressed trepidations that *Daubert*'s emphasis on empirical testability, scientific falsifiability, and error rates poses serious trouble for the forensic sciences.

It must be pointed out that *Frye, Daubert,* and *Kumho* are legal guidelines for admissibility, not scientific standards for reliability. This means that judges are free to use any or all of the guidelines of either when assessing expertise and determining expert admissibility. It also means that they are free to ignore them as well. As explained in Blinka (2006; pp. 221–222):

[T]rial judges are granted enormously broad discretion in determining whether the trier of fact may profit from expert assistance and, if so, the precise form and content of that assistance. The witness's qualifications present the range of possible assistance from which the judge will select, a discretionary determination guided by the limited gatekeeping function. The options may range from total exclusion (this witness has nothing to add) to exposition or opinion testimony.

Moreover, because these are legal standards and not scientific ones, imposed inconsistently on forensic experts by the court, more than a few forensic scientists have expressed dissent over some of the prongs of *Daubert*. For informed discussions of these issues, see Thornton (1994) and Chisum and Turvey (2011).

The Role of Experts
As a general rule, opinions are not allowed from witnesses giving evidence in court; they are allowed to speak only regarding what they have perceived with their senses, not what they make of or believe about their perceptions. The reason for this general rule is to protect the court from opinions masquerading

as fact. That is, if all witnesses were allowed to give their opinions openly, the judge and jury may be tempted to simply accept said opinions rather than drawing their own conclusions based on the facts of the case (Keane, 2006).

There are a few exceptions to this general rule. One such exception is expert testimony, which is the allowance for an appropriately qualified expert to give his or her opinion on a matter that would otherwise remain confusing or elusive to the court. That is, expert opinion evidence is admitted when a subject comes into question during the proceedings that the court does not have the specialized knowledge required to make an informed decision about (Keane, 2006; Murphy, 2008). Put simply (Keane, 2006; p. 553), "the opinion evidence of an expert is only admissible on a matter calling for expertise."

Despite the fact that expert opinion evidence is routinely allowed into court, the goals of the general rule prohibiting opinions remain. Subsequently, measures are taken to ensure that the triers of fact are not usurped by expert testimony and that they come to their own conclusions based on all the facts of the case. Ensuring this objectivity is theoretically done in many ways. It is generally a question of education, training, and experience; whether or not the sum of one or more of these has made the witness competent enough to give expert evidence. Demonstrable expertise may come in the form of peer-reviewed research and publications, advanced training, organizational memberships, educational qualifications such as degrees and diplomas, or it may be wholly experiential (Roberts and Zuckerman, 2004). It is, however, important to recognize this as an area of discretion on the part of the judge, where virtually anyone having more than common knowledge on a subject could be deemed an expert depending on the case.

The role of the expert within the court seems fairly straightforward, theoretically speaking. Experts are meant to educate the court regarding their areas of specialized knowledge: to provide not only the results of any examinations performed but what they mean. In theory, experts are meant to remain objective and balanced regardless of the fact that one side or the other may be paying for their time.

By and large, expert witnesses are expected to be honest, avoid advocacy, and remain objective. For some, this is clearly understood and routinely accomplished. For others, it is not. Apart from overt instances of conscious forensic fraud[10] on the part of duplicitous examiners who fabricate evidence, credentials, or findings, there are also subconscious influences pressing forensic examiners. These are referred to as *observer effects*, ignorance of which can be detrimental to any forensic examination.

---

[10]See generally Turvey (2003) and Turvey (2013).

Examiner Bias

Observer effects should be of particular concern to forensic examiners. Their role involves the recognition, documentation, and interpretation of physical and behavioral evidence. If their examinations are distorted in any fashion, the results can be catastrophic for everyone concerned—from the investigation to the courtroom.

Victimological evidence in particular is charged with emotional and political content. One part of this is the natural sympathy that certain victims evoke—especially those who are inherently vulnerable (e.g., children, the elderly, the physically challenged, the mentally ill, or the developmentally disabled). This can affect the emotions and judgment of anyone concerned. Another part is the negative social stigma that may be associated with other victim populations (e.g., drug addicts, the homeless, incarcerated felons). Investigators and forensic examiners must contend with not only their own biases when dealing with these groups, but also the biases of others who interject themselves into the equation (e.g., colleagues, supervisors, attorneys, judges, political figures, and even the general public). Sometimes these biases are out in the open and easily recognized, and sometimes they are not.

Taylor (in Roberts and Zuckerman, 2004; p. 297) explains eloquently that "it is often quite surprising to see with what facility and to what an extent [expert witnesses'] views can be made to correspond with the wishes or the interests of the parties who call them. They do not, indeed, willfully misrepresent what they think, but their judgments become so warped by regarding the subject in one point of view, that, even when conscientiously disposed, they are incapable of forming an independent opinion." This is a reference to what cognitive psychologists have termed *observer effects*. As Professor D. Michael Risinger and colleagues (2002) explained in their groundbreaking article on observer effects in forensic science, many different forms of observer effects can bias the forensic examiner (p. 9): "At the most general level, observer effects are errors of apprehension, recording, recall, computation, or interpretation that result from some trait or state of the observer."

These covert biases are more concerning than deliberate fraud and misconduct because they are often misperceived or even thought of as beneficial and therefore tend to go undetected. Consequently, in order to blunt their impact, scientists and researchers must be aware that these influences exist and can indeed significantly influence their analyses. Once conceded, they can be studied and understood; once understood, they can be addressed and even mitigated. The vast majority of scientific disciplines accept the need to blunt examiner bias and observer effects as a given, and it is reflected in their published research. Put simply, "[s]ensitivity to the problems of observer effects has become integral to the modern scientific method" (Risinger et al., 2002; p. 6). Forensic examiners must be equally vigilant.

The Term Victim

One of the contextual issues influencing observer effects specific to victimology is the very term *victim*. As should be clear from the preceding chapters, this word is used inconsistently and can be highly politicized. It also tends to carry with it certain assumptions.

First, use of the term *victim* by a professional or on an official form or document suggests to others that the person being described is, in fact, a victim. This may or may not be the case. The "victim" complainants and allegations may have been investigated and confirmed, or they may not. Use of the term *victim* implies that there has indeed been a crime or that there has been harm suffered; this may, in fact, be a matter that has yet to be determined in court. Subsequently, unless there has been an unequivocal determination prior to a legal action (e.g., a medico-legal investigation establishing that a death is, in fact, a homicide), the objective forensic examiner will prefer to use the term *alleged victim* or *complainant* to preserve an objective mindset.

Additionally, according to Williams (2004), the word *victim* tends to suggest, or evoke, the image of positive characteristics, for example (adapted from Williams, 2004; p. 101):

- The individual is blameless of the crime;
- The person is deserving of sympathy and should be absolved;
- The person deserves compensation;
- The person has a right to expect that his or her transgressor be fully punished;
- The individual is a good person;
- The person is honest;
- The person is morally superior;
- His or her view of the crime and what should be done about it should be given precedence over the views of others, even professionals in the system.

These endowments are problematic in that they can influence the interpretation of the physical and behavioral evidence in favor of the victim, which is undesirable for those with a truth-seeking mission.

Professionals who are required to make interpretations regarding victim evidence may embrace one or more of the preceding as an inviolate assumption, consciously or subconsciously. To preserve these assumptions, they might even be tempted to gloss over, ignore, or even conceal unfavorable victim information.[11]

---

[11]See the preface to the first edition of this text, and the example of forensic nurse Wendy Gladstone; she falsified a report to conceal unfavorable victim mental health information collected as part of a standard patient history during intake. She regarded this as her duty, to protect the victim from attack by the defense and to help secure the prosecution of the criminal defendants involved. She viewed her fraud as noble and necessary, and she was not held professionally accountable for it by anyone.

As explained in Cooley and Turvey (2011), these subconscious effects are as follows (pp. 62–63):

> As cognitive psychologists have documented, tested, and proven repeatedly, "[T]he scientific observer [is] an imperfectly calibrated instrument" (Rosenthal, 1966, p. 3). Imperfections stem from the fact that subtle forms of bias, whether conscious or unconscious, can easily contaminate what appears outwardly to be an objective undertaking. These distortions are caused by, among other things, observer effects. This particular form of bias is present when results of a forensic examination are distorted by the context and mental state of the forensic scientist, to include subconscious expectations and desires.
>
> Identifying and curtailing observer effects are considerable tasks when one takes into account the forensic community's affiliation with both law enforcement and the prosecution. Specifically, this association has fashioned an atmosphere in which an unsettling number of forensic professionals have all but abandoned objectivity and have become completely partial to the prosecution's objectives, goals, and philosophies. They may even go so far as to regard this association as virtuous and heroic, and believe any alternative philosophy to be morally bankrupt. So strong is the influence of this association between forensic science and law enforcement that some forensic scientists have deliberately fabricated evidence, or testified falsely, so that the prosecution might prove its case; however, this is the extreme end of the spectrum.
>
> It is fair to say that the majority of forensic science practitioners acknowledge the existence of overt forms of conscious bias. That is, they generally recognize and condemn forensic ignorance, forensic fraud, and evidence fabricators when they are dragged into the light and exposed for all to see. When asked, most can recount specific instances they've seen or learned of, some involving severe consequences for the forensic scientist involved and others involving no consequences.
>
> The forensic science community is attenuated to the potential for extreme forms of outright fraud and overt bias, especially given widespread coverage of the increased and repeated major crime lab scandals since the mid-1960s. However, it tends to be wholly unaware when it comes to understanding and accepting that well-documented forms of covert bias can taint even the most impartial scientific examinations. This remains true even with the publication of the NAS report (Edwards and Gotsonis, 2009[...]), as too many forensic scientists have failed to read it or be questioned about its findings under oath. This is disheartening for the simple reason that covert and subconscious biases represent a far greater threat to the forensic community than the small percentage of overtly biased, dishonest, or fraudulent forensic examiners.

Ultimately, any conscious or subconscious assumptions about the victim as an inherently good and honest person (or conversely as an inherently bad and duplicitous person) can affect the context under which related evidence is viewed—bringing bias and prejudice into the decision-making process. This may hinder the ability of forensic examiners to remain impartial and unemotional in their analysis. It may also lead to the presentation of inaccurate victim evidence before the judge, jury, and community, causing an unwarranted verdict or sentence.

Emotional Identification

Another contextual issue influencing observer effects specific to victimology is the emotion that is necessarily involved. Learning about victims and the harm they have suffered can be emotionally difficult. It can leave investigators, attorneys, judges, juries, and the community as a whole with intense feelings of shock, anger, sympathy, and sadness. They may even seek to embrace victim perspectives, and over-identify with victim suffering because of what they believe to be similar experiences in their own personal life.

Certainly, the forensic examiner is not immune to similar sentimental responses. When information comes directly from a victim during an interview or on the witness stand, the impact may be even greater. Heightened sensitivity in this regard can create examiner expectation that is yet another form of observer effects, as explained in Risinger et al., (2002; pp. 24–26):

> There also is an extensive literature on "need-determined perception," that is, how an emotionally heightened or "hot" motivational state, as distinct from a "cool" cognitive expectation, affects what the observer perceives. If even the mildest of expectations can affect perception, then it is not surprising to find that where an observer has strong motivation to see something, perhaps a motivation springing from hope or anger, reinforced by role-defined desires, that something has an increased likelihood of being "seen." And to be sure, scientists and their assistants may have strong hopes about what it is that they will "merely observe." ...
>
>   Many individuals have attitudes toward what they are observing and harbor a preference for one outcome over another. Other observers, perhaps less committed to the data and more committed to the uses to which an observation will be put, might be even more susceptible to observer effects. Here, research on the effects of the perceived role of the observer becomes relevant once again. Research on need-determined perception shows that in general the world appears different to people who have a desire to see it in different ways, and how different the world appears is related to the intensity of that desire.

...[O]bserver effects may occur at any of several stages of observation, from the initial observation to the conclusions drawn about what was observed. The errors at each of these stages may be described as follows:

- Errors of Apprehending (errors that occur at the stage of initial perception);
- Errors of Recording (errors that creep in at the stage where what is observed is recorded, assuming a record beyond memory is even made);
- Errors of Memory (errors that are induced by both desires and the need for schematic consistency, and that escalate over time when memory is relied on);
- Errors of Computation (errors that occur when correct observations accurately recorded or remembered are transformed into incorrect results when calculations are performed on them); and
- Errors of Interpretation (errors that occur when examiners draw incorrect conclusions from the data).

In the case of errors of interpretation, the criteria for the "true" values of the underlying observations are often so vague, ephemeral, and submerged in the interpretation, that one often cannot discover the inaccuracy in the interpretative conclusion. Interestingly, this most error prone circumstance corresponds to the realm of the expert testifying in a legal proceeding: the expert's "opinion." It is exactly where stimuli are most on the border of accurate perception and classification that conditions most favor errors of interpretation. The more ambiguous and ill-defined the stimulus and the more frustrated or motivated the observer, the more likely one or more observer effects will occur, resulting in an inaccurate result.

When it comes to emotion there is little doubt that it is difficult if not impossible to disregard the way we feel. Even in the most strong-willed individuals, our true feelings may subtly or grossly influence the way we behave and communicate, the way we collect and examine evidence, and the interpretations that can result. Despite strong emotions, it is imperative that the greatest effort be made to weigh all the information available, check whether theories are supported or refuted, and remain objective in seeking and explaining the truth. Recognizing that it can be a problem is the first and most important step—as this opens the door to seeking remedy.

It is also clear that emotions can affect the way that evidence is collected, presented, and viewed in court. In fact, those charged with presenting the evidence may purposely offer emotional evidence as a way to advocate for their position—to sway a judge or jury when the evidence alone does not take them far enough. This is where the forensic examiner has great value in cooling such zealous interpretations—as an objective foil.

THE ROLE OF FORENSIC VICTIMOLOGY

In cases in which victim actions, history, or demeanor is relevant to legal proceedings, forensic examiners may be asked to examine victim-oriented behavioral evidence and contextualize it before the trier of fact. This is the *forensic* aspect of forensic victimology.[12] As has been discussed, the rules of admissibility vary from state to state, court to court, and judge to judge—as admissibility of victimology evidence is made by the court on an individual basis and based on a sometimes-unique interpretation of the law.

The question arises as to the role of victimology in this venue. In general, forensic examiners should conduct themselves as both scientist and educator. It is their role to provide a cooling effect to the often-heated issues surrounding victim-oriented behavioral evidence. They must examine the evidence impartially, through the lens of the scientific method, and render conclusions related to victimology in accordance with their findings. When necessary, they must be able to explain their findings to the court and show how they achieved them.

For the small percentage of cases that do go to trial, there is an unavoidable vulnerability to the culmination of errors, improper motivations, and the zeal of advocates on either side of the courtroom. This is particularly true of information related to the victim. As described in preceding chapters, victimological information can be compiled ineptly, reported inaccurately, or provided in a biased manner—and that is when it is collected at all. The misinformation that follows may combine during court proceedings to have a tremendous impact. Bad information can create a snowball effect: errors and omissions in the original information provided to police lead to errors in the investigation; leading to problems in the case assembled against the accused; leading to mistakes in the charges handed down and how the case is brought by the prosecution; leading to false perceptions by the judge, jury, and media. All these can have influence over whether or not a defendant is convicted and how he or she is sentenced.

---

[12]The single feature that distinguishes forensic examiners from all others in the field is the expectation that they may be asked to provide expert testimony regarding their findings in a court of law. If they conduct examinations and render findings without this expectation hanging over their work, it is not being done in a forensic context, and subsequent conclusions may not be prepared with the same standards of confidence or certainty. Worse, findings may be overly confident, without the required scientific restraint.

Generally speaking, one purpose of forensic victimology is to help prevent this snowball effect from happening. Victimological information should be gathered objectively and consistently, and then used to describe or evaluate the victims and their circumstances so that judges and juries are privy to information that may be relevant to their decisions. In this context, direct questions must be asked: was the victim using drugs; does the victim have a history of falsely reporting crime; what was the extent of the victim's physical injuries; was the victim conscious during the attack; does the victim have a history of taking rides from strangers or letting strangers into his or her home; does the victim lock his or her door at night? The judge, who determines what is legally admissible, decides the issue of relevance for these and similarly themed questions. Then, as already discussed, the judge makes a ruling: sometimes everything about a victim is admissible, sometimes nothing, and sometimes the court "splits the baby" by admitting a percentage of victim information.

The more accurate and complete the victim information provided, the clearer the context of the crime. This is an investigative axiom. During an investigation, everything about the victim must be learned and documented, with nothing treated as trivial. Unfortunately, there is a tendency on the part of some investigators to avoid gathering some or all of the victimology, to deprive the court of contextual information that might sway their findings against prevailing case theories. The court should view this practice with dismay, as informed decisions about what to admit and what to keep out cannot be made in the absence of a complete investigative effort and record.

As already discussed in this chapter, presenting victimological information in court involves a different standard from the investigative effort. Investigative victimology gathers everything; the court decides admissibility based on that record in the context of the collective issues in a case. Typically, victimological evidence must serve a particular purpose related to a legal issue to be admissible. For example, victimological information may demonstrate that a crime has actually occurred or that the elements of this case meet the definition of the charges brought against the accused. Information about the victim will undoubtedly contextualize the crime and help to reconstruct exactly what took place and in what order. Information about the victim may also allow the judge and jury to better understand who the victim is/was, why that person was targeted, how the victim was acquired and harmed, and most importantly by whom. On the other hand, if there is a specific reason to doubt the victim's credibility or the accuracy of particular statements, victimology may be introduced at trial to bring this to light. These are just some of the many possible scenarios, but the theme remains clear: to be admissible in court, victimology must be relevant to a factual matter or legal question, and not simply part of a smear campaign.

Legal versus Scientific Sufficiency

At this point we need to put ourselves back on track and distinguish between legal and scientific sufficiency of evidence. The standards for a given judge in a given courtroom in a given state are important because they dictate what the victimologist may testify to in a particular case. However, these legal standards have no hold over a victimologist's methods and science. In other words, what is sufficiently reliable for legal purposes may not be sufficiently reliable for inclusion in a victimology. It is the forensic examiner's responsibility to know the difference—in order to make it clear to the court when necessary.

As explained in Thornton (1994; p. 476):

> Although there is a forensic science profession in the United States, and although many of us spend much of our time in courts of law, we have for the most part been passive spectators to the court decisions that deal with the admissibility of scientific evidence. In one sense, this is as it should be. It is the job of the law, and not of science, to determine how science is to be used in the courts. But in another sense, our passivity has served both ourselves and the legal system poorly. It is the job of science, and not of law, to determine what is good science and what is not.

And (p. 483):

> Every scientist understands that there are courts of law. By and large, they are accorded respect. I am not as certain that every lawyer understands that there are courts of science as well. They are not as easily identified because they do not exist in a particular point in space, nor is there one man or woman in a black robe that symbolizes the court, nor a marble anteroom outside smelling of urine and industrial strength disinfectant. Courts of science are constructs of the mind, which bring clarity and coherency to scientific and technical matters. They are built not of marble, but from the scientific method. Every scientist is expected to serve as his or her own presiding judge, and if a costume is necessary, it is a white lab coat instead of a black robe. But these courts have certain rules also, just as courts of law. And the scientist who declines to practice his or her profession by the rules of science will soon find that he or she has earned only the derision of his or her colleagues, and eventually finds that he or she cannot continue to practice at all.

A threshold evidentiary and admissibility issue is whether statements made by the victim, or about the victim, are of sufficient quality to be used in a court proceeding. Consider the case of James Sherman, a police officer in Newport

News, Virginia, on trial for sexually abusing a teenage girl. As explained in Zielinski (2008):

> Attorneys for James Sherman presented 10 motions to Williamsburg–James City County Circuit Judge Samuel Powell Tuesday. Sherman, 40, is charged with aggravated sexual battery and indecent liberties with a child in connection with the abuse of the teen at a James City County apartment between July 2005 and July 2006.
>
> Sherman's attorney Marc Messier said that the girl testified in a deposition that the allegations she made against Sherman were false, but then testified at the preliminary hearing that he had in fact touched her inappropriately on multiple occasions. He said it is inadmissible to use perjured testimony to secure a criminal conviction, and that the victim's testimony should be suppressed.
>
> "I don't know that anybody can know which to believe at this point," Messier said. "The fact is, we have perjury." Williamsburg–James City County Commonwealth's Attorney Nate Green admitted that the girl had lied under oath, but said prosecutors believe her statement at the preliminary hearing was true and that her testimony at trial would not be perjury.
>
> Powell took the motion under advisement Tuesday so that he could read relevant case law dealing with the issue.

Is the victim a reliable source of information in this case, and is her testimony admissible? These are two very separate questions. For the court, both answers are a matter of law, admissibility, and precedent. After much research, answers and interpretations of the law can be clear to murky depending on the jurist and jurisdiction.

For the forensic examiner, however, the law is not a factor, and the second question is irrelevant to a victimological analysis. The first issues with any evidence are *sufficiency* and *reliability*. Is the evidence provided in a victim's statement or testimony of sufficient quantity and quality (reliability) to form the basis of forensic conclusions? Here, the answer is clearly no. The question is not whether the victim was lying under oath, but when.

In circumstances in which the victim statements cannot be trusted, for whatever reason, forensic examiners have a clear professional duty. They must warn, or advise, that any findings based solely on the word of an untrustworthy victim may not rise to the level of reliability required for the purposes of forensic analysis and subsequent expert testimony. While contradictory or inherently dubious victim statements may have investigative utility, they are not reliable enough to stand on their own for the purpose of rendering forensic opinions or conclusions. Such a advisements may be of great value in a legal proceeding, especially if the unreliable victim statement is deemed admissible.

Expert Victimologists

As discussed throughout this text, and explained at the beginning of this chapter, victimology comes in at trial as evidence through a number of professional and expert witnesses. Though certainly not an exclusive list, the following are common examples.

Forensic Criminologists

Forensic criminologists are those who study, examine, and interpret the biological, social, behavioral, and/or cognitive aspects of crime and criminality and testify about it in a court of law (Ferguson, Petherick, and Turvey, 2010). Their role in court is well documented, as discussed in Anderson and Winfree (1987; p. 13):

> The presence of criminologists in the court as expert witnesses offering testimony on a broad range of criminal justice practices and procedures, or criminological testimony in criminal trials, has included, and continues to include evidence provided by forensic criminologists trained in criminalistics.... Experts are available for every imaginable type of physical evidence and are usually qualified as expert witnesses based on training and experience....
>
> More recently, owing largely to the expansion of the academic field of criminal justice..., to the increased liability of actions of its criminal justice personnel..., and to social issues on key constitutional issues..., behavioral scientists and social scientists with criminological or criminal justice expertise have increasingly been asked to appear as expert witnesses.

Though it actually covers many applied sub-specialities (including forensic victimology), the term *forensic criminologist* most often refers to those with more academic or research-oriented credentials.

Forensic Pathologists

In cases involving violent or unexpected death, a medical examiner or coroner will examine a decedent's body to determine the nature in which that person interacted with his or her environment in such a manner as to cause to death. Using a blend of medical and forensic knowledge, *forensic pathologists* assign a non-diagnostic but forensic determination as to the manner of death, whether it be natural, accidental, suicide, homicide, or undetermined. In making such determinations, the three most important things are *history, history,* and *history*. As stated clearly and succinctly in the National Institute of Justice manual *Death Investigation: A Guide for the Scene Investigator* (NIJ, 1999; p. 39):

> Establishing a decedent profile includes documenting a discovery[13] history and circumstances surrounding the discovery. The basic

---

[13]*Discovery* refers to documents and other evidence that must by disclosed by one side of a legal dispute to the other as a strict matter of law.

profile will dictate subsequent levels of investigation, jurisdiction, and authority. The focus (breadth/depth) of further investigation is dependent on this information.

Victim history and lifestyle information are therefore gathered as part of a competent medico-legal investigation and then incorporated into forensic findings. Subsequently, forensic pathologists regularly offer testimony about victim event history (based on injuries), medical history, and lifestyle to support their conclusions regarding the cause and manner of death. In fact, in every homicide trial that involves a body (only a rare few will not), the medical examiner will be there to testify about the victim and his or her demise.

Medical Professionals

In cases that involve actual or potential non-lethal victim injury, such as rape, assault, and attempted homicide, the victim will be taken to an emergency room or clinic and examined by staff. Typically, this staff includes paramedics, emergency room physicians, nurses, and sexual assault nurse examiners. Each of these medical professionals must take a complete victim history and write a report that covers the nature of their examinations, findings, and any medical care provided (see Chapter 5). They may even be required to document the victim's injuries or lack thereof with charts and photographs. At trial, medical professionals may be called on by the prosecution or defense to explain what they did, what they didn't do, what they found, and what it means.

Toxicologists

A *forensic toxicologist* examines the victim's biological fluids, hair, and organs to determine the presence or absence of drugs and their metabolites; chemicals such as ethanol and other volatile substances; carbon monoxide and other gases; metals and other toxic chemicals; and evaluates their role in causing death or modifying behavior. Samples are taken from the victim subsequent to an autopsy or as part of a medical examination, in accordance with agency-specific protocols and the law. At trial, a forensic toxicologist may testify as to whether certain drugs or chemicals were present in the victim, at what levels, and what those levels mean in the case at hand. For example, if there is alcohol, was the victim legally drunk or necessarily impaired? Was there poison in the victim's system, and how long did it take to accumulate? If there were drugs present, were they consistent with therapeutic levels of prescription medication or over-dose levels of illicit narcotics? And how long had the victim been taking or abusing the drugs found in his or her system?

In cases involving victim death, toxicology is standard except when inept forensic examiners fail to request it. However, in non-death cases, many police investigators will actively work to prevent this kind of examination from being performed. The reason is that the presence of alcohol or other drugs in the victim's system at the time of the crime may be used to accurately suggest a lack of victim reliability. Victim toxicology should be standard in all criminal cases. Its absence may suggest bias, ignorance, or perhaps budgetary constraints.

Mental Health Professionals

Victims of crime may have a history of mental health issues prior to an attack, or they may develop mental health issues subsequently. Also, the court may request a mental health evaluation of victims. In any case, victims may be seeing a psychologist, psychiatrist, counselor, or some other mental health professional. Their mental health issues and any related treatment might have a direct bearing on the case at hand. Testimony from mental health professionals can include everything from a victim's general state of mind and awareness to details regarding uncharged acts involving intimates to the precise nature of the psychological and emotional harm that an attack may have caused. As discussed in Chapter 8, "Psychological Aspects of Victimology," this may also involve testimony regarding any number of victim syndromes. For an example of examiner bias as it relates to forensic medical professionals and the purposeful concealment of victim mental health history, see the preface of this text.

Crime Scene Analysts and Criminal Profilers

Victimology is an essential component in the crime scene analysis and related criminal profiling process (Turvey, 2011). Consequently, crime scene analysts and criminal profilers may be called upon to perform examinations that incorporate victimology into their findings for investigative and forensic purposes. This may be to assist with modus operandi analysis, case linkage, or motivational analysis or simply to offer an opinion regarding the victim's risk or exposure to various kinds of harm or loss.

CASE EXAMPLE:

Polite v. Doubleview (2012)

In 2012, the author was contacted by plaintiff's attorneys Richard Jones and Nathan Tyrone out of Atlanta, Georgia. They were representing Nathan Polite, a young black man who was attacked while walking home to his apartment from a nearby gas station convenience store (see Figures 18-4 and 18-5). As a result of his injury, a single gunshot wound to the back, he became a paraplegic with limited walking ability.

The plaintiff's attorneys argued that the attack on Mr. Polite occurred in large part because of the negligence of the property owners where Mr. Polite lived: that they

knew of recent similar attacks on their tenants; that they ignored a breach in the fence where tenants had been attacked; that the concerns of their own on-site security personnel regarding these issues had been ignored; and that they did not warn their tenants regarding these issues.

The defense argued that Mr. Polite incurred the attack in large part because of his personal background; because of his involvement with the hip-hop music industry (e.g., he ran a small recording studio out of his home); and that he was therefore likely targeted by gang members. In specific, they argued that the use of bleach

CASE EXAMPLE: *CONTINUED*

FIGURE 18-4
Crime scene photo taken by the DeKalb County Police Department shows the gate in the fence from the Chevron Station side. Nathan Polite was attacked on the opposite side of the gate, as he walked down the path toward the Stonebridge Apartments.

FIGURE 18-5
Nathan Polite's shoes were found on that path by police, approaching the Stonebridge Apartments parking lot.

during the attack was strong evidence the attack was gang-related because this was a known gang tactic.[14]

The author was asked to examine the modus operandi in this case and the victimology to assess, among other things, whether the victim was specifically targeted by his attackers. It should be noted that as of this writing the case remains unsolved. The author's report, in which victimology featured heavily, was as follows (Turvey, 2012):

Modus Operandi Analysis
Forensic Solutions, LLC

Continued

CASE EXAMPLE: *CONTINUED*

P.O. Box 2175,
Sitka, Alaska 99835
Ph: (907) 738-5121
For: Attorney Richard Jones
Richard Jones Law Firm
1117 Perimeter Center West, Suite N-114
Atlanta, GA 30338
Ph: 770-671-1730
Fax: 770-671-8137
Examiner: Brent E. Turvey, MS
Date: April 22, 2012
Case: *Nathaniel Polite v. Doubleview Ventures, LLC and Westdale Asset Management, LTD.* No. 09A05619-4
Victim: Nathaniel Polite

PURPOSE

The purpose of this report is to provide examination results related to the modus operandi used by two unknown offenders in the attempted robbery and shooting of Nathan Polite on the evening of May 30, 2007, at his apartment complex (the Stonebridge Apartments) in Stone Mountain, Georgia.

Modus operandi (MO) is a Latin term that means *method of operating*. It refers to the manner in which a crime has been committed (Gross, 1924, p. 478).

MATERIALS

The examiner was provided with, and relied upon, at least the following materials from the Richard Jones Law Firm:

1. DeKalb County Police Department Incident Reports
2. Crime Scene Photos;
3. DeKalb Medical records re: Nathaniel Polite;
4. Grady Health System records re: Nathaniel Polite;
5. Service call records from DeKalb County Dept. of Public Safety related to this case, requested September 4, 2008;
6. Service call records from DeKalb County Dept. of Public Safety related to this case, requested October 2, 2008;
7. Complaint and interrogatories re: *Nathaniel Polite v. Doubleview Ventures, LLC and Westdale Asset Management, LTD.,* No. 09A05619-4;
8. Deposition of Nathaniel Polite dated Nov. 17, 2009;
9. Preliminary report of Norman Bates, Esq., dated July 23, 2010;
10. Affidavit of Det. Charles Lyda, DeKalb County Police Department, CID/Gang Unit, date September 9, 2010.

FINDINGS

The findings in this case have been made in comportment with the literature on Modus Operandi Analysis, detailed in Chisum and Turvey (2011), Ferguson, Petherick and Turvey (2010), and Turvey (2011), as well as the education, training, research, and experience of this examiner.

1. The attack in this case was planned, but not the victim. This finding is based on at least the following:
   a. Two offenders were involved in the attack of Mr. Polite, requiring advanced discussion, agreement, and coordination of crime related efforts.
   b. The location of the attack was a strategically chosen bottleneck located behind the Chevron station (a place of commerce). This area is characterized by a fence that had been opened to allow foot traffic between the Stonebridge Apartments and the area to the rear of the Chevron station—out of plain sight from either.
   c. The offenders chose positioning on either side of the fence on the Stonebridge Apartments side. Given that Mr. Polite did not see the offenders on his way to the Chevron Station, they must have waited, identified him as suitable target, and then positioned themselves after he passed to lay in wait.
   d. The offenders thought to bring a cup of bleach for use during the attack.
   e. The offenders thought to bring a gun for use during the attack.
   f. Prior to the attack of Mr. Polite, there had been multiple profit-motivated assaults at that precise location involving multiple armed offenders. On May 11, 2007, there were two such attacks: one at 4:40am and another at 5:00pm.

CASE EXAMPLE: *CONTINUED*

g. Mr. Polite's schedule was not routine at the time of the attack, as he was not regularly employed and kept no regular appointments. Consequently, his movements could not be anticipated. There is no evidence that the attackers were in that area all day long waiting for a particular victim (e.g., witness statements); rather the evidence suggests that the offenders could have been returning to a place where prior success was experienced.

2. The attack in this case involved bleach thrown in the face of the victim as a blinding agent—a precautionary act. This finding is based on at least the following:

a. One of the offenders threw a cup of bleach in the victim's face and eyes immediately prior to the shooting.

b. Bleach is a widely used chemical known for properties as both a cleaner and an irritant.

c. Bleach is commonly associated with the following when applied to the face in the context of criminal activity:

- a precautionary cleanser used by offenders to remove blood and gunpowder evidence from the face;
- a precautionary irritant thrown into the eyes of victims at the onset of an attack, to prevent an offender's eventual identification as a suspect—often related to profit motivation and in association with firearms use;
- an offensive attack during the course of a domestic altercation, akin to spitting or throwing any available drink or liquid on a victim as an act of disgust;
- a defensive attack during the course of a domestic altercation, to create an opportunity for escape;
- an offensive attack during the course of bullying or hate crimes; and
- a means of torture, poured over the victim's face and eyes, and in some cases involving forced ingestion.

d. Bleach is not commonly associated with gang related activity of any kind.

e. Bleach is not necessarily associated with stranger or non-stranger crimes; it is associated with both.

f. There is no evidence to suggest that bleach was used in an attempt to clean up evidence in this case.

g. There is no evidence to suggest that bleach was used to torture the victim in this case.

h. There is no evidence to suggest that this case involves bullying or a hate crime.

i. There is no evidence to suggest that this case involves a domestic component.

j. The evidence suggests that the bleach was thrown into the victim's face as a precautionary act, to prevent the victim from being able to see his attackers and identify them at a later date.

k. This finding is supported by finding No. 3.

3. The attack in this case involved an attempted homicide by shooting—a precautionary act. This finding is based on at least the following:

a. After the attackers threw bleach into the victim's face, he immediately screamed for the help of his friends nearby and ran towards them in the parking lot of the apartment complex.

b. While running away from his attackers, and before they could rob him, the attackers shot the victim in the back. This was most likely intended to eliminate a living witness and serve as a warning to anyone that might try and come after them.

c. The evidence suggests that the attackers did not pursue the victim after shooting him because of the attention brought by his screaming, the sound of the gunshot, and the nearness of his friends in the parking lot of the apartment complex.

Based in part on the combined testimony of the author as an expert on offender modus operandi; security expert Norman Bates; Det. Charles Lyda of the DeKalb County Police Department Gang Unit; and the defendant's own security guard, the jury found for the plaintiff in the sum of $5.25 million (Niesse, 2012). The case is now under appeal.

---

[14]*This defense theory, while certainly interesting, has no basis in reality. No expert witnesses were presented by either side at trial to substantiate such a connection. This includes the local law enforcement gang expert, who testified for the plaintiff.*

SUMMARY

In a criminal trial, the prosecutor serves the interests of the state and not the victim. The role of the victim at trial is therefore not necessarily one of partnership with the prosecutor, but rather one of performance for the judge and jury. He or she serves to help establish certain elements of the crime through his or her evidence of injury and any related testimony. However, once a guilty verdict has been achieved, the victim or his or her family may have some influence over sentencing through the delivery of victim impact statements.

Victim information and related professional attitudes can influence its presentation and admissibility. Forensic victimology may serve a very important role in the legal process with respect to cooling the emotional content that victim information brings to the legal process through objective examination and interpretation. However, the court, for various reasons relating to admissibility, may curtail victim information and any related expert testimony. In reacting to blunt subconscious bias, forensic victimologists must understand that they serve a scientific standard of evidentiary reliability and not a legal one, regardless of what the court decides will get before the jury.

QUESTIONS

1. What are *rape shield laws?* What are some of the problems associated with these laws?
2. Summarize the current debate between victim and offender advocated regarding the use of victim impact statements.
3. Describe three pieces of information that victim impact statements usually contain.
4. Name and describe two common examples of expert witnesses in victimology.
5. Define *relevance* as it pertains to victimological information.

REFERENCES

Anderson, P., Winfree, L.T., 1987. Expert Witnesses: Criminologists in the Courtroom. State University of New York Press, Albany.

Berger, V., 1977. Man's trial, women's tribulation: rape cases in the courtroom. Columbia Law Review 7, 1–103.

Blinka, D., 2006. Expert testimony and the relevancy rule in the age of Daubert. Marquette Law Review 90 (2), 173–226.

Bopp, W., Schultz, D., 1972. Principles of American Law Enforcement and Criminal Justice. Charles C. Thomas, Springfield, IL.

Booth v. Maryland, 1987. 482 U.S. Supreme Court, 496.

Chisum, W.J., Turvey, B., 2011. Crime Reconstruction, second ed. Elsevier Science, San Diego.

Cooley, C., 2011. Crime reconstruction: expert testimony and the law. In: Chisum, W.J., Turvey, B. (Eds.), Crime Reconstruction, second ed. Elsevier Science, San Diego.

Cooley, C., Turvey, B., 2011. Observer Effects and Examiner Bias: Psychological Influences on the Forensic Examiner. In: Chisum, W.J., Turvey, B. (Eds.), Crime Reconstruction, second ed. Elsevier Science, San Diego.

Crowder, S., Turvey, B., 2013. Ethical Justice: Applied Issues for Criminal Justice Students and Professionals. Elsevier Science, San Diego.

Curry, C., 2013. Jodi Arias admits enjoying some sex, maintains she 'felt like a prostitute.' ABC News, February 26; Available at: http://abcnews.go.com/US/jodi-arias-admits-enjoying-sex-maintains-felt-prostitute/story?id=18598761#

Flowe, H., Ebbesen, E., Putcha-Bhagavatula, A., 2007. Rape shield laws and sexual behavior evidence: effects of consent level and women's sexual history on rape allegations. Law and Human Behavior 31 (2), April; 159–175.

Grabosky, P., 1987. Victims. In: Bastan, J., Richardson, M., Reynolds, C., Zdenkowski, G. (Eds.), The Criminal Justice System, Pluto Press, Sydney.

Gross, H., 1924. Criminal Investigation. Sweet and Maxwell, London.

Gruber, A., 2003. Victim wrongs: the case for a general criminal defense based on wrongful victim behavior in an era of victims' rights. Temple Law Review 76, Winter; 645–738.

Guthrie, C., 2007. Misjudging. Nevada Law Journal 7, Spring; 420–456.

Guthrie, C., Rachlinski, J., Wistrich, A., 2007. Blinking on the bench: how judges decide cases. Cornell Law Review 93, November; 1–43.

Kappeler, V., 2006. Critical Issues in Police Civil Liability, fourth ed. Waveland Press, Long Grove, IL.

Keane, A., 2006. The Modern Law of Evidence, sixth ed. Oxford University Press, London.

Kilpatrick, D., Otto, R., 1987. Constitutionally guaranteed participation in criminal justice proceedings for victims: potential effects of psychological functioning. Wayne Law Review 34, 7–28.

Kleinig, J., 1996. The Ethics of Policing, Cambridge University Press, New York.

Kuhn, P., 2006. Victim impact statements in capital sentencing and Humphries v. Ozmint—do "worthless" defendants pay a higher price. New England Journal on Criminal and Civil Confinement 32, Summer; 251–278.

Murphy, P., 2008. Murphy on Evidence, tenth ed. Oxford University Press, New York.

Myers, B., Green , E., 2004. The Prejudicial nature of Victim Impact Statements. Psychology, Public Policy, and Law 10, 492–511.

National Institute of Justice, 1999. Death Investigation: A Guide for the Scene Investigator, Research Report NCJ 167568. NIJ, Washington, DC.

Niesse, M., 2012. 5.25M verdict in DeKalb shooting. Daily Report, November 24; Available at: http://www.tyronelaw.com/files/451021302_polite_verdict.pdf

Pokorak, J., 2007. Rape victims and prosecutors: the inevitable ethical conflict of de facto client/attorney relationships. South Texas Law Review, Spring, 695–732.

Reaves, B., 2006. Violent Felons in Large Urban Counties, Washington DC: BJS, NCJ 205289, July.

Risinger, D.M., Saks, M., Thompson, W., Rosenthal, R., 2002. The Daubert/Kumho implications of observer effects in forensic science: hidden problems of expectation and suggestion. California Law Review 90 (1), January; 1–56.

Roberts, P., Zuckerman, A., 2004. Criminal Evidence. Oxford University Press, New York.

Saks, M., Faigman, D., Kaye, D., Sanders, D., 2004. Admissibility of scientific evidence. In: Saks, M., Faigman, D., Kaye, D., Sanders, D. (Eds.), Annotated Scientific Evidence Reference Manual, West Publishing, St. Paul, MN.

SATF, 2009. False Reports and Case Unfounding, Attorney General's Sexual Assault Task Force, State of Oregon, Position Paper, January 22.

Savino, J., Turvey, B., 2011. Rape Investigation Handbook, second ed. Elsevier Science, San Diego.

Simmons, R., 2007. Private criminal justice. Wake Forest Law Review 47, Winter; 911–990.

Simonich, M., 2013. New Mexico case puts rape-shield law on trial, but undercurrent is about kids out of control. The Daily Times, April 26; Available at: http://www.daily-times.com/farmington-opinion/ci_23118223/new-mexico-case-puts-rape-shield-law-trial

Sullivan, J., 1977. Introduction to Police Science, third ed. McGraw-Hill, New York.

Thornton, J., 1994. Courts of law v. Courts of science: a forensic scientist's reaction to Daubert. Shepard's Expert and Scientific Quarterly 1 (3), Winter; 475–485.

Turvey, B., 2003. Forensic frauds: a study of 42 cases. Journal of Behavioral Profiling 4 (1).

Turvey, B., 2011. Criminal Profiling: An Introduction to Behavioral Evidence Analysis, fourth ed. Elsevier Science, San Diego.

Turvey, B., 2012. Modus operandi analysis report. Nathaniel Polite v. Doubleview Ventures, LLC and Westdale Asset Management, LTD., Case No. 09A05619–4, April 22.

Turvey, B., 2013. Forensic Fraud: Evaluating Law Enforcement and Forensic Science Cultures in the Context of Examiner Misconduct. Elsevier Science, San Diego.

Turvey, B., Ferguson, C., 2010. Victimology at trial. In: Turvey, B., Petherick, W., Ferguson, C. (Eds.), Forensic Criminology, Elsevier Science, San Diego.

Wallace, H., 1998. Victimology: Legal, Psychological and Social Perspectives. Allyn & Bacon, Needham Heights.

Williams, B., 1999. Working with Victims of Crime: Policies, Politics, and Practices. Athenaeum Press, London.

Williams, K., 2004. Textbook on Criminology. Oxford University Press, New York.

Zielinski, D., 2008. Victim in sexual abuse trial commits perjury. DailyPress.com, January 23; Available at: http://www.dailypress.com/news/local/williamsburg/dp-news_sherman_0123jan23,0,6314781.story

CHAPTER 19

Miscarriages of Justice: Victims of the Criminal Justice System

Brent E. Turvey

KEY TERMS

Alford pleas A type of plea that allows defendants who do not wish to risk their fates at trial to plead guilty while simultaneously asserting their innocence.

Conviction integrity units Units intended to re-examine, and in some cases re-investigate, claims of actual innocence in post-conviction.

Forensic expert A professional who has been qualified by the court to give opinion-oriented testimony in relation to his or her area of education, training, or experience.

Forensic science commissions Groups intended to serve as watchdog organizations to investigate allegations of fraud, misconduct, and negligence in the local forensic science community.

Legal truth The current disposition of the court or law on a particular matter.

Miscarriage of justice A general term used to describe the inequity that occurs when victims or offenders do not receive fair treatment by the justice system, often resulting in a legal outcome that is not in their favor.

Scientific fact Something that is not in dispute, having been established by scientific examination and testing.

Wrongful conviction A particular miscarriage of justice in which a defendant is found legally guilty in court, by a judge or jury, despite being factually innocent of the crime.

In this textbook, we have discussed victims who suffer at the hands of friends, family members, co-workers, and strangers. The intended role of the criminal justice system in these instances is that of impartial arbitrator—to decide who did what, if the law has been broken, and then determine a fair punishment. Law enforcement is meant to investigate the facts; forensic examiners are meant to analyze evidence and explain its meaning in court; prosecutors are meant to seek justice; defense attorneys are meant to defend their clients; and judges are meant to impartially render the law to preserve the rights of all parties.

However, the criminal justice system is not always fair and impartial. Sometimes those working in the criminal justice system act in a manner that is, ultimately, unjust. Consequently, a criminal defendant can become a victim of bias, corruption, ignorance, error, and even indifference. When this occurs, it is referred to as a *miscarriage of justice*. As explained in Naughton (2005), current

559

Forensic Victimology. http://dx.doi.org/10.1016/B978-0-12-408084-3.00019-3

definitions of what precisely constitutes a miscarriage are both legalistic and retrospective (p. 165):

> One of the defining features of the study of miscarriages of justice is that whatever allegations of wrongful criminal conviction there may be, a miscarriage of justice cannot be said to have occurred unless, and until, the appeal courts quash a criminal conviction. For instance, the Birmingham Six (Mullin 1986)—perhaps one of the most notable cases in recent times—had two unsuccessful appeals before they successfully overturned their criminal convictions and were officially acknowledged as miscarriage-of-justice victims. This renders the study of miscarriages of justice inherently legalistic and retrospective. 'Legalistic,' as miscarriages of justice are wholly determined by the rules and procedures of the appeal courts—if those rules and procedures change, then the way in which miscarriages of justice are defined and quantified will also change. 'Retrospective,' as there is no way of knowing about how many wrongful convictions will be overturned in the future or how many are in the process of being overturned. They remain 'alleged' miscarriages of justice until they pass the test and achieve a successful appeal.

This passage is useful, but its author ignores the reality that miscarriages of justice take many forms.

It is possible to harm a factually innocent suspect or defendant without convicting him or her of a crime. Damage is incurred short of a wrongful conviction by means of the emotional and financial costs related to arrest and detention, malicious prosecution, and related defamation of defendant character. This is accomplished by means of investigative apathy and incompetence, false and erroneous testimony, evidence tampering, forensic error, forensic fraud, ineffective assistance of defense counsel (incompetent lawyering), prosecutorial misconduct, jury misconduct, judicial misconduct, and overall ignorance of the law (see, generally, Crowder and Turvey, 2013). Any of these and more can result in a miscarriage of justice.

A *wrongful conviction* is a particular miscarriage of justice in which a defendant is found legally guilty in court, by a judge or jury (aka the trier of fact), despite being factually innocent of the crime. Wrongful convictions can happen intentionally, at the hands of one or more concerted or fragmented individuals looking to subvert justice. In some cases this will involve the implication of a specific factually innocent defendant (or defendants). In other cases, it will involve actively concealing the truth, leaving the remaining facts to implicate who they will.

However, wrongful convictions can also occur despite the best intentions of everyone involved. In these cases, justice is not intentionally sabotaged. The wrong person becomes the target of an investigation and subsequent prosecution due to unintended and unforeseen failures in one or more parts of the process. When this happens, factually innocent defendants become the collateral victims of crime.

The goals of this chapter are to dispel prevailing myths and rhetoric connected with the nature and causes of miscarriages in general, wrongful convictions in specific, and to bring those harmed by the criminal justice system to their rightful place at the criminal justice table—as victims of crime. It is also written to educate forensic examiners regarding the consequences of their efforts and eventual testimony. As such, it is best treated as a primer to the issues presented, most which demand far more in-depth coverage.

A HISTORICAL PERSPECTIVE

That miscarriages of justice can and do occur is not a revelation made possible by modern scientific advances in suspect identification. Historically, courts of law, even when tempered by juries and adversarial systems, have made errors. It is, in fact, safe to say that miscarriages of justice and wrongful convictions have been a feature of each and every court that has taken to the task of passing judgment.

The Bible

Consider the Biblical example of Joseph and Potiphar's wife, memorialized in Guido Reni's oil on canvas rendering from about 1631 A.D. (see Figure 19-1). The story goes (Genesis 39:7–20) that Joseph, a slave, had repeatedly rebuffed the sexual advances of his master's wife. She was, unfortunately, persistent and not to be denied. On one occasion, she was able to get hold of Joseph's garment as he tried to leave the house—and he ran out without it.

Angered by his refusals, she staged her bedroom, with his garment, to appear as though Joseph had raped her. She then reported Joseph's "crime" to the men of her household, who in turn informed her husband. Her husband, Potiphar, was also a captain of Pharaoh's guard. Needless to say, Joseph went right to prison for a crime that he did not commit, as Potiphar was likely in no position to doubt his wife.

Though distant in time and largely unsubstantiated, this example is representative of a particular source of wrongful convictions still found in courtrooms today: the false accuser. That it exists in a text written thousands of years ago, likely as a cautionary tale, is not without significance.

FIGURE 19-1
Guido Reni's "Joseph and Potiphar's Wife," 1631.

The Three Perrys

As suggested in the beginning of this section, there is a tendency to view wrongful convictions as a modern revelation—with DNA providing the certainty needed to demonstrate actual innocence when circumstances permit. However, the literature makes it clear that such thinking ignores a well-documented history of both wrongful convictions and executions. Consider the case of the three Perrys in England, as detailed in Smith (2005; pp. 1189–1192):

> By some accounts, legal observers only discovered the problem of wrongful execution in the past two decades, when the increased availability and accuracy of DNA testing brought the problem of wrongful conviction—and the even more shocking prospect of wrongful execution—to public attention. In truth, wrongful execution cast a specter over Anglo-American criminal justice administration from the seventeenth through the early nineteenth centuries. During this period, English and American legal commentators confronted the sobering possibility not only that persons might be executed

wrongfully, but that they undeniably had been—at times for committing offenses that had never occurred at all....

On August 16, 1660, William Harrison, the steward of Lady Campden, left his home in Gloucestershire, England, for a nearby town to collect some rents. By eight or nine o'clock that night, the seventy-year-old Harrison still had not returned from his rounds. Harrison's wife sent her servant, a fourteen-year-old boy named John Perry, to look for her husband—but to no avail. The following morning, Harrison's son Edward took up the search. After meeting up with the servant boy John, Edward discovered his father's hat and collar near a road in a "hackt," "cut," and "bloody" state. Although the townspeople of Campden "haste[ne]d...in multitudes to search for...[Harrison's] body," they managed to turn up nothing.

Suspicion soon fell upon John, who was brought before a justice of the peace (JP) the following day. The boy claimed that, on the night of Harrison's disappearance, he had begun his search in earnest but had been "afraid to go forwards" because of the "dark" and, instead, had returned to rest in his master's "hen-roost." At around midnight, John had ventured forth once again but had "lost his way" in a "great mist" and "so lay the rest of the night under a hedge." When he awoke the next day, he went to a neighboring town, spoke to some people there, and later met up with Edward. Four other persons who appeared before the JP corroborated John's story. Nonetheless, the JP committed John to custody.

Once confined, the young boy began to talk. He claimed to some of his interlocutors that a "tinker" had killed Harrison, to others that "a gentleman's servant...had robbed and murdered him," and to "others again...that [Harrison] was murdered, and hid in a bean-rick." As these stories proliferated, John was once again brought before the JP, a week after his initial commitment. This time, he told a more chilling story. He now claimed that his mother, Joan, and brother, Richard, had lain in wait for Harrison on the night of Harrison's disappearance, strangled him, and robbed him of his money bags. John also claimed to have heard his mother and brother discuss throwing Harrison's body "into the great sink" —a bog near a local mill. Additional searches, however, failed to turn up Harrison's body.

When the JP interrogated Joan and Richard, both denied any wrongdoing. But at the next meeting of the Gloucestershire assizes in September 1660, a pair of indictments were brought against the three Perrys: the first, for breaking into Harrison's house the previous year, a crime in which John—in his apparent mania to confess—had also implicated the whole family; and the second, for robbing and murdering Harrison on the night of his disappearance. The Perrys pleaded guilty to the first charge, begged for a pardon, and received it. The presiding judge refused to send the second charge to the jury because the body of Harrison still had not been found.

Unfortunately, the Perrys' troubles did not end—for John continued to talk. Not only did he persist in swearing that his mother and brother had killed Harrison, but he now claimed that the two had "attempted to poison him in…jail, so that he durst neither eat nor drink with them." At the Gloucestershire assizes in Spring 1661, a second indictment for murder was brought against the three Perrys. Suddenly John—apparently coming to his senses—insisted that, at the time of his previous confessions, he was "mad, and knew not what he said." Joan and Robert, for their part, desperately continued to protest their innocence. Although Harrison's body still had not been found—in "the great sink" or anywhere else—a new assize judge, Sir Robert Hyde, permitted the case to go to a jury. The jury duly pronounced all three members of the family guilty and Joan, Richard, and John Perry were promptly hanged and gibbeted on Broadway Hill near Campden.

So ended the lives of the three Perrys. But two years after their executions, a "wondrous" event occurred: William Harrison returned to Gloucestershire, claiming to have been attacked on the night of his disappearance by an unknown man on horseback, pressed to serve on a sailing ship, sold into slavery in Turkey, and ultimately spirited back to England by way of Lisbon.

This example is also representative of a particular source of wrongful convictions that persists in the modern justice system: the false confession.

The Boorn Brothers

The United States is not immune from a similar history. Consider the case of the Boorn brothers, as detailed in Smith (2005; pp. 1205–1206):

In 1812, Russell Colvin, a local eccentric prone to wandering, disappeared from his home in Manchester, Vermont. His brothers-in-law, Jesse and Stephen Boorn, were suspected of Colvin's disappearance, but the body of Colvin, the supposed victim, could not be found. After seven years had passed, and long after initial suspicion had dissipated from the brothers, a relative of the two suspects claimed to have experienced a dream in which Colvin had appeared to him.

Interest in Colvin's disappearance and presumed murder revived and, during the course of a renewed investigation, a dog uncovered some bones believed to be those of Colvin. Upon the basis of this new "evidence," which seemed, by the "scientific" standards of the day, to demonstrate conclusively that Colvin had been killed, Jesse Boorn was imprisoned. Thereafter, a convicted forger in an adjacent cell claimed to the authorities that Jesse had confessed. When confronted with his alleged jailhouse statement, Jesse placed the blame on his brother Stephen, who had relocated to New York and was apparently believed by Jesse to be outside the jurisdiction of the Vermont courts. Tracked down and arrested in New York, Stephen ultimately confessed to killing Colvin in self-defense, likely concluding— quite sensibly— that the decision of Jesse to accuse him of Colvin's killing rendered his prospects for acquittal rather dim. Instead, both brothers were tried, convicted, and sentenced to death. Although the Vermont legislature commuted Jesse's sentence to life imprisonment, it declined to respite the sentence of Stephen—seemingly, the more culpable of the two.

Supporters of the condemned man then undertook a concerted effort to find Colvin, placing advertisements in regional newspapers containing descriptions of the man they believed to be merely missing, and not dead. Shortly before Stephen Boorn was to have been executed, Colvin miraculously re-emerged after a resident of New York City had read the description of Colvin in a local newspaper and notified the Boorns' representatives that a man fitting Colvin's description was living in New Jersey. Colvin's "triumphant" return to Vermont secured the release of both of his erstwhile "killers."

This example is also representative of a particular source of wrongful convictions that persists in the modern justice system: the jailhouse informant.

Gary Dotson

In modern history, the first person to be exonerated of a criminal conviction with DNA evidence was Gary Dotson, in the 1980s (see Figure 19-2). In 1979,

FIGURE 19-2
Gary Dotson sitting with Cathleen Crowell Webb, in 1985, after Ms. Webb recanted her statement.

Dotson had been wrongly convicted and incarcerated for a rape that never happened. Details are taken from Connors, et al. (1996; pp. 52–53):

> Gary Dotson (Chicago, Illinois)
>
> Factual background. On the evening of July 9, 1977, the complainant was walking home from work when two men forced her into the back seat of a car and raped her. She also testified that one of the men tried to write words on her stomach using a broken beer bottle. She was then pushed from the car onto the street.
>
> In July 1979 Gary Dotson was convicted of aggravated kidnapping and rape.
>
> He was sentenced to not less than 25 and not more than 50 years.
>
> Prosecutor's evidence at trial. The prosecution's case included the following evidence:
>
> - A composite sketch of the defendant, which the complainant helped with, was prepared by the police.
> - The victim identified Dotson from a police mug book.
> - Dotson was identified by the victim from a police lineup.
> - The State's expert serologist testified that the semen on the victim's undergarment came from a type B secretor and that the defendant was a type B secretor. (It was later reported that the State's serologist failed to disclose that the victim was also a type B secretor.)[1]
> - Testimony was presented that a pubic hair removed from the victim's underwear was similar to the defendant's and dissimilar to the victim's.
>
> Postconviction challenges. In March 1985 the victim recanted her testimony.
>
> She said she had fabricated the rape to hide a legitimate sexual encounter with her boyfriend. Dotson contended that the victim's recantation of testimony constituted grounds to vacate the original sentence. At the hearing on Dotson's motion for a new trial, the same judge from the original trial refused to order a new trial. His reasoning

---

[1] As explained in the commentary by Rowe (1996; pp. xvi–xvii): …the forensic serologist who testified against Gary Dotson failed to disclose that, because the alleged victim was also a type B secretor, the fraction of the male population that could have contributed the semen found on the vaginal swabs exceeded 60 percent, making the serological evidence in the case probative of very little. In this instance, the prosecution's expert witness failed to volunteer potentially exculpatory information but did not actually lie under oath. The failure of forensic experts to be forthcoming about the limits of inclusionary evidence, by clearly and accurately explaining the context of statistical probabilities, remains a problem to this day—particularly in the field of DNA.

was that the complainant was more believable in her original testimony than in her recantation.

The governor accepted authority for the case and held a session of the Illinois Prisoner Review Board. The governor stated that he did not believe the victim's recantation and refused to pardon Dotson. On May 12, 1985, however, the governor commuted Dotson's sentence to the 6 years he had already served, pending good behavior. In 1987 the governor revoked Dotson's parole after Dotson was accused by his wife of assaulting her. The Appellate Court of Illinois affirmed Dotson's conviction on November 12, 1987 (516 N.E.2d 718). On Christmas Eve 1987 the governor granted Dotson a "last chance parole." Two days later, Dotson was arrested in a barroom fight, and his parole was revoked. In 1988 Dotson's new attorney had DNA tests conducted that were not available at the time of the alleged rape.

DNA results. A sample of semen from the victim's underwear was sent to Dr. Alec Jeffreys in England for RFLP analysis. The sample was badly degraded, however, and results were inconclusive. Samples were then sent to Forensic Science Associates in Richmond, California. The lab performed PCR DQ alpha tests that showed that the semen on the victim's undergarments could not have come from Dotson but could have come from the victim's boyfriend.

Conclusion. The chief judge of the Cook County Criminal Court ruled that Dotson was entitled to a new trial. The State attorney's office, however, decided not to prosecute based on the victim's lack of credibility and the DNA test results. Dotson's conviction was overturned on August 14, 1989, after he had served a total of 8 years.

Since Dotson's exoneration, the number of convicted defendants freed as the direct result of DNA testing has steadily grown. Almost every week a new wrongful conviction is recognized by the courts, which results in another exonerated defendant. As of this writing, according to the Innocence Project,[2] there have been at least 306 DNA exonerations in the United States.

NOMOTHETICALLY SPEAKING: THE AGGREGATE

There are more than a few criminal justice practitioners who cling to the notion that wrongful convictions in the modern criminal justice system are either rare and therefore irrelevant, or that they are an acceptable cost of living in a free society. Not surprisingly, such opinions tend to come from those with a vested professional interest in the absolute certainty of legal convictions, namely law

---

[2] See http://www.innocenceproject.org/know/.

enforcement investigators, state-employed forensic practitioners, prosecutors, and judges.[3] As explained in Bernhard (2004; p. 716):

> Bias against those who have been accused and reluctance to accept the possibility of mistake color prosecutorial attitudes.... Even when DNA evidence clearly exonerates, prosecutors have trouble admitting that they convicted the wrong person.

Risinger (2007) refers to some of those with such extremist views as *Paleyites* (pp. 763–768):

> Paleyites, whom I have named after the early exponent of this position, the 18th-century proto-utilitarian the Rev. William Paley, believe that, even though it is wrong to convict an innocent person, such convictions not only are inevitable in a human system, but represent the necessary social price of maintaining sufficient criminal law enforcement to provide an appropriate level of security for the public in general. Hence, one should not be moved by the prospect of wrongful conviction to take actions that would reduce such convictions, no matter how common, at the cost of reducing convictions of the guilty to a dysfunctional level. Paleyites tend to be conservative, in the sense that any changes to current ways of conducting the criminal justice process, proposed for their supposed effect on protecting the innocent, will be presumed so counterproductive in their effect on convicting the guilty that they will be opposed....
>
> Traditionally, a certain stripe of Paleyite has also denied that wrongful convictions happen at all, or, that if they happen, they happen so rarely that worrying about them is like worrying about being struck by a meteorite. The reasons assigned for this assumed near-perfection in regard to false-positive error have generally been the numerous layers of filtration involved in the pre-trial system, and the general fairness of the adversary trial itself, with its formal requirement that the prosecution prove guilt beyond a reasonable doubt.
>
> Such a position is very difficult to take in the era of DNA exonerations.

As explained similarly by another legal scholar (Uphoff, 2006; p. 838):

---

[3]It bears explaining that many in the judiciary are former prosecutors, if not former police officers. That is to say, some judges come to the profession with a particular background and mindset. Some are able to overcome this. Others are not. In any case, judges are paid to deliver a fair and balanced interpretation of the law without prejudice to the defendant. However, if they allow injustices in their court by act or omission, this reflects poorly on their judgment, for lack of a better word. Consequently, they have a vested interest in keeping secure any decisions and convictions that have been attained in their courtroom. Admitting to a miscarriage may cut against this interest.

The growing number of DNA exonerations and the attendant publicity surrounding these cases and other wrongful convictions sound an increasingly loud discordant note in the normal chorus of praise for the American criminal justice system.

However, one study of wrongful convictions offers perhaps the best overall insight, noting that (at the time) over 208 post-conviction DNA exonerations had occurred in cases of rape and homicide since 1989 (Garrett, 2008; pp. 56–57):

> Postconviction DNA testing changed the landscape of criminal justice in the United States. Actors in the criminal system long doubted whether courts ever wrongly convicted people; for example, Judge Learned Hand famously called "the ghost of the innocent man convicted...an unreal dream." With the benefit of DNA testing, we now know our courts have convicted innocent people and have even sentenced some to death. This has happened, as Justice Souter recently noted, "in numbers never imagined before the development of DNA tests."
>
> ...Exoneration cases have altered the ways judges, lawyers, legislators, the public, and scholars perceive the criminal system's accuracy.

Accordingly, the author agrees that the continuously mounting volume of overturned convictions has made such denials appear not just untenable and naïve, but too often they suggest belligerent ignorance.

Research

The question persists: How often does the court get it wrong? Where is the data to answer this question? First, there is no centralized database from which to draw these numbers; each of the United States, even each individual county, keeps and maintains data regarding wrongful convictions, or fails to do so, in its own way. Second, the available numbers are limited to capital cases and some rape cases for which DNA evidence has been preserved and for which the judiciary has permitted post-conviction review. This makes available data a narrow sample of the total cases.

Having said all that, the available numbers aren't encouraging.

Rape-Homicide Exoneration Rate in the United States

One study determined that the minimum factually wrongful conviction rate (exoneration rate) for rape-homicide alone, in the 1980s, was about 5% (Risinger, 2007). Regarding these findings, it is explained (p. 780):

> Whatever the depth (or shallowness) of one's emotional or moral response to a 3–5% factual innocence error rate in a significant set of

real-world capital cases, it is hard to characterize it as de minimis, or to fairly say that it represents a "remote" possibility of conviction of the innocent. Paleyites often depend on the tenability of such assertions either to make themselves feel better, or to convince the general mass of people that there is no systemic problem of wrongful conviction to be considered, or both....

In addition, Paleyites will find little to comfort them regarding claims that such exonerations are demonstrations of "the system working," or that reversals through the ordinary appellate process take care of the problem of wrongful conviction.

This is consistent with the findings of another study conducted by *Chicago Tribune* reporters Ken Armstrong and Maurice Possley. In 1999, they produced a five-part series reporting on their national study of approximately 11,000 court rulings over 36 years. They found 381 defendants who had their homicide convictions reversed due to prosecutorial misconduct alone (Joy, 2006).

Wrongful Convictions in the United States: 1989–2003

A more inclusive study of exonerations in the United States from 1989 through 2003 (Gross, et al., 2005) provides better detail (p. 524):

Overall, we found 340 exonerations, 327 men and 13 women; 144 of them were cleared by DNA evidence, 196 by other means. With a handful of exceptions, they had been in prison for years. More than half had served terms of ten years or more; 80% had been imprisoned for at least five years. As a group, they had spent more than 3400 years in prison for crimes for which they should never have been convicted—an average of more than ten years each.

Rather than offering a total percentage estimate of wrongful convictions for the time frame examined, this research concluded that for a number of reasons such a task is not feasible, offering an estimate of knowns instead. It also explains where the holes are in the data and, to some extent, why (p. 551):

We can't come close to estimating the number of false convictions that occur in the United States, but the accumulating mass of exonerations gives us a glimpse of what we're missing. We have located 340 exonerations from 1989 through 2003, not counting hundreds of additional exonerated defendants in the Tulia and Rampart scandals and other mass exonerations, or more than seventy convicted childcare sex abuse defendants. Almost all the individual exonerations that we know about are clustered in two crimes, rape and murder. They are surrounded by widening circles of categories of cases with false convictions that have not been detected: rape convictions that have not been reexamined with DNA evidence; robberies, for which DNA identification is useless; murder cases that are ignored because the defendants were not sentenced to death; assault and drug convictions that are forgotten entirely. Any plausible guess at the total number of miscarriages of justice in America in the last fifteen years must be in the thousands, perhaps tens of thousands.

Based on the casework and research of this author, this estimate of the total number of wrongful convictions in the United States appears conservative.

Death Penalty Miscarriage Rate in the United States: 1973–1995

More disturbing is the known miscarriage/error rate for cases of the most serious nature, in which one would expect the best efforts to be made by all involved. This was established by the first study of its kind, conducted on 4,578 state capital (death penalty) cases between 1973 and 1995 (Liebman, et al., 2000; pp. 1846–1850):

Six years in the making, our central findings thus far are these:

- Between 1973 and 1995, approximately 5,760 death sentences were imposed in the United States. Only 313 (5.4%; one in 19) of those resulted in an execution during the period.
- Of the 5,760 death sentences imposed in the study period, 4,578 (79%) were finally reviewed on "direct appeal" by a state high court. Of those, 1,885 (41%) were thrown out on the basis of "serious error" (error that substantially undermines the reliability of the outcome).
- Most of the remainder of the death sentences were then inspected by state post-conviction courts. Although incomplete, our data (reported in A Broken System) reveal that state post-conviction review is an important source of review in some states, including Florida, Georgia, Indiana, Maryland, Mississippi, and North Carolina. In Maryland, for example, at least 52% of capital judgments reviewed in state post-conviction proceedings during the study period were overturned due to serious error; the same was true for at least 25% of the capital judgments that were similarly reviewed in Indiana, and at least 20% of those reviewed in Mississippi.
- Of the death sentences that survived state direct and post-conviction review, 599 were finally reviewed on a first habeas corpus petition during the 23-year study period. Of those 599, 237 (40%) were overturned due to serious error.
- The "overall success rate" of capital judgments undergoing judicial inspection, and its converse, the "overall error-rate," are crucial factors in assessing the efficiency of our capital punishment system. The "overall success rate" is the proportion of capital

judgments that underwent, and passed, the three-stage judicial inspection process during the study period. The "overall error rate" is the frequency with which capital judgments that underwent full inspection were overturned at one of the three stages due to serious error. Nationally, over the entire 1973–1995 period, the overall error-rate in our capital punishment system was 68%.

- Because "serious error" is error that substantially undermines the reliability of the guilt finding or death sentence imposed at trial, each instance of that error warrants public concern. The most common errors found at the state post-conviction stage (where our data are most complete) are (1) egregiously incompetent defense lawyering (accounting for 37% of the state post-conviction reversals), and (2) prosecutorial suppression of evidence that the defendant is innocent or does not deserve the death penalty (accounting for another 16%—or 19%, when all forms of law enforcement misconduct are considered). These two violations count as "serious," and thus warrant reversal, only when there is a "reasonable probability" that, but for the responsible lawyer's miscues, the outcome of the trial would have been different.

The result of very high rates of serious, reversible error among capital convictions and sentences, and very low rates of capital reconviction and resentencing, is the severe attrition of capital judgments.

This means that in the most serious cases, those in which the death penalty was imposed, the court's sentence was overturned approximately 68% of the time because it was wrong—either because of actual innocence or the identification of some other miscarriage of justice causing the sentence to be reduced or vacated entirely.

CAUSAL FACTORS

As already stated at the beginning of this chapter, there are multiple potential origins for any wrongful conviction. Described in Garrett (2008), based on a study of 200 post-conviction DNA exonerations, eyewitness identification and false or misleading forensic evidence top the list (p. 60):[4]

---

[4]In describing a study of DNA exonerations published by the Innocence Project, Joy (2006) ranks the causes of wrongful convictions with similar results: After mistaken identification, the other most common factors leading to wrongful convictions in the first seventy DNA exonerations were: serology inclusion (forty cases), police misconduct (thirty-eight cases), prosecutorial misconduct (thirty-four cases), defective or fraudulent science (twenty-six cases), bad defense lawyering (twenty-three cases), microscopic hair comparison matches (twenty-one cases), false witness testimony (seventeen cases), informants or jailhouse snitches (sixteen cases), and false confessions (fifteen cases).

All were convicted of rape or murder, and all but the nine who pleaded guilty were convicted after a trial. A few predictable types of unreliable or false evidence supported these convictions. The vast majority of the exonerees (79%) were convicted based on eyewitness testimony; we now know that all of these eyewitnesses were incorrect. Fifty-seven percent were convicted based on forensic evidence, chiefly serological analysis and microscopic hair comparison. Eighteen percent were convicted based on informant testimony and 16% of exonerees falsely confessed.

Though not a complete list, causal factors in wrongful convictions tend to include one or more of the following:

1. Incorrect eyewitness identification
2. False or misleading expert testimony
3. Misrepresented or misunderstood evidence
4. False confessions
5. False testimony from "jailhouse" informants
6. Ineffective/incompetent defense counsel
7. Prosecutorial misconduct

For the purposes of this work, we confine our discussion to the top contributors: incorrect eyewitness identification and false or misleading forensic evidence. However, the examples adduced tread into other causes.

Incorrect Eyewitness Identification

Eyewitness identifications occur when witness to a crime, or crime-related event, provides a report to authorities that he or she recognizes a person or his or her physical features, such that the witnesses can unequivocally name the person, or accurately "recognize" that person, at a later time. Either the eyewitness knows the person, has regular contact with him or her, or recalls the person to such a level of detail that he or she is able to point out the person to authorities in public, pick the person out of a physical line-up, or pick the person out of a photo line-up.

Myriad studies have explored the strengths and weaknesses of eyewitness identification. At the end of the day, it all comes down to the artfulness of pattern recognition and the tenuousness of human memory. Basically, sometimes eyewitnesses are wrong. As already provided, this fact is the leading cause of wrongful convictions. As explained in Fradella (2006; p. 4):

> There is no truly accurate way to know how frequently mistaken identifications result in wrongful convictions. But, decades of

research on the topic have consistently found that mistaken identification is the leading cause of wrongful convictions. In fact, it is so common that it practically rivals the sum of all other errors that lead to wrongful conviction. For example, between seventy-five and eighty-five percent of the convictions overturned by DNA evidence have involved a mistaken eyewitness. This is likely due to the fact, as the Supreme Court has observed, that "despite its inherent unreliability, much eyewitness identification evidence has a powerful impact on juries…. All evidence points rather strikingly to the conclusion that there is almost nothing more convincing than a live human being who takes the stand, points a finger at the defendant, and says, 'That's the one!'" Yet, studies have repeatedly shown a roughly forty percent rate of mistaken identifications. In spite of this, nearly 80,000 suspects are targeted every year based on an eyewitness identification.

The problems with eyewitness identifications, from a legal/forensic and cognitive perspective, are described in Overbeck (2005), which provides a tour of the confounding variables (pp. 1805–1904):

> Few kinds of evidence are as compelling, or as damning, as eyewitness testimony: A human being, frequently a victim, takes the stand, looks at the defendant, and says, "He did it." Eyewitness testimony is a staple element of criminal cases. In 1999, eyewitness identifications led to 75,000 prosecutions in the United States….
>
> From a jury's perspective, eyewitness testimony is one of the most persuasive forms of evidence. Nevertheless, psychological studies have indicated that even the most sincere eyewitnesses are frequently inaccurate. Various factors, such as the passage of time, the introduction of new information, and the identification procedures used by the police, can influence the accuracy of eyewitness accounts. Many jurors are unaware of the weaknesses of eyewitness testimony, and thus routinely over credit it, which can lead to wrongful convictions.
>
> A. Juror Reliance on Eyewitnesses
>
> Eyewitness testimony can be extremely persuasive in the courtroom, particularly in criminal trials. In an experimental setting, the introduction of eyewitness testimony has been shown to increase conviction rates dramatically. In mock trials conducted by Elizabeth Loftus, jurors were four times more likely to convict when they heard eyewitness testimony than when they did not. Even when a defense attorney attacked the witness's credibility on cross-examination, conviction rates remained very high.

This study indicates that jurors place substantial weight on eyewitness identification. In fact, jurors place more weight on eyewitness testimony than on many other types of evidence, including fingerprint evidence. Therefore, it is of paramount importance that witnesses are accurate, or at least that jurors are able to detect when they are inaccurate. Unfortunately, neither occurs often.

B. Eyewitnesses Are Frequently Inaccurate

Lawyers and judges have long been concerned with eyewitness accuracy. In an oft-cited passage from *United States v. Wade*, the Supreme Court noted that "the vagaries of eyewitness identification are well-known; the annals of criminal law are rife with instances of mistaken identification." Since the 1970s, a growing body of psychological research has been available to add to the debate. Some of the major psychological findings are outlined below.

1. Accuracy of Memories Over Time

One factor that can influence eyewitness accuracy is the simple passage of time. Memory does not diminish at a uniform rate. Rather, we forget at a rapid rate immediately following an event, and the rate of forgetting then diminishes over time. This is called the "forgetting curve." Thus, even if an eyewitness testifies shortly after an event, her memory may already be substantially diminished.

Furthermore, what happens in the time between the observation and the recall of an event can influence, and even change, a person's memory of it. Witnesses frequently encounter new information after they experience an event. This information can come from other witnesses, investigators, attorneys, or any number of other sources. Post-event information can enhance or compromise a witness's memory. For example, suggesting a fact, such as the presence of a stop sign at the scene of an accident, greatly increases a witness's chances of remembering it, whether it was there or not.

If witnesses encounter additional information that conflicts with their memory of an event, and therefore cannot be easily assimilated into the existing memory, they will compromise between the new information and the information they remember, creating a new memory. Sometimes compromise is impossible, such as when a witness sees a stop sign but is later told it was a yield sign. Witnesses will then frequently "adjust" their memories to be consistent with the subsequent information, rather than with what they originally perceived.

2. Stress, Violence, and Weapon Focus

Stress can affect a witness's original perception of an event as well as her subsequent recall of the event. Stress and other forms of emotional provocation can improve perception to some extent, but when stress levels get too high, they can impair a witness's ability to assess the situation accurately. Violence is one major factor that causes stress for eyewitnesses of crimes, particularly victims. Researchers have found that both men and women recall violent events with much less accuracy than non-violent ones. The presence of a weapon further undermines a witness's ability to remember events. Witnesses focus on the weapon more frequently and for longer periods than other objects in the scene. This phenomenon is called "weapon focus." As a result of weapon focus, witnesses spend less time focusing on other details of the crime, including the appearance of the assailant. This may result in less accurate eyewitness identifications.

3. Witness Confidence

Common sense may suggest that the more confident a witness is, the more likely it is that her memory is accurate. However, psychological research has shown little or no correlation between eyewitness confidence and accuracy. In some studies, researchers asked eyewitnesses how confident they were in their ability to make a positive identification before viewing a lineup. This pre-identification confidence proved to be a poor predictor of the witnesses's actual ability to identify the correct suspect in the lineup. Other studies asked eyewitnesses about their confidence levels after they had viewed a lineup and made an identification. The correlation between post-identification confidence and accuracy was only slightly higher than that for pre-identification confidence. Some studies have shown no relationship at all between confidence and accuracy, and some even suggest a negative correlation—that witnesses can be more confident when they are inaccurate than when they are accurate.

In addition, witness confidence is subject to outside influences. Witnesses who are questioned repeatedly become more confident in their accounts, regardless of accuracy. Those who are told they have identified the "correct" suspect also become more confident. Similarly, briefing eyewitnesses about cross-examination—including the likelihood that opposing counsel will attempt to discredit them—increases eyewitness confidence, accuracy notwithstanding. Furthermore, if a witness believes that she is not the only eyewitness, information about another witness's identification can have a dramatic effect on her confidence.

Taken together, this research indicates that although juries often consider eyewitness confidence in weighing credibility, confidence is an unreliable indicator of accuracy, and can be influenced by factors bearing no relation to the accuracy of a witness's identification.

4. Unconscious Transference

The phenomenon of unconscious transference occurs when a witness has seen an individual in one situation, and then incorrectly recalls seeing that person in a second situation. For example, a person in a lineup may look familiar to the witness, and the witness may unconsciously interpret this familiarity as stemming from the crime. The familiar person may, however, only have been an innocent bystander, someone the witness saw just prior to the crime, or even someone the witness saw at an entirely different time from the crime. An illustration of this point from an early study involved a railroad ticket agent who identified a sailor as the person who held him up at gunpoint. The sailor had an airtight alibi. It turned out that the sailor was stationed at a base near the railroad, and the ticket agent had sold him tickets on several prior occasions. The ticket agent recognized his face, and remembered him as the perpetrator. This could happen in any eyewitness identification situation, but is particularly likely in situations where witnesses view more than one photo array or lineup. An eyewitness may see someone for the first time in an initial lineup, but if that same person is present in a second lineup, the witness could "unconsciously transfer his or her visualization of the subject…and incorrectly identify the subject in the second lineup."

5. Cross-Racial Identifications

People are generally better at recognizing the faces of people who are the same race as they are. Witnesses identify same-race faces correctly more often, and falsely identify them less often. There is substantial psychological research to support the existence of this phenomenon, but there is little indication of why this is the case. One theory is that people have more experience with their own race, and therefore are better able to recognize same-race faces than different-race faces. However, numerous studies have shown that witnesses with substantial exposure to another race were no better at recognizing different-race faces. Another theory is that racial prejudice may influence eyewitness identification of different-race faces, but psychological research has found that racial attitudes have no impact on accuracy. Regardless of the cause, reduced accuracy in cross-race identifications is highly relevant in any trial involving an eyewitness of a different race than the defendant.

C. Juries Do Not Know That Eyewitnesses Are Inaccurate

Perhaps most importantly, psychological studies also illustrate that most people do not have a good understanding of the factors that influence the accuracy of eyewitness identifications. A number of studies have focused on potential jurors' understanding—or misunderstanding—of these factors. These studies, conducted across different populations, indicate that potential jurors generally do not understand the influence these factors have. For example, only slightly more than half of the Americans surveyed were aware that people have more difficulty identifying people of other races than people of their own race. Potential jurors are similarly unaware that viewing a person's picture in a photo array will increase the chances of picking that person out of a lineup. Furthermore, many people surveyed grossly overestimated a witness's ability to retain memories. These results offer a glimpse into lay misperception about eyewitness accuracy.

Rather than focusing on awareness of various factors, many recent studies seek to evaluate how well jurors actually judge eyewitness accuracy. In these studies, mock jurors read descriptions of prior eyewitness identification studies, and are asked to predict the accuracy of the resulting eyewitness identifications. For example, the mock jurors are told that in the prior study, the witnesses observed a "crime" and later made an eyewitness identification. The mock jurors are also told about any variables involved, for instance that some of the witnesses would see a perpetrator of their own race, and that some would see a perpetrator of a different race, or that some witnesses had seen the perpetrator appear in prior lineups. The mock jurors then predict the accuracy of the eyewitness identifications, based on the witness's particular conditions. Across several studies, the mock jurors repeatedly predicted a higher level of accuracy than the witnesses had actually demonstrated in the previous experiments. These prediction studies indicate that jurors consistently overestimate the accuracy of eyewitness identifications. Given the relationship between faulty eyewitness identifications and false convictions, educating juries about the weaknesses of eyewitness testimony is extremely important.

Based on these considerations, it is not unreasonable to argue that providing any forensic interpretations on eyewitness testimony alone is a substandard practice—requiring an assumption of accuracy and reliability that is not warranted. Eyewitness statements should be considered as part of a forensic analysis only when they can at least in part be corroborated by the established facts, or a reconstruction of the physical evidence.

CASE EXAMPLE:

A Perfect Storm of Causal Factors

Consider the case of Ronald Williamson out of Ada, Oklahoma. Taken from the court record (*Williamson v. Ward*, 1997):

> The murder occurred in 1982 in the small town of Ada, Oklahoma. The victim, twenty-one year old Debra Sue Carter, was found dead in her apartment. The door had been broken open and the crime scene showed signs of a struggle. The police found a washcloth forced into Ms. Carter's mouth and a ligature around her neck. The police concluded that Ms. Carter had been sexually assaulted, and suffocated. The police recovered latent fingerprints, hair, and body fluids from the scene, and found a bloody fingerprint on the wall of the bedroom in which the body was located. The only latent prints identified were those of the victim and an Ada police detective who investigated the crime. In a 1983 report, a state fingerprint expert concluded that the bloody print did not match that of the victim or of Mr. Williamson, who was a suspect by that time.
>
> Ms. Carter had worked at the Coachlight Club. The murder took place after she left the Club in the early morning hours of December 8, 1982. Mr. Williamson was known to frequent the Club with Dennis Fritz, and one witness placed Mr. Williamson at the Club the night of the murder. Mr. Williamson was first interviewed by the authorities in March 1983. He denied any involvement and agreed to provide hair and saliva samples. His mother stated that he was home by 10:00 p.m. the night of the murder. Mr. Williamson was interviewed several additional times in 1983 by both the Ada police and agents from the Oklahoma State Bureau of Investigation (OSBI), and he took two inconclusive polygraph examinations. He continued to assert that he knew nothing about the crime.
>
> From October 1984 through January 1985, Mr. Williamson was incarcerated in the Pontotoc County Jail on an unrelated bad-check charge. In August 1985, Charles W. Amos of the Mental Health Services of Southern Oklahoma determined that Mr. Williamson was not competent to stand trial on this charge, and in September the state district judge in that case ruled him incompetent and sent him to Eastern State Hospital. In October, Dr. R.D. Garcia, Chief Forensic Psychiatrist at Eastern State Hospital, issued an opinion stating that Mr. Williamson was competent and returned him for trial. In February 1986, Terri Holland, who had been incarcerated in the Pontotoc County Jail while Mr. Williamson was held there a year earlier, informed the District Attorney that she had heard Mr. Williamson confess to the murder when they were in jail together. On May 1, 1987, the victim's body was exhumed and another set of her fingerprints was obtained. The state fingerprint expert then changed his opinion and concluded that the bloody print found on the bedroom matched that of the victim. Mr. Williamson was arrested on May 8. On May 9, after being held in the Pontotoc County Jail for twenty-four hours, Mr. Williamson gave a statement to Agent Gary Rogers of the OSBI describing a dream in which he had committed the murder. Mr. Williamson also related the contents of a similar dream to a Pontotoc County jailor on May 22. Neither of these statements was recorded. In September 1987, another man, Ricky Jo Simmons, confessed to killing Ms. Carter in a statement that was videotaped by police. Mr. Williamson was tried and convicted in April 1988.

Details regarding Mr. Williamson's defense, trial, and exoneration are taken from Uphoff (2006; pp. 763–764):

> Ronald Williamson was one indigent defendant who had no choice but to go to trial with an attorney who was woefully unprepared to do so. His attorney, W.B. Ward, was a sole practitioner appointed to defend Williamson

Continued

CASE EXAMPLE: *CONTINUED*

in a capital murder case. His appointed co-counsel withdrew shortly before trial so Ward tried the case alone. He did not receive any investigative or expert services and was paid a total of $3,200 for his efforts. Ward explained to the trial judge that he had to make a living and could not spend any more time than was necessary on this case. Unfortunately, the time Ward spent investigating Williamson's case was far from adequate. Despite being aware of some of Williamson's psychiatric history, Ward failed to investigate his mental condition. Had he done so, he would have discovered that Williamson had a long history of mental illness that left him delusional with a distorted perception of reality. Although Williamson's dream confession to the police was a major part of the prosecution's case, Ward failed to challenge it and the jury never learned of Williamson's mental condition. Nor did the jury learn that another man, Ricky Simmons, confessed to the crime. Based on his dream confession, the testimony of a jailhouse informant, and some questionable hair comparison testimony,

the jury convicted Williamson at trial and sentenced him to death.

Five days before Williamson was to be executed, the federal district court issued a stay and subsequently overturned his conviction. Based on counsel's inept performance, the Tenth Circuit Court of Appeals agreed that Williamson's conviction should be reversed and ordered a new trial. While he was awaiting retrial, Williamson's DNA was tested and he was cleared of any involvement in the murder.

This case involved a false confession inferred from a dream (not the first such case by any stretch), a jailhouse informant, misleading scientific testimony, ineffective defense counsel, and concealment of potentially exculpatory evidence from the jury—namely the actual confession of Ricky Simmons.

It also highlights the failure of the court system to provide adequate funding in a capital murder case, for defense counsel or private forensic experts. As such, it underscores the reality that causal factors can surround a case and attack it from all directions. This weighs more in favor of an overall systemic influence on the initial wrongful conviction and death sentence than merely a series of honest mistakes.

FORENSIC EXPERTS AND WRONGFUL CONVICTIONS

As careful students will note from chasing down the references at the end of this chapter, much has been written on the subject of wrongful convictions. Its history, extent, causes, victims, and costs are much debated in the literature. Yet very little in the way of conciliatory writing or coverage actually comes from those in the forensic community who have participated in wrongful convictions, nor have those in the forensic community engaged in significant self-reflection on the subject (for a discussion, see, generally, Turvey, 2013).

More disturbing, there is a portion of the forensic community that does not dwell on its role in the courtroom—as though this is strictly a place of laws, lawyers, and lawyering where they have no say about what is said. We see it in forensic examiners who have heard of but not actually read *Brady v. Maryland* (1963) and *Melendez-Diaz v. Massachusetts* (2009)—with no understanding of when they must show up in court and what they are lawfully required to disclose; we see it in forensic examiners who consider it the responsibility of attorneys to ask them the right questions in order to unlock favorable testimony—with no perceived duty to prevent false impressions being left in the minds of jurors about the limitations of their findings; we see it in forensic examiners who are illiterate with respect to the laws of evidence and professional ethical standards that bind them when giving expert testimony; we see it in forensic examiners who cling to unreal claims of forensic infallibility, despite being unable to define the scientific method or how they applied it to their findings when asked under oath. Such indifference to the rules of science and law is nothing short of contempt toward the criminal justice system itself and one's role in it. Such indifference is the hallmark of faulty forensic science in wrongful convictions.

Thornton (1994) provides a warning meant primarily for those forensic examiners who do not understand their role in court, or that the mandates of science require a great deal more than the court may want or require (p. 483):

> Every scientist understands that there are courts of law. By and large, they are accorded respect. I am not as certain that every lawyer understands that there are courts of science as well. They are not as easily identified because they do not exist in a particular point in space, nor is there one man or woman in a black robe that symbolizes the court, nor a marble anteroom outside smelling of urine and industrial strength disinfectant. Courts of science are constructs of the mind which bring clarity and coherency to scientific and technical matters. They are built not of marble, but from the scientific method. Every scientist is expected to serve as his or her own presiding judge, and if a costume is necessary, it is a white lab coat instead of a black robe. But these courts have certain rules also, just as courts of law. And the scientist who declines to practice his or her profession by the rules of science will soon find that he or she has earned only the derision of his or her colleagues, and eventually finds that he or she cannot continue to practice at all.
>
> A scientist who cannot practice successfully in the courts of science has no business in the courts of law.

Forensic examiners, consequently, have a duty to know and practice within the bounds of the law, as well as within scientific standards. This requires knowing the letter and spirit of both.

Scientific Fact versus Legal Truth

Despite the bizarre positions of some jurists, the superior court (aka trial court) is not the final arbiter of fact. Rather, it determines legal facts and truths—until the next legal cycle. Any position to the contrary ignores the reality of the appellate court, which can reverse superior court decisions. It also ignores state supreme courts, which can reverse the appellate court. From a truth-seeking standpoint, it also ignores the aforementioned advent of DNA exonerations, proving every day that many in the United States are found legally guilty in court while being factually innocent of the crime.

In this way, we cleave scientific fact from legal truth. As we have learned, *legal truth* is a function of the prevailing judgments in a given court that are susceptible to review, revision, and even reversal. It is a matter of law, which is dynamic. *Scientific fact* is determined using the scientific method and exists in a sphere independent of the court. No legal finding can change a scientific fact; it can only rule on its admissibility. However, the opposite occurs on a regular basis.

A fairly useful discussion regarding the intersection of law and science is provided in Thornton (1983), as well as a reminder regarding the abuse of scientific testimony (pp. 86–88):

> Law and science on occasion have conflicting goals, each having developed in response to different social and intellectual needs. The goal of law is the just resolution of human conflict, while the goal of science traditionally has been cast, although perhaps too smugly, as the search for "truth." Certainly there is nothing intrinsically dichotomous in the pursuit of these goals; the court or jury strives in good faith to determine the truth in a given situation as a way to resolve conflicts. But proof is viewed somewhat differently by law and science, as is the application of logic and the perception of societal values.
>
> Numerous writers have commented on these differences, including Glanville Williams in his *Proof of Guilt* (1958): "The principles of [the legal system] are not the product of scientific observation, but embody a system of values. These values do not necessarily have to be changed with the march of knowledge of the material world.... The rule conferring upon an accused the right not to be questioned...may be a good or a bad rule, [but it] has certainly not been made better or worse by the invention of printing or the aeroplane."
>
> ...
>
> How, then, do these differences between law and science lead to abuse of forensic science? They do simply because all the players want to win and are likely to use any ethical means at their disposal to do so. The attorneys in a case are aligned with only one side, and it is entirely appropriate under the adversary system for them to advocate a particular point of view, even without full and fair disclosure of all relevant facts. Subject only to the rules of evidence, the rules of

procedure, and the Code of Professional Responsibility, attorneys are free to manipulate scientific evidence to maximize the opportunity for their side to prevail. Not only is behavior of this sort countenanced by the law, it is the ethical responsibility of counsel to attempt to do so.

With this in mind, forensic examiners must not only anticipate but rather expect that their findings and related testimony will be, at best, misrepresented by attorneys making arguments on both sides once they have left the witness stand. It is consequently their scientific obligation to report findings and testify in such a manner as to prevent this from happening whenever possible (Turvey, 2013).

Faulty Forensics

The defining quality of a *forensic expert* is the possibility that he or she will be called upon to present his or her findings, under penalty of perjury, in a court of law. Subsequently, the forensic expert will be asked to explain to the court what those findings mean and how he or she came to them. Those experts whose work does not bring them into court are not forensic in nature. As provided in Thornton and Peterson (2007; p. 3):

> The single feature that distinguishes forensic scientists from any other scientist is the certain expectation that they will appear in court and testify to their findings and offer an opinion as to the significance of those findings. The forensic scientist will testify not only to what things are, but to what things mean. Forensic science is science exercised on behalf of the law in the just resolution of conflict.

The unique role of the forensic expert is that of educator to attorneys, judges, and juries. The trust extended to such experts by the court under these circumstances is not trivial. Results of their examinations and any related opinions can greatly influence the outcome of a trial. In civil matters, reputations and fortunes may be lost or won. In criminal matters, nothing less than the life and liberty of the accused is at stake. A convincing forensic expert with favorable findings or opinions can be terribly compelling to a judge or jury, and thus tip the scales for either side.

The majority of forensic scientists and other forensic experts take their court responsibilities seriously, and the quality of their work reflects integrity to the evidence. Of course, flaws and fallibility are arguably an integral facet of human nature, and subsequently every human endeavor. They are to be expected, admitted, and addressed. However, the ongoing research of this author continues to uncover a steady stream of forensic experts willing to provide sworn expert testimony or reports to the court that contain deceptive or misleading findings and opinions. Separate from error born of accident and human fallibility, these are instances of forensic fraud. As described in Thompson (2000):

> In addition to honest mistakes born of incompetence and overwork, there are continuously uncovered examples of fraud: the lab analyst, believing that the verdict justifies the means, willing to lie on the stand or fake test results.

As discussed in Turvey (2013; p. 5): "*Forensic fraud* occurs when forensic examiners provide sworn testimony, opinions, or documents (e.g., affidavits, reports, or professional resumes) bound for court that contain deceptive or misleading information, findings, opinions, or conclusions, deliberately offered in order to secure an unfair or unlawful gain." Forensic fraud is not a matter to be taken lightly. As discussed in Saks (2001), it is a breach of both professional ethics and the law:

> Where a proffered expert knows himself or herself to be a quack or otherwise to be offering false testimony, the situation is like that of any other witness who is perpetrating a fraud on the court. Such acts are illegal as well as unethical.

A fraudulent expert of any kind is certainly unreliable, and certainly not to be extended the trust and confidence of the court. Such an expert betrays the trust of his or her client, the court, and the public and contributes directly to the victimization of the innocent. But we must remember that the fraudulent expert is more than just a liar, and more than just unreliable; he or she is also criminal.

Furthermore, forensic fraud has consequences. As explained in Turvey (2013; p. 116): "Forensic fraud has an undeniably devastating impact: it destroys the reputations of the forensic examiners involved, if not their careers; it erodes public confidence in the institutions where they are employed; it can result in overturned convictions, individual and institutional liability, and costly civil judgments; and it is corrosive to the collective faith in the justice system as a whole." The expenses related to forensic fraud are incalculable, but discussed generally in Turvey (2013), which provides that there is (p. 189) "a significant impact with respect to expenses necessarily related to reviewing [affected] cases and hiring/training new employees incurred by employers; a significant impact on the financial cost and credibility to the justice system related to cases that must be overturned and perhaps retried; a significant impact on forensic services as laboratory caseloads must be shifted due to suspensions, terminations, and closures; and a significant impact on the financial cost to those individuals, agencies, and governments that incur civil liability."

As described, the consequences of forensic fraud for all concerned are weighty, to say nothing of the potential contributions to wrongful convictions. As a result, those of authority within forensic communities (institutions, agencies, and organizations) continue to downplay instances of demonstrable forensic fraud as isolated events rather than a significant problem. Certainly biased toward protecting the forensic professions from criticism, this may not be the most accurate interpretation.[5]

Consider the findings published in Cooley (2007; pp. 390–395):

> Contrary to what many forensic examiners profess, there is an unmistakable correlation between overturned convictions and erroneous and/or fraudulent forensic science. To date, there have been 204 convictions thrown out or overturned because post-conviction DNA tests either conclusively exonerated a previously convicted person or cast such serious doubts on the State's case the State moved to have the defendant released and all charges dismissed. While a number of these flawed convictions stem from eyewitness misidentifications, false confessions, jailhouse snitches, and incompetent defense counsel, there is a discernible association between these cases and defective and/or fraudulent forensic science.
>
> In many of these cases, forensic examiners, particularly hair analysts, offered opinions which new DNA tests later proved wrong. Besides hair misidentifications, convictions have been vacated or overturned due to misidentified fingerprints, fabricated fingerprints, misleading testimony, misinterpreted firearms evidence, miscalculated DNA statistics, forensic fraud, misinterpreted drug evidence, misidentified bite marks, faulty blood testing, misinterpreted burn patterns, misidentified earprints, misidentified handwriting, and erroneous autopsy conclusions. More significantly, courts have vacated death sentences and capital convictions because of botched autopsies, misleading testimony, misidentified bootprints, erroneous burn pattern interpretations, misidentified hair evidence, misidentified bite marks, forensic fraud, and erroneous firearms identifications. Additionally, innocent people have been wrongly accused of serious offenses like murder, rape, and train bombings because of misidentified fingerprints, misidentified firearms, misidentified shoe prints, misidentified bite marks, erroneously interpreted burn patterns, and misinterpreted autopsy results. Likewise, there are several cases currently pending in state post-conviction or federal habeas corpus which not only raise significant questions regarding the defendant's guilt and/or death sentence, but the forensic evidence used to secure the conviction,

---

[5]The only published research of forensic fraud (Turvey, 2003; and Turvey, 2013) found that forensic fraud was committed primarily on behalf of the prosecution, and most often by law enforcement crime lab personnel. This suggests that bias is associated with employment by the police or prosecution.

death sentence, or both. Finally, there is evidence that suggests erroneous or unsubstantiated forensic science played a role in an innocent person's execution.

While many of these errors can and will be labeled as honest human errors, this does not diminish the fact that an unacceptable number of errors could have been avoided had the forensic science community: (1) been properly funded; (2) conducted adequate research; and (3) properly trained its examiners. Besides being emotionally and psychologically devastating for the wrongly accused or convicted person and the victims, wrongful accusations and convictions are economically disastrous because they typically generate extensive litigation resulting in large financial settlements.

These findings are echoed more recently by research published in Garrett (2008; pp. 81–86):

Forensic evidence was the second leading type of evidence supporting these erroneous convictions. In many cases, little more than flimsy forensic evidence supported the conviction. Some had more than one type introduced. One hundred and thirteen cases (57%) involved introduction of forensic evidence at trial, with serological analysis of blood or semen the most common (79 cases), followed by expert comparison of hair evidence (43 cases), soil comparison (5 cases), DNA tests (3 cases), bite mark evidence (3 cases), fingerprint evidence (2 cases), dog scent identification (2 cases), spectrographic voice evidence (1 case), shoe prints (1 case), and fiber comparison (1 case).

The forensic evidence was often fairly central to the prosecution's case even though it may have been known to have limited probative power at the time of trial. For example, exonerations in cases involving serology may not show misconduct, but rather either the limitations of old-fashioned serology as compared with more advanced DNA testing technology or unintentional error in conducting such testing. Serological testing sorts individuals into just a handful of different blood types, typically using the A, B, and H antigens, each shared by high percentages of the population; for example, approximately 40% of the population possesses only the H antigen, making them the O type. In contrast, DNA testing can provide random match probabilities greater than all humans who have ever lived (for example, one in 100 trillion).

Despite its relative lack of probative power, serological evidence was often all that law enforcement could use at the time of the investigation. In this group of cases, which chiefly consist of rape convictions in the pre-DNA era, serological evidence was the most common type of forensic evidence introduced at trial, and it typically involved analysis of materials from a rape kit prepared after an assault.

Serological evidence was usually not the only evidence at trial—though in one case the serological evidence was the central evidence at trial and in another case serology and hair evidence were the central evidence at trial. In forty-six of the exonerees' cases (23%), there was an eyewitness identification added to the serological evidence. In four cases, the serology was added to a confession. In three more it was added to alleged self-inculpatory remarks. In two cases, the serological evidence was added to informant testimony. Thus, despite its typical lack of probative power, serological evidence often bolstered other evidence at trial.

Many, and perhaps most, cases, however, appear to have involved not merely use of evidence with limited probative value, but the improper use of then-existing forensic science. To a surprising extent, the forensic testimony at trial was improper based on science at the time. A preliminary review of serological testimony during these exonerees' trials disclosed that more than half involved improper testimony by forensic examiners.

The second most common type of evidence in these cases, visual hair comparison testimony, is notoriously unreliable. Absent any data regarding probabilities that hair or fiber may match visually, experts can make only a subjective assessment whether two hairs or two fibers are "consistent" and share similarities. Forty-three cases (22%) involved false visual hair or fiber comparison. Hair evidence was used in forty-two cases. In some cases that visual hair comparison evidence was particularly central to the prosecution's case. Calvin Scott spent twenty years behind bars based largely on hair comparison evidence alone, in a case where the victim did not get a good look at her attacker and could not identify Scott. In eleven cases, visual hair comparison testimony was added to eyewitness testimony as evidence of identity. In five cases, hair comparison testimony and an informant were presented at trial.

Just as with the serological cases, a preliminary review suggests that microscopic hair comparison testimony at trial often distorted or misstated the forensic evidence to inflate its probative significance. Errors were due not merely to the underlying unreliability of visual hair comparison, but were at a minimum compounded by improper and misleading testimony regarding comparisons conducted. Most commonly, state experts mischaracterized their results by purporting to "match" hairs or constructing the probability of such a match, rather than merely visually comparing hairs and either observing certain similarities or excluding any common source. For example, in the case of Paul D. Kordonowy, convicted of rape where the victim did not see her assailant, the conviction rested on forensic evidence. Montana Forensic Science Laboratory specialist Arnold Melnikoff did not correctly explain the lack of probative power of hair comparison. Instead, he testified that he could distinguish head hairs in 99 of 100 cases, telling the jury that Kordonowy's hair and blood type matched those found at the scene. In fact, an enzyme in the blood sample did not match Kordonowy, nor did the hairs, and yet Melnikoff's testimony contributed to Kordonowy's wrongful imprisonment for thirteen years. Melnikoff was later fired, but not before he falsified testimony in at least one other case. In the case of Jimmy Ray Bromgard, Melnikoff used made-up probabilities that he then improperly multiplied as follows: "[T]he odds were one in one hundred that two people would have head hair or pubic hair so similar that they could not be distinguished by microscopic comparison and the odds of both head and pubic hair from two people being indistinguishable would be about one in ten thousand."...

Each of three cases in which faulty DNA evidence was introduced at trial involved experts who offered misleading testimony and mischaracterized their own laboratory reports. Two cases involved improper analysis and testimony that resulted in false inclusions. In one case, that of Gilbert Alejandro, the criminalist claimed a DNA match even though neither he nor anyone else had even conducted the DNA testing.

Bite mark evidence, also notoriously unreliable, was relied on in three cases, in one providing the only evidence of guilt in a capital case. The forensic evidence was rarely challenged with any success on appeal or postconviction, though six exonerees obtained reversals based on challenges to forensic evidence at trial. None of the 113 persons who were convicted based on forensic evidence raised a fabrication of evidence claim under the Due Process Clause. However, some exonerees raised state evidence law claims (15), ineffective assistance claims (11), or prosecutorial misconduct claims (2) to challenge the forensic evidence introduced at trial. These figures represent a total of twenty-five exonerees, or 32% of the seventy-seven cases with written decisions involving convictions based on forensic evidence. One reason for the dearth of challenges to forensic evidence may be that indigent defendants could not afford to hire a forensic expert. Indigent defendants frequently fail to receive funding for such independent experts. Thus, until the DNA testing was done, these exonerees may simply have been unable to show that the forensic evidence at trial was false or unreliable.

In the first published study of scientific testimony by prosecution experts in cases where the defendant was eventually exonerated, Garrett and Neufeld (2009) reviewed the transcripts from 137 trials. They found the following (pp. 1–2):

[I]n the bulk of these trials of innocent defendants—82 cases or 60%— forensic analysts called by the prosecution provided invalid testimony at trial—that is, testimony with conclusions misstating empirical data or wholly unsupported by empirical data. This was not the testimony of a mere handful of analysts: this set of trials included invalid testimony by 72 forensic analysts called by the prosecution and employed by 52 laboratories, practices, or hospitals from 25 states. Unfortunately, the adversarial process largely failed to police this invalid testimony. Defense counsel rarely cross-examined analysts concerning invalid testimony and rarely obtained experts of their own. In the few cases in which invalid forensic science was challenged, judges seldom provided relief.

Examining trial testimony did not reveal the entire picture, however. The authors discovered, upon evaluating "post-conviction review, investigations, or civil discovery" (p. 14), that 13 (10%) of the 137 cases also involved withholding of exculpatory evidence. This included 3 cases that did not involve invalid testimony. Consequently, 85 (63%) of the 137 cases under review involved either invalid scientific testimony or the withholding of exculpatory evidence.

The nature of invalid forensic science testimony reported in Garrett and Neufeld (2009) included the following:

- Non-probative evidence presented as probative
- Exculpatory evidence discounted
- Inaccurate frequency or statistic presented
- Statistic provided without empirical support
- Non-numerical statements provided without empirical support
- Conclusion that evidence originated from defendant without empirical support

With respect to the types of forensic examinations that involved invalid testimony in the 137 cases reviewed (with 10 cases involving more than one type of forensic examination), Garrett and Neufeld (2009) reported the following frequency data:

- Serology: 100 cases reviewed; 57 cases involved invalid testimony
- Hair comparison: 65 cases reviewed; 25 cases involved invalid testimony
- Bite mark comparison: 6 cases reviewed; 4 cases involved invalid testimony
- DNA testing: 11 cases reviewed; 3 cases involved invalid testimony
- Fingerprint comparison: 13 cases reviewed; 1 case involved invalid testimony
- Shoe print comparison: 3 cases reviewed; 1 case involved invalid testimony
- Voice comparison: 1 case reviewed; 1 case involved invalid testimony
- Soil comparison: 6 cases reviewed; 0 cases involved invalid testimony

While not delving into the issue of intent such that accusations of fraud might be levied beyond examiner ignorance and incompetence, this study (1) identifies invalid scientific testimony and the withholding of exculpatory evidence, as significant factors in wrongful convictions; and (2) identifies those specific forensic science examinations and testimony that have caused the most harm to innocent defendants.

The preceding, in concert with the research presented in Turvey (2013), paints an extremely disparaging picture of the forensic community. This includes consideration of forensic practitioners who refuse to concede or address flawed or fraudulent science, those in the criminal justice system that have all but lost faith in forensic experts, and those who count on the willingness of forensic examiners to be exploited. Until these issues are put on the table for serious discussion and specific remedies are brought to bear, those in the forensic community can and will be measured by the weakest links among them with respect to competence and ethics.

CASE EXAMPLE:

Timothy Masters

Consider the case of Timothy L. Masters from Ft. Collins, Colorado, convicted for the 1987 murder of 37-year-old Peggy Hettrick—a crime Masters would have had to commit when he was 15 years old (see Figure 19-3). Taken entirely from the court record in *Colorado v. Masters* (2001):

Late one night in 1987, as the victim walked along a road near a field adjacent to defendant's home, she was subjected to an apparent surprise attack and was stabbed in the back by a person wielding a knife with a five-inch blade. She was dragged more than a hundred feet into the open field and was found by a passerby the next morning. When found, the body had been partially disrobed and had been sexually mutilated with a very sharp instrument, possibly a scalpel. Scratches were evident on one side of her face, and a pool of blood surrounded her body.

During the investigation that morning, police contacted defendant's father at home. Since defendant's bedroom faced the field, and the victim's body could be seen from his bedroom window, the police contacted the fifteen-year-old defendant at his high school concerning the possibility that he had seen the body on his way to school. When the police detective first spoke to defendant and asked him if he knew why the detective was there, defendant nodded and stated that "it had been bothering him" and that he thought he had seen a body as he was walking to catch the bus. He explained that he did not report it because he believed the body to be a mannequin.

Because of his failure immediately to report the victim's body, defendant became a suspect. A consensual search of defendant's bedroom revealed a large collection of survival knives with long blades, one containing a scalpel in its handle, a fillet knife, a machete, and a ninja sword, as well as a suitcase containing pornographic depictions of female anatomy and a large number of drawings and narratives.

These latter written materials had been created by defendant and depicted surprise attacks, gruesome death scenes, and scenes of violence and sex. Some of the drawings depicted persons with scratches across their cheeks with pools of blood surrounding them, and there were scenes of torture, cutting of body parts, and depictions of survival knives with long blades.

CASE EXAMPLE: *CONTINUED*

FIGURE 19-3
The body of Peggy Hettrick, 37, was found in a field. She had been stabbed to death.

A consensual search of defendant's locker and backpack revealed additional drawings and narratives, including two maps of the field and surrounding area and a drawing of a body being dragged by another person.

The murder had taken place almost exactly four years following the death of defendant's mother. Both the victim and the mother had wavy red hair. Defendant did not know the victim, but admitted that he might have seen her around the neighborhood; they lived in the same area and shopped at the same Albertson's supermarket.

During an interrogation following a *Miranda* advisement and waiver, a detective stated to defendant that stabbing someone with a serrated edged knife would cause a lot of damage. Defendant replied, "Yeah, but it would be tough to pull it back out."

Defendant also had stated that the victim was wearing pink shoes. The victim's socks were in fact pink but could not be seen at the crime scene because of the positioning of the body and the arrangement of the clothing.

The detective asked defendant if he had any suggestions concerning investigation

Continued

CASE EXAMPLE: *CONTINUED*

of the case, and defendant said to check the ditch under a particular bridge. Six months later, a survival knife with a serrated edge was found in the ditch very close to the bridge. The coroner opined at trial that the serration on that knife could account for the irregularity in the stab wound in the victim's back that he had observed upon autopsy.

The police investigation did not find any blood matching the victim's on any of defendant's clothing or property. Also, there was no fiber evidence that would link defendant to the murder, and there was no property of the victim or any severed body parts found in defendant's possession. As a result, no charges were filed, and the murder remained unsolved.

Ten years later, the police department consulted a forensic psychologist with expertise in the area of "sexual homicides." The psychologist reviewed the drawings and narratives that defendant had produced, together with the other evidence in the case, and prepared reports containing his opinion. He opined that defendant had killed the victim and, by doing so, had symbolically killed his own mother.

Based on this and the other evidence, defendant was arrested and charged with first degree murder in 1998. The police obtained a search warrant and seized additional drawings and narratives defendant had created following the crime.

By a motion *in limine*, defendant sought to bar the psychologist's testimony and to preclude admission of the drawings and narratives under CRE 404(b). At a hearing on the motion, the psychologist testified at length regarding research in the area of sexual homicide. The psychologist stated that a sexual homicide, *i.e.*, one in which there is sexual activity by the perpetrator, is generally preceded by a triggering event in the emotional life of the perpetrator. He explained that fantasy is the motivation behind sexual

homicides and that a perpetrator's fantasies become a rehearsal for his commission of the crime. He described in detail five different categories of such fantasies and opined how defendant's drawings and narratives fit into each of the five categories.

He opined that the materials reflected a preference for surprise attack, rather than a ruse or seduction; that the materials exhibited "piquerism," *i.e.*, stabbing and slicing as the means of sexually penetrating the victim's body, as demonstrated by defendant's preoccupation with knives and cutting; that the victim resembled defendant's mother in age and hair color, and the killing occurred almost exactly four years after the defendant's mother had died; that the victim was a stranger or, at most, a casual acquaintance; and that defendant perceived himself as a warrior character without empathy or feeling who engaged, through fictional narratives and pictures, in a variety of killings.

The court admitted the drawings and narratives under CRE 404(b), but limited the expert's testimony. The court permitted the psychologist to testify about the concept of sexual homicide and the associated concepts of triggering events, fantasy, and rehearsal fantasy, and allowed him to describe evidence that fit its characteristics. The expert, however, was precluded from giving an opinion that this was a sexual homicide, that defendant fit the characteristics of a sexual homicide perpetrator, that defendant committed the crime, or that any drawing or narrative was evidence that defendant had committed this crime. He was also permitted to testify hypothetically concerning the type of event that might be a trigger for a sexual homicide and to give an opinion that a drawing or narrative defendant had created was an example of one of the categories noted.

Among the other testimony presented at trial was that of defendant's high school teacher and a counselor, who were permitted

CASE EXAMPLE: *CONTINUED*

to testify concerning an incident at school that had happened approximately one month before the victim's murder. The prosecution theorized that this incident was a triggering event for the murder.

According to the court record, the expert hired by the prosecution in this case was Dr. J. Reid Meloy. As explained in Campbell (2008):

Meloy came onto the case in late 1997 after famed FBI criminal profiler Roy Hazelwood recommended him to Fort Collins Police Det. Jim Broderick. Broderick, now a lieutenant, needed professional validity for his theory that Masters' voluminous drawings and short stories not only provided the motive for the brutal 1987 stabbing murder and sexual mutilation of Peggy Hettrick, but the evidence as well.

Meloy seemed happy to oblige. Broderick provided him with crime scene videotapes, police interviews with Masters, police reports, photographs, maps and transcripts. He sent him more than 2,000 pages of Masters' productions. When all was said and done, Meloy was paid more than $52,700 for his work on the case.

…Meloy was interviewed for a 2000 documentary about the case that appeared on the A&E Network's "Cold Case Files." The show is an uncritical ode to how Meloy, Broderick, Gilmore and Blair joined forces to crack the case using something akin to mentalism.

"After spending six months on the case, I felt I understood the motivations for this homicide and that I had become convinced that Timothy Masters was the individual that had committed this homicide," Meloy said on the show.

For Meloy, Masters' drawings represented a "fantasy rehearsal" for the crime, especially a doodle on Masters' math homework of a knife-wielding hand cutting a diamond shape that Meloy interpreted as a vagina, "which may have been a rehearsal of the genital mutilation," as he wrote in his first report to Broderick.

Equally damning in Meloy's interpretation was a picture Masters drew the day after he saw Hettrick's body. It depicted one figure dragging another, which was apparently wounded or dead, from behind. The wounded figure was riddled with arrows and blood seemed to flow from its back.

The figure's heels dug furrows in the ground similar to furrows found where Hettrick's body was dumped.

Entirely discounting the presence of the arrows—which had nothing whatsoever to do with the murder—Meloy wrote in his report that this picture represented the crime as it actually happened.

"This is not a drawing of the crime scene as seen by Tim Masters on the morning of Feb. 11 as he went to school," Meloy wrote. "This is an accurate and vivid drawing of the homicide as it is occurring. It is unlikely that Tim Masters could have inferred such criminal behavior by just viewing the corpse, unless he was an experienced forensic investigator. It is much more likely, in my opinion, that he was drawing the crime to rekindle his memory of the sexual homicide he committed the day before."

Although these two depictions were the most critical in bolstering the prosecution's case, Meloy told the A&E interviewer that the sheer volume of Masters' productions also implicated him.

"Lt. Broderick provided me with approximately 2,200 pages of drawings and narratives produced by this young man before and immediately after the homicide," he said on the TV show. "This is a voluminous amount of material. In my 18 years of doing this kind of work I have never seen such voluminous productions by a suspect in a sexual homicide. And that tells us he was preoccupied with sexual violence, with violence, with sexually sadistic images, with images of domination and degradation of women, and he was also fascinated by knives."

Continued

CASE EXAMPLE: *CONTINUED*

Jolene Blair also commented about this on the show. "It wasn't just the fact that he had these drawings…but the number, the sheer number we found," she said. "What we needed to do is demonstrate that this wasn't just a passing fancy of this kid, this was complete obsession with death, specifically the death of a woman, and try to draw parallels between the drawings and our crime scene."

In court, the jury was bombarded with Masters' scary pictures that were shown on a large video monitor while Meloy pointed out features of them that he testified showed pairing of sex and violence; evidence of "picquerism," the sadistic pleasure derived from stabbing; degradation of women; and fascination with weapons and death.

In his first report to Broderick, Meloy wrote that Masters killed Hettrick because he felt abandoned by his mother, who died unexpectedly almost exactly four years to the day before the murder. He opined that her death, an "emotionally distant" relationship with his father who spent a lot of time away from home while on active duty in the Navy, the departure of his sister from their home to join the U.S. Army, and his retreat into a fantasy world combined to create a boiling kettle of latent violence just waiting to erupt.

"A retreat into such a compensatory narcissistic fantasy world, replete with sexuality and violence, works for a while, but at a great cost," Meloy wrote. "The unexpressed rage continues, depression may ensue, and anger toward women as sources of both pain (abandonment) and erotic stimulation builds."

Peggy Hettrick's random appearance on the road near Masters' house as she walked home from a Fort Collins tavern—according to the prosecution's theory of events—proved the tragic tipping point for this troubled person, in Meloy's view.

"Sexual homicide represents the solution, particularly in the form it took in this case: If I kill a woman, she cannot abandon me;

if I desexualize her (genital mutilation) she cannot stimulate me," he wrote. "These are not conscious thoughts for Tim Masters, but likely represent the unconscious beliefs that drove his behavior the night of Feb. 11, 1987, when he killed and sexually mutilated Peggy Hettrick, a victim of choice and opportunity. Ms. Hettrick represented all Women (sic) to Tim Masters."

On March 26, 1999, a Larimer County jury convicted Masters of first-degree murder, and he was sentenced to life in prison. Two subsequent appeals failed. However, in 2008, DNA testing exonerated him of the crime (see Figures 19-4 and 19-5). As explained in Hughes (2008):

[S]pecial prosecutors appointed to review that case concluded that DNA found on Hettrick's body matches someone else, and excludes the now-deceased Dr. Richard Hammond, another potential suspect.

"It is our belief as special prosecutors in this case that the new evidence meets the constitutional requirements of Rule 35C. That requires a vacation of the original conviction and sentence and entitles Mr. Masters to a new trial," said Adams County District Attorney Don Quick at a hastily called Denver press conference Friday.

Legal observers said it was unlikely that Masters would be tried again in the case.

Quick was appointed as an outside prosecutor because Masters' bid for a new trial centered on accusations that Fort Collins police and Larimer County prosecutors withheld evidence during his case. The two prosecutors in the original case are now Larimer County judges, and the lead police investigator, Lt. Jim Broderick, now runs the police department's Internal Affairs unit.

Several years ago, a new defense team took up Masters' cause and recently submitted DNA evidence found on Hettrick's clothing for independent analysis in The Netherlands.

On Jan. 15, defense lawyers turned over the profile gleaned from that DNA to prosecutors, who compared it with a partial sample they

CASE EXAMPLE: *CONTINUED*

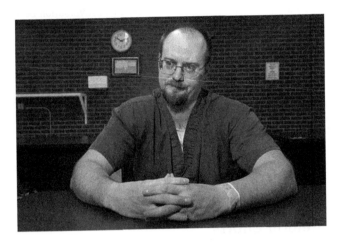

FIGURE 19-4
Timothy Masters, convicted in no small part by his drawings, was freed from prison after his sentence was vacated.

FIGURE 19-5
Masters was released on January 22, 2008.

had developed. The Dutch [DNA] profilers are expected to be at Tuesday's court hearing.

On Friday, after several hours of discussion with officials from the Colorado Bureau of Investigation, Quick decided the new evidence

entitled Masters to a new trial—and demanded further investigation.

The Master's case is far from over, however, as those involved are now under close scrutiny. Among other wrong-doings, the defense team has accused the prosecution of

Continued

CASE EXAMPLE: *CONTINUED*

withholding reports and opinions of experts with contrary opinions, withholding Dr. Meloy's report, and failing to investigate alternate suspects. As explained in Pilsner (2008):

> [The 19th Judicial District Attorney's Office in Weld County] has spent the past few months reviewing Fort Collins Police Lt. Jim Broderick and his actions while investigating Masters for the 1986 murder of Peggy Hettrick.
>
> ...
>
> Broderick faces allegations that he lied while under oath on the stand, illegally taped a conversation between Masters and his father and failed to turn over some of the documents that could have assisted in Masters' defense.
>
> The prosecutors in the Masters case, Terry Gilmore and Jolene Blair, also are being investigated by the state Supreme Court's Office of Attorney Regulation for any misconduct they might have committed during Masters' prosecution.

As of this writing, no other further action has been taken against those accused of misconduct in this case.

Reform Efforts

In an effort to address the overwhelming and costly tide of DNA exonerations and related exoneree lawsuits, which can fetch millions in a civil action against the state, some governments have begun to take steps. This includes the development of Conviction Integrity Units, the development of forensic science commissions, and the previously unheard-of criminal prosecution of district attorneys.

Conviction Integrity Units

A few states and prosecutor's offices have established the equivalent of *Conviction Integrity Units*. These units are intended to re-examine and, in some cases, re-investigate claims of actual innocence in post-conviction. The first such unit was established by District Attorney Craig Watkins of Dallas County, Texas, in July 2007. Other DA's offices followed, including the Brooklyn DA's office in New York—which refers to itself as "the do-over unit" (Hamill, 2013).

Forensic Science Commissions

A few states have funded *forensic science commissions*. They are intended to serve as watchdog organizations to investigate allegations of fraud, misconduct, and negligence in the local forensic science community. They also make recommendations to the legislature. Both Texas and New York have established such statewide commissions.

Criminal Prosecutions for DAs

In a very few cases involving highly publicized miscarriages of justice, there have been equally high-profile criminal prosecutions of the district attorneys responsible. One of the most well-known examples would be dismissal of charges in the Duke LaCrosse case. The case was ultimately dismissed as a false allegation, with the overzealous prosecutor in charge, Mike NiFong, disbarred and convicted of criminal contempt of court. He worked with forensic scientists to hide evidence of suspect guilt and made improper inflammatory statements to the press to bolster his case.

In 2013, the State of Texas passed the Morton Act in response to the high-profile exoneration of Michael Morton and an ongoing investigation into the former prosecutor who oversaw his wrongful conviction, state District Judge Ken Anderson of Williamson County. As reported in Grissom (2013):

> Morton was convicted in 1987 of murdering his wife in Austin. He was exonerated and released from prison in 2011 after DNA testing linked another man to the crime. Morton's lawyers say that Anderson violated Brady rules by withholding crucial evidence that could have pointed to the real killer and prevented the innocent Morton from spending 25 years in prison. Anderson has denied wrongdoing.
>
> "This is a huge first step," Morton said in an interview outside the House gallery. "It will prevent all sorts of abuse." Morton and his wife, Cynthia, looked on as legislators unanimously approved the measures with little discussion. Lawmakers gave him a standing ovation when Thompson introduced him to the chamber. Since his release, Morton has lobbied lawmakers to enact reforms that would prevent his tragedy from befalling others.
>
> In the five decades since the high court issued its Brady ruling, most states have approved laws that require both prosecutors and defense lawyers to exchange evidence. Texas state law, however, does not require prosecutors to provide evidence unless ordered by a court do so.
>
> Under Senate Bill 1611, by state Sens. Rodney Ellis, D-Houston, and Robert Duncan, R-Lubbock, prosecutors would be required to turn over evidence both before trial and after it begins. Senate Bill 825, by state Sen. John Whitmire, D-Houston, would extend the statute of limitations for offenses involving evidence suppression by district attorneys. Under current law, the four-year statute of limitations begins when such offenses occur. Whitmire's bill would start the clock on the statute of limitations at the time a wrongfully convicted defendant is released from prison.

In April 2013, a judge ruled that former Williamson County District Attorney Ken Anderson hid evidence and "acted to defraud the trial court and Morton's defense lawyers, resulting in an innocent man serving almost 25 years in prison" (Lindell, 2013). Subsequently, a warrant was issued for then Judge Anderson's arrest, and he was booked into jail for his offenses; he was released on bail. As of this writing, this case is still making its way through the legal system in Texas.

FREEDOM FOR THE WEST MEMPHIS THREE

Rather than admit fault in one of the most egregious wrongful conviction cases in its history, involving prosecutorial misconduct and faulty forensics alike, the state of Arkansas hashed out a cynical no-fault solution to avoid impending civil liability.

In 1994, Damien Echols, Jason Baldwin, and Jessie Misskelley Jr. (who would come to be referred to as the West Memphis Three; see Figure 19-6) were convicted of murdering three eight-year-old boys: Stevie Branch, Michael Moore, and Christopher Byers. Mr. Echols, tried separately from the other two defendants, received the death penalty. Mr. Misskelley received life plus 20 years, and Mr. Baldwin received life. Throughout the trials, they maintained their innocence.

However, this was not a typical investigation and prosecution. There was sparse funding for the defense during the original trials, and the evidence against the defendants was not just circumstantial but deeply flawed. Other compounding factors included ignorant/ untrained law enforcement investigators; a phony set of false confessions achieved by dubious means and immediately recanted; inflammatory pre-trial publicity against the defendants regarding phony and contrived evidence of satanic rituals; a hostile community (with a lack of venue change); and inappropriately close relationships between the prosecutors, the trial judge, and defense attorneys. To say nothing of the observation that the defense attorneys were not truly murder experienced or death qualified to the level that one would expect (if at all).

Disclosure

This author became involved in the case during post-conviction review. By a twist of fate, he was the first forensic scientist to be hired by the defense to examine the evidence, evaluate the investigation, and reconstruct the crime—ultimately going so far as to offer a profile of the offender responsible (in response to the under-informed and generally inaccurate profile prepared by the FBI's BAU, which was at the time supervised by John Douglas). The author found some pertinent things that had been missed and pointed the defense in some important new directions.

In late October of 1998, the author testified under oath to findings regarding the biased and inept investigation conducted by the police, the flawed conclusions that had been reached about the physical evidence, and the uninformed theories of the case that had been allowed to be put before the jury without competent refutation. This along with other forensic experts for the defense (a forensic pathologist and a forensic odontologist), as part of a Rule 37 hearing to establish that three defendants

FIGURE 19-6
Damien Echols, Jessie Misskelley Jr., and Jason Baldwin pictured at the time of their arrests.

FREEDOM FOR THE WEST MEMPHIS THREE *CONTINUED*

had suffered from Ineffective Assistance of Counsel (IAC). This to support the legal argument that they should be given a new trial with more adequate representation.

This attempt to get a new trial quickly failed. None of us on the ground in West Memphis back in 1998 were surprised. The same judge who appointed defense attorneys, denied funding, and presided over the original trials (David Burnett) also made a point of presiding over every post-conviction hearing. In grading the quality of his own work, it was a foregone conclusion that Judge Burnett would never agree that he had acted improperly, denied vital funding to the defense, or appointed unqualified defense attorneys to represent the defendants.

It is also worth noting that this 1998 post-conviction hearing and the events leading up to it were partially documented in the second of two documentary films about the case by Joe Berlinger and Bruce Sinofsky: *Paradise Lost 2: Revelations.*

New Evidence, a New Judge, and a Devil's Deal

After ten years of investigation, with multiple state's witnesses having recanted, with new DNA testing that points to other suspects, and with a completely new legal team at work, the West Memphis Three were set free on August 19, 2011. The circumstances that led up to their release and the devil's deal that was struck with prosecutors to gain their freedom were a sudden shock to the system for all those out of the legal loop, the author included.

This deal came about because a new judge, David Laser, would be presiding over an evidentiary hearing set for December 2011. The hearing was intended to be a review of all the newly discovered evidence in the case. Scott Ellington, prosecuting attorney for the 2nd Judicial District, made it clear at the time that he believed Judge Laser would have overturned the convictions and granted all three defendants new trials. Moreover, Mr. Ellington believed that those trials would likely result in acquittals for all the defendants (Jared, 2011). The fear of this eventuality, and the cost of wrongful conviction lawsuits, weighed heavily in the decision to make a plea deal before the December hearing, Ellington explained (Jared, 2011).

The devil's deal was this: all three defendants would have their convictions vacated so long as they each agreed to immediately enter an *Alford plea,* at

which point they would be sentenced to time served and released after 18 years of imprisonment.

This unorthodox development has many asking an important question: what's an Alford plea? It also has some ignoring this difficult legal concept and merely stating that the West Memphis Three have pleaded guilty in exchange for release. Having worked as a forensic scientist and testified in courtrooms around the United States since 1996, the author has encountered such plea deals only a few times. Each use was different. Some discussion is warranted, without which it is difficult to understand the kind of justice that has been achieved in this case, if any.

Alford Plea

A useful history of the *Alford plea* is offered in Redlich and Ozdogru (2009; pp. 468–469):

> In brief, Alford pleas allow defendants who do not wish to risk their fates at trial to plead guilty while simultaneously asserting their innocence.
>
> In 1963, Henry C. Alford was accused of first-degree murder in North Carolina. Alford was an African American man in the South at the height of the civil rights movement. His lawyer, who was just a few years out of law school at the time, recently stated it was a case fraught with racial overtones (Barksdale, 2007).
>
> Alford went to visit a prostitute at a drink house and allegedly got into a fight with Nathaniel Young. Young was later killed from a shotgun blast. Despite Alford's claims of innocence, there was seemingly strong evidence of his guilt. Specifically, although there was no eyewitness to the crime, there were witnesses who claimed that shortly before the murder, Alford returned home to get his gun, stated he was going to kill the victim, and then upon returning home, stated that he carried out the killing. Alford also had a lengthy criminal history, including a prior conviction for murder.
>
> At his arraignment, Alford was expected to plead guilty but then testified that he did not kill Young and was pleading guilty only

Continued

FREEDOM FOR THE WEST MEMPHIS THREE *CONTINUED*

to avoid the death penalty. Specifically, Alford stated, "I pleaded guilty on second degree murder because they said there is too much evidence, but I ain't shot no man, but I take the fault for the other man. We never had an argument in our life and I just pleaded guilty because they said if I didn't they would gas me for it, and that is all."

After some discussion that Alford indeed spoke with his attorney and family members about his decision to plead and that he had been informed of his rights, the following exchange occurred between Alford and his attorney:

Attorney: "And you authorized me to tender a plea of guilty to second degree murder before the court?"

Alford: "Yes, sir."

Attorney: "And in doing that, that you have again affirmed your decision on that point?"

Alford: "Well, I'm still pleading that you all got me to plead guilty. I plead the other way, circumstantial evidence; that the jury will prosecute me on—on the second. You told me to plead guilty, right. I don't—I'm not guilty but I plead guilty."

According to published news reports at the time, Alford was unable to read or write (Barksdale, 2007). Despite his claims of innocence, the trial judge allowed Alford to enter a guilty plea and sentenced him to the maximum 30 years for second degree murder. Alford then repeatedly sought relief. Alford's conviction was eventually overturned by the Fourth Circuit Court of Appeals, but then re-affirmed in the now famous Supreme Court decision, *North Carolina v. Alford*, U.S. 400 25 (1970). In this six to three decision, the court recognized that while there are usually two components of pleading guilty—the waiver of the right to a trial and the admission of guilt—the latter is not a constitutional requisite to imposing a criminal sanction. In his dissent, Justice Brennan remarked that Alford was "so

gripped by fear of the death penalty that his decision to plead guilty was not voluntary but was the product of duress as much so as choice reflecting physical coercion" (p. 40). As a result of this landmark decision, defendants can now enter "Alford pleas" (sometimes called "best-interest pleas" or, in New York, Serrano pleas) when they claim to be innocent but perceive their chances for acquittal at trial to be too much of a risk. Alford died in prison in 1975.

According to the U.S. Supreme Court's ruling in *North Carolina v. Alford* (1970): "An individual accused of crime may voluntarily, knowingly, and understandingly consent to the imposition of a prison sentence even if he is unwilling or unable to admit his participation in the acts constituting the crime." The Alford plea is intended as a unique sub-class of guilty plea, where a defendant maintains his or her innocence while simultaneously admitting that the state might be able to convict him or her at trial. In doing so, the defendant accepts the penalties associated with an admission of guilt while declaring his or her innocence—in other words, "pleading guilty without admitting factual guilt" (Gooch, 2010; p. 1757). By contrast, a stronger sub-class of the guilty plea, wherein the court levies legal penalties associated with guilt and the defendant admits neither guilt nor innocence, is the *nolo* or *no contest* plea. These sub-pleas are not, by any stretch, the same as a straightforward admission of guilt, and suggesting otherwise conceals important factual realities.

It is important to recall at this point that scientific fact and legal truths are not at all the same thing, governed by very different rules and realities (Thornton and Peterson, 2007). *Scientific fact* refers to information and events that have been established based on a broad factual record to a reasonable degree of objective scientific certainty by scientists using the scientific method. *Legal truth* refers to information and events that have been established by a court ruling based on a narrow factual record—at the discretion of a judge and/or jury. This is why factually innocent people can get convicted of crimes they did not commit, and the factually guilty can avoid being convicted, depending on what is presented in the courtroom and how it is perceived.

FREEDOM FOR THE WEST MEMPHIS THREE *CONTINUED*

A Strong Factual Basis

A distinguishing feature of the Alford Plea is the requirement of a strong factual basis for accepting the legal consequences of guilt. In other words, as explained in Natapoff (2008; p. 986):

> The Alford court noted that the guilty plea in that case was acceptable in part because the trial court had before it a "strong factual basis for the plea" and "telling evidence of guilt." In other words, even where a defendant declines to invoke the adversarial process in order to contest the government's information, waiver is not enough: guilt still requires some supporting information.

The judge, in accepting an Alford Plea, is required to ensure that such a factual basis exists. As explained in Redlich and Ozdogru (2009; p. 470):

> In theory, courts are supposed to find a sufficient factual basis of guilt before allowing the plea. Although Alford pleas are guilty pleas, with traditional guilty pleas the admission of guilt via the plea itself or the in-court allocution serves as the factual basis. With Alford pleas, however, because the person insists on innocence, the judge must determine there is sufficient evidence of guilt in order to allow the plea. However, as Shipley (1987) argues, 'sufficient' was never defined, guidelines were never forthcoming, and as a result, the pleas are accepted—or not accepted—for a variety of reasons, with differential standards applied. Further, the judge often relies on a summary of the evidence provided only by the state without a similar summary provided by the defense (Shipley, 1987).

This would suggest that while the requirement exists, it is weak in practice because of the necessity of the Alford plea in making certain expedient plea deals.

Alford and the West Memphis Three

The plea deal in this case has been described as the release of hostages in exchange for immunity (from civil wrongful conviction lawsuits). This is an accurate analogy in the author's view. However, questions remain as to whether an Alford plea makes sense for these defendants, under these circumstances (see Figure 19-7).

From the defendants' perspectives, the answer must be an unwavering "yes." Any improvement in their

FIGURE 19-7
Damien Echols, Jessie Misskelley Jr., and Jason Baldwin pictured with their attorneys at the time of their release, at a press conference, on August 19, 2011.

Continued

FREEDOM FOR THE WEST MEMPHIS THREE *CONTINUED*

circumstances at all is an order of magnitude greater than anything that has happened, from a legal perspective, in the past 18 years. Being released and free to live out their lives while still relatively young is also something that is difficult to put a price on. In addition, it allows the defendants to proclaim their innocence and continue legal battles while not constrained by incarceration.

From the perspective of the prosecution, the Alford plea also makes sense. It allows them to claim victory and declare the legal guilt of the defendants without admitting to any of the wrongdoing that the case is well known for. And this is where we run into problems:

1. Alford requires a strong factual basis for guilt to be provided by the prosecution. Given that the state's key witnesses have recanted at this point, that no physical evidence connects the defendants with the crime, and that strong physical evidence suggests other suspects, this Alford requirement is not met. This is actually not my opinion, but the opinion of Scott Ellington, prosecuting attorney for the 2nd Judicial District. He made it very clear in his statement to the press that the lack of evidence and witnesses made acquittals a very real possibility— which is why he agreed to the Alford plea deal.

2. Scott Ellington also made it clear that part of the reason for the plea deal was to avoid having to make massive payouts that would necessarily result from wrongful conviction lawsuits. He even started to do the math in his press conference, counting into the tens of millions. He even stated, explicitly, this decision was based on the math. This would seem to indicate a complete lack of confidence in the state's case.

3. Despite acknowledging the utter absence of evidence of guilt (other than the ability to secure a conviction when the deck is stacked), and that the convictions were likely going to be overturned, Mr. Ellington,

the States' Attorney General, and now the governor of Arkansas have all made clear that they stand behind the convictions and that no further inquiry is required. This position is at odds with the clearly stated reasons for making the deal in the first place— fear of lawsuits and cost (as so eloquently stated by Peter Jackson in his response to the verdicts: "So the West Memphis three are finally released"). And with the anticipated findings of the Judge Laser.

4. Without acknowledging the problems that led to the wrongful convictions of these individuals, reforms will not be possible and further harm may be done by those that have been protected by this deal. And there are many.

It is easy to understand the state's internally conflicted positions as an example of cognitive bias reified. However, this makes their lack of logic no less acceptable. In this case, justice has indeed been negotiated—by extorting Alford pleas from the defendants in exchange for their freedom.

We should expect more from our justice system. In point of fact, we need more from our justice system. Otherwise, we teach our legal professionals and our politicians that justice can be negotiated, and that it is better to save face than admit wrong and let actual criminals escape justice. If those responsible for this plea actually believe that they have let guilty defendants walk free, then it is an affront to justice. The same is true if they are simply making a deal to save face. In either case, it would seem that they are generally unfit for public service.

From the perspectives of criminal justice practitioners and the general public, this agreement should be unacceptable—not just in terms of what an Alford plea legally requires, but what we require from our public servants as well. We should, as they say, consider not just what we kill with these kinds of agreements, but also what we protect and let live.

SUMMARY

Wrongful convictions are not rare. Nor are they a recent historical phenomenon. Known wrongful conviction rates since the 1980s make clear that they actually exist at a volume and frequency that can no longer be denied, ignored, or defended. Although the lead cause if faulty eyewitness identification, forensic error, and fraud are closing the gap at second place. More often than not, these errors and related forensic misconduct tend to favor the prosecution. Consequently, to avoid such bias, forensic victimologists are warned to adopt a scientific mandate with practice standards that embrace objectivity and reliability, and to refrain from report, testimony, or conduct that contributes to furthering the problem—if they wish to be worthy of any trust afforded by the criminal justice system. In an effort to address the overwhelming and costly tide of DNA exonerations and related exoneree lawsuits, some governments have begun to take steps, including the developing of Conviction Integrity Units, the development of forensic science commissions, and the previously unheard-of criminal prosecution of district attorneys.

QUESTIONS

1. True or False: Wrongful convictions can occur despite the best intentions of everyone involved.
2. What are some factors that may lead to false convictions?
3. Explain the difference between *scientific fact* and *legal truth*.
4. What are three factors that can influence the accuracy of eyewitness testimony?
5. List three consequences of forensic fraud.
6. What steps have governments begun to take in an effort to address the overwhelming and costly tide of DNA exonerations and related exoneree lawsuits?
7. Explain when an *Alford plea* would be used by a defendant.

REFERENCES

Barksdale, T., 2007. Piedmont profile—(Not) guilty: Lawyer in case that led to Alford plea says he worried about later questions. Winston Salem Journal, Retrieved June 5, 2007 from http://www.accessmylibrary.com/coms2/summary_0286-30144461_ITM

Bernhard, A., 2004. Justice still fails: a review of recent efforts to compensate individuals who have been unjustly convicted and later exonerated. Drake Law Review 52, Summer; 703–738.

Brady v. Maryland, 1963. U.S. Supreme Court, No. 490 (373 U.S. 83). Decided May 13, 1963.

Campbell, G., 2008. The Tim Masters case: chasing Reid Meloy. Fort Collins Now, February 1; Available at: http://www.fortcollinsnow.com/article/20080201/NEWS/297958975

Colorado v. Masters, 2001. Colorado Court of Appeals, Div. IV., No. 99CA0896. (33 P.3d 1191) Denied March 22, 2001.

Connors, E., Lundregan, T., Miller, N., McEwen, T., 1996. Convicted by Juries, Exonerated by Science: Case Studies in the Use of DNA Evidence to Establish Innocence After Trial. National Institute of Justice, Office of Justice Programs, U.S. Department of Justice, Washington DC, NCJ 161258, June.

Cooley, C., 2007. Forensic science and capital punishment reform: an "intellectually honest" assessment. George Mason University Civil Rights Law Journal 17, Spring; 299–422.

Crowder, S., Turvey, B., 2013. Ethical Justice: Applied Issues for Criminal Justice Students and Professionals. Elsevier Science, San Diego.

Fradella, H., 2006. Why judges should admit expert testimony on the unreliability of eyewitness testimony. Federal Courts Law Review 3, June; 1–46.

Garrett, B., 2008. Judging innocence. Columbia Law Review 108, January; 55–142.

Garrett, B., Neufeld, P., 2009. Invalid Forensic Science Testimony and Wrongful Convictions. Virginia Law Review 95 (1), 1–97.

Gooch, A., 2010. Admitting guilt by professing innocence: when sentence enhancements based on *Alford*. Vanderbilt Law Review 63 (6), 1755–1792.

Grissom, B., 2013. Morton Act, DA accountability bill head to Perry. The Texas Tribune, May 14; http://www.texastribune.org/2013/05/14/house-approves-morton-act-sanctions-prosecutors/

Gross, S., Jacoby, K., Matheson, D., Montgomery, N., Patil, S., 2005. Exonerations in the United States, 1989 through 2003. Journal of Criminal Law and Criminology 95, Winter; 523–559.

Hamill, D., 2013. Brooklyn district attorney's Conviction Integrity Unit reviews possible wrong verdicts to make sure they got it right. New York Daily News, March 25; http://www.nydailynews.com/new-york/hamill-b-klyn-reviews-wrong-convictions-article-1.1298934

Hughes, T., 2008. Masters to go free: prosecutor moves to vacate conviction after DNA linked to former boyfriend. The Fort Collins Coloradoan, January 19; Available at: http://www.coloradoan.com/apps/pbcs.dll/article?AID=/20080119/NEWS01/801190361/1002/CUSTOMERSERVICE02

Jared, G., 2011. Prosecutor: 'We made right call' in WM3 case. Paragould Daily Press, August 23; http://www.paragoulddailypress.com/articles/2011/08/23/local_news/doc4e53ab9e3ee7f111086957.txt

Joy, P., 2006. The relationship between prosecutorial misconduct and wrongful convictions: shaping remedies for a broken system. Wisconsin Law Review, 399–429.

Liebman, J., Rifkind, S., West, V., Lloyd, J., 2000. Capital attrition: error rates in capital cases, 1973–1995. Texas Law Review 78, June; 1839–1865.

Lindell, C., 2013. Judge finds that Anderson hid evidence in Morton murder trial. The Austin Statesman, April 19; http://www.statesman.com/news/news/local/ken-anderson-court-of-inquiry-resumes/nXRLm/

Melendez-Diaz v. Massachusetts, 2009. U.S. Supreme Court. Case No. 07–591, June 25.

Natapoff, A., 2008. Deregulating guilt: the information culture of the criminal system. Cardozo Law Review 30 (3), 965–1021.

Naughton, M., 2005. Redefining miscarriages of justice. British Journal of Criminology 45, March; 165–179.

North Carolina v. Alford (1970) 400 U.S. Supreme Court 25.

Overbeck, J., 2005. Beyond admissibility: a practical look at the use of eyewitness expert testimony in the federal courts. New York University Law Review 80, December; 1895–1920.

Pilsner, J., 2008. Review continues into actions of lead Masters investigator. The Reporter-Herald, May 3; http://www.reporterherald.com/news_story.asp?ID=16561

Redlich, A., Ozdogru, A., 2009. Alford pleas in the age of innocence. Behavioral Sciences and the Law 27, 467–488.

Risinger, D.M., 2007. Innocents convicted: an empirically justified factual wrongful conviction rate. Journal of Criminal Law and Criminology, Spring, 761–804.

Rowe, W., 1996. Commentary by Walter F. Rowe. In: Connors, E., Lundregan, T., Miller, N., McEwen, T. (Eds.), Convicted by Juries, Exonerated by Science: Case Studies in the Use of DNA Evidence to Establish Innocence After Trial, National Institute of Justice, Office of Justice Programs, U.S. Department of Justice, Washington DCNCJ 161258, June.

Saks, M., 2001. Scientific evidence and the ethical obligations of attorneys. Cleveland State Law Review 49 (3), 421–438.

Shipley, C.J., 1987. The Alford plea: a necessary but unpredictable tool for the criminal defendant. Iowa Law Review 72, 1063–1089.

Smith, B. "The history of wrongful execution, " Hastings Law Journal, 56, June; 1185–1233.

Thompson, C., 2000. Crime bomb: police crime labs are churning out tainted evidence—and nobody's doing anything about it. November 22 SFBG.com.

Thornton, J., 1994. Courts of law v. Courts of science: a forensic scientist's reaction to Daubert. Shepard's Expert and Scientific Quarterly 1 (3), Winter; 475–485.

Thornton, J., Peterson, J., 2007. The general assumptions and rationale of forensic identification. In: Faigman, D., Kaye, D., Saks, M., Sanders, J. (Eds.), Modern Scientific Evidence: The Law and Science of Expert Testimony, Vol. 1. West Publishing Group, St. Paul, MN.

Thornton, J., 1983. Uses and abuses of forensic science. In: Thomas, W. (Ed.), Science and Law: An Essential Alliance, Westview Press, Boulder, pp. 79–90.

Turvey, B., 2003. Forensic frauds: a study of 42 cases. Journal of Behavioral Profiling, April, 4 (1).

Turvey, B., 2013. Forensic Fraud: Evaluating Law Enforcement and Forensic Science Cultures in the Context of Examiner Misconduct. Elsevier Science, San Diego.

Uphoff, R.J., Convicting the Innocent: Aberration or Systemic Problem? Wisconsin Law Review, Forthcoming; U of Missouri-Columbia School of Law Legal Studies Research Paper No. 2006-20, http://papers.ssrn.com/sol3/papers.cfm?abstract_id=912310

Williamson v. Ward, United States Court of Appeals, Tenth Circuit, No. 95–7141, April 10, 1997 (110 F.3d 1508, 97 CJ C.A.R. 516).

Index

Note: Page numbers with "f" denote figures; "t" tables; "b" boxes.

607